UNIVERSITY LIBR/
UW-STEVENS POI

W9-CIM-063

The Politics of
International Organizations
Patterns and Insights

The Politics of
International Organizations
Patterns and Insights

Edited by

Paul F. Diehl
University of Georgia

Dorsey Press
Chicago, Illinois 60604

© RICHARD D. IRWIN, INC., 1989

All rights reserved. No part of this publication may be reproduced, stored in a retrieval system, or transmitted, in any form or by any means, electronic, mechanical, photocopying, recording, or otherwise, without the prior written permission of the publisher.

Acquisitions editor: Leo A. W. Wiegman
Project editor: Gladys True
Production manager: Bette Ittersagen
Cover Design: Leon Bolognese & Associates
Compositor: Weimer Typesetting Co., Inc.
Typeface: 10/12 Times Roman
Printer: Malloy Lithographing, Inc.

Library of Congress Cataloging-in-Publication Data

The Politics of international organizations: patterns and insights / edited by Paul F. Diehl.
    p. cm.
    ISBN 0-256-06840-2 (pbk.): $18.00
    1. International agencies. 2. International relations.
I. Diehl, Paul F. (Paul Francis)
JX1995.P585 1989
341.2—dc19   88–12091

Printed in the United States of America
1 2 3 4 5 6 7 8 9 0 ML 5 4 3 2 1 0 9 8

JX
1995
.P585
1989

Preface

International organizations are a relatively new phenomenon in international relations. Yet, in today's interdependent world, they play a vital and expanding role in a wide variety of activities. Some of the earlier books on international organizations focused exclusively on the United Nations and its role in security affairs. Over time, the actual functions performed by international organizations spread well beyond security affairs and involved more than the United Nations.

In selecting the readings that follow, I was guided by several principles. First, I wanted to present readings that showed this diversity of activities carried out by international organizations. Accordingly, this book contains articles on how international organizations undertake actions in international trade, development, human rights, relief services, and many other fields beyond their traditional role in security affairs. Second, I wanted the reader to be aware that the United Nations, while very important, is not the only international organization with a significant role in international relations. Thus, I've chosen articles that look at the activities of the International Monetary Fund, the International Committee of the Red Cross, and the World Health Organization, among others.

Beyond expanding the scope of traditional anthologies on international organizations, I've made an effort to ensure that the readings here represent the best and most recent scholarship in the field. Economic and political analysis, in particular, have a short shelf life in the rapidly evolving international system. Thus, with a few exceptions, the articles in this collection were originally published within the last decade, and their analyses retain their relevance today. Each of the selections also was originally published in a book or leading academic journal. This ensures that, unlike a magazine article, the selections here have undergone anonymous peer review before being published; hence the reader will be exposed to the works of some of the leading scholars in the field of international organizations.

Finally, although this book is composed of scholarly articles, it should be accessible to undergraduates, graduate students, and scholars alike. There is a tendency in any academic discipline for some scholars to address a very narrow audience, using particular phrases and methods of analyses that are not adequately explained for the general readership. Each of the selections here was selected and edited to assist all readers in understanding the politics of international organizations.

I benefited greatly from several individuals in the preparation of this manuscript. Leo A. W. Wiegman of Dorsey Press deserves credit for encouraging me to pursue this project. At every stage of the editing process, he provided timely advice and assistance. My research assistant Nikos Zahariadis was instrumental in the identification and collection of these articles; he also proved to be an able editor of the introductory sections, as did my colleague Christopher Allen. The Department of Political Science at the University of Georgia provided the clerical help necessary in this project. In particular, Bridget Pilcher was indispensable with her fast and accurate typing.

Finally, I owe a debt of gratitude to those of my colleagues at other universities who read and commented on this manuscript at different stages of preparation, namely, Harold Jacobson, Robert Jordan, Joseph Lepgold, Jack C. Plano, and Robert E. Riggs. I adopted many of their suggestions and am grateful for their help, although final responsibility for the manuscript rests with me.

Paul F. Diehl

Contents

LIST OF FIGURES

LIST OF TABLES

CHAPTER I

Introduction

There are two predominant views of international organizations among the general public. The first is a cynical view that emphasizes the dramatic rhetoric and seeming inability to deal with vital problems that are said to characterize international organizations and the United Nations in particular. According to this view, international organizations should be treated as insignificant actors on the international stage. The other view is an idealistic one. Those who hold this view envisage global solutions to the major problems facing the world today, without recognition of the constraints imposed by state sovereignty. Most of the naive calls for world government are products of this view. An understanding of international organizations probably requires that neither view be accepted in its entirety, nor be wholly rejected. International organizations are neither irrelevant nor omnipotent in global politics. They play important roles in international relations, but their influence varies according to the issue area and situation confronted.

This book is designed so that the reader gains a balanced and realistic view of international organizations. In this way, the selections in this collection dispel a number of myths. Narrow views about how international organizations make decisions or respond to conflict are called into question. An understanding of international organizations requires the correct knowledge of how, where, and why they operate. Only then can we learn to recognize their limitations as well as their possibilities. We begin the study of international organizations by briefly tracing the origins of the present United Nations system.

The League of Nations was formed following World War I, and it represented an attempt at international cooperative efforts to prevent war. The breakdown of the League system in the 1930s was the product of many factors. Yet, the failure of will by the major powers of the era and the unwieldy requirements for concerted action certainly were the primary causes. As with most initial experiments, the results were far from ideal, but the total effort gives some basis for optimism. In the case of the League, it was not able to prevent World War II, but it did provide

1

a means for cooperation and consultation among states on a variety of issues not confined to security matters, although this was the major purpose for which it was created.

It is, therefore, perhaps not surprising that world leaders sought to form another general international organization at the conclusion of World War II. The occurrence of war has generally had a stimulating effect on the development of international organizations in the modern era.[1] What may be surprising to some is the similarity between the League of Nations and its successor, the United Nations.[2] The Security Council and the General Assembly had comparable antecedents under the League system. Furthermore, the United Nations was also predicated on the assumption that continued cooperation among the victorious coalition in the previous war would insure global stability. One might think that given the League experience, the United Nations would suffer similar setbacks. Although the United Nations and its affiliated agencies have not achieved most of the goals set out in its Charter, neither have they been insignificant in dealing with many of the most pressing problems in the world. This can be attributed to the radically differing environments faced by the League and the United Nations.

After 1945, the international system was structured in a bipolar fashion, with each superpower retaining an interest in maintaining its status. Consequently, there has been little pressure for the rapid systemic upheaval that characterized the periods prior to the world wars. This does not imply that conflict has abated; rather, such conflict has been more limited and less threatening to the international system or the existence of the United Nations. Second, there seems to be a greater recognition in the last forty years of a need for cooperation among states. The ideas behind the United Nations are not new ones, but the prospects of global devastation from nuclear war or environmental alteration have been sufficient to prompt a greater commitment to international organizations. It has become clear that various problems, such as pollution, hunger, and nuclear proliferation, are not amenable to action by only one or several states.

Finally, the United Nations has acquired a symbolic importance that the League of Nations lacked. States feel obligated to justify their actions before the main bodies of the United Nations, even when they may appear contrary to the Charter principles. As the United States did during the Cuban Missile Crisis, states may use the United Nations as a means to legitimize their actions or policy positions.[3] Most important, however, states are exceedingly hesitant to withdraw from membership in the United Nations, even when that organization's actions appear contrary to their national interests. Such reluctance prevents the debilitating loss of significant actors that plagued the League during most of its existence.

The United Nations and its affiliates are the most significant international organizations, but they are hardly the only ones. In this century, the number of international organizations has grown exponentially. The current number approaches 5,000.[4] The list includes a wide range of memberships and purposes, and they vary in significance from the Inter-American Tropical Tuna Commission to the World Bank.

One method of classifying international organizations is according to their membership potential and scope of purpose.[5] International organizations can either be designed for universal membership, potentially including all states in the world, or the membership may be limited, as are many regional organizations. We may also classify international organizations according to the breadth of their concerns. Specific purpose organizations may be confined to one problem, such as the SEATO Medical Research Laboratory, or one issue area, such as the Food and Agriculture Organization. A general purpose organization is concerned with a variety of problems in several issue areas. Most international organizations are nongovernmental entities in the limited membership, specific purpose category. Although reference is occasionally made to these bodies in the readings, most of our attention is directed at intergovernmental organizations of a general membership variety. As the only universal membership, general purpose organization, the United Nations gets much of our attention.

This first section provides an overview to the study of international organizations. The next section of this book focuses on the various theoretical approaches to the study of international organizations. It is evident that the ways analysts have studied international organizations have changed dramatically over the last 40 or more years. The reader is especially advised to note the description and critique of regime analysis. This approach is currently the most prominent in the field, and accordingly, some of the remaining articles in this book adopt that framework. The third section is devoted to the patterns of cooperation that exist in international organizations. The reader will note both the extent and depth of involvement of states in such entities. Furthermore, the degree of cooperative behavior in international organizations may surprise some who regard international organizations merely as hostile debating societies.

The fourth section details the decision-making processes of international organizations. The range of activities and the bureaucratic actors and processes that are often hidden from public view are revealed in these selections. Furthermore, proposals to change the most visible aspect of decisionmaking—voting—are assessed.

After the first four sections, the reader will have a broad view of the place of international organizations in the world system and the patterns of their activities. Armed with this understanding, the reader is now directed to the actions of international organizations in three major issue areas: peace and security, economic, and social and humanitarian. In Sections V through VII, one can appreciate the number of organizations involved, the scope of activities undertaken, and the variation in effectiveness across organizations and issue areas. While the first four sections highlight common patterns in international organizations, the next three sections provide more details and reveal the diversity of the bodies.

The peace and security articles provide an historical overview and some empirical evidence on the effectiveness of international organizations in the period since 1945. One article focuses on the most successful approach to peace used by international organizations, the deployment of peacekeeping forces. The economic section details the major organizations and processes in this issue area. Much of the growth in the importance of international organizations has taken place in this area. Articles on the General Agreement on Tariffs and Trade (GATT), the World Bank, and the International Monetary Fund reveal the current state of the world economic system. Articles on the New International Economic Order (NIEO) and the United Nations Conference on Trade and Development (UNCTAD) reveal the desires of some states to change the system and the barriers that stand in their way. With respect to social and humanitarian issues, international organizations are an integral part of several controversial activities, including the monitoring of human rights behavior and the regulation of consumer products across national boundaries.

The eighth section moves away from the previous focus on universal and public international organizations. The first selection addresses the regional organizations, the European Economic Community (EEC) and the Council for Mutual Economic Assistance (CMEA or Comecon) and their interrelationship. The other article looks at the activities of the best-known private international organization, the International Committee of the Red Cross (ICRC).

I do not believe that any discussion of international organizations is complete without evaluating the relationship of the United States with the United Nations. Accordingly, the ninth and final section explores the basis of the U.S.-U.N. relationship with new insights on the convergence of interests between the two. This should provide some different perspectives on the ongoing debate concerning the importance of the United Nations to American foreign policy goals.

Before proceeding to these issues, the book begins with a brief essay on the roles of international organizations in global politics. Charles Pentland identifies three central roles of organizations. Consistent with a cynical viewpoint, he first points out that international organizations may be used as tools of a state's foreign policy in order to achieve national interest. Yet, international organizations are more than policy instruments in the manipulative hands of member states. Pentland additionally notes that international organizations can also modify the behavior of states and even function as semiautonomous actors in international relations. Thus, this first article not only broadly defines the place of international organizations on the world stage, but also suggests that simplistic views of international organizations are unlikely to be accurate ones.

NOTES

1. See J. David Singer and Michael Wallace, "International Government Organizations and the Preservation of Peace, 1816–1964" *International Organization*, 24 (1970): 520–547.
2. For a definitive comparison, see Leland Goodrich, "From League of Nations to United Nations" *International Organization*, 1 (1947): 3–21.
3. Ernst Haas, "Collective Legitimization as a Political Function of the United Nations" *International Organization*, 20 (1966): 367–379.
4. Harold Jacobson, *Networks of Interdependence*, 2nd edition (New York: Random House, 1984), 36–53.
5. *Ibid*, 11–13.

1

INTERNATIONAL ORGANIZATIONS AND THEIR ROLES

Charles Pentland

What roles do international organizations play in the international system, and what kinds of organizations—in terms of types of activity and patterns of membership—play those roles most prominently? In the sections that follow, we shall examine in turn three of the roles most widely attributed to international organizations: (1) instruments of national policy, (2) systematic modifiers of states' behavior, and (3) autonomous international actors.

SOURCE: Reprinted with permission of The Free Press, a Division of Macmillan, Inc., from *World Politics*, James Rosenav, Kenneth W. Thompson, Gavin Boyd, Editors. Copyright © 1976 by The Free Press.

INTERNATIONAL ORGANIZATIONS AS INSTRUMENTS OF POLICY

As instruments for the collective pursuit of foreign policy goals, international organizations are subject to evaluation by member states in terms of their utility. From national capitals the whole field of international organizations is likely to be perceived as an array of more or less useful pieces of machinery through which to enhance national policy aims. This instrumental outlook means that, as with other modalities of foreign policy, the national policymaker weighs the costs and benefits (insofar as they can be estimated) of participating in an international organization or attempting to mobilize it for specific purposes. Such utilitarian calculations are made both by small states pursuing policy goals through coalitions and by major powers which may by themselves be able decisively to influence the organization's performance.

Clearly states vary greatly in their ability to mobilize and manage international organizations for the pursuit of their foreign policy goals, and organizations in turn vary in the degree to which they can be so used. Major powers can often determine if organizations will be active at all in areas of interest to them. In regional organizations especially, a hegemonic state can usually be assured of sufficient small power backing to permit it to manage the organization toward acceptable decisions. Its calculations will tend to center less on the probability of creating a winning coalition around itself (this being assumed) than on the relative virtues of multilateral and unilateral action. For smaller powers, largely incapable of effective unilateral action and much less sure of their ability to create winning coalitions to control the multilateral setting, the calculations have to be more subtle and complex.

Important for both great and small powers are the power disparities embodied in the organization and the degree to which any working consensus created among the members is likely to be compatible with their particular interests. A good measure of the power relationship is the "presence" of the state in the organization, reflected in its contribution of finances and personnel, its demands for action, and its level of participation in decision making. The degree of compatibility between the working consensus of the organization and the state's interests can be seen in the responsiveness of the organization's policy decisions and executive actions to the state's original demands. . . . Cases of evident domination of an international organization by a single state remain exceptional. For most states, using international organizations to pursue foreign policy objectives means collaboration, not manipulation (although the distinction can sometimes be rather fine). The emphasis is less on individually "managing" the organization toward certain ends and more on working to create or maintain coalitions which can collectively generate and oversee organizational policy and collectively share in its benefits. . . .

The important coalition patterns in the UN have not reflected the perceived difference between big power and small power interests. The most institutionalized coalitions are the caucusing groups—the Eastern European states, the Arab states, the Latin Americans, the African and Asian states, and the "Western European and other" grouping—which meet regularly to elect bloc "representatives" to various UN organs and sometimes to concert policy on issues of substance. Among these formally designated blocs the degree of cohesion varies considerably. That of the Soviet bloc has been consistently high for all sessions on nearly all issues; the Latin American states have also been remarkably likeminded. For the other groups, cohesion is considerably lower.[1] In fact the usefulness of such regional designations is exhausted rather quickly in analyzing General Assembly voting, since they obscure the great amount of coalition formation which takes place across regional lines—particularly on cold war, development, and decolonization issues. An inductive analysis of General Assembly voting suggests that the members divide into six groupings for which geographical or "pro-West, pro-Soviet" labels are quite inappropriate, and which support each other to differing degrees on different substantive issues.[2]

It is nevertheless true that the composition of the prevalent "winning coalition" in the United Nations has changed, to the point that many observers argue that the organization has moved from being an instrument of American policy (wielded with the support of Western Europe, Latin America, and a handful of other states) to being the captive of the underdeveloped, anticolonial states of Asia and Africa (usually aided by Latin America and the Soviet bloc). The voting power of this group of states was evident, for example, in the passing of General Assembly resolution 1514(XV) of 1960, which set out more uncompromising demands for further rapid decolonization than most Western states felt they could realistically accept. . . .

Of course, massive General Assembly majorities and elaborate new programs do not by themselves indicate that the UN has become the policy instrument of a cohesive underdeveloped, anticolonial majority of its members. Certainly the organization's priorities and preoccupations have changed radically.

---

[1] R. O. Keohane, "Political Influence in the General Assembly," *International Conciliation,* vol. 557 (March 1966), pp. 10–11 (table 1).

[2] H. R. Alker, Jr. and B. M. Russett, *World Politics in the General Assembly* (New Haven, Conn.: Yale University Press, 1965). See also B. M. Russett "Discovering Voting Groups in the United Nations," *American Political Science Review,* vol. 60 (June 1966), pp. 327–339.

But so far the increased organizational presence of the Third World has not been matched by effective, concrete policy outcomes: the organization's responsiveness is largely verbal and symbolic, and is likely to remain so as long as the Western states, which control the purse strings, the bulk of the world's military force, and its few remaining colonies, remain determined in the face of what they deem empty rhetoric or irresponsible "voting machines." Moreover, the Third World is not as cohesive as the voting totals suggest. Attitudes toward development, decolonization, and other issues vary widely, as do the political strengths of the Third World countries within their coalitions. Hence the payoffs of successful action by these coalitions are rarely distributed evenly, and the cost-benefit calculus concerning the UN as a policy instrument can produce divergent conclusions. Some states will choose to emphasize collective Third World action through the General Assembly; others will opt for regional solutions (mobilizing the OAU against southern African racism, forming regional common markets for economic development); and others still will make their own deals with the rich countries. The UN option is rarely dropped entirely, but the costs of solidarity and UN diplomacy may appear greater, and the benefits less (or more remote), than those accruing to more exclusive regional arrangements sometimes involving dependence on a great power. . . .

In general, regional organizations do not provide us with much clear evidence, in terms of the relative "presence" of member states or the responsiveness of policy outcomes to their interests, to suggest that coalitions of certain states consistently benefit disproportionately from these organizations' activities. In most cases the coalitions formed are shifting in composition. The process of political influence through which states pursue their foreign policy interests in these organizations thus tends to take place in something approaching a pluralistic setting.

To sum up, it is comparatively rarely that international organizations serve directly as controlled, effective instruments of one state's foreign policy. In these rare cases the dominant state's support for, and demands on, the organization will far outstrip those of any other member; it will have ready-made majorities of its clientele to determine the outcome of all decisions it considers important; and the actions of the organization will amount to putting a multilateral gloss on a unilateral interest. The cold war alliances, the UN on rare occasions such as the Korean action, and the OAS are about the only international organizations which fit this pattern to any notable extent. It is worth adding that smaller members of a hegemonic organization may find this situation the most rational in terms of their own policy goals. The theory of "collective goods" suggests that the small can in fact "exploit" the large, since the marginal cost of producing the good (such as security or wealth) shared by all members of the organization is lowest for the hegemonic state. Collective goods "may be provided to an almost 'optimal' degree in a group in which one member is very much larger than all the other members."[3] The cost-benefit calculus, then, does not necessarily indicate that collaboration on an egalitarian basis is always the best for a small state seeking to maximize foreign policy goals. Sometimes, to use international organizations as foreign policy instruments may be, in effect, to "use" the hegemonic state. At other times, it may mean establishing a dominant coalition which controls decisions and allocates the proceeds among its members.

But generally, to speak of international organizations as instruments of state policy is to stress the element of "free" intergovernmental collaboration toward shared or convergent objectives. In an increasingly interdependent world, unilateralism is impossible because "more and more goods are becoming collective at the international level."[4] The calculus of utility for most states, therefore, is concerned neither with the pros and cons of collaboration *per se* nor with the probabilities of successfully manipulating any organization. Rather it is concerned with ongoing judgments about the responsiveness of various organizations in providing the state with an acceptable share of the collective goods produced, and about the optimum amount of resources to commit to their common production. These calculations are rarely all that visible or precise, but the occasional surfacing of debates over the American contribution to the UN budget or over what constitutes a "just return" from the European Community should remind us of their continuing importance for the functioning of international organizations.

INTERNATIONAL ORGANIZATIONS AS SYSTEMIC MODIFIERS OF STATE BEHAVIOR

Since "instruments" are supposed to be neutral and to lack any life or direction but that imparted by their users, the thrust of the first perspective on international organizations is to minimize their status as independent entities in the international system. Viewed as re-

---

[3]B. M. Russett and J. D. Sullivan, "Collective Goods and International Organization," *International Organization,* 25 (Autumn 1971), p. 853. Collective goods are goods from the benefits of which it is not feasible to exclude those who do not pay a share of the costs, and the consumption of which by one actor does not lead to a reduced supply for others (p. 846). For critical comments on the application of this model to international organizations, see W. Loehr, "Collective Goods and International Cooperation: Comments," *International Organization,* vol. 27 (Summer 1973), pp. 421–430.

[4]Russett and Sullivan, op. cit., p. 849.

straints on the behavior of states, however, international organizations begin to take on a life of their own as part of the landscape of the international system. From this perspective international organizations are not seen as actors in their own right, equivalent to and interacting with states; rather they are institutional channels, obstacles, and aids collectively created by states which modify the traditionally *laissez-faire* character of their relationships.

As such, international organizations become an institutional manifestation of the general set of restraints placed on states by the international system. Their effectiveness as modifiers of state behavior will depend to a great extent on the general structural pattern of this system. Four aspects of this structural pattern are commonly singled out as important in this respect: (1) the degree of polarization, (2) the power and status hierarchies, (3) the linkage of central system and regional subsystems, and (4) the degree of transnational interdependence. Tight bipolarity, in which every state is bound to one bloc or the other, is the least congenial setting for global international organizations, although it may give rise to hegemonic or regional institutions within each bloc as means of control or internal conflict resolution. Between the blocs, however, accommodation and interaction tend to be limited to the leaders, whose bilateral dealings give little role to a global organization. Multipolarity, on the other hand, increases states' freedom of maneuver and the variety of their interactions, while the absence of clientelistic bloc structures means they must pursue collective goods through wider collaboration.[5]

Second, the influence of international organizations is likely to be greater to the extent that power, wealth, and status are distributed evenly among the states. If there are huge disparities between one state and all the rest, international organizations are likely to be instruments of hegemonic control, restraining all states but the superpower. If there are several large states which are in basic agreement about the international order, the organization becomes an instrument of oligarchic control. Only a relatively egalitarian system permits a truly collective system of restraint to operate, since the capa-

---

[5]On the implications of patterns of polarization for international organization, see M. A. Kaplan, *System and Process in International Politics* (New York: Wiley, 1957), chap. 3. On the related question of the stability of various types of systems, see K. N. Waltz, "The Stability of a Bipolar World," *Daedalus,* vol. 93 (Summer 1964), pp. 881–909, K. W. Deutsch and J. D. Singer, "Multipolar Power Systems and International Stability," *World Politics,* vol. 16 (April 1964), pp. 390–406, and R. N. Rosecrance, "Bipolarity, Multipolarity and the Future," *Journal of Conflict Resolution,* vol. 10 (September 1966), pp. 314–327.

bilities of potential violators are less likely to outweigh those of the rest of the community of states.[6]

Concerning the optimum relationship between global system and regional subsystem, different arguments are defensible. One, which stresses "islands of peace" and "division of labor," suggests that discontinuities between the two levels actually aid international organizations. Conflicts can be localized within regional organizations and dealt with by the states most directly concerned. The other argument stresses the "indivisibility of peace" and points to the superior resources of the global organizations, as well as the dangers of balkanization. In this view the intensification of regional interactions among states is liable to paralyze global organizations.[7]

The development of transnational interdependence, finally, is usually held to be a vital underpinning for international organizations. Steadily growing flows of goods, services, money, people, and ideas between countries represent that fabric which stands to be damaged or destroyed should the states'

collective system of self-control fail. We might expect, then, that organizations which follow particularly intense patterns of interdependence would draw the greatest degree of commitment and compliance from their member states.[8] This commitment and compliance would probably be a product not so much of legal or coercive restraints as of a process of socialization occurring among political, economic, and administrative elites as they interacted with each other in a multilateral context. International organizations, in short, can restrain states by means of internalized norms as well as the more evident external pressures. . . .

INTERNATIONAL ORGANIZATIONS AS ACTORS

Viewed as restraints on the behavior of states, international organizations begin to take on independent life. But it is a limited sort of independence: the organizations are created and sustained by the states in a collective act of self-limitation or self-enhancement, and there is certainly no expectation

---

[6]The optimum setting for a collective security system is one of considerable diffusion of power among states with approximately equal resources. See I. M. Claude, *Swords into Plowshares*, 4th ed. (New York: Random House, 1971), pp. 256–259.

[7]For a positive view of regionalist trends and the role of regional organizations, see L. H. Miller, "The Prospects for Order through Regional Security," in C. E. Black and R. A. Falk, *The Future of the International Legal Order*, vol. I (Princeton, N.J.: Princeton University Press, 1969), pp. 556–594. More skeptical is P. E. Jacob, A. L. Atherton, and A. M. Wallenstein, *The Dynamics of International Organization*, rev. ed. (Homewood, Ill.: Dorsey, 1972). chaps. 7 and 21, especially pp. 689–694.

[8]On interdependence generally, see O. R. Young, "Interdependencies in World Politics," *International Journal*, vol. 24 (Autumn 1969), pp. 726–750.

that they will come to coexist with, or even supersede, their creators as the dominant actors in the international system. In the postwar period, however, it has become apparent that some international organizations promise (or threaten, depending on one's perspective) to do just this. At present their numbers are fewer than some would claim, but their implications are far-reaching for the future of international politics.

Becoming an actor means, essentially, to achieve some degree of autonomy and some capacity to influence other actors. Autonomy is the product of what Schmitter calls "organizational development," or a "process whereby an initially dependent system, created by a set of actors representing different and relatively independent nation-states, acquires the capabilities of a self-maintaining and self-steering system, one whose course cannot be predicted solely from knowledge of its environment."[9] A capacity to influence other actors (or, indeed, to resist influences from other actors) is based on resources—expert information, finances, decision-making capacity, popular support or legitimacy, enforcement capabilities, and diplomatic skills—which accrue independently to the organization. To analyze international organizations in these terms is not necessarily to assume the inevita-

bility or desirability of their challenging the supremacy of the nation-state, or indeed even to assume that such organizational development necessarily occurs at the expense of the national autonomy. It is simply to recognize that some international organizations are more highly developed than others and that their impact on the international system is thus rather more forceful.

The UN system has four important assets which provide it with varying degrees of political influence. These are regulatory authority, executive capacity, expertise, and legitimacy. The first two are on balance rather more important for the UN's narrower technical agencies; the latter two are increasingly evident in its work in economic management and development. *Regulation* is largely confined to technical agencies, especially in such fields as communications, transportation, and health, which, as Gregg observes, "are no respectors of political boundaries." The rules laid down by organizations like ITU, UPU, ICAO, and WHO "are binding and they are observed, almost reflexively."[10] In other areas the rules are less comprehensive, and acceptance and enforcement less certain. In some cases the rules themselves are purely the product of intergovernmental negotiation, although on

---

[9]P. C. Schmitter, "The 'Organizational Development' of International Organizations," *International Organization,* vol. 25 (Autumn 1971), p. 918.

[10]R. W. Gregg, "UN Economic, Social and Technical Activities," in J. Barros (ed.), *The United Nations: Past, Present, and Future* (New York: Free Press, 1972), p. 224.

technical matters the outcome need not be low-level agreement; in other cases (WHO is a good example) the expertise commanded by the Secretariat is a major source of regulations.[11] In most cases, finally, enforcement power is negligible in the face of deviant governments. Sanctions available to some organizations include publicity and denial of access to resources or information, but in more technical areas perhaps the most effective curb is the state's own awareness of the high cost to all—including itself—of a breakdown in the regulatory regime.

By *executive capacity* is meant what Skolnikoff describes as "operation."[12] To a limited extent in the management of resources and technology, somewhat more in research and development, and most of all in technical assistance and in the financial operations of the IMF and the World Bank group, UN agencies (and, indeed, other international organizations like Intelsat and OECD) have acquired the expertise and the organizational apparatus to perform tasks for which national institutions lack the capacity. As with regulation, these tasks are delegated by governments, but because of their technical and transnational nature the delegation is virtually irrevocable.

Expertise is a major and growing asset for low political organizations. Gregg is surely right to remark that the UN's contribution to knowledge in the economic, social, and technical fields "has been so great and so fundamentally important as a basis for future efforts . . . that if the United Nations system should cease to exist tomorrow, at least these research and informational services would have to be reinstituted at once."[13] As the costs of research and communication of knowledge increase, all states can be expected to rely more on this kind of pooled effort. For poorer countries, there has never been much alternative.

Legitimacy, finally, accrues to most of these low political organizations essentially as a reflection of satisfaction with the services they perform. These judgments are normally the business of member governments, of course, but since the economic, technical, and social activities of such organizations give them frequent contact with groups and individuals as well, it is plausible to consider, as functionalists do, that some individual awareness and loyalty begins to fix on them as well.[14] But if legitimacy thus tends to have a "functionally specific" quality in connection with the more technical agencies, it is of a much

---

[11]E. B. Skolnikoff, *The International Imperatives of Technology,* (Berkeley: University of California, Institute of International Studies, Research Series, no. 16), p. 104.

[12]Ibid., pp. 114–116.

[13]Gregg, in Barros (ed.), op. cit., p. 222.

[14]J. P. Sewell, *Functionalism and World Politics* (Princeton, N.J.: Princeton University Press, 1966), pp. 48–49, 58–63.

more general and pervasive character with the development agencies. The less developed countries are nearly unanimous in demanding a greater role for the UN in the whole development assistance enterprise. For many of them, too, the UN is already a major functional and political presence in their domestic societies, through the field representatives of the UN Development Program, the World Bank group, and the specialized agencies. Donor countries, on the other hand, have traditionally been unenthusiastic about multilateral economic assistance. . . .

CONCLUSIONS

International organizations are of interest to the statesman and the theorist of world politics because of the variety of roles they play in the international system and the widely differing interpretations which can be attached to those roles. First, international organizations are used by states, individually or collectively, as instruments of foreign policy. Second, they act, by their very presence in the system, to modify states' behavior. Third, they sometimes achieve a degree of autonomy and influence as political actors in their own right. The fact that most international organizations are perceived or expected—from a variety of perspectives—to play two or possibly all three of these roles simultaneously underlines that the roles are not mutually exclusive and in fact may at times be mutually reinforcing.

Observers of, or participants in, international organizations may have divergent expectations as to their future development. Accordingly, they may apply different standards in measuring an organization's success or failure. But on such organizations' contribution to the complexity of the international system there is little disagreement. If international organizations alleviate some problems for states, they also create new ones. And if, for the theorist, they do not yet seriously challenge the traditional state-centered model of the international system, they do complicate and compromise it somewhat.

CHAPTER II

The Study of International Organizations

International organizations are a relatively new phenomenon, with the League of Nations being the first universal, general purpose organization. The study of international organizations is perhaps even more recent. It was not until the 1930s that David Mitrany published his first classic book on functionalism. It was not until 1947 that an academic journal, entitled *International Organization,* devoted to the subject, first appeared. Yet, over this brief period, scholars have changed dramatically the way they study international organizations. This series of articles traces the evolution of those changes and offers differing opinions on one of the dominant modes of analysis today: regime analysis.

Kratochwil and Ruggie trace the development of international organizations as a field of study. Not surprisingly, early studies focused on the institutional characteristics of these new international actors; scholars of American and foreign governments were pursuing a similar focus during this time. Gradually, as Kratochwil and Ruggie argue, the focus shifted to the processes and roles of international organizations. In the last decade, however, regime analysis has become a preeminent method of analysis. What is an international regime and how did regime analysis come about?

An international regime is composed of sets of explicit or implicit principles, norms, rules, and decision-making procedures around which actor expectations converge in a given area of international relations and which may help to coordinate their behavior. There are numerous examples of international regimes. The international trade regime, based largely on the General Agreement on Tariffs and Trade (GATT), and the ocean regime, based on the Law of the Sea Treaty, are but two examples. Regimes do not necessarily have to be based on formal agreements; an international energy regime, for example, may emerge from custom rather than treaties between states. International organizations enter the picture to the extent that they can perform a variety of roles in the context of an international regime. They may be instrumental in the creation of a regime, by providing the forum in which the regime is defined or negotiated or as an instrument by which regular patterns of behavior are created. Many times, international organizations may be the culmination of a process of regime definition. At other points, international organizations may be the mechanism by which regime procedures are regulated (as in the Non-Proliferation regime) or adapted (as has been attempted in the United Nations Conference on Trade and Development).

International organizations are increasingly involved in global affairs, but not all efforts at international cooperation are taking place within an international organization framework. Therefore, focusing only on international organizations leads analysts to miss many important patterns of interstate interaction within a given issue area. Regime analysis can capture the behavior of states and other actors in that issue area as well as the role of international organizations.

The Young article provides the definitive framework by which to identify and analyze international regimes. Included is a scheme by which to define the procedures and mechanisms for implementation for each regime. Furthermore, the processes by which regimes are created and transformed are discussed. This article provides the basic building blocks by which an analyst can identify, classify, and assess an international regime in a given issue area. The reader will note that regime analysis is used in several of the substantive articles in this collection, including those by Haas and Sikkink.

Since the time that Young wrote his article, the use of regime analysis has expanded, becoming a common framework in many studies of international organizations and international political economy. Yet, the scheme is still a controversial one. Susan Strange gives a spirited critique of regime analysis, focusing on the vagueness of the regime concept and its bias toward the status quo, among other points. The reader should not be too hasty in drawing judgments about regime analysis from this article. Many of the criticisms cited are best understood as reflections of the underdevelopment of this method of analysis. Strange implicitly offers a valid set of challenges to scholars using international regime analysis that they must work to refine further this framework. If regime analysis is more than a passing fad, as is now evidently the case, the reader will eventually see this method of analysis improved as it permeates the discipline.

2

INTERNATIONAL ORGANIZATION: THE STATE OF THE ART

Friedrich Kratochwil and John Gerard Ruggie

International organization as a field of study has had its ups and downs throughout the post-World War II era and throughout this century for that matter. In the interwar period, the fate of the field reflected the fate of the world it studied: a creative burst of work on "international government" after 1919, followed by a period of more cautious reassessment approaching the 1930s, and a gradual decline into irrelevance if not obscurity thereafter. Although they sometimes intersected, the fate of theory and the fate of practice were never all that closely linked after World War II. Indeed, it is possible to argue, with only slight exaggeration, that in recent years they have become inversely related: the academic study of international organization is more interesting, vibrant, and even compelling than ever before, whereas the world of actual international organizations has deteriorated in efficacy and performance. Today, international organization as a field of study is an area where the action is; few would so characterize international organizations as a field of practice.

Our purpose in this article is to try to figure out how and why the doctors can be thriving when the patient is moribund. To anticipate the answer without, we hope, unduly straining the metaphor, the reason is that the leading doctors have become biochemists and have stopped treating and in most cases even seeing patients. In the process, however, new discoveries have been made, new diagnostic techniques have been developed, and our understanding has deepened, raising the possibility of more effective treatment in the long run.

What we are suggesting, to pose the issue more directly, is that students of international organization have shifted their focus systematically away from international institutions, toward broader forms of international institutionalized behavior. . . . This evolution has brought the field to its current focus on the concept of international regimes. To fully realize its potential, the research program must now seek to resolve some serious anomalies in the regime approach and to link up the informal ordering devices of international regimes with

SOURCE: Reprinted from *International Organization*, Vol. 40, No. 4, 1986. Friedrich Kratochwil and John Ruggie, "International Organization: A State of the Art on an Art of the State," by permission of The MIT Press, Cambridge, Massachusetts. © 1986 by the World Peace Foundation and the Massachusetts Institute of Technology.

the formal institutional mechanisms of international organizations.

In the first section of this article, we present a review of the literature in order to trace its evolution. This review draws heavily on articles published in *International Organization,* the leading journal in the field since its first appearance in 1947, and a source that not only reflects but in considerable measure is also responsible for the evolution of the field. The second section critiques the currently prevalent epistemological practices in regime analysis and points toward lines of inquiry which might enhance the productive potential of the concept as an analytical tool. Finally, we briefly suggest a means of systematically linking up regimes and formal organizations in a manner that is already implicit in the literature.

PROGRESSIVE ANALYTICAL SHIFTS

As a field of study, international organization has always concerned itself with the same phenomenon: in the words of a 1931 text, it is an attempt to describe and explain "how the modern Society of Nations governs itself."[1] In that text, the essence of government was assumed to comprise the coordination of group activities so as to conduct the public business, and the particular feature distinguishing international government was taken to lie in the necessity that it be consistent with national sovereignty. Few contemporary students of international organization would want to alter this definition substantially.[2]

However, there have been identifiable shifts in how the phenomenon of international governance has been conceived, especially since World War II—so much so that the field is often described as being in permanent search of its own "dependent variable." Our reading of the literature reveals four major analytical foci, which we would place in roughly the following logical—and more or less chronological—order.

Formal Institutions

The first is a formal institutional focus. Within it, the assumption was made or the premise was implicit that (1) international governance is whatever international organizations do; and (2) the formal attributes of international organizations, such as their charters, voting procedures, committee structures, and the like, account for what they do. To the extent that the actual operation of institutions was explored, the frame of reference was their constitutional mandate,

---

[1]Edmund C. Mower, *International Government* (Boston: Heath, 1931).

[2]The basic terms of the definition are entirely compatible with the most recent theoretical work in the field, Robert O. Keohane, *After Hegemony* (Princeton: Princeton University Press, 1984). The precise meaning of the terms of course has changed significantly, as we shall see presently.

and the purpose of the exercise was to discover how closely it was approximated.[3]

Institutional Processes

The second analytical focus concerns the actual decision-making processes within international organizations. The assumption was gradually abandoned that the formal arrangements of international organizations explain what they do. This perspective originally emerged in the attempt to come to grips with the increasingly obvious discrepancies between constitutional designs and organizational practices. Some writers argued that the formal arrangements and objectives remained relevant and appropriate but were undermined or obstructed by such political considerations as cold war rivalry and such institutional factors as the veto in the UN Security Council, bloc voting in the UN General Assembly, and the like.[4] Others contended that the original designs themselves were unrealistic and needed to be changed.[5]

Over time, this perspective became more generalized, to explore overall patterns of influence shaping organizational outcomes.[6] The sources of influence which have been investigated include the power and prestige of individual states, the formation and functioning of the group system, organizational leadership positions, and bureaucratic politics. The outcomes that analysts have sought to explain have ranged from specific resolutions, programs, and budgets, to broader voting alignment and the general orientation of one or more international institutions.

---

[3]A distinguished contribution to this literature is Leland M. Goodrich and Anne P. Simons, *The United Nations and the Maintenance of International Peace and Security* (Washington, D.C.: Brookings, 1955). See also Klaus Knorr, "The Bretton Woods Institutions in Transition," *International Organization* [hereafter cited as *IO*] 2 (February 1948); Walter R. Sharp, "The Institutional Framework for Technical Assistance," *IO* 7 (August 1953); and Henri Rolin, "The International Court of Justice and Domestic Jurisdiction," *IO* 8 (February 1954).

[4]Norman J. Padelford, "The Use of the Veto," *IO* 2 (June 1948); Raymond Dennett, "Politics in the Security Council," *IO* 3 (August 1949); M. Margaret Ball, "Bloc Voting in the General Assembly," *IO* 5 (February 1951); Allan Hovey, Jr., "Obstructionism and the Rules of the General Assembly," *IO* 5 (August 1951); and Arlette Moldaver, "Repertoire of the Veto in the Security Council, 1946–1956," *IO* 11 (Spring 1957).

[5]See, among others, Sir Gladwyn Jebb, "The Role of the United Nations," *IO* 6 (November 1952); A. Loveday, "Suggestions for the Reform of UN Economic and Social Machinery," *IO* 7 (August 1953); Wytze Corter, "GATT after Six Years: An Appraisal," *IO* 8 (February 1954); Lawrence S. Finkelstein, "Reviewing the UN Charter," *IO* 9 (May 1955); Robert E. Riggs, "Overselling the UN Charter—Fact or Myth," *IO* 14 (Spring 1960); and Inis L. Claude, Jr., "The Management of Power in the Changing United Nations," *IO* 15 (Spring 1961).

[6]The most comprehensive work in this genre remains Robert W. Cox and Harold K. Jacobson, eds., *The Anatomy of Influence: Decision Making in International Organization* (New Haven: Yale University Press, 1973).

Organizational Role

In this third perspective, another assumption of the formal institutionalist approach was abandoned, namely, that international governance *is* whatever international organizations *do*. Instead, the focus shifted to the actual and potential roles of international organizations in a more broadly conceived process of international governance.[7] This perspective in turn subsumes three distinct clusters.

In the first cluster, the emphasis was on the roles of international organizations in the resolution of substantive international problems.

Preventive diplomacy and peace-keeping were two such roles in the area of peace and security,[8] nuclear safeguarding by the International Atomic Energy Agency (IAEA) was another.[9] Facilitating decolonization received a good deal of attention in the political realm,[10] providing multilateral development assistance in the economic realm.[11] The potential role of international organizations in restructuring North-South relations preoccupied a substantial number of scholars throughout the 1970s,[12] as did the possible contributions of international organizations to managing the so-called global commons.[13]

---

[7]Inis L. Claude's landmark text, *Swords into Plowshares* (New York: Random House, 1959), both signaled and contributed to this shift.

[8]Lincoln P. Bloomfield, ed., *International Force—A Symposium, IO* 17 (Spring 1973); James M. Boyd, "Cyprus: Episode in Peacekeeping," *IO* 20 (Winter 1966); Robert O. Matthews, "The Suez Canal Dispute: A Case Study in Peaceful Settlement," *IO* 21 (Winter 1967); Yashpal Tandon, "Consensus and Authority behind UN Peacekeeping Operations," *IO* 21 (Spring 1967); David P. Forsythe, "United Nations Intervention in Conflict Situations Revisited: A Framework for Analysis," *IO* 23 (Winter 1969); John Gerard Ruggie, "Contingencies, Constraints, and Collective Security: Perspectives on UN Involvement in International Disputes," *IO* 28 (Summer 1974); and Ernst B. Haas, "Regime Decay: Conflict Management and International Organization, 1945–1981," *IO* 37 (Spring 1983).

[9]Robert E. Pendley and Lawrence Scheinman, "International Safeguarding as Institutionalized Collective Behavior," in John Gerard Ruggie and Ernst B. Haas, eds., special issue on international responses to technology, *IO* 29 (Summer 1975); and Joseph S. Nye, "Maintaining a Non-Proliferation Regime," in George H. Quester, ed., special issue on nuclear nonproliferation, *IO* 35 (Winter 1981).

[10]Ernst B. Haas, "The Attempt to Terminate Colonization: Acceptance of the UN Trusteeship System," *IO* 7 (February 1953); John Fletcher-Cooke, "Some Reflections on the International Trusteeship System," *IO* 13 (Summer 1959); Harold K. Jacobson, "The United Nations and Colonialism: A Tentative Appraisal," *IO* 16 (Winter 1962); and David A. Kay, "The Politics of Decolonization: The New Nations and the United Nations Political Process," *IO* 21 (Autumn 1967).

[11]Richard N. Gardner and Max F. Millikan, eds., special issue on international agencies and economic development, *IO* 22 (Winter 1968).

[12]Among many other sources, see Branislav Gosovic and John Gerard Ruggie, "On the Creation of a New International Economic Order: Issue Linkage and the Seventh Special Session of the UN General Assembly," *IO* 30 (Spring 1976).

[13]David A. Kay and Eugene B. Skolnikoff, eds., special issue on international institutions and the environmental crisis, *IO* 26 (Spring 1972); Ruggie and Haas, eds., spe-

Most recently, analysts have challenged the presumption that the roles of international organizations in this regard are invariably positive; indeed, they have accused international organizations of occasionally exacerbating the problems they are designed to help resolve.[14]

The second cluster of the organizational-role perspective shifted the focus away from the solution of substantive problems per se, toward certain long-term institutional consequences of the failure to solve substantive problems through the available institutional means. This, of course, was the integrationist focus, particularly the neofunctionalist variety.[15] It was fueled by the fact that the jurisdictional scope of both the state and existing international organiza-

tions was increasingly outstripped by the functional scope of international problems. And it sought to explore the extent to which institutional adaptations to this fact might be conducive to the emergence of political forms "beyond the nation state."[16] Neofunctionalists assigned a major role in this process to international organizations, not simply as passive recipients of new tasks and authority but as active agents of "task expansion" and "spillover."[17] Other approaches concerned themselves less with institutional changes than with attitudinal changes, whether among national elites, international delegates, or mass publics.[18]

The third cluster within the organizational-role perspective began with a critique of the transfor-

---

cial issue, *IO* 29 (Summer 1975); and Per Magnus Wijkman, "Managing the Global Commons," *IO* 36 (Summer 1982).

[14]The most extreme form of this criticism recently has come from the political right in the United States; cf. Burton Yale Pines, ed., *A World without the U.N.: What Would Happen If the United Nations Shut Down* (Washington, D.C.: Heritage Foundation, 1984). But the same position has long been an article of faith on the political left as well; cf. Cheryl Payer, "The Perpetuation of Dependence: The IMF and the Third World," *Monthly Review* 23 (September 1971), and Payer, "The World Bank and the Small Farmers," *Journal of Peace Research* 16, no. 2 (1979); and the special issue of *Development Dialogue,* no. 2 (1980).

[15]Various approaches to the study of integration were summarized and assessed in Leon N. Lindberg and Stuart A. Scheingold, eds., special issue on regional integration, *IO* 24 (Autumn 1970).

[16]Ernst B. Haas, *Beyond the Nation State: Functionalism and International Organization* (Stanford: Stanford University Press, 1964).

[17]In addition to Haas, ibid., see Philippe C. Schmitter, "Three Neo-Functionalist Hypotheses about International Integration," *IO* 23 (Winter 1969); Leon N. Lindberg and Stuart A. Scheingold, *Europe's Would-Be Polity: Patterns of Change in the European Community* (Englewood Cliffs, N.J.: Prentice-Hall, 1970); Joseph S. Nye, *Peace in Parts: Integration and Conflict in Regional Organization* (Boston: Little, Brown, 1971). For a critique of the neofunctionalist model, see Roger D. Hansen "Regional Integration: Reflection on a Decade of Theoretical Efforts," *World Politics* 21 (January 1969).

[18]Henry H. Kerr, Jr., "Changing Attitudes through International Participation: European Parliamentarians and Integration," *IO* 27 (Winter 1973); Peter Wolf, "Interna-

mational expectations of integration theory and then shifted the focus onto a more general concern with how international institutions "reflect and to some extent magnify or modify" the characteristic features of the international system.[19] Here, international organizations have been viewed as potential dispensers of collective legitimacy,[20] vehicles in the international politics of agenda formation,[21] forums for the creation of transgovernmental coalitions as well as instruments of transgovernmental policy coordination,[22] and as means through which the global dominance structure is enhanced or can possibly come to be undermined.[23]

The theme that unifies all works of this genre is that the process of global governance is not coterminous with the activities of international organizations but that these organizations do play some role in that broader process. The objective was to identify their role.

International Regimes

The current preoccupation in the field is with the phenomenon of international regimes. Regimes are broadly defined as governing arrangements constructed by states to coordinate their expectations and organize aspects of international behavior in various issue-

---

tional Organizations and Attitude Change: A Re-examination of the Functionalist Approach," *IO* 27 (Summer 1973); David A. Karns, "The Effect of Interparliamentary Meetings on the Foreign Policy Attitudes of the United States Congressmen," *IO* 31 (Summer 1977); and Ronald Inglehart, "Public Opinion and Regional Integration," *IO* 24 (Autumn 1970).

[19]The phrase is Stanley Hoffmann's in "International Organization and the International System" *IO* 24 (Summer 1970). A similar position was advanced earlier by Oran R. Young, "The United Nations and the International System," *IO* 22 (Autumn 1968).

[20]Inis L. Claude, Jr., "Collective Legitimization as a Political Function of the United Nations," *IO* 20 (Summer 1966); cf. Jerome Slater, "The Limits of Legitimization in International Organizations: The Organization of American States and the Dominican Crisis," *IO* 23 (Winter 1969).

[21]A representative sampling would include Kay and Skolnikoff, eds., special issue, *IO* 26 (Spring 1972); Robert Russell, "Transgovernmental Interaction in the International Monetary System, 1960–1972," *IO* 27 (Autumn 1973); Thomas Weiss and Robert Jordan, "Bureaucratic Politics and the World Food Conference," *World Politics* 28 (April 1976); Raymond F. Hopkins, "The International Role of 'Domestic' Bureaucracy," *IO* 30 (Summer 1976); and John Gerard Ruggie, "On the Problem of 'The Global Problematique': What Roles for International Organizations?" *Alternatives* 5 (January 1980).

[22]The major analytical piece initiating this genre was Robert O. Keohane and Joseph S. Nye, "Transgovernmental Relations and International Organizations," *World Politics* 27 (October 1974); cf. their earlier edited work on transnational relations and world politics, *IO* 25 (Summer 1971).

[23]Robert Cox's recent work has been at the forefront of exploring this aspect of international organization: "Labor and Hegemony," *IO* 31 (Summer 1977); "The Crisis of World Order and the Problem of International Organization in the 1980's," *International Journal* 35 (Spring 1980); and "Gramsci, Hegemony and International Relations: An Essay in Method," *Millenium: Journal of International Studies* 12 (Summer 1983).

areas. They thus comprise a normative element, state practice, and organizational roles.[24] Examples include the trade regime, the monetary regime, the oceans regime, and others. The focus on regimes was a direct response both to the intellectual odyssey that we have just traced as well as to certain developments in the world of international relations from the 1970s on.

When the presumed identity between international organizations and international governance was explicitly rejected, the precise roles of organizations *in* international governance became a central concern. But, apart from the focus on integration, no overarching conception was developed *of* international governance itself. And the integrationists themselves soon abandoned their early notions, ending up with a formulation of integration that did little more than recapitulate the condition of interdependence which was assumed to trigger integration in the first place.[25] Thus, for a time the field of international organization lacked any systematic conception of its traditional analytical core: international governance. The introduction of

the concept of regimes reflected an attempt to fill this void. International regimes were thought to express both the parameters and the perimeters of international governance.[26]

The impact of international affairs during the 1970s and beyond came in the form of an anomaly for which no ready-made explanation was at hand. Important changes occurred in the international system, associated with the relative decline of U.S. hegemony: the achievement of nuclear parity by the Soviet Union; the economic resurgence of Europe and Japan; the success of OPEC together with the severe international economic dislocations that followed it. Specific agreements that had been negotiated after World War II were violated, and institutional arrangements, in money and trade above all, came under enormous strain. Yet—and here is the anomaly—governments on the whole did not respond to the difficulties confronting them in beggar-thy-neighbor terms. Neither systemic factors nor formal institutions alone apparently could account for this outcome. One way to resolve the anomaly was to ques-

---

[24]The most extensive analytical exploration of the concept may be found in Stephen D. Krasner, ed., *International Regimes* (Ithaca, N.Y.: Cornell University Press, 1983), most of which was first published as a special issue of *IO* in Spring 1982. Page references will be to the book.

[25]Robert O. Keohane and Joseph S. Nye, "International Interdependence and Integration," in Fred I. Greenstein and Nelson W. Polsby, eds., *Handbook of Political Science,* vol. 8 (Reading, Mass.: Addison-Wesley, 1975). The point is also implicit in Ernst Haas's self-criticism, "Turbulent Fields and the Theory of Regional Integration," *IO* 30 (Spring 1976).

[26]John Gerard Ruggie, "International Responses to Technology: Concepts and Trends," *IO* 29 (Summer 1975).

tion the extent to which U.S. hegemony in point of fact had eroded.[27] Another, and by no means entirely incompatible route, was via the concept of international regimes. The argument was advanced that regimes continued in some measure to constrain and condition the behavior of states toward one another, despite systemic change and institutional erosion. In this light, international regimes were seen to enjoy a degree of relative autonomy, though of an unknown duration.[28] In sum, in order to resolve both disciplinary and real-world puzzles, the process of international governance has come to be associated with the concept of international regimes, occupying an ontological space somewhere between the level of formal institutions on the one hand and systemic factors on the other. . . .

These shifts in analytical foci of course have never been complete; not everyone in the field at any one time works within the same perspective, and once introduced into the field no perspective ever disappears altogether.

PROBLEMS IN THE PRACTICE OF REGIME ANALYSIS

One of the major criticisms made of the regimes concept is its "wooliness" and "imprecision."[29] The point is well taken. There is no agreement in the literature even on such basic issues as boundary conditions: Where does one regime end and another begin? What is the threshold between nonregime and regime? Embedding regimes in "meta-regimes," or "nesting" one within another, typifies the problem; it does not resolve it.[30] The same is true of the proposal that any set of patterned or conventionalized behavior be considered as prima facie evidence for the existence of a regime.[31]

The only cure for wooliness and imprecision is, of course, to make the concept of regimes less so. Definitions can still be refined, but only up to a point. . . . Ultimately, there exists no external Archimedian point from which regimes can be viewed as they "truly" are. This is so because regimes are conceptual

---

[27]This is the tack taken by Susan Strange, "Still an Extraordinary Power: America's Role in a Global Monetary System," in Raymond E. Lombra and William E. Witte, eds., *Political Economy of International and Domestic Monetary Relations* (Ames: Iowa State University Press, 1982); and Bruce Russett, "The Mysterious Case of Vanishing Hegemony: Or, Is Mark Twain Really Dead?" *IO* 39 (Spring 1985).

[28]See Krasner, "Introduction," *International Regimes,* and Keohane, *After Hegemony,* for discussions of this thesis.

[29]See Susan Strange, in this collection.

[30]This route is taken by Vinod K. Aggarwal, *Liberal Protectionism: The International Politics of Organized Textile Trade* (Berkeley: University of California Press, 1985).

[31]Oran R. Young, "Regime Dynamics: The Rise and Fall of International Regimes," in Krasner, ed., *International Regimes.*

creations, not concrete entities. As with any analytical construction in the human sciences, the concept of regimes will reflect commonsense understandings, actor preferences, and the particular purposes for which analyses are undertaken. Ultimately, therefore, the concept of regimes, like the concept of "power," or "state," or "revolution," will remain a "contestable concept...."[32]

REGIMES AND ORGANIZATIONS

The progressive shift in the literature toward the study of international regimes has been guided by an abiding concern with the structures and processes of international governance. Despite remaining problems with this framework of analysis, . . . a great deal has been accomplished in a relatively short span of time. Along the way, however, . . . international institutions of a formal kind have been left behind. This fact is of academic interest because of the ever-present danger of theory getting out of touch with practice. But it is also of more than academic interest. The secretary general of the United Nations, to cite but one serious practical instance, has lamented that the malfunctioning of that institution seriously inhibits interstate collab-

oration in the peace and security field.[33] This is not the place to take up detailed institutional shortcomings in the world of international organizations. Nor would we be the ones to propose a return to the institutionalist approaches of yesteryear. Nevertheless, in order for the research program of international regimes *both* to contribute to ongoing policy concerns *and* better reflect the complex and sometimes ambiguous policy realm, it is necessary to link up regimes in some fashion with the formal mechanisms through which real-world actors operate. In point of fact, the outlines of such linkages are already implicit in the regime approach.

There has been a great deal of interest in the regimes literature recently in what can be described as the "organizational-design" approach. The key issue underlying this approach is to discern what range of international policy problems can best be handled by different kinds of institutional arrangements, such as simple norms of coordination, the reallocation of international property rights, or authoritative control through formal organizations. For example, an international fishing authority would probably be less appropriate and less able to avoid the early exhaustion of fisheries' stock than would

---

[32]On "contestable concepts," see William Connally, *The Terms of Political Discourse*, 2d ed. (Princeton: Princeton University Press, 1983).

[33]United Nations, *Report of the Secretary-General on the Work of the Organization*, 1982 (A/37/1).

the ascription of exclusive property rights to states. Where problems of liability enter the picture, however, as in ship-based pollution, authoritative procedures for settling disputes would become necessary. The work of Oliver Williamson and William Ouchi is very suggestive here, demonstrating the relative efficacy of the institutionalization of behavior through "hierarchies" versus through transaction-based informal means.[34] Robert Keohane has pioneered this territory in his "functional" theory of international regimes, from which organizational designs can be similarly derived.[35]

Three additional dimensions of the organizational-design issue would be emphasized. The intersubjective basis of international regimes suggests that *transparency* of actor behavior and expectations within regimes is one of their core requirements. And, as has been shown in such diverse issue-areas as international trade, investment, nuclear nonproliferation, and human rights, international organizations can be particularly effective instruments by which to create such transparency.[36] The appropriate design of the mechanisms by which international organizations do so, therefore, should be given every bit as much consideration as the design of the mechanisms of substantive problem solving.

The second is *legitimation*. A regime can be perfectly rationally designed but erode because its legitimacy is undermined.[37] Or a regime that is a logical nonstarter can be

---

[34]Oliver Williamson, *Markets and Hierarchies* (New York: Free, 1975), and William Ouchi and Oliver Williamson, "The Markets and Hierarchies Program of Research: Origins, Implications, Prospects," in William Joyce and Andrew van de Ven, eds., *Organization Design* (New York: Wiley, 1981). From the legal literature, see Guido Calabresi and Douglas Melamed, "Property Rules, Liability Rules, and Inalienability: One View of the Cathedral," *Harvard Law Review* 85 (April 1972); Philip Heyemann, "The Problem of Coordination: Bargaining with Rules," *Harvard Law Review* 86 (March 1973); and Susan Rose-Ackerman, "Inalienability and the Theory of Property Rights," *Columbia Law Review* 85 (June 1985).

[35]Keohane, *After Hegemony*. Some policy recommendations that flow from the approach are spelled out by Robert O. Keohane and Joseph S. Nye, "Two Cheers for Multilateralism," *Foreign Policy* 60 (Fall 1985).

[36]The GATT multilateral surveillance mechanisms are, of course, its chief institutional means of establishing intersubjectively acceptable interpretations of what actors are up to. For a treatment of investment which highlights this dimension, see Charles Lipson, *Standing Guard: Protecting Foreign Capital in the Nineteenth and Twentieth Centuries* (Berkeley: University of California Press, 1985); for nonproliferation, see Nye, "Maintaining a Nonproliferation Regime," and for human rights, John Gerard Ruggie, "Human Rights and the Future International Community," *Daedalus* 112 (Fall 1983). The impact of intergovernmental information systems is analyzed by Ernst B. Haas and John Gerard Ruggie, "What Message in the Medium of Information Systems?" *International Studies Quarterly* 26 (June 1982).

[37]Puchala and Hopkins, "International Regimes," in Krasner, ed., *International Regimes*, discuss the decline of colonialism in terms that include this dimension.

the object of endless negotiations because a significant constituency views its aims to be legitimate.[38] If a regime enjoys both it is described as being "stable" or "hegemonic." The important point to note is that international organizations, because of their trappings of universality, are the major venue within which the global legitimation struggle over international regimes is carried out today. Work in this genre goes back at least to Inis Claude and includes important recent contributions by Robert Cox and Stephen Krasner.[39]

The third dimension we would describe as *epistemic*. Stephen Toulmin has posed the issue well: "The problem of human understanding is a twofold one. Man knows, and he is also conscious that he knows. We acquire, possess, and make use of our knowledge; but at the same time, we are aware of our own activities as knowers."[40] In the international arena, neither the processes whereby knowledge becomes more extensive nor the means whereby reflection on knowledge deepens are passive or automatic. They are intensely political. And for better or for worse, international organizations have maneuvered themselves into the position of being the vehicle through which both types of knowledge enter onto the international agenda.[41] As Ernst Haas has sought to show in his seminal work, in these processes of global epistemic politics lie the seeds of the future demand for international regimes.[42]

In short, the institutional-design approach, complemented by a concern with transparency creation, the legitimation struggle, and epistemic politics, can push the heuristic fruitfulness of the regime research program "forward" yet another step, linking it "back" to the study of international organizations.

---

[38]The New International Economics Order is a prime example.

[39]See Claude, "Collective Legitimization"; Cox, "Labor and Hegemony," "The Crisis of World Order," and "Gramsci, Hegemony, and International Relations"; and Krasner, *Structural Conflict*.

[40]Toulmin, *Human Understanding*, p. 1.

[41]Ruggie analyzes this process in "On the Problem of 'The Global Problematique.'"

[42]Haas, "Words Can Hurt You," and Haas, "Why Collaborate? Issue-Linkage and International Regimes," *World Politics* 32 (April 1980).

3

INTERNATIONAL REGIMES: PROBLEMS OF CONCEPT FORMATION

Oran R. Young

We live in a world of international regimes. Some of them deal with monetary issues (for example, the Bretton Woods system); others govern international trade in commodities (for example, the coffee agreement). Some regimes serve to manage the use of natural resources at the international level (for example, the international arrangements for whaling) or to advance the cause of conservation (for example, the agreement on polar bears). Still other regimes address problems pertaining to the control of armaments at the international level (for example, the partial test-ban system) or to the management of power within the international community (for example, the neutralization agreement for Switzerland). And there are some international regimes that encompass several issues within well-defined geographical areas (for example, the Spitzbergen agreement and the arrangement for Antarctica).

International regimes vary greatly in terms of functional scope, domain, and membership. Functionally, they range from the narrow purview of the polar bear agreement to the broad concerns of the treaties on Antarctica and outer space. The area covered may be as small as the highly restricted domain of the regime for fur seals in the North Pacific or as far-flung as that of the global regimes for international air transport (the ICAO/IATA system) or for the control of nuclear testing. A similar diversity occurs with respect to membership: the range runs from two or three members (as in the regime for high-seas fishing established under the International North Pacific Fisheries Convention) to well over a hundred members (as in the partial nuclear test-ban system). What is most striking, however, is the sheer number of international regimes. Far from being unusual, they are common throughout the international system. . . .

THE CORE CONCEPT

Regimes are social institutions governing the actions of those interested in specifiable activities (or meaningful sets of activities). As such, they are recognized patterns of practice around which expecta-

SOURCE: Oran R. Young, "International Regimes: Problems of Concept Formation," *World Politics*, Vol. 32, No. 3 (April, 1980). Copyright © 1980 by Princeton University Press. Reprinted with permission of Princeton University Press.

tions converge. It follows that regimes are social structures. It is important not to mistake them for functions, though the operation of regimes frequently contributes to the fulfillment of certain functions. Like other structures, regimes may be more or less formally articulated, and they may or may not be accompanied by explicit organizational arrangements.

International regimes pertain to activities of interest to members of the international system. Typically, these activities take place entirely outside the jurisdictional boundaries of sovereign states (for example, deep seabed mining), or cut across international jurisdictional boundaries (for example, high-seas fishing), or involve actions having a direct impact on the interests of two or more members of the international community (for example, major adjustments in exchange rates). In formal terms, the members of international regimes are always sovereign states, though the parties carrying out the actions governed by international regimes are often private entities (for example, fishing companies, banks, or private airlines). Implementing the terms of international regimes therefore involves a two-step procedure, a feature that is not characteristic of regimes at the domestic level.[1]

The mere existence of a regime will lend an element of orderliness to the activity it governs. But there is no reason to assume that regimes will guide human actions toward well-defined substantive goals such as enduring peace, economic efficiency, or maximum sustained yields from renewable resources. The concept "regime" contains no intrinsic metaphysical or teleological orientation, though actors involved in the creation or reform of any given regime will often attempt to shape its contents with clearcut goals in mind.[2] It is, however, possible to enumerate several components that every international regime will possess.

1. The Substantive Component

The core of every international regime is a collection of rights and rules. They may be more or less extensive or formally articulated, but some such institutional arrangements will structure the opportunities of the actors interested in a given activity, and their exact content will be a matter of intense interest to these actors. . . .

Several differentiable categories of rights are prominent in interna-

---

[1]Among other things, it will often prove necessary to rely on domestic courts to enforce the rights and rules incorporated in international regimes. See Richard A. Falk, *The Role of Domestic Courts in the International Legal Order* (Syracuse, N.Y.: Syracuse University Press, 1964).

[2]Actors will virtually never operate behind a Rawlsian "veil of ignorance" in real-world situations. See John Rawls, *A Theory of Justice* (Cambridge: Harvard University Press, 1971), chap. III.

tional regimes. Property rights may take the form of private property rights (for example, rights to commodities traded internationally) or common property rights (for example, rights to airspace or high-seas fisheries).[3] Because of the prevalence of common property arrangements at the international level, international regimes often emphasize the development of use-and-enjoyment rights. These may be exclusive in nature (for example, the right to exploit a given tract on the deep seabed), or they may be explicitly formulated in non-exclusive terms (for example, the right to use certain international straits).[4] But all such rights are designed to ensure the availability of key resources to actors under conditions in which private ownership is infeasible. International regimes may also encompass an assortment of other types of rights, including the right to protection against certain forms of aggression, the right to receive specified benefits from international transactions or productive operations, the right to trade on favorable terms with other members of the international community, and the right to participate in making collective decisions under the terms of a given regime. . . .

. . . In some societies, for instance, there are near-universal rules enjoining individuals to tell the truth and to keep promises in their dealings with other members of the society. A rule may be directed toward some clearly designated group, as in the case of ethical prescriptions relating to the behavior of teachers, doctors, or lawyers. Or a rule may focus on some specific activity, as in the case of prescriptions pertaining to civil aviation or maritime commerce. Of course, the existence of an acknowledged rule does not guarantee that the members of the subject group will always comply with its requirements. Even in well-ordered societies, noncompliance with rules is a common occurrence.

Among the numerous rules associated with international regimes, three general categories are particularly prominent. First, there are use rules. For example, members of the ICAO/IATA system are required to follow certain safety rules in using international airspace; those engaged in high seas fishing should abide by rules pertaining to the conservation of fish stocks; and those using international sea lanes are subject to rules designed to maximize safety and to minimize marine pollution. Frequently, such use rules take the form of limitations on the exercise of rights. Just as rights commonly safeguard the

---

[3]Consult, among others, Eirik Furubotn and Svetozar Pejovich, "Property Rights and Economic Theory: A Survey of Recent Literature," *Journal of Economic Literature*, x, No. 4 (1972), 1137–62.

[4]The result might be described as a system of "restricted" common property; see J. H. Dales, *Pollution, Property, and Prices* (Toronto: University of Toronto Press, 1968), 61–65.

freedom of actors to behave in certain ways, rules often spell out restrictions on the freedom of actors to do as they wish.[5] Liability rules constitute a second category. They spell out the locus and extent of liability in cases of (usually unintended) injury to others arising from the actions of individual parties under the terms of a regime. They range from rules concerning compensation for expropriation of foreign investments under various circumstances to rules pertaining to responsibility for cleaning up maritime environments in the wake of accidents.[6] Finally, international regimes often specify a variety of procedural rules, which deal with the handling of disputes or the operation of explicit organizations associated with the regimes. . . .

Regulations and incentive systems will be used less extensively in conjunction with international regimes than with regimes operating at the national or subnational level. They require the existence of some public agency possessing a measure of authority and power; such agencies are far less characteristic of highly decentralized social systems like the international system than of the more centralized

systems that are common at the national level. Nevertheless, international regimes accompanied by explicit organizations can and sometimes do employ these devices. For example, the International Monetary Fund has promulgated extensive regulations pertaining to the drawing rights of individual members, and the proposed International Seabed Authority would be able to regulate production of manganese nodules to implement more general rules concerning such matters as the impact of deep seabed mining on the world nickel market.[7]

2. The Procedural Component

Although collections of rights and rules form the substantive core of international regimes, they are not the only components of such regimes. A procedural component encompasses recognized arrangements for resolving situations requiring social or collective choices. Situations of this type arise whenever it is necessary or desirable to aggregate the (non-identical) preferences of two or more individual actors into a group choice.[8] Such problems occur in most social sys-

---

[5]See G. H. von Wright, *Norm and Actions* (New York: Humanities Press, 1963).

[6]On liability rules and their significance, compare R. H. Coase, "The Problem of Social Cost," *Journal of Law and Economics,* III (October 1960), 1–44, and Guido Calabresi and A. Douglas Melamed, "Property Rules, Liability Rules, and Inalienability: One View of the Cathedral," *Harvard Law Review,* Vol. 85 (April 1972), 1089–1128.

[7]See, for example, Robert Z. Aliber, *The International Money Game* (New York: Basic Books, 1976).

[8]For a general analysis of social choice, see A. K. Sen, *Collective Choice and Social Welfare* (San Francisco: Freeman, 1970).

tems; they range from the selection of individuals to fill top positions to establishing the terms of trade for exchange relationships and deciding on the distribution of valued goods and services.

Several types of problems requiring social choices can be expected to arise within the framework of an operative international regime.[9] Some of these will involve the allocation of factors of production (for example, deep seabed mining tracts, total allowable catches in the fisheries, and segments of the global radio spectrum). Such problems will be especially difficult to solve at the international level due to the prevalence of common rather than private property. Other social choice problems will relate to issues with explicit distributive implications (for example, decisions relating to adjustments in exchange rates or royalties in connection with deep seabed mining). Collective choices will also be required in settling disputes. Typically, these will arise from efforts to apply general rights and rules to the complexities of real-world situations. Nor does this exhaust the range of problems of social choice that can be expected to emerge continually under the terms of international regimes. Thus, there will be cases in which group decisions are necessary to determine the sorts of research activities to permit in an area like Antarctica,

to resolve conflicts between different uses of the same resource, and to organize collective sanctions aimed at obtaining compliance with the rights and rules of an international regime.

Social choice mechanisms are institutional arrangements specialized to the resolution of problems of social choice arising within the framework of particular regimes. Like other components of regimes, these mechanisms may be more or less formalized, and it is typical for a regime to make use of several at the same time. The range of these mechanisms is wide, encompassing such devices as the "law of capture," markets, voting systems, bargaining, administrative decision making, adjudication, unilateral action backed by coercion, and organized violence.[10] Certain conditions are required for the effective operation of each of these mechanisms; we may therefore assume that individual mechanisms will be associated primarily with particular types of social systems. The most striking features of the international system in this connection are its relatively small number of formal members and its high level of decentralization with respect to the distribution of power and authority. Social choice mechanisms characteristic of systems of this type are the "law of capture," bargaining, various forms of coercion,

---

[9]Problems of social choice pertaining to the selection and reform of international regimes *per se* are discussed in a later section of this essay.

[10]The classic study (focusing on voting systems) is Kenneth Arrow, *Social Choice and Individual Values* (2d ed.; New York: Wiley, 1963).

and, to a lesser degree, markets. We should therefore expect important problems of social choice arising in international regimes to be handled through these procedures.[11] Still, procedures involving voting and administrative decision making will not be altogether absent in international regimes. Voting, for example, is of some significance in cases like the International Monetary Fund and the ICAO/IATA system. But there can be no doubt that unilateral claims, bargaining, and coercion are central to the processes of reaching social choices within most international regimes.

It is also worth noting that some regimes do not possess social choice mechanisms of their own. They may rely upon the institutional arrangements of larger social structures in dealing with problems of social choice, or they may share mechanisms with other regimes. Such situations are common in cases where adjudication or voting is employed in reaching collective choices. For example, the same courts may resolve conflicts of interest pertaining to civil liberties, business activities, and land use. In principle, the International Court of Justice of the General Assembly of the United Nations could be employed to deal with many social choice problems arising under specific international regimes. In practice, however, various combinations of bargaining and coercion geared to the problems of specific regimes constitute the norm at the international level.

3. Implementation

Smoothly functioning international regimes are difficult to achieve.[12] Rights are not always respected, and even widely acknowledged rules are violated with some frequency. Nor is it reasonable to assume that the relevant actors will simply accept the outcomes generated by social choice mechanisms as authoritative, and abide by them. Accordingly, it is important to think about the effectiveness of international regimes,[13] and this suggests an examination of compliance mechanisms as a third major component of these regimes.

Any discussion of compliance must deal with the issue of incentives. What are the benefits and costs of complying with rights and rules, in contrast to violating them? How do individual actors decide whether to comply with the substantive provisions of international regimes? There is a tendency to assume that the typical actor will vi-

---

[11]Young, "Anarchy and Social Choice: Reflections on the International Polity," *World Politics*, xxx (January 1978), 241–63.

[12]That is, reality seldom approximates the condition of "perfect compliance" discussed in Rawls (fn. 2), 351.

[13]For a similar observation about domestic problems, see A. Myrick Freeman, "Environmental Management as a Regulatory Process," Discussion Paper D-4, *Resources for the Future,* January 1977.

olate such provisions so long as the probability of being caught in specific instances is low—a line of reasoning which implies that the availability of effective enforcement procedures is essential to the achievement of compliance. But this argument appears to be quite wide of the mark in many real-world situations. It is not difficult to identify circumstances in which considerations of self-interest will lead to compliance, especially in conjunction with long-run perspectives on iterative behavior. Further, there is no reason to assume that individual actors make large numbers of discrete benefit/cost calculations relating to compliance with the provisions of international regimes. Actors will often develop general rules or policies in this realm, and it seems reasonable to expect that long-term socialization as well as feelings of obligation will play an important role in the articulation of these rules.[14]

A compliance mechanism is any institution or set of institutions publicly authorized to pursue compliance with the substantive provisions of a regime, or with the outcomes generated by its social choice mechanisms. The image that comes to mind here is one of formal governmental agencies, and such agencies are no doubt the classic institutions specializing in the achievement of compliance. But less formal compliance mechanisms are common, and highly decentralized social systems, such as the international system, typically rely upon them.[15] The result is apt to be a heavy emphasis on self-interest calculations coupled with publicly recognized procedures for self-help in the redress of wrongs.[16] Alternatively, the outcome may involve reliance on arrangements in which explicit agencies are employed to gather information and to inspect the actions of individual actors, but decentralized procedures are retained for the application of sanctions (for example, the ICAO/IATA system and many of the regional fisheries regimes).[17]

From the point of view of the members of a regime, the development of compliance mechanisms poses an investment problem. Any expenditure of resources on such mechanisms will generate opportunity costs, and declining marginal returns from such investments will virtually always become pronounced before perfect compliance

[14]For an intriguing empirical example, see Abram Chayes, "An Enquiry into the Workings of Arms Control Agreements," *Harvard Law Review,* Vol. 85, No. 5 (1975), 905–69.

[15]Young, *Compliance and Public Authority, A Theory with International Applications* (Baltimore: The Johns Hopkins University Press, 1979), esp. chaps. 4 and 5.

[16]For empirical examples, see Lucy Mair, *Primitive Government* (Bloomington, Ind.: Indiana University Press, 1977), esp. chap. 1.

[17]Ronald S. Tauber, "The Enforcement of IATA Agreements," *Harvard International Law Journal,* x, No. 1 (1969), 1–33.

is reached. Accordingly, it is safe to assume that the members of a regime will rarely attempt to develop compliance mechanisms capable of eliminating violations altogether. Exactly where equilibrium will occur with respect to these investment decisions depends on the assumptions made about the members of international regimes. In view of the decentralization of responsibility that goes with the decentralization of power and authority in the international system, however, it seems safe to conclude that underinvestment in compliance mechanisms will be characteristic of international regimes.[18] Still, various types of compliance mechanisms do occur at the international level,[19] and such mechanisms must be accepted as a third major component of international regimes.

Several clarifying observations are in order in closing this section. It is possible to argue that some regime must always be present with respect to any given activity: regimes can vary greatly in extent, and extreme cases can simply be treated as null regimes. Thus, the arrangement for high-seas fishing prior to World War II might be described as a regime based on unrestricted common property and the procedure known as the "law of capture," rather than as a situation lacking any operative regime.[20] But this line of reasoning leads to serious problems. Sometimes activities are initiated *de novo* in the absence of prior experience (for example, international satellite broadcasting or deep seabed mining). In such cases, we would have to develop some fictions about latent or tacit regimes to avoid the conclusion that there are situations in which no regime is present. Further, existing regimes sometimes break down, leaving a confused and inchoate situation with respect to some activity (for example, the current situation regarding the territorial sea).[21] Here too, the concept would have to be stretched excessively to assert the continued existence of a regime. Additionally, avoiding the temptation to assume the presence of some

---

[18]International regimes, like other social institutions, will ordinarily exhibit the attributes of collective goods (that is, non-excludability and jointness of supply) to a high degree. For further discussion of the problems of supplying collective goods, see Mancur Olson, Jr., *The Logic of Collective Action* (Cambridge: Harvard University Press, 1965).

[19]For a variety of examples, see William T. Burke, Richard Legatski, and William W. Woodhead, *National and International Law Enforcement in the Ocean* (Seattle: University of Washington Press, 1975).

[20]Francis T. Christy and Anthony Scott, *The Common Wealth in Ocean Fisheries* (Baltimore: The Johns Hopkins University Press, 1965).

[21]For the background of earlier efforts to reach agreement on a regime for the territorial sea, consult Philip C. Jessup, "The United Nations Conference on the Law of the Sea," in *Essays on International Law from the Columbia Law Review* (New York: Columbia University Press, 1965), 197–231.

regime in conjunction with every specifiable activity will facilitate later discussions of the origins of regimes and of regime transformation.

In analyzing international regimes, there is a tendency to focus on highly coherent and internally consistent constructs. Yet, real-world regimes are typically unsystematic and ambiguous, incorporating elements derived from several analytic constructs. This divergence between the ideal types articulated by students of regimes and the more inchoate regimes in operation in real-world situations is partly attributable to misunderstandings by those who make decisions about regimes. Much of it, however, arises from two other factors. The development of an international regime usually involves intense bargaining and the hammering out of critical compromises among the interested actors. . . . Furthermore, international regimes generally evolve and change over time in response to various economic and political pressures. This is true even of regimes initially formulated comprehensively in some sort of "constitutional" contract. With the passage of time, regimes generally acquire additional features and become less consistent internally. The point of these remarks is neither to criticize existing regimes nor to argue that the examination of ideal types is unimportant in conjunction with the development of international regimes. But a failure to bear in mind the distinction between ideal types and reality is bound to lead to confusion.[22]

Finally, there is a difference between the conditions required for the effective operation of an international regime and the consequences resulting from its operation. To illustrate, consider a regime governing international trade in some commodity based on private property rights and a competitive market. The conditions necessary to ensure effective operation of such a regime include the availability of information about potential trades, a willingness to accept the terms of trade dictated by the market, and an absence of natural monopolies.[23] The consequences of the operation of the regime, by contrast, relate to the extent to which it yields economically efficient outcomes; the degree to which it produces social costs or neighborhood effects; the attractiveness of the results in distributive terms; and so forth. Both the conditions for operation and the consequences of operation are central issues in the analysis of international regimes. But it is important to differentiate clearly between them, as well as to

---

[22]On the relationship between ideal types and reality, with special reference to the theory of games, see Anatol Rapoport, *Two-Person Game Theory* (Ann Arbor: University of Michigan Press, 1966), 186–214.

[23]For a succinct and clearly written discussion of such conditions, see Robert Haveman, *The Economics of the Public Sector* (New York: Wiley, 1976), 22–27.

bear in mind that both these issues are separable from efforts to characterize the institutional content of an international regime.

REGIMES IN OPERATION

Having examined the analytic content of the concept "regime," with special reference to the international system, let me turn to some of the major features of regimes as they occur in real-world situations.

1. Varieties of Regimes

Variety with respect to extent, formality, direction, and coherence is a prominent feature of international regimes. Sometimes these differences are attributable to underlying philosophical orientations. For example, regimes resting on socialist premises will encompass more extensive collections of rules as well as more explicit efforts to direct behavior toward the achievement of goals than *laissez-faire* regimes that emphasize decentralized decision making and autonomy for individual actors. In other cases, variations arise from the character of specific bargains struck in the processes of setting up regimes, or from the particular patterns of institutional evolution over time.

The extent of a regime is a matter of the number and restrictiveness of its rights and rules. At one extreme is the case of unlimited *laissez-faire,* in which the actors are completely free to do as they please without even the constraints of a system of property or use rights.[24] At the other extreme are arrangements emphasizing central planning and detailed rules governing the actions of individual members. Between these extremes lie various mixed cases that are differentiable in terms of the extent to which they include rights and rules restricting the autonomy of the actors. International regimes tend to be less restrictive than domestic ones, but they do not generally approximate the extreme of unlimited *laissez-faire*.

International regimes vary greatly in the extent to which they are laid out in formal agreements, conventions, or treaties. For example, the current regime for Antarctica is formalized to a greater degree than the neutralization arrangements for Switzerland. As in domestic settings, moreover, it is common for informal understandings to arise within the framework established by the formal structure of an international regime. Such understandings may serve either to provide interpretations of ambiguous aspects of the formal arrangements (for example, the notion of maximum sustained yield in conjunction with the marine fisheries),

---

[24]A regime for some natural resource with no private property rights, no liability rules, and allocation based on the principle known as the "law of capture" might approximate this extreme case.

or to supplement formal arrangements by dealing with issues that they fail to cover (for example, the treatment of nuclear technology under the terms of the partial nuclear test-ban regime). Though it may be helpful, formalization is clearly not a necessary condition for the effective operation of international regimes. There are informal regimes that have been generally successful, and there are formal arrangements that have produced unimpressive results (for example, several of the commodity agreements).[25]

Regimes are directed to the extent that they exert pressure on their members to act in conformity with some clear-cut social goal. Various goals are feasible—including economic efficiency, the preservation of ecosystems, distributive justice, and so forth. Even where there is agreement in principle about the pursuit of some social goal, however, it may prove difficult to meet under real-world conditions. For example, the goal of "optimum" yield with respect to the marine fisheries is notoriously difficult to fulfill in reality.[26] Additionally, when a regime is directed toward the achievement of several goals at once, close attention must

be paid to the determination of trade-offs among these goals.[27] In the absence of systematic efforts to construct trade-off functions, any apparent directedness of a regime encompassing two or more distinct goals will be an illusion.

Coherence refers to the degree to which the elements of an international regime are internally consistent. Severe internal contradictions are common in real-world regimes, even in cases where they have been articulated in more or less explicit "constitutional" contracts. For example, there are often contradictions between use rights for marine resources and rights vested in adjacent coastal states to exclude outsiders. Similarly, conflicts commonly arise between the alleged requirements of indivisible state sovereignty and the obligations imposed by the rules of international regimes. It is not hard to account for these elements of incoherence in terms of the compromises necessary to achieve initial acceptance of a regime, or in terms of the piecemeal evolution of regimes over time in response to changing political, economic, and social forces. But the widespread occurrence of incoherence means that we must beware of relying too heavily on

---

[25]United Nations, *International Compensation for Fluctuations in Commodity Trade* (New York: United Nations, 1961).

[26]P. A. Larkin, "An Epitaph for the Concept of Maximum Sustained Yield," *Transactions of the American Fisheries Society,* Vol. 106 (January 1977), 1–11.

[27]On the economic approach to such trade-offs, see Richard Zeckhauser and Elmer Shaefer, "Public Policy and Normative Economic Theory," in Raymond A. Bauer and Kenneth J. Gergen, eds., *The Study of Policy Formation* (New York: Free Press, 1968), 27–101.

neat analytic constructs in interpreting real-world situations, and that we must learn to cope with the existence of contradictions.

2. Explicit Organization

All regimes, even highly decentralized private-enterprise arrangements, are social institutions, but they need not be accompanied by explicit organizational arrangements with their own personnel, budgets, physical facilities, and so forth. Effective regimes lacking explicit organizational arrangements are common to "primitive" societies,[28] but they are by no means confined to societies of this type. For example, free-enterprise systems making use of competitive markets are classic cases of social institutions performing vital functions in society in the absence of explicit organization.[29] Many other social institutions—such as those governing manners, dress, and intergenerational relations—serve to structure behavior effectively with little need for explicit organization. Although it is undoubtedly true that international regimes characteristically involve fewer explicit organizational arrangements than domestic regimes, it is important not to carry this generalization too far. The explicit organizations associated with the international monetary regime are certainly not trivial, and the organizational arrangements contemplated in conjunction with the International Seabed Authority are quite complex.

Even where a need for explicit organization is apparent, regimes may make use of organizational structures created for other purposes, or associated with a more comprehensive public authority, in preference to establishing autonomous arrangements of their own. Such situations are common at the domestic level: regimes regularly turn over tasks that involve information gathering, inspection, dispute settlement, and enforcement to agencies specializing in these matters, so that they will not require court systems or police forces of their own. At the international level, this practice appears to be far less common. Situations in which substantive regimes could benefit from such arrangements occur frequently enough. For example, arms-control regimes could make use of more general inspection procedures, and the ICAO/IATA system could rely on some larger authority to enforce its rules.[30] But comprehensive organizational capabilities are either lacking or severely underdeveloped in the international community. Thus, the United Nations is hardly capable of inspecting activities carried out under the regime for Antarctica or resolving disputes per-

---

[28]Mair (fn. 16), Part I.

[29]See Haveman (fn. 23), 21, for a description of markets in precisely these terms.

[30]See Richard A. Falk and Richard Barnet, eds., *Security in Disarmament* (Princeton: Princeton University Press, 1965), as well as Tauber (fn. 17).

taining to deep seabed mining. In the international system, therefore, individual regimes are not tightly linked, even though they often lack extensive organizational arrangements in their own right.

Perhaps the most obvious and compelling reason to endow regimes with explicit organizational arrangements is to resolve problems of interpretation and dispute settlement.[31] But there are several other tasks that are difficult to accomplish without such organizations. For instance, it may be desirable to conduct research and to monitor various activities in order to determine whether rights and rules need to be adjusted to deal with changing conditions. Such problems are common with respect to the management of fisheries, the stabilization of commodity trade, and the handling of oil spills. Whenever revenues must be collected and disposed of, some organizational arrangements will be required. For example, a regime for deep seabed mining that requires leaseholders to make regular royalty payments can hardly function without some organization to handle the resultant funds. Moreover, explicit organizational arrangements often become important in dealing with problems of social choice and compliance that are outside the realm of dispute settlement. The exploitation of fish stocks purely on the basis of the "law of capture" requires no explicit organization, but the need for organization arises as soon as regulations limiting harvests, quotas, or entry schemes are introduced. The same holds true of compliance. Some regimes (for example, the partial test-ban regime) are able to resolve their basic problems of compliance without creating explicit organizations. But with the introduction of systematic surveillance or formal sanctions, the establishment of explicit organizations becomes a necessity.

The emergence of explicit organizational arrangements raises a range of classic questions that are just as pressing at the international as at the domestic level. How much autonomy, vis-à-vis other centers of authority in the social system, should the organizations possess? What sorts of decision rules and procedures should be adopted in conjunction with these organizations? How much discretion should the organizations have to make changes that affect the substantive content or the procedural character of the regime itself? How should the organizations be financed: where should their revenues come from, and how should they be raised? How should the organizations be staffed? What sorts of physical facilities should the organizations have, and where should these facil-

---

[31]This is, for example, the classic argument developed by Locke and similar contractarians concerning the origins of government. See John Locke, *The Second Treatise of Government,* paragraphs 123–131.

ities be located? The answers to all these questions can affect the impact that any given regime has on its members. It is therefore to be expected that these issues will be fought over vigorously—not only at the outset, but also during the whole period over which the regime is effective. To the extent that explicit organizational arrangements are less important in international regimes than in domestic ones, this sort of contention will be less pervasive at the international level. Nevertheless, it is impossible to make sense out of recent negotiations relating to international monetary arrangements, deep seabed mining, or the allocation of the broadcast frequency spectrum without paying careful attention to these questions of organizational design.[32]

3. Policy Instruments

Policy instruments are elements of regimes that are subject to deliberate or planned manipulation in the interests of achieving social goals. Such instruments can operate at different levels of generality. Thus, changes in bundles of property rights, the introduction of restrictive regulations, and decisions concerning individual applications for loans or mining licenses may all be treated as matters involving the use of policy instruments, but they obviously address problems occurring at different levels of generality. Policy instruments are also apt to be articulated in terms that are specific to individual regimes or types of regimes. Thus, the determination of allowable catches, as well as decisions concerning the opening and closing of harvest areas, are standard issues involving policy instruments in fisheries regimes. Adjustments of exchange rates or the issuance of broadcast licenses are common policy instruments in other regimes.[33]

At the international level, a key distinction concerns the extent to which the use of policy instruments requires the existence of explicit organizational arrangements. For example, it is possible to redefine the contents of rights and rules at occasional assemblies of the members of a regime; it may even be possible to do so by means of unilateral actions on the part of some members of a regime to which others subsequently conform on a *de facto* basis. Policy instruments of this sort will have an obvious appeal in highly decentralized social systems. This appeal may account for the current tendency to respond to problems relating to international maritime regimes by redrawing jurisdictional boundaries (that is, shifting from the domain of international com-

---

[32]See, for example, Michael Hardy, "The Implications of Alternative Solutions for Regulating the Exploitation of Seabed Minerals," *International Organization*, XXXI, No. 2 (1977), 313–42.

[33]For further discussion, see Giandomenico Majone, "Choice among Policy Instruments for Pollution Control," *Policy Analysis*, II (Fall 1976), 589–613.

mon property to the domain of national property) rather than by agreeing to specific rules for the use of common property resources at the international level.[34] Jurisdictional changes can be pursued unilaterally; they do not generate requirements for new international organizations. The creation of use rules for common property resources, by contrast, is apt to require the development of explicit organizations, though the results produced may be more equitable than those arising from shifts in jurisdictional boundaries.[35]

Nonetheless, policy instruments suitable for use by explicit organizations are not altogether lacking in connection with international regimes. The International Whaling Commission has the authority to adjust annual harvest quotas for individual species of great whales. The International Monetary Fund can lay down specific conditions in granting loans to countries experiencing currency problems. The International Coffee Agreement allows for the allocation of export shares among its members. And the International Seabed Authority would be able to make use of a relatively complex system of permits and licenses to regulate the production of manganese nodules from the deep seabed. The ability of these organizations to reach autonomous decisions about the use of such instruments may be severely limited. Moreover, compliance can become a major problem in the use of such instruments (for example, export quotas for coffee).[36] But these facts do not suggest a qualitative distinction between the use of policy instruments in international regimes and their use in domestic regimes.[37] In short, though the use of these instruments is limited by the characteristic weaknesses of explicit organizations associated with international regimes, the instruments are by no means irrelevant at the international level.

REGIME DYNAMICS

Like other social institutions, international regimes are products of human interactions and the convergence of expectations among groups of interested actors. They are not autonomous entities waiting

---

[34]Recent changes in regimes for marine fisheries arising from unilateral extensions of jurisdiction on the part of coastal states exemplify this prospect. In the case of the United States, the transition was accomplished through the passage of the Fishery Conservation and Management Act of 1976 (PL 94–265).

[35]For a case in point, consult the analysis of the proposed International Seabed Authority, in Young, "International Resource Regimes."

[36]Bart S. Fisher, "Enforcing Export Quota Commodity Agreements," *Harvard International Law Journal,* XII, No. 3 (1971), 401–35.

[37]It is not necessary to subscribe to Marxian precepts to realize that domestic as well as international regimes may be heavily influenced by actors who are, in principle, subject to regulation under the terms of these regimes. In fact, this is the central insight of the "capture" theory of regulation.

to be discovered by actors searching for institutional arrangements to govern their activities. Nor are they like natural rights, possessing some normative status independent of the evaluations of the affected actors.

It is significant that regimes arise from the actions of *groups* of actors.[38] Sometimes social institutions of this type emerge and function effectively without any deliberate effort on the part of individual participants. That is the idea underlying the "invisible hand" conception of markets, in which it is suggested that groups of individuals— each vigorously pursuing his own self-interest—will interact in such a way as to produce socially desirable outcomes (for example, economic efficiency). But invisible-hand mechanisms cannot generally be counted on to yield effective international regimes. The conditions necessary to produce such outcomes are highly specialized even in the realm of straightforward economic transactions.[39] In the international arena, the pursuit of individual self-interest commonly leads to outcomes that are socially undesirable; even conscious efforts to coordinate the actions of individual actors frequently run afoul of severe conflicts of interest.[40]

Since regimes are human arti-facts, there will be no physical barriers to their creation and reform. But change—especially guided change—is not necessarily easy to achieve in this realm. Social institutions frequently prove resistant to change, even when they generate outcomes that are widely regarded as undesirable. Existing institutions are familiar constructs, while new arrangements require actors to learn unfamiliar procedures and to accept (initially) unknown outcomes. Further, guided change requires not only the destruction of existing institutions, but also the coordination of expectations around some new focal point. In view of the prevalence of conflicts of interest regarding problems of international coordination, it is fair to assume that a convergence of expectations around new institutional arrangements will often be slow in coming. What is more, social institutions are complex entities, which typically encompass a number of informal as well as formal elements. Consequently, deliberate efforts to adjust a regime run the risk of doing more harm than good; they may produce disruptive consequences that were neither foreseen nor intended by those advocating the specific changes. Although not all initiatives along these lines are doomed to failure,

---

[38]Compare this view with the analysis of conventions in David K. Lewis, *Convention: A Philosophical Study* (Cambridge: Harvard University Press, 1969).

[39]For a more optimistic assessment of invisible-hand mechanisms see Robert Nozick, *Anarchy, State, and Utopia* (New York: Basic Books, 1974), 18–25.

[40]Thomas C. Schelling, "On the Ecology of Micromotives," *The Public Interest*, No. 25 (Fall 1971), 61–98.

naive hopes concerning the efficacy of social engineering in this realm abound among policy makers and students of international relations alike.[41]

1. Origins of Regimes

It is helpful to differentiate three channels or tracks in the emergence of international regimes. There is, to begin with, the contractarian track. The actors interested in some activity (or their authorized representatives) may meet for the explicit purpose of negotiating a "constitutional" contract laying out a regime to govern the activity in question.[42] The regime for Antarctica that was agreed upon in 1959 exemplifies this track; the effort to work out a comprehensive international regime for the oceans constitutes a far more ambitious attempt to engage in regime construction on a contractarian basis.[43]

An alternative approach can be described as the evolutionary track: social institutions sometimes arise either from widespread practice over time or as a consequence of dramatic unilateral actions that are subsequently accepted by others on a *de facto* basis. In general, regimes governing the use of marine resources have traditionally originated in this fashion. More specifically, the post-1945 regime for the continental shelves exemplifies this pattern.[44]

In an intermediate process of regime construction, which might be labeled the piecemeal track, actors sometimes reach agreement on one or more components of a regime without entering into a comprehensive social contract regarding the activity in question. A common justification for this approach rests on the (dubious) argument that the introduction of one or several regime components will initiate a process of task expansion or "spillover" that will lead over time to the emergence of a more comprehensive and coherent regime.[45] Prominent ex-

---

[41]This point of view may seem conservative (in the Burkean sense), but surely it is more than that. There are similar themes in many of the anarchist criticisms of Marxian or authoritarian socialism, as well as in many contemporary expressions of libertarianism. Skepticism about the efficacy of social engineering, therefore, is not a good indicator of ideological orientation.

[42]On the concept of a "constitutional" contract, see James M. Buchanan, *The Limits of Liberty* (Chicago: University of Chicago Press, 1975), esp. chap. 4.

[43]Howard Taubenfeld, "A Treaty for Antarctica," *International Conciliation,* No. 531 (1961), and Edward Miles, "The Structure and Effects of the Decision Process in the Seabed Committee and the Third United Nations Conference on the Law of the Sea," *International Organization,* XXXI, No. 2 (1977), 159–234.

[44]Note that it was formalized or codified in the 1958 Geneva Convention on the Outer Continental Shelf. For relevant background, see Jessup (fn. 21).

[45]Leon Lindberg and Stuart Scheingold, eds., *Regional Integration: Theory and Practice* (Cambridge: Harvard University Press, 1971).

amples of this piecemeal track at the international level include many of the regional fisheries regimes (for example, ICNAF or INPFC), as well as the institutional arrangements relating to marine pollution.

There can be no doubt that the evolutionary track will be followed more often than the contractarian track in highly decentralized social systems like the international system. These systems lack authoritative procedures for dealing with regimes; it is often difficult even to determine the pertinent set of actors to deal with the development of a regime. At the same time, group size undoubtedly makes a difference within the class of highly decentralized systems. It is possible to identify cases in which small groups of actors have been able to reach contractarian bargains even in highly decentralized systems, but such bargains are extremely difficult to reach in systems that are both highly decentralized and large with respect to number of members. To illustrate, the 12 original signatories to the Antarctica Treaty of 1959 were able to reach agreement on a relatively comprehensive regime for Antarctica, but in the United Nations Conference on the Law of the Sea (UNCLOS) the combination of decentralization and large numbers led to fundamental difficulties in working out a meaningful "constitutional" contract covering the oceans.

Does it make a difference whether the institutional arrangements governing a given activity emerge along one or another of these tracks? Contractarian processes offer the distinct advantage of producing explicit arrangements that are incorporated into documents (such as treaties or conventions) which become part of the public record available for consultation. But the articulation on a "constitutional" contract is not always an unmixed blessing, even when it is politically feasible to persuade the actors to accept it. Agreements of this type may be explicit, but they are frequently couched in ambiguous language designed to obscure irreconcilable conflicts of interest among the actors.[46] Moreover, actors frequently indicate superficial acquiescence in arrangements to which they do not intend to abide in practice. In such cases, the promulgation of a "constitutional" contract purporting to spell out a regime for some activity will not only generate confusion; it is also apt to breed disillusionment and cynicism among the members of the relevant social system. Despite their obvious initial drawbacks, international regimes emerging from evolutionary

---

[46]On the resulting problems of treaty interpretation in international law, see Myres S. McDougal, Harold D. Lasswell, and James C. Miller, *The Interpretation of Agreements and World Order* (New Haven: Yale University Press, 1967).

processes may yield results that are preferable to those arising from a contractarian approach gone sour.

In the piecemeal approach, the critical issue concerns the likelihood that the introduction of one or several regime components will actually generate substantial task expansion of "spillover." Although the approach seems to offer opportunities for deliberate or planned development of international regimes where contractarian procedures are politically infeasible,[47] actual experience is not reassuring. With respect to regional economic and political integration, where the notion has been investigated most thoroughly, the available evidence offers no assurance that the logic of functionalism can be counted on to yield significant results.[48] What is more, the piecemeal track may lead to severe problems of incoherence when little spillover occurs: it may leave a trail of half-formed regimes with little if anything to recommend them.

2. Regime Transformation

International regimes do not become static constructs even after they are fully developed. They undergo continuous transformation in response to shifts in their political, economic, and social environments. Significant alterations may occur with respect to the content of a regime's rights and rules, the character of its social choice mechanisms, or the nature of its compliance mechanisms. It would be arbitrary to identify some critical point of transition at which such alterations yield a qualitative change in the sense of one regime disappearing and another one taking its place. Rather, my objective in this discussion is to identify the processes through which international regimes change, and to comment on institutional procedures for handling these changes.

It is possible to differentiate several types of pressure for transformation in international regimes. In some cases, there are fundamental changes in the nature of the relevant activity. For example, shifts from light to heavy usage have generated major problems for traditional regimes in the marine fisheries; and the advent of communications satellites has raised significant problems affecting the preexisting regime for international broadcasting. In other cases, pressures for change arise from the dissatisfaction of some actor or class of actors with the distributive consequences of a prevailing regime. The unilateral imposition in recent years of 200-mile fishery jurisdictions on the part of numerous coastal states constitutes a dramatic illustration

---

[47]The classic early expression of this reasoning appears in David Mitrany, *A Working Peace System* (London: Royal Institute of International Affairs, 1943).

[48]Leon Lindberg and Stuart Scheingold, *Europe's Would-Be Polity* (Englewood Cliffs, N.J.: Prentice-Hall, 1970).

of this type of regime change. A third type of pressure for major alterations is a desire to introduce a systematic or coherent regime to replace a chaotic or inchoate regime. The basic idea here is to streamline or rationalize a regime that has grown ambiguous or contradictory in the course of evolution.[49]. . .

Regimes frequently anticipate pressures for change through the articulation of transformation rules. These are institutional arrangements specifying how pressures for change are to be treated, what steps must be taken to bring about alterations in a regime, and what decision rule is to be employed as a standard for determining when proposed changes are to be accepted. Transformation rules may vary greatly with respect to their stringency (the extent to which they make it easy or difficult to get alterations accepted), and there is no reason to assume that those wishing to change a regime will always abide by the terms of such rules. Nevertheless, the existence of a set of transformation rules—even if they are not always followed in practice—is likely to structure efforts to alter regimes. Regardless of the precise content of the rules, they will not be neutral in their impact on the interests of the actors affected by a regime.[50] Transfor-

mation rules will determine what skills (such as bargaining, legislative coalition building, legal reasoning) will be essential in efforts to alter a given regime, and actors will never be equal in the possession of these skills, or ease of access to them. It follows that the promulgation of transformation rules for an international regime will be treated as an important matter, and that members of the regime will promote the acceptance of rules they expect to favor their own interests over time.

Guided reform of social institutions is a difficult process in all social systems, especially in the presence of rapid political, economic, and social changes. But the difficulties are unusually severe in systems that, like the international system, are highly decentralized in their distribution of authority and power. Such systems lack routinized procedures (for example, legislative mechanisms) capable of accommodating pressures for institutional change. Where the number of members is small and the system has been in operation a long time, it may be possible to solve such problems through regularized bargaining processes. Where the number of actors is large and their interests are heterogeneous, however, the transaction costs associated with

---

[49]The distinction between this type of pressure and redistributive pressure frequently becomes blurred in practice because it is politically more acceptable to cloak redistributive desires in the guise of promoting good management practices. Numerous illustrations of this phenomenon can be found in the debates over the American Fishery Conservation and Management Act of 1976.

[50]See Young (fn. 11), 260–62.

efforts to transform international regimes will be substantial; it may prove impossible to arrive at clear-cut outcomes without resorting to highly coercive practices—either in the form of unilateral actions taken in disregard of the interests of others, or in the form of efforts to impose changes on others in the absence of their voluntary consent.

3. Change and Social Choice

Like all social institutions, international regimes exhibit the attributes of collective goods to a high degree.[51] Therefore, no markets will arise in international regimes *per se,* though there may be markets in entry permits for fishing, pollution rights, licenses for deep seabed mining, and so forth. Since regimes never yield neutral results, it is safe to assume that interested parties will express non-identical preferences with respect to both the initial development and the subsequent reform of these social institutions. Moreover, the expected impact of international regimes is generally great enough to deter the affected actors from consigning matters relating to their development and alteration to administrative experts. Under the circumstances, regime dynamics typically revolve around processes of social choice or procedures through which conflicting preferences concerning institutional arrangements can be aggregated into collective decisions. Again, a particularly clear illustration of this phenomenon can be seen in the complex negotiations concerning the institutional features of the proposed International Seabed Authority.[52]

In the highly decentralized environment of the international system, the prescribed procedure for resolving such problems of social choice is to resort to multilateral bargaining within the framework of an international conference. However, conflicts of interest among major actors or groups of actors are typically severe. There is no effective tradition that puts pressure on interested parties who find themselves in the minority to accept the preferences of majority coalitions.[53] Since actors commonly mistrust the performance of institutional arrangements (to the point of attempting to resolve all potential issues during the phase of re-

---

[51]This argument is set forth clearly in Olson (fn. 18), for the general case of social institutions.

[52]Compare the views expressed in Young, "International Resource Regimes" with those advanced in Ross D. Eckert, "Exploitation of Deep Ocean Minerals: Regulatory Mechanisms and United States Policy," *Journal of Law and Economics,* XVII (April 1974), 143–77.

[53]Some analysts favor unanimity as a decision rule, especially at the level of "constitutional" contracts: see James M. Buchanan and Gordon Tullock, *The Calculus of Consent* (Ann Arbor: University of Michigan Press, 1962). Rawls (fn. 2) suggests that individuals contemplating principles of justice in the "original position" would reach unanimous agreement.

gime formation), multilateral bargaining is often a costly method of resolving problems of social choice relating to international regimes; sometimes it fails to yield any clearcut outcomes altogether.

Two alternative methods exist for dealing with the development and alteration of international regimes. In some situations, small groups of actors possessing strong and generally compatible interests in a particular activity band together to work out an acceptable set of arrangements to govern that activity. The existing regimes for Antarctica, whaling, and fishing in the northeastern Atlantic are all products of this method of handling problems of social choice. . . .

The other method involves dramatic unilateral action on the part of one or a few powerful actors. Under suitable conditions, this process will lead to *de facto* conformity on the part of others in the same way that price leadership operates to produce coordinated behavior in certain oligopolistic industries. Both the existing regime for the outer continental shelves and the regime for the marine fisheries have arisen largely in this

fashion, and the postwar international monetary regime may be considered a product of American dominance in the aftermath of the war.[54]. . .

Any given case of regime development or alteration at the international level will undoubtedly be governed by the configuration of power among the interested actors.[55] The resultant dynamics are much like those occurring in oligopolistic industries. Where one actor is clearly dominant, unilateral actions are likely to loom large in the processes of regime construction and reform. Where several actors share power as well as a strong interest in the activity, by contrast, regimes are likely to emerge from bargains struck among small groups of key players.[56]

CONCLUSION

Although there is great variation among international regimes, they are all social institutions. Among other things, this suggests that regimes are dependent upon the maintenance of convergent expectations among actors; formalization is not a necessary condition for

---

[54]See, for example, Robert Gilpin, "The Politics of Transnational Economic Relations," *International Organization,* XXV, No. 3 (1971), 398–419.

[55]For a review of recent thinking about power in international relations, see David A. Baldwin, "Power Analysis and World Politics: New Trends versus Old Tendencies," *World Politics,* XXXI (January 1979), 161–94.

[56]For a more extensive development of the analogy between oligopolistic industries and international relations, see Young, "The Perils of Odysseus: On Constructing Theories of International Relations," in Raymond Tanter and Richard H. Ullman, eds., *Theory and Practice in International Relations* (Princeton: Princeton University Press, 1972), 190–95.

the effective operation of regimes, and regimes are always created rather than discovered. Undoubtedly, these attributes account for certain methodological problems that arise regularly in efforts to study international regimes systematically. But the recognition of these attributes is a prerequisite for the achievement of any analytic success in this realm.

In closing, I would like to lay out an agenda of questions that should be considered in the analysis of any international regime:

1. *Institutional character.* What are the central rights, rules, and social choice procedures of the regime? How do they interact with the behavior of individual actors to produce a stream of outcomes?

2. *Jurisdictional boundaries.* What is the coverage of the regime with respect to functional scope, areal domain, and membership? To what extent is this coverage optimal under the prevailing conditions?

3. *Conditions for operation.* What conditions are necessary for the regime to work at all? Under what conditions will the operation of the regime yield particularly desirable results (for example, economic efficiency or equity)?

4. *Consequences of operation.* What sorts of outcomes (either individual or collective) can the regime be expected to produce? What are appropriate criteria of evaluation in this context?

5. *Regime dynamics.* How did the regime come into existence, and what is the likelihood of its experiencing major alterations in the foreseeable future? Does the regime include transformation rules and are they likely to be effective?

4

CAVE! HIC DRAGONES:
A CRITIQUE OF REGIME ANALYSIS

Susan Strange

Instead of asking what makes regimes and how they affect behavior, [this article] seeks to raise more fundamental questions. In particular, it queries whether the concept of regime is really useful to students of international political economy or world politics; and whether it may not even be actually negative in its influence, obfuscating and confusing instead of clarifying and illuminating, and distorting by concealing bias instead of revealing and removing it.

It challenges the validity and usefulness of the regime concept on five separate counts. These lead to two further and secondary (in the sense of indirect), but no less important grounds for expressing the doubt whether further work of this kind ought to be encouraged by names as well-known and distinguished as the contributors to this volume. The five counts (or "dragons" to watch out for) are first, that the study of regimes is, for the most part, a fad, one of those shifts of fashion not too difficult to explain as a temporary reaction to events in the real world but in itself making little in the way of a long-term con-

tribution to knowledge. Second, it is imprecise and woolly. Third, it is value-biased, as dangerous as loaded dice. Fourth, it distorts by overemphasizing the static and underemphasizing the dynamic element of change in world politics. And fifth, it is narrowminded, rooted in a state-centric paradigm that limits vision of a wider reality.

Two indirect criticisms—not so much of the concept itself as of the tendency to give it exaggerated attention—follow from these five points. One is that it leads to a study of world politics that deals predominantly with the status quo, and tends to exclude hidden agendas and to leave unheard or unheeded complaints, whether they come from the underprivileged, the disfranchised or the unborn, about the way the system works. In short, it ignores the vast area of nonregimes that lies beyond the ken of international bureaucracies and diplomatic bargaining. The other is that it persists in looking for an all-pervasive pattern of political behavior in world politics, a "general theory" that will provide a nice, neat, and above all simple explanation of the

---

The title translates as "Beware! here be dragons!"—an inscription often found on pre-Columbian maps of the world beyond Europe.

SOURCE: Reprinted from *International Organization*, Vol. 36, No. 2, 1982, Susan Strange, *"Cave! hic dragones:* A Critique of Regime Analysis," by permission of The MIT Press, Cambridge, Massachusetts. © 1982 by the Massachusetts Institute of Technology.

past and an easy means to predict the future. Despite all the accumulated evidence of decades of work in international relations and international history (economic as well as political) that no such pattern exists, it encourages yet another generation of impressionable young hopefuls to set off with high hopes and firm resolve in the vain search for an El Dorado. . . .

FIVE CRITICISMS OF THE CONCEPT OF REGIMES

A Passing Fad?

The first of my dragons, or pitfalls for the unwary, is that concern with regimes may be a passing fad. A European cannot help making the point that concern with regime formation and breakdown is very much an American academic fashion. . . . Europeans concerned with matters of strategy and security are usually not the same as those who write about structures affecting economic development, trade, and money, or with the prospects for particular regimes or sectors. Even the future of Europe itself never dominated the interests of so large a group of scholars in Europe as it did, for a time, the American academic community. Perhaps Europeans are not generalist enough; perhaps having picked a field to work in, they are inclined to stick to it too rigidly. And conversely, perhaps Americans are more subject to fads and fashions in academic inquiry than Europeans, more apt to conform and to join in

behind the trendsetters of the times. Many Europeans, I think, believe so, though most are too polite to say it. They have watched American enthusiasm wax and wane for systems analysis, for behavioralism, for integration theory, and even for quantitative methods indiscriminately applied. The fashion for integration theory started with the perceived U.S. need for a reliable junior partner in Europe, and how to nurture the European Communities to this end was important. The quantitative fashion is easily explained by a combination of the availability of computer time and the finance to support it and of the ambition of political scientists to gain as much kudos and influence with policy makers as the economists and others who had led the way down the quantitative path. Further back we can see how international relations as a field of study separate from politics and history itself developed in direct response to the horrors of two world wars and the threat of a third. And, later, collective goods theories responded to the debates about burden-sharing in NATO, just as monetarism and supply-side economics gained a hearing only when the conditions of the 1970s cast doubts on Keynesian remedies for recession, unemployment, and inflation.

The current fashion for regimes arises, I would suggest, from certain, somewhat subjective perceptions in many American minds. One such perception was that a number of external "shocks," on top of internal troubles like Watergate and Jimmy Carter, had accelerated a serious decline in American power. In contrast to the nationalist, reactionary response of many Reaganites, liberal, internationalist academics asked how the damage could be minimized by restoring or repairing or reforming the mechanisms of multilateral management—"regimes." A second subjective perception was that there was some sort of mystery about the uneven performance and predicament of international organizations. This was a connecting theme in Keohane and Nye's influential *Power and Interdependence,* which struck responsive chords far and wide.

But the objective reality behind both perceptions was surely far less dramatic. In European eyes, the "decline" arises partly from an original overestimation of America's capacity to remake the whole world in the image of the U.S.A. In this vision, Washington was the center of the system, a kind of keep in the baronial castle of capitalism, from which radiated military, monetary, commercial, and technological as well as purely political channels carrying the values of American polity, economy, and society down through the hierarchy of allies and friends, classes and cultural cousins, out to the ends of the earth. The new kind of global empire, under the protection of American nuclear power, did not need territorial expansion. It could be achieved by a combination of military alliances and a world economy opened up to trade, investment, and information.

This special form of nonterritorial imperalism is something that many American academics, brought up as liberals and internationalists, find hard to recognize. U.S. hegemony, while it is as nonterritorial as Britain's India in the days of John Company or Britain's Egypt after 1886, is still a form of imperialism. The fact that this nonterritorial empire extends more widely and is even more tolerant of the pretensions of petty principalities than Britain was of those of the maharajahs merely means that it is larger and more secure. It is not much affected by temporary shocks or setbacks. Yet Americans are inhibited about acknowledging their imperialism. It was a Frenchman who titled his book about American foreign policy *The Imperial Republic.*[1]

Moreover, Americans have often seemed to exaggerate the "shocks" of the 1970s and the extent of change in U.S.-Soviet or U.S.-OPEC relations. Nobody else saw the pre-1971 world as being quite so stable and ordered as Americans did. Certainly for Third-Worlders, who had by then lived through two or three recent cycles of boom and slump in the price of their country's

---

[1]Raymond Aron, *The Imperial Republic: The U.S. and the World, 1945–1973* (Englewood Cliffs, N.J.: Prentice-Hall, 1974).

major exports—whether coffee, co-coa, tin, copper, sugar or ba-nanas—plus perhaps a civil war and a revolution or two, the "oil-price shock" was hardly the epoch-making break with the stable, com-fortable, predictable past that it seemed to many Americans. If one has been accustomed for as long as one can remember to national plans and purposes being frustrated and brought to nothing by exogenous changes in the market, in technol-ogy or in the international political situation between the superpow-ers—over none of which your own government has had the slightest control—then a bit more disorder in a disorderly world comes as no great surprise.

To non-American eyes therefore, there is something quite exagger-ated in the weeping and wailing and wringing of American hands over the fall of the imperial republic. This is not how it looks to us in Europe, in Japan, in Latin Amer-ica, or even in the Middle East. True, there is the nuclear parity of the Soviet Union. And there is the depreciated value of the dollar in terms of gold, of goods, and of other currencies. But the first is not the only factor in the continuing domi-nant importance to the security structure of the balance of power between the two superpowers, and the second is far more a sign of the abuse of power than it is of the loss of power. The dollar, good or bad, still dominates the world of inter-national finance. Money markets and other markets in the United States still lead and others still fol-low; European bankrupts blame American interest rates. If the authority of the United States appears to have weakened, it is largely because the markets and their operators have been given freedom and license by the same state to profit from an integrated world economy. If Frankenstein's monster is feared to be out of con-trol, that looks to non-Americans more like a proof of Frankenstein's power to create such a monster in the first place. The change in the balance of public and private power still leaves the United States as the undisputed hegemon of the system.[2]

To sum up, the fashion for regime analysis may not simply be, as Stein suggests,[3] rehash of old academic debates under a new and jazzier name—a sort of intellectual mutton dressed up as lamb—so that the pushy new professors of the 1980s can have the same old arguments as

---

[2]For a more extended discussion of this rather basic question, see my "Still an Ex-traordinary Power," in Ray Lombra and Bill Witte, eds., *The Political Economy of International and Domestic Monetary Relations* (Ames: Iowa State University Press, 1982); James Petras and Morris Morley, "The U.S. Imperial State," mimeo (March 1980); and David Calleo, "Inflation and Defense," *Foreign Affairs* (Winter 1980).

[3]See Arthur Stein, "Coordination and Collaboration: Regimes in an Anarchic World" in Stephen Krasner (ed.) *International Regimes* (Ithaca, N.Y.: Cornell University Press, 1983), p. 116.

their elders but can flatter themselves that they are breaking new ground by using a new jargon. It is also an intellectual reaction to the objective reality.

In a broad, structuralist view (and using the broader definition of the term) of the structures of global security, of a global credit system, of the global welfare system (i.e., aid and other resource transfers) and the global knowledge and communications system, there seems far less sign of a falling-off in American power. Where decline exists, it is a falling-off in the country's power and will to intervene with world market mechanisms (from Eurodollar lending to the grain trade) rather than significant change in the distribution of military or economic power to the favor of other states. Such change as there is, has been more internal than international.

The second subjective perception on the part of Americans that I wish to address is that there is some mystery about the rather uneven performance in recent times of many international arrangements and organizations. While some lie becalmed and inactive, like sailing ships in the doldrums, others hum with activity, are given new tasks, and are recognized as playing a vital role in the functioning of the system. I would personally count the GATT, FAO, and UNESCO in the first group, the World Bank and the regional banks, the BIS, and IMCO in the second. The IMF holds a middle position: it has largely lost its universal role but

has found an important but more specialized usefulness in relation to indebted developing countries.

The mixed record of international organizations really does need explaining. But Americans have been curiously reluctant, to my mind at least, to distinguish between the three somewhat different purposes served by international organizations. These can broadly be identified as *strategic* (i.e., serving as instruments of the structural strategy and foreign policy of the dominant state or states); as *adaptive* (i.e., providing the necessary multilateral agreement on whatever arrangements are necessary to allow states to enjoy the political luxury of national autonomy without sacrificing the economic dividends of world markets and production structures); and as *symbolic* (i.e., allowing everybody to declare themselves in favor of truth, beauty, goodness, and world community, while leaving governments free to pursue national self-interests and to do exactly as they wish).

In the early postwar period, most international organizations served all three purposes at once. They were strategic in the sense that they served as instruments of the structural strategies of the United States. Also, they were often adaptive in that they allowed the United States and the other industrialized countries like Britain, Germany, France, and Japan to enjoy both economic growth and political autonomy. Finally, many organizations were at the same time symbolic in that they expressed and partially satisfied the universal yearning for a "better world" without doing anything substantial to bring it about.

In recent years the political purposes served by institutions for their members have tended to be less well balanced; some have become predominantly strategic, some predominantly adaptive, and others predominantly symbolic. This has happened because, where once the United States was able to dominate organizations like the United Nations, it can no longer do so because of the inflation of membership and the increasing divergence between rich and poor over fundamentals. Only a few organizations still serve U.S. strategic purposes better than bilateral diplomacy can serve them; they are either top-level political meetings or they deal with military or monetary matters in which the U.S. still disposes of predominant power. In other organizations the tendency toward symbolism, expressed in a proliferation of Declarations, Charters, Codes of Conduct, and other rather empty texts, has strengthened as the ability to reach agreement on positive action to solve real global problems has weakened. This applies especially to the United Nations and many of its subsidiary bodies, to UNCTAD, IDA, and many of the specialized agencies. The one growth area is the adaptive function. The integration of the world economy and the advance of technology have created new problems, but they also have often enlarged the possibility of reaching agreement as well as the perceived need to find a solution. Such predominantly adaptive institutions are often monetary (IBRD, IFC, BIS) or technical (ITU, IMCO, WMO).

Imprecision

The second dragon is imprecision of terminology. "Regime" is yet one more woolly concept that is a fertile source of discussion simply because people mean different things when they use it. At its worst, woolliness leads to the same sort of euphemistic Newspeak that George Orwell warned us would be in general use by 1984. The Soviet Union calls the main medium for the suppression of information *Pravda* (Truth), and refers to the "sovereign independence of socialist states" as the principle governing its relations with its East European "partners." In the United States scholars have brought "interdependence" into general use when what they were describing was actually highly asymmetrical and uneven dependence or vulnerability. In the same way, though more deliberately, IBM public relations advisers invented and brought into general and unthinking use the term "multinational corporation" to describe an enterprise doing worldwide business from a strong national base.

Experience with the use of these and other, equally woolly words warns us that where they do not actually mislead and misrepresent, they often serve to confuse and disorient us. "Integration" is one example of an overused word loosely taken to imply all sorts of other developments such as convergence as well as the susceptibility of "integrated" economies to common trends and pressures—a mistake that had to be painstakingly remedied by careful, pragmatic research.[4]

"Regime" is used to mean many different things. In the Keohane and Nye formulation ("networks of rules, norms and procedures that regularize behavior and control its effects")[5] it is taken to mean something quite narrow—explicit or implicit internationally agreed arrangements, usually executed with the help of an international organization—even though Keohane himself distinguishes between regimes and specific agreements. Whereas other formulations emphasize "decision-making procedures around which actors' expectations converge," the concept of regime can be so broadened as to mean almost any fairly stable distribution of the power to influence outcomes. In Keohane and Nye's formulation, the subsequent questions amount to little more than the old chestnut, "Can international institutions change state behavior?" The second definition reformulates all the old questions about power and the exercise of power in the international system. So, if—despite a rather significant effort by realist and pluralist authors to reach agreement—there is no fundamental consensus about the answer to the question, "What is a regime?", obviously there is not going to be much useful or substantial convergence of conclusions about the answers to the other questions concerning their making and unmaking.

Why, one might ask, has there been such concerted effort to stretch the elasticity of meaning to such extremes? I can only suppose that scholars, who by calling, interest, and experience are themselves "internationalist" in aspiration, are (perhaps unconsciously) performing a kind of symbolic ritual against the disruption of the international order, and do so just because they are also, by virtue of their profession, more aware than most of the order's tenuousness.

Value Bias

The third point to be wary of is that the term regime is value-loaded; it implies certain things that ought not to be taken for granted. As has often happened before in the study of international relations, this comes of trying to apply a term derived from the observation of national politics to international or to world politics.

Let us begin with semantics. The word "regime" is French, and it has two common meanings. In everyday language it means a diet, an or-

---

[4]Yao-so Hu, *Europe under Stress* (forthcoming).
[5]Robert Keohane and Joseph Nye, *Power and Interdependence* (Boston: Little, Brown, 1977).

dered, purposive plan of eating, exercising, and living. A regime is usually imposed on the patient by some medical or other authority with the aim of achieving better health. A regime must be recognizably the same when undertaken by different individuals, at different times, and in different places. It must also be practiced over an extended period of time; to eat no pastry one day but to gorge the next is not to follow a regime. Nor does one follow a regime if one eats pastry when in Paris but not in Marseilles. Those who keep to a diet for a day or two and abandon it are hardly judged to be under the discipline of a regime.

Based on the same broad principles of regularity, discipline, authority, and purpose, the second meaning is political: the government of a society by an individual, a dynasty, party or group that wields effective power over the rest of society. Regime in this sense is more often used pejoratively than with approval—the "ancien regime," the "Franco regime," the "Stalin regime," but seldom the "Truman" or "Kennedy" regime, or the "Attlee" or "Macmillan," the "Mackenzie King" or the "Menzies" regime. The word is more often used of forms of government that are inherently authoritarian, capricious, and even unjust. Regimes need be neither benign nor consistent. It may be (as in the case of Idi Amin, "Papa Doc" Duvallier or Jean-Bedel Bokassa) that the power of the regime is neither benign nor just. But at least in a given regime, everyone knows and understands where power resides and whose interest is served by it; and thus, whence to expect either preferment or punishment, imprisonment or other kinds of trouble. In short, government, rulership, and authority are the essence of the word, not consensus, nor justice, nor efficiency in administration.

What could be more different from the unstable, kaleidoscopic pattern of international arrangements between states? The title (if not all of the content) of Hedley Bull's book, *The Anarchical Society,* well describes the general state of the international system. Within that system, as Bull and others have observed, it is true that there is more order, regularity of behavior, and general observance of custom and convention than the pure realist expecting the unremitting violence of the jungle might suppose. But by and large the world Bull and other writers describe is characterized in all its main outlines not by discipline and authority, but by the absence of government, by the precariousness of peace and order, by the dispersion not the concentration of authority, by the weakness of law, and by the large number of unsolved problems and unresolved conflicts over what should be done, how it should be done, and who should do it.

Above all, a single recognized locus of power over time is the one attribute that the international system so conspicuously lacks.

All those international arrangements dignified by the label regime are only too easily upset when either the balance of bargaining power or the perception of national interest (or both together) change among those states who negotiate them. In general, moreover, all the areas in which regimes in a national context exercise the central attributes of political discipline are precisely those in which corresponding international arrangements that might conceivably be dignified with the title are conspicuous by their absence. There is no world army to maintain order. There is no authority to decide how much economic production shall be public and how much shall be privately owned and managed. We have no world central bank to regulate the creation of credit and access to it, nor a world court to act as the ultimate arbiter of legal disputes that also have political consequences. There is nothing resembling a world tax system to decide who should pay for public goods—whenever the slightest hint of any of these is breathed in diplomatic circles, state governments have all their defenses at the ready to reject even the most modest encroachment on what they regard as their national prerogatives.

The analogy with national governments implied by the use of the word regime, therefore, is inherently false. It consequently holds a highly distorting mirror to reality.

Not only does using this word regime distort reality by implying an exaggerated measure of predictability and order in the system as it is, it is also value-loaded in that it takes for granted that what everyone wants is more and better regimes, that greater order and managed interdependence should be the collective goal. . . . There is a whole literature that denies that order is "the most fundamental concern" and that says that the objectives of Third World policy should be to achieve freedom from dependency and to enhance national identity and freer choice by practicing "uncoupling" or delinking or (yet another woolly buzz-word) by "collective self-reliance."

Now, these ideas may be unclear and half-formed. But in view of the Islamic revival and the newfound self-confidence of several newly industrialized countries (NICs), it would be patently unwise for any scholar to follow a line of inquiry that overlooks them. Let us never forget the folly of League of Nations reformers, busily drafting new blueprints while Hitler and Mussolini lit fires under the whole system. Should we not ask whether this too does not indicate an essentially conservative attitude biased toward the status quo. Is it not just another unthinking response to fear of the consequences of change? Yet is not political activity as often directed by the desire to achieve change, to get more justice and more freedom from a system, as it is by the desire to get more wealth or to assure security for the haves by reinforcing order?

Too Static a View

The fourth dragon to beware is that the notion of a regime—for the semantic reasons indicated earlier—tends to exaggerate the static quality of arrangements for managing the international system and introducing some confidence in the future of anarchy, some order out of uncertainty. In sum, it produces stills, not movies. And the reality, surely, is highly dynamic, as can fairly easily be demonstrated by reference to each of the three main areas for regimes considered in this collection: security, trade, and money.

For the last thirty-five years, the international security regime (if it can be so called) has not been derived from Chapter VII of the U.N. Charter, which remains as unchanged as it is irrelevant. It has rested on the balance of power between the superpowers. In order to maintain that balance, each has engaged in a continuing and escalating accumulation of weapons and has found it necessary periodically to assert its dominance in particular frontier areas—Hungary, Czechoslovakia, and Afghanistan for the one and South Korea, Guatemala, Vietnam, and El Salvador for the other. Each has also had to be prepared when necessary (but, fortunately, less frequently) to engage in direct confrontation with the other. And no one was ever able to predict with any certainty when such escalation in armaments, such interventions or confrontations were going to be thought necessary to preserve the balance, nor what the outcome would be. Attempts to "quick-freeze" even parts of an essentially fluid relationship have been singularly unsuccessful and unconvincing, as witness the fate of the SALT agreements, the European Security Conference, and the Non-Proliferation Treaty.

In monetary matters, facile generalizations about "the Bretton Woods regime" abound—but they bear little resemblance to the reality. It is easily forgotten that the original Articles of Agreement were never fully implemented, that there was a long "transition period" in which most of the proposed arrangements were put on ice, and that hardly a year went by in the entire postwar period when some substantial change was not made (tacitly or explicitly) in the way the rules were applied and in the way the system functioned. Consider the major changes: barring the West European countries from access to the Fund; providing them with a multilateral payments system through the European Payments Union; arranging a concerted launch into currency convertibility; reopening the major international commodity and capital markets; finding ways to support the pound sterling. All these and subsequent decisions were taken by national governments, and especially by the U.S. government, in response to their changing perceptions of national interest or else in deference to volatile market forces that thay either could not or would not control.

Arrangements governing international trade have been just as changeable and rather less uniform. Different principles and rules governed trade between market economies and the socialist or centrally planned economies, while various forms of preferential market access were practiced between European countries and their former colonies and much the same results were achieved between the United States and Canada or Latin America through direct investment. Among the European countries, first in the OEEC and then in EFTA and the EC, preferential systems within the system were not only tolerated but encouraged. The tariff reductions negotiated through the GATT were only one part of a complex governing structure of arrangements, international and national, and even these (as all the historians of commercial diplomacy have shown) were subject to constant revision, reinterpretation, and renegotiation.

The trade "regime" was thus neither constant nor continuous over time, either between partners or between sectors. The weakness of the arrangements as a system for maintaining order and defining norms seems to me strikingly illustrated by the total absence of continuity or order in the important matter of the competitive use of export credit—often government guaranteed and subsidized—in order to increase market shares. No one system of rules has governed how much finance on what terms and for how long can be obtained for an international exchange, and attempts to make collective agreements to standardize terms (notably through the Berne Union) have repeatedly broken down.

The changeable nature of all these international arrangements behind the blank institutional facade often results from the impact of the two very important factors that regime analysis seems to me ill-suited to cope with: technology and markets. Both are apt to bring important changes in the distribution of costs and benefits, risks and opportunities to national economies and other groups, and therefore to cause national governments to change their minds about which rules or norms of behavior should be reinforced and observed and which should be disregarded and changed.

Some of the consequences of technological change on international arrangements are very easily perceived, others less so. It is clear that many longstanding arrangements regarding fishing rights were based on assumptions that became invalid when freezing, sonar, and improved ship design altered the basic factors governing supply and demand. It is also clear that satellites, computers, and video technology have created a host of new problems in the field of information and communication, problems for which no adequate multilateral arrangements have been devised. New technology in chemicals, liquid natural gas, nuclear power, and oil production from under the sea—to mention only a few well-known areas—is dramatically increasing the risks involved in production, trade, and use. These risks become (more or less) acceptable thanks to the possibility of insuring against them. But though this has political consequences—imposing the cost of insurance as a kind of entrance tax on participation in the world market economy—the fact that no structure or process exists for resolving the conflicts of interest that ensue is an inadequately appreciated new aspect of the international system.

Technology also contributes to the process of economic concentration, reflected in the daily dose of company takeovers, through the mounting cost of replacing old technology with new and the extended leadtime between investment decisions and production results. Inevitably, the economic concentration so encouraged affects freedom of access to world markets and thus to the distributive consequences in world society. The nationalist, protectionist, defensive attitudes of states today are as much a response to technical changes and their perceived consequences as they are to stagnation and instability in world markets.

Since the chain of cause and effect so often originates in technology and markets, passing through national policy decisions to emerge as negotiating postures in multilateral discussions, it follows that attention to the end result—an international arrangement of some sort—is apt to overlook most of the determining factors on which agreement may, in brief, rest.

The search for common factors and for general rules (or even axioms), which is of the essence of regime analysis, is therefore bound to be long, exhausting, and probably disappointing. Many articles abound in general conclusions about regimes, their nature, the conditions favoring their creation, maintenance, and change, and many of the generalizations seem at first reading logically plausible— but only if one does not examine their assumptions too closely. My objection is that these assumptions are frequently unwarranted.

State-centeredness

The final but by no means least important warning is that attention to these regime questions leaves the study of international political economy far too constrained by the self-imposed limits of the state-centered paradigm. It asks, what are the prevailing arrangements discussed and observed among governments, thus implying that the important and significant political issues are those with which governments are concerned. Nationally, this is fairly near the truth. Democratic governments have to respond to whatever issues voters feel are important if they wish to survive, and even the most authoritarian governments cannot in the long run remain indifferent to deep discontents or divisions of opinion in the societies they rule. But internationally, this is not so. The matters on which governments, through international organizations, negotiate and make arrangements are not necessarily the issues that even they regard as most important, still less the issues that the mass of individuals regards as crucial. Attention to regimes therefore accords to governments far too much of the right to define the agenda of academic study and directs the attention of scholars mainly to those issues that government officials find significant and important. If academics submit too much to this sort of imperceptible pressure, they abdicate responsibility for the one task for which the independent scholar has every comparative advantage, the development of a philosophy of international relations or international political economy that will not only explain and illuminate but will point a road ahead and inspire action to follow it.

Thus regime analysis risks overvaluing the positive and undervaluing the negative aspects of international cooperation. It encourages academics to practice a kind of analytical *chiaroscuro* that leaves in shadow all the aspects of the international economy where no regimes exist and where each state elects to go its own way, while highlighting the areas of agreement where some norms and customs are generally acknowledged. It consequently gives the false impression (always argued by the neofunctionalists) that international regimes are indeed slowly advancing against the forces of disorder and anarchy. Now it is only too easy, as we all know, to be misled by the proliferation of international associations and organizations, by the multiplication of declarations and documents, into concluding that there is indeed increasing positive action. The reality is that there are more

areas and issues of nonagreement and controversy than there are areas of agreement. On most of the basic social issues that have to do with the rights and responsibilities of individuals to each other and to the state—on whether abortion, bribery, drink or drug pushing or passing information, for example, is a crime or not—there is no kind of international regime. Nor is there a regime on many of the corresponding questions of the rights and responsibilities of states toward individuals and toward other states.

In reality, furthermore, the highlighted issues are sometimes less important than those in shadow. In the summer of 1980, for example, INMARSAT announced with pride an agreement on the terms on which U.S.-built satellites and expensive receiving equipment on board ship can be combined to usher in a new Future Global Maritime Distress and Safety System, whereby a ship's distress call is automatically received all over a given area by simply pressing a button. For the large tankers and others who can afford the equipment, this will certainly be a significant advance; not so for small coasters and fishing boats. In the same year, though, millions died prematurely through lack of any effective regime for the relief of disaster or famine. Meanwhile, the Executive Directors of the International Money Fund can reach agreement on a further increase in quotas, but not on the general principles governing the rescheduling of national foreign debts.

Moreover, many of the so-called regimes over which the international organizations preside turn out under closer examination to be agreements to disagree. The IMF amendments to the Articles of Agreement, for example, which legitimized the resort to managed floating exchange rates, are no more than a recognition of states' determination to decide for themselves what strategy and tactics to follow in the light of market conditions. To call this a "regime" is to pervert the language. So it is to call the various "voluntary" export restrictive arrangements bilaterally negotiated with Japan by other parties to the GATT "a multilateral regime." Since 1978 the Multi-Fibre "Agreement," too, has been little more, in effect, than an agreement to disagree. Similarly, UNESCO's debate on freedom and control of information through the press and the media resulted not in an international regime but in a bitter agreement to disagree.

One good and rather obvious reason why there is a rather large number of issues in which international organizations preside over a dialogue of the deaf is simply that the political trend within states is towards greater and greater intervention in markets and greater state responsibility for social and economic conditions, while the major postwar agreements for liberal regimes tended the other way and bound states to negative, noninterventionist policies that would increase the openness of the world economy.

In a closely integrated world economic system, this same trend leads to the other aspect of reality that attention to regimes obscures, and especially so when regimes are closely defined as being based on a group of actors standing in a characteristic relationship to each other. This is the trend to the transnational regulation of activities in one state by authorities in another, authorities that may be, and often are, state agencies such as the U.S. Civil Aeronautics Authority, the Department of Justice or the Food and Drug Administration. There is seldom any predictable pattern of "interaction" or awareness of contextual limitations to be found in such regulation.

Other neglected types of transnational authority include private bodies like industrial cartels and professional associations or special "private" and semiautonomous bodies like Lloyds of London, which exercises an authority delegated to it by the British government. This club of rich "names," underwriters, and brokers presides over the world's largest insurance and reinsurance market, and consequently earns three-quarters of its income from worldwide operations. By converting all sorts of outlandish risks into costs (the premiums on which its income depends), Lloyds plays a uniquely important part in the smooth functioning of a world market economy.

By now the limits on vision that may be encouraged as a secondary consequence of attention to regimes analysis have been implied. The aspects of political economy that it tends to overlook constitute the errors of omission that it risks incurring. I do not say that, therefore, *all* regime analyses commit these errors of omission; I can think of a number that have labored hard to avoid them. But the inherent hazard remains. They should not have to labor so hard to avoid the traps, and if there is a path to bypass them altogether it should be investigated.

The second indirect reason for skepticism about the value of regime analysis is that it persists in the assumption that somewhere there exists that El Dorado of social science, a general theory capable of universal application to all times and places and all issues, which is waiting to be discovered by an inspired, intrepid treasure-hunter. I confess I have never been convinced of this; and the more I know of political economy, the more skeptical I become. If (as so many books in international relations have concluded) we need better "tools of analysis," it is not because we will be able to dig up golden nuggets with them. Those nuggets— the great truths about human society and human endeavor—were all discovered long ago. What we need are constant reminders so that we do not forget them.

CHAPTER III

Patterns of Cooperation in International Organizations

Membership in international organizations is voluntary. Before states or private groups decide to join an organization, they assess the costs and benefits of membership as opposed to those incurred by *not* joining the organization. For example, joining the International Monetary Fund (IMF) runs the risk of the organization requiring domestic economic restrictions, which can be regarded as invasions of national sovereignty, as a condition for assistance with balance of payments or larger debt problems. Yet, membership in the IMF is a prerequisite for World Bank membership, with its commensurate benefits for national development loans. Thus, initially, international organization members must perceive some overall benefit to collaboration in the issue area(s) of the particular organization. In this section, we explore two questions. First, we focus on state decisions to join international organizations, seeking to ascertain how extensive those membership patterns are across space and time. Second, we are concerned with the level of cooperative behavior of states after their decision to join. Specifically, do states exhibit more cooperative behavior inside or outside international organizations?

The most prominent theoretical approach to our understanding of the creation and growth of international organizations is functionalism. Functionalism posits that the growth of technology and mass political participation in states will create pressures for those states to cooperate in international organizations. Increasing interdependence leads states to cooperate in order to solve common problems and to take advantage of the greater efficiency (similar to economies of scale) from such cooperation. Functionalism envisions that states begin cooperation in technical, relatively noncontroversial (in a political sense) areas; these are often referred to as *low politics* issues. The organizations formed are very specialized and generally have limited membership. In later stages, cooperation in these limited areas may expand and spill over into more controversial issues (security or *high politics* issues).

In the first selection, Jacobson, Reisinger, and Mathers explore the growth of international organizations and state membership in those organizations. In particular, they are concerned with whether the patterns uncovered are consistent with the expectations of functionalist theory.

They discover that a state's propensity to join an international organization is related to its economic and political development, as well as to the number of years it has been a part of the international system. Such findings are consistent with the functionalist notions that technological growth and increased political participation, which are coterminus with development, are associated with growth in the number and scope of international organizations. The extent of the growth that has occurred in limited membership, nongovernmental organizations (INGOs) is also consistent with functionalist expectations. The authors conclude their essay with some predictions on the future growth of international organizations and a warning that new ways must be discovered to deal with a world containing a more densely woven web of increasing numbers of international organizations.

If states are more willing than ever before to join international organizations, are they also more cooperative in those organizations? Or are patterns of conflict and cooperation in international affairs mirrored in international organizations? James McCormick tries to answer these questions in his essay by comparing the proportion of cooperative behavior between states in international governmental organizations (IGOs) and states outside of those forums. There is some supporting evidence to suggest that there may be greater cooperation in IGOs. First, several studies link an attitudinal change toward more cooperative behavior to participation in international forums. In addition, the act of joining an international organization signifies some common interest and the expectation of cooperation for mutual benefit among the members. McCormick first points out that over two thirds of international interactions between states can be labeled cooperative. Nevertheless, cooperative behavior is more prevalent in international organizations, especially global organizations dealing with low politics issues.

In summary, these two articles reveal that national entanglements in international organizations are widespread and growing. Furthermore, those entanglements can lead to a greater level of cooperation between states than is present in the normal course of international relations.

5

NATIONAL ENTANGLEMENTS IN INTERNATIONAL GOVERNMENTAL ORGANIZATIONS

Harold K. Jacobson
William M. Reisinger
Todd Mathers

The global political system now contains more than 1,000 international governmental organizations (IGOs) of one type or another, and states are deeply entangled in this expanding web. Denmark heads the list by belonging to 164 IGOs; 19 states are members of 100 or more, and the mean number of memberships held by member states of the Group of 77, the Third World Caucus, is over 61. The entanglement of states and international governmental organizations has rapidly increased. The United Nations and its related agencies, the European communities, the Organization of American States, and the North Atlantic Treaty Organization are well known, but states have joined together and created a great many more formal institutional structures than those prominent examples. This study describes the growing web of IGOs, analyzes the propensity of states to join them, and assesses the broad consequences of a state's total IGO memberships for its economic performance and conflict behavior. It then raises questions about the implications for international relations of a continuation of the multiplying entanglement between states and IGOs, particularly in light of the apparent resistance to this trend evidenced by the U.S. and British withdrawal from the United Nations Educational, Scientific and Cultural Organization (UNESCO).

FUNCTIONALISM AS AN EXPLANATION

The theory of "functionalism," developed by David Mitrany (1933, 1966) and his followers, remains virtually the only corpus of scholarship about IGOs that offers general explanations of why states create and join such organizations, and what the consequences of this would be. Mitrany and others also saw their version of functionalism as a prescription to guide the development of the global political system. Because their version of functionalism is the only theoretical persuasion available to guide this analysis, it will be the point of departure.

Functionalism maintains that states create and join international governmental organizations be-

SOURCE: American Political Science Review, Vol. 80, No. 1 March, 1986.

cause of two broad historical tendencies that date from the nineteenth century: the extension and deepening of political participation within states, and the continual advance of technology. Functionalism argues that mass participation in political life will inexorably increase, that general populations everywhere are primarily interested in increasing their own standard of living, and that mass participation will make economic welfare the dominant concern of governments. Functionalism also argues that technology offers immense possibilities for improving living standards, but that international cooperation is essential to take full advantage of the opportunities provided by technology; states are simply too small. In the perspective of functionalism, IGOs are the consequence of political pressures and technological opportunities.

Functionalism would expect and prefer that the membership and mandates of an IGO be determined by the problem at issue; the overwhelming majority of IGOs would and should have limited memberships and specific mandates. The point of establishing an IGO, according to functionalism, is to facilitate international cooperation with respect to a specific technical issue, not to establish a general political authority with broad scope and domain.

Functionalism postulates that entanglement in a web of IGOs will make states less bellicose. Given the pressures to join IGOs, and the economic benefits presumably gained from membership and participation in them, states would be loathe to jeopardize these benefits by escalating interstate disagreements to violent conflicts that would inevitably destroy IGOs. Moreover, the increased opportunities for communication that IGOs provide should make it easier for states to avoid or settle disagreements before they reach the stage of violent conflict. States ought to have an incentive to reach agreement because, presumably, they have a common interest in economic expansion.

To what extent do the international governmental organizations in the contemporary global political system and the interaction between them and their member states conform to these functionalist tenets? How adequate is functionalism as an overall explanation for the pervasiveness of IGOs? This analysis examines the validity of functionalist tenets and assesses the extent to which functionalism must be supplemented for a full comprehension of the phenomenon of IGOs. It also raises questions about the adequacy of functionalism as a prescriptive guide to the future development of the global political system.

THE UNIVERSE OF IGOs

As a first stage in the analysis, it is necessary to describe the web of international governmental organizations as it currently exists. The basic source for information about the number and characteristics of

IGOs is the *Yearbook of International Organizations,* which is published periodically by the Union of International Associations (UIA) in Brussels.[1] The data used in this analysis are derived from the nineteenth edition, which was published in 1981 (UIA, 1981).

Starting with the nineteenth edition, the *Yearbook* divides the organizations that are included into two major categories and four subcategories. The number of IGOs included in each subcategory in the 1981 *Yearbook* are:[2]

I. Conventional International
    Bodies
    A. Federations of International
        Organizations   1
    B. Universal Membership
        Organizations   31
    C. Inter-Continental
        Organizations   48
    D. Regionally Delimited
        Organizations   264

II. Other International Bodies
    E. Emanations and
        Semi-Autonomous
        Bodies   405
    F. Organizations of
        Special Form   287
    G. Internationally Oriented
        National Bodies   39
    H. Inactive or Dissolved
        Bodies   _____26_

Total   1101

In addition, seven organizations listed in the *Yearbook* had been proposed, but were not yet in existence in 1981. Including these, 1108 IGOs are listed in the *Yearbook,* 1,075 of which were active in 1981.

The only IGO included in subcategory A is the United Nations. The United Nations' specialized agencies and other similar agencies comprise subcategory B. The International Exhibition Bureau and the International Olive Oil Council are examples of the type of organization included in subcategory C. The European communities are the most prominent of the organizations included in subcategory D.

The 344 organizations included in subcategories A through D are indisputably IGOs. The 731 organizations included in subcategories E through G have a more ambiguous status. Subcategory E includes such organizations as the United Nations Conference on Trade and Development, which, though it is a creation of the United Nations, has a larger budget, staff, and program than most of the organizations listed in subcategories C and D. It also includes some bodies, such as the U.N.'s Joint Inspection Unit, that because of their small size or apparent lack of autonomy are more questionable cases. Organizations such as the Integrated Global Services System and the Joint Nordic Organization for Lappish Culture and Reindeer Husbandry are included in subcategory F. The first is an offshoot of UNESCO and the second of the Nordic Council, but both are more than suborgans, and in their characteristics resemble many of the organizations included in subcategories C and D. Subcategory G includes many of the joint ventures set up by the member states of the Council for Mutual Economic Assistance (CMEA), as well as such bodies as the Nigeria-Niger Joint Commission for Cooperation. . . .

True to the prediction and preference of functionalism, the overwhelming majority of the IGOs that are included in the data set and could be classified according to their function and membership have specific mandates and limited memberships: 96.8% have functionally defined specific mandates, and 80.6% limit their membership according to one or another criteria. Of the total, 54.1% have mandates related to economic matters, and 56.4% limit their membership according to geographic criteria.

THE DYNAMIC EVOLUTION OF THE WEB OF IGOs

The preceding description provides an initial guide to the nature of the web of IGOs, but it is necessary to go beyond this. A sense of the dynamic processes involved in the creation of the web of IGOs can be gained from an analysis of the past, and trends from the past can be projected to foreshow likely developments if these trends continued unabated.

The analysis can be structured conveniently according to four periods. The first period starts in 1815, the year the Napoleonic Wars ended and the first IGO, the Central Commission for the Navigation of the Rhine, was created. It ends in 1914 with the outbreak of World War I. The second period starts in 1915 and ends in 1939, with the outbreak of World War II. The third period begins in 1940 and ends in 1959. This is the period of World War II and the construction of the postwar international order. The final period starts in 1960 and ends in 1981, the last year for which data were available for inclusion in this analysis.

The rationale for breaking the post-World War II period in 1960 is that 17 states, the largest number ever, gained independence in 1960. By 1960, it was clear that colonialism was doomed and the nation-state system would be extended to the entire globe. As of 1959 there were 90 independent states in the globe political system, 69 of which had been in existence in 1945 when the postwar period began. Between 1960 and 1981, 70 more would be added. Starting in 1960, decolonization fundamentally altered the global political system, at least in terms of the number of independent states included within it. The emergence of the new states led to an explosion in the membership of those IGOs that had come into existence before 1960 and—as will be seen—in the number of IGOs.

With the use of this periodization, several trends become apparent. Before examining these trends, however, it is important to emphasize that most IGOs are relatively recent creations. Of the 880 IGOs for which the date of founding is available, 94.1% were established after 1939, and 70.3% were established from 1960 through 1981. This pace of multiplication is astounding, and showed no sign of slowing. Indeed, more than 40% additional organizations were created in the decade of the 1970s ($n = 354$) than were created in the 1960s ($n = 250$).

The first notable trend is that progressively relatively fewer IGOs met the Union of International Associations criteria for being "conventional international bodies"; that is, for inclusion in the first four subcategories in the *Yearbook*. Sixty-five percent ($n = 13$) met these criteria in the period 1815–1914, 59.4% ($n = 19$) in the period 1915–1939, 47.1% ($n = 98$) in the period 1940–1959), and 31.8% ($n = 199$) in the period 1960–1981. By far the largest share of the increase in other international bodies was accounted for by IGOs in subcategories E and F, which tend to be organizations that owe their existence to decisions of organizations already existing.

Stating the trend in another way, with the passage of time IGOs created more and more offshoots. The obvious advantage of this practice is that often all that is required to create a new IGO is a majority vote, not a new treaty that would require signature and ratification to take effect. Governments of states may also believe that it will be easier for them to keep track of IGOs that are offshoots of other IGOs than those that are totally disconnected from any existing structure. Whatever the reason, a large portion of the increase of IGOs since 1960 has been in the UIA category "other

international bodies." The pace of creation of IGOs in the UIA category "conventional international bodies" reached a peak in the 1960s when 110 were established; only 86 were created in the period 1970–1981.

A second notable trend is the significant difference between the distribution of types of membership criteria for the international governmental organizations that were founded prior to 1940 and for those that were founded starting that year. The proportion of IGOs founded before 1940 that have no criteria in their constitutions limiting membership to particular political, geographic, economic, or cultural groups of states is much higher than it is for IGOs founded later.

This does not mean that in the years since World War II began states have not formed a large number of IGOs with potentially universal membership. Twenty-five such organizations were founded prior to 1940, and 143 starting that year. The absolute number for the post-World War II era is impressively high. What it does mean is that after World War II began, limited-membership IGOs multiplied much more rapidly than those with potentially universal memberships. Starting in 1940, more than 80% of the IGOs that have been founded and were still in existence in 1981 limited their membership according to some criterion. In total, 682 limited-membership organizations were established during this period, and the real number is undoubtedly higher, since the UIA does not have founding dates for all IGOs. Geography has always been the criterion most frequently used for limiting membership, and this continues to be the case.

This trend should be interpreted in light of the fact that the sovereign states of the nineteenth and early twentieth centuries were much more homogeneous than they are in the late twentieth century. A universal-membership organization formed in the earlier years had a much less diverse membership then than it does now or would have if it were formed in the present period.

That the relative proportion of IGOs that could have universal membership should fall off is logical. It would not be surprising if there were some upper limit on the number of universal membership IGOs that could be included in a global political system, even though this limit might be flexible over time.

Another factor is that as decolonization proceeded in the post-World War II period, and the number of sovereign states grew at an explosive rate, the opportunities for creating limited-membership IGOs also expanded rapidly. Organizations could be created both among new states and among new and old states. International bodies could make possible the continuation and extension of activities that were organized within the framework of a single sovereignty in the colonial era.

A consequence of the trend favoring limited-membership IGOs in the post-World War II period is that organizations established from 1940 on tend to have significantly smaller numbers of members than those established prior to this date. The mean number of member states of IGOs in the latter category is 42.9, while that of those in the former category is 20.4.

To explore further the trend of an increasing proportion of limited-membership IGOs, it is useful to categorize states in order to see the extent to which different types of states have formed exclusive IGOs. A threefold categorization based on broad political and economic alignments divides states among those that are members of the Organization for Economic Cooperation and Development (OECD),[3] those that are members of the Warsaw Treaty Organization (WTO),[4] and those that do not belong to either of these organizations, a group that for this reason is called "Other."

These three categories are mutually exclusive and roughly place states into the groupings that are used in conventional political analyses. The members of OECD are those that are customarily referred to as the "West," and the members of WTO are those that are usually referred to as the "Soviet bloc" or group. The residual category of "Other" includes those states that are referred to as the Third World.[5]

Of the 563 IGOs for which membership information is available, 103 were comprised exclusively of states that were members of OECD; 28 exclusively of states that were members of WTO; and 178 exclusively of other states. Most of the Western IGOs were the basic agencies and offshoots of: the OECD, the North Atlantic Treaty Organization, the European communities, and the Nordic Council. Beyond the Warsaw Treaty Organization itself, the 28 Soviet-group IGOs were primarily derivatives of the Council for Mutual Economic Assistance (CMEA).[6] CMEA includes three non-European states, Cuba, Mongolia, and Vietnam, that for most purposes of this analysis are included in the "Other" category. In 1981 there were 38 IGOs comprised exclusively of CMEA members; these included the 28 comprised exclusively of WTO members.

The IGOs that were comprised exclusively of states in the category "Other" were less likely to be derivatives of other organizations than those comprised exclusively of OECD and WTO states. Of the IGOs comprised only of states in the category "Other," 58.6% were in the UIA category of "conventional international bodies," while only 47.1% of the OECD-only IGOs and 42.9% of the WTO-only IGOs were in this category. The economically more advanced Western and Soviet-group states have been refining their existing relationships through establishing additional organizations, albeit often subsidiary ones, while Third World states have been establishing relatively more new relationships and consequently more new primary organizations.

Since 1960, more IGOs comprised exclusively of states in the category "Other" have been established than IGOs of any other type. In the 1960s and 1970s, they accounted for about 40% of the IGOs formed in each decade. During the 1970s, these states began to create substantial numbers of IGOs in the UIA category "other international bodies"; they created 39 of these and 35 "conventional international bodies." By the 1970s, Western states were creating more than three UIA secondary-category IGOs for every one primary-category IGO that they established.

IGOs comprised solely of states in the category "Other" offer the greatest potential for growth in the near future. In 1981, only slightly more than one such organization existed for each state in this category, while there were more than three WTO-only IGOs and more than four OECD-only IGOs for each state in those categories. States in the category "Other" could expand considerably the number of "conventional international bodies" among themselves, and they could increase the ratio between IGOs of this type and "other international bodies," moving toward the level established by the Western states. The evidence of the 1960s and the 1970s is that states in the "Other" category are moving in these directions.

There were also 104 IGOs in existence in 1981 that were comprised of states from both the OECD and "Other" groupings; they did not include any members from the WTO group. Thirty-one of these organizations were established in the

1960s, in the immediate aftermath of decolonization, and 22 in the 1970s. Many of these organizations could be regarded as providing elements of the framework of the world market economy.

The third notable trend is a tendency toward greater differentiation and variety in the mandates of the IGOs that have been established since 1939. While this trend is not as pronounced as the other two, it nevertheless is important. In the 1940s and 1950s, an unprecedentedly large number of organizations that were established—28, or 13.5% of the total—had mandates dealing with security. Starting in the 1960s, progressively larger numbers of newly formed IGOs had mandates in the social field. This expansion of the numbers of IGOs with mandates to deal with social issues was most marked among OECD-only IGOs, although the "Other" group also moved to establish relatively more IGOs with social mandates. The record of the Soviet group is somewhat different. Only one of the 28 WTO-only IGOs has a mandate to deal with social issues; it was established in the 1970s. The Warsaw Treaty Organization's mandate is security; the remaining 26 (92.9%) of the WTO-only IGOs have economic mandates. Table 1 shows the distribution by function of the IGOs that were established starting in 1960 and were comprised exclusively of members of one or another group.

The growing differentiation of IGOs reflects a widely observed tendency toward specialization in political institutions. Security organizations were so relatively

TABLE 1   Distribution by Function of IGOs Comprised Exclusively of Members of Particular Political-Economic Groups Established from 1960 through 1981 (in percentages)

Function	Group[a]		
	OECD	WTO	Other
General	4.5	0	3.8
Economic	47.0	96.0	73.7
Social	47.0	4.0	18.8
Security	1.5	0	3.8
	100.0	100.0	100.1
No. of cases	66	25	133

Chi Square = 29.28
Cramer's Phi = .26
Sig. = .00

[a]OECD = Organization for Economic Cooperation; WTO = Warsaw Treaty Organization.

prominent in the 1940s and 1950s because the post-World War II political order was being created. This order has been relatively stable since those years, as is reflected in the fact that only 3.1% ($n = 19$) of the IGOs established in the period starting in 1960 have security mandates. The increasing focus on social issues mirrors the focus on such issues that developed within states, particularly the advanced industrial Western countries, in the 1960s.

With their overwhelming concentration on economic issues, WTO-only IGOs stand apart from the general trend. Beyond the basic security commitment of the Warsaw Treaty, the Soviet-group states appear to have been almost inexorably drawn into economic cooperation, but they either have little desire or little necessity for institutionalized inter-governmental cooperation in other areas. The CMEA-only organizations are also heavily concentrated in the economic area (92.1%, $n = 35$).

In sum, the web of IGOs in existence in 1981 was dense and complex. Although functionalist tenets accurately describe the broad characteristics of the web and its dynamic evolution, one must go beyond functionalism for a more detailed description and for a fuller understanding of the growth of the web. The basic dynamic forces in the global political system—the urge to create a new order in the aftermath of a destructive war and decolonization—had a strong impact on the processes and course of

institution building, as one would expect. IGOs are, after all, instruments of states, and states are likely to follow policies in this sphere that are similar and related to those that they follow in other spheres. The evolution of the web of IGOs also reflects an internal development within states: the greater attention paid by governments to social issues. An important exception to this trend, however, is the paucity of WTO-only IGOs directed toward social issues.

THE PROPENSITY OF STATES TO JOIN IGOs

The analysis so far has indicated that states belong to varying numbers of international governmental organizations. Now that the web of IGOs has been described, this varying propensity of states to join these organizations can be analyzed in detail. Functionalist tenets again provide the point of departure.

To give an indication of the varying propensity of states to be members of IGOs, Table 2 lists the 26 states that held the highest number of IGO memberships in 1981. For each state, it gives both the total number of full and associate memberships in all categories of IGOs, and the number of full memberships in "conventional international bodies." Denmark's leading the list is explained by the fact that its unique position as a member of both the European communities and the Nordic Council gives it an unusual opportunity to belong to a

TABLE 2 States with the Highest Number of IGO Memberships

Rank Order	State	Full and Associate Memberships in All Categories of IGOs	Full Memberships in UIA[a] Principal Category IGOs
1	Denmark	164	91
2	France	155	95
3	Norway	154	86
4	Sweden	153	87
5	United Kingdom	140	83
6	Finland	139	78
7	Federal Republic of Germany	135	83
8	The Netherlands	131	82
9	Belgium	127	77
10	Italy	124	72
11	United States	122	67
12	Spain	113	76
13	Canada	110	69
14	Japan	106	63
15	Iceland	105	54
16.5	Australia	104	67
16.5	Soviet Union	104	67
18	India	102	61
19	Brazil	100	60
20	Poland	99	69
21	Algeria	96	57
22.5	Austria	95	62
22.5	Yugoslavia	95	58
25	Egypt	94	60
25	Mexico	94	56
25	Switzerland	94	65

[a]UIA = Union of International Associations.

large number of "other international bodies."

Fourteen of the 26 states, including all of those in the top 10, are from Western Europe; 3 are from Eastern Europe and 3 from Asia and the Middle East; 2 are from North America and 2 from Latin America; and 1 is from Africa and 1 from Oceania. These membership data reflect the fact that the IGO web is most dense and complex in Western Europe, where it began with the creation of the Central Commission for the Navigation of the Rhine in 1815. What is most impressive about this list of 26 states and the participation of states in

IGOs more generally, however, is the extent to which the web has become global. Even Vanuatu, which just gained independence in 1981, held 11 IGO memberships that year, 4 of which were in "conventional international bodies." Joining IGOs has become among the first actions that governments take as soon as sovereignty is gained.

Functionalism argues that states will be propelled to join IGOs because popular pressures to increase living standards will lead their governments to engage in international collaboration to take advantage of the opportunities that technology offers to respond constructively to these pressures. Following this argument, one would expect that states with more opportunities for popular pressures to be expressed and at higher levels of technological development would belong to a relatively greater number of IGOs. The extent of party competition is an appropriate indicator for the first variable, and per capita gross national product (GNP) is an appropriate indicator for the second. For this analysis, Freedom House's fourfold classification of states in 1980 as (1) multiparty, (2) dominant-party, (3) one-party, and (4) no-party (Gastil, 1981) is used to indicate the extent of party competition. The per capita GNP figures used are those for 1980 published by the World Bank in its *World Bank Atlas 1982* (IBRD, 1982a).

True to the functionalist argument, party competition and per capita GNP do predict IGO

memberships.[7] An ordinary least squares regression with these two independent variables produces an equation with $R^2 = .29$ ($n = 160$, sig. $= .00$). The functionalist argument is supported, but less than 30% of the variance is explained, which leads to a quest for further factors that might influence the propensity of states to belong to IGOs.

Since the phenomenon of decolonization proved so important in the growth of the web of IGOs, it could also be an important factor in explaining the propensity of states to belong to IGOs. At the most basic level, the longer a state has had sovereignty the more opportunities it would have had to join IGOs. Since more than 90% of the IGOs in the global political system were established after World War II, it seems appropriate to assume that the exact order of states coming to independence in the nineteenth century or early twentieth century, or even earlier, would have little bearing on their propensity to belong to IGOs in the late twentieth century. Thus years of sovereignty—or of membership in the global political system—are measured starting in 1945. Since the data used in the analysis are for 1981, this independent variable has values from 0 to 37, 0 being for territories that did not have sovereignty in 1981, and 37 being for states that gained sovereignty in 1945 or earlier.

Traditional thought about world politics has always accorded special status to great powers. Given their presumed propensity to be extensively involved in world politics, one would expect greater powers to have more IGO memberships than lesser powers. GNP is the most convenient single indicator of power. The GNP figures used here are also taken from the *World Bank Atlas, 1982*.

Adding date of entry into the global political system and power to the two independent variables used previously sharply improves the explanatory power of the ordinary least squares equation. With the four variables included, the equation is:

IGO Memberships =
$$36.29 + 1.43 \text{ System Years}$$
$$(5.33) \quad (.14)$$
$$+ \ .002 \text{ Per Capita GNP}$$
$$(.00)$$
$$- \ 4.43 \text{ Party Competition} + .00002 \text{ GNP}$$
$$(1.34) \qquad\qquad (.00)$$

$R^2 = .61$; standard error of estimate = 1961; and level of significance = .00. (The partial coefficients are unstandardized; numbers in parentheses are standard errors.)

This equation explains more than 60% of the variance.[8] . . . Years in the global political system is the most powerful predictor. An ordinary least squares regression equation with it as the sole independent variable yields $R^2 = .46$, larger than the R^2 of the equation utilizing the two independent variables suggested by functionalist tenets.

The effects of the four independent variables in the regression equation can be understood more clearly by interpreting the coefficients in terms of the measurement of the independent variables. According to the equation, each additional year a state has been in the global political system increases its total number of IGO memberships by 1.4; each additional 100 dollars in per capita GNP increases the total by 1.8; each step toward a multiparty system increases the total by 4.4; and, each additional 10 billion dollars in GNP increases the total by 1.6. . . .

FUNCTIONALISM AND THE FUTURE EVOLUTION OF THE WEB OF IGOs

Functionalism provided a good point of departure for an examination of the multiplying entanglement between states and IGOs in the latter half of the twentieth century. It gave reliable initial guidance about the type of IGOs that would be established, the factors that would propel states toward IGO membership, and the consequences of IGO membership for the economic performance and conflict behavior of states. Yet functionalism fell short of providing a comprehensive explanation. It had to be supplemented by traditional explanations of international politics.

The evolving web of international governmental organizations has modified the global political system, as functionalism argued that it would, but it has not yet radically transformed this system, as functionalism hoped would happen. The radical transformation may yet come. In the meantime, however, international governmental organizations, in addition to modifying the political system, institutionalize aspects of traditional international politics.

The evolution of the web of IGOs has been affected by the broad historical currents of world politics, as well as by the dynamics foreseen by functionalism. Decolonization explains much of what has happened, and surely the exclusive organizations established by both Western states and members of the Soviet group owe their origins in part to the deep rift between these two groupings stemming from the Cold War.

Probably the multiplying entanglement between states and IGOs will continue in the immediate future, and perhaps even at the same dizzying pace. The complexity of modern life creates many pressures for states to establish additional IGOs. What has happened so far demonstrates the overwhelming sense of governments throughout the world that states no longer provide large enough frameworks for tackling pressing problems. As for modalities, there are not many barriers to the continuing generation of IGO offshoots. Finally, simply on the basis of mathematical possibilities, there are enormous opportunities for creating IGOs among Third World states. The regression equation developed here would predict that as the GNP and per capita GNP of Third World states rises, and if the competition of political parties within them increases, the number of IGOs to which each Third World state belongs will increase substantially. If the IGO web were to become as dense in the Third World as it already is in the West, the total number of IGOs would have to be multiplied several times.

The mere statement of these possibilities raises an issue that will have to be faced. The functionalist persuasion was enunciated and became popular before a dense web of IGOs existed; it provided an important impulse toward creating this web. The evolution of the web, however, cannot continue indefinitely on the basis of early basic ideas. States in the contemporary global political system on the average already belong to one IGO for every 356,490 of their inhabitants. The ratio is considerably more extreme for countries with numerically limited populations. For New Zealand it is one IGO for every 42,466; for Cape Verde, one for every 11,571; for Jordan, one for every 43,108; and for Costa Rica, one for every 28,013. Even for as populous a country as the United States, that belongs to fewer than the predicted number of organizations, the ratio is one for every 1,865,900. If the United States finds it administratively trying to formulate constructive policies for the organizations to which it belongs, as it does, what must the situation be like for countries that belong to proportionately more IGOs and have much smaller bureaucracies?

In most countries a relatively small number of bureaucrats along with a few delegates are charged with the responsibility of overseeing the work of and formulating policies for some 60 international governmental organizations. The impossibility of doing these tasks well in such circumstances is obvious. When the majority of states in an IGO are in such a position, the control of the direction of the organization can easily drift to the secretariat or to a minority of activist delegates who can muster majority support. States, and particularly those that provide the greatest financial support, can easily lose control. The United States and other Western countries allege that this has happened in UNESCO, and the U.S. and British withdrawal from UNESCO is a result of deep disagreement with the policies of the organization. Whatever the wisdom of the U.S. and U.K. decisions in this particular instance, there is a general problem. Somehow the multiplying entanglement of states and IGOs will have to take account of administrative realities and possibilities.

Functionalist theory expresses a preference for international governmental organizations becoming relatively autonomous from the states that comprise them. Functionalist theory sees such relatively autonomous IGOs gradually guiding states. UNESCO, which became relatively autonomous, could demonstrate the unreality of this vision. Given the fact of national control over resources, IGOs are at some risk when they ignore the preferences of the most powerful states. To do so may make them irrelevant to contemporary affairs, or, more seriously, could jeopardize their existence.

It is clear that creative ideas that go beyond functionalism are needed to guide the future evolution of the web of international governmental organizations. Such ideas will have to take into account and build on the empirical evidence presented here. Ways need to be discovered for effectively, constructively, and reliably engaging states in the web of IGOs that is continually being woven even more densely.

NOTES

1. The *Yearbook* contains information about both international governmental and international nongovernmental organizations. The first edition of the *Yearbook* was published in 1909, and the most recent in 1983. The information contained in the *Yearbook* comes from responses to a questionnaire sent to the secretariats of international organizations by the Union of International Associations. The amount of information contained in the *Yearbook* about each IGO thus varies. There is a headquarters address for virtually all the IGOs that are listed, the date of founding for almost 80%, the member states for some 50%, the size of the staff for 12%, and the size of the budget for less than 3%.

2. Curiously, the numbers in the summary statistics included in the nineteenth edition do not correspond with the number of organizations that are actually listed. There are more IGOs listed in subcategories D through F of the *Yearbook*, and fewer in categories C and

G, than the summary statistics indicate. In addition, some organizations that have been inactive or are dissolved are included in categories B through G of the listing, and as mentioned in the text, these categories also include some IGOs that had been proposed but were not yet in existence in 1981. These latter organizations have been placed in a separate category, I, in the data set.

3. The members of the OECD are Austria, Australia, Belgium, Canada, Denmark, Finland, France, Federal Republic of Germany, Greece, Iceland, Ireland, Italy, Japan, Luxembourg, the Netherlands, New Zealand, Norway, Portugal, Spain, Sweden, Switzerland, Turkey, the United Kingdom, and the United States of America.

4. The members of the Warsaw Treaty Organization for the purposes of this analysis are Bulgaria, the Byelorussia Soviet Socialist Republic, Czechoslovakia, the German Democratic Republic, Hungary, Poland, Romania, the Ukrainian Soviet Socialist Republic, and the Union of Soviet Socialist Republics. Byelorussia and the Ukraine are not formally members of WTO, but they are members of several IGOs, and since they are part of the Soviet Union, which is a member of WTO, it seems appropriate to include them in this category.

5. It includes the 121 states that were members of the Group of 77 in 1981, and 50 other states and territories. Some of the 50 were not independent, but they nevertheless belonged to various IGOs, and thus should not be excluded from analyses. Were they independent, they probably would join the Group of 77, as indeed some of them have done after gaining independence in the years since 1981. The 50 also includes some small European sovereignties and other states such as Israel, Taiwan, and South Africa that are difficult to classify. All of these states need to be included in some group, and the latter group of states that are difficult to classify resembles the states in the "Other" category with respect to economic characteristics more than it resembles those in the OECD or WTO categories. The categories are used in the descriptions that follow, so that the inclusion of any particular state is not necessary: when IGOs composed exclusively of "Other" states are described, these bodies in fact seldom include those states that are difficult to classify.

6. The members of CMEA are Bulgaria, Cuba, Czechoslovakia, the German Democratic Republic, Hungary, Mongolia, Poland, Romania, the Union of Soviet Socialist Republics, and Vietnam.

7. In this analysis, the term "IGO memberships" is defined as including both full and associate memberships in organizations in both of UIA's categories. States' IGO membership using this inclusive definition correlate almost perfectly the total arrived at using various narrower definitions. The generalizations derived from analyses using the most inclusive definition would also be valid if a more restrictive definition were preferred.

8. Using states' full memberships only in IGOs included in the UIA category of conventional international organizations as the dependent variable yields a very similar equation.

REFERENCES

Gastil, Raymond D. 1981. The Comparative Survey of Freedom—The Ninth Year. *Freedom at Issue*, 59:3–18.

International Bank for Reconstruction and Development (IBRD). 1982a. *World Bank Atlas, 1982*. Washington, D.C.

Mitrany, David. 1933. *The Progress of International Government*. New Haven: Yale University Press.

Mitrany, David. 1966. *A Working Peace System*. Chicago: Quadrangle.

Union of International Associations (UIA). 1981. *Yearbook of International Organizations, 1981*. 19th ed. Brussels.

6

INTERGOVERNMENTAL ORGANIZATIONS AND COOPERATION AMONG NATIONS

James M. McCormick

International organizations are increasingly a prominent feature of international politics today. Both intergovernmental organizations (IGOs) and nongovernmental organizations (NGOs) have grown at a rapid rate in recent years (Angell, 1969; Kegley and Rochester, 1971; Pentland, 1976). Although numerous studies have described this organizational growth, few have evaluated the behavior of nations within these organizations. Nonetheless, a usual assumption in much of the literature is that international organizations provide the conditions conducive to greater cooperation and interdependence among nations. In addition, some argue that such common organizational ties set in motion forces that produce cooperative interstate behavior in areas not originally envisioned by the organizational tasks. Yet such assertions are largely untested.[1] In the research reported here, we examine empirically the levels of cooperative behavior of nations inside and outside intergovernmental organizations (IGOs) and assess the extent to which levels of cooperation differ across

SOURCE: Reprinted from the *International Studies Quarterly*, Vol. 24, No. 1, March 1980, 75–98, with permission of the International Studies Association, Byrnes International Center, University of South Carolina, Columbia, S.C. 29208 USA.

[1]For some important attempts to test this notion, see Caporaso (1970, 1972) and Dolan (1975). The classic studies on this phenomenon are provided by Mitrany (1966) and Haas (1958, 1964).

types of IGOs and across types of nations. Our aim is to begin to evaluate empirically intergovernmental organizations as vehicles of interstate cooperation.

SOME THEORETICAL CONSIDERATIONS

Two types of previous research provide a theoretical basis for contending that international organizations would likely lead to greater cooperative behavior among states: (1) studies that posit attitudinal change among participants within international organizations and (2) research that links this attitudinal change to behavior modification among states. For instance, a number of systematic studies of international organizations (Alger, 1963, 1966; Matecki, 1957; Best, 1960) have noted that the contacts among states within such a confined setting have an important impact on the participants' attitudes toward one another.[2] This contact can result in a more positive level of affect among the representatives. In his *Peace on the March*, Robert Angell explains this process in terms of a theory of small group behavior:

One of the best demonstrated theories is that contacts made in small intimate groups tend to produce favorable attitudes toward one another among the members. . . . This proposition rests upon the findings of several social psycholo-

gists that intimate association leads to "taking the role of the other," to put oneself in the other's shoes, and hence of sharing his values and aspirations to some degree [1969: 30 as quoted in Kegley and Rochester, 1971: 405].

Moreover, at least three studies provide additional empirical support for this socialization argument. Riggs (1977) finds that significant attitude change toward international cooperation occurs among congressmen and senators attending the UN General Assembly as U.S. delegates. Karns (1977) also reports that attendance at interparliamentary group meetings by members of Congress did alter their foreign policy attitudes. In an earlier study, Volgy and Quistgaard (1975) demonstrate that learning experiences within the United Nations (as measured by nations taking certain roles within the organization or by taking cues from regional counterparts) did relate closely to the degree of "support for world order" (Angell, 1973) by these states.

While Angell, Alger, Riggs, and others have thus suggested that international organizations provide the forum for attitude change, they do not explicitly link it to the change in behavior between states. Fortunately, Coplin (1971) and Pentland (1976) provide such a tie. In discussing international organizations and interstate bargaining,

---

[2]For a dissenting view on international organizations and attitude change, see Wolf (1973), Bonham (1970), and Jacobson (1967). For a useful summary of the literature on the socialization process within international organizations, see Peck (1978).

Coplin states that such organizations may have come to serve as "sets of norms, operating at an implicit level" (1971: 300) for member nations. In turn, this set of norms "encourages states to regulate themselves in conflict bargaining relationships" (1971: 300). Coplin thus sees a linkage between attitudinal change (via the internalization of organizational norms) and behavioral change (via the bargaining among states). Similarly, Pentland suggests that organizational constraints do serve as systemic modifiers of state behavior, particularly in those cases in which states have internalized norms "through a process of socialization occurring among political, economic, and administrative elites as they interacted with each other in a multilateral context" (1976: 641).

Thus, an underlying two-step process seems to be operating within international organizations: (1) Interpersonal contacts within international organizations will likely produce positive attitudes among the participants; and (2) such attitudinal change, in turn, will provide the conditions conducive to accommodation (and thus cooperation) among member-states. Accordingly, it seems plausible to argue that the behavior of states inside IGOs would be significantly more cooperative than the behavior of states outside of them.

Little systematic evidence exists, however, on whether foreign policy behavior conducted within such organizations is really different from that conducted by other means. Such evidence is necessary if we are to draw any conclusion about the role that international organizations play as forums for fostering cooperative activities. Therefore, the first task of this article is to present some aggregate data on foreign policy cooperation inside one type of international organization—the intergovernmental organization (IGO)[3]—and compare it to the foreign policy cooperation conducted outside of such organizations. Going further though, we also compare the degree of cooperation within global, regional, "low politics," and "high politics" organizations to see the extent to which the type of IGO is associated with differing levels of international cooperation. Based on the regionalist (Nye, 1971) and the functionalist (Mitrany, 1966; Haas, 1964) arguments, we would expect the

---

[3]IGOs were chosen for examination because they are more clearly recognized as arenas for foreign policy behavior by nations than are nongovernmental organizations (NGOs).

An important analytic point needs to be addressed at this juncture. The fact that states employ international organizations obviously reflects a cooperative response among nations. However, our concern is what occurs beyond this initial step. Moreover, we believe these questions are empirical ones and ones that have important implications for various theoretical arguments regarding international organizations. These arguments are developed below.

regional organizations and low politics organizations to be greater forums of interstate cooperation than global organizations and high politics organizations. The reasoning here is relatively straightforward. Regional organizations, as contrasted to global organizations, are usually composed of states that have political, economic, and cultural similarities. Thus, cooperation would be more easily obtainable in such a homogeneous setting than it would be in the heterogeneous setting of global organizations. Likewise, low politics organizations would generate greater cooperation than high politics organizations because the former are established to perform technical and noncontroversial "functions" or "tasks" (e.g., joint economic or social welfare tasks), while the latter tend to deal with political and military matters—matters that tend to arouse conflict among states.

To ascertain whether it might be the type of state which accounts for the level of cooperation inside and outside IGOs, we examine the relative size and level of economic development of the nations that act within these various forums.[4]

Based upon previous research on these attributes in international politics, we would expect that small states would tend to be less cooperative than large states in their behavior inside IGOs (and outside of them, too). This line of reasoning is based on East's (1973) "alternative model" of small state behavior. East (1973: 559–560) contends that small states with few resources available for allocation to foreign affairs and with a limited bureaucracy tend to perceive events and developments in the international system more slowly. Thus, when they do enter into a situation, there is less time to engage in early, low-level ambiguous behavior. As a consequence, they tend to emphasize actions (deeds) at the expense of diplomacy (words), risk at the expense of caution, and conflict at the expense of cooperation.[5] Assuming the validity of this view, small states would thus tend to act less cooperatively than large states. Nonetheless, given our view of IGOs as cooperation-generating forums, we would still expect the levels of cooperation inside IGOs to be greater than outside of IGOs for those small states.

For the development dimension,

---

[4]For a discussion of the centrality of these two attributes in analyzing nation behavior, see Sullivan (1976: 102–141) and Moore (1974: 251–267). Moreover, a recent study by Sullivan (1978) highlights the utility of national attributes in assessing national support for world order.

[5]A more traditional view of small state behavior might well argue that small states would act more cooperatively in international forums, because such organizations may assist them in obtaining their foreign policy goals—weak as they are in terms of relative international power. By this reasoning, small states would be relatively more cooperative than large states in IGOs. Our data base will allow us to evaluate both of these views of small state behavior.

we would expect that the developing states would be less cooperative than developed states both inside and outside IGOs. This assertion is based upon reasoning similar to that which was advanced for the differences between large and small states. Developing states do not have many resources to monitor international events and thus have to be more judicious in their selection of foreign policy actions. Thus, these states are likely to act in a manner similar to small states. There is another reason for this developed/developing difference. In the past, developed states have tended to strongly influence the operation of IGOs; thus, cooperation within these forums by such states might well be expected. Conversely, developing states find themselves in a less advantageous position in IGOs and would be more likely to challenge the status quo (thus generating more conflict) in these arenas.[6] In short, the actions of these states inside IGOs would be more conflictual and less cooperative than those of developed states. Finally, and like our earlier argument on the size dimension, we would expect that the levels of cooperation by developing states inside IGOs would be greater than outside IGOs, because IGOs are still cooperation-generating forums.

DATA AND METHOD

The data base for this study is the CREON (Comparative Research on the Events of Nations) data set. The CREON data consist of 11,665 foreign policy events initiated by 35 nations gathered during randomly selected quarters (January-March, April-June, July-September, or October-December) for the years 1959–1968. . . .

This particular data set was well suited for our purposes because it coded foreign policy activity in two important ways: (1) whether a nation's foreign policy behavior (or event) occurred inside the context of an international organization or outside of it and (2) what type of activity took place inside or outside these international forums.

. . . When an action occurred within a specific IGO, we recoded that IGO by geographical and functional type.[7] The geographical distinction was made between organizations that were either global or regional in membership. Such a dis-

---

[6]Other findings on international organization behavior by developed and developing states suggest a hypothesis that is exactly opposite of this reasoning. Vincent (cited in Sullivan, 1976: 115) characterizes highly developed states' behavior as "negative" and "oppositional" within the UN General Assembly. This view would suggest that *developed* states would be more conflict-prone than developing states within such international forums. Again, our data analysis allows us to assess both sets of arguments.

[7]These two categories were chosen because they have direct relevance for evaluating the regionalist and functionalist arguments in the rest of the research. Additionally, a more exacting breakdown of IGOs would greatly reduce the number in each group and would thus make any analysis more difficult.

tinction was usually self-evident when surveying the membership lists. The only difficulty arose over organizations that were *quasi-regional*—member-states primarily from one region but including at least one nonregional member-state.[8] A decision was made, however, to include these organizations within the regional category. The functional classification also divided the IGOs into two groups: Each IGO was classified as either a "high politics" organization—one dealing primarily with political and military affairs—or a "low politics" organization—one dealing with economic, technical or social-cultural concerns.[9]

Another research decision was made regarding the foreign policy actions coded by the CREON investigators. First, we collapsed their 35 categories into 8 broad groups following East's (1973: 569–570) scheme. . . . The 8 groups consisted of 3 verbal statement categories (of evelution, desire, and intent) and a nonverbal deed category, with each subdivided by a conflict and cooperation dimension. Second, we collapsed 4 of the categories into what we labeled "cooperative behavior" and the other 4 categories into what we labeled "conflictual behavior." The 3 cooperative verbal categories and the 1 cooperative deed category formed the "cooperative behavior" while the 3 conflictual verbal categories and the 1 conflictual deed category formed the "conflictual behavior."[10] Percentages were then computed on the extent of cooperative behavior for a given nation or set of nations inside the recoded IGO groups—i.e., global, regional, high politics, or low politics organizations—or outside of them. It is important to note that the percentages we shall report are the mean percentages of cooperative behav-

---

[8]This research decision was made because there were only a limited number of "quasi-regional" organizations in our data and because, by collapsing these IGOs into the regional category, we could more easily test the regionalist argument. For a discussion of "quasi-regional" organizations, see Nye (1971: 8).

[9]The classification of "high politics" and "low politics" IGOs is largely based upon Pentland's (1976: 628–629) discussion of types of international organizations. He identifies four types of organizations: (1) diplomatic-military, (2) economic management or development, (3) technical, and (4) social or cultural. The first category formed our "high politics" organizations, and the latter three formed the "low politics" organizations. For a complete discussion of the procedures used in categorizing each IGO, see McCormick and Kihl (1979: 497).

[10]One final research design decision was made in order to calculate meaningfully the cooperative/conflictual percentages. For inclusion in our analysis, a nation had to initiate at least ten foreign policy events in the forum under examination (whether inside a particular IGO or outside IGO). This cut-off point was chosen to reduce the possibility that a very few actions of a nation in either the cooperative or noncooperative category could skew the overall results of our analysis. We should add that most states had much greater numbers of events in any forum than this lower limit of ten. Nonetheless, this lower bound did require the exclusion of some nations from the regional and regional low politics analyses.

ior for the appropriate category. These figures were calculated by averaging the mean percentages for each individual nation. Such a measure is more meaningful than simply calculating the mean level of cooperation, because it takes into account the relative contribution of each nation. For example, nations with substantial cooperative behavior could disproportionately skew the results when only the behavior itself is the unit of analysis. Such an outcome is less likely when the nation is used as the unit of analysis.

FINDINGS

Cooperative Behavior and IGOs

According to the data presented in Table 1, the behavior of the CREON nations inside IGOs is sig-

nificantly more cooperative than their behavior outside IGOs. On the average, 85% of the behavior inside IGOs is cooperative, compared to roughly 70% of the behavior outside of them. Such differences in cooperative behavior should not be surprising based upon our earlier arguments. Additionally, though, Mansbach et al. (1976: 282–283) point out that IGOs are creations of nation-states and are thus set up to facilitate coordination among them. Consequently, one would expect to see greater levels of cooperation in these forums than in other arenas. What is surprising from these results, however, is the great magnitude of interstate cooperation in both arenas—both inside and outside IGOs. Apparently, the considerable amount of cooperation among nations is too easily

TABLE 1   Percentage of Cooperative Behavior Outside and Within IGOs by the CREON Nations

	Mean Level of Cooperative Behavior[a]
Outside IGOs	69.7% (N = 35)
Within IGOs	84.5% (N = 35)[b]
Global	88.2% (N = 34)
Regional	74.2% (N = 29)
High Politics	81.1% (N = 34)
Low Politics	91.9% (N = 34)[c]

a. Entries represent the mean percentages of cooperative behavior for the appropriate category. These were computed by averaging the mean percentages for each nation across the data set.
b. Difference of means test is significant beyond the .001 level for the outside/within comparison.
c. Difference of means tests were calculated for all combination of types of IGOs (six in total). All were significant at the .01 level except for the regional/high politics comparison (.03 level) and the global/low politics comparison (.06 level).

SOURCE: Table 1 and all subsequent tables were calculated from the CREON (Comparative Research on the Events of Nations) data set, 1959–1968 (Hermann et al., 1973).

overlooked in an international system that so often concentrates attention on the level of conflict among states.

Levels of cooperation in types of IGOs also prove to be significantly different from one another. (Also see Table 1.) The low politics IGOs have the highest levels of cooperation with an average score of 92%, while the global IGOs have the next highest with an average score of 88%. Next in line are the high politics IGOs with 81%, and, quite surprisingly, the regional IGOs have the lowest mean score at 74%. In the main, these results suggest that even inside IGOs, the type of forum is important in affecting the level of cooperation among the CREON states.

Furthermore, these results provide some empirical evaluation of the functionalist and regionalist arguments about international organizations. They seem to confirm the functionalist argument; the low politics organizations do indeed prove to be the arenas of most coopera-

tion among the four types examined. Technical, noncontroversial issues (issues usually discussed in low politics organizations) are more likely to result in cooperative responses among the participants.[11] However, our results are not as promising for the regionalist position. In fact, these arenas exhibit less cooperation than global organizations—the arenas to which they are usually compared—and even lower cooperation scores than the high politics organizations. Thus, despite the fact that regional organizations tend to have greater levels of social, cultural, and political homogeneity than do global organizations, this has apparently not resulted in greater levels of cooperation in such organizations.[12]

NATIONAL ATTRIBUTES AND COOPERATIVE IGO BEHAVIOR

Table 2 shows the percentage of cooperative behavior inside and outside IGOs, after controlling for

---

[11]For an excellent summary and critique of the functionalist thesis, see Pentland (1973). Also see Mitrany (1966), Haas (1964), and Sewell (1966) for standard treatments of functionalism.

[12]These results are not inconsistent with Butterworth's (1976) findings on 146 cases brought before and handled by international organizations from 1946 to 1971. First of all, he found that somewhat more conflictual cases are submitted to the United Nations (the global organization) than to regional organizations, but that the former has a somewhat stronger impact in handling such cases than the latter. He later demonstrates that an important reason for this difference in impact is that more consensus is required in regional organizations in order to take action than in the global organizations. Applying these results to our present concern for cooperation within IGOs, it would therefore be consistent with his argument to find more cooperative behavior in global organizations than in regional ones, since efforts at the disposition of disputes in the former is apparently less rancorous than in the latter. For other recent studies comparing the relative effectiveness of regional and global organizations, see Butterworth (1978) and Haas et al. (1972).

TABLE 2   Percentage of Cooperative Behavior Within and Outside IGOs for the CREON Nations by Size and Development[a]

	Within IGOs	Outside IGOs
A. BY SIZE		
Small States	85.9%[b]	70.2%
	(N = 23)	(N = 23)
Large States	82.0%	68.7%
	(N = 12)	(N = 12)
B. BY DEVELOPMENT		
Developed States	85.9%	68.5%
	(N = 20)	(N = 20)
Developing States	82.7%	71.3%
	(N = 15)	(N = 15)
C. BY SIZE AND DEVELOPMENT		
Small Developed	88.4%	64.7%
	(N = 11)	(N = 11)
Small Developing	83.6%	75.3%
	(N = 12)	(N = 12)
Large Developed	82.9%	73.1%
	(N = 9)	(N = 9)
Large Developing	79.0%	55.4%
	(N = 3)	(N = 3)

a. The percentages shown in the tables represent the averages of the mean percentages for each nation in the categories shown. In subsequent tables, a similar procedure was used, but nations with no or little activity within a particular grouping were not used in the analysis.
b. Difference of means and one-way analysis of variance tests were used throughout the analysis. Because there was not always homogeneity of variances, the Kruskal-Wallis one-way analysis of variance test by ranks was employed. All results were insignificant except as where otherwise noted.

size and development of the participant states. These data fail to support our earlier arguments about differences among types of states and levels of cooperative behavior inside and outside international organizations. Although some differences exist between small and large states and between developed and developing nations, neither attribute discriminates among levels of cooperative behavior in a significant way. Even when we control for both of these factors (see part C of Table 2), the differences in cooperation among the four types of states remain small and statistically insignificant, ranging from 79% for large developing states to 88% for small developed ones.

When we examine the behavior within IGOs by the national attribute characteristics, we do find some differences. Although the low

TABLE 3   Percentage of Cooperative Behavior Within Functional IGOs for the CREON Nations by Size and Development

	High Politics IGOs	*Low Politics IGOs*
	A. BY SIZE	
Small States	82.1% (N = 22)	93.0% (N = 23)
Large States	79.4% (N = 12)	89.6% (N = 11)
	B. BY DEVELOPMENT	
Developed States	83.3% (N = 19)	90.6% (N = 20)
Developing States	78.4% (N = 15)	93.8% (N = 14)
	C. BY SIZE AND DEVELOPMENT	
Small Developed	85.7% (N = 10)	92.3% (N = 11)
Small Developing	79.1% (N = 12)	93.6% (N = 12)
Large Developed	80.7% (N = 9)	88.4% (N = 9)
Large Developing	75.4% (N = 3)	95.1% (N = 2)

politics and high politics IGOs fail to produce any significant differences in the level of cooperation by the size and development dimensions, this is not entirely the case for the geographical IGOs (Tables 3 and 4). The size dimension differentiates cooperative behavior for both regional and global IGOs, while the development dimension is only discriminating for the regional IGOs. For the size dimension, we find that the small states tend to act more cooperatively in the global IGOs, while the large states tend to act more cooperatively in the regional IGOs. For the development dimension, the developed states tend to act more cooperatively than the developing states. These findings are generally consistent with

our earlier arguments about national attributes, except for the size results in the global IGOs.[13] But these results provide only limited support for the role of national attributes, confined as they are primarily to one type of IGO. Moreover, our next analysis clarifies (and weakens) even these apparent relationships.

Combining size and development into a fourfold classification and examining both geographical and functional IGOs, we obtain significant results only for the regional IGOs. However, these results help us specify the extent to which the type of state differentiates cooperative behavior. As part C of Table 4 indicates, it is not exactly the size or development dimension that dis-

---

[13]In fact, the results for the global IGOs are more consistent with Vincent's (1968, 1971) findings that small and weak states tend to act more cooperatively in international organizations.

TABLE 4   Percentage of Cooperative Behavior Within Geographical IGOs for the CREON Nations by Size and Development

	Global IGOs	*Regional IGOs*
	A. BY SIZE	
Small States	91.5% (N = 22)	71.3% (N = 20)
Large States	82.1% (N = 12)[a]	80.6% (N = 9)[b]
	B. BY DEVELOPMENT	
Developed States	87.7% (N = 19)	81.2% (N = 16)
Developing States	88.7% (N = 15)	65.5% (N = 13)[c]
	C. BY SIZE AND DEVELOPMENT	
Small Developed	90.9% (N = 10)	83.2% (N = 9)
Small Developing	91.9% (N = 12)	61.5% (N = 11)
Large Developed	84.1% (N = 9)	78.7% (N = 7)
Large Developing	76.0% (N = 3)	87.6% (N = 2)[d]

a. Difference of means test for the size dimension within global IGOs is significant at the .009 level for the pooled variance estimate and at the .055 level for the separate variance estimate.

b. Difference of means test for size dimension within regional IGOs is significant at the .035 level for the separate variance estimate but not significant (.111) for the pooled variance estimate.

c. Difference of means test for development dimension within regional IGOs is significant beyond .01 level.

d. One-way analysis of variance (Kruskal-Wallis test) by size and development is significant beyond the .01 level for the regional IGOs.

tinguishes the states' behavior within regional IGOs; instead, it appears that the differences we detected can be largely attributed to the behavior pattern of the small developing states. Although the cooperation scores for the other states are within a narrow range, only the small developing states have appreciably different (and lower) cooperation scores. Such a discovery considerably weakens any argument about substantial differences between types of states even within regional IGOs.

In a further effort to evaluate the utility of national attributes for delineating IGO cooperation, we divide the IGOs into four types (global high, global low, regional high, and regional low) and then examine each by the four types of states. Table 5 presents these results.[14] We find some differences by type of state within global high politics IGOs and global low politics

[14]Because not all *types* of states (particularly the small and large developing ones) acted sufficiently within the regional low politics organizations, it was not possible to carry out the analysis of variance for this set of IGOs.

TABLE 5   Percentage of Cooperative Behavior Within Geographical and Functional IGOs for the CREON Nations by Size and Development

| | Type of IGO[a] | | |
	Global High	Global Low	Regional High
Small			
Developing	90.5% (N = 12)	93.4% (N = 12)	60.0% (N = 11)[b]
Small Developed	91.9% (N = 9)	90.7% (N = 10)	73.5% (N = 8)
Large			
Developing	74.9% (N = 3)	94.6% (N = 2)	86.0% (N = 2)
Large Developed	82.4% (N = 8)	85.6% (N = 9)	74.0% (N = 7)

a. Because not all CREON nations acted within regional low politics IGOs, it was not possible to analyze differences in cooperative behavior by size and development.
b. One-way analysis of variance (Kruskal-Wallis test) by size and development is significant at the .02 level for the regional high politics IGOs.

IGOs. Small states are more cooperative in the former, while developing states are more cooperative in the latter. Neither of these differences proves to be significant with our analysis of variance test. Only for the regional high politics organizations do we find significant differences. The large developing states are most cooperative in these forums, both types of developed states act at about the same level of cooperation in these arenas, and the small developing states are considerably less cooperative. Although the significant differences for this set of IGOs cannot be wholly attributed to the behavior of the small developing states, the overall pattern is similar to what we discovered in the regional IGO analysis. In sum, though, this more refined analysis of IGOs and types of states does not alter the thrust of our results to this point: National attribute characteristics have only limited utility in differentiating the level of cooperative behavior in IGOs.

CONCLUSION

Although we need to caution the reader about pushing our results too far (owing to the aggregate level of our analysis and the limitations of our data set), nonetheless, two important substantive and theoretical findings on IGO cooperation deserve further comment. On a substantive level, we first confirmed the conventional view that foreign policy cooperation inside IGOs is greater than cooperation outside these forums. We also discovered, however, that while cooperative behavior is found in all types of IGOs, the degree of cooperation differs among the various types of organizations. Although the low politics and the global IGOs show particularly high levels of cooperation among the nations in our sample, the regional organizations produce significantly lower levels. In fact, these latter organizations produced the lowest levels of co-operation of the four types examined. Such a result seems to call into question the regionalist argument as an approach to interstate cooperation. Moreover, it is especially significant in light of the fact that regional organizations grew more rapidly than did global organizations in the decade of the 1960s and were often characterized as holding considerable promise for regulating interstate conflict (Nye, 1971).[15] From our aggregate analysis, however, these organizations fail to support this description very strongly.

Second, we found that the national attributes of the participating states were not very useful in discriminating among levels of cooperation in the various IGOs. It was primarily for the regional IGOs, and specifically the regional high politics IGOs, that we found some significant differences by type of state. Upon closer inspection, we discovered that a good portion of this result can be attributed to the behavior of one set of states—the small developing states. This group of states apparently sees the regional organizations less as arenas of cooperation and more as arenas of regional rivalries. Overall, then,

the type of state proved less important in understanding interstate co-operation in IGOs than simply knowing the type of IGO in which a state was participating. On a theoretical level, this finding tends to support the view that a single national attribute (or even a combination of these attributes) does not possess much explanatory power when analyzing foreign policy behavior. As Sullivan (1976) concluded after reviewing a vast amount of writing on national attributes:

> Simple theoretical linkages between internal attributes, or domestic sources, and external behavior do not exist. Rather, very specific linkages need to be formulated into the theoretical structure of national attribute theory, and even these—the research here strongly suggests—do not play a *large* part in differential foreign policy behavior [1976: 135].

Such statements aptly characterize the national attribute analyses in this study. . . .

In this analysis, we have treated all issues taken up inside and outside IGOs as if they were of equal importance; this is obviously not the case. Consequently, all of our results may not hold across all issue areas, or more accurately, they may only apply for particular kinds of issues. Unfortunately, we cannot address such concerns with our

---

[15]This commentary should not suggest that cooperation within regional organizations is low, but only that cooperation within other IGO forums is greater. As a consequence, the other forums seem to provide greater possibilities for fostering interstate cooperation.

present analysis. Similarly, we have not identified the specific kinds of conditions that move nations toward cooperation in IGOs. It may well be that not only are issues important, but contextual factors also may prove to be central to cooperative outcomes. Finally, we have not evaluated the impact that cooperative (or noncooperative) outcomes have had on stability and change in the international system. That is, do outcomes in IGOs make a "difference" in international politics? It is these problems that future work on IGOs and interstate behavior might fruitfully address.

REFERENCES

Alger, C. F. (1966) "Personal contact in international organizations," in H. C. Kelman (ed.) International Behavior: A Social-Psychological Analysis. New York: Holt, Rinehart & Winston.

—— (1963) "United Nations participation as a learning experience." Public Opinion Q. 27 (Fall): 411–426.

Angell, R. C. (1973) "National support for world order: a research report." J. of Conflict Resolution 17 (September): 429–454.

—— (1969) Peace on the March: Transnational Participation. New York: Litton.

Best, G. (1960) "Diplomacy in the United Nations." Ph.D. dissertation, Northwestern University.

Bonham, G. M. (1970) "Participation in regional parliamentary assemblies: effects on attitudes of Scandinavian parliamentarians." J. of Common Market Studies 8 (June): 325–336.

Butterworth, R. L. (1978) Moderation from Management: International Organizations and Peace. Pittsburgh: University Center for International Studies.

—— (1976) "Organizing collective security: the UN Charter's Chapter VIII in practice." World Politics 28 (January): 197–222.

Caporaso, J. A. (1972) Functionalism and Regional Integration: A Logical and Empirical Assessment. Sage Professional Papers in International Studies, 02–004. Beverly Hills, CA: Sage.

—— (1970) "Encapsulated integrative patterns vs. spillover: the cases of transport integration in the European Economic Communities." Int. Studies Q. 14 (December): 361–394.

Coplin, W. D. (1971) "International organization in the future international bargaining: a theoretical projection." J. of Int. Affairs 55 (Summer): 287–301.

Dolan, M. B. (1975) "The study of regional organization: a quantitative analysis of the neo-functionalist and systemic approaches." Int. Studies Q. 19 (September): 285–315.

East, M. A. (1973) "Size and foreign policy behavior: a test of two models." World Politics 25 (July): 556–576.

Haas, E. B. (1964) Beyond the Nation-State. Stanford: Stanford Univ. Press.

—— (1958) The Uniting of Europe. Stanford: Stanford Univ. Press.

—— R. L. Butterworth, and J. S. Nye (1972) Conflict Management by International Organizations. Morristown, NJ: General Learning Press.

Hermann, C. F., M. A. East, M. G. Hermann, B. G. Salmore, and S. A. Salmore (1975) "Comparative research on the events of nations codebook." Inter-University Consortium for Political Research, Ann Arbor.

—— (1973) CREON: A Foreign Events Data Set. Sage Professional Papers in International Studies, 02–024. Beverly Hills, CA: Sage.

Jacobson, H. K. (1967) "Deriving data from delegates to international assemblies: a research note." Int. Organization 21 (Summer): 592–613.

Karns, D. A. (1977) "The effect of interparliamentary meetings on the foreign policy attitudes of United States Congressmen." Int. Organization 31 (Summer): 497–513.

Kegley, C. W., Jr. and J. M. Rochester (1971) "Assessing the impact of trends on the international system: the growth of intergovernmental organizations," pp. 401–411 in W. D. Coplin and C. W. Kegley, Jr. (eds.) A Multi-Method Introduction to International Politics. Chicago: Markham.

Mansbach, R. W., Y. H. Ferguson, and D. E. Lampert (1976) The Web of World Politics. Englewood Cliffs, NJ: Prentice-Hall.

Matecki, B. E. (1957) Establishment of the International Finance Corporation and the United States Policy. Princeton, NJ: Princeton Univ. Press.

McCormick, J. M. and Y. W. Kihl (1979) "Intergovernmental organizations and foreign policy behavior: some empirical findings." Amer. Pol. Sci. Rev. 73 (June): 494–504.

Mitrany, D. (1966) A Working Peace System. Chicago: Quadrangle Books.

Moore, D. W. (1974) "National attributes and nation typologies: a look at the Rosenau genotypes," pp. 251–267 in J. N. Rosenau (ed.) Comparing Foreign Policies: Theories, Findings, and Methods. New York: Halsted.

Nye, J. S. (1971) Peace in Parts. Boston: Little, Brown.

Peck, R. (1978) "Socialization of permanent representatives in the UN? some evidence." Presented at the 1978 Annual Meeting of the International Studies Association, Washington, DC, February.

Pentland, C. (1976) "International organizations," pp. 624–659 in J. N. Rosenau, K. W. Thompson, and G. Boyd (eds.) World Politics. New York: Free Press.

—— (1973) International Theory and European Integration. New York: Free Press.

Riggs, R. E. (1977) "One small step for functionalism: UN participation and congressional attitude change." Int. Organization 31 (Summer): 515–539.

Sewell, J. P. (1966) Functionalism and World Politics. Princeton, NJ: Princeton Univ. Press.

Sullivan, M. P. (1978) "International organizations and world order: a reappraisal. J. of Conflict Resolution 22 (March): 105–120.

—— (1976) International Relations: Theories and Evidence. Englewood Cliffs, NJ: Prentice-Hall.

Vincent, J. E. (1971) "Predicting voting patterns in the general assembly." Amer. Pol. Sci. Rev. 65 (June): 471–498.

—— (1968) "National attributes as predictors of delegate attitudes at the United Nations." Amer. Pol. Sci. Rev. 62 (September): 916–931.

Volgy, T. J. and J. E. Quistgaard (1975) "Learning about the value of global cooperation: role-taking in the United Nations as a predictor of world mindedness." J. of Conflict Resolution 19 (June): 349–376.

Wolf, P. (1973) "International organization and attitude change: a re-examination of the functionalist approach." Int. Organization 27 (Summer): 347–371.

CHAPTER IV

Decisionmaking

The common public perception of decisionmaking in international organizations is a narrow one. Many see the decision process confined to formal, roll-call votes on symbolic resolutions by member states in a large legislative session; the various General Assembly resolutions are some familiar examples of activities that seem to confirm this perception. In this section, we hope to dispel this myth and give the reader a more sophisticated view of the activities and processes of international organizations.

The first article in this section, by Cox and Jacobson, provides a framework to analyze the decision-making processes of international organizations. First, it is evident that the decisions and activities of international organizations are not confined to formal votes. Cox and Jacobson present a taxonomy of seven different kinds of decisions, which include well-known symbolic actions such as equating Zionism with racism. Yet, they also include supervisory decisions; for example, the International Atomic Energy Agency (IAEA) conducts inspections of nuclear facilities throughout the world.

Just as the decisions of international organizations involve more than symbolic actions, so too does the process of decisionmaking involve more than delegates from member states. Cox and Jacobson also identify a set of seven actors that play varying roles in the decision-making process. These actors include the executive heads of the organizations and members of the mass media, in addition to the delegates appointed by their national governments. The actual influence of a particular actor depends on the organization and the situation at hand, but the authors correctly point out that personal attributes of the individual can exercise a great impact. The dynamic leadership of Dag Hammarskjold was a critical factor in the peacekeeping missions carried out by the United Nations during the late 1950s and early 1960s.

Finally, it is evident from the Feld and Jordan selection that not all the decisions of international organizations occur in formal legislative sessions. These authors demonstrate that many international organizations have subsidiary organs that are crucial in the decisions of the organization. The United Nations has an extensive committee system divided along the lines of issue areas. Other organizations have comparable arrangements for developing policy. For example, major decisions of the International Monetary Fund (IMF) actually are worked out in meetings of that organization's board of executive directors, which does not include representatives of all IMF members. Indeed, it further might be argued that the executive board only ratifies decisions worked out in consultations between the industrialized states in the Group of Ten. Therefore, focusing only on the activities in the plenary organs of an international organization results in missing the processes and coalitions by which the formal decisions were made.

Feld and Jordan also investigate two other important aspects of decisionmaking in international organizations. First, they outline the character of the bureaucracy and international civil service in the performance of organization tasks. Then, in a later section, the authors detail several important strategies, including the calling of special conferences, used by actors in the decision-making process. Again, studying only public sessions of an international organization provides a superficial view and one that is of limited value in understanding the development and selection of policy alternatives.

Although formal voting is not the only aspect of decisionmaking in international organizations, it is often an important component. Many international organizations adhere to the "one state-one vote" standard. This results in a situation whereby micro-states such as Tuvalu have the same theoretical voting strength as the People's Republic of China. In other organizations, such as the IMF and World Bank, votes are weighted according to criteria such as economic wealth or level of budgetary contributions. At different times, the United States and other Western states have demanded a greater voice in the decisionmaking of the United Nations General Assembly. That body bases its voting allocation on the concept of sovereign equality, the effect of which is that each state receives one vote. This demand is often based on the disproportionate amount of the organization's budget contributed by Western states.

William Dixon provides an analysis of the impact that changes in the General Assembly voting scheme would have on the power of various blocs in the United Nations. He concludes that all the proposed alternatives would result in a net loss of voting power for the so-called Third World bloc. Yet, he points out that the mere increase in the number of votes for a given bloc of states does not necessarily increase the effective voting power they have in influencing decision outcomes. The implication is that changing the one state-one vote system in the General Assembly will not necessarily bring all the benefits hoped for by the

Western bloc. Indeed, no matter how one defines each state's "fair" share of votes, there are inevitable advantages and disadvantages in voting power that are attendant to each scheme.

The activities of international organizations and the actors who influence those actions are varied. An understanding of the complex decision-making process is one key to understanding the behavior and impact of international organizations in a given issue area.

7

THE FRAMEWORK FOR INQUIRY

Robert Cox and Harold Jacobson

Decision making in international organizations occurs within a context comprising the functions, the institutional framework and basic procedures, and the historical development of the agency. Because both the decision-making processes and the distribution of influence are initially shaped by these factors, considering them is an essential first stage in any analysis.

Given the nature of the international system, the creation of an international organization requires concrete action by states. Usually, although not always, such actions are consecrated in a treaty. In any case, understanding must be achieved about what is to be done and how.

International organizations have been set up to perform a variety of tasks: keeping the peace, promoting economic development, allocating the radio frequency spectrum, reducing obstacles to trade, ensuring that technology is used only for peaceful purposes, and facilitating the maintenance of stable exchange rates—to name only a few. While a certain level of agreement about what it is to do is necessary when an international organization is created, all parties need not share the same conception of the agreement. On the contrary, there are often sharp differences, and these differences can provide essential clues to future dynamic developments in international organizations.

Nor does an agreement about what an organization is to do necessarily represent all the ambitions nursed by the parties to the agreement concerning the ultimate functions of the organization. Many

SOURCE: Reprinted from Robert Cox and Harold Jacobson, *The Anatomy of Influence* (New Haven: Yale University Press, 1973). Copyright © Yale University Press.

states may look upon international organizations principally as instruments for preserving their hegemony or improving their status. Moreover, personal motives, for example the wish to occupy top jobs, can operate along with considerations of state interests in creating new international agencies. Such motivations as these, whether expressed or unexpressed, are also important in shaping later developments in international organizations.

Whatever their specific tasks and fields of activity, international organizations can be divided into two broad categories according to the way in which they perform these tasks. Some organizations are established to provide a forum or framework for negotiations and decisions, others to provide specific services. This dichotomy establishes two ideal types: the *forum organization* and the *service organization*. Organizations in the first category provide a framework for member states to carry on many different activities ranging from the exchange of views to the negotiation of binding legal instruments. States also often use such forums for the collective legitimation of their policies or for propaganda. Organizations in the second category conduct activities themselves; they provide common or individual services or both. Inclusion in this second group depends upon who conducts the services. If the services are carried out directly by individual states, even though they may

have been agreed to within the framework of an international organization, that agency would not belong in the service category. The organization itself must carry out the services. An agency that collects, analyzes, and disseminates information would fit into this category unless the information were intended mainly to facilitate discussions within the framework of the organization, in which case it would be classified as a forum organization.

In reality, of course, many international organizations fall into both categories. ILO, for example, has an extensive technical assistance program, but it also provides a framework for the negotiation of International Labor Conventions. Similarly ITU, UNESCO, WHO, IAEA, and IMF execute services in their own right and at the same time provide frameworks for discussions and negotiations among their member states.

The distinction nevertheless has meaning, and the distribution of an agency's endeavors between the two types of activity may significantly affect patterns of decision making and influence. On the most elementary level, the more an organization leans toward service, the larger its international bureaucracy and the greater the bureaucracy's potential role in certain types of decision making. This classification scheme also provides helpful clues about how an organization can be studied—particularly what bodies of theory developed in other contexts might be most germane. Organizational theory can have great relevance for understanding decision making in service organizations, and the more strongly an agency tends in this direction, the more directly applicable this body of theory is. Conversely, theories about negotiation, such as game theory, can be extremely helpful in analyzing decision-making patterns in forum organizations.

This distinction between forum and service organizations relates to the way in which agencies perform their functions, not to the importance these functions have for member states and not to the authority possessed by the agencies. Whatever their mode of activity, the importance and authority of different organizations varies, and different states perceive them in different terms. An agency that is regarded as crucial by one state may be considered trivial by another, and there is similar variance in the responsiveness of states to the decisions of international organizations. These differences too are important.

They are immediately apparent when one examines the structure of international organizations. The formal powers of the organization and its organs, the extent of regionalism, the forms of representation, the voting procedures, and the organization of the international bureaucracy, all tend to be prescribed at the time an international agency is formed. The initial understanding about how an international organization is to perform its functions inevitably represents compromises among conflicting points of view; all parties must be given some incentives to participate. If an organization is to have functions that might affect significant values, those in control of these values will generally demand structural and procedural devices to ensure for themselves the means of exerting special influence. How far they will press their demands and how successful they will be will depend upon the configuration of forces they face at the time. They might be dissuaded from pressing their claims too far by actual and potential counterclaims in the same functional area or in another. In general, the broader the mandate of the organization, the more likely will be such counterclaims. Conscience or conceptions of long-run self-interest can also serve as moderating forces. Whatever the outcome, these initial understandings provide the basic rules for subsequent decision making.

In some instances the parties to an agreement establishing an international organization will not only prescribe the structures and procedures for decision making but also attempt to specify doctrines according to which decisions should be taken. Thus the constitutional documents of IMF and GATT contain detailed codes of conduct, and the charters of several other international agencies tend in this direction. The more they lean toward such specification, the more the organizations' activities are likely to be set in a particular mold and the harder it will be to shift their direction.

Regardless of the rigidity of their charters, though, once international organizations are established, in many instances they evolve in ways that could not have been foreseen by their founders. To some extent this is because the interests and intentions of the member states change over time, sometimes because of developments within states or in relations among states. Moreover, states may modify their interests and intentions with respect to international organizations as a consequence of participation in them. As in other contexts interaction among actors can result in changed views. In addition, international bureaucracies created to serve international organizations may add new ambitions to those of the states: from the pursuit of specific technical goals the aim might be extended to the desire to make international relations more peaceful or to redistribute the wealth between rich and poor countries. Thus, once established, organizations take on a life of their own and develop their own inner dynamics.

Many of the major changes that take place in international organizations can be identified and measured in terms of the organizations' activities and accomplishments. An organization may change in its functions, either with respect to subject matter—by adding new areas of action or abandoning old ones—or with respect to modes of action—

by switching, for example, from forum to service activities. Changes in functions can be traced in the programs of international organizations. There may be changes in the scale of operations, significant increases or, though not so likely, decreases in programs, for which budgets may provide an indicator. There may also be changes in the authority of an organization, either because members become more responsive to its decisions or because the organization begins to make enactments of a new kind that place more demands upon members. There is no necessary correlation between growth in scale and growth in authority; an organization's budget might grow at the same time that its importance for member states or its authority declined. Finally, there may be changes in the relative importance of an international organization within the issue-area or areas with which it is concerned. The extent to which the organization performs essential functions within the issue-area is relevant here. The existence or creation of another rival organization with overlapping jurisdiction would be an indication of significant change in this respect. Changes of the kinds suggested here may be explained by changes in membership of the organization, in the top personnel of the organization's bureaucracy, in the matters preoccupying member states, or in the new currents of ideas that may emerge.

Changes may be gradual, but one must watch for sudden discontinuities in an organization's history, significant changes in direction that could be termed turning points. Such turning points might occur in relation to any of the features mentioned in the previous paragraph—functions, scale, authority, or importance in the issue-area. They may also arise from dramatic and important changes in input—for example, in the intentions of major participants or in the membership of the organization. What constitutes a turning point is the abruptness, the unpredictability of a significant change, "an impulse which breaks through, untrammelled by the past."[1] . . .

DECISION MAKING: A TAXONOMICAL ANALYSIS

Once the context provided by the functions, structure, and historical evolution of an agency is known, one can begin to consider patterns of decision making and the distribution of influence. For this purpose it is useful to classify decisions. . . .

This taxonomy divides decisions of international organizations into seven categories: representational, symbolic, boundary, programmatic, rule-creating, rule-supervisory, and operational.

Representational decisions affect membership in the organization and representation on internal bodies. They include decisions concerning the admission and exclusion of members, validation of credentials, determination of representation on executive organs and committees, and the manner in which the secretariat is composed, especially at the higher level.

Symbolic decisions are primarily tests of how opinions are aligned; no practical consequences in the form of actions flow directly from these decisions. The intention in symbolic issues is to test the acceptability of goals or ideologies intensely espoused by one group of actors or the legitimacy of long-accepted norms of dominant elites. In some cases these goals or ideologies may relate to broad issues of international politics, in others, to matters specific to the organization's field. In an organization with a mandate in the economic field, decolonization might be an example of a broad issue; improving the lot of developing countries would be an example of a goal specifically related to an organization. Some decisions that might fall within the definitions of other categories may be considered primarily symbolic; but as soon as the direct consequences of the decisions become appreciable, as for example in the controversies over the representation and participation of the communist states in ILO, these decisions fall into another category, in this instance, representational. The criteria for classification as symbolic are thus: the positive one of symbolic intention on the part of the decision makers; and the negative one of the absence of significant practical consequences flowing directly from the decision. The absence of direct consequences does not mean that symbolic decisions are unimportant. On the contrary, in the long run they may have profound consequences because of their effects on the milieu within which international relations are conducted.

This category of decisions can be singled out in order to test the hypothesis that symbolic issues tend to become acute during periods when the organization is adjusting to major changes in the environment that may entail shifts in the structure of influence and in the basic goals and policies of the organization. Such decisions may thus provide a particularly sensitive measure of changes in the internal distribution of influence.

Boundary decisions concern the organization's external relations with other international and regional structures on the matter of (1) their respective scopes, (2) cooperation among organizations, and (3) initiatives taken in one organization to provoke activity in another. . . . GATT and UNCTAD share overlapping jurisdictions, and to a lesser extent the same situation also exists among other organizations. When this occurs, boundary problems inevitably arise.

Programmatic decisions concern the strategic allocation of the organization's resources among different types of activity—the principal types are forum or service—and different fields of activity, which tend to be specific to each individual agency. Allocations usually result from negotiations among the

actors concerning the main goals and division of emphasis among the programs of the organization. Budgets are often the framework within which the programmatic decisions are taken.

Rule-creating decisions define rules or norms bearing upon matters within the substantive scope of the organization. The outcome of the decisions may in some cases be formal instruments such as conventions, agreements, or resolutions. Illustrations of decisions covered in this category include GATT's activity in the negotiation of agreements for tariff reductions, the establishment of Special Drawing Rights by the IMF, as well as the preparing of labor and health conventions by ILO and WHO. Rules may also be created in less formal ways; for example, speeches by the executive head or others that may never explicitly be the subject of votes may nonetheless articulate widely shared norms or goals with which the organization may come to be identified in the minds of many of its constituents. Such actions may in significant cases be considered as rule-creating decisions.

Some rule-creating decisions may resemble programmatic decisions because they seem to imply that certain priorities should be followed in making allocations; but decisions are considered to be programmatic only when they include a definition of priorities specifically for purposes of allocation, or, as is more usual, when they make an actual allocation in terms of budget or personnel.

Rule-supervisory decisions concern the application of approved rules by those subject to them. These decisions may involve various procedures ranging from highly structured to extremely subtle ones. The process of rule supervision passes through several stages, and organizations may develop distinct procedures for each of these stages.[2] The first stage is detection or gathering information about the observance or ignoring of rules. For example, are states complying with the frequency allocations agreed to within ITU? the standards set in International Labor Conventions? the safeguard provisions of IAEA? or the nondiscriminatory trading rules of GATT? Detection may be performed by states acting unilaterally or jointly, by the international bureaucracy, by a private panel, or by some combination of these.

Verifying whether or not the rules are observed is the second stage. This function may also be performed in various ways. Decisions could be entrusted to experts, to the international bureaucracy, or to representatives of member states, to list the most obvious alternatives. Proceedings could be public or private.

The final stage in rule supervision is applying sanctions or punishments for the violation of rules or awarding privileges for compliance with them. As in the other stages decisions about penalties and rewards can be made in several ways.

Operational decisions relate to the providing of services by the organization or the use of its resources in accordance with approved rules, policies, or programs. Examples are decisions about projects for specific technical assistance undertaken by UNESCO or other agencies or the granting of loans by IMF. They are essentially tactical allocations of resources made within broad strategic (programmatic) allocations. Frequently, such tactical, operational decisions are made largely between representatives of individual states and the international bureaucracy. In such decisions criteria referring to the pursuit of general goals may be diluted as a consequence of pressures for services and the need to retain clients' support.

Operational decisions may lead cumulatively to programmatic decisions. The inclusion of a program in an agency budget may be the culmination of a process in which the initiative came originally from an operational decision by the executive head or a segment of the international bureaucracy.

The extent to which operational decisions are effectively subordinated to programmatic decisions may indicate the degree of control that the executive head exercises over the bureaucracy. Weak control may lead to a dispersal of activities, which strengthens the relations between particular clients and segments of the bureaucracy but weakens the overall directing of resources. Strong control may give the executive head greater initiative to enlarge the tasks and enhance the autonomy of the organization.

In order to describe how decisions are usually arrived at for each of these categories of decision in a particular international organization, it will be useful to classify the actors involved, to consider the ways in which they may exercise influence, and to list the modes of decision making that may be employed.

The actors in international organizations may be classified according to the following categories:

1. Representatives of national governments (who may be appointed by various ministries)
2. Representatives of national and international private associations (including interest groups and commercial enterprises)
3. The executive heads of organizations
4. High officials and other members of the bureaucracy of each organization
5. Individuals who serve in their own capacity formally or informally as advisers
6. Representatives of other international organizations
7. Employees of the mass media

Of course, not all of these classes of actors will be active in all organizations. For each category of decisions, however, the actors will fall into one or more of these classes, and it is important to know which of these categories of actors typi-

cally have the most influence on the outcome. . . .

ACTORS AND THEIR SOURCE OF INFLUENCE

As conceived in this study, the actors are individuals who participate directly in the decisions of an international organization. The power of actors—that is, their capacity to exercise influence—is derived both from their position or office and from their personal characteristics. The representatives of some states or the occupants of some positions within international organizations will be important in certain decisions regardless of who they are. Even in these cases, though, the personal characteristics of individuals can enhance or diminish the power that would normally accrue to someone in their position. For example, Ambassador Goldberg had considerable power in the United Nations because he was the United States representative, but some of his power was also attributable to his personal qualities and skills as a negotiator and to his political connections.

Position includes as potentiality the resources of the collectivity represented by the individual and the priority given by the authorities of the collectivity to the use of these resources for influence in the organization. These resources can be of different orders: states may possess economic and military strength, which may be accorded deference in certain decisions; high international officials may command information and recognition, which allows them the initiative in proposing action or resolving conflict. Every position also carries with it its own history of previous attitudes and actions that predispose the behavior of the incumbent in certain directions; it includes also certain limitations in the form of binding instructions imposed by higher authorities in the collectivities represented.

Personal characteristics include skills necessary to carry out the duties and exploit the possibilities of a position: mobilizing the resources of the collectivity represented to achieve influence in the organization, shaping instructions for performing the duties of the position, and influencing the behavior of other actors.

An actor's power or his capacity to exercise influence is thus compounded of his position and his personal attributes. For the sake of clarity the relationship can be expressed in symbolic form:

$$P \pm A = C$$

Position or office (P) modified by (in this formula, plus or minus) personal attributes (A) equals the power or the capacity (C) of the individual actor. C is a function of P and also a function of A, but P and A vary independently. Although the form in which this symbolic statement is written assumes that A will add to or detract from P, in some circumstances the relationship may be multiplicative or more complex. This equation is not intended to create an illusion of precise mathematical treatment. Some of the concepts have not been, and probably cannot be, represented in a numerical form that would lend itself to mathematical application.

Among the personal attributes that might enhance an individual's power in an international organization are his personal charisma, ideological legitimacy, administrative competence, expert knowledge, long association with an organization, negotiating ability, and ability to persist in intransigence. The personal status he has acquired outside the organization through such things as wealth, election to an important office, scientific achievements, and possession of significant influence in an important collectivity will also affect his power. The advantages of these personal attributes vary with organizations. For example, negotiating ability might be especially valuable in organizations like GATT where consensus must be achieved, while the ability to persist in intransigence might be a telling factor in UNCTAD if the outcome was to be a declaratory resolution.

An actor's power attributable to his position may be represented symbolically here as:

$$X_C (G \pm S) = P$$

That is, the capability of the position of an actor (P) is a function of the priority (X_C) that the authorities of the collectivity attach to converting their capabilities in international affairs generally (G), as modified by their capabilities in the specific field of the organization in question *(S)* into influence in the organization. This anticipates somewhat the discussion of the components of the general and the specific capabilities of states to be presented in the next section, dealing with the environment, but it should be noted here that other kinds of power besides material power are included. Thus this symbolic statement can be used for other collectivities as well as states.

Substituting the components of the actor's position for *P,* the symbolic statement for an actor's power is:

$$X_C (G \pm S) \pm A = C$$

Like the authorities of the collectivities they represent, actors also exercise judgment about the conversion of their capabilities into influence. Here, we are referring to active influence in the sense discussed in the previous section. For both the individual actor and the authorities of the collectivity, the decision whether or not they should seek to use available resources to gain influence will depend upon several factors, including the intensity of their feelings about the issues at stake and their estimates of the probability and the costs of obtaining their goals. In estimating such probabilities actors make assumptions about the influence of others as well as about the likely extent of opposition and support. If they seek to exercise influence, the degree of their success will depend on how all the other influences within the organization are distributed on the issue at stake. For ex-

ample, when faced with a united opposition, the representative of a powerful state might find it impossible to achieve an objective, whereas in other circumstances he would succeed easily.

Obviously, the influence that an individual actor actually exercises in an international organization may differ considerably from his capacity or power. Putting it in abbreviated fashion, the influence of an individual actor *(I)* is the result of his power *(C)* as modified by his decision to attempt to convert his power into influence (X_a) and by the distribution of all other influences within the organization on a particular issue *(D)*. Symbolically, this can be expressed as:

$$X_a \cdot C \cdot D = I$$

The distribution of all other influences includes the pattern of alignments on a particular issue, as well as how other actors feel about it, the weight of their opinions, and their power. Thus it includes those who would support, oppose, or be indifferent. It also includes the deference accorded to the actor in question by other actors.

As the focal point of analysis shifts from the capacities of actors to their influence, attention must be given to their attitudes and perceptions and more broadly to process. Attitudes and perceptions are crucially important factors affecting actors' behavior; they have an effect, among other things, on whether or not the actors will seek to convert their capacities into influence. Process, the working out of strategies to obtain goals, the building of alliances, coalitions, and consensus, determines the configuration of forces within an organization.

The fundamental questions concerning attitudes and perceptions are how actors see the organization in question and how they understand its purposes and potentialities, particularly in terms of their own interests and objectives. The distribution and interplay between personal goals and public goals must be investigated in this connection. Personal goals involve such things as jobs, prestige, and tourism. There is every reason to suspect that personal goals play as great a part in international as in national or local politics. Public goals include those relating to both the substantive concerns of the organization and the interests of the collectivities that the actors represent. Concern for survival and growth of the organization as a whole or of subunits might be derived either from public or personal goals. Actors may have different points of view formed by their experience and professional training, as lawyers, economists, scientists, or engineers, for example, which mold their attitudes in certain directions. Actors may be grouped according to common perceptions of the organization and according to the intensity of their commitment to the organization and its goals.

A particularly significant case of regularities in perceptions and attitudes takes the form of organizational ideology. As defined here, an organizational ideology would contain—

1. An interpretation of the environment as it relates to action by the organization
2. Specification of goals to be attained in the environment
3. A strategy of action for attaining these goals

Organization ideologies might be narrow or broad. Functionalism is an ideology that is applicable to international organizations representing a variety of objectives. (The precise nature of these objectives is largely irrelevant, but they must be specific.) Functionalism stresses developing collaboration among states with regard to specific objectives as a means of gradually eroding the authority of nation-states in favor of world institutions. Marxist and populist ideologies compete with functionalism as other broad interpretations of the aims and strategies of international organizations. International organizations are seen in the Marxist view as expressing power relations between socialist and capitalist blocs; to the populist, they appear as a means of exerting pressure by the numerous poor upon the few rich. Along with these broad organizational ideologies are narrower and more task-oriented ideologies. Thus "education for development" is an ideology of UNESCO and to some extent ILO, and nondiscrimination or the most favored nation are ideologies of GATT and IMF. It is of interest to ascertain whether such organizational ideologies exist, how they came into being, and how widely they are shared. Other important questions are whether they are especially linked with certain actors, whether they are publicized, and whether competing organizational ideologies exist.

Perceptions and attitudes are particularly important in identifying who pushes for what. No one assumes, however, that attitudes and perceptions impel actors in only one direction. On the contrary, actors may often be subject to conflicting pressures, and one of the reasons why special attention is given to organizational ideologies is to see the extent to which these pressures act counter to other motivational forces. A particularly interesting question is whether dual loyalties emerge with some actors, leading them not only to represent the views of their collectivity in the organization but also to exert influence on their collectivity in line with the consensus reached by the organization or in conformity with organizational ideology.

The formal structures and procedures of the organization are the institutional constraints within which the strategies of the actors are developed. But when attitudes are translated into strategies within these formal constraints, the actors create additional and often informal structures.

These structures created in the political process itself may be studied in various ways. In the first place, we look for persistent groupings of actors.[3] These may be formal groupings such as caucuses or informal networks involving an in-group or establishment of actors who occupy key positions and who normally consult among each other about important decisions. Persistent groupings may enhance or decrease the possibility of an individual actor's exercising influence. An actor may find it easier to attain his objectives because of his membership in a coalition, or an opposing coalition may place obstructions in his path.

Such groupings determine, secondly, the configurations of influence within organizations, which may take forms approximating (1) unanimity; (2) one dominant coalition, possibly led by a dominant actor; (3) polarization between two rival coalitions; (4) a larger number of alliances, none of which dominates; or (5) crosscutting cleavages on different issues with no general pattern. The coalition policies of executive heads and members of international bureaucracies, as well as those of national representatives, are important factors determining these configurations.

Finally, there is the identification of elites made up of influential individual participants, elites that cut across groupings and configurations and thus show the stratification of influence in the organization. It is by knowing who is most influential that we can infer which resources are the most significant determinants of influence. . . .

The purpose of trying to measure influence goes beyond simply wishing to know which particular actors have the most influence at any particular time. Finding out more about the characteristics and sources of influence of each of the most influential actors is one step toward inferring more generally the relative importance of different sources of influence in different international organizations. What other sources of influence compete most effectively with a position as representative of a powerful state? In which organizations do administrative competency or expert ability carry most weight? Which give preeminence to ideological legitimacy, that is, the definition and articulation of an ideological position, whether in the form of an organizational ideology or of one of the major ideologies of world politics?

Analyzing the backgrounds of the most influential actors and the roads they have followed to gain influence should give some clues to the relative importance of various personal attributes and should help to single out the positions or offices that are most likely to be springboards to influence. In some organizations these may be membership on the executive board; in others, posts in the secretariat. Some study of persons without influence may also be revealing, particularly if they might have been expected to be influential because of their positions. . . .

ENVIRONMENTAL IMPACTS

The next step is to isolate that influence which is attributable to environment. International organizations are aspects of international relations or more broadly of world

politics. To understand international organizations we must devise a framework that will make the decisions and actions taken through them intelligible in the context of events where they originate and which they may affect. International organizations are thought of in this study as systems that are not fully autonomous, but rather are subject to environmental forces that become major constraints upon the determinants of decisions.

These decisions, it is assumed, will reflect a pattern of expectations and demands that can be perceived in the world situation, for example, the desire of states for greater security from external violence or for freedom from unilateral domination by one powerful country, or the desire for redistribution of the world's resources or for widespread acceptance of some particular principles of political organization or ideology. The pattern of expectations and demands—in particular, the relative strength of different demands—and the extent of compatibility or of conflict among different demands—is in turn assumed to be determined by certain objectively ascertainable conditions in the world, including the relative military and economic power of states, their level of economic development and social mobilization, governmental effectiveness, and the basic principles of organization of different polities.

Three major variables describe the general environment: the stratification of state power, the economic and political characteristics of states, and the patterns of alignment and conflict among states. . . . In the consideration of the first variable it is assumed that some relationship exists between the power of a state in international affairs generally and its power in international organizations. Since power is a primary factor in influence, there is likely to be a connection between a state's power in relation to other states and its influence in international organizations generally. The point of considering the stratification of power is to explore this relationship. We would expect the United States and the USSR, as powerful states, to have greater influence than Canada, Sweden, or India in any international organization, irrespective of its functional field; and we would expect Canada, Sweden, or India to have greater influence over decisions than Nicaragua, Gabon, or Cambodia.

The second major variable in the description of the general environment is the distribution of states according to their economic and political characteristics. Here it is assumed that the economic development of a state is important in determining the demands the state will place on an international organization, especially the type and priority of services demanded—for example, whether it would prefer an organization to be a clearinghouse for information or an agency for redistributing the world's wealth.

It has also frequently been assumed that the internal polity of a state affects such aspects of its behavior in international organizations as its style of participation, its degree of commitment to the organizations, and its responsiveness to their decisions. International organizations have sometimes been seen as the creations of democratic states in their own image. Their assemblies have been compared figuratively with the elected assemblies of democratic polities—as parliaments of mankind. The ideals of international organization have been seen as the logical extension of the ideals of democracy—universal respect for the rights of the individual and the need to provide opportunities for his social fulfillment. But in practice can we find any discernible differences in the way democratic and nondemocratic states behave in and toward international organizations? . . .

Two dimensions of polities are particularly significant. In the first place, it is important to know whether the polity is democratic in the sense that there is a regularly accepted and reasonably orderly competition for political power. Second, when countries cannot be described as democratic in this sense, it is important to know whether the state is one that is in the hands of a revolutionary group seeking to mobilize the population with the aim of transforming society to fit its own ideology or whether it belongs in a third class, those where a more conservative group holds the reins and is preserving in broad outlines the existing structure of social power and wealth. These three types are called *competitive, mobilizing,* and *authoritarian*. It should be stressed that the criteria distinguishing them relate to internal politics, not to external alignments. The classification is designed to help uncover any meaningful relations between the internal character of the state's polity and its external behavior, particularly in international organizations.

Another set of questions arises in this connection. It has often been thought characteristic of revolutionary governments that they use foreign policy issues as a means of mobilizing domestic support. Will it, then, be found that the mobilizing regimes are most active in initiating and supporting symbolic decisions in international organizations? Will these regimes be more concerned than others that symbolic decisions and rule-creating or rule-supervisory decisions conform with their ideologies?

It may be assumed that authoritarian regimes care less whether the positions they take in international organizations reflect the characteristics of the regime. They can tolerate a hiatus between the principles they formally support in an international forum and their practices at home precisely because their populations are not mobilized and articulate on the issues involved, and the regimes are not seeking to mobilize them. Ideological consistency will thus be less important for authoritarian regimes than for polities concerned with mobilization. In regard to competitive polities, it is often assumed that such polities are more penetrable, "open" societies and thus more likely to acquiesce in the authority of international organizations. There is more likelihood that groups within these societies will protest failures to observe international obligations. . . .

Patterns of conflicts and alignments on major world political and ideological issues constitute the third variable used to describe the general environment. It is assumed that these patterns will have some effect on decision making in international organizations even when the subject matter of particular decisions may seem remote from the conflicts in which world political alignments originated. For example, many technical issues have acquired political overtones because of the East-West conflict. On the other hand, classical functionalist theory would have predicted that the more technical an issue is the more likely the chances are of avoiding the complications of politics. Thus the exact effect of these patterns on particular types of decisions at particular times and in particular organizations has to be considered.

Most international organizations also operate in the context of an environment that is specific to the organization. For example, decision making in GATT is undoubtedly affected by the position of states in the world economy—their share in world trade and the proportion of their GNP derived from trade. The specific environment is conceived in quite broad terms to include such things as technological developments affecting communications in the case of ITU, and articulated bodies of opinion like labor movements in that of ILO. Two concepts developed with regard to the general environment can be applied to the specific environment: the stratification of power (or capabilities) and the pattern of alignments and conflicts. . . .

The environment specific to an international organization may be either linked with or independent of the general environment. In most instances there is probably some relationship, but its strength will vary with different fields. The relation between decision making and the general specific environments can be examined empirically. One or the other could be more important, and the specific environment could act as an intervening variable. . . . Just as each organization has a specific environment, so it may be argued has each issue-area, or even—at the limit—each decision. The concept of specific environment can be applied with some flexibility.

NOTES

1. The phrase is from Geoffrey Barraclough, *History in a Changing World* (Oxford: Basil Blackwell, 1955), pp. 183–84. Barraclough was referring to "three great turning points when European society swung upwards on to a new plane" (p. 79). The same concept can be applied in the microcosmic history of international organizations.

2. The stages outlined here were suggested by the work of Fred C. Iklé. See especially his *Alternative Approaches to the International Organization of Disarmament* (Santa Monica, Calif.: RAND Corporation, 1962).

3. Various attempts have already been made to identify groupings. See especially Chadwick F. Alger, "Interaction in a Committee of the United Nations General Assembly," in *Quantitative International Politics,* ed. J. David Singer (New York: Free Press, 1968), pp. 51–84; Arend Lijphart, "The Analysis of Bloc Voting in the General Assembly," *American Political Science Review* 57 (December 1963): 902–17; and Bruce M. Russett, "Discovering Voting Groups in the United Nations," *American Political Science Review* 60 (June 1966): 327–39. However, neither participants' observations of interactions in a committee room nor the analysis of roll call votes, the two techniques involved in these attempts, fully measures what is involved in the concept of persistent groupings of actors used here. Among other things neither gives adequate attention to actors who are not representatives of states.

8

PATTERNS OF DECISIONMAKING IN INTERNATIONAL ORGANIZATIONS

Werner Feld and Robert Jordan

THE RANGE OF INSTITUTIONAL PATTERNS

IGO Administration

All contemporary IGOs have a secretariat as the basic administrative organ, although the name for this organ may vary. For example, in some IGOs the name "bureau" is used—a case in point is the Universal Postal Union (UPU); in the European Communities it is the commission that is in charge of administration.

The executive head of an IGO may be called the secretary-general, as in the case of the United Nations, or president, the title of the head of the EC Commission. Director-general is another title for a chief administrator and this is used for the chief of the secretariat of the General Agreement on Tariffs and Trade (GATT), and throughout the United Nations.[1] It is important to note that these chief administrative officers often also have important executive functions that either flow from provisions in the constituent treaties (Article 99 of the U.N. Charter) or from the development of continuing practices such as those that have occurred in the case of GATT's director-general.

Plenary Organs

A large majority of IGOs have plenary organs on which all member-states are represented. Historically, these organs were known as conferences, going back to the Congress of Vienna, and this designation continues to be used today as exemplified by the General Conference of the ILO and UNESCO. Other names for plenary organs are congress (the Universal Postal Union and World Meteorological Organization use this term), assembly (the United Nations and the Council of Europe), and parliament (the European Communities).

The frequency of plenary organ meetings varies with the kind of function for which the IGO was created. Some plenary organs meet only once every five years—Universal Postal Union (UPU) and International Telecommunication Union (ITU)—while the European Parliament meets now four to five times

SOURCE: *International Organizations: A Comparative Approach,* by Werner Feld and Robert Jordan with Leon Hurwitz (copyright © Praeger Publishers, New York, 1983), pp. 85–92; 94–97, 133–136; 139–145. Edited and reprinted with permission.

each year and the U.N. General Assembly at least once a year, but this session lasts from September through mid-December. There also has been the tendency for the General Assembly to have resumed sessions sometime in the following year.

Plenary organs normally engage in deliberations on broad policy questions and make appropriate recommendations to member-states and IGO administrators. However, in some cases they become involved in IGO management or make proposals on more detailed issues. For example, the ITU Plenipotentiary Conference establishes the budget for the organization for the next five years,[2] the U.N. General Assembly, whether convened in general or special session, often makes detailed recommendations on economic matters such as the resolutions embracing the so-called New International Economic Order (NIEO) and the Consultative Assembly of the Council of Europe makes specific proposals on draft conventions of various kinds. In many cases, the plenary organs review and act on the work of standing committees whose membership is open to all members.

Organs of Limited Composition

The executive functions of management in an IGO are often performed by a council or an executive board or committee with limited membership. The members are elected usually by the plenary organ(s) of the IGO, and it is not unusual for stiff competition to arise between different member-states that want to be represented on these councils or boards, especially if they wield considerable power. The Security Council of the United Nations provides a prime example for such competition; in order to accommodate as many member-states as possible for the ten two-year terms of the non-permanent members of the council, the term has been split into two single-year terms.[3]

The size of the limited composition organs varies. The U.N. Economic and Social Council (ECOSOC) consists of 54 members, the ILO Governing Body has 40 representatives, ICAO 27, UNESCO 24, and the Inter-Governmental Maritime Organization (IMO) is composed of 16 members. It is interesting to note that some constituent treaties contain guidelines for the selection of council members. It is expected that the members should come from states with important interests in the subject matter for which IGO was created. . . .

Finally, it is important to point out that in regional organizations, councils as executive organs are composed of representatives of all member-states. This is the case in the EC Council of Ministers, in NATO, in the Standing Committee of the Association of South East Asian Nations and others. The reason is the small number of member-states normally found in regional organizations.

In most cases the organs of limited composition meet monthly or more frequently since they are engaged in the day-to-day operations of their IGO. Usually, they are authorized to set up subordinate committees or working groups on various issue areas to help them in managing the IGO's task performance. In regional IGOs these committees and other groups may not always have representation from all the states that compose the membership of the higher council. An example is NATO's Nuclear Planning Group, a seven-state suborgan ultimately responsible to the NATO Council.

Adjudicatory Organs

Only a few IGOs have adjudicatory organs. The United Nations has both the International Court of Justice in The Hague and the Secretariat's Administrative Tribunal. In terms of decisions rendered and complied with, the latter might have a better record caused mainly by its considerable involvement in intra-U.N. matters. In the European Communities the Court of Justice is a very viable adjudicatory organ that has rendered more than 1000 judgments and opinions since its establishment in 1953. The European Court of Human Rights is associated with the Council of Europe; the number of cases decided by this judicial body has remained small although its decisions have had a significant impact on administrations throughout Europe. The institutional framework of the East African Common Market had included a Court of Appeal, but with the demise of that organization the court has become inoperative, if,

indeed, it ever was used. It is interesting to note that the Convention on the Law-of-the-Sea envisages the creation of an International Tribunal connected with the regime of the Enterprise that would be charged with the deep-seabed mining of the oceans. This suggests that as the number of IGOs and the scope of their activities expands further, we might witness the creation of additional adjudicative organs.

If we look at the many IGOs existing in the world today, we can observe a great variety of institutional frameworks. On the one hand, there are the very extensive and intricate frameworks of the United Nations and the European Communities, whose institutions are housed in skyscrapers and many other buildings in different cities and states. On the other hand, we can observe much smaller IGO structures, much less complicated, in political organizations such as the OAU and ASEAN, and even more so in smaller technical IGOs such as ICAO.

What are some of the basic factors that determine the extent and intricacy of an IGO's institutional framework? We believe that perhaps the most important factor is the scope and complexity of the tasks to be performed by the IGO. In some cases these tasks are in several issue areas, as is the case with the United Nations whose concerns range from dispute settlement and conflict resolution to economic and social development. In others, they require the issuance of detailed regulations for the management of various economic sectors—the best example is the EC and its detailed operation of the Common Agricultural Policy (CAP).

Another influential factor seems to be the kind of politics involved in the operation of particular IGOs—low politics or high politics. The former refers primarily to economic matters and technical problems, while the latter deals with strategic issues and political matters significantly affecting the national welfare. Although the distinction between low and high politics at times becomes blurred, we hypothesize that in low-politics areas, the more far-reaching and specific the tasks to be performed by an IGO the more extensive and comprehensive is the institutional framework; whereas, if the tasks to be carried out are relatively narrow, only a moderate framework is used. In high politics, we posit that if multiple tasks are to be performed, the framework will be extensive with attempts made to portion out functions in accordance with different perceived needs; on the other hand, if the tasks for the IGO are limited, the framework will be relatively simple although the issues involved may touch on the survival of the member-states. . . . In actuality, IGO institutional frameworks do not always fit tidily into any schema. The United Nations is generally a high-politics IGO with multiple tasks (peace keeping and concern for the global economy), but it also performs low-politics tasks, primarily through the specialized and affiliated agencies. NATO's high-politics task is limited, while the EC's is basically a multiple low-politics IGO with some high-politics aspirations. The Universal Postal Union is a typical low-politics IGO with narrow tasks.

TASK PERFORMANCE

The fundamental mission of IGO institutions is the management of cooperation in various fields in order to carry out the tasks for which the IGO was created. This involves the search for compromises in conflictual situations whose origins may have been military, political, and/or economic. It also involves the coordination of the member-states' national policies and activities in economic and security issue areas as far as it is needed to assure the success of the IGO's assigned functions, under the powers transferred to the institutions.[4]

Depending on the issue area with which the IGO is concerned, the institutional framework must provide the appropriate means for its task performance. This includes the necessary physical facilities for deliberation, consultation, and negotiations within and among institutions and between member-state governments and institutions.

The instrumentalities for task performance vary from IGO to IGO. However, all IGOs collect information on their issue areas and disseminate it to relevant institutional parties and to the member-states (usually through the governments but sometimes also directly to the people). The higher the quality of the information disseminated, the more it can contribute to the success of deliberations, consultations, and possible negotiations within the institutional framework. The Bank for International Settlements (BIS) is a good example of an IGO that generates a high quality of information with resulting success in task performance.

Another important instrumentality authorized for many IGOs is the formulation of pertinent policies. In some IGOs such as the United Nations and the EC, several institutions participate in policy making. The implementation of these policies is, in many if not most cases, carried out by member-state agencies; member governments opposed to the policies are therefore likely to forego implementation. However, in the EC limited implementation is performed by the Commission in the agricultural and anti-trust sectors, and both the International Monetary Fund (IMF) and the International Bank for Reconstruction and Development (better known as the World Bank) also implement their own policies by granting or refusing loans for different projects, although in the latter case, local bank officials may help in the implementation. Another example is the monitoring function of the International Atomic Energy Agency (IAEA), whose inspectors make checks of nuclear power facilities in member-states to prevent the use of fission-able materials for the production of nuclear weapons. . . .

Regardless whether IGOs themselves carry out the implementation of their policies or whether this task is handled by the member governments, IGOs must be concerned with the supervision of the implementation process. In crisis situations, the power to investigate and to report to the major political organ reflects this function; for other IGO tasks, monitoring events and preparing reports for discussion and dissemination serve the function of supervision of policy implementation. This is therefore a very significant dimension of task performance, but at times it may be difficult to achieve as it may impinge on what member governments consider their national prerogatives or even is seen as interference in their domestic affairs. Indeed, the scope and success of IGO policy making and the successful supervision of the implementation process depends on the perceptions of the member governments as to how far IGO policies promote or hinder the attainment of national priority goals and important objectives of nongovernmental actors in the individual member-states.

Less stringent institutional instrumentalities for task performance, yet not unimportant and often effective, are nonbinding recommendations and resolutions. Obviously, they do not have to be heeded by any government objecting to them, but the repeated passage of recommendations, especially in a politically visible body such as the U.N. General Assembly, is bound to affect world opinion and thereby could influence the decision-making processes of member governments in opposition.

Finally, in some cases IGO institutions are authorized to render judgments regarding obscure or ambiguous, factual or legal situations. For example, the U.N. Security Council may have to issue a judgment as to whether an act by a state is a violation of international peace, or the EC Commission must make a determination as to whether the behavior of a company in the Common Market constitutes an infringement of the EEC or ECSC antitrust provisions. The authority to make such findings is a significant instrument in the United Nations' or EC's performance of its various tasks.

MANAGEMENT EFFICIENCY

Management efficiency in the task performance of an IGO is high if its institutions have a good record in attaining desired outcomes. This, in turn, requires superior knowledge of cause-effect relationships and of political, social, and economic environmental elements in the issue areas in which a particular IGO is involved. The more limited this knowledge, the greater are the difficulties for goal achievements.[5] Task performance is also likely to be improved, or at least not likely to be impaired, if the relevant institutions can adjust themselves to

constraints and contingencies not controlled by the IGO itself.

An important element in achieving good task performance is the leadership quality of the executive head of IGO institutions. According to Robert W. Cox, the executive head plays a big role in converting an IGO conceived as a framework for multilateral diplomacy into one that is an autonomous actor in the international system.[6] However, there are also significant constraints on the executive's leadership ability to bring about full management efficiency. These included bureaucratic immobilism, increasing client control benefiting from intrabureaucratic balances of influences, and the patterns of conflict and national power alignments that make it difficult to mobilize uncommitted supporters for particular IGOs.

Of course the greatest thing an executive head can do for improving task performance efficiency is to alter the policies of the member-states so that they conform more with the decisions and interests of the IGO. In order to do this he must have: "(1) access to domestic groups having influence; (2) adequate intelligence concerning their goals and perceptions; and (3) ability to manipulate international action so that these groups can perceive an identity of interest" with the IGO.[7] Such a strategy is likely to work best in a pluralistic national political system and most states do not fall into this category. But even in pluralistic politics this is a difficult undertaking, except perhaps in small states. The president of the EC Commission has not been successful in persuading the larger EC member-states of this identity of interests, nor has the U.N. secretary-general been able to do this as far as the United States and other major powers are concerned. The coincidence of IGO member-state interests fluctuates according to the larger world political environment in which both rest.

Another factor affecting the efficiency of IGO task performance is the organizational structure of institutions. The EC Commission, which has grown tremendously between 1958 and 1976, has been declining in efficiency. Edouard Poullet and Gerard Deprez, who have made a careful study of the Commission's administrative efficiency, stress that "the multiplication and differentiations of principal administrative units [especially directorates-general and directorates] have contributed to the compartmentalization of policies and made the means for the coordination needed more numerous and expensive."[8] They conclude that the organizational pattern that has gradually developed has been imposed upon it by events and external pressure. They believe, however, that it represents in effect nothing other than the perpetuation of a simple hierarchical model which was well suited to a small organization, but is poorly suited to a large organization operating within a very complex system, which is what the EC

now represents.[9] The consequence of the resulting organizational pattern of the Commission has been the breakdown of the organization internally into separate subsystems, each acting for its own account, defending its own interests, having recourse to its own policies, and coexisting rather than interacting with the others.[10] Efforts at restructuring the United Nations have also met with only limited success. . . .

CHARACTERISTICS OF AN INTERNATIONAL CIVIL SERVICE

The traditional concept of a truly international civil service is that it must serve the interests of the organization as a whole.[11] This concept can be said to consist of four basic principles. The first, and probably the most crucial, principle is that of loyalty: the employees of an IGO must shed their national loyalties to some extent and consider only the interests of the IGO that employs them in carrying out their professional responsibilities. A corollary to this first principle is that international civil servants, while in international employment, should not receive instructions of any kind from their own governments or attempt to represent the interests of their national governments in any manner.

The second principle is that of impartiality. International civil servants are to be administrators, not politicians. It is their function to implement conscientiously decisions that were reached elsewhere, and to avoid involvement in the controversy that often surrounds IGO decision making if at all possible. International civil servants should be apolitical in the sense that they will willingly implement whatever policy decisions are reached by the governing political bodies or organs (that is, those composed of representatives of the member-states). This principle is more easily practiced by nationals from the industrial democracies, where the capacity of the state to control a person's right to free speech and expression is circumscribed.

A third principle is that of independence. Independence, in the sense of international secretariats being independent of political pressure from any national government or group of member-states, is implied by the first principle discussed above. But the principle of independence of the international civil service has a very important organizational dimension as well. It has been suggested that for any international secretariat to maintain its independence, it must be composed of career civil servants who enjoy a considerable degree of job security. Hence, career or indefinite contracts should be given to international civil servants so that they can feel confident that if they promote the best interests of the organization, they will be free from retribution or from removal from office for political reasons. The expectation is that a predominantly career civil service would thus fa-

cilitate the creation of an international identity, or esprit de corps. In contrast, individuals seconded (on leave of absence from their national governments) to an IGO on a fixed-term contract would find it difficult not to retain their national political self-consciousness, and thus, (so the argument goes) would not develop the same type of nonnational attitudes and behavior patterns as individuals who knew that they were immune from the worry that their official actions could influence their subsequent national career fortunes.

The fourth and final principle relates to recruitment practices. Those persons who still adhere to the traditional concept of an international civil service, maintain that individuals should be recruited primarily on the basis of merit, "primarily" because it is recognized that a certain amount of geographical representation (or distribution) is also a prerequisite. The rationale for geographic representation is that IGOs basically reflect a common effort of the member-states, and nationals of all states should participate as civil servants in this effort. Consequently, because of decolonization and the rapid increase in new states, a form of international affirmative action has taken hold in the United Nations and many other IGOs, whereby the newer member-states have claimed that geographical distribution should be equal to or even take priority over, merit and objective criteria of personal competence. States that have been the major financial contributors in such affected IGOs and that obviously have something to lose in terms of the numbers (and rank) of their nationals in the various secretariats, have protested this preoccupation with geographical representation.

The creation of IGO institutions and the employment of civil servants in these institutions have as their major purpose to accomplish the tasks for which the IGOs were created. The attainment of this goal requires national and multinational decision making that form the basis of IGO policies and implementing actions. For a comparative analysis and evaluation of IGO decision- and policy-making processes we will examine in the following pages the voting systems used in IGOs; the scope and level of decisions authorized in the constituent treaties; special strategies used in IGO decision making such as bloc voting or package deals; and the implementation and evaluation of decisions. . . .

VOTING SYSTEMS

Majority Rule

There is a clear historical trend away from the rule of unanimity to majority rule in decisions made within IGOs. In the course of drafting the Covenant of the League of Nations, Lord Robert Cecil declared that "all international decisions must, by the nature of things, be unanimous."[12] Therefore, it is not surprising that in the Covenant the unanimity rule was generally preserved, although some explicit exceptions were made in which majority voting sufficed. These exceptions included procedural questions, the admission of new members, and other instances in Assembly voting and even in a few situations in Council decisions.[13] In the United Nations, majority vote has become the rule in most bodies except the Security Council. In the General Assembly the basic rule is that a simple majority is sufficient unless the decision to be made deals with an important question (Article 18).

Majority rule also prevails in the specialized agencies of the United Nations. In fact, because of the technical nature of their task performance, so-called public unions, some of which were the predecessors of these agencies—for example the Universal Postal Union formed in 1894—employed majority rule much earlier than the IGOs.[14] On the other hand, unanimity (or, rather, the absence of a negative vote) remains the basic rule in the Committee of Ministers in the Council of Europe, the Council of the OECD, the Council of the Arab League, COMECON, the Political Consultative Committee of the Warsaw Treaty Organization (WTO) and the NATO Council. In the Council of Ministers of the EC unanimity is basically retained when prospective decisions affect the vital interests of member-states.

At times there are differences in the voting system depending on whether procedural or substantive issues are involved. In the latter case, the majority requirements are often a two-thirds vote rather than a simple majority. There are also instances when continuing practices may change voting systems and this change develops into customary law.

VARIATIONS IN THE EQUALITY OF VOTING POWER

If one were to follow strictly the principle of cosovereign equality, each member-state of an IGO should have the same voting power. However, in the real world of unequal power distribution and considering the concern of especially the large states to retain as much of their political freedom of action as possible, some means had to be found to deviate from this principle. One way has been to allow a state extra representation through assigning sovereign status to territorial units within a state. This was the reason for admitting Byelorussia and the Ukraine to full status as member-states in the United Nations. It is reasonable to assume that these two states usually vote the same way as does the Soviet Union.

Another means of breaking the principle of one state-one vote is weighting the votes of IGO members. This has been defined as a system that assigns to members of IGOs votes proportioned on the basis of predetermined relevant criteria.[15] Such criteria may be the financial contributions of member-

states to the IGO as is done in the World Bank, the International Monetary Fund (IMF), and the International Development Association (IDA), or the size and economic power of the member-states as exemplified in the voting arrangements of the Council of Ministers of the EC. Under this arrangement, the four largest members (France, West Germany, Italy, and the United Kingdom) have ten votes each; Belgium, Greece, and The Netherlands, have five each; Denmark and Ireland three each; and Luxembourg two.[16] . . .

Finally, the one state-one vote principle is circumvented when some member-states are given a veto power over decisions. The obvious case is the U.N. Security Council where the five permanent members (the United States, Soviet Union, China, Great Britain, and France) can veto any substantive decision of the council.

In summarizing our discussion of voting systems, it appears that the more technical or perhaps low politics the issue areas in which an IGO is concerned, the greater the chances that simple majorities are employed for the approval of decisions. Conversely, the more high politics are involved in particular decision making within IGOs, the greater is the tendency to insist on unanimity in voting. In this way, it is not likely that perceived vital interests of member-states may be adversely affected. Where the issues are very general, such as those that compose the NIEO, reliance on consensus decision making has helped to paper over real and specific differences that have hampered effective implementation.

THE SCOPE AND LEVEL OF DECISIONS

The term decision in our discussion covers all types of action taken by vote, whether framed as resolution, recommendation, directive, or other description. Most decisions are not automatically binding on the member-states of an IGO; indeed the majority may be nonbinding and often programmatic, especially as far as those in the U.N. family are concerned.

Decisions may be rendered at different levels of an IGO's activities. Usually, decisions at lower levels, for example in committees, will become building blocks for the decisions at the top levels. The international political significance of decisions of IGOs depends in large part on the level where it has been made although in some cases— such as the large body of anti-apartheid resolutions passed in U.N. organs—the higher political level has not resulted in a significant change in national policies. On the other hand, a resolution by the U.N. Economic and Social Council (ECOSOC) on some development issue will gain considerably in importance if endorsed by an appropriate resolution in the U.N. General Assembly. Also, a decision of the European Parliament will have saliency only if the EC Council of Ministers adopts it and gives it political and legal support.

The circle of decision makers in IGOs does not only consist of IGO civil servants. While these individuals, especially those in high or top executive positions, play the main roles in decisions made in the secretariats or the organs they serve, in the plenary bodies and councils of the organization it is the representatives of the member governments who, as the appointed delegates of their governments, has the prime responsibility in the decision-making process. In some cases, these individuals, who may either be national civil servants or legislators or ad hoc appointees, may also participate in preliminary decisions, either in IGO committees, their diplomatic missions at the seat of the IGO, or in committees composed of mission staffs such as the Committee of Permanent Representatives serving the EC or the Council of Permanent Representatives of NATO. In some instances, a government may use representatives of interest groups or commercial enterprises as participants at various levels in the IGO decision-making process. This method is often employed by the United States and offers splendid opportunities to interest groups and enterprises to influence directly the IGO decision-making process. The ILO is the most obvious case in point.

In many IGO decisions, the economic and political stakes are high and therefore the utilization of appropriate strategies may be crucial.

This may require launching particular initiatives by some participants in the decision-making process, expressing support for these initiatives by others, or seeking to kill them by still another group of actors. Others again may serve as power brokers or consensus builders depending on the particular interests pursued by governments and private groups.[17] . . .

SPECIAL STRATEGIES IN DECISION MAKING

Special strategies in IGO decision making are employed by the IGO leadership, international civil servants, and member governments and are designed to attain important goals in which these actors are particularly interested. These strategies may include the utilization of conferences first to prepare and then to vote on relevant issues, the use of special sessions in various deliberative IGO bodies, the repeated introduction and passage of the same pertinent resolution first in subsidiary bodies and later in such top-level plenary bodies as the U.N. General Assembly, proposals by IGO executives for package deals in stalemated negotiations, and the formation of voting blocs by states with common or converging interests.

Conference and Related Strategies

Since the emergence of the Third World as a major bargaining force in the international political process, there has been a tendency to view conference diplomacy as a primary strategy to achieve the goals of the Group of 77. Thus, challenges to the global status quo have been expressed multilaterally through IGOs, as well as through other forms of coalitions. Single-issue, or ad hoc, conferences have received a great deal of attention in this regard. They have been utilized, mostly but not always under the sponsorship of the United Nations, to give expression to the desires of the Third World for a change in international economic relationships. These conferences have been charged to consider such particular issues as food, population, energy, the role of women, and science and technology for development. Their value has been summarized thus:

If one views global, ad hoc conferences as vehicles for the interaction of public and private, national and international bureaucracies, an appropriate question to ask is, "What would have happened without the conference?" Our answer lies in investigating the two important functions of these conferences: 1. to give publicity to an issue-area and to change the dominant attitudes surrounding the definition of the issue-area; 2. to initiate actions designed to alleviate the problem by an agreement on how to strengthen the existing institutions or an agreement on new and more appropriate institutional machinery.[18]

A second strategy in conference decision making is the use of special sessions of the U.N. General

Assembly to take up important issues outside its normal program of work or traditional U.N. Charter responsibilities. The special sessions on disarmament, held in 1978 and 1982, could be considered in this category, as also can the sixth (1974) and seventh (1975) special sessions dealing with New International Economic Order (NIEO) issues, and even possibly the U.N. General Assembly's Committee of the Whole, which was charged in 1980 with reconciling the issues that comprise the so-called North-South dialogue, but which had to report in 1980 to another special session its inability to do so.[19]

Probably the apex of the use of the General Assembly as a special-issue negotiating forum was the eleventh special session, held in August 1981, presumably to launch global negotiations that theretofore had not succeeded in other forums. The reason for the failure of this session, therefore, can be traced to the general inability of intergovernmental conferences—whether ad hoc, specialized agency sponsored, or General Assembly special sessions—to resolve issues of immense complexity and that address the vital interests of major participating states. . . .

A third strategy in promoting particular goals through appropriate decisions is the practice in the United Nations of making use of subsidiary bodies, or of the specialized agencies, to serve as the convenor of a conference and to provide the secretariat. This was done,

for example, for the World Employment Conference of 1976 for which the ILO was the convenor, and for the World Conference on Agrarian Reform and Rural Development of 1979 for which the FAO was the convenor.

Resolutions introduced and approved by basically sympathetic delegates to these conferences and subsidiary bodies are then moved to higher bodies for further approval and ultimately are presented to the U.N. General Assembly for consideration. Given the substantial Third World majority in the Assembly, it is not surprising that these resolutions are adopted in that body, receiving thereby the highest legitimacy within the U.N. framework.

A final step in the use of General Assembly resolutions is the movement toward global negotiations in the Assembly. The hopes (so far unrealized) of the developing states that compose the Group of 77 has been that through such negotiations their economic and political objectives will find acceptance by the industrialized states, perhaps with the help of a sympathetic global public opinion.

While we have focused here on the United Nations, the three strategies conceivably can also be employed in regional IGOs if they have a hierarchical structure as has the U.N. family of IGOs. However, success depends also on the distribution of decision-making powers to subsidiary organs and on the fervor with which conflicting interests are pursued. Hence, a regional IGO such as the OAS might be suitable for the employment of these strategies.

"Package Deals"

When negotiations on an important issue are stalled in an IGO and votes on that issue either cannot be scheduled or are likely to be inconclusive, package deals can be and have been used successfully by the executive heads of an IGO, or by the conference chairman or president, to break the stalemate and achieve an acceptable outcome of the negotiations. A reason for such success is the comprehensive knowledge possessed by the IGO executive regarding all elements of the issue, which enables him and his colleagues to prepare a solution with an acceptable distribution of gains and concessions for all parties. Such package deals have become a stock-in-trade of the EC Commission over the years, and has been employed successfully on several occasions by the director-general of GATT.[20] But these IGOs may be only the best examples; package deals may be found in other IGOs as well.

Somewhat similar to proposals of a package deal is the utilization of a chairman's text to galvanize consensus and movement on outstanding issues, mostly in working groups set up by U.N. bodies and specialized agencies. The chairman of such a group will formulate a proposed text for an international convention such as an accord on the code of conduct for the transfer of technology. This tool, which may contain agreed and nonagreed portions of articles and clauses of the prospective convention, can serve as a stimulus for further negotiations by the parties involved and has been effective in reaching final consensus on contested parts of the convention.

VOTING BLOCS

Although the term "voting bloc" is frequently used in the literature when voting in the U.N. General Assembly or in other plenary bodies is discussed, the term "caucusing group" might be more appropriate because continuous solid bloc voting is rare except perhaps with respect to the Soviet Union and the East European states. A bloc may be defined as a group of states that meet regularly in caucus, has some degree of formal organization, and is concerned with substantive issues and related procedural matters that may come to a vote in plenary IGO organs.[21] These groupings include the developing states (the Group of 77), which may be broken down further into Afro-Asian, Latin American, and other Third World regional units. Another group is the EC states, sometimes voting with other Western states such as the United States, Canada, and Japan and, of course, another bloc is composed of the Soviet Union and the so-called People's Democracies (but not the People's Republic of China).

Group cohesion in voting depends on the issues and caucus leadership. Anticolonialism and the NIEO have been powerful stimulants to coalesce Third World states. Caucus leadership is closely related to persuasive skill, careful presentation of issues and possible outcomes, and the charisma of the caucus leader. It is interesting to note that the United States and the Soviet Union voted more often against the majority in the U.N. General Assembly than most U.N. members.

While it is important in both theoretical and practical terms to understand the political and economic implications of voting patterns in IGO plenary organs as well as to comprehend the reasons for these patterns, it would be even more valuable if one could predict future voting outcomes in IGO institutions. Jack E. Vincent has attempted to correlate national attributes of member-states with their voting record in the General Assembly. His findings are that a state's degree of economic development is one of the most important predictors of future voting behavior. With respect to attitudes toward the work and task performance of the United Nations, this might signify that highly developed states may be inclined to show negative tendencies because their capabilities and resources are already high and contributions of IGOs to these capabilities might be relatively insignificant. On the other hand, economically underdeveloped states are more apt to want to expand the work of IGOs because it offers prospects of substantial improvement of their capabilities. Other important attributes according to Vincent are democracy as the political system used in particular states and relations with the United States.[22]

OUTPUT IMPLEMENTATIONS

An important question to be explored in more detail relates to the tools that an IGO can use to implement decisions and the degree of effectiveness of the implementation method. Several methods are available to IGOs; the constituent treaties specify which method can be employed in particular circumstances and not all methods are permitted for all IGOs. In many cases, member-state agencies or bureaucracies (both public and private) must be used by IGOs to implement decisions and policies.

Member-states concerned that the balance between national and IGO policy making should favor their governments may not consider that the effectiveness of implementation is the most desirable objective, since it may undermine national prerogatives. The history of disarmament and arms control negotiations bears eloquent witness to this observation. Even in low-politics issue areas, states may have only a limited interest in seeing the functionalist logic work too successfully unless the tasks to be performed by the IGO institutions are completely beyond the reach of their capabilities or are perceived as relatively unimportant.

The least circumscribed method for IGO output implementation is the dissemination of information. The effectiveness of this method depends on the issue area. The more technical the subject or issue areas and the less political they are, the better chances for its effectiveness, and for its acceptability to IGO member-states. Information on health matters or agricultural production by the World Health Organization or the Food and Agricultural Organization (FAO) are cases in point. The use of U.N. agencies to disseminate such political information as apartheid and South Africa, or the plight of the Palestinians and Israel, has aroused resistance and opposition.

A recommendation, which is normally nonbinding, is a method through which an IGO can move things forward, especially if the same recommendation is passed again and again. In particular, if a recommendation is approved by an important body such as the U.N. General Assembly, it can have a decisive effect on world public opinion. Opponents will be pushed in a corner when the same recommendation is passed with increasing majorities and it will take a strongly-held view of a member-state for that state to remain in the opposition year after year. The votes recommending the expulsion of South Africa from the U.N. General Assembly, if not from U.N. membership, and the recent rec-

ommended sanctions against Israel to punish that state for the annexation of the Golan Heights are indicative of the problem. . . .

Directives authorizing IGOs to issue an enforceable order are not frequent. The U.N. Charter's Chapter VII grants the Security Council such authority, but of course five U.N. member-states have veto rights in the Council. Moreover, actual enforcement action of an order has never been undertaken. Furthermore, the use of Article 19 of the Charter to compel financing of peace-keeping operations authorized by the Security Council has not been successful.[23] In the EC system, however, directives as implementing tools for policy decision are used more often and in most cases member governments comply.

While directives, wherever authorized, are addressed to the member governments, a very few IGOs are empowered to implement policies with regulations (ordinances) that are directly binding on member-states without positive implementing legislation or decrees by the national parliaments or executive administrations. The prominent examples of this type of output implementation are the ECSC and EEC. In this kind of a legal situation, the member governments and the nongovernmental actors must keep a very watchful eye on the entire IGO decision-making process in order to assure that their major interests are protected and their various national policy goals enhanced as much as possible. Indeed, in some cases member governments may be anxious to frustrate completely the IGO implementation process if they are dissatisfied with a decision.

NOTES

1. For a summary discussion of the origins of the office of secretary-general, see Robert S. Jordan, "The Influence of the British Secretariat Tradition on the Formation of the League of Nations," in *International Administration: Its Evolution and Contemporary Applications,* ed., Robert S. Jordan (New York: Oxford University Press, 1971). See also Robert S. Jordan, ed., *Dag Hammarskjöld Reconsidered: The U.N. Secretary-General as a Force in World Politics* (Durham, N.C.: Carolina Academic Press, 1983).
2. D. W. Bowett, *The Law of International Institutions* (New York: Praeger, 1963), p. 108.
3. For an elaboration on the powers and functions of the Security Council, see Davidson Nicol, ed., *The United Nations Security Council: Towards Greater Effectiveness* (New York: United Nations Institute for Training and Research, 1982).
4. See in this connection James M. McCormick, "Intergovernmental Organizations and Cooperation Among Nations," *International Studies Quarterly* 24 (March 1980), pp. 75–95.
5. See James D. Thompson, *Organizations in Action* (New York: McGraw-Hill, 1967), pp. 14–24, 159–60.
6. Robert W. Cox, "The Executive Head: An Essay on Leadership in International Organizations," *International Organization* 23 (Spring 1969), pp. 205–30.
7. Ibid., p. 230.
8. Christoph Sasse, Edouard Poullet, David Coombes, Gerard Deprez, *Decision Making in the European Community* (New York: Praeger, 1977), p. 176.
9. Ibid., p. 178.
10. Ibid., p. 157. See also Hans J. Michelmann, *Organizational Effectiveness in a Multinational Bureaucracy* (Westmead, England: Saxon House, Teakfield Limited, 1978).
11. Portions of this section are derived from chapter 1 of Norman A. Graham and Robert S. Jordan, eds., *The International Civil Service: Changing Role and Concepts,* (New York: Pergamon Press, 1980). See also Sydney D. Bailey, *The Secretariat of the United Nations* (New York: Carnegie Endowment for International Peace, 1962).
12. Quoted in D. W. Bowett, op. cit., p. 326.
13. Articles 1, 5, 15, 16 of the Covenant.
14. Bowett, op. cit., p. 327.
15. Ibid.
16. Articles 148 (2) EEC Treaty, 118 (2) EURATOM Treaty, and 28 (4) ECSC Treaty as amended.
17. See Robert W. Cox and Harold K. Jacobson, *The Anatomy of Influence* (New Haven, Conn.: Yale University Press, 1973), p. 12.
18. Thomas G. Weiss and Robert S. Jordan, *The World Food Conference and Global Problem Solving* (New York: Praeger, 1976), p. 4.
19. For a review of the somewhat tortured progress of the negotiations between North and South, see Robert S. Jordan, "Why an

NIEO: The View From the Third World," in *The Emerging International Economic Order: Dynamic Processes, Constraints and Opportunities,* eds. Harold K. Jacobson and Dusan Sidjanski (Beverly Hills, Calif.: Sage, 1982). See also George A. Codding, "Influence in International Conferences," *International Organization* 35 (Autumn 1981).

20. Regarding the action by GATT's Director-General Mr. Wyndham White at the end of the Kennedy Round negotiations, see Werner Feld, *The European Community in World Affairs,* (Port Washington, N.Y.: Alfred, 1976), p. 184.

21. For somewhat similar definitions see Thomas Hovet, Jr., *Bloc Voting in the United Nations* (Cambridge, Mass.: Harvard University Press, 1960), p. 31 and Jack C. Plano and Robert E. Riggs, *Forging World Order* (New York: Macmillan, 1967), p. 148. See also

Weiss and Jordan, op. cit., p. 27ff. for a discussion of bloc voting definitions in U.N. conferences; for a discussion of caucusing within conferences, see ibid., p. 110ff.

22. Jack E. Vincent, "Predicting Voting Patterns in the General Assembly," *American Political Science Review* 65 (June 1971), pp. 471–95; "National Attributes as Predictors of Delegate Attitudes at the United Nations," *American Political Science Review* 62 (September 1968), pp. 916–32; "An Application of Attributes Theory to General Assembly Voting Patterns, and Some Implications," *International Organization* 26 (Summer 1972), pp. 551–82.

23. See Joel Larus, ed., *From Collective Security to Preventive Diplomacy* (New York: Wiley, 1965), p. 490ff. for a discussion of the state of affairs toward financing U.N. peacekeeping as a result of the Congo crisis.

9

THE EVALUATION OF WEIGHTED VOTING SCHEMES FOR THE UNITED NATIONS GENERAL ASSEMBLY

William J. Dixon

INTRODUCTION

Vanuatu and Belize, the United Nations' two newest members, have a combined population of only about one-quarter of a million people, and yet each wields a vote in the General Assembly equal to that of the most populous and most powerful states. This is simply the most recent manifestation of the twin

SOURCE: Reprinted from the *International Studies Quarterly,* Vol. 27, No. 3, 1983, with the permission of the International Studies Association, Byrnes International Center, University of South Carolina, Columbia, S.C. 29208 USA.

processes of decolonization and universalization. And it is also material for those who claim that Assembly decision-making procedures have been 'distorted' by the influx of micro-state members. It has been calculated, for example, that member countries representing less than 4 per cent of the world's population can constitute a simple majority and that only about 8 per cent need be represented in a two-thirds majority (Perusse, 1982). Of the various measures proposed to rectify this situation, the simplest involve the weighting of Assembly votes.[1]

Weighted voting is not a novel idea, of course; it has long been used by the World Bank Group and several European regional organizations. Nor is it merely the stepchild of those who would create a more popularly representative world body—on at least two occasions the U.S. government has privately examined the weighting of UN votes, presumably as a way to contain an increasingly hostile Third World majority.[2] It is somewhat surprising, then, that the most significant feature of weighted voting systems—the underlying distribution of voting power—has received so little attention from students of international organization.[3]

Previous studies of General Assembly representation (Barret and Newcombe, 1968; Newcombe *et al.*, 1971 and 1977; Perusse, 1982) have failed to acknowledge a fundamental truth about weighted voting systems derived from the theory of games, namely, that the distribution of voting power is seldom proportional to the distribution of votes (e.g., Shapley and Shubik, 1954; Riker and Shapley, 1968; Brams, 1975; Fischer and Schotter, 1978; Holler, 1982). Thus, to assert that the political acceptability of an alternative representational formula depends on the number of votes it distributes to member-states is to overlook an extremely crucial point. The present effort avoids this problem by first showing that votes and voting power are not equivalent concepts. The concept of voting power is then operationalized and applied to the bloc distribution of General Assembly votes under 14 weighting formulas which deviate from the current one state-one vote procedure. In this respect, this research updates and significantly revises an earlier study of weighted voting systems by Newcombe *et al.* (1971).

POWER UNDER WEIGHTED VOTING

The ostensible aim of any representational formula, whether applied in a domestic legislature or an international body, is an *equitable* distribution of voting power. To have said that is, of course, to have said very little. The one state-one vote system presently used in the General Assembly and many other international organizations is perfectly equitable under the classical doctrine of sovereign equality. Even if one rejects the present system, there remain at least two fundamentally different standards of equity on which to base the allocation of voting strength in an international organization. A principle of representational democracy or populism would require apportioning votes on the basis of population size; the principle of power, on the other hand, would lead to a weighting scheme based on some measure of political power or influence.

As the authors of an earlier study rightly observed, adherence to some abstract principle of justice may have little to do with member governments' acceptance of an alternative representational formula in the General Assembly. They argued that 'the most acceptable compromise [among available weighting schemes] would seem to be the achievement of a "balance," in which none of the major blocs is placed in a permanent minority . . .' (Newcombe et al., 1971: 465). By this criterion a weighting scheme is considered acceptable to the extent that it approximates an equal distribution of voting power among the existing blocs. These authors operationalized balance as the difference in the numbers of votes controlled by the Assembly's principal blocs under a given weighting formula. One variant of this procedure subsumed all blocs into pro-Western and anti-Western coalitions, and then defined balance as the simple difference in the number of votes available to the opposing sides. An alternative technique utilizing three main blocs measured balance as the summation of the absolute differences in votes among all three. In each case the smaller

these differences, the more 'balanced'—and therefore more acceptable—the particular formula under consideration.[4]

The difficulty with this formulation is its explicit assumption that a bloc's voting power is proportional to the number of votes it controls under the constitutional rules. To see why this assumption is erroneous, it is necessary to consider the meaning of power in the context of a voting body. Of the numerous approaches to the definition of power, those focusing on actors' relationships with one another are probably the most familiar and widely accepted among political scientists.[5] This 'control over actors' approach can lead to unsettling results when applied to collectivities that make decisions by voting. For instance, in a large collectivity where each member has a single vote and no member can control the vote of any other member, this approach would suggest that no one has any power when, in fact, each member has an equal chance to influence the outcome (Banzhaf, 1965). An alternative view of power, the 'control over outcomes' approach, is able to capture this feature of voting situations. Moreover, it has been shown repeatedly that under conditions of weighted voting, power over outcomes is seldom proportional to the number of votes members control (e.g., Banzhaf, 1965; Riker and Shapley, 1968). This apparent paradox can be illustrated by a simple example. Consider a voting body with three members whose votes are weighted by

3, 2, and 2. Under a decision rule requiring a simple majority (i.e., 4 out of 7 votes), *any* combination of two members is sufficient to enact (or block) a collective decision. In this example, each member shares an *equal* chance of determining the outcome despite an *unequal* allocation of votes.

The balance criterion advanced by Newcombe *et al.* (1971) is an attempt to gauge the uniformity of voting strength among blocs under various weighting proposals. It has been shown, however, that the raw number of votes cast by a bloc may not be indicative of that bloc's actual control over voting outcomes. In general, voting power in a collectivity is related to the number of votes held by an individual member only within the larger context of: (a) the number of votes available to other members; and (b) the decision rule adopted by the voting body.

Voting Power Indice

Formal voting power in a collectivity is that measure of influence over outcomes which derives from the formal constitutional rules alone. Note that certain behavioral sources of influence which might ordinarily be expected to operate in actual voting situations—e.g., use of side payments, threats of coercion, individual expertise or seniority—are specifically excluded from assessments of formal power in a voting context.[6] More explicitly, it is assumed that members are able to affect outcomes only through their vote(s); that each member

votes without regard to the actions of any other member; and that each voting situation is considered in complete isolation from every other situation. Under these circumstances a member has power to the extent that his vote is likely to be decisive in determining the collective decision.

One measure of voting power has been developed by Banzhaf (1965; 1966) to study the representational characteristics of weighted voting bodies. By Banzhaf's method, formal voting power is indicated by the number of times an individual can change his or her vote and thereby change the collective outcome by transforming a coalition from winning to losing or vice versa. A coalition is simply a distinct voting combination irrespective of the particular arrangement of the members or the sequence in which they joined. In order for a single member of a coalition to determine the outcome the coalition must have started out as a minimal winning coalition; moreover, more than one member may be critical to any given coalition. If we define a *swing* (Straffin, 1977) for any member i to be a winning coalition in which i's membership is necessary for it to remain winning, the swing is a potential defection which is critical to the collective outcome. The Banzhaf index, β, for i is then given by

$$\beta = \frac{\text{total swings for } i}{\text{total swings for all } i} \quad (2)$$

It is clear that the Banzhaf index is a *normalized* measure; that is, the values for all members of a collectivity always sum to unity. Note, too, that the swings accumulated in the Banzhaf index encompass two different types of critical defections: those from the 'aye' coalition and those from the opposing 'nay' coalition. Conceptually, these two types of swings are quite distinct. A member's potential defection from a minimal winning 'aye' coalition represents a negative or preventive use of power by being sufficient to block the passage of an action. Of course, defection from a minimal winning 'nay' coalition has the opposite effect by assuring passage of a collective measure. Since the number of potential 'aye' defections for any member will always equal the number of potential 'nay' defections, these two aspects of formal voting power cannot be differentiated in Banzhaf's formulation.[7]

ALTERNATIVE WEIGHTING FORMULAS

The Banzhaf power index will be applied to the vote distribution resulting from each of 15 different representational formulas summarized in Table 1. These weighted voting proposals were assembled from various sources by Barret and Newcombe (1968) and analyzed across the first 18 Assembly sessions by Newcombe et al. (1971). Original authors and the Newcombe et al. designation number are provided to aid identification; full citations can be found in Newcombe et al. (1971).

For convenience the alternative weighting schemes can be grouped into three broad categories. The first is based exclusively on population and includes formulas 2 through 6. Formula 2 allocates votes in direct proportion to population size whereas the others in this category attempt to moderate the vast disparities in voting strength that would be entailed by the direct population formula. One technique (3 and 4) assigns votes according to arbitrary brackets on population size. A second method (5 and 6) achieves a similar effect by utilizing root functions to discount extremely large magnitudes.

A second general category encompassing formulas, 7, 8, 9 and 10 focuses on some aspect of power or wealth as the basis for granting voting privileges in the General Assembly. The assessment formula (8) would be a natural choice of the Western states since it takes into account their indispensable contributions to the organization's budget. Similarly, formula 7 assigns votes based on GDP, which for present purposes can be taken as a rough indication of a state's power.[8] Of course, it is to be expected that formulas 7 and 8 will produce quite similar results given that assessments are generally proportional to GDP. Formulas 9 and 10 represent further modifications of the straight assessment formula by allocating each member a minimum of five votes. Both schemes further depreciate the effects of assessment differences through a weighting factor chosen to yield a sum total of 1000 votes.

The final set of formulas (11, 12, 13, 14 and 15) utilize a combination of weighting factors. In each case

TABLE 1   Formulas for Weighting UN Votes.[a]

Formula Number	Brief Description	Author(s)	Designation in Newcombe et al.
1.	One state, one vote	Present system	(1.)
2.	Proportional to population	—	(2.)
3.	Bracketed relative population (30 votes to 4 largest countries; 15 to next 8; 6 to next 20; 4 to next 30; 2 to next 34; 1 to rest)	Clark & Sohn	(5.)
4.	Bracketed absolute population (30 votes to countries > 140 million; 16 to 40–140 million; 8 to 20–40; 5 to 5–20; 3 to 1.5–5; 2 to 0.5–1.5; 1 to < 0.5)	Clark & Sohn	(6.)
5.	Square root of population	Millard, Penrose, Riker & Shapley	(7.)
6.	Cube root of population	Millard	(8.)
7.	Proportional to GDP[b]	—	(4.)
8.	Proportional to UN assessment	Manno	(3.)
9.	Linear function of assessment ($ax + 5$; x = assessment, 5 = minimum vote)	Manno	(10.)
10.	Nonlinear function of assessment ($c \log x = 5$; x = assessment, 5 = minimum vote)	Manno	(12.)
11.	Population + UN assessment[c]	Dulles, Newfang, Wilcox & Marcy, Manno, Adams	(15.)
12.	Population + GDP[b,c]	Sohn	(16.)
13.	Log population + log GDP[b]	World Service Federation	(17.)
14.	Population + energy consumption	Betchov	(18.)
15.	Population × square root of GDP per capita[b]	Alcock	(20.)

[a]Adapted from Newcombe et al. (1971:455).
[b]GDP substituted for GNP in original.
[c]Applied proportionally rather than with arbitrary brackets.

population is incorporated along with another property intended to register a state's power or wealth. Formulas 11 and 12 are similar in that both assign votes in direct proportion to the sum of population and assessment (11) or GDP (12). The latter scheme is modified in formula 13 by the application of logarithms as a way to discount extreme values. Population disparities are counterbalanced by total energy consumption in formula 14. The final weighting scheme, 15, compensates for population differences by distributing votes according to the product of population and the square root of GDP per capita.

AN APPLICATION TO VOTING BLOCS

The analysis of formal power in a collectivity normally proceeds by assigning each member a prescribed number of votes under a given weighting formula and then calculating individual power values according to the overall distribution of assigned votes and the prevailing decision rule. This procedure presents few difficulties when applied to the small voting bodies (e.g., the Security Council) and hypothetical committees favored as illustrative examples in many expository treatments of voting power. Indeed, if the size of a collectivity is sufficiently small, say three to five members, the required calculations may be so transparent that not even paper and pencil are needed to carry them out. As a voting body increases in size, however, the complexity and tedium of the calculations can quickly become an overwhelming obstacle. A body of only ten members can produce more than 1000 such outcomes while 25 members implies upwards of 33 million. Clearly, then, an empirical application to the 150 or so members of the contemporary General Assembly is no trivial task, even by modern computing standards.

It is apparent that the smaller the size of a voting body, the simpler the analysis of voting power. To take advantage of this logic within the empirical context of the General Assembly, this inquiry focuses on the power of aggregate voting *blocs* rather than individual voting *members*. This shift in units of analysis has the effect of reducing the composite size of the Assembly by treating blocs *as if* they were constituent members. In fact, from the standpoint of the power calculus, a voting bloc is analytically equivalent to an individual member. To understand this equivalence it is necessary to understand the power of joint action.

When an individual joins with other members of a voting body in a coalition or voting bloc, the combined power of the group is augmented beyond the simple summation of its constituent members' power (Coleman, 1971). To see why this is so, notice that when votes are not weighted each member's power value is equal to $1/n$ in an n-member collectivity. An individual belonging to, say, a six member voting body will control $1/6$ of all potential swings, a proportion yielding a Banzhaf value of 0.167. Now, if two members of this body were to join forces their two votes together would actually account for *more* than $1/3$ of all swings—that is, more than the combined swings of the two individual members. This is because the formation of a bloc has the effect of reconstituting the original voting body by diminishing its size and establishing a weighting of votes. Thus, a two-member bloc in a collectivity of six equally weighted members is tantamount to a five-member body with one member possessing two votes. The Banzhaf value of our two-member bloc would be 0.385, yielding a net increase of 0.03 for each member and a decrease in the power of the remaining four individuals to 0.154. In general, then, for the purpose of calculating bloc voting power a bloc must be treated as if it were an individual member of a collectivity.

All of this should not be taken to mean that blocs are *in fact* unitary actors. With the possible exception of the Soviet bloc, such a proposition clearly contradicts the reality of General Assembly voting. Nor are blocs conceived as 'the equivalent, in embryonic form, of world political parties in an embryonic world parliament . . .' (Newcombe *et al.*, 1971: 453). Rather, a bloc level analysis is employed merely as a simplifying device, albeit one that preserves the essential point that votes and voting power are empirically, as well as conceptually, distinct. Analysis of blocs also permits a more efficient presentation of results and provides some measure of comparability between this study and the earlier investigation by Newcombe *et al.* (1971). . . .

The bloc structure of UN General Assembly voting has been delineated most recently by Powers (1980). This analysis encompassed all 196 committee and plenary session roll call votes recorded for the 143 member states attending the 30th Assembly. . . . The present

study employs Powers' results with the added provision that a state must have participated in no fewer than 60 per cent of the recorded votes to qualify for membership in any bloc. This requirement reduced the number of blocs to five.[9] Any state whose voting pattern qualified it for membership in two blocs is counted under both, although in subsequent analyses it is weighted only one-half in each bloc.

The bloc distribution of votes under the various weighting formulas is displayed in Table 2.[10] Column one indicates that the current rule allotting one vote to each member (formula 1) provides a plurality—though one considerably short of a simple majority—to states identified as the Developing World. The Western and Muslim communities control approximately the same number of votes, as do Latin America and the Soviet bloc. Note, too, that fully 11.7 per cent of the states lack sufficient regularity in their voting behavior to be reliably classified as a bloc member, although this does not preclude them from aligning with some identifiable blocs more than others. This also suggests the need for some caution in interpreting the figures in Table 2. Except for the remarkable consistency of the Soviet bloc, there is enough within-bloc variability in the classified states' voting patterns to permit defections by roughly one half of each bloc's members more than one half of the time.[11] Thus, Table 2 should be taken as an indication of overall trends in alignments during the 30th session and not as an exact measure of bloc votes on any particular issue.

Empirical Results

Banzhaf power values were calculated for each voting bloc under each of the 15 weighting formulas identified in Table 1. As noted above, blocs were treated as though they were unitary actors with votes apportioned according to the distributions specified in Table 2. Before proceeding to the results, two caveats bear explicit mention. The first has to do with the disposition of the unclassified states. The voting patterns of these states are distinct from any of the established blocs, but they are also distinct enough from one another that they cannot be grouped together as a single entity. To include these states individually, however, would be to unnecessarily complicate both the analysis and the interpretation of results. Therefore, the unclassified states were excluded from the calculation of voting power indices.

Second, the voting alignments used in this analysis should not be regarded as immutable under the various weighting schemes. To the extent that bloc voting patterns are motivated by shared concerns and common positions on world issues, the present alignment structure should remain unaffected by a change in representational formulas.[12] Nevertheless, it must be recognized that adoption of a weighting procedure would also revise each state's value to a developing coalition and this could alter some states' voting behavior quite dra-

matically depending on the particular issues involved, the kinds of rewards being offered, and so forth.[13] Simply put, the weighting of votes alone may be sufficient to change the bloc structure of UN voting. Those states voting on the margins of an established bloc—that is, states sharing less than, say, 50 per cent voting variance with their bloc—would appear to be most susceptible to influences of this sort. Although it would be interesting to explore the kinds of alignment changes that might be expected under various weighting schemes, this question must be left for future research. In sum, there is no assurance that the composition of individual blocs or even the overall bloc structure would remain intact under any of the alternative representational formulas examined here.

Bloc power values under a simple majority decision rule are presented for each of the 15 voting formulas in Table 3. It is immediately evident that only six different power distributions are derived from the 15 formulas. An examination of these power values reveals that the one state-one vote procedure (formula 1) is far more favorable to the Developing World than is indicated by the simple allocation of votes in Table 2. Moreover, the disparities in nonweighted vote totals among the remaining four blocs only masks an underlying equivalence in voting power. While it is not surprising that every one of the alternative voting systems has the effect of reducing the power of the Developing

TABLE 2 Allocation of Votes under 15 Voting Formulas

							Voting Formula								
Bloc	No. 1	No. 2	No. 3	No. 4	No. 5	No. 6	No. 7	No. 8	No. 9	No. 10	No. 11	No. 12	No. 13	No. 14	No. 15
Developing World	38.3	35.1	30.9	32.4	33.9	35.6	11.7	8.9	29.5	34.1	22.4	24.8	33.6	24.2	24.0
Western Community	16.0	17.7	22.2	22.1	19.5	18.7	66.0	66.9	32.1	21.9	41.4	39.0	21.0	36.2	41.5
Muslim Community	18.4	14.8	19.3	19.3	19.5	19.4	3.7	1.9	13.4	17.5	8.5	9.9	18.7	9.5	8.7
Latin America	7.8	1.7	4.2	5.3	5.0	6.2	0.9	0.7	5.7	7.1	1.1	1.4	7.3	1.3	1.5
Soviet Bloc	7.8	9.7	10.5	8.8	8.9	8.2	13.0	17.4	9.8	7.8	13.4	11.1	8.5	15.0	13.7
Unclassified	11.7	21.0	12.8	12.1	13.2	11.9	4.6	4.2	9.5	11.6	13.1	13.8	11.0	13.8	10.6
Total	100%	100%	99.9%	100%	100%	100%	99.9%	100%	100%	100.1%	100%	99.9%	100%	100%	100%

Cell entries indicate the percentage of General Assembly votes controlled by each bloc under the designated weighting formula. Formula numbers correspond to those given in Table 1. Totals deviating from 100% are due to rounding error.

World, the degree of attenuation is at times quite unexpected. For instance, the cube root of population formula (6) apportions this bloc only 3 per cent fewer votes than the present system, but the corresponding power index is almost halved. Note, too, that identical voting weights do not necessarily yield equivalent power index values under different weighting schemes. Formula 10 (nonlinear function of assessment) provides the Soviet bloc with less power than it has under the present system despite the fact that its proportion of votes by the two formulas is exactly the same. Clearly, then, vote allocation performs rather poorly as an indicator of control over voting outcomes. Just how poorly is the question to be considered next.

Riker and Shapley (1968) have devised an index of bias in weighted voting systems designated the 'power ratio' or p. The ratio can be calculated for any measure of voting power provided that its values sum to unity over all members. The power ratio may be defined symbolically as

$$\rho = \beta \div \frac{\omega}{W} \qquad (6)$$

Where β is the power value, ω is the nominal voting strength of an individual member, and W is the total number of votes in the collectivity. Thus, the power ratio will equal 1 when a member's share of voting power is identical to its share of votes. Magnitudes greater than 1 indicate more power than is warranted by the member's relative weight whereas values less than 1 reveal just the reverse.

Table 4 displays power ratios for each of the voting procedures under consideration. The power ratios listed in column one confirm our

TABLE 3   Banzhaf Power Values under 15 Voting Formulas

Bloc	Voting formula					
	No. 1	No. 2	Nos. 3,4, 5,6,10&13	Nos. 7&8	No. 9	Nos. 11, 12,14&15
Developing World	0.636	0.500	0.385	0.000	0.231	0.167
Western Community	0.091	0.167	0.231	1.000	0.385	0.500
Muslim Community	0.091	0.167	0.231	0.000	0.231	0.167
Latin America	0.091	0.000	0.077	0.000	0.077	0.000
Soviet Bloc	0.091	0.167	0.077	0.000	0.077	0.167

Power index values computed for a five member voting body under a simple majority decision rule. Bloc vote allocations are displayed in Table 2.

TABLE 4 Power Ratios under 15 Voting Formulas

Bloc							Voting Formula								
	No. 1	No. 2	No. 3	No. 4	No. 5	No. 6	No. 7	No. 8	No. 9	No. 10	No. 11	No. 12	No. 13	No. 14	No. 15
Developing World	1.466	1.125	1.086	1.044	0.986	0.953	0.000	0.000	0.709	0.998	0.648	0.580	1.020	0.595	0.622
Western Community	0.502	0.745	0.907	0.919	1.028	1.088	1.000	1.000	1.085	0.932	1.050	1.105	0.979	1.191	1.077
Muslim Community	0.437	0.891	1.044	1.052	1.028	1.049	0.000	0.000	1.560	1.167	1.707	1.454	1.099	1.515	1.716
Latin America	1.030	0.000	1.599	1.277	1.337	1.094	0.000	0.000	1.223	0.959	0.000	0.000	0.939	0.000	0.000
Soviet Bloc	1.030	1.360	0.639	0.769	0.751	0.827	0.000	0.000	0.711	0.873	1.083	1.297	0.806	0.960	1.090

The power ratio is adapted from Riker and Shapley (1968). Unclassified states are excluded from the calculation of relative weights used in the power ratio.

earlier observation that the present voting system is especially favorable to the countries of the Developing World. What was not obvious before, however, was the relatively advantaged positions of Latin America and the Soviet Bloc. Formulas 6 (cube root of population) and 13 (log population + log GDP) appear to produce the least discrepancy between power and nominal weight while formulas 7 (GDP) and 8 (assessment) are highly biased due to their total concentration of power in a single bloc. But perhaps the most striking feature of the entire table is the failure of *any* representational formula to distribute voting power in proportion to its allocation of votes.

CONCLUSION

Our results raise some interesting questions regarding the political acceptability of alternative representational formulas for the UN General Assembly. Consider the concept of 'balance,' the evaluation criterion with which this study began. It may be that the balanced distribution of voting strength sought by Newcombe et al. (1971) is no longer an appropriate objective for a larger and more diversified Assembly in which the major blocs differ by such huge magnitudes on the representational criteria used to allocate votes under existing weighting proposals.[14] But even if the balance criterion itself is of questionable durability, the assumption underlying it—that the political acceptability of a weighting procedure is contingent upon

the resulting distribution of voting strength—is not. That is to say, an alternative representational formula is likely to be acceptable to the extent that it places each individual member or bloc in its 'rightful' position in comparison with others. A major stumbling point, of course, is that individual political considerations are bound to produce widely divergent views regarding the acceptability of the various formulas.

So much is obvious. But the problems with weighted voting go much deeper than the political differences over which particular system offers the 'fairest' method of representation. With no intention of diminishing the intractability of this issue, let us suppose for the moment that some standard of representation can be found that is agreeable to most members.[15] Historically, such weighted representational systems have been implemented by manipulating simple vote allocations. But, as has been shown, weighted voting procedures ordinarily do not distribute votes and voting power in direct proportion to one another. In practice, then, weighted voting systems generally fail to distribute actual influence in the manner prescribed by the established representational standard. Moreover, once the distinction between nominal voting strength and voting power is understood, a weighting system of this sort could hardly be considered politically acceptable.

This particular difficulty, however, would seem to stem more from a naive understanding of the voting process than from an inherent inability of the weighting mechanism to reapportion voting power. The obvious solution to this problem would be to design a weighting scheme to allocate votes in whatever way necessary to achieve the desired distribution of power. Although there is no direct functional relationship between votes and voting power, it is possible to *approximate* a prescribed power distribution by allocating votes through a kind of 'backward search.' That is, rather than the usual sequence which begins with raw votes and calculates power values, such a procedure would work backwards from *a priori* power values to derive an allocation of votes. In the case of the UN General Assembly this solution is complicated by almost annual increases in membership and the practice of relying on two different decision rules.

Assuming that our hypothetical weighting system is technically feasible, its implementation almost surely will require a seemingly arbitrary allocation of votes in order to establish the requisite distribution of power. And herein lies a second problem. Recall that voting power is an abstract concept grounded in long-run probabilities; actual votes, on the other hand, provide a more tangible indicator of influence encountered virtually every day the Assembly is in session. After all, it is the number of votes that makes the difference between winning and losing. Actual votes also serve as a convenient basis for comparison with others and with the intended representational standard. For these reasons, then, votes are likely to retain some symbolic importance even though they are only indirectly related to voting power. This suggests that vote allocations, although less critical than voting power, may still have some impact on member-states' evaluation of the weighting formulas. Therefore, insofar as the allocation of concrete votes bears less than a perfect relationship to the criterion for representation, the political acceptability of a weighting scheme is left in doubt.

Even if the apparent arbitrariness of vote allocations is within the bounds of acceptability, another feature of this representational system—the distribution of power ratios—may not be. When votes are treated merely as an instrument for distributing power rather than as a direct means of influence, the correspondence between votes and power will exhibit some unevenness, and anything less than a perfect correspondence between votes and power yields a power ratio other than unity. Furthermore, because the power ratio is a ratio of two proportions there will always be some values above unity and some values below.[16] Once again appearances are important. In this case, power ratios greater than unity give the appearance of preferential treatment in the sense that some members' votes seem to 'count' more than those of other members. This may be a trivial concern so long as actual power is distributed correctly; nevertheless, the image of some votes being worth more than other votes is not likely to inspire confidence in a voting procedure.

The principal conclusion to emerge from this analysis is that weighted voting is a highly problematic method for adjusting the representational structure of a voting body such as the UN General Assembly. Previous studies of weighted voting in the UN have underestimated the extent of these problems by focusing on actual vote allocations to the exclusion of voting power. Because votes and voting power are seldom proportional under conditions of weighted voting, the political acceptability of an alternative representational system is likely to depend on more than just the allocation of votes. In particular, a formula is likely to be acceptable to a broad range of members only if it firstly, distributes voting power in a generally satisfactory manner and secondly, counts all votes equally, that is, delivers virtually identical power ratios to most members. The prospect of a weighting system meeting both of these conditions is remote at best.

NOTES

1. Other procedural reforms advocated by the US Department of State include counting abstentions in the vote totals when computing majorities and introducing a non-voting membership category of 'Associate States' to accommodate the micro-states ('Report of the Secretary of State to the President on Reform and Restructuring of the United Nations System,' Washington, DC, February, 1978 cited in Bedjaoui, 1981: 242, fn. 30). Several study groups have made similar recommendations; for a review, see Alger (1973).

2. One occurred as early as 1963 (US Department of State, 'Weighted Voting in the United Nations,' Washington, DC, 1963 cited in Newcombe *et al.*, 1971: 465, fn. 19). The second was completed in 1978 ('Report of the Secretary of State . . .' cited in Bedjaoui, 1981: 242, fn. 30). A more recent instance of US Government interest in weighted voting concerned the proposed International Seabed Authority. Rejection of the US weighted voting scheme is reported to be one of the reasons the Reagan Administration refused to accept the long awaited Law of the Sea Treaty (Ratiner, 1982).

3. A major exception is the UN Security Council. Indeed, the Council's unorthodox voting system has made a favorite example in discussions of formal voting power (e.g., Shapley and Shubik, 1954; Coleman, 1971; Brams, 1976; Junn and Park, 1977; Junn, 1983). Other international organizations analyzed from this perspective include the European Community (Brams and Affuso, 1976) and the International Monetary Fund (Fischer and Schotter, 1978).

4. Balance, of course is not the only standard by which such voting schemes might be judged. For example, Newcombe *et al.* (1971) also considered 'additivity' and 'future representation by population.' Additivity refers to the stability of overall voting strength in cases of fragmentation or unifica-

tion of member states. Future representation by population derives from the democratic tradition that all persons have a right to equal representation. Application of this criterion is modified by the assumption that at some future date standards of living will tend to even out rendering aggregate indicators such as national income, energy consumption, and UN assessment proportional to population. For other possible criteria, see Newcombe *et al.* (1977).

5. The literature on power is very large indeed. For useful reviews of power in international relations see Baldwin (1979) or Hart (1976).

6. For a measure of power which incorporates both formal and behavioral sources of influence see Harsanyi (1962).

7. For every critical 'aye' defection there is a complementary critical 'nay' defection regardless of the decision rule being used. A switch from a minimal winning 'aye' coalition renders the 'nay' coalition minimal winning; a switch back to the 'aye' coalition just reverses the process and once again makes the 'aye' coalition minimal winning.

8. Formulas 7, 12, 13 and 15 were originally based on GNP. This analysis employs GDP because it is the measure of gross product used in the UN's system of national accounting.

9. The sixth bloc identified in Power's (1980) analysis accounted for just 2 per cent of the variance and contained only China and Albania. The latter was absent for about one-half of the roll calls thus disqualifying it from bloc membership. Since no bloc can have less than two members, this posed a problem regarding the classification of China. Two alternatives were available: to treat China as an unclassified state or to join it to an existing bloc. The former option would have left an exceedingly large proportion of weighted votes unclassified under any of the population based formulas. Therefore, China was placed in its next highest loading (0.47) bloc—the Developing World. For further justification of this decision, see Chai (1979). Other member states dropped due to excessive absences are the Bahamas, Cambodia, Cape Verde Islands, Central African Republic, the Comoros, Gambia, Guatemala, Guinea-Bissau, Haiti, Maldives, Paraguay, Sao Tome and Principe, Surinam and Yemen.

10. The data utilized here are for 1973 and were obtained from the *Cross-National Time-Series Data Archive* originally collected by Banks and made available by the Inter-University Consortium for Political and Social Research. Neither the collector of the data nor the Consortium bears any responsibility for the analysis or interpretation presented here.

11. This has to do with the criterion for bloc membership. Because a loading of only 0.50 or better is required for a state to be included in a bloc, there is generally a substantial amount of variance in each state's voting behavior left unaccounted for by its bloc membership(s). In fact, approximately one half of the members in the Developing World, Muslim Community, and Latin American blocs load below 0.71, the minimum required for one half of a state's var-

iance to be congruent with bloc variance.

12. For evidence that attributes such as economic development or political ideology do play a role in UN voting behavior see Vincent (1971, 1973) and Moore (1975).

13. Although there is now a large literature on coalition formation, the classic statement of this process is found in Riker (1962).

14. Even a very rough balance may be difficult to justify given the current Assembly's bloc structure. For instance, the Latin American bloc could hardly claim an equal share of voting power under any of the population based formulas when it represents only about 2 per cent of the world's inhabitants.

15. Naturally, agreement on a general principle of representation need not imply agreement on the operational criteria for implementing it. An instructive analogy would seem to be the perennial controversy over the UN scale of assessments. Distributing the financial burden according to member states' capacity to pay is seldom contested as a guiding principle. In practice, however, the Committee on Contributions has had little success in devising an objective measure of capacity to pay that is agreeable to all major groups of states. For further discussion of this issue see Renninger *et al.* (1982).

16. Unless, of course, all power ratios are exactly equal to unity.

REFERENCES

Alger, C. F. (1973) 'The United States in the United Nations.' *International Organization* 27 (1): 1–23.

Baldwin, D. A. (1979) 'Power Analysis in World Politics: New Trends versus Old Tendencies.' *World Politics* 31(2): 160–94.

Banzhaf, J. F., III (1965) 'Weighted Voting Doesn't Work: A Mathematical Analysis.' *Rutgers Law Review* 19(2): 317–43.

Banzhaf, J. F., III (1966) 'Multimember Electoral Districts—Do They Violate the "One Man, One Vote" Principle?' *Yale Law Journal* 75(8): 1309–88.

Barret, C. and H. Newcombe (1968) 'Weighted Voting in International Organizations.' *Peace Research Reviews* 2(2).

Bedjaoui, M. (1981) 'A Third World View of International Organization: Action Toward a New International Economic Order,' pp. 207–45 in Georges Abi-Saab (ed.) *The Concept of International Organization.* Paris: Unesco.

Brams, S. J. (1975) *Game Theory in Political Science.* New York: Free Press.

Brams, S. J. (1976) *Paradoxes in Politics.* New York: Free Press.

Brams, S. J. and P. J. Affuso (1976) 'Power and Size: A New Paradox.' *Theory and Decision* 7(1):29–56.

Chai, T. R. (1979) 'Chinese Policy Towards the Third World and the Superpowers in the UN General Assembly 1971–1977: A Voting Analysis.' *International Organization* 33(3):391–402.

Coleman, J. S. (1971) 'Control of Collectivities and the Power of a Collectivity to Act,' pp. 277–287 in Bernhardt Lieberman (ed.) *Social Choice.* New York: Gordon and Breach.

Fischer, D. and A. Schotter (1978) 'The Inevitability of the "Paradox of Redistribution" in the Allocation of Voting Weights.' *Public Choice* 33(2): 49–67.

Harsanyi, J. C. (1962) 'Measurement of Social Power in n-Person Reciprocal Power Situations.' *Behavioral Science* 7(1):81–91.

Hart, J. (1976) 'Three Approaches to the Measurement of Power in International Relations.' *International Organization* 30(2):289–305.

Holler, M. J. (ed.) (1982) *Power, Voting, and Voting Power*. Würzburg-Wein, West Germany: Physica-Verlag.

Junn, R. S. (1983) 'Voting in the United Nations Security Council.' *International Interactions* 9(4):315–52.

Junn, R. S. and T. W. Park (1977) 'Calculus of Voting Power in the U.N. Security Council.' *Social Science Quarterly* 58(1):104–10.

Moore, D. W. (1975) 'Repredicting Voting Patterns in the General Assembly: A Methodological Note.' *International Studies Quarterly* 19(2):199–211.

Newcombe, H., J. Wert and A. Newcombe (1971) 'Comparison of Weighted Voting Formulas for the United Nations,' *World Politics* 23(3):452–92.

Newcombe, H., C. Young and E. Sinaiko (1977) 'Alternative Pasts: A Study of Weighted Voting at the United Nations.' *International Organization* 31(3):579–86.

Perusse, R. I. (1982) 'One Man, One Vote and the United Nations,' paper delivered at the Annual Meeting of the International Studies Association, Cincinnati.

Powers, R. J. (1980) 'United Nations Voting Alignments: A New Equilibrium?' *Western Political Quarterly* 33(2):167–84.

Ratiner, L. S. (1982) 'The Law of the Sea: A Crossroads for American Foreign Policy.' *Foreign Affairs* 60(5):1006–21.

Renninger, J. P. with D. Donaghue, P. Geib, H Perez and W. van Nispen Tot Sevenaer (1982) 'Assessing the United Nations Scale of Assessments: Is It Fair? Is It Equitable?' Policy and Efficacy Studies No. 9. New York: United Nations Institute for Training and Research.

Riker, W. H. (1962) *The Theory of Political Coalitions*. New Haven: Yale University Press.

Riker, W. H. and L. S. Shapley (1968) 'Weighted Voting: A Mathematical Analysis for Instrumental Judgements,' pp. 199–216 in J. Roland Pennock and John W. Chapman (eds.) *NOMOS X: Representation*. New York: Atherton Press.

Shapley, L. S. and M. Shubik (1954) 'A Method for Evaluating the Distribution of Power in a Committee System.' *American Political Science Review* 48(3):787–92.

Straffin, P. D., Jr. (1977) 'Homogeneity, Independence, and Power Indices.' *Public Choice* 30: 107–17.

Vincent, J. E. (1971) 'Predicting Voting Patterns in the General Assembly.' *American Political Science Review* 65(2):471–98.

Vincent, J. E. (1973) 'An Application of Attribute Theory to General Assembly Voting Patterns and Some Implications.' *International Organization* 16(3):551–82.

CHAPTER V

Peace and Security Affairs

It is easy for a cynic to discount the role of international organizations in peace and security affairs. State sovereignty is still predominant, and nothing resembling an international police force is on the horizon. Furthermore, the collective security provisions in Chapter Seven of the U.N. Charter (see Appendix B) have either never been fully implemented or have been abandoned in the face of serious disagreement in the Security Council.

Although international organizations have not prevented war as originally hoped, the cynical view ignores their role as significant actors in ameliorating the level and scope of global conflicts. First, it might be noted that NATO and the Warsaw Pact are international organizations committed to deterring war, thus forming the backbone of the rivalry between East and West, especially on the European continent. Second, several of the most important arms control agreements were negotiated under the auspices of international organizations; the Non-Proliferation Treaty and the Partial Test Ban Treaty are the most notable examples. Third, international organizations attempt to ensure peaceful resolution of disputes in all areas of the world today.

The previous three points highlight the evolution of international organizations in the security area over the past forty years. Alliances between states have become increasingly formalized through international organizations. Thus, even though international collective security has not been actualized, regional collective security of a sort is alive and well. Additionally, international organizations often serve as the centerpiece of attempts to settle protracted international disputes. For example, the most frequent suggestion for a Middle East peace has involved a U.N.-sponsored conference among the interested parties. Finally, international organizations have become semiautonomous actors in their pursuit of peaceful resolution of conflict. The means of intervention vary from peacekeeping to mediation; yet, the scope has expanded beyond the traditional fact-finding missions.

Although international organizations are important actors in trying to resolve global conflict, they are far from being completely effective in that pursuit. Part of the reason may be that international organizations usually become involved only after one or more of the disputants has threatened or actually used military force. At this stage, it becomes very difficult to resolve the dispute without further violence. Despite being slow to deal with a developing crisis or war, international organizations have a better success rate in limiting or terminating conflict than might be assumed. Wilkenfeld and Brecher examine United Nations involvement in crises for the period 1945–1975. They find that the United Nations was involved in 59% of all crises, and their frequency of involvement was even greater in the most serious of those conflicts. Surprisingly, the United Nations was most successful in stopping hostilities and achieving a settlement when the situation involved full-scale war. This indicates that international organizations are far from irrelevant in the most serious threats to peace in the world.

In his article, Paul Diehl focuses on the most prominent and, some say, most successful strategy employed by international organizations: peacekeeping. It is clear from his analysis, however, that peacekeeping is not an appropriate strategy for all situations. It might be noted that even when peacekeeping is successful in stopping the fighting, it provides little or no guide on how to resolve the underlying sources of conflict between the disputants. The deployment of peacekeeping troops for almost a quarter of a century in Cyprus illustrates the inherent problem of what to do after the fighting stops.

If the first two articles in this section define the parameters for success of international organizations in this issue area, then the final selection by Haas is a little more sobering. Looking at the effectiveness of the United Nations and some regional organizations across time, he uncovers some disturbing trends. The success rate of international organizations in international disputes has declined since 1970. Furthermore, Haas notes a decay in the established norms and procedures (i.e. regime) for handling disputes in international organizations. Haas traces the evolution of the international security regime across four distinct periods. He also cites several reasons for the important changes that have occurred; this will further temper any optimism from the first two selections.

Collectively, these three articles should convey to the reader that international organizations are far from inactive or irrelevant in international disputes, but their involvement is not as yet evolving to constitute a more pervasive or effective influence in peace and security affairs. Perhaps the Soviet Union's new commitment to support United Nations operations in this issue area will be the beginning of a reversal to the gloomy patterns noted in the Haas article.

10

INTERNATIONAL CRISES, 1945–1975:
THE UN DIMENSION

Jonathan Wilkenfeld and Michael Brecher

The involvement of third parties in the search for pacific settlement of disputes has been an enduring—some would add necessary—part of world politics in the twentieth century. It received initial quasi-institutional expression at The Hague Peace Conferences of 1899 and 1907. It was enshrined in the Covenant of the League of Nations (Articles 11–13, 15, 17) and, after World War II, in the United Nations Charter (Chapter VI). A legitimate role in international disputes was also assumed by regional organizations such as the Organization of American States, the League of Arab States, the Organization of African Unity, and also security organizations like NATO and the Warsaw Pact and, to a lesser extent, political bodies like the Council of Europe. Individual states, notably the major powers of the interwar period and the superpowers since 1945, have also been involved in the resolution of conflicts, crises, and disputes among other states.

Third party intervention has been defined as 'any action taken by an actor that is not a direct party to the crisis, that is designed to re-duce or remove one or more of the problems of the bargaining relationship and, therefore, to facilitate the termination of the crisis itself' (Young, 1967:34). The rationale for such intervention derives from the essentially anarchic character of the international system and, more generally, from conflict resolution relating to all human relations. Parties to a dispute can often achieve accommodation only by the involvement of a 'disinterested' person or institution—or by arbitration or adjudication on the part of quasi-legal and legal bodies with the full authority of a universally accepted regime. Such authority, present in most domestic political institutions, is conspicuously absent in the global international system. Moreover, given the unequal distribution of capabilities and resources, and the autonomy of political decision-making, disputes among states carry the potential of more dangerous spillover, affecting the fragile stability of the global system or one of its subsystems. In the absence of authoritative institutions and binding rules for the resolution of disputes, state actors have granted in-

SOURCE: Reprinted from the *International Studies Quarterly*, Vol. 28, No. 1, 1984, with permission of the International Studies Association, Byrnes International Center, University of South Carolina, Columbia, S.C. 29208 USA.

ternational organizations the power to seek pacific settlement and, where violence occurs, to restore international peace and security (Article 16 of the League Covenant and Chapter VII of the UN Charter). This involvement is usually initiated by member-states in quest of legitimation and support for their claims.

The institutional sources of third party intervention in international disputes are thus very broad: global, regional and security organizations, superpowers and major powers, and on occasion, lesser actors as well. So too is the scope of third party activity. This may be viewed along a scale of involvement, beginning with no discussion of an approach, complaint or request by one or more members, followed by discussion without decision, and decision without provision for action. These activities are verbal and passive in form, with no commitments. Greater involvement is evident in an array of field operations, 'the "acid test" of the concern of the world's governments for world peace. Field operations imply the expenditure of time, money, reputations, and even lives away from organization (or third state) headquarters' (Haas, Butterworth and Nye, 1972:36). This too may be modest, such as fact-finding in a dispute, an offer of good offices, even a willingness to mediate or suggest a formula for conciliation. Mediation may, however, extend to proposing the specific terms of a compromise solu-tion. Still higher on the scale of involvement is a call for economic and/or military sanctions. Highest is a direct military presence to maintain a fragile cease-fire, armistice or peace agreement, such as truce supervision through the placing of observers in the contested territory, the stationing of a peacekeeping force in a neutral zone between the parties, and, at the apex of involvement, the use of emergency military forces to interpose and/or monitor compliance.

In the present paper, our attention shifts from disputes and wars in general to a more narrow focus on international crisis. Third parties can take on a variety of functions in international crisis situations. In a very useful summary of these functions, based primarily on the work of Young (1967) and Touval (1975), Bobrow (1981), makes the following points:

In principle, third parties can contribute to crisis regulations and settlement in two ways. First, they can make a direct positive contribution. Familiar examples include focusing the parties on a particular termination agreement, devising a formula to avoid hard issues, providing an agenda, and manipulating timing. Second, third parties can work to weaken constraints on the primary parties; that is, they can make it easier for the primary parties to do what they would in some sense like to do anyway. Third parties do this by lowering the net costs associated with a more flexible bargaining position, including the internal political penalties. In effect, third parties provide face-saving assistance for the primary conflict participants. They may do so by providing rationalizations for the disavowal of previous stands, by certifying the benefits of an agreement, and by providing insurance against the risks should an agreement fail.

Third party intervention will be restricted in this analysis to the activity of the UN in crisis management.[1] Our point of departure is the International Crisis Behavior Project (ICB) definition of a crisis for a state as a situational change in its external or internal environment which triggers three interrelated perceptions by its decisionmakers: threat to basic values; a sense of finite time for response to those threats; and a rise in the likelihood of its involvement in some form of military hostilities before the threat has been overcome (Brecher, 1977:43–44). The presence of these three images indicates the existence of a crisis for a specific state, which is designated a crisis actor.[2]

While the above notion of crisis suffices when attention is focused on the behavior of individual state decisionmaking units, third party intervention occurs at the level of the international crisis as a whole. Thus, actor cases may be grouped into clusters or international crises, whose members are seized by a common issue (e.g., US, UK, France, USSR in the Berlin Blockade Crisis of 1948; India, Pakistan, Bangladesh in their 1971 crisis-war; Egypt, Israel, Syria, US, USSR in the 1973 Middle East Crisis). Apart from a shared issue, what demarcates an international crisis is that its duration extends from the first increase in stress, the product of the three specified perceptions for an actor in an issue grouping, to the last decline of stress to its normal, pre-crisis level among the actors in such a group. The majority of international crises comprise at least two crisis actors, whose decision-makers manifest the three perceptions of threat, time, and war likelihood. However, there are also single state international crises, comprising one crisis actor, with the presence of one or more involved actors, whose decisionmakers may have intitiated the crisis and, in any event, are involved but do not perceive *all* three conditions noted earlier as applying to themselves (e.g., Dominican Republic in a 1947 crisis with Guatemala, with the latter as an involved actor; Egypt, in its 1955 Baghdad Pact Crisis, with the UK, US, Iraq and Turkey as involved actors; Portugal in its Goa Crisis the same year, with India as an involved actor). Since UN involvement in an international crisis presupposes a disagreement between two or more states, a single state international crisis, with the involved adversarial actor specified, fits the category of third party cases. Grouped by issue and rising/declining stress levels, the ICB Project has identified 160 international crises for the 1945–1975 period. It is this set of cases which will provide the data base for our examination of the role of the UN in international crises.

THE ROLE OF THE UN IN INTERNATIONAL CRISES, 1945-1975

Throughout the current analysis, our attention will focus on three aspects of UN intervention in crises. First, we will be concerned with the level of such involvement in terms of the specific organs (Security Council, General Assembly, Secretary-General) which take an active role in crisis management. Second, we will be interested in the extent to which resolute action (i.e., resolutions authorizing member action, observer or emergency military forces) or non-resolute action (i.e., fact-finding missions, good offices, mediation) was undertaken. Third, we will assess the effectiveness of the UN in abating the crisis, that is, in preventing hostilities or contributing to crisis termination. UN activity was considered to have been effective when such activity was the single most important factor in crisis abatement, or when such activity had an important impact, along with action by other international actors.

Before proceeding to a discussion of hypotheses relevant to the role of the UN in international crises, it would be useful to examine briefly the empirical record of the UN in terms of crisis intervention. The UN became involved in 95 of the 160 cases of international crises in the 1945-1975 period, constituting some 59% of the total.[3] Furthermore, our data indicate that the UN was considered to have been effective in terms of crisis abate-

ment in only 18% of all the international crises. Table 1 presents a yearly breakdown in terms of the number of crises per year, the number of crises in which the UN became involved, and the number of cases in which its actions were judged to have been effective in terms of crisis abatement.

At first glance, the record speaks for itself, and would hardly seem to justify the rather elaborate analysis called for in order to properly evaluate the hypotheses we will present. The UN became involved in only slightly more than half of all crises which occurred in the international system, and of these cases, was judged to be effective in only one-third. It is, however, possible to note some trends in these data, and it is the explanations for these trends which we will try to pin down as our analysis proceeds.

The peak periods of crisis for the international system as a whole occurred roughly in the years 1947-48, 1957-58, 1960-65, 1968-69, 1973, and 1975. With some exceptions—notably 1957, 1962, 1973—UN activity peaked in roughly the same periods. UN effectiveness more often than not followed its own course throughout this period, showing particular strengths in 1947-48, 1958, 1963, 1965, and 1971. Thus, while the volume of UN activity in crises has increased from an average of 2.78 interventions per year in the bipolar period of 1945-1962 to an average of 4.15 interventions per year in the 1963-75 polycentric period, the effectiveness of such intervention has re-

TABLE 1   UN Involvement in International Crises, 1945–1975

Years	Total Number of Crises	Number of Crises in which U.N. Active	U.N. Active as Percent of Total	Number of Crises in which U.N. Effective	U.N. Effective as Percent of Total
1945	2	2	100	1	50
1946	3	1	33	1	33
1947	8	4	50	2	25
1948	9	7	77	3	33
1949	3	0	0	0	0
1950	3	3	100	0	0
1951	3	3	100	1	33
1952	1	0	0	0	0
1953	5	3	60	0	0
1954	2	1	50	0	0
1955	6	2	33	1	17
1956	4	3	75	1	25
1957	7	3	43	0	0
1958	8	5	63	2	25
1959	4	1	25	0	0
1960	7	4	57	1	14
1961	11	5	45	2	18
1962	6	2	33	1	17
1963	10	5	50	2	20
1964	8	5	62	0	0
1965	6	6	100	2	33
1966	2	2	100	0	0
1967	2	2	100	1	50
1968	7	6	86	0	0
1969	6	3	50	1	17
1970	5	3	60	1	20
1971	5	3	60	2	40
1972	3	1	33	0	0
1973	6	2	33	1	17
1974	2	2	100	1	50
1975	6	6	100	1	17
	160	95	59	28	18

mained relatively constant at slightly less than one effective intervention per year for the entire period.

Clearly, we must look more closely at a number of factors which have a bearing on the gross trends observed here. While the initial findings are discouraging (in terms of an effective role for the UN in international peace and security), we must now turn to an evaluation of sets of hypotheses in order to fill out the picture.

As noted above, while third party intervention in international disputes and crises can range from that of universal international organizations, such as the UN and the League of Nations, to regional organizations, such as the OAS and the OAU, and individual nation-states, such as the superpowers, the present paper focuses exclusively on the UN. In this regard, two general research questions guide our current analysis.

1. What is the relationship between the attributes of international crises and the extent, substance and effectiveness of UN activity?

2. Under what conditions is UN intervention in international crises likely to lead to favorable outcomes?

In the sections below we will examine these questions in some detail and propose several hypotheses for examination in the analysis section of this paper.

Crisis Attributes and UN Intervention

Data reveal that the UN became active in barely half of the 160 international crises spanning the 1945 to 1975 period. Given the clear mandate of the UN in the area of international conflict and crisis, what explains this relatively low involvement? On the surface, it could be plausibly argued that the UN, as the universal organization with a primary interest in the maintenance of international peace and security, will become involved in those situations which pose the most serious threat to peace and security. Traditionally, this threat has been judged in terms of such indicators as the extent of violence, the number of participants, and the involvement of major powers and superpowers. In this regard, the first research hypothesis may be formally stated as follows:

Hypothesis 1:
The more serious the international crisis, the more likely it is that the UN will intervene.[4]

The concept of *seriousness of crisis* may be operationalized in several ways. The following indicators will be used in the present study.

Number of Crisis Actors: Generally, one might expect that the larger the number of states participating in a crisis situation, the more serious that situation is in terms of the peace and security of the international system. In fact, such seriousness may increase geometrically rather than linearly as the number of crisis actors increases, posing problems for the bargaining and negotiation process (Coase, 1960, 1981; Avaizian and Callen, 1981; Creary and Wilkenfeld, 1983). Thus, the first subhypothesis may be stated as follows:

Hypothesis 1a:
The larger the number of crisis actors, the more likely it is that the UN will become involved.

Severity of Violence: Severity refers to the subsequent employment of violence by the actors as a crisis management technique. While a variety of crisis management techniques may be employed by actors, ranging from negotiation and other pacific methods, those crises characterized as serious usually exhibit a degree of violence in crisis management. Hence, the second subhypothesis is as follows:

Hypothesis 1b:

> *The more severe the violence employed as a crisis management technique, the more likely it is that the UN will become involved.*

Superpower Involvement: While involvement by superpowers in crises will almost automatically imply seriousness, there are clearly gradations in such an assessment. The most serious of such situations are those in which the US and the USSR are both directly involved as actors. Less serious are cases in which only a single superpower is a crisis actor, and situations in which superpower involvement is limited to the political, economic, or propaganda levels (for an analysis of superpower crisis management behavior, see Wilkenfeld and Brecher, 1982a). The final subhypothesis of this section is as follows:

Hypothesis 1c:

> *The higher the level of superpower involvement in a crisis, the more likely it is that the UN will become involved.*

UN Intervention and Crisis Outcomes

The second major question dealt with in this study focuses on the extent to which UN intervention affects crisis outcomes. In particular, we are concerned with identifying the conditions under which UN involvement in a crisis is likely to lead to favorable outcomes, both from the point of view of the individual actors (in terms of their own goals and satisfaction levels and in terms of the peace and security of the international system in general (defusion of tensions). In this regard, we are guided by the following general hypothesis:

Hypothesis 2:

> *The more active the UN is in an international crisis, the more likely it is that outcomes will be favorable to the participants and the international system in general.*

The concept of *favorable outcome* will be operationalized in terms of the following indicator.

Termination in Agreement: It is our contention that one way to evaluate the outcome of a crisis is by the extent to which the parties achieve some form of agreement. Crisis resolution might be achieved formally through treaties, armistices, or cease-fires, as well as semi-formally as in letters or oral declarations. The thrust of UN activity in crises is usually to incorporate the terms of a solution into a formal document, such as a Security Council resolution or a General Assembly report of the results of good offices, fact-finding missions, or mediation efforts. The following, more specific, subhypothesis will guide our analysis. . . .

Along with the hypothesized favorable results to accrue from UN intervention in crises, we must also deal with at least two unintended (and not necessarily positive) consequences of such intervention. Thus, the process by which an agreement among the parties is hammered out may result both in the necessity for compromise in terms of the objectives of the crisis actors (and hence a more indecisive outcome) and in the dragging out of the termination process itself. The following subhypotheses deal with these unintended consequences:

Hypothesis 2a:
The more active the UN is in an international crisis, the more likely it is that outcomes will be indecisive.

Hypothesis 2b:
The more active the UN is in an international crisis, the more likely it is that the duration of the crisis will be extended.

We now turn to the analysis of the data and the evaluation of our hypotheses pertaining to UN interventions in international crises for the 1945–1975 period.

ANALYSIS

Crisis Characteristics and UN Intervention

Our first set of analyses evaluate hypotheses dealing with the seriousness of international crises and the propensity of the UN to intervene. We will assess the extent to which our four indicators of seriousness—crisis management technique, severity of violence, number of actors, and superpower involvement—explain whether or not the UN was likely to have become involved in an international crisis during the 1945–1975 period. As we proceed, we will also provide information, where relevant, as to the type of UN activity involved, the most active UN organ, and the overall effectiveness of such activity. Finally, we will conclude this section with profiles of cases which meet the criteria of seriousness of crisis and UN involvement, and attempt to draw some conclusions regarding the effectiveness of the UN in terms of crisis abatement.

We have already discussed the indicators of seriousness of crisis in some detail. Our central dependent variable in this section is UN activity. For purposes of this analysis, UN activity will be dichotomized as follows. Low-level activity includes general activity, activity of sub-organs and specialized committees, and Secretary-General activity. High-level activity includes the activity of the General Assembly and the Security Council. Where the strength of the findings for aggregate UN activity warrants further elaboration, we will provide some additional detail on the activities of the different UN organs, the nature of such activity, and its effectiveness in terms of crisis abatement.

Table 2 presents findings on the relationship between techniques of crisis management employed by the actors in a crisis and the extent of UN activity. Three general types of management techniques are available to individual crisis actors: negotiation and other pacific techniques; non-violent military techniques; and violent military techniques. It is interesting to note that violence was employed as the principal crisis management technique in 95 cases or 60% of the total.

The findings reveal that the UN was most likely to become involved when either negotiation or violence were employed by the actors as the principal crisis management techniques. Furthermore, such UN activity was likely to be at the highest levels, i.e., Security Council or General Assembly. Interestingly, it is the cases where neither negotiations nor violence were employed that exhibited the least tendency for UN activity. This may be due to the fact that both violent and negotiation-related crisis management techniques require interaction with other actors whereas non-violent military techniques such as threats, manoeuvres, redisposition of forces, and mobilizations are domestic policy decisions generally beyond the jurisdiction of the UN. Among these latter cases are the crises resulting from increasing USSR influence in Eastern Europe

TABLE 2   Crisis Management Technique and UN Activity

		U.N. Activity			
		No U.N. Activity	Low-Level U.N. Activity	High-Level U.N. Activity	
Crisis management technique	Negotiation and other pacific CMT	16 41%	7 18%	16 41%	39 24%
	Non-violent military CMT	16 62%	6 23%	4 15%	26 16%
	Violent military CMT	33 35%	19 20%	43 45%	95 60%
		65 41%	32 20%	63 39%	160

$$\chi^2 = 8.48; \ p = 0.08$$

in the immediate post-World War II period: Poland 1946, Hungary 1946, Czechoslovakia 1947 and 1948, and the threat to Yugoslavia in 1949. We also find that the UN was more likely to act in a resolute manner in crises characterized by violence or negotiation than it was in non-violent military situations.

In terms of effectiveness, while the levels were generally low, the UN appeared to be far more effective in crises in which violent or non-violent military crisis management techniques were employed than it was when negotiation and other pacific crisis management techniques were employed. That is, of the 28 cases in which UN intervention was judged to be effective, 21 of those cases (75%) involved violent military crisis management techniques. This latter finding con-trasts sharply with Haas, Butterworth and Nye (1972:26), who found that the 'UN is not strikingly effective in managing disputes . . . in terms of the violence level . . .' Among cases with violent crisis management techniques, we find that high-level UN involvement was more effective than low-level involvement.

Turning to Table 3, we examine the relationship between the severity of violence employed as a crisis management technique and the extent of UN activity. Here our reasoning is that it is not merely the existence of violence which compels UN activity, but it is also the nature of that violence, or its severity. Values range from no violence, minor clashes, serious clashes, and finally to full scale war. With one exception (Hungary 1956), all wars

TABLE 3   Severity of Violence and UN Activity

		U.N. Activity			
		No U.N. Activity	Low-Level U.N. Activity	High-Level U.N. Activity	
	No violence	28 51%	10 18%	17 31%	55 35%
Severity of vio-lence	Minor clashes	17 65%	2 8%	7 27%	26 16%
	Serious clashes	17 36%	11 23%	19 41%	47 29%
	Full-scale war	3 9%	9 28%	20 63%	32 20%
		65 41%	32 20%	63 39%	160

$$\chi^2 = 23.05; \; p = 0.00$$

listed by Small and Singer (1982) for the 1945–1975 period appear as crisis cases on the ICB list in which full-scale war occurred. The ICB list is somewhat larger (32 cases) since a number of wars produced several distinct clusters (India–Pakistan—3, Israel Independence—2, Korea—2, Yemen—4, Vietnam—8).

The results show a sharp contrast in UN involvement between crises involving full scale war, on the one hand, and those involving either no violence or low levels of violence, on the other. That is, among the 32 cases of full scale war, only three (9%)—India–China 1962, Black September 1970, and US–North Vietnam 1972—showed no UN activity at all. The comparable figures for no UN involvement are 51% when no violence occurred, 65% when minor clashes occurred, and 36% when serious clashes occurred. High-level UN involvement occurred in 63% of all crises involving full scale war. UN activity was classified as resolute in 59% of full scale wars in which it became involved, whereas resolute UN activity occurred in only 33% of all other cases. Finally, UN activity was effective in crisis abatement in 45% of the full scale war cases in which it intervened, as compared with a 22% effectiveness rate for other cases. Among the cases of full scale war in which the UN was effective were India–Pakistan 1947–49, 1965, 1971, Israel Independence 1948–49, Suez 1956, Middle East War 1973, and Cyprus 1975. It should be noted that in 9 of the 13 cases of effective UN action in full scale wars, the Security Council was the active organ.[5]

Table 4 explores the relationship between the number of actors in a crisis and the extent of UN activity. Single actor cases are those in which the adversarial state (or

TABLE 4   Number of Crisis Actors and UN Activity

		U.N. Activity			
		No U.N. Activity	Low-Level U.N. Activity	High-Level U.N. Activity	
	Single actor	32 62%	5 9%	15 29%	52 32%
Number of actors	2-3 actors	28 41%	17 25%	23 34%	68 43%
	4 + actors	5 12%	10 25%	25 63%	40 25%
		65 41%	32 20%	63 39%	160

$$\chi^2 = 24.97; \ p = 0.00$$

TABLE 5   Extent of Superpower Involvement and UN Activity

		U.N. Activity			
		No U.N. Activity	Low-Level U.N. Activity	High-Level U.N. Activity	
	Neither SP involved	22 65%	3 9%	9 26%	34 21%
Superpower involvement	US or USSR minor involvement	24 31%	22 29%	31 40%	77 48%
	US or USSR crisis actor	17 44%	5 12%	17 44%	39 25%
	US and USSR crisis actors	2 20%	2 20%	6 60%	10 6%
		65 41%	32 20%	63 39%	160

$$x^2 = 16.35; \ p = 0.01$$

states) is not itself experiencing a crisis. The largest international crises in this data set involve six actors, and include the Middle East crises of 1948, 1956, and 1967, the Berlin Wall crisis of 1961, and the Czech crisis of 1968. We have hypothesized that the larger the number of actors in a crisis, the more serious the crisis in terms of its implications for peace and security in the international system, and hence the greater the likelihood of UN involvement.

The findings clearly reveal that UN involvement becomes more probable as the number of crisis actors increases. Sixty-three percent of all large crises (four or more actors) elicited high-level UN activity, as compared with 34% of two- and three-actor cases and 29% of

one-actor cases. The number of actors in the crisis does not appear to be related to either resolute UN action or effectiveness in crisis abatement.

The final portion of this analysis deals with the relationship between the extent of superpower involvement and the likelihood of UN activity. In Table 5, we rank order the crises in terms of the degree of superpower involvement, ranging from cases of no involvement by either superpower, cases of minor involvement by the US and/or the USSR (political, propaganda, covert, military) cases in which one of the superpowers was a crisis actor, and finally cases in which both superpowers were crisis actors. It should be noted that in the ICB data set for the 1945–1975 period, the following ten crises involved both superpowers as actors: Iran Hegemony 1945–46, Berlin Blockade 1948–49, Korea October 1950, Suez 1956, Berlin Deadline 1958, Berlin Wall 1961, Cuban Missiles 1962, Congo 1964, Six Day War 1967, and Middle East War 1973.

Table 5 reveals a strong trend in the hypothesized direction; that is, as the level of involvement of the superpowers increased, the probability of UN involvement also increased. (In this regard, see Pelcovits and Kramer 1976). Moreover, the higher the level of superpower involvement, the higher the level of UN activity, with six of the ten joint US/USSR crises indicating either Security Council or General Assembly activity. The exceptions were the Berlin Wall Crisis 1961 and the Congo (Stanleyville) Crisis 1964, in which there was no UN activity, and the Berlin Deadline 1958 and the Cuban Missile Crisis 1962, in which there was Secretary-General activity. Further elaboration indicates that resolute UN activity was far more probable in crises in which both superpowers were actors (75%) than in crises exhibiting lower level superpower involvement (38%). Effective UN action was also more probable in superpower confrontation cases than in others, with an effectiveness rate of 50% (four cases—Iran Hegemony 1945–46, Suez 1956, Cuban Missiles 1962, Middle East War 1973). The higher effectiveness rate for cases of high superpower involvement runs counter to conventional wisdom concerning UN ac-

tivity, as expressed, for example, in Nicholas' observation that 'in a major confrontation of the U.S.A. and the U.S.S.R. the U.N.'s role is necessarily a marginal one' (1971:65).

To summarize, we have noted that all indicators of seriousness of crisis are related to UN intervention. That is, as seriousness increases, the likelihood of UN intervention increases, the most potent UN organs—the Security Council and the General Assembly—are likely to become involved, UN activity is more likely to be resolute in form, and the overall effectiveness of the UN in crisis abatement increases. It will be useful to identify the specific international crises which meet virtually all the conditions of seriousness set forth in our hypotheses. That is, these cases exhibited violent crisis management techniques, and large numbers of actors[6] and, at the same time, showed UN intervention. Six cases meet all of these criteria: Israel Independence 1948–49, Korea June 1950, Korea October 1950, Suez 1956, War of Attrition 1970, and India/Pakistan 1971. There were no cases which exhibited this highest level of seriousness and in which the UN did not intervene. This confirms an earlier finding by Haas, Butterworth and Nye (1972:5), to the effect that 'the overwhelming bulk of the more intense disputes was referred to international organizations.'[7] It is also worth noting that in three of the six cases noted above—Israel Independence 1948–49, Suez 1956, and India/Pakistan 1971—UN activity was judged to have been effective in terms of crisis abatement. In the next section, we will explore additional aspects of UN activity, particularly as they pertain to the outcomes of crises.

UN Intervention and Crisis Outcomes

Thus far we have been concerned with the relationship between the seriousness of an international crisis and the propensity of the UN to become involved. In this section our focus shifts to an assessment of the impact of UN involvement on the outcomes of crises. In an earlier section, we hypothesized that the more active the UN was in a crisis, the more likely it was that outcomes favorable to the crisis actors and the international system in general would result. Favorable outcomes for the participants were operationalized in terms of the achievement of agreement at the point of crisis termination and the degree of participant satisfaction with the outcome. From a systemic perspective, a favorable outcome was defined in terms of the long-term reduction in tension among the participants. As was the case with the previous analyses, our attention will focus primarily on the manner in which the extent of UN activity had an impact on these indicators of favorableness of outcome.

In Table 6, we examine the relationship between level of UN activity and form of outcome. 'Agreement' denotes both formal agreements, such as treaties, armistices, and cease-fires, as well as semi-formal agreements, such as letters and oral declarations. 'Tacit' agreements are mutual understandings by adversaries, neither written nor stated. The 'no agreement' category groups crises which terminated through unilateral acts, as well as those which simply faded, with no known termination date and no agreement among the adver-

TABLE 6   UN Activity and Form of Crisis Outcome

		Form of Outcome			
		Agreement	Tacit	No Agreement	
	No UN activity	23 36%	12 18%	30 46%	65 41%
UN activity	Low-level UN activity	16 50%	4 12%	12 38%	32 20%
	High-level UN activity	38 60%	6 10%	19 30%	63 39%
		77 48%	22 14%	61 38%	160

$$x^2 = 8.22; \ p = 0.08$$

saries. The data reveal that 48% of all crises in the 1945–1975 period terminated in agreement, 14% in tacit agreement, and 38% terminated with no agreement of any sort among the contending parties.

We observe a moderate relationship between the level of UN activity and the tendency toward termination in agreement. While 60% of the cases in which high-level UN involvement occurred terminated in agreement, only 50% of the low-level UN involvement cases and 36% of the no involvement cases terminated in agreement. Tacit agreement was more likely when the UN was not involved, that is, the existence of UN activity in a crisis increased the likelihood of more formal agreement among the parties. Finally, efforts to reach some form of agreement failed in one third of cases in which the UN was involved, but in almost one half of no UN involvement cases. Among the more prominent crises in which high-level UN activity failed to result in agreement among the parties were Palestine Partition 1947, Korea June 1950, Guatemala 1953–54, Hungary 1956, Bay of Pigs 1961, Gulf of Tonkin 1964, Rhodesia 1965, and Sahara 1975.

Additional analysis of the cases in which some UN activity was recorded indicates that when such activity was resolute (i.e., Security Council or General Assembly resolution, emergency forces, military forces), the achievement of an agreement was facilitated. Furthermore, in those cases where recorded UN activity was viewed as effective, a greater tendency toward agreement among the parties was in evidence (75% agreement versus 49% agreement).

It should be recalled that along with the favorable outcomes hypothesized to follow from UN intervention in crises, we also anticipated at least two unintended and unfavorable consequences of UN action: indecisive outcomes and an extended crisis period. In Table 7 we examine the relationship between UN activity and the substance of the crisis outcome. Crisis outcomes are classified as follows: 'compromise' indicates that some or all of the parties exhibited partial achievement of basic goals, 'stalemate' indicates no effect on basic goals, and 'victory or defeat' indicate the total achievement or non-achievement of goals. Compromise or stalemate are taken as indicators of indecisive outcomes, while victory and defeat are taken as decisive.

The table reveals that while diverse levels of UN activity (or inactivity) appear to produce equal levels of decisive outcomes (50%), significant differences exist for the two types of ambiguous outcomes. Thus, high-level UN activity (Security Council or General Assembly) resulted in 32% compromise and 16% stalemate, whereas low-level UN activity resulted in only 12% compromise and 38% stalemate. Furthermore, differentiating between resolute and non-resolute UN action does not help to explain differences in the substance of crisis outcome. Finally, in those cases

TABLE 7   UN Activity and Substance of Outcome

		Substance of Outcome			
		Compromise	Stalemate	Victory or Defeat	
	No UN activity	13 20%	18 28%	34 52%	65 41%
UN activity	Low-level UN activity	4 12%	12 38%	16 50%	32 20%
	High-level UN activity	20 32%	10 16%	33 52%	63 39%
		37 23%	40 25%	83 52%	160

$$x^2 = 8.18; \; p = 0.08$$

TABLE 8   UN Activity and Duration of Crisis

		Crisis Duration			
		0-31 Days	32-60 Days	61+ Days	
	No UN activity	26 43%	9 15%	25 42%	60 40%
UN activity	Low-level UN activity	7 23%	6 20%	17 57%	30 20%
	High-level UN activity	15 25%	6 10%	39 65%	60 40%
		48 32%	21 14%	81 54%	150

$$\chi^2 = 8.60; \; p = 0.07$$

where UN activity was judged to be effective, definitive outcomes were more likely than ambiguous ones.

The final portion of this analysis deals with the relationship between UN activity and the duration of a crisis.[8] Crisis duration is measured from the initial trigger date for the first actor in an international crisis to the final termination date in the crisis. The results in Table 8 indicate a clear positive relationship between the level of UN activity and duration of crisis, as originally hypothesized. It would probably be unwise to draw causal conclusions from this finding, since many of the shorter crises were over before the UN could become involved. In other words, crises must be of a certain duration before the UN can be mobilized to take action. Neither resolute action nor effectiveness appear to be related to duration.

SUMMARY AND CONCLUSION

By way of summary, let us return to the original hypotheses upon which these analyses were based and evaluate their overall ability to explain aspects of UN intervention in international crises. In the first hypothesis, we proposed that the UN was more likely to intervene in crises when a serious threat to the peace and security of the international system and its member units existed. Virtually all of the indicators of seriousness showed moderate to strong relationships with UN intervention, and all were in the predicted direction. The major findings are summarized below.

1. Violent crisis management techniques were employed by actors in 60% of all international crises. The more violent the crisis management technique employed, the greater was the likelihood of UN intervention.

2. The UN was active in 29 of the 32 cases involving full scale war, and was effective in 13 cases.

3. The larger the number of actors in a crisis, the greater was the likelihood of UN intervention.

4. As the level of superpower involvement in a crisis increased, the likelihood of UN intervention also increased. Six of the ten cases in which both superpowers were crisis actors exhibited Security Council or General Assembly activity, while only 38% of all other cases showed such high-level UN activity.

In general then, these findings show that while the UN intervened in only 59% of all crises, its rate of intervention in those crises which we could characterize as serious was actually quite a bit higher. Furthermore, while the UN was effective in terms of its contribution to crisis abatement in only 18% of all crises, this figure is considerably higher among the most serious crises, and particularly those in which full scale war was involved (45%). Finally, in those crises with high scores on the indicators of seriousness, high-level UN activity (Security Council and General Assembly) was more effective in crisis abatement than was low-level UN activity. Haas (1983: 206), in his study of disputes, also finds that the most intense disputes are most likely to be managed by the UN. Furthermore, he finds that 45% of the cases involving active warfare showed a moderate or great impact for the UN. Those findings concerning UN intervention in international crises are more encouraging than those with which we began this analysis.

Our second hypothesis was concerned with the impact of UN intervention on crisis outcomes. More specifically, we proposed that UN intervention would foster greater agreement and satisfaction among the parties and tend to result in overall tension reduction among the crisis actors. On the other hand, we also hypothesized that UN intervention would tend to promote indecisive outcomes (i.e., compromise or stalemate) and crises of longer duration. Once again, we summarize the major findings:

1. During the 1945–1975 period, 48% of all crises terminated in agreement among the parties. Cases exhibiting UN intervention were far more likely to terminate in agreement than were cases in which no UN intervention took place.

2. Outcomes involving compromise among the parties constituted 23% of total crises for the period. Compromise outcomes were most likely when high-level UN activity was involved.

3. The higher the level of UN activity, the longer was the duration of the crisis from trigger to termination.

Thus, our findings regarding crisis outcomes also point to the fact that the UN has perhaps been unfairly maligned. At least insofar as agreements are concerned, UN intervention seems to have facilitated their achievement. However, in other measures of outcomes such as the satisfaction of the parties and the tendency toward tension reduction, UN intervention did not seem to make a substantial difference. In short, while the UN appeared to have generated agreements, it displayed a very mixed record as a crisis manager.

NOTES

1. Later, in a larger inquiry into third parties and crisis management from 1930 to 1980, we propose to add: the multi-power system of the thirties; the involvement of the League of Nations and other regional organizations as crisis managers; and the role of major powers and superpowers in international crises.

2. A more extended discussion of the nature of the ICB Project and its ultimate objectives can be found in Brecher and Wilkenfeld (1982).

3. In a recent study of conflict management by international and regional organizations, Haas (1983) focuses on a set of 282 *disputes* between 1945 and 1981, of which 123 or 44% made the agenda of the United Nations. Thus, while the 59% figure for UN involvement in *crises* is relatively low, it reflects a better rate of UN involvement than is the case for disputes in general.

4. Finlayson and Zacher (1980) suggest that alignment configuration is an important factor in determining whether or not the UN will become involved in a particular crisis. In essence, they suggest that the one type of conflict which is most likely to evoke UN attention is that involving threats or acts of force by aligned against non-aligned states. While we find this notion intriguing, its implications are beyond the scope of the present analysis. Similarly, Wilkenfeld and

Brecher (1982b) explore the extent to which different types of system polarity in the 1945–1975 period have affected on the extent, nature, and effectiveness of UN intervention. That analysis, too, is beyond the scope of the present paper.

5. For a more detailed discussion of the factors contributing to UN effectiveness in general, and Security Council effectiveness in particular, see Slawitsky (1982).

6. Although superpower involvement was analyzed in this section as one of the indicators of seriousness of crisis, it will be excluded in this profile since its inclusion would restrict us to only those cases in which the US and USSR were both crisis actors.

7. In an analysis of conflict managers in general for the period 1945–1975, Butterworth (1978) found that a set of indicators including major war, lesser issues, intractability, and inequality, did not aid in explaining whether or not conflict managers would become involved. His findings run counter to those presented here for UN activity in crises, where indicators of seriousness help explain UN activity.

8. Ten cases could not be analyzed here, since the precise date of termination was unknown.

REFERENCES

Avaizian, V. A. and J. L. Callen (1981) 'The Coase Theorem and the Empty Core.' *Journal of Law and Economics* 24: 175–181.

Bobrow, D. B. (1981) 'The Perspective of Great Power Foreign Policy: Steps in Context,' in J. Rubin (ed.) *Dynamics of Third Party Intervention: Kissinger and the Middle East.* New York: Praeger.

Brecher, M. (1977) 'Toward a Theory of International Crisis Behavior.' *International Studies Quarterly* 21: 39–74.

Brecher, M. and J. Wilkenfeld (1982) 'Crises in World Politics,' *World Politics* 34: 380–417.

Butterworth, R. L. (1976) *Managing Interstate Conflict: Data with Synopses.* Pittsburgh: University Center of International Studies.

Coase, R. H. (1960) 'The Problem of Social Cost.' *Journal of Law and Economics* 3: 1–44.

Coase, R. H. (1981) 'The Coase Theorem and the Empty Core: A Comment.' *Journal of Law and Economics* 24: 183–187.

Creary, P. J. and J. Wilkenfeld (1983) 'Structural Factors in International Crisis Behavior,' presented at the Peace Science Society (International) Meeting, Illinois.

Finlayson, J. A. and M. W. Zacher (1980) *The United Nations and Collective Security: Retrospect and Prospect.* United Nations Association of America.

Haas, E. B. (1983) 'Regime Decay: Conflict Management and International Organizations, 1945–1981.' *International Organization* 37: 189–256.

Haas, E. B., R. L. Butterworth and J. S. Nye (1972) *Conflict Management by International Organizations.* Morristown: General Learning Press.

Nicholas, H. G. (1971) *The United Nations.* New York: Oxford University Press.

Slawitsky, B. (1982) 'UN Activity and the Pace of Crisis Abatement.' MA Thesis, The Hebrew University.

Small, M. and J. D. Singer (1982) *Resort to Arms: International and Civil Wars, 1816–1980.* Beverly Hills: Sage.

Touval, S. (1975) 'Biased Intermediaries: Theoretical and Historical Considerations.' *Jerusalem Journal of International Relations* 1, 1: 51–70.

Wilkenfeld, J. and M. Brecher (1982a) 'Superpower Crisis Management Behavior' in C. W. Kegley and P. J. McGowan (eds) *Foreign Policy: US/USSR, Sage International Yearbook of Foreign Policy Studies, VIII.* Beverly Hills: Sage.

Wilkenfeld, J. and M. Brecher (1982b) 'Crisis Management, 1945–1975: The UN Dimension.' Paper presented at the XII World Congress of the International Political Science Association.

Young, O. R. (1967) *The Intermediaries: Third Parties in International Crises.* Princeton: Princeton University Press.

11

THE CONDITIONS FOR SUCCESS IN PEACEKEEPING OPERATIONS

Paul F. Diehl

. . . The gradual abandonment of a collective security strategy [has] led the U.N. to seek other means to insure international peace and security. The Suez Crisis presented the United Nations with a difficult problem. Observation forces were insufficient to ensure disengagement and collective enforcement action would risk a confrontation between four world powers. The solution was to create the United Nations Emergency Force (UNEF) to facilitate withdrawal of troops, prevent a recurrence of hostilities, and act as a barrier separating the protagonists. A new strategy of "peacekeeping" had been created. . . .

The primary goal of a peacekeeping operation is to halt armed conflict or prevent its recurrence. It achieves this goal by acting as a physical barrier between hostile parties and monitoring their military movements. A secondary purpose of peacekeeping is to create a stable environment for negotia-

---

SOURCE: Edited and abridged with permission from *Political Science Quarterly*.

tions, which could lead to resolution of the underlying conflict. The operation can defuse tensions between the parties by giving each side time to "cool-off" without fear of imminent attack. In theory, this should make them more willing to negotiate and offer concessions.

If peacekeeping operations are effective, they can help resolve conflict without bloodshed—a valuable accomplishment indeed. Nevertheless, no approach to peace is ideally suited to every situation. One approach may be a complete success under one set of conditions, but a total failure under another. Variations in the implementation of a program can also influence success rates. The purpose of this paper is to identify and analyze the conditions that contribute to the effectiveness of peacekeeping operations. Our initial focus is on the characteristics of the operations themselves; the elements of organization, impartiality, and logistics, among others, are considered. Secondly, the level of cooperative behavior exhibited by interested parties is assessed, as is its impact on the operations' effectiveness. From an analysis of this multiplicity of factors in a comparative case study, we hope to gain a more complete picture of when and how peacekeeping operations should be used. . . .

We have decided to concentrate on six peacekeeping operations, including the earliest and most recent examples: The United Nations Emergency Force, with operations conducted after the Suez Crisis (UNEF I) and following the Yom Kippur War (UNEF II); the United Nations Operations in the Congo (ONUC); the United Nations Peacekeeping Force in Cyprus (UNFICYP); the United Nations Interim Force in Lebanon (UNIFIL); and the Multinational Force of American, British, French, and Italian troops stationed in Beirut (MNF).

The selection of these cases was guided by a number of principles. First, we wished to focus on those operations that were deployed to maintain cease-fires with military interposition forces. Consequently, we ignore observer and other civilian forces. In the instances, the performance of those missions played only a minor role in the maintenance of peace. Secondly, we looked only at operations that were sent to conflicts prior to final resolution of the dispute between the parties. Because some significant conflict remains, we are better able to assess the impact of the operations on conflict reduction and peace maintenance. Finally, we purposely ignored operations that resembled occupying forces more than peacekeeping troops and whose purpose was to preserve the hegemony of a regional power. Examples of such operations were the InterAmerican Peace Force (IAPF) in the Dominican Republic and the Syrian intervention in Lebanon following the 1975 Civil War. We are then left with the six operations noted above that are consistent with our purposes. Besides confining our analysis to those operations that neatly correspond to the goals of preventive diplomacy, we have chosen our sample so that it has a number of attractive features.

First, the sample enables the analyst to consider international intervention in two different settings: civil and interstate conflict. The sample cases include operations sent into an area wrecked by internal instability, as well as those that concerned themselves primarily with the separation of warring states. Another feature of the sample is that different operations within the same geographic area, (the Middle East) involving many of the same protagonists, can be compared. In effect, the environmental context is held constant to some extent, and the effect of differences in the conduct of the operations can be assessed. Indeed, two different segments of the same operation (UNEF I and UNEF II) make for almost a perfect analysis of this kind.

Finally, comparisons are possible between operations conducted by an international organization and one conducted by a multilateral grouping of nations without international sanction. Whether peacekeeping should become a primary option in national foreign policy or whether such operations should be exclusive to international bodies can be judged.

It should be noted that estimating a peacekeeping operation's success is a difficult problem. It seems to

us, however, that a successful operation should achieve two things in particular. First, the operation should prevent a renewal of armed hostilities between the disputing parties. Maintaining the cease-fire is its primary function and a prerequisite to attempts at reconciling the protagonists. Secondly, the peacekeeping operation should facilitate a final, peaceful resolution to the dispute. This often can be a monumental task, and the blame for failure cannot always rest solely on the operation itself. Nevertheless, unless the underlying sources of conflict are resolved, the threat of renewed war is always present. Thus, in evaluating each operation, we focus primarily on the first criterion of success, but [still] recognize the importance of the second. . . .

INTERNAL FACTORS

In this section, we look at the internal operations of the peacekeeping mission and determine their effect on its success or failure. It is not our intention to focus on all aspects of a peacekeeping operation, but rather to concentrate on the non-trivial elements that could affect whether the mission's purpose is achieved or not. The five factors below are those most frequently cited in reports, debates, and scholarly works on preventive diplomacy. In addition, our analysis of the six cases indicates that these factors deserve consideration, if only to dispel or confirm some of the conventional wisdom surrounding peacekeeping.

Financing

Peacekeeping operations can be quite expensive; money is needed for supplies, equipment, salaries, and various administrative costs. In the United Nations system, peacekeeping operations are not funded from the regular budget. They require a special authorization from the organization or rely on voluntary contributions. When groups of nations form a peacekeeping mission, appropriations are dependent upon each national contribution, subject to the constraint of domestic political forces. Financing is a problem for any collective action, particularly when the coercive mechanism to enforce contributions is weak.[1] A peacekeeping operation could be terminated prematurely if its source of funding were cut off. Its area of operation or its efficiency could also be severely limited if funds were insufficient.

Almost all of the U.N. operations studied here had difficulties with financing. Operating expenses exceeded expectations, and there was a persistent problem with nations refusing to contribute their assessed share. At the end of 1983, the debt from peacekeeping was approximately $205 million, or 68 percent of total U.N. indebtedness. Attempts to rectify the problem have failed. In 1964, the United States attempted to suspend non-contributing members under Article 19 of the Charter. When the U.S. withdrew its effort, the only legal means of pressuring recalcitrant members was effectively abandoned for political considerations. The MNF endured threats of a cutoff of funds by the Congress of the United States, but was apparently unaffected by the financial actions of other countries in the consortium.

Although the operations experienced financial difficulties, these did not seem to adversely affect the conduct of missions. Large deficits did not prevent the U.N. from continuing the operations and the consequences of the financial problems were minor. For example, UNEF II was unable to purchase certain mine-sweeping equipment because of financial constraints. The U.N. operations benefitted from large voluntary contributions from some nations. These tended to hold down the deficits and allowed the operations to continue. A notable exception among the operations was ONUC. It was a very expensive operation, and the high cost produced constant pressure to complete the mission. It may be that this pressure encouraged the U.N. to use military force against Katanga and thereby complete its mission. Financial considerations were certainly important in the decision to withdraw from the Congo even though some analysts thought it wise to continue the mission for a little while longer.

Overall, finances were an irritating problem for peacekeeping missions, but in no case were any of the operations seriously hampered by the difficulty. Financial support of a peacekeeping operation is, to some degree, a barometer of the political support for the operation. Financial problems themselves apparently will not jeopardize the effectiveness of preventive diplomacy, but they could be the official cause of death were enough political support withdrawn.

Geography

Another consideration in the success or failure of preventive diplomacy is the locus of development. Where the operation is located can influence the effectiveness of its patrols. If the size of the area is great, the monitoring of conflicting parties' actions could be problematic; the margin for error in detection and verification would increase. The vulnerability of the peacekeeping forces to hostile fire also could damage their effectiveness and possibly draw them into the military struggle.

In our six cases, geographic considerations were important in the success or failure of each operation. The most successful operations had certain geographic advantages. The two UNEF missions were located in mostly desert terrain in sparsely populated areas. This allowed for easy observation of military movements and infiltration attempts. This advantage clearly outweighed the minor problems encountered with desert transportation. UNFICYP was fortunate to be located on an island separated from Greece and Turkey, who might

have more easily instigated trouble had they been contiguous by land to Cyprus. In these three instances, geography assisted in the prevention of conflict.

A number of general rules can be derived by looking at those missions that were less than successful. First, when the peacekeeping troops did not separate the combatants by a significant distance, the results were adverse. The French troops in the MNF were stationed at the so-called Green Line separating East and West Beirut. Their presence was not enough to halt sniper fire or artillery attack over their heads. The buffer zone was much too narrow to effectively separate the rival militias. UNIFIL encountered a similar problem over a larger geographic area as political considerations prevented it from taking its desired positions. They were unable to prevent rocket attacks or retaliatory raids by either the Israelis or the Palestinians as each side was still close enough to do damage to the other.

Another geographic problem concerned logistics. If the area of deployment did not permit easy observation of the combatants, problems could arise. UNIFIL had to patrol a very rural portion of Lebanon, and it was rather easy for guerilla fighters to infiltrate the area. ONUC operated in such a large geographic area that it was difficult to monitor all the activities around them, much less supply their own troops in an orderly fashion. A final rule is that the vulnerability of peacekeeping positions to attack can undermine their neutrality and complicate their mission. The MNF forces of the Americans and French were located in areas open to attack. The French position has already been mentioned. The American position was at the Beirut airport on low ground and subject to attack from the surrounding hills. The attacks on French and American positions led them to take an active role in combat, contrary to the basic principles of preventive diplomacy.

In general, geographic considerations were important to the success of peacekeeping missions. It appears that the peacekeeping forces ideally should be placed in an area that is relatively invulnerable, yet is easy to patrol and separates the combatants at a distance capable of preventing armed exchanges. Nevertheless, a favorable location is no guarantee that the mission will turn out well (as is evident from the remainder of the paper). At best, one might hope that a particular deployment will prevent violent incidents that could escalate and renew the warfare.

Clarity of the Mandate

A frequently cited problem, especially in light of the truck-bomb tragedy in Lebanon, is the absence of a clear mandate for a peacekeeping mission.[2] A clearly-defined mandate restricts the latitude of action given the mission, thereby limiting both the controversy of possible actions and the potential manipulation of the force by interested parties. A clear mandate also may generate greater public support in that the populace can identify and understand the purpose of the operation.

In practice, the most successful missions have begun with clear mandates. Nevertheless, the causal links between mandate clarity and operation success are not clear. Some missions had problems emanating from their mandates, but it is not evident whether these were sufficient to do serious damage. The MNF had very few guidelines to follow in its second deployment.[3] American forces had no clear idea of what to do beyond holding down positions around the airport.[4] This not only undermined public and Congressional support, but perhaps led the force to undertake military actions that were inconsistent with the concept of peacekeeping. ONUC also experienced some problems because of its mandate. The Secretary-General was granted enormous power in the conduct of that operation, and his actions led to an erosion of support for the mission among U.N. members. Furthermore, the ONUC mandate was modified several times, leading to confusion and additional erosion of support.

It is evident from these six cases that a clear mandate is useful for a peacekeeping operation. Yet, that clarity is often only a reflection of the underlying political consensus on the mission. A clear mandate often can generate little support in the deliberative bodies that authorize such operations. In controversial situations, some operations would never have taken place without a vague mandate. The operations that had a vague mandate can attribute their major problems to something other than the mandate itself. In short, the importance of a clear mandate is probably overestimated as it is merely a surrogate for the political consensus underlying it.

Command and Control

Any organizational program needs to have a smooth method of operation. A peacekeeping mission can be jeopardized if it makes mistakes, cannot carry out its duties effectively, or lacks coordination. The most common command and control problem in over six cases was language. By organizing forces from many different nations, it was often difficult for commanders to communicate on a one-to-one basis (much less in any larger aggregation) with their subordinates.

A central command can solve coordination problems, and four of our sample operations were set up in this fashion. ONUC was somewhat disorganized because it lacked a central command.[5] It did, however, have a coordinating body to ensure the forces were not working at cross purposes. ONUC's only problem occurred when it was unclear who gave orders for a particular maneuver during the operation. The MNF was linked only

through liaison officers. The sharing of intelligence and the mapping of joint strategy correspondingly suffered.

Most peacekeeping operations have run smoothly, with command and control problems affecting the efficiency, but not the overall success, of the missions. Language problems can be cumbersome, but there is an inherent tradeoff in making a peacekeeping force representative versus making it efficient. Most of the command and control problems should dissipate in the future.[6] From the benefits of experience, the U.N. can now send trained personnel into the field and choose from among many experienced individuals to direct the peacekeeping units. Should any collective effort be launched by a group of nations, they too should learn from the mistakes of the MNF. Other than an unprecedented case of complete incompetence, command and control problems are unlikely to ruin a peacekeeping operation.

Neutrality

An essential component of the preventive diplomacy strategy is that the forces should not work to the benefit of either side. Historically, military personnel from nonaligned countries were used to guarantee this neutrality. Two informal rules have arisen in choosing troops for the peacekeeping force. The first is to never allow forces from a state involved in the conflict to participate in the operation. A second rule is to bar troop contributions from major power nations (or their allies). In these ways, it was hoped that the conflicting parties would regard the peacekeeping forces as unbiased and disinterested. Because the host state's consent is necessary to deploy peacekeeping forces, the failure of the host state to approve a particular force composition prevents that operation from taking place.

In our sample, those operations that were staffed almost entirely from disinterested, non-aligned nations had the least difficulty. Nevertheless, we found the Cyprus operation was equally effective, despite being composed primarily of troops from NATO countries, including those of ex-colonial power Britain. This seems to indicate that troops from non-aligned countries are not a prerequisite for success. Nevertheless, they are no guarantee of it either; Israel claimed UNIFIL was guilty of aiding the Palestinian cause and took violent action. The MNF operation had terrible difficulties arising from the perceived unfairness of the troops. Many of the factions in Lebanon regarded U.S. troops as supporters of their two principal enemies in the dispute, the Gemayel government and Israel. This immediately subjected the forces to distrust and later to hostile fire. These suspicions seemed to be confirmed when the U.S. helped train Lebanese government troops and shelled surrounding villages. The French encountered a similar response from the militias. The Italian contingent was regarded as neutral by all sides, owing to its behavior during the operation (which included numerous humanitarian acts) and the political stance of its government. As a result, they generally were not the subject of protest or attack.

Overall, drawing peacekeeping personnel from non-aligned countries is desirable, but is not a necessary condition for successful completion of the mission. Neutrality in peacekeeping is determined more by behavior and situation than by force composition. To the extent that the troops' behavior is perceived as biased and undermines the cooperation between conflicting parties, the peacekeeping mission could be ruined. Furthermore, troops supplied by a given country may be regarded as neutral in one situation (e.g., Tanzanian troops in Latin America), but not necessarily under a different scenario (e.g., the same troops in Namibia). All things being equal, however, a non-aligned force is more desirable than any other. The non-aligned force is more likely to be accepted by all sides and will be less likely to take actions that may be interpreted as unfair by one or more of the parties.

RELEVANT ACTORS

Common sense and the previous analysis tell us that the manner in which a peacekeeping operation is conducted is not the sole determinant of success or failure. In this section, we consider the behavior of a number of relevant actors, with an eye to estimating their impact on peacekeeping operations. First, we investigate the actions of the primary disputants or host state(s) in the conflict. We then consider other states, which may be regional powers or neighboring countries that take an active role in the conflict. Because peacekeeping operations often deal with instability in the host state(s), we also analyze the behavior of sub-national groups. Finally, the policies of the superpowers are weighed. They have the global power, not to mention a dominant role in the Security Council, to dramatically influence a peacekeeping mission.

Primary Disputants

Before peacekeeping troops are deployed on a nation's territory, they must have the consent of that nation's government. If it is an interstate conflict, the other disputant(s) must usually agree to refrain from military force. A successful peacekeeping operation, however, depends on more than this initial level of cooperation. It would seem that the conflicting states also must not try to exploit the peacekeeping troops for their own advantage and refrain from incidents that could lead to a return of open warfare. If one side is not sincere in its support of peacekeeping or changes its policy over the course of the operation, the mission could be doomed.[7]

In practice, the maintenance of cooperation between the primary disputants has not been a severe

problem. In both UNEF operations, Egypt was generally cooperative with the peacekeeping forces. Israel demonstrated a less cooperative attitude, but at no time did they initiate violent opposition. The disagreements were minor disputes concerning the use of troops from nations that did not recognize the Israeli state. The other operations had similar results, as the host state(s) usually did little to hinder the mission. In one instance, the Cyprus National Guard blocked access to certain areas, but this problem was short-lived. The major exception to this pattern of cooperative behavior was Israel's actions toward UNIFIL. Israel initially refused to turn over territory where the UNIFIL forces would patrol. Their subsequent behavior, including the 1982 invasion, showed a complete disregard of the force and its mission.

We tend to agree with David Wainhouse that "where cooperation of the parties is not sustained and whole-hearted, a positive result will be difficult to obtain."[8] Nevertheless, the initial level of agreement needed to establish the force has usually persisted; problems from the primary disputants have not been empirically important in the failure of the missions. Our analysis has discovered that while cooperation from the disputants is a necessary condition for success, it is not a sufficient one. This is particularly relevant when the host state has a very weak government. Although the Congolese government supported ONUC, the split among factions prevented it from fully aiding the operation. The Lebanese government support for UNIFIL and MNF had little impact because that government did not have *de facto* control over the areas where the troops were deployed. To identify the sources of failure for peacekeeping, it is necessary to consider the behavior of other actors.

Third Party States

Third party intervention can play a prominent role in international conflict. Allies of the conflicting parties may take certain actions (e.g., supplying arms, diplomatic pressure) that may assist or hinder resolution of the conflict. Peacekeeping operations are subject to these same benefits and constraints. Neighboring states or regional powers may have a stake in the outcome of the conflict and consequently may take actions in support of or contrary to the goals of the peacekeeping mission.

Among our sample cases, five involved significant intervention by third party states. UNEF II was the only operation that was not significantly affected by the actions of a third party state. It may be coincidental, but this mission not only kept the peace, the conflict was resolved by treaty. The other operations all experienced negative effects from the actions of other states. UNEF I was terminated after Syria and Jordan pressured Egypt into joining their military action against Israel. It is unlikely

without that pressure Egypt would have expelled the peacekeeping force and gone to war with Israel at that time. In the Congo, Belgium encouraged the secessionist movement, and Belgian mercenaries joined in the armed struggle. A similar situation occurred in Cyprus as Turkey promoted the founding of a secessionist Turkish-Cypriot state on the island. On various occasions, they also made threats against the Greek majority there. The peacekeeping operations were severely jeopardized or complicated in each case.

Not surprisingly, the failed missions (MNF and UNIFIL) faced strong opposition from neighboring states. Syria played a critical role in each operation's downfall. Syria supplied weapons and other support to PLO fighters in southern Lebanon, helping them to infiltrate UNIFIL lines and attack Israeli positions. Syria opposed MNF through its allies among the factions in Beirut. They supplied weapons and pressured the Shi'ite and Druse factions not to accept a solution involving the MNF. There is also some indication that Syria, Iran, and possibly Libya had a hand in supporting terrorist attacks against the peacekeeping forces. Given its influence in Lebanon, Syria could have been a positive influence for MNF, but its actions were a major factor in the mission's failure.

It was difficult to detect any positive pressure in support of peacekeeping from this kind of analyis. Third party intervention was primarily negative and proved critical in damaging certain operations. Yet, this non-cooperation from third party states is not automatically fatal to a mission. For example, UNFICYP survived despite the actions of Turkey. A peacekeeping operation can be destroyed if the third party state encourages violence from another state or subnational group and/or undertakes violence itself. A large portion of the blame for the UNIFIL and MNF failures must be borne not by the primary disputants, but rather by hostile third states.

Sub-national Groups

Just as other states might influence peacekeeping operations, so too might sub-national groups in the host or neighboring states. The behavior of these groups could be particularly important when peacekeeping forces are thrust into areas of internal instability. Preventive diplomacy may be viewed unfavorably by groups seeking to topple the government of the host state; preservation of peace and the status quo favors the established government.

Sub-national groups played little role in either UNEF operations, but were detrimental in the other operations. The PLO never really accepted UNIFIL, claiming that Palestinians had a right to operate in the disputed area. Consequently, they smuggled weapons into UNIFIL's patrol area and launched attacks against Israeli targets. Following the 1982 invasion, UNIFIL has continued to have dif-

ficulty dealing with uncooperative local militias, particularly the SLA. ONUC faced problems from the Katanga independence movement and various tribal groups that supported factional leaders in the central government.

Perhaps the best example of how sub-national groups can destroy a peacekeeping operation is the tragedy of the MNF. Lebanon consisted of a large number of competing factions, none of which actually supported their presence. Even the Christian Phalangists were less than enthusiastic about the operation, as they continued battles with Moslem factions. The Shi'ite and Druse factions opposed the MNF; they felt the MNF was a shield for the Gemayel government. Part of their demands for a resolution to the conflict was a withdrawal of the peacekeeping forces. Terrorist groups were at times just as damaging as those of third party states. When those states and sub-national groups acted in unison to undermine the operation, not even the support of the host state could save the operation. Whether peacekeeping is even an appropriate mechanism for resolving internal conflict is questionable.

Superpowers

An analysis of peacekeeping success should not ignore the behavior of another group of third parties—the superpowers. The U.S. and the Soviet Union (along with the other three permanent members of the

Security Council) have the power to veto a resolution that initially authorizes a U.N. peacekeeping operation. Because the initial authorization is usually for a specified time period, the operation and its mandate will again be subject to that power if renewal is necessary. Beyond their powers in the United Nations, the superpowers can use their political, economic, and military power to influence the actors in the area of conflict. In these ways, the superpowers have the potential to rescue or destroy peacekeeping operations.

The United States has proved quite helpful to the cause of preventive diplomacy. Its political support was often the driving force behind the creation of peacekeeping operations. Later, the U.S. provided logistical support and other voluntary contributions to keep the operations running smoothly. Its support of the MNF troops, through the bombing of suspected terrorist bases, proved counter-productive as it increased hostility against the operation. The Soviet Union was reluctant to offer political and financial support for ONUC and other operations, but demonstrated little active opposition in the way of military action or vetoing resolutions. It did resupply Syria during the MNF's operation and vetoed a resolution authorizing a U.N. force to replace MNF. Yet, the MNF was too badly damaged already to say that the Soviets' actions were decisive.

It is easy to attribute a great deal of influence to the superpowers in any area of world politics. Nevertheless, in the U.N. peacekeeping operations studied here, their actual influence was less than conventional wisdom might predict. The superpowers clearly played an important role in setting up some of these operations.[9] Of particular note was their ability to halt the 1973 Mideast war and install UNEF II forces. The success of the operations once in place, however, was only marginally affected by superpower behavior. At best, they helped supply the operations and gave them some political support. At worst, they complicated an operation's efficiency and increased its controversy. The superpowers have a great potential to do good or harm to peacekeeping. While their behavior must be considered in any evaluation of peacekeeping, we have found that thus far, their actual influence has been overrated.

CONCLUSIONS

International peacekeeping has had a mixed record of success over the past thirty years. The main reason for the failure of peacekeeping operations has been the opposition of third party states and subnational groups. By refusing to stop violent activity and in some cases attacking the peacekeeping forces, these two sets of actors can undermine a whole operation. The failure of UNIFIL and MNF can be attributed to this as can many of the problems encountered by other operations. This leaves us with something of a tautology: peacekeeping is successful only when all parties wish to stop fighting. Peacekeeping forces can do certain things (e.g., remain neutral) to ensure that the desire for peace continues. Nevertheless, peacekeeping will fail or be severely damaged if peace is not initially desired by all parties.

Although the primary disputants and the superpowers each had a great deal of power to destroy a peacekeeping operation, our study revealed that neither group generally took strong action in opposition to the operation. To set up a peacekeeping force, the host state(s) must grant its (their) approval, indicating some desire to stop fighting. If the peacekeeping force was organized by the United Nations, the Security Council would likely have to approve it; superpower acquiescence is the minimum requirement for this. Therefore, once a peacekeeping operation is authorized, there is already confirmation that it is not opposed by the primary disputants or the superpowers. Operations opposed by either of these two groups will likely never come into being.

The internal characteristics of a peacekeeping operation were generally found to have a relatively minor impact on the mission's success. A clear mandate was useful, but hardly critical in determining the outcome. When the mandate was vague, the underlying political consensus was already shaky, and the mission experienced support problems with the various interested parties. The same conclusion is appropriate with respect to the financing and organization of the peacekeeping force. Problems with funding and command structure served to make the operation less efficient, but not necessarily less successful. Budget deficits were ameliorated by voluntary contributions or ignored. Command and control difficulties were never serious enough to jeopardize any of the operations.

Two aspects of the operations did have an impact on their success: geography and neutrality. Peacekeeping operations performed best when their areas of deployment adequately separated the combatants, were fairly invulnerable to attack, and permitted easy observation. The absence of these conditions undermined confidence in the operation and allowed minor incidents to escalate. The neutrality of the peacekeeping forces was also significant. If the peacekeeping force is perceived as biased, support from interested parties was likely to be withheld or withdrawn. As we have seen, this is enough to ruin the operation. Neutral behavior is not always linked with non-aligned force composition. The likelihood, however, that a force composed from non-aligned countries will take action favoring one party (or be perceived as doing so) is much less.

From these findings, we can draw a few guidelines regarding the use of a preventive diplomacy strategy.[10] Peacekeeping is most appropriate in a conflict in which all parties are willing to halt hostilities and accept a peacekeeping force.

Consideration must be given to more than just the primary disputants; other interested states and sub-national groups deserve attention. If these latter two actors oppose the operation, then the peacekeeping option might be reconsidered unless the opposition is minor or would not involve violent activity. This criterion may confine peacekeeping operations to conflicts that involve relatively few actors, as the probability of consensus will decrease as the number of interested parties increases.

Implementation by an international organization is to be preferred to a multilateral grouping of nations. The U.N., in particular, now has extensive experience with peacekeeping and is more likely to conduct an efficient operation. More importantly, however, an international organization will be better able to acquire consent from the host state(s) and approval from interested parties.[11] It is not that a multinational peacekeeping force cannot succeed, but rather problems with perceived bias (justified or otherwise) will be more likely and its moral authority will not be as great.

Once it has been established that the relevant actors will support a peacekeeping operation, the U.N. command should give special attention to taking a proper geographic position as well as continuing their policy of neutral force composition. Although the issues of mandate, financing, and command should not be ignored, neither should problems with them hold up the operation.

The findings of this study do more than confirm conventional wisdom about peacekeeping, although in some cases they do that too. The importance of the mandate and the role of the superpowers is considerably less than has been assumed. Analysts have also probably overestimated the importance of the primary disputants and the operation's command structure once there is an agreed-upon ceasefire. Yet, as is prominent in the literature on conflict and peacekeeping, the importance of third parties, neutrality, and geography is reaffirmed. Regardless of whether the guidelines laid down here conform to prior expectations about peacekeeping, they bear repetition. We know that policymakers too often ignore or forget these guidelines, with the MNF being the most recent example of neglect. According to these guidelines, the number of peacekeeping operations would be limited, but the rate of success should be positively affected. . . .

Some Final Notes

As final notes, we offer a few caveats and considerations on this analysis of preventive diplomacy. We are limited in anticipating how and where the peacekeeping strategy might be applied next. The superpowers did not play a critical role in the five U.N. operations studied here, but this is not to say that they can not or will not in the future. In addition, a multinational operation sponsored by non-aligned countries (such as Finland or Sweden) may offer a more desirable alternative than those offered here. Without empirical referents, such a judgment is premature. The future may breed new variations of peacekeeping that overcome the difficulties cited. It is our sincere hope that it does.

Finally, we have seemed to imply that no peacekeeping operation is better than an unsuccessful one. But, is this really correct? If peacekeeping can halt fighting and stop bloodshed, even for a short time, is this enough to justify a peacekeeping operation? The answer requires a value judgement. How a failed mission affects future operations is an empirical question. Both deserve serious consideration.

NOTES

1. The classic analysis of this problem is given in Mancur Olson, *The Logic of Collective Action*. Cambridge: Harvard University Press, 1965.
2. For example, both Naomi Weinberger, "Peacekeeping Options in Lebanon," *The Middle East Journal*, 37, 3 (1983): 341–369 and Richard Nelson, "Multinational Peacekeeping in the Middle East and the United Nations Model," *International Affairs*, 61, 1 (Winter 1984–85): 67–89, give primary importance to this factor.
3. Unlike a U.N. operation, there is no authorizing resolution stating the mandate of MNF's operation.

The closest one comes to a statement of the mandate came from Deputy Press Secretary Speakes:

"The MNF is to provide an interposition force at agreed locations and thereby provide the MNF presence requested by the Government of Lebanon to assist it and Lebanon's armed forces in the Beirut area" (quote taken from *Public Papers of the President of the United States: Ronald Reagan*, Book II, Washington: GPO, 1983: a 1202).

This is still vague and quite in contrast to the first deployment of MNF, when the guidelines for supervising PLO withdrawal were fairly specific.

4. Problems with the mandate were complicated by the lack of training in peacekeeping measures for the military personnel. MNF troops were primarily combat personnel, unaccustomed to holding down a defensive position without firing at an enemy force. For a description of peacekeeping training, see Richard Swift, "United Nations Military Training for Peace," *International Organization*, 28, 2 (1974): 267–280.
5. An elaboration on ONUC's problem in this regard is given by Lincoln Bloomfield, "Political Control of International Forces in Dealing with Problems of Local Instability" in Arthur Waskow, *Quis Custodiet?: Controlling the Police in a Disarmed World*. Washington: Peace Research Institute, 1963: Appendix E.
6. An excellent operations manual detailing the mechanics of setting up and conducting a peacekeeping operation is International Peace

Academy, *Peacekeeper's Handbook*. New York: Pergamon Press, 1984.

7. Of course, if the host state formally withdraws consent, the space operation is terminated. This occurred in 1967 as Egypt asked UNEF I forces to leave. Despite some suggestions to the contrary by members of the international community, U Thant complied with this request. See Jack Garvey, "United Nations Peacekeeping and Host State Consent" *American Journal of International Law,* 64, 1 (1970): 241–269.

8. David Wainhouse, *International Peace Observation*. Baltimore: Johns Hopkins University Press, 1966:557.

9. Nathan Pelcovits and Kevin Kramer, "Local Conflict and U.N. Peacekeeping: The Uses of Computerized Data," *International Studies Quarterly,* 20, 4 (1976): 533–552 reports a strong correlation between superpower intervention in a conflict and the use of peacekeeping. This demonstrates that the superpowers are also an indirect stimulus for peacekeeping operations, beyond their more direct role in the U.N. Security Council.

10. Although we look at peacekeeping operations as presently constituted, there have been many proposals for improvement. Representative of these efforts and ideas are Indar Jit Rikhye, *The Theory and Practice of Peacekeeping*. New York: St. Martin's Press, 1984; and Alastair Taylor, "Peacekeeping: The International Context" in Canadian Institute of International Affairs, *Peacekeeping: International Challenge and Canadian Response* Ontario: Canadian Institute of International Affairs, 1968: 1–40.

11. Certain nations, such as Israel and South Africa, may object to peacekeeping operations directed by the United Nations, owing to the perceived bias of that institution toward their interests. In that event, a multinational force may be more appropriate. In general, however, its advantages over a U.N. force are minimal; see Frank Gregory, *The Multinational Force: Aid or Obstacle to Conflict Resolution*. Conflict Study, no. 170. Institute for the Study of Conflict. London: Eastern Press, 1984.

12

CONFLICT MANAGEMENT AND INTERNATIONAL ORGANIZATIONS, 1945–1981

Ernst B. Haas

If no less an expert than the Secretary-General of the United Nations, Javier Perez de Cuellar, declares that the United Nations "often finds itself unable to take decisive action to resolve conflicts and its resolutions are increasingly defied or ignored by those who feel themselves strong enough to do so," we might reasonably think that general disillusionment with the organization is fully justified.[1] The Arab-Israeli conflict, South African repression and aggression, Cyprus, unrest in Southeast Asia, and the Kashmir dispute have been on the UN agenda almost since its inception. Nor have the conditions underlying these conflicts—arms races, insecurity, racial discrimination, demand for scarce resources, and mutually incompatible claims for national self-determination—been improved by collective action.

Yet it would be erroneous to claim that "the United Nations has failed" just because the record in the 1970s might show some marked change over the previous twenty

five years. Before correcting the error, however, the particulars of the decline must be admitted. First, the record of the United Nations and of the Organization of American States (OAS) in abating, isolating, and settling disputes among its members, as well as in stopping hostilities, has worsened sharply since 1970. Second, that decline has not been compensated for by a proportional improvement in the success of the conflict management activities of the Arab League and the Organization of African Unity. Third, recent efforts to manage conflicts in Timor, Lebanon, Cambodia, Angola, Namibia, the Falkland Islands, and the Shatt-el-Arab have been characterized more by rhetorical posturing than by efforts to maintain or restore peace. Fourth, instead of routinized mediation and peacekeeping activities, large public conferences have become the preferred way of managing conflict. Finally, the major powers no longer exercise leadership in conflict management, the role of secretariats has declined, and fi-

SOURCE: Reprinted from *International Organization*, Vol. 32, No. 2, Ernst Haas, "Regime Decay: Conflict Management and International Organizations, 1945–1981," by permission of The MIT Press, Cambridge, Massachusetts. Copyright © 1983 by the World Peace Foundation and the Massachusetts Institute of Technology.

[1]Annual report of the UN Secretary-General, as quoted in the *New York Times,* 7 September 1982.

nancial and political disagreements militate against the mounting of operations to keep the peace and supervise truce agreements.

1. IS COLLECTIVE CONFLICT MANAGEMENT A FAILED REGIME?

The common impression that collective conflict management has failed derives from the mistaken notion that the United Nations and the regional organizations are autonomous entities, set up to coerce or cajole states into substituting cooperation for conflict. Indeed, the very idea that cooperation is the opposite of conflict is a misconception in which professional analysts as well as the lay public widely indulge. The United Nations or the OAS cannot "fail," but their members can behave in such a fashion toward one another as to give life to the principles, norms, rules, and procedures enshrined in these organizations—or they can fail to do so.

These organizations were created to moderate conflict. (It bears repeating that conflict among states was and is taken as a given; conflict is, after all, almost a synonym for politics.) They were designed to reduce "collective insecurity dilem-

mas" stemming from their members' antagonistic striving for individual security.[2] While they stress concerted action by some or all members as the desirable method for managing conflict, this is a long way from institutionalizing "cooperation" as a principle of behavior to substitute for managed conflict. To insist that the success of the United Nations must mean the victory of cooperation over conflict is to interpret world politics as an all-or-nothing game.

Collective conflict management is an aspect of foreign policy; it does not replace foreign policy. Diplomacy and action in the United Nations or a regional organization provide another way of implementing foreign policy. Far from transcending the objectives that states consider to be their national interests, conflict management organizations are forums for realizing these interests when action outside the organizations is either not possible or not desired. Action by the organizations never monopolizes the possibilities open to states; action outside them is usually possible and sometimes preferred. It is, of course, true that many in 1945 expected that the cumulative channeling of national objectives into these organizations would eventu-

---

[2]The term is borrowed from Hayward R. Alker Jr., James Bennett, and Dwain Medford, "Generalized Precedent Logics for Resolving Insecurity Dilemmas," *International Interactions* 7, 2 (1980), p. 166. In the tradition of research of artificial intelligence, Alker and his associates seek to determine by modeling the implicit (and possibly explicit) reflective logical procedures the member states follow in bringing about (or failing to bring about) cumulative conflict-management practices. Alker claims the breakpoint in UN history toward declining institutionalization occurred in the aftermath of the Congo operation (around 1963), whereas my data suggest the decline started around 1970. See the literature he cites.

ally lead to the institutionalized resolution of all interstate conflict by means of routinized procedures. Bilateral conflict would be moderated as the techniques of third-party intercession became accepted and the organizations might thus develop into autonomous agencies. Freed from continuing dependence on their member governments they would become actors on the international stage in their own right and thus properly become the targets of judgments of success and failure, much like autonomous bureaucratic agencies at the national level. We know this did not happen; we wish to know what occurred instead. . . .

The Argument

I intend to show that talk of the "failure of the United Nations" and of other entities as "organizations" is misleading and inaccurate. Failure as compared to what? Is there more intolerable conflict today as compared to 1950 or 1970? Are non-institutionalized modes of managing conflict more successful than they were? I argue that "decay" is a more appropriate image for describing what has happened. Decay implies the gradual disintegration of a previously routinized pattern of conduct. If the concept of regime has bean reasonably successful in describing such processes in other issue-areas, we ought to make the attempt to show its utility in the field of collective insecurity and its management. If the concept proves useful in this, the most demanding of issue-areas, its utility in other

arenas of world politics will be all the more persuasive. Seen in this light, collective conflict management provides the limiting case for determining the overall applicability of the regime concept. It might give us a tool for describing the growth, stability, decay, or death of complex routines of behavior that cut across international organizations and take in only a portion of the total mandate of each organization.

My argument, furthermore, seeks to demonstrate just how decay came about. This requires a historical and statistical description of the effectiveness and the coherence of the regime, assuming, of course, that the existence of a regime can be demonstrated successfully. *Effectiveness* consists of the ability of member-states to use the routines enshrined in principles, norms, rules, and procedures to moderate successfully the conflicts referred to the organizations; it also involves the ability to persuade members to refer the bulk of their disputes to the organizations instead of seeking unilateral or bilateral solutions. Effectiveness thus consists of a wide scope of activity matched with high success in management. The *coherence* of a regime consists of the mutual complementarity of its principles, norms, rules, and procedures—the support these components give one another. Effectiveness captures performance and behavior, coherence captures the institutional routines that are designed to channel behavior.

Given the well-known lag between behavior and institutions we cannot expect to map the life of the regime as if there were a perfect covariation between effectiveness and coherence. If the concept has any utility, however, we can expect that movement will be roughly in the same direction. This allows us to posit four possibilities in observing the "life" of regimes. Regime "growth" occurs when effectiveness and coherence increase in tandem. "Stability" prevails if the initial level of performance remains steady and is matched by an unchanging adjustment between the components. "Death" occurs when scope declines even though the regime may remain successful with respect to the remaining disputes referred to it and even though the coherence remains the same; of course success and coherence may also decline. "Decay," finally, is the situation in which both effectiveness and coherence decline but not necessarily in such a fashion that scope, success, and mutual complementarity of regime components covary perfectly.

My final task is to explain why decay occurred after a period of growth and after a decade of seeming stability. I shall examine several hypotheses, which are far from mutually exclusive:

1. Decline in effectiveness and coherence is due to the waning hegemony of the United States in world politics; earlier success was associated with active American leadership.

2. Decline in effectiveness and coherence in the United Nations is due to the increase in the number of voting blocs and the fragmentation of common interests and consensus among them. Winning coalitions on issues that earlier commanded big majorities can no longer be formed.

3. Winning coalitions and a wide consensus were associated with the predominance of the Cold War and decolonization as metaissues. The decline in salience of the metaissues implies a fragmentation of concern with conflict.

4. The remaining metaissues create an incentive for resolving conflicts in regional organizations rather than in the United Nations in order to isolate conflicts from global infection.

These hypotheses lead to a corollary: if hypotheses 3 and 4 are correct, the members of the regime should show greater tolerance of unresolved conflict than was earlier the case. Reduced regime coherence ought to be associated with greater toleration of conflicts seen as nonthreatening.

Before undertaking these examinations I present the data on the disputes and describe the variables used in their analysis.

2. DATA AND VARIABLES

The Regime

The regime is comprised of the conflict management routines of the United Nations, the Organization of American States (OAS), the Arab League (AL), the Organization of African Unity (OAU), and the Council of Europe (CE). According to the UN Charter, members were to refer certain types of disputes to appropriate regional organizations and make arrangements for coordination between the regionals and the United Nations. The constitutions of most regional organizations contain similar professions of adherence to global principles, norms, rules, and procedures.

The regional organizations also serve as alliances, much like the North Atlantic Treaty and Warsaw Pact (which also have "organizations"). I confine my analysis to disputes that pit the members of the regional organizations against one another. I exclude disputes between them and extraregional powers because these tap the organizations' role as alliances rather than as collective security arrangements. Other tabulations in the analysis do, however, capture such disputes.

Data Base

The data base for the study of the regime is a set of 282 "disputes" that occurred between July 1945 and September 1981. A dispute is a specific grievance between two or more states about a specific subject involving an allegation that a norm of the regime has been violated. Thus "imperialism," "the Cold War," "racism," and "the threat of the arms race" are not disputes. Of the 282, 79 were not referred to any international organization, 123 made the agenda of the United Nations, 28 went to the OAS, 25 to the OAU, 22 to the Arab League, and 5 to the Council of Europe. Since it was impossible to construct a universe of all disputes that were not referred, the nonreferred set contains only disputes in which at least some fighting occurred, that is, the most serious conflicts that remained outside the scope of the regime.[3] Double counting exists in the sense that 20 disputes were referred to the United Nations and to a re-

---

[3]Robert L. Butterworth, Joseph S. Nye, and I created the data set for the period 1945–70; we reported it in Haas, Butterworth, and Nye, *Conflict Management by International Organizations* (Morristown, N.J.: General Learning Press, 1972). The definition of "dispute," the specification of variables used in the analysis, and the coding procedures are described there and in the Appendix; I used the same definitions and procedures in this study. Data for the period 1971–78 were taken from Robert L. Butterworth, *Managing Interstate Conflict* (Pittsburgh: University Center for International Studies, University of Pittsburgh, 1976) and from Butterworth's unpublished manuscript, "Managing International Conflict" (1980). I am responsible for preparing data for the period since 1978 and for mistakes in coding and interpretation throughout. Disputes are credited to the five-year period during which they were first referred to the organization and are counted only once, even if they remained on the agenda during subsequent periods and even if success came about in a later period. Certain long-lived disputes were broken up according to coding rules described in Haas, Butterworth, and Nye, *Conflict Management,* notably those between Israel and the Arab states, the Kashmir dispute, and the situation in South Africa. Butterworth compared computations of success based on the present method with the alternative of crediting success

TABLE 1   All Disputes Involving Military Operations and Fighting
(N = 217), in Percent

| | Total N | Referrals by Era | | | | | |
| | | To UN | | To Regionals | | Nonreferred | |
		N	%	N	%	N	%
1945–50	24	10	42	1	4	13	54
1951–55	20	9	45	4	20	7	35
1956–60	26	9	35	5	19	12	46
1961–65	49	21	43	15	30	13	27
1966–70	21	12	57	4	19	5	24
1971–75	25	8	32	8	32	9	36
1976–81	52	18	35	14	27	20	38
1945–81	217	87	40	51	24	79	36

Note: Excludes double-counting of disputes referred to more than one organization. Most successful organization is credited.

gional organization, and that 3 disputes were referred both to the OAU and to the Arab League. Table 1 summarize[s] the distribution over time of the disputes that involved military activity and their referral to the respective forums.[4]

Each of the 203 disputes that appeared on the agenda of the United Nations and the five regionals was coded in terms of ten large variables. Each of these was then broken down into several smaller categories, some in the form of scales. One group of large variables seeks to capture the salience of the dispute—its seriousness in challenging peace. Another seeks to place each dispute in the overall context of world politics. The final set deals with the manner by which the membership managed the conflict.

to the period in which it actually occurred. He found that the two curves were hardly distinguishable.

[4]The Ns in various tables will differ according to need. Comparisons between referred and nonreferred disputes will use an N of 217 or below. Some tables will use only referred disputes that involved military activity, i.e., an N of 87 for the United Nations and 51 for the regionals out of total Ns of 123 and 80 respectively. The total number of disputes referred to the United Nations and the regionals was somewhat higher. I excluded disputes in which no management action was possible since there was nothing for the organization to do short of enforcement. In other instances the parties appealed to the organization for propaganda reasons and expected no action. Examples of disputes excluded are the Eichmann abduction, the Baghdad reactor raid, and various airplane incidents pitting the United States against the USSR. There were 23 excluded disputes for the United Nations, 4 for the regionals.

The Dependent Variable: Success

Unlike regimes that deal with economic and scientific issues, a regime that manages conflict takes for granted that the norms enjoining members to settle their disputes peacefully and to abstain from the use of force will be violated. Hence the prevalence of violations does not provide de facto evidence that no regime exists; the failure of the rules and procedures to limit or punish violations, however, does. But even if it is true that the regime's success in managing conflict is not very impressive, some questions remain: lack of success as compared to what? Is it a matter of consistent failure or does the record show change over time?

Conflict may be successfully managed in various ways. I label these various ways of being successful "abatement," "isolation," "settlement," and "stopping hostilities." Every dispute is capable of being settled and abated but not every dispute was judged likely to escalate beyond the initial parties and, obviously, hostilities cannot be stopped if the dispute did not involve any fighting. Each dispute was scored on whether the organization was somewhat successful on each of the dimensions applicable to the dispute, whether it scored a great impact, or whether no impact of any kind was discernible. A score of one hundred means that the organization made a *major* contribution on *all* applicable dimensions during the period in question; a score of zero means that not even

limited impact on a single dimension could be observed.

The aggregate success of the United Nations since its inception is 23, as compared to 34 for the OAS, 20 for the OAU, 15 for the Arab League, and 18 for the Council of Europe. Figure 1 shows a decay curve for the United Nations and suggests a pattern of stability for the regionals.

3. EFFECTIVENESS OF THE REGIME

Effectiveness: Scope and Success

We now have to determine whether the record of referrals to the international organizations warrants the conclusion that, at least for a period of time, they were made responsible for managing the bulk of the disputes that arose in world politics. Sixty four percent of all disputes involving military operations were so referred; the number rises to 72 percent if we consider only the more serious disputes. However, the pattern varies a good deal over time. The United Nations' share of these referrals declined to one third during the 1970s from a high of 57 percent in the previous five-year period. Yet during the most recent five years, 62 percent of the more serious disputes still found their way to the UN agenda while only 5 percent remained non-referred. Of all disputes involving military operations, the number of disputes not referred to the regime fell from a high of over one half in 1945–50 to 24 percent in

FIGURE 1   Success by Era, United Nations (N = 123),
Left, and Regional Organizations (N = 80), Right

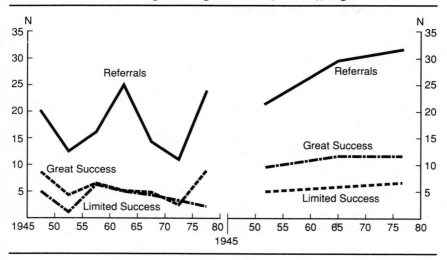

TABLE 2   Attributes of Referred and Nonreferred Disputes
(percent of caseload, N = 217)

Variable	UN	Regionals	Nonreferred
Intensity: high	65	45	37
Warfare: high	30	24	14
Spread: regional/global	23	38	22
Issue: Cold-War/decol.	55	20	61
Parties: Cold-War aligned	65	47	66
Parties: super/large	46	18	45

1966–70, only to rise again to over one third since that time. Again, however, the resurgence of extra-regime disputes is less pronounced when we restrict our attention to the more serious disputes. Moreover, some of the decline in the United Nations' share was absorbed by the regional organizations.

It appears, therefore, that the scope of the regime is declining even though it continues to dominate the universe of interstate conflict. This decline is made more concrete when we pinpoint the characteristics of the UN caseload and compare it with nonreferred disputes. Table 2 contrasts the cases on the organizational agenda

FIGURE 2   Referrals and Success by Era, United Nations (N = 123), Left, and Regional Organizations (N = 80), Right

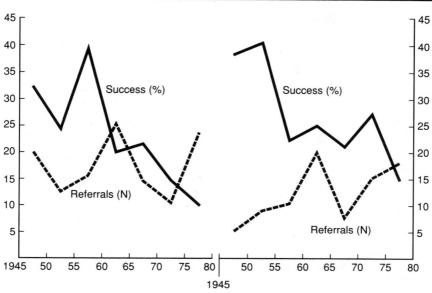

and the cases that were not referred to the regime in terms of their threat to world peace.

While disputes referred to the United Nations were more threatening than the nonreferred disputes in terms of intensity and amount of fighting, the same is not true with respect to other characteristics. The nonreferred cases include more Cold War and decolonization cases, while the shares are about the same in terms of spread, alignment, and power of the disputants. We can safely conclude, however, that the cases dealt with in the regime are the more serious ones and are numerically preponderant.

How successful were the organizations in managing this caseload?

The decline in UN success is presented in Figure 2 (left), that of the regionals in Figure 2 (right). The record of the regionals aggregates the differential successes of the various organizations. The caseload of the Council of Europe has been very small, about one dispute per era. The OAS accounts for most of the decline in success, since that organization always scored above 33 percent before 1970 but dropped to 25 percent in 1975 and to 17 percent by 1981. The Arab League, however, improved its performance over the years even though its most recent score was only 19 percent. The OAU, finally, progressed from 17 percent in 1965 to 30 percent in 1971–75, only to drop back

FIGURE 3   Dimensions of Failure, United Nations (N = 63), in Percent

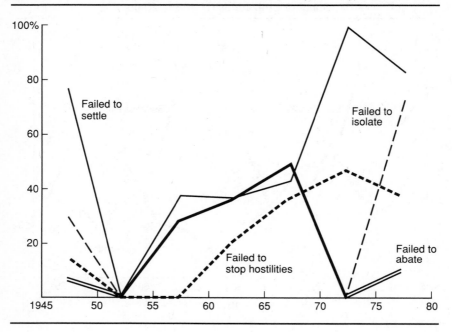

to 10 percent in the most recent period. There is no question that the general record of the regionals matches the decay in UN success since 1975.

When we turn to the dimensions of possible success (Figure 3), however, we see that failure on one of the dimensions does not necessarily imply failure on all. Figure 3 uses the universe of 63 disputes in which the United Nations scored limited or great impact. Most of the instances of successful settlement occurred before 1970.[5] Success in isolating conflicts has also de-

[5]The cases of "great" success in settling disputes: Indonesian independence, status of British Togoland, status of Cyrenaica, removal of KMT troops from Burma, West Irian, Suez war, status of British Cameroon. Thai/Cambodian border (1959–60). Congo independence, status of African High Commission Territories, status of Ifni.

Cases of "limited" success: Corfu Channel, French withdrawal from Levant, status of Namibia, Russian wives, Palestine truce (1949–56), China Sea piracy, Algerian independence, Israel borders (1957–67), Wadi Halfa, Buraimi Oasis, Laos civil war (1959–62), Moroccan-Mauritanian border (1960–61), Kuwait independence, Sarawak/Sabah, Tutsi restoration attempt, Panama Canal 1, Falkland Islands, Katanga exiles, Arab-Israeli confrontation (1967–73), Equatorial Guinea independence, Bahrein independence, Panama Canal 2, Chilean repression, Farakka barrage, Transkei border, South

clined, but less dramatically.[6] The United Nations' record in stopping hostilities remains high, though it worsened after 1965.[7] Abatement, clearly the least demanding activity in the management of conflict, has been quite good throughout the life of the organization. Decay does not yet amount to irrelevance.[8]

But that time may come. I compared the eventual outcome of the 79 nonreferred disputes with 75 disputes involving military operations that were referred to the United Nations but which it did not manage with any degree of success. I considered as failures all disputes that remain unsettled, that petered out without resolution, and that resulted in the victory of one party. Successful resolution could be achieved either by mediation or by bilateral negotiation outside the United Nations. The results appear in Figure 4. Until the period 1965–70 even "failed" UN cases were set-tled peacefully more often than were nonreferred disputes; since that time, the reverse has been true.

Correlates of Decay: The United Nations

To the extent that interpretations can be offered without looking at specific disputes and without allowing for situations specific to certain eras—such as the personality of secretaries-general or the overall turbulence of the global system—success for the United Nations over its entire history has ten characteristics.

1. The most intense disputes are the most likely to be managed. Insignificant and very low-intensity disputes can be marginally influenced. Disputes in the intermediate levels of intensity seem to be the most difficult to manage.

African race policies (1976–), Western Sahara war, Benin coup, Burmese refugees, Israeli raids in Lebanon (1978–82), U.S. hostages in Iran.

[6]The case of "great" success in isolating disputes: Corfu Channel, Greek civil war, Azerbaijan, Kashmir secession, Kashmir negotiations, Korean negotiations (1951–53), Suez war, status of British Cameroon, Sakiet raid, Lebanon/Jordan civil wars (1958), Bizerta, status of African High Commission Territories, independence of South Yemen, Cyprus civil war, status of Panama Canal, second Kashmir war, Iran expansion in Persian Gulf (1969–75), Turkish invasion of Cyprus, Benin coup, Litani River war.

[7]The cases of "great" success in stopping hostilities: Korean negotiations (1951–53), West Irian, Congo independence, Cyprus civil war, Iran expansion in the Persian Gulf (1969–75).

[8]High and very high intensity cases that the United Nations failed to manage though they were referred: Korean War (1950–51), Soviet intervention in Hungary, status of Portuguese colonies, Cuban missile crisis, repression in South Africa (1962–76), Yemen civil war, Portuguese Guinea, status of Rhodesia, Vietnam war, Eritrean independence, Rhodesia-Zambia border fighting, status of Timor, repression in Israeli-occupied territories, South African attacks on Angola, Rhodesia-Mozambique border fighting, invasion of Kampuchea, repression in El Salvador, Afghanistan.

FIGURE 4 Eventual Resolution of Failed UN and Nonreferred Disputes (N = 154), in Percent

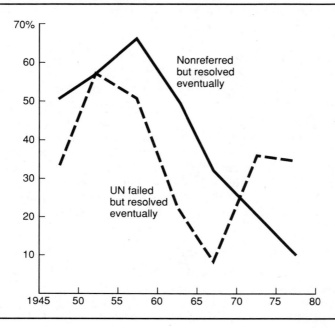

2. Unfortunately, the findings for intense disputes do not match the performance of the United Nations with respect to the seriousness of the fighting. Only 45 percent of the cases involving active warfare were managed, though the United Nations' impact tended to be moderate or great. Success comes more readily when the fighting is very limited, though then the impact is usually slight. It also seems clear that cases which did not involve fighting were not taken very seriously.

3. However, the most contagious disputes are the ones most frequently influenced by the United Nations, very often with great success. Disputes that the neighbors of the main contending parties are about to enter actively are the most difficult to manage, whereas it seems relatively simple to score some minimal impact on purely bilateral disputes.

4. Decolonization disputes are most readily managed. Cold War disputes very rarely (and then with minimal impact), while disputes not related to the metaissues show a very indifferent rate of success.

5. Cold War alignments complicate the management of conflict considerably.

6. Disputes involving the superpowers are very rarely managed with success, but cases pitting the weakest UN members against each other do not fare so well either. Disputes involving middle powers such as Argentina, Mexico, Egypt, Pakistan, the Netherlands, Belgium, and Spain yield most easily to UN action.

7. Strong decisions bring results. However, the failure to make a decision does not necessarily imply the failure of conflict management.

8. Energetic measures to enforce a truce and to separate the contestants bring results, overwhelmingly with great success. But small-scale mediation and conciliation also pay off over half the time. However, we must recall that many of the instances of "no operation" were such as to make field missions inappropriate or impossible.

9. Weak powers make poor leaders but more powerful states do not do much better. When the superpowers happen to exercise their leadership together, of course, they are usually successful. The single most effective mode of leadership is the initiative of the Secretary-General, acting either alone or in concert with one of the larger states.

10. No effective action is possible without a wide or very wide consensus among the members.

There is an appreciable difference between situations in which a major impact was scored and those in which a marginal one was scored. Major impact is correlated with active warfare, decolonization issues (until 1965), disputes involving super and large powers (until 1970), strong decisions, large operations, and the leadership of the Secretary-General. These add up to a very restrictive profile of disputes on which the United Nations had a major impact. Much more versatility, however, is suggested by the cases in which we observe only minor impact. Instances of marginal effectiveness are spread over a wide spectrum of dispute attributes and modes of management. If the membership is sufficiently concerned, it appears, the United Nations may still make a limited difference in a wide variety of circumstances even though the members will tend not to use it in decisively abating, isolating, or settling their disputes.

Can the United Nations' decline in success and scope since 1970 be correlated with any of the variables for describing salience? The decline in effectiveness accompanies an increase in the number of high-intensity disputes; hence one wonders why success was high in earlier periods with high-intensity conflicts. Moreover, the decay in the regime's effectiveness continued in the face of a decline in the incidence of disputes with major fighting since the relatively successful 1966–70 period and matches a trend toward more localized disputes. While decay cannot be explained exclusively in terms of the changing salience of conflict, it appears as if a decline in salience induces the members to tolerate conflict rather than to manage it.

A similar explanation of this decay seems to be associated with the changing global context in which disputes arise. Increasing failure is correlated with the decline of the Cold War and of decolonization disputes with the prevalence of parties not aligned with a Cold War bloc, and with a trend toward more conflict among the smaller member states. Marginality with respect to the major issues of world politics appears to go with regime decay.

These trends are reflected in the management practices of the United Nations.[9] Since 1970, the United Nations has often substituted rhetoric for action. Resolutions that authorize operations continue to be passed but less often than before. The relative inactivity of the United Nations in recent years was exceeded only during the height of the Cold War. Yet small field operations continue to be popular and even the number of truce-observation and peacekeeping operations did not decline sharply until 1975. By contrast, the change

in the pattern of leadership is very striking. After 1965 the United States and the Soviet Union seldom sought to lead unilaterally though they still occasionally launch joint initiatives. It should be noted that the apparent lack of American leadership between 1955 and 1960 is misleading: this was the era of initiatives launched by Dag Hammarskjold, usually with the active support of the United States. Under Kurt Waldheim the office of the Secretary-General became less prominent, abandoning the leadership role to the very powers whose conflicts increasingly dominated the agenda. These variables, rather than the relatively unchanging pattern of consensus, seem to account for the decline in energy. . . .

Do Regional Organizations Complement the United Nations?

While the OAS seems to be undergoing decay, the Arab League, the OAU, and the Council of Europe seem to have entered a period of stability after initial periods of failure.[10] In the aggregate and with the exception of the period

---

[9]For descriptions of the major disputes referred to international organizations and of the methods of conflict management applied to them see David W. Wainhouse et al., *International Peace Observation* (Baltimore: Johns Hopkins University Press, 1966) and *International Peacekeeping at the Crossroads* (Baltimore: Johns Hopkins University Press, 1973); Leon Gordenke, *The United Nations Secretary-General and the Maintenance of Peace* (New York: Columbia University Press, 1967); Mark W. Zacher, *Dag Hammarskjold's United Nations* (New York: Columbia University Press, 1970) and his *International Conflicts and Collective Security, 1946–77* (New York: Praeger, 1979).

[10]OAS cases are discussed in Gordon Connell-Smith, *The Inter-American System* (New York: Oxford University Press, 1966); Joseph S. Nye, *Peace in Parts* (Boston: Little, Brown, 1971).[10] Arab League cases are discussed in Hussein A. Hassouna, *The*

1971–75, regional organizations were given cases that were far less intense than those the United Nations addressed. Warfare was rarely aimed at defeating or conquering the enemy. However, extraregional states were often on the point of entering disputes in Africa and the Middle East, though the same was not true in the western hemisphere. Over 80 percent of the cases involved neither decolonization nor the Cold War; only 30 percent pitted members of Cold War alliances against each other; civil strife accounted for 56 percent of the caseload. Naturally, given the membership of these organizations, the bulk of the disputes involved only the smallest states. In short, the regional record of success exceeds that of the United Nations in some of the contextual categories in which UN performance has been weak.

Our excursion into the regional organizations' record in managing conflict is justified by the hypothesis that regional organizations have a specialized capability for dealing with relatively localized, low-intensity disputes and thus complement the overall mandate of the United Nations. It is also justified by the fact that organizational decay does not seem to strike all collective security organizations evenly. What,

then, distinguished the regional organizations from the United Nations in terms of leadership, consensus, and operations?

OAS

For the OAS the watershed occurred in 1965, with the authorization of a peacekeeping force led by the United States and the Dominican Republic that a substantial minority of member states opposed. Their challenge progressively undermined the earlier consensus on norms because, as left-leaning governments came and went in Latin America, the early congruence of the collective security and anticommunist norms eroded. Before 1965 the United States was able successfully to justify OAS intervention in disputes that pitted right against left by pointing to the Soviet threat; after 1965 it was no longer able to conflate the two principles so readily because a substantial number of other governments refused to acquiesce.

Before 1965 the United States used the OAS effectively in the furtherance of its own objectives, which then coincided with the perceived interests of most of the other members. The organization did well in insignificant as well as in moderately intense disputes, in cases of limited fighting as well as

---

League of Arab States and Regional Disputes (Dobbs Ferry, N.Y.: Oceana, 1975); Robert W. Macdonald, *The League of Arab States* (Princeton: Princeton University Press, 1965). OAU cases are discussed in Jon Woronoff, *Organizing African Unity* (Metuchen, N.J.: Scarecrow, 1970); R. David Meyers, "Intraregional Conflict Management by the Organization of African Unity," *International Organization* 28 (Summer 1974), pp. 345–76.

in disputes without fighting. It did even better when war was waged seriously. It coped better with bilateral and local than with regional disputes but even there the record was good. The United States also did well in using the OAS to restrain Cuban forays into other Caribbean countries. The OAS scored successes against members in all the categories of the power hierarchy. Strong decisions predominated but even deliberations that resulted in no formal decision at all scored limited impacts. Small-scale operations, usually a conciliation commission of the Permanent Council in which certain perennial diplomats played the key roles, regularly scored limited successes, though most of the major successes required large-scale operations (as in the Dominican Republic and the Honduran-Nicaraguan border dispute). And the United States acted as the leader, financier, and furnisher of military support half of the time.

Much of this changed after 1965. Mexico and Venezuela challenged the U.S. leadership successfully with respect to Cuba and the Sandinista revolt in Nicaragua. Jamaica, Panama, and the Andean countries are no longer reliable clients. Conciliation commissions no longer score easy successes because they now reflect the deep-seated divisions among the member governments; fewer strong decisions are made and far fewer field operations are attempted. New referrals have declined sharply and success has dropped from 38 to 17 percent. American leadership has all but disappeared while that of the middle powers is rising; consensus remains tenuous. Before 1965, the United States was the object of complaints 14 percent of the time, but that figure rose to 33 percent after 1965. Certainly, the experience of the OAS since 1965 confounds the hypothesis that the regional organization complements the United Nations, though before 1965 its record provides considerable support for the notion. Now the two are decaying in tandem.

Arab League

Membership in the Arab League expanded gradually from the core of Mid-eastern Arab states to include all of North Africa. Mauritania, the Palestine Liberation Organization, and even Somalia. The success rate of the League was dismal in its first decade, improved during the 1960s, and stabilized at 19 percent in 1976–81. Improvement in performance went with increasing intensity of disputes, more active warfare, and greater threats of infection by regional and global confrontations. Since 1970, improved performance also covaries with increased Cold War alignments of the disputants. In the earlier period, most of the inter-Arab disputes were not directly linked to superpower rivalry in the Middle East. But as the Arab states increasingly split into "moderate" and "radical" camps, considerations of Cold War alignments became more prominent. Presumably, the increasing success—albeit at a very modest level—of the Arab League is related to the desire of member states to isolate the region from global infection. Limited success in containing the Lebanese civil war before 1982 and great success in stopping two wars between the Yemens provide support for this interpretation. Increasing consensus has made possible the mounting of relatively large-scale operations in the 1970s.

Leadership emerges as the most powerful variable to explain the change. At first, Egypt sought to exercise hegemonic influence. The Secretary-General, always an Egyptian until the 1970s, was extremely active even though he had no clear constitutional mandate and was widely perceived to act in the interests of Egypt. Iraq sought to challenge Egyptian hegemony from time to time and during the 1950s factions would form around the two leaders; hence, Egypt was ineffective as a conflict manager. In later years, Saudi Arabia assumed a quiet hegemonic rule. Following the Camp David agreements Egypt was expelled from the League, headquarters were moved to Tunis, and a Tunisian became Secretary-General. He has not sought an active role for himself. Saudi Arabia continues to finance most of the Arab League's operations and to provide the diplomatic initiatives required to manage conflict. Since everything seems to depend on momentary constellations of hegemony in the League, it would be risky to project current stability into the future.

OAU

The effectiveness of the OAU has oscillated more dramatically than that of the Arab League, from a success score of 22 percent in 1966–70 to 30 percent in the following lustrum, only to slide back to 10 percent since 1976. During the 1970s its task became heavier: African wars became more deadly, disputes spread more widely in the region as well as outside, and the disputing parties were increasingly aligned with one of the sides in the Cold War. During the first period, one half of the disputes grew out of civil wars and revolutions; during the second the number fell marginally, to six out of fourteen. Still, performance improved at first, decisions became stronger, and one large operation was attempted in Chad. A look at the identity of the cases may suggest why.

The number of strong decisions does not differ much between the two periods, but their impact does. The OAU failed to manage the Nigerian and Zairean civil wars during the first era, though it helped to moderate the border dispute between Somalia and its neighbors. When governments feel they can win a civil war, often with external help, they reject OAU intervention. Thus, during the second period, Ethiopia rebuffed the OAU's attempt to manage the Ogaden and Eritrean wars, and disputes of this type remain outside the OAU's competence. On the other hand, the OAU's strong decisions after 1970 did moderate the impact of Amin's coup in Uganda and the effort in 1975 to overthrow the government of Benin, stopped the genocide in Burundi, and aided in getting Libya out of Chad.

While the OAU is not able to mount more small-scale operations than in the past, the ones it does launch have become more effective. Such operations follow a routinized pattern. The president of the Conference of Heads of States first attempts mediation on his own or in the company of a small committee composed of heads of states. Failing this, the dispute may be discussed in the full Conference in order to strengthen the hand of the mediators. During the 1960s, the Secretary-General sought an active role as conflict manager, a role strongly resisted by member states of more conservative views and opposed to Pan Africanism. Succeeding secretaries-general have been more modest, leaving the management role to heads of state. While leadership was diffused, the fact that there is neither a strong executive head nor a hegemonic state (Nigeria's leadership role being intermittent) compels the OAU to seek American and French assistance whenever operations are contemplated. The OAU is incapable of mounting and financing operations on its own and its success, when mediation by heads of state proves insufficient, continues to depend on extraregional actors. When these actors' goals in isolating African conflicts from the global context happen to coincide with the OAU membership's, management action

complementing that of the United Nations is possible.

Are Regional Organizations Successful at UN Expense?

We would characterize the global conflict management regime as a set of competing organizations and forces if we were to arrive at the conclusion that the United Nations and the regionals are rivals for the same kinds of cases. What does the record of the effectiveness of the regionals have to tell us on that score?

An examination of the twenty disputes submitted both to the United Nations and to one or more of the regionals allows one judgment of relative effectiveness. A study of disputes that went to the United Nations but match the profile of "typical" referrals to regional organizations permits another. Typically, disputes referred to a regional organization before 1965 involved minimal fighting, were of low intensity, and had not spread beyond the neighbors of the antagonists. Few global metaissues were involved, the parties were small or middle powers, and they were either nonaligned or members of the same Cold War bloc. If regionals consistently outperform the United Nations in managing such conflicts we would have to conclude that their specialized competence complemented that of the United Nations. The record suggests that this did not happen with any degree of consistency, even though the OAS

before 1965 performed in accordance with the ideal division of
labor.

After 1965 the profile of disputes
submitted to the regionals no longer
differed systematically from the
United Nations' caseload. The organizations became competitors
for the same task and the regionals
did outperform the United Nations
in three out of seven cases, as opposed to five out of thirteen before
1965. Thus the global regime is decaying in another sense: its constituent organizations have become
rivals.

The same conclusion emerges
from a second test. There were
eight disputes referred to the
United Nations that "normally"
should have gone to the OAS and
the Council of Europe, all after
1963; in four of these the United
Nations scored successes, in a
sense at the expense of regional organizations because the parties did
not trust them. Hence we must conclude not only that the regionals are
increasingly successful at UN expense but also that the reverse is
true. There is no global division of
labor among conflict management
agencies now and there probably
never was one.[11]

Conclusion

The aggregate success scored by
most international organizations in
managing conflicts has declined
steadily after 1970. Success diminished with the advent of disputes
among small and middle powers
that did not relate to decolonization
and the Cold War; the domination
of the procedure by small and middle powers who are nonaligned with
respect to the Cold War; the increasing average intensity of disputes; and the increasing incidence
of disputes of local significance.
These aspects of the international
environment in which conflicts
arose, in turn, resulted in behaviors
characterized by the reluctance of
most organizations to adopt sub-
stantively meaningful decisions;
the absence of prominent leadership by the superpowers; and the
decline of leadership by the Secretary-General. Put slightly differ-
ently, the historical record suggests
that collective efforts to manage
conflict tend to thrive when disputes are perceived to threaten
global peace but that they languish
when disputes are scattered and
relatively unconnected to global
concerns. The corollary of this

[11]This confirms Robert Butterworth's finding. See his "Organizing Collective Security: The UN Charter's Chapter VIII in Practice," *World Politics* 28 (January 1976), pp.
197–222. Five of the eight cases involved aspects of the confrontation between Greece
and Turkey; the other three were Caribbean disputes to which the United States was a
party. For additional evidence that states do not consistently coordinate policy in the
United Nations with what is done in regional organizations see Ernst B. Haas and
Edward T. Rowe, "Regional Organizations in the United Nations: Is There Externali-
zation?" *International Studies Quarterly* 17 (March 1973).

finding is the tendency on the part of some regional organizations to be increasingly effective in managing conflicts that do threaten to infect the region with a global ailment. Since some disputes of global significance continue to be referred to the United Nations and since states apparently are unwilling to have the United Nations confront them energetically, the members of the OAU and the Arab League seek to compensate by upgrading regional activity. This interpretation is strengthened by the finding that the number of high-intensity disputes not referred to any organization has declined sharply since 1975.

4. COHERENCE OF THE REGIME

Change in Regime Coherence

Such are the facts of recent history. They suggest that the actors on the stage of world politics have learned little; or, perhaps, they have learned to manage conflict without needing an effective regime. After all, the sharp rise in international disputes since 1975 (after many ups and downs since 1945) has led neither to nuclear nor to a big conventional war. Before coming to any such conclusion, however, we have to show what happened to the regime during the process of decay. This requires us to summarize changes in principles, norms, rules, and procedures in such a way as to throw into relief the differences in pattern between the relatively successful initial

twenty-five years and the more recent era of relative failure. And this leads us to a crucial question: why did improvements in regime coherence mapped during the first period not lead to their stabilization in the second?

Principles may change for a number of reasons, such as the appearance of a large number of new actors whose beliefs about causation and rectitude differ from the original membership's because of the emergence of new demands and of different expectations of behavior. If these demands and expectations prevail and agreement on new principles can be achieved, the regime "grows." If, however, the old and the new actors cannot agree, the regime "dies." Evidence of the death of a regime includes the withdrawal of large numbers of members or of a few important members, nonpayment of contributions, systematic absence from meetings, or consistent violations of norms by most of the members. The United Nations is not often plagued by such behavior. In all formal ways, the regime continues to exist and its scope remains wide. But it neither grew nor stabilized after 1970; the attributes of decay become crucial for understanding. Decay must be studied by looking at the changing coherence of norms, rules, and procedures in relation to principles. Norms may require adaptation for two reasons. It may become apparent that the initial fit between norms and principles was poor and that norms must be adjusted to serve principles better. In addition, the initial coherence among norms may have been deficient. The same is also true of rules and procedures. Each component may suffer from poor adjustment to the next "higher" component or with respect to the other rules and procedures. Moreover, the lack of fit may occur because of initial design flaws or because the next higher component is changing. Rules and procedures may require adaptation because norms are changing or even if norms remain constant.

Thus the coherence of a regime increases if norms that were initially poorly adjusted to one another are later made more mutually supportive; it decreases if norms are progressively permitted to contradict one another. Unless new norms improve the principles, a change in norms undermines the regime. Coherence decreases when the new norms tend to make the principle of collective security more problematic.

Regime Components and the United Nations

The subsequent discussion focuses on changes in the United Nations and neglects the regional organizations. We have seen that, despite the original regime norms, the regionals were progressively detached from UN procedures. Their development as separate entities further underlines the decay of the original regime.

Mapping changes in regime components is a tedious business, justified only if we take seriously our commitment as students of regimes to the concepts we have developed for these studies. There is no justification for using the terms unless we take the trouble to demonstrate what they can tell us about historical events. Nevertheless, we ought not to expect a perfect match between changes in regime components and the ups and downs in regime effectiveness. Principles, norms, rules, and procedures do not change even in five-year increments. Earlier changes are rarely repealed in later periods; they linger on as new changes are superimposed on them.

If we isolate certain features of UN practice, the historical record breaks down into four eras, though they overlap a bit. The features of interest are the overall pattern of polarity in world politics; the salience of the Cold War in world politics and the alignments among states that show up in UN behavior as a result; leadership exercised by the Cold War superpowers in the United Nations; and the consensus among the other members they are able to mobilize. The combination of these four features gives us eras I shall label "the concert" (1945–47 and occasionally thereafter), "permissive enforcement with balancing" (1948–55), "permissive engagement" (1956–70), and—despite my best efforts to find a pattern—a rather chaotic period of "no pattern" at all since 1970. The initial period of "the concert" corresponds to the regime components found in the UN Charter, which I have described earlier. Changes in components, therefore, must be analyzed with the concert as the baseline. In the terminology used by Mark Zacher, the trajectory of the regime ran from a principle of consensus to one of competition.[12] While that competition in turn corresponded to a discernible pattern for over twenty years, my evidence suggests that this is no longer the case. Table 3 shows the changes.

Concert

Under the dominance of the idea of the concert, the Security Council ruled the regime. The five permanent members sanctioned all action; their failure to agree implied inaction. They alone were to enforce the norms. But this implied—since each had the veto—that either they were expected to be in agreement on almost everything or that they would keep disputes among themselves off the agenda and confine the UN caseload to disputes of no great salience in their foreign policies. In short, the United Nations under the aegis of the concert assumed consensus on world order issues among the permanent members, leadership by the superpowers, and their ability to mobilize appropriate majorities on their behalf. It also implied the absence of polarity or, more accurately, a unipolar system under the hegemony of the United States in which others acquiesced. With the advent of the Cold War and bipolarity as a fact of life, none of these assumptions and conditions remained relevant. If no new norms and rules had been invented after 1947, the Cold War would have condemned the United Nations to death then and there.

The initial period was one of the United Nations' most successful. The fact that Cold War alignments did not interfere with its impact in Indonesia, the Levant, Azerbaijan, and Palestine is partly accounted for by the Soviet Union's not insisting on the logic of the veto and accepting the strong leadership of the United States. The Soviet Union's restraint enabled the concert to function, a condition no doubt helped by a convergence of its interests with America's.

Permissive Enforcement with Balancing

The Greek civil war and the Korean war spelled the end of the concert; they implied the advent of tight bipolarity and full Cold War alignments inside and outside the United Nations, and the United States commanded a two-thirds majority by virtue of the alignments. The reciprocity of the implication of "mutual abstention" in the use of the United Nations by the superpowers gave way to its em-

---

[12]See Zacher, *International Conflicts*. Zacher studied the same disputes as I, though using an N of 116, asking under what circumstances the United Nations managed to intervene with success. He defines success, unlike me, as the ability to halt aggression. He found that the United Nations achieves success most frequently in disputes pitting a nonaligned member against a member of a Cold War alliance (when the victim was nonaligned). Scrutiny of actual cases discloses that Zacher's instances of success are identical with the cases I identify as dominated by the issue of decolonization. Whether issue or alignment is the more powerful predictor cannot be settled without considering the additional variables I introduce.

TABLE 3   Change in UN Regime Components

Concert 1945–47	Permissive Enforcement with Balancing 1948–55	Permissive Engagement 1956–70	No Pattern 1971–81
PRINCIPLES			
Collective security	No change	No change	No change
Sovereign equality	No change	No change	No change
Treaties binding	No change	"Unjust treaties" may not be binding	As in 1956–70
Reciprocity in benefits	Upset by use of UN for Cold War	Upset by use of UN for decolonization	As in 1948–70
NORMS			
Membership criteria	No change	Universality supercedes restrictions of Art. 4	"Racist states" may be ineligible; liberation groups may be eligible
Domestic jurisdiction	Disregarded with inclusion of human rights issues	Disregarded further with inclusion of colonial civil wars	As in 1948–70
Self-defense limited by Art. 51	Disregarded as Security Council's monitoring power is not used	As in 1948–55	As in 1948–70
Regional arrangements	Regional organizations used to sidestep UN	As in 1948–55	Regional organizations sometimes complement UN
Privileged role of big powers	Sidestepped via "Uniting for Peace" procedure by using General Assembly	As in 1948–55 but not always	As in 1948–70 but less often
No use of force, peaceful settlement, mutual assistance in case of violations	Recourse to "Uniting for Peace" procedure	"Peacekeeping" as intermediate technique between peaceful settlement and enforcement; use of General Assembly	Decline of peacekeeping; special sessions/ conferences of General Assembly

TABLE 3   *(continued)*

Concert 1945–47	Permissive Enforcement with Balancing 1948–55	Permissive Engagement 1956–70	No Pattern 1971–81
RULES			
Graduated steps for peaceful settlement (Chap. 6)	General Assembly committees assume role of Security Council	Peacekeeping blurs distinction between Chaps. 6 and 7; Art. 39 avoided	As in 1948–70
Enforcement via Security Council	Noninvocation of Arts. 39, 40. No use of Military Staff Committee	As in 1948–55; label of "aggressor" avoided	As in 1948–70
Big power standby forces	Disregarded; ad hoc voluntary forces for fighting and truce observation	Some routinization of ad hoc voluntary forces for peacekeeping and truce observation	Decline of routinization
General Assembly role in collective security (Arts. 10–14)	Upgraded via "Uniting for Peace" recommendation only	As in 1948–55	Intensified with ad hoc conferences to deal with crises; recommendations only
Obligatory financial contributions	No change	Dispute over payments of peacekeeping expenses; voluntary contributions	Formula for combining obligatory with voluntary payments
ICJ decisions enforceable by Security Council	Disregarded	Disregarded	Disregarded
PROCEDURES			
General Assembly can only recommend	No change	No change	No change
General Assembly role on membership, choice of Secretary-General	No change	No change	No change

TABLE 3 *(concluded)*

	Permissive Enforcement with Balancing 1948–55	Permissive Engagement 1956–70	No Pattern 1971–81
Concert 1945–47			
Security Council can block new members, Secretary-General	No change	No change	No change
Security Council voting	Permanent members fail to abstain in votes on disputes to which they are party	Double-veto disused; abstention by permanent member not a veto; consensus procedure	As in 1948–70
Secretary-General's role in peacekeeping and mediation (Art. 99)	Attempt to use Art. 99 ends in resignation of Secretary-General	Secretary-General acquires right to use his permanent representative as mediator; propose recruit and maintain peacekeeping forces; build supporting voting coalitions	As in 1956–70 but used more sparingly

ployment for Cold War purposes. The membership applications of states suspected of joining either alignment were blocked. The Soviet Union considered the Secretary-General a lackey of the West. After the predictable Soviet response to American dominance—the use of the veto in crises such as the Greek and Korean wars—the United States used its overwhelming majority to initiate the "Uniting for Peace" norm (and its associated rules and procedures) by shifting collective security operations from the Security Council to the General Assembly. While the impact of the United Nations on conflict management declined after 1950, it remained a respectable 24 percent.

The authorization of enforcement measures by the General Assembly remained "permissive" because it carried no binding force; a vote merely authorized states willing to undertake an operation to do so. The Assembly legitimizes a decision by a state or an alliance, making the United Nations an adjunct of the alliance—or so it would be if the norm were permitted to work unchecked. The Korean war and its eventual settlement, however, suggest that the norm of permissive enforcement dominates only as long as the two-thirds majority of the sponsoring states remains unimpaired. If some states change their minds and decide to attempt mediation or conciliation between the antagonists, permissive enforcement yields to "balancing." Obviously, the antagonists would not consent to balancing unless they had decided on their own that a continuation of the conflict was undesirable. During the period 1948–1955, then, this combination of circumstances prevented the United Nations from becoming simply an appendage of one superpower, like the OAS.

Permissive Engagement

The changes in regime components initiated during the late 1940s and the early 1950s were expanded and routinized between 1956 and 1965, a period that saw some of the United Nations' more dramatic successes and included a success score of 40 percent in 1956–60. Tight bipolarity gave way to a much looser constellation of forces as the nonaligned movement was organized and as the large number of newly independent states joined neither alliance, acquiring after 1960 a two-thirds majority in the United Nations. At the same time the internal cohesion of both Cold War alliances declined and, for reasons unrelated to the United Nations, the salience of the Cold War ebbed, resulting in the first detente after the Cuban missile crisis. The dissolution of colonial empires was at the top of the international conflict agenda and dominated the UN

caseload, though this trend interacted with Cold War considerations in some instances. Furthermore, this context provided the opportunity for Dag Hammarskjold's "quiet diplomacy," the engagement of the United Nations under "Uniting for Peace" auspices but no longer under the exclusive aegis of the United States and the West. The enlarged membership gave the Secretary-General the opportunity to base UN intervention on shifting coalitions of supporting states, often including the United States as an enthusiastic backer. The Soviets, while sometimes on the losing end of these coalitions, nevertheless reduced their use of the veto from an annual average of .9 between 1945 and 1955 to .7 for this period (as opposed to .4 for the period after 1970).

The shift in the principle of reciprocity, highlighting the rights of colonized peoples, implied several adjustments in norms, rules, and procedures. Decolonization spurred the change in the membership and domestic jurisdiction norms. It was also responsible for continuing the shift to the General Assembly of responsibility for active conflict management. And that shift made possible the adjustments in the "no force" and "mutual assistance" norms that gave the Secretary-General the opportunity to invent peacekeeping as a technique straddling the pacific settlement of disputes and the prevention of armed attacks and acts of aggression.

Rules were adjusted to serve the changed norms through the avoidance of the Charter-sanctioned distinction between the steps envisaged in Charter Chapters 6 and 7 (again through the invention of peacekeeping and the "Uniting for Peace" resolution); the price paid for the shift, however, was the serious controversy over obligatory payments, as states outside the Secretary-General's coalitions refused to contribute. Increasing regime coherence was by no means linear and uniform.

Procedural adjustments responded only in part to these changes in norms and rules. The procedures in the Security Council for selecting commissions and committees to aid the Secretary-General's upgraded role in conflict management derive from the change in rules. So do the routines for recruiting, organizing, deploying, and supplying national peacekeeping forces, as well as for negotiating agreements guaranteeing their rights of action and access. However, the change in decision-making procedure in the Security Council was due to a waning Cold War, not to changes in rules.

On balance, then, the United Nations became more coherent as a conflict manager by the early 1960s. The hierarchy of interlocking norms, rules, and procedures became more mutually supportive and better able to serve the principles once the principle of reciprocity had been changed. Institutional evolution occurred because of the short-term, self-interested behavior of the actors. Why, then, did it fail to stabilize?

The seeming growth of the regime, as evidenced by improved coherence among its components and its effectiveness during the 1956–60 era, led to a very precarious stability in the 1960s. Success dropped to 20 percent by 1965, though it rose again to 24 percent between 1966 and 1970. The very adaptation of the norms to the altered principle of reciprocity made some of the original rules inappropriate and their successors more ambiguous. The norms dealing with regionalism and self-defense were, in effect, sacrificed to the new principle. The nonreciprocal relationship between the European colonial powers and their Third World challengers undermined the rules on binding financial contributions. Firmly earmarked standby military forces became a victim of the "Uniting for Peace" resolution and of the ad hoc peacekeeping mechanism; and that mechanism became unreliable because of the dispute over financing.

The record of the International Court of Justice offers further striking evidence of failure in the mutual reinforcement of rules. The Charter lists judicial settlement as a form of pacific settlement and calls for Security Council enforcement of awards by the Court.[13] The actual record, however, is dismal.

---

[13]I considered 20 judgments and advisory opinions of the Court that dealt with disputes also on the political agenda of the United Nations. They break down as follows

Because the active involvement of the General Assembly depended on the existence of an appropriate coalition, predictable and consistent adherence to new rules and procedures of conflict management could not be attained. Conversely, when concert-like conditions made it possible, the Security Council could function with the active leadership of the Secretary-General, but only on occasion. While the Secretary-General's role looked like an important increase in regime coherence, the enactment of that role remained in practice entirely dependent on the political alignments triggered by a given dispute and the extraordinary personality of Dag Hammarskjold. U Thant, though he attempted to play the same role until 1965, was unable to routinize and stabilize the procedure.

The Current Era: No Pattern

No fundamental change in the components of the regime occurred after 1970. Institutional innovations made earlier continued to be used. Rules and procedures that had gone by the wayside were not revived. Yet the regime was less coherent in several ways. Universality of membership became a source of discord as it was extended de facto to the Palestine Liberation Organization and the South West African People's Organization; the watered-down domestic jurisdiction norm was applied asymmetrically to burden colonial and right-wing governments; its further extension to human rights concerns was aimed mostly at Israel and South Africa. The Security Council continued to be sidestepped on occasion, primarily to restrain Israel, South Africa, and white-ruled Rhodesia. Earlier adaptations were not used when Indonesia conquered Timor, China attacked Vietnam, Vietnam invaded Kampuchea, Iraq moved into Iran, India aided secessionist Bangladesh, and several Middle East countries fueled the civil wars in Eritrea and Chad. A double standard seemed to prevail in conflict management as the membership was less inclined to intervene energetically in conflicts among Third World nations, even though it continued to make use of the regime rules and procedures, as they had evolved in decolonization cases, in disputes involving Israel.

One explanation lies in the changing nature of alignments and

---

with respect to implementation: 8 cases declared moot, jurisdiction or standing of complainant declined, withdrawn, pending; in 3 cases, judgment implemented; in 9 cases, judgment not implemented. The implemented judgments are the Haya de la Torre asylum, Honduras-Nicaraguan border, and the Temple of Preah Vihear cases. The nonimplemented judgments are in these cases: Corfu Channel, first Southwest Africa, Anglo-Iranian Oil Company, Portuguese colonies in India, UN peacekeeping expenses, third Southwest Africa, Icelandic fisheries, Western Sahara, Iranian hostages. No decision rendered since 1962 has been implemented. Until then the number of implemented and nonimplemented judgments was about the same in each five-year period. The four advisory opinions used were really proxy adversary cases.

consensus, which in turn represents a major shift in the international environment. During the period before 1965, the nonaligned states were fewer in number and less united on issues. They became numerically dominant after 1965 as some Latin American and African states previously aligned with the United States joined them. The Non-Aligned Movement as a whole gained cohesion from its program for a New International Economic Order. (The fact that most nonaligned states also depend for favors on their oil-rich colleagues is not irrelevant.) Another reason lies in the decline of metaissues: the Cold War and decolonization gave way to disputes that involved issues specific to the antagonists in a given conflict. The additional fact that superpower leadership was muted goes hand in hand with the decline of polarity—the disintegration of the loose bipolar clusters into a congeries of unstable blocs that must tolerate crossovers among their members on a case-to-case basis. Under these circumstances even a Secretary-General more resourceful than Kurt Waldheim would have had trouble taking up the slack in leadership.

While many of these conditions were also visible during the relatively successful years between 1966 and 1970, leadership, consensus, and alignment mark the difference from the current period. The 1966–70 period saw the advent of issues other than the Cold War and decolonization, the emergence of middle and small powers as the main contestants, and a rise in the intensity of warfare, especially in local and bilateral disputes—all characteristic as well of the period since 1970. On the other hand, leadership by the Secretary-General was still significant then, one or both of the contestants in disputes was still a member of a Cold War coalition 71 percent of the time, and consensus was at its highest point in UN history. Hence there was still room for permissive engagement. There may still be now, since the components of the regime have not changed much. But the overt commitment of the member states gives little evidence of the necessary interests. Conflict management behavior, then, mirrors the fact that the nonaligned majority can agree on collective action when a dispute triggers the issue of racism or zionism; but the nonaligned cannot be expected to be similarly united when wars among their own members are at issue. The permanent members of the Security Council take sides or urge action only when their own interests are involved— as in the Middle East and Cyprus. The result is a United Nations whose members are fundamentally divided on the importance of conflict management as a task. The norms have not disappeared, the rules remain in effect, and the procedures continue to be used; but the members cannot agree on the circumstances under which they ought to be applied. One consequence is the remarkable use of international peacekeeping forces in the Sinai and Lebanon since 1978, which avoids UN procedures. Another is the invited intervention of extracontinental forces in Africa, again in disregard of previously used procedures. The regime has not died, but it has decayed.

5. WHY DID THE REGIME DECAY?

Before we consider the explanatory persuasiveness of the hypotheses advanced in the introduction, a prior question requires an answer: did the decline in effectiveness match the decline in coherence and did it match an increase in the ability of states to manage their conflicts peacefully outside the regime?... The United Nations lagged behind bilateral and extraorganizational success in managing conflict during the height of the Cold War and during the period of declining permissive engagement; it performed better than the extraorganizational efforts of states in five out of seven periods, including the most recent decade. There is no dominantly inverse relationship. This finding provides further evidence that obituaries for the United Nations are premature. Why did improvements in coherence not always correspond to improved performance? The same two five-year periods impair the perfect match. Improvements in coherence in 1951–55 were achieved in defiance of the Soviet Union, whose policy was also responsible for preventing additional success in conflict management; this situation was reversed in the next period, because

the Soviets accommodated themselves to the regime's changes. In 1961–65 the previous improvements in coherence were stabilized but performance declined anyway. By 1970, effectiveness and regime coherence were moving in tandem— downward. Clearly there is a lag between institutional innovation and stability and the behavior of states with respect to conflict management.

Declining American Hegemony?

One popular explanation for the decay of the United Nations is the so-called "declining hegemony" thesis. Hegemony may be conceived as the national capability to advance long-range visions of world order (such as the notion of collective security and other UN principles) by working with the preponderant resources available to the hegemon for the success of institutions charged with that task. In addition a hegemon would be expected to make side payments to reluctant coalition partners unwilling to follow the hegemon's lead spontaneously; and the hegemon is expected to forego its own short-range interests in favor of the final goal.

It is undeniable that the success of the United Nations until the early 1960s was due in large measure to American leadership, pressure, and support. Most institutional innovations were initiated by the United States or its close allies, the bulk of UN conflict management policy and procedures was consistent with American interests, and the United States offered side payments in the form of shouldering annually up to 33 percent of the organization's regular budget and sometimes as much as 50 percent of the technical assistance and humanitarian relief funds. Why, then, is the declining hegemony argument inconclusive?

The United States began to declare its reluctance to make these side payments in 1962, with the insistence that peacekeeping expenses be paid by all members in proportion to their share of the regular budget contributions. It became more strident in 1965, with the insistence that the American contribution to the regular budget be kept to 25 percent annually. However, UN effectiveness *improved* after 1965, albeit not for long. The support the United States could garner in the General Assembly declined sharply after 1960; however, this occurred too soon to be consistent with the hypothesis and the same is true for the data summarizing U.S. support of and satisfaction with UN decisions. True, the divergence between UN decisions and U.S. preferences grew after 1960; but U.S. satisfaction never fell below 54 percent and *rose* again after 1965, even though overall UN effectiveness declined. This was not a bad showing for a fading hegemon.

The niggardliness of the United States with respect to financial contributions can hardly be blamed on a declining economic position, since the sums in question are paltry. Moreover, the U.S. contribution to the UN Emergency Force in the Sinai remained at 37 percent per year until 1967 (from a high of 47% in 1957). The United States paid between one half and one third of the Congo force's expenses every year between 1960 and 1964. Contributions to the force in Cyprus hovered around 40 percent per year until 1971; they rose to 50 percent for the period 1973–78.[14] On the other hand, the expenses for the three UN forces separating Israel from the Arabs since 1974 have been borne by the regular UN budget, a signal victory for the American position. In short, when it suited American interests there was a willingness to pay for UN operations in excess of the declared ceiling on contributions.

One source of the mismatch between overall declining hegemony and the continuing U.S. role in the United Nations may be in the confounding of hegemony with influence. My data on leadership clearly show that the United States no longer tried very hard to impose its conflict management preferences after 1955, though Dag Hammarskjold largely assumed those preferences for the United States for

---

[14]Data through 1971 taken from Wainhouse et al., *International Peacekeeping at the Crossroads,* pp. 535–36; data since 1971 collected from the annual reports of the UN Board of Auditors. I thank Professor M. J. Peterson for pointing me to this source.

another six years. Furthermore, after 1965 the United States had to resort to the veto to defend its interests. Was this inevitable? If the failure to exercise consistent leadership is to be associated with declining overall hegemony, it happened much too soon. Declining influence probably resulted from the appointment in the 1970s of a number of permanent representatives (Moynihan, Young, Kirkpatrick) chosen less for their abilities to build supporting coalitions than to propound America's displeasure with the Third World majority's economic and racial demands or to demonstrate America's support for national self-determination. It is quite possible that more diplomatically conservative representatives (Scranton, McHenry) could, if given the time, have reasserted American influence in building coalitions.

Unstable Alignments, Shattered Consensus

The notion of declining American influence is entirely compatible with a second hypothesis about the decay of the United Nations. As the number of voting blocs increases the simple distinction between U.S. and Soviet allies loses its salience as a constraint on behavior. It also means that, as there are more sets of national interests to be brought under a single hat, consensus comes about with greater difficulty. Therefore, winning coalitions have become more difficult to build.

This hypothesis also assumes that the early successes of the United Nations are largely explicable in terms of the importance of alignments. While effective conflict management could not be expected in situations pitting the opposing Cold War coalitions against one another, conflict management was quite possible when a member of one alignment faced a nonaligned antagonist. Moreover, this hypothesis suggests that UN effectiveness would remain respectable as long as the parties to dispute are superpowers, large powers, or smaller states under the diplomatic and military influence of a superpower. Nonaligned small states, however, escape these constraints. The increasing numbers would thus complicate conflict management because they are not reliable coalition partners and do not necessarily share the objectives of other states sufficiently to be part of a stable consensus. While the main nonimplementers of UN decisions were until 1970 the members of Cold War alignments, this is no longer true. Now the nonaligned middle and smaller powers are the culprits. In the most recent periods, the earlier explanatory power of alignments in predicting UN involvement *and* UN success no longer holds. The diplomatic and military texture of the world has perhaps grown too complex for effective collective security practices.

The Decline of Metaissues

This explanation is, in turn, entirely consistent with another hypothesis: regime effectiveness and coherence are associated with a small number of metaissues around which consensus could be built. Once these metaissues lose their relevance and if no new overarching concern develops, conflict management becomes less effective.

Decay is associated with the advent of nonaligned smaller states as the main antagonists; so is the increasing incidence of issues other than decolonization and the Cold War. The successes scored by the United Nations before 1970 were heavily concentrated on managing conflicts associated with colonial liberation movements. Now, few remain and they are recalcitrant cases. On the other hand, civil wars among rival movements in new countries, though perhaps supported by other states, cannot be considered as cases of decolonization. Global conflict may be increasing, but the issues over which countries disagree no longer fit the earlier categories. The regime has become the victim of the trend.

The Attempt to Achieve Regional Isolation

The decay of the United Nations and of the OAS has been accompanied by a slight increase in the effectiveness of the Arab League and a temporary spurt in the effectiveness of the OAU. These developments have been associated with an increase in disputes that threaten the intervention of distant and even extraregional powers and a spreading of the dispute beyond the immediate antagonists and their neighbors. This pattern suggests that, in Africa and in the Middle East, states are making an attempt to manage their conflicts in such a manner as to head off foreign intervention on a large scale, though not always successfully. It is unlikely, in view of the earlier histories of the OAU and the League, that the attempt would be made if the United Nations were perceived as an effective forum for guaranteeing isolation of disputes. Hence the decay of the United Nations with respect to consensus, the unstable alignment pattern, and the decline of metaissues are consistent with the hypothesis that these regional organizations now seek to compensate for the deficiencies of global arrangements.

Tolerance of Unresolved Conflict

These four hypotheses imply that the members of the regime display a far more tolerant attitude toward the nonresolution of conflict than the original principles and norms of the regime might have suggested, a situation predictable from the confirmation of the hypotheses. The principle of collective security is the principle of "all for one"; each state's insecurity is potentially of concern to all states. The decay of the regime demonstrates that belief in this principle has weakened during the almost forty years that have elapsed since World War II. Tolerance for the nonresolution of many conflicts, or acceptance of a certain permanent amount of conflict, is but the corollary of this weakened belief.[15] Does regime decay therefore mean that states have become indifferent to conflict and its collective management, that they have learned nothing since 1965?

The conclusion that nothing has been learned can be justified only if we assume that the purpose of the regime was to create a new international order of peace, to transform the international system of sovereign states into a supranational system ruled by the superpowers and a few large states, and to turn the United Nations and the regional entities into a single autonomous organization charged with enforcing that supranationalism. Even if, in 1945, it was hoped that the regime would prevent (or at least limit) the use of force in all of international relations, this hope was soon scaled down to the expectation of limiting only those conflicts that, because of their potential destructiveness, threaten the system of independent states. The regime was soon turned into the in-

strument for tripling the number of sovereign entities. Many of them were and are motivated by the same fear of collective insecurity that elicited the creation of the regime. The old system was reenforced, not transcended, and given the principles of the regime no new order could come from the old. No autonomous organizations developed in the field of conflict management because the members did not wish them to develop. We cannot blame the United Nations or its members for not learning an institutional lesson that calls for moral perfectibility as the metaprinciple of the evolution of international relations.

The toleration of relatively low levels of conflict, however, is itself a lesson that has been learned. No conflict that threatens the system of independent states has emerged since 1945. Even the Cold War was managed, at least until now. Governments in the 1970s have learned to tolerate a level of conflict that does not threaten the system as a whole, while the United Nations and regional organizations continue to be effective in abating many conflicts and settling a few. Regime decay is not incompatible with learning lessons at another level of consciousness. The toleration of conflict that remains diffused, con-

---

[15]Interviews with 125 high officials of the UN Secretariat and high-level members of permanent delegations to the United Nations suggest that peace is valued *less* highly as a UN objective than social justice and economic welfare, ranking ahead only of environmental protection. Moreover, the relative indifference to peace covaries with age: the younger are less concerned with peace. See Christine Sylvester, "UN Elites: Perspective on Peace," *Journal of Peace Research* 17, 4 (1980), pp. 305–24.

fined to weak states, and removed to the periphery of politics and geography may be a second-best solution to the problem of war. But it is better than making every conflict a matter of principle. Rousseau's metaphor of the staghunt retains all of its evocative power: hunting hares separately may not be as good as hunting a stag through collective effort, but it beats starving to death.

CHAPTER VI

Economic Issues

Following World War II, the international economic system was redefined by the agreements at Bretton Woods. The Bretton Woods system came to rest on three pillars: the International Monetary Fund (IMF), the World Bank, and the General Agreement on Tariffs and Trade (GATT). The IMF was designed to deal with currency exchange and balance of payments problems stemming from international trade. The World Bank was created to assist in the development process of member-states, specifically to arrange for loans to facilitate economic projects. GATT was the mechanism by which states could resolve disputes and increase the volume of international trade through the lifting of national restrictions.

There have been several important changes in the Bretton Woods system in the last forty years. For example, floating currency exchange rates have replaced fixed rates pegged to gold, and the IMF and World Bank now perform some of the other's functions. Yet, the Bretton Woods system remains largely intact. The major debates in international organizations center on whether that system should be changed further and in what ways.

The Bretton Woods system was designed by Western and largely developed states committed to the principles of capitalism; most Third World states had not yet achieved independence. The institutions underlying the system are still largely controlled by the Western economic powers, either through formal voting procedures or by virtue of their collective power in international economic relations. Third World states have argued that the current system is, at worst, designed to perpetuate the dominance of the Western countries or, at best, not designed to meet the needs of less developed states. It is the disagreement between the states of the North and the South that has increasingly dominated the agendas of international economic bodies during the past quarter century.

In order to understand the North-South conflict, it is appropriate to consider the changes in the system advocated by the Third World. Many of these demands for change have been lumped into what has been called the New International Economic Order (NIEO). Rather than a set list of policies or a definitive program, NIEO is a loose collection of often vaguely defined ideas and proposals on how the international economic system might be altered to meet Third World needs. In the first article of this section, Craig Murphy traces the history of the NIEO movement and in his words "what the Third World wants." The rest of the articles in this section at least implicitly refer back to the bases of this article.

At first glance, one might be tempted to dismiss the article by Jahangir Amuzegar as the work of an apologist for the IMF; indeed, the author is the former executive director of that organization. Nevertheless, Amuzegar provides not only a summary of the major complaints lodged against the IMF by many Third World critics, but he also does more than simply rebut the claims. At several points, he acknowledges shortcomings in the organization and identifies some possibilities for improvement. At other junctures, he effectively addresses the complaints and allows the reader to gain a more balanced view of the controversy. Finlayson and Zacher detail in their article the components of an international trade regime based on the norms and procedures established by GATT. In that article, one can ascertain not only the norms underlying the regime, but also how they have changed over time. Furthermore, the North-South conflict is apparent over a number of operational norms.

Although there is considerable debate over the current structure of the international economic system, it is not clear whether dramatic changes will be implemented. The last two articles in this section highlight the resistance to change. Ascher looks at the microdecision-making level in the World Bank. It is evident from his analysis that the bureaucracy at the World Bank has dramatic influence in setting that organization's policies. It is also apparent that the staff members are resistant to change, especially along the lines of the NIEO, which would politicize some of the economic decisions of the organization. Bureaucratic resistance is not the only impediment to change. The United Nations Conference on Trade and Development (UNCTAD) was an organization created by and invested with a Third World voting majority. It was thought that this organization would promote development in a manner consistent with the needs of the Third World. As Ramsay notes in his essay, UNCTAD has largely not fulfilled its potential. He argues that problems inside and outside UNCTAD have widened the gap between rich and poor rather than narrowing it as intended. His analysis of UNCTAD is insightful for understanding the shortcomings of the organization, but many of his criticisms are applicable to other international organizations as well.

13

WHAT THE THIRD WORLD WANTS: AN INTERPRETATION OF THE DEVELOPMENT AND MEANING OF THE NEW INTERNATIONAL ECONOMIC ORDER IDEOLOGY

Craig N. Murphy

In this article I argue that the New Order ideology results from 'consciousness raising,' and the recognition of real problems. It further suggests that Third World leaders came to their views responsibly and that international regimes can be transformed through the opening of communications that responsible global negotiations would assure. Such negotiations would in themselves serve to test the model further. . . .

THE CORE OF THE NEW INTERNATIONAL ECONOMIC ORDER IDEOLOGY

The story about what Third World governments want to achieve through their support of the NIEO ideology logically begins in the 1940s. Even though Asian, Latin American, and African states agreed with many of the principles underlying the 'new economic order' that was then being created, many of the Third World's views about post-war regimes were not taken into account in the formation of that 'new order.' During World War II, and immediately before, most of the independent governments of Latin America and the semi-autonomous local governments in Asia and Africa pursued development plans supported by interventionist foreign economic policies, including a whole range of trade and currency restrictions.[1] During the War and at its end, however, what would later be Third World governments preferred a vision of post-war international economic institutions that would allow national regulation of international economic relations while seeing to it that those national regulations conflicted with each other as little as possible.[2]

In the 1940s, this vision of the post-war institutions was, if anything, the dominant view worldwide. Representatives of the national government of Argentina and the native government of India could find what Fred Block (1977) calls 'national capitalist' spokesmen from countries like Britain and Australia agreeing that interna-

SOURCE: Reprinted from the *International Studies Quarterly,* Vol. 27, No. 1, 1983, with permission of the International Studies Association, Byrnes International Center, University of South Carolina, Columbia, S.C. 29208 USA.

tional institutions should approve of national regulation of the economy and should only serve to make the regulations that different governments desired, compatible. And, of course, Soviet officials, representing an economy that required regulation, sang the same tune.

That tune was not pleasing to the most powerful people in the most powerful country at the end of the War. The most significant American policy makers imagined post-war economic institutions as agencies that would aim to abolish national restrictions on the international economy rather than merely regulate them (*see* Gardner, 1964: 195).

The American vision became the blueprint for the institutions. Socialist states whose economies required regulation never became active members of the post-war system. Other states that had been wealthy prior to World War II went along with the development of increasingly liberal regimes because the United States assured the liberal system work by giving the previously rich market states the opportunity to reconstruct their economies.[3] Latin America and the independent and colonial areas in Asia and Africa went along with the system, while unconvinced of its value for them. But without any alternative for managing some of the global money, finance, and trade problems that they, as much as the Europeans or North Americans, felt should be managed globally, they conceded to the American vision.

The key problem confronted by Asian, African, and Latin American policy makers in the late 1940s, the problem that led to the adoption of the ideas that became the core of the New Order ideology, was how to argue for and justify those restrictions upon strictly liberal international exchange that they had used in the past and might want to continue to use as part of their industrial development policies.

The ideological milieu of the 1940s, especially within the international organizations and meetings on economic matters, really provided only two possible justifications.

1. A 'scientific' principle. If it could be shown that such economic restrictions would be the most efficient way to achieve specific economic goals, like national industrial development, then those policies could be justified by principles of economic science alone. It was to this sort of principle that Keynes and many other economists appealed when they supported the 'national capitalist' vision of post-war regimes (Block, 1977: 7–8).[4]

2. The other justification was based upon notions concerning the rights of sovereign states and their duties toward one another. These ideas were new; they had been developed during international discussions about the creation of the United Nations and the operation of the wartime 'United and Associated Nations,' the antifascist alliance.

Unlike appeals to economic science, appeals to various economic rights and duties of states never required that they be understood as the most rational principles possible; those policies had only to be the ones that could achieve some set of goals that governments were said to have the sovereign right to formulate for themselves. Supporting those goals could even be considered the *duty* of other states. The most significant version of the economic rights and duties of states formulated at the end of the War was expressed by officials of the United Nations Relief and Rehabilitation Administration (UNRRA). They argued that each state had the duty to aid the economic development of every other state, that this aid should be given no matter what political and economic disagreements a country might have with another country's economic ideology or economic policies (e.g., it was the duty of a capitalist state to aid the economic development of socialist states), and that the material extent of this obligation was directly proportional to the material differences in life from one country to another; every state had duties to aid all those states where people were materially less advantaged.[5]

In the late 1940s, Latin American, Asian, and African officials invoked the principles of states' economic rights and duties rather than the scientific principle. They made this choice because the notions about the rights and duties would

not only suggest that they had a right to employ illiberal policies, those ideas could also justify Latin American, Asian, and African claims for direct international material aid for their industrial development plans, aid similar to that given to the previously wealthy war-torn nations through UNRRA and the American Marshall Plan (Brown, 1950: 136; the *Economist*, 8 May, 1948: 782). At the earliest meetings of the United Nations, and throughout the 1940s and 50s, representatives from what would become the Third World argued both for new international economic regimes that would regulate rather than abolish national interventions *and* they argued that aid similar to that being given to Europe should be given to Asia, Africa, and Latin America, because such aid was required of wealthy states as their duty to poorer states. They justified both claims by citing UN statements defining states' rights and duties and by citing the short-lived UNRRA precedent. Latin American officials, in particular, argued that it was only fair that aid be given to them because they had contributed to European reconstruction through UNRRA in response to American appeals to the economic rights and duties of states.[6]

Thus, the core of the NIEO was formed in the 1940s when the prewar 'Third World' goal of achieving national industrial development by using as wide a range of national economic policy tools as possible appeared to be thwarted by the liberal international economic regimes that were being created. At the same time, Third World governments had available to them a particularly attractive justification for the policies that they wanted to pursue. That justification had been treated as a legitimate one by the supporters of the liberal order when they created UNRRA and later aid systems. And, more significantly, that justification suggested that other states had *moral* obligations to aid the industrial development plans that Third World states advocated. By 1950 this moral justification was already being reiterated at every international meeting on economic matters attended by delegates from Asia, Africa, and Latin America. Around it grew the entire New Order ideology.

ANALYIS OF THE WORLD ECONOMY: RESPONSE TO UNANTICIPATED PROBLEMS

Almost any conversation about the growth of the Third World's NIEO ideology brings up Raul Prebisch, his ideas about terms of trade shifting against products produced in the Third World, and his ideas about the structures of the global economy impeding Third World industrial development. Prebisch's analysis of the world economy has been invoked for the past 20 years by almost every Third World government spokesman on international economic matters. As such, his analysis was the first ma-

jor addition to those simple precepts that formed the core of the NIEO ideology.

The best way to understand why Prebisch's ideas became so important is to look at what most Third World policy makers were concerned with when they first started talking in the terms of that analysis. Although Prebisch wrote his seminal work (1950) in the late 1940s, examination of General Assembly Second (Economic) Committee debates shows that Prebisch's ideas did not become a consistent topic of general UN debate until the mid-1950s. And they did not become 'the Third World position' in the General Assembly, until the early 1960s. This timing is significant: Prebisch's ideas were not adopted as the Third World position earlier simply because they were completely compelling in their own right.

Third World governments began to adopt Prebisch's views when they first faced specific problems that those ideas helped them understand. The first time Prebisch's ideas entered the General Assembly debate they were linked to something Prebisch hardly would have been able to discuss in 1949— the effects that the formation and (later) depletion of strategic stockpiles of raw materials in the North had on Third World economies. Yet, those Northern, Korean War-era policies certainly represented an example of the situation that Prebisch wrote about: institutions at the core of the world economy having more influence on the world economy than institutions in the periphery.[7]

By the early 1960s, the Third World's trade problems included others similar to those associated with the North's use of strategic stockpiles. Since the War, while worldwide trade had expanded at unprecedented rates and had fueled world economic growth, just as the founders of the post-war system had intended, the Third World's percentage of this trade had declined. That was, if anything, just the opposite of what was expected (Pincus, 1965: 126–27). By the early 1960s most Third World governments felt cheated out of the trade-induced growth that the rich nations enjoyed just as some of the same officials had felt cheated out of the growth that could have been encouraged by continuous trade in raw materials at stable prices had it not been for the Northern stockpiling.

In response to the problem of the declining Third World trade share, most Third World representatives in the General Assembly and in GATT[8] began to articulate their resentment in the language of Prebisch's analysis. This ideological package brought with it some additional ideas like the notion that the relative value of Third World trade with the North had been declining for some time (a notion that proved to be debatable). But Prebisch's ideas certainly were not the only ones available at the time. Southern officials could have explained their economic problems in terms of the 'cultural constraints on development' popularly cited by many early Northern development economists (e.g., Rostow, 1953, 1960: 12). Instead, Third World representatives appealed to the economic rights and duties of states, and held that every government had a right to choose an economic development plan compatible with its cultural context, and that all nations should support such plans. For the South, the idea that the international community should identify 'cultural impediments to development' was ridiculous. Third World governments could have looked to domestic structures impeding development, such as those identified by Gunnar Myrdal (1956), and many states did. But such domestic structures could not become the *shared* Third World explanation for their trade income problem simply because other shared principles allowed any Southern government to reject such an explanation as being applicable to *its* domestic economy.

More significantly, Third World leaders now had an alternative *global* explanation of the source of their problems. And while supporters of the post-war system were just as upset about the declining Third World trade share, the GATT's 1958 report on the problem, written by liberal economist Gottfried Haberler, directly blamed the developed states for the declining Third World share of trade (Friedeberg, 1969: 53–56). Northern trade policies, like those associated with strategic stockpiling, created tariff and nontariff barriers to increasing the Third World's share of trade. The free trade system was not to blame according to the GATT report, but the exceptions to the system, which had been granted mostly to Northern states, were.

Why did the Prebisch thesis rather than the 'Haberler thesis' become the center of Third World New Order policy analysis? The answer has little to do with the comparative accuracy, sufficiency, or elegance of the two theses. In fact, both theories explained that key issue in exactly the same way: it was the result of the West's greater power to influence international economic relations. A new manifestation of an old pattern, said Prebisch. A violation of recently achieved liberalizations that should benefit all, said Haberler. Both theses provide sufficient explanation of the declining Third World trade share. Haberler's 'saves' liberal trade theory, easily one of the most elegant ideas any social scientist has ever invented. And Haberler's thesis certainly identifies the immediate problems of the 1960s in a more concrete way than Prebisch's ideas, invented to explain 50 years of Latin American underdevelopment, do. Why, then, did the Third World reject the Haberler thesis? Apparently Prebisch's ideas were preferable to Haberler's simply because they did not contradict the core of the New Order ideology. They were compatible with the notion that national regulation of international economic exchange was

desirable. Haberler's ideas were not.

Of course, a supporter of Haberler's point of view could argue, as many did and still do, that the core of the Third World's new ideology was irrational and that an increasingly liberal world economic system was better for everyone than a system of internationally regulated national regulations of the world economy, but someone from the Third World could counter that such a fact had never been proved: the system the Third World wanted had never been tried, and the operating system was not total liberalism, but only a partial liberalism, and only one part of a system that even liberals admitted discriminated against the Third World because power was concentrated in the North.

THE GROUP OF 77 AND THE DEMOCRATIZATION OF INTERNATIONAL RELATIONS

Prebisch's analysis of the world economy had become the official position of the growing Third World alliance by the first UNCTAD in 1964. The South presented a set of 'trade principles' based on Prebisch's views, and the vote on these demonstrated the sharp division between North and South (Moss and Winton, 1976: 43–51). Adding Prebisch's views to the Third World's ideological consensus meant more than adding an explanation of some of the unanticipated problems experienced by the Third World, it meant adding a primarily political analysis of what should be done about Third World economic problems.

The logical starting place of Prebisch's analysis, the most significant independent variable in his model of the world political economy, is the difference between the power to influence economic decisions in the center and in the periphery of the world economy. People in the center can influence most global economic decisions; people in the periphery cannot. Accepting Prebisch's thesis meant constantly searching for *new* Third World powers to influence economic relations. It meant, for example, considering the creation of producer's alliances as a legitimate way to carry out some international economic policies[9] and it meant actively and self-consciously pursuing Third World unity not only through the regional economic development schemes Prebisch's followers then supported (Cardoso, 1977), but also through more conscious development of the alliance's ideology.[10] In short, accepting Prebisch's ideas meant looking for ways to change institutions that structured and governed international trade by shifting the power over those institutions to the South.

In the late 1960s then, the South articulated its desire to gain more power over international institutions in a 'political analysis,' a view of how international economic regimes can and should be changed. Third World governments argued for the 'democratization' of international relations, meaning by that two very different, and somewhat contradictory things.

1. On the one hand, Third World officials meant that international institutions should be used to 'energize' public opinion in developed countries to support Third World goals.[11]

2. On the other hand, Third World governments argued for making more, binding international decisions 'democratically,' that is, on the basis of a one-nation, one-vote principle.[12]

The apparent contradiction of the Third World position lies in the contradictory justifications that *could* be used for these two different 'democratic' policies. Stressing the importance of public opinion suggests that popular sovereignty legitimates political decisions. Popular sovereignty could lead to very different decisions than rules based on the principle of the equal sovereignty of states, the principle that could be called upon to justify the other half of the Third World's plan for 'democratizing' international relations.

This apparent contradiction can be explained by the fact that the desire for these 'democratizing' policies reflected only a Third World desire for greater power over international economic relations and not prior principles about how decisions can be made justly. It was an extension of a policy analysis which said that the Third World should try to get more power over international economic relations in order to achieve those truly central goals of economic development. These were simply two different ways to get more power.

The mercantilist version of the American common wisdom correctly identifies this 'structural power interest' in the Third World but the common wisdom is wrong about where this interest comes from. It is not the result of some permanent inherent interest that states or individuals have in gaining or maintaining power over others, an interest that perhaps would best be masked by more pleasant ideas like 'popular sovereignty.' The conscious Third World desire for greater power over international economic decisions came as part of the analysis they adopted to help them understand and cope with a real, practical problem. Even when Third World officials in the United Nations argued that the organization should try to influence Northern public opinion, very few Southern representatives invoked 'popular sovereignty' as a justification (or mask). Most only said that they believed public opinion actually influenced decisions made by Northern governments and that they wanted the majority of the states in the United Nations to have indirect influence over those decisions.[13]

Certainly, Third World governments justified the one-nation, one-vote and UNCTAD conciliation decision-making procedures on the basis of the equal rights and duties of states, the only principles that have been at the core of the Third World ideology since it was first in-

vented. But that does not mean that arguments for such 'democratic' forms of decision making are merely a mask for the South's interest in collectively developing the power to structure international economic relations. If the South were looking for a mask under which to hide such a power interest there are principles more appealing to the North than one-nation, one-vote that could be used. For example, the South could have argued for greater influence by invoking the old claim of democratic theory mentioned earlier—the claim that greater Third World input would have assured that more of the potential problems with economic regimes could have been anticipated and avoided. Southern states did not invoke that argument because Third World governments were not *only* seeking more collective power over international economic relations. They were also still seeking that world where states would have those equal economic rights and duties, the world they had wanted since the end of World War II. And they remained quite willing to justify their proposals with their fundamental principles despite the fact that Northern governments rejected their moral force.

REITERATING THE MORAL BASIS FOR THE NIEO: RESPONSE TO UNANTICIPATED OPPORTUNITIES

The early years of the Third World's self-conscious attempts to gain greater power over international economic relations hardly suggested that the alliance gathered under the new ideology would ever achieve its goal. By the late 1960s the alliance had begun to fragment.

The alliance reunified between 1971 and 1974, seizing the opportunities created by the breakdown of the Bretton Woods system to patch-up an ideological split. In doing so, the South added a final, significant (and most often misunderstood)[14] notion to their collective ideology. This was the notion that Northern states owe something to the South as back-payments for past colonialism.

That notion was hardly new in 1971. It had split the alliance ever since more radical African governments, such as those of Guinea (UN, 1961: 49) and of Nkrumah's Ghana (UN, 1960: 35) first took it up. If restitution for colonialism were to be the only grounds for reforms in international economic institutions, then those Third World states that did not have a long experience of colonialism (e.g., Ethiopia, Liberia, or Argentina) could claim no right to have the institutions changed to serve their own national interests. If restitution (even for both colonialism and neocolonialism) defined the only duties of wealthy states, then some states where people were wealthy probably had *no* duty to aid poorer nations; it would be hard to identify a significant level of colonialism or neocolonialism practiced by (say) Norway, Finland, or Poland.[15]

By 1970 the debate over restitution helped split the South into 'radical' and 'moderate' camps. The radical camp included mostly Asian and African nations, non-aligned states, states that were recently independent, and other states that supported the restitution ethic. The moderate camp tended to be Latin American, aligned with the West, and included some states that had been independent longer, where people were relatively better off and whose governments rarely talked about the need for restitution for colonialism.[16]

By 1975 the issue was resolved: In the 'Charter of Economic Rights and Duties of States' (Moss and Winton, 1976: 902–06) Third World governments agreed, as they had in the 1940s, that the equal rights and duties of states made it incumbent upon all states to aid the economic development of every other state along the path chosen by its government. Nevertheless, in the debate over the NIEO, *all* Southern states began to tell former colonizers and 'neocolonialists' that they were required, by a principle of restitution, to *negotiate* the creation of a New Order.[17]

This manipulation of justifications and the resulting reunification of the Third World behind all elements of its long-standing ethic was not the result of some individual's brilliant solution to a logical problem, nor was it the result of direct bargaining and exchanges of concessions among those Third World governments that had different interests. Certainly some individuals were important—perhaps the Mexican delegate who appears in UN records as the first to raise the idea that certain Northern policies made it incumbent upon the North to negotiate a new order (UN, 1971: 79) and certainly Mexico's President, who put the 'Charter' itself on the Third World agenda. Nonetheless, those individuals could not have acted without having contemplated the political opportunities created by the first signs that the post-war global economic institutions were breaking down.

Those institutions started to break down, as Block (1977) illustrates, because of a series of problems affecting the wealthy market states, problems that the founders had not been able to anticipate and problems severe enough to lead the United States to renounce part of its leadership role in monetary matters and apply some trade restrictions universally in order to try to get some other wealthy states to bear some of the burdens of regime maintenance. These American actions, taken at the end of the summer of 1971, allowed the unity of the Third World to reemerge with a vengeance in that autumn's General Assembly session when both radical and moderate Third World governments claimed rights to receive compensation from the United States for the adverse effects of the new American economic policy. Third World governments expressed their demands not as calls for simple material transfer, but said (echoing the Mexican delegate) that because the United States had ended the effective life of the post-war economic regimes, it now had a responsibility to the Third World to negotiate the creation of new regimes (UN, 1972: 27–98).

At the same time, individual oil producers and, later, OPEC as a whole, seized upon the West's growing oil dependence on some Third World states to make greater exactions. This was something not taken into account by the architects of the post-war institutions, even though the dependence of their nations on Third World oil was created, in part, by the post-war prosperity that the system helped create. With the unity of the Third World already reaffirmed, the oil price increases of 1973 and 1974 were met with enthusiasm across the South, much to the surprise and chagrin of policy makers in the North who had predicted Southern responses based on the common wisdom and knowledge of immediate Third World economic interests which were, in fact, disastrously affected by the rising prices (Singh, 1977: 6–9).

The oil price increases created a Western interest in discussing some reforms of international economic regimes with some Third World countries. The Group of 77 used that opportunity to present its entire package of proposals for a New Order once again. Surprised by the coherence and unity of Third World support for that presentation at the United Nations in 1974, many Westerners for the first time started to try to figure out what it was that the Third World wanted.

APPROPRIATE POLITICAL ACTION IN RESPONSE TO THIRD WORLD DEMANDS

What *does* the Third World want? This reading of the way the New Order ideology developed suggests that the Group of 77 wants more power over international economic regimes in order to assure that Third World countries get all the advantages of trade-induced growth that they can. Third World governments want to take part in the creation and maintenance of stable international economic regimes which would coordinate, rather than abolish, national regulations of foreign economic relations. The South believes that such national regulations are sometimes necessary, or at least useful, ways to encourage industrial development, but it also believes, just as firmly, that stable, effective international regimes are essential as well. Of course tensions and differences of opinion divide Southern governments. Now, as has always been the case, when richer Third World states face no immediate economic crises that might make them want to use trade restrictions,

they still remain interested in having the global system of coordination move toward greater liberalism. They want the North to reduce barriers to Southern industrial exports. All Third World governments, it seems, argue that international coordination of current development-related economic restrictions is a must.

One way to test these conclusions would be for Northern supporters of current regimes to unite with other states in the North and actively engage Southern governments in serious debates about how existing international economic regimes should be reformed. The history offered here of how the South came to its views, while not suggesting those views are fully justified or that the process of their development was wholly rational, does indicate that those views developed in response to real problems and that they are held in good faith. Those social theorists who provide the best arguments for recognizing the role that ideology can play in shaping social history suggest that, when we are confused about what someone means while still believing that he is acting competently and in good faith, the most efficient way to understand his interests is to ask him and to clarify them while at the same time demonstrating our willingness to cooperate with him to do things to our mutual interest.[18] That means negotiating.

Camps and Gwin's (1981) proposals for reforming international economic regimes, written under the auspices of the Council on Foreign Relations, suggest both a good idea for a new international economic order that might be acceptable to the Third World and the Northern states, and a good idea for a reasonable attitude that Northern policy makers might take toward Third World proposals. Camps and Gwin note, for example, that a vision of a world without national restrictions on international economic exchange has proved to be too optimistic, and will probably remain so. Thus, even those with a commitment to international liberalism must accept that truly effective international economic regimes should be more widely recognized as legitimate, and more justly coordinated with respect to national attempts to regulate than present regimes are. The United States' position on this fundamental issue has grown a lot closer to the Third World's, and the chances for real cooperation are that much better for it.[19]

Of course, those who believe the liberal version of the American common wisdom about the New Order ideology would not trust Third World governments to negotiate with wisdom and in good faith. Assuming that all governments should, and do, act 'rationally' on the basis of simple power and economic interests, the incompetence of Third World governments— 'proven' to liberals by Southern attachment to imperfect economic analyses—means that Third

World states would be unreliable partners in any new international economic order. The deviousness of many Third World governments—'proven' to liberals by Southern calls for 'democratizing' and 'equalizing' international economic relations while they were unwilling to democratize and equalize domestic economic relations— shows they could not negotiate in good faith.

We need not be so pessimistic. As mercantilists Krasner (1981) and Tucker (1977) both say, Third World governments have fairly good reasons for the New Order positions they have adopted. We can go even further: the history of the adoption of those beliefs suggests that those good Third World reasons are not just tactical. The theories embodied in the New Order ideology may not explain the underdevelopment of the Third World as coherently as other theories do, and they may have been adopted under the ideological constraint of prior consensus, but Third World advocates of the New Order were trying to understand real problems and they selected one of a number of equally flawed theories to do so. Likewise, even if some Third World states do advocate popular sovereignty and greater economic equality among individuals, those positions have no more been part of the ideology shared by the *alliance* which is dedicated to creating the New Order than they were part of the ideology of the alliance which created the United Nations system in the first place. Lack of concern for social democratic values may mean a government is inegalitarian or authoritarian. It need not mean a government is devious.

The mercantilists who think the Third World has good reasons for its New Order ideology, yet still maintain that the North should avoid New Order discussions, may be right. But their argument must be based on their assumptions about the ways international regimes work most effectively and not on their interpretations of Third World views. But those assumptions are also open to question. As yet, no one has done the research necessary to find out who is really right: the statists who relate the stability of international regimes to the degree they accurately reflect an underlying power structure, or those who think learning and shared ideas are more important.

NOTES

1. On Latin America *see* Gardner (1964: 109–32, 195–216) and on countries in the British Empire and Commonwealth, Bell (1958: 260–63).

2. Rothschild (1944) gives a prescient Keynesian justification for the poorer states' views. American trade negotiator Clair Wilcox's book (1949) remains the most readily available discussion of the postwar economic conferences where the Asian, Latin American, and few free African states began to state shared views.

3. Such, at least, was the view the London *Economist* took in the name of Europe after the Marshall Plan was developed (17 July, 1948: 90) and after having ridiculed the United States throughout the months between the end of the War and the development of the Plan (*see* the *Economist*, 26 Oct. 1945: 652; 22 Nov. 1947: 828).

4. Keynes's speech at the first World Bank/IMF governors' meeting exemplifies the argument (Horsefield, 1969: 123).

5. *See* UNRRA Director Fiorello La Guardia's defense of these principles (UN, 1946: 51).

6. *See* e.g. Argentina (UN, 1946: 8); Brazil (UN, 1946: 89); India (UN, 1947: 46); in a speech by later UNCTAD official and Pearson Commission member Roberto de Oliveira Campos: Brazil (UN, 1948: 168–69); and George Hakim in proposing the outline of what would become proposals for the Special UN fund for Economic Development: Lebanon (UN, 1949: 9). As these citations demonstrate, and Wilcox affirms (1949: 42), in the 1940s the Third World tended to be 'led' by the larger and wealthier states from each region. Later the most ideologically committed governments in the South would be more active and thus also appear to lead, joining but not displacing the large and wealthy states (Hart, 1982: chapter 4).

7. *See* e.g. Brazil (UN, 1950: 138), Egypt (UN, 1951: 19).

See Nwekwe's (1980: 94–107) discussion of the politics in the GATT. Nwekwe, a Nigerian, calls his discussion of the Third World response in the GATT to falling trade shares 'The Nigerian Initiative of 1961' and notes (p. 99) that Gosovic and Ruggie (1976) were apparently unaware of how the Nigerian action in the GATT was a direct antecedent of the calls for a New Order in 1974. Nwekwe's claim of Nigerian initiation of the New Order debate, while uncharacteristically simplistic, is evidence of the degree to which New Order ideas are taken very seriously by many scholars and public officials from the Third World and serves as an example of a growing genre—statements by Third World nationalist leaders and scholars attributing a special role to their particular country in creating the NIEO ideology.

8. *See* e.g. Saudi Arabia (UN, 1960: 100) and Colombia (UN, 1960: 114).

9. A statement made by Alfonso Patino of Colombia in 1963 is typical:

   Against blind respect for those (market) forces and against anachronistic trade restrictions imposed by the strongest against the weakest ranges the vigorous new ideology which inspired the convening of the (UNCTAD) conference. That ideology, which we must specify further, will constitute a new phase in the age-old struggle for the liberation of peoples and respect for human dignity (UN, 1963: 27).

10. E.g. Indonesia (UN, 1968: 2) and Tanzania (UN, 1969: 30).

11. See the Cairo Declaration of 1964 (Moss and Winton, 1976: 94) and Gosovic (1972: 57).

12. Only one state in the General Assembly challenged these proposals. Sudan objected, but only because they might not work (UN, 1969: 19). Nonetheless, an inter-Third World debate on democratic principles would have been possible. Chinweizu's (1975) account explains why (say) Sudan and Tanzania would have had different views about whether domestic democracy was good in 1969 while illustrating why few Third World governments would have then agreed with the Sudanese who were unusual in asserting that public opinion was not a major force shaping the policies of developed market states.

13. *See* e.g. MacPhee's (1979) response to Bronfenbrenner's (1976) article. Bronfenbrenner had (incorrectly) argued that the Third World position was based on an ethic of reparations. MacPhee (correctly) points out that this view has never been central to the South's position but then (incorrectly) goes on to say that the reparations argument had never been raised by UNCTAD.

14. MacPhee (1979) notes that the most important states accepting this reparations notion are Eastern European (*see* Moss and Winton, 1976: 204–07, 310–14).

15. Compare the Asian-African dominated declaration of the nonaligned (Moss and Winton, 1976: 194–205) to the Latin American influenced plan for the 1970s development decade (Moss and Winton, 1976: 856–67).

16. For a humorous account of this position *see* Ul Haq, 1976: 140–41.

17. Habermas writes about the basic efficiency of dialogue as a means of resolving confusions in his long essay on scientific methodology (1971), and in his later discussions of communication and the development of society (1979). Perwin's (1975) critique of the first essay correctly points out that for dialogue to work the people engaged in it must have faith in each other and, moreover, need to be

involved in a real, concrete relationship, acting together and not just talking.

18. While Camps and Gwin's view would be compatible with much of the NIEO Ideology and with the views of many Northern governments many issues would remain to be debated and bargained over before there could be a NIEO. A New Order resulting from such negotiations would, by no means, signal the end of basically liberal economic relations among nations or the end of a basically capitalist world-system. These are points that can perhaps be brought home best by reviewing Shoup and Minter's (1977: 264–72) radical critique of the earliest published version of Camp's argument and by noting the degree to which what she argues for is similar to what Third World spokesmen demand. Within the framework of the capitalist world-economy as a whole, the ideas behind calls for a NIEO constitute a reformist ideology and not a revolutionary one, despite what both some of the New Order's advocates and some of its conservative critics sometimes say. The compatibility of New Order views with many of Camp's views neither suggests that the New Order is merely a Third World elite sell-out, as some radicals would believe, nor that people like Camps and Gwin are sellouts to the Third World, as some American conservatives claim. Rather, that compatibility may suggest that both New Order advocates and Camps and Gwin, as well as others with similar views, like the Brandt Independent Commission (1980) or former World Bank official Paul Streeten (1981), are doing just what they say they are doing: looking for the best North-South compromise now possible.

REFERENCES

Bell, P. (1958) *The Sterling Area in the Post-War World*. Oxford: Oxford University Press.

Block, F. (1977) *The Origins of International Economic Disorder*. Berkeley: University of California Press.

Bronfenbrenner, M. (1976) 'Predatory Poverty on the Offensive: The UNCTAD Record.' *Economic Development and Cultural Change* 24:825–31.

Brown, W. A. Jr. (1950) *The United States and the Restoration of World Trade*. Washington: Brookings.

Camps, M. and C. Gwin (1981) *Collective Management: Reform of Global Economic Organization*. New York: McGraw-Hill.

Cardoso, F. (1977) 'The Originality of a Copy: CEPAL and the Idea of Development.' *CEPAL Review* 2nd Half: 7–40.

Chinwizu (1975) 'The Cult of Liberal Democracy,' in *The West and the Rest of Us*. New York: Random House.

Friedeberg, A. S. (1969) *UNCTAD 1964: The Theory of the Peripheral Economy at the Center of Global Discussion*. Rotterdam: University of Rotterdam Press.

Gardner, L. C. (1964) *Economic Aspects of New Deal Diplomacy*. Madison: University of Wisconsin Press.

Gosovic, B. (1972) *UNCTAD: Conflict and Compromise*. Leiden: A. W. Sifthoff.

Gosovic, B. and J. Ruggie (1976) 'On the Creation of the New International Economic Order: Issue Linkage and the Seventh Special Session of the United Nations General Assembly.' *International Organization* 30, 2:309–345.

Habermas, J. (1971) 'Knowledge and Human Interests: A General Perspective,' in *Knowledge and Human Interests*. Boston: Beacon.

Habermas, J. (1979) *Communication and the Evolution of Society*. Boston: Beacon.

Hart, J. (1982) *Political Forces in the Global Economy: Explaining Negotiations for the New International Economic Order*. London: Macmillan.

Horsefield, J. K. (1969) *The International Monetary Fund: 1945–1965*. Washington: IMF.

Independent Commission (1980) *North-South: A Programme for Survival*. Cambridge: MIT Press.

Krasner, S. (1974) 'Oil is the Exception.' *Foreign Policy* No. 14: 68–83.

Krasner, S. (1980) 'The United Nations and the Struggle for Control of North-South Relations.' Unpublished paper. Department of Political Science, University of California, Los Angeles.

Krasner, S. (1981) 'Transforming International Regimes: What the Third World Wants and Why.' *International Studies Quarterly* 25: 119–48.

MacPhee, C. (1979) 'Martin Bronfenbrenner on UNCTAD and the GSP.' *Economic Development and Cultural Change* 27:357–63.

Moss, A. and H. Winton (1976) *A New International Economic Order: Selected Documents, 1945–1975*. New York: UNIPUB.

Myrdal, G. (1956) *Development and Underdevelopment*. Cairo: National Bank of Egypt.

Nwekwe, G. A. (1980) *Harmonization of African Foreign Policies 1955–1975: The Political Economy of African Diplomacy*. African Research Studies No. 14. Boston: African Studies Center, Boston University.

Perwin, C. (1975) 'Habermas and Psychoanalytic Epistemology.' Paper presented at the annual meeting of the Southern Political Science Association.

Pincus, J. (1967) *Trade, Aid, and Development*. New York: Council on Foreign Relations.

Prebisch, R. (1950) *The Economic Development of Latin America and Its Principle Problems*. Lake Success: United Nations.

Rostow, W. W. (1953, 1960) *The Process of Economic Growth*. Oxford: Oxford University Press.

Rothschild, K. W. (1944) 'The Small Nation in World Trade.' *Economic Journal* 54: 26–37.

Shoup, L. H. and W. Minter (1977) *Imperial Brain Trust,* New York: Monthly Review Press.

Singh, J. S. (1977) *A New International Economic Order*. New York: Praeger.

Streeten, P. (1981) 'Constructive Responses to the North-South Dialogue,' in Edwin Reuben (ed.), *The Challenge of the New International*

Economic Order. Boulder: Westview.

Tucker, R. W. (1977) *The Inequality of Nations.* New York: Basic Books.

Ul Haq, M. (1976) *The Poverty Curtain.* New York: Columbia University Press.

UN General Assembly (1946–1974) , *Summary Records of the Meetings the Second (Economic) Committee.*

Wilcox, C. (1949) *A Charter for World Trade.* New York: Macmillan.

14

THE IMF UNDER FIRE

by Jahangir Amuzegar

The global economic challenges of the 1980s—the colossal debt overhang, wild swings in exchange rates, and continued imbalances in external payments—have presented the International Monetary Fund (IMF) with the immense task of devising orderly and effective solutions. And they have focused unprecedented attention on the organization. Thrown suddenly and inadvertently into the epicenter of the world economic crises after the 1973–1974 oil price shocks, the IMF has gradually, and erroneously, come to be seen as the world's master economic troubleshooter. A limited-purpose organization, conceived in 1944 to deal with 1930s-style exchange and payments problems, the Fund has recently been pushed by circumstances into becoming a super-

agency in charge of the global debt and development problems of the 1970s and 1980s—tasks for which it has neither adequate expertise nor sufficient resources.

The IMF still enjoys the support and respect of many multinational economic organizations, bankers, business leaders, government officials, and academics in both industrialized and developing countries. But misconceptions and unrealistic expectations have prompted harsh and often distorted criticisms from other quarters, especially the media.

Initially confined to some left-leaning fringe elements in the Third World, recent attacks on the Fund have been echoed by a curious coalition—including some U.N. agencies—that defies both North-South and Left-Right divides.

SOURCE: Jahangir Amuzegar, "The IMF Under Fire." Reprinted with permission from *Foreign Policy* 64 (Fall 1986). Copyright © 1986 by the Carnegie Endowment for International Peace.

Critics from the less-developed countries (LDCs) and their supporters paint the IMF as a highly rigid, single-minded, biased institution dominated by a cabal of industrial countries. These critics accuse the Fund of following a narrow, free-market approach to external imbalances and contend that the Fund shows little or no concern that its adjustment policies often cripple economic growth and further skew income distribution in Third World countries. They also think that the IMF is cruelly indifferent to the social and political consequences of its stabilization programs.

Fund detractors in industrialized countries criticize the IMF for being insufficiently market oriented; for helping noncapitalist and anti-Western countries; and for progressively evolving into a soft-headed foreign-aid agency.

Some observers from both sides of the North-South divide claim that Fund-supported adjustment programs, by checking demand in many countries simultaneously, give a deflationary bias to the world economy as a whole.

Some skeptics see no useful role for the IMF under the present world economic order. A few believe that the Fund's existence blocks the Third World's economic interests; others argue that, in a world of floating exchange rates, the IMF—which was devised to ensure currency stability—has no part left to play. A hodgepodge of consumerists, religious activists, and neo-liberals oppose the Fund because the IMF allegedly bails out big multinational banks, favors the rich, helps big business, and supports dictatorial regimes. Some old-line conservatives and free-market ideologues disapprove of the IMF because they generally oppose public intervention of any kind in the economy. And monetarist critics of the U.S. Federal Reserve Bank would like to dismantle anything that seems like an international central bank.

There are Western analysts who believe that Fund programs and facilities—increasingly tailored for and used by the LDCs—no longer benefit industrialized countries. Other radical critics, such as the political economist Cheryl Payer, believe that only a radical restructuring of the international economic system will solve today's international economic problems. They believe that Fund assistance frustrates the very type of economic discipline and financial autonomy LDCs need to break out of "imperialism's grip."[1]

Many analysts, by contrast, urge major reforms of the Fund. Some conservatives want the IMF to be stricter with borrowing countries. Their liberal counterparts emphasize creating a more Third World-oriented Fund.

---

[1]See, for example, Cheryl Payer, *The Debt Trap* (New York: Monthly Review Press, 1975).

Five aspects of the relationship between the IMF and its LDC clients dominate the debate over the organization: the Fund's philosophy and principal objectives; its approach to economic stabilization in deficit countries; the conditions attached to the use of Fund resources; the costs of domestic economic adjustment; and the IMF's alleged biases in the application of its policies and programs.

Critics accuse the IMF of deviating from its principles and objectives as contained in its Articles of Agreement. They include a call for "the promotion and maintenance of high levels of employment and real income." The Fund, they argue, favors internal and external stability in deficit member countries at the expense of economic growth and full employment. Most LDC-oriented critics would like to see the IMF facilitate capital flows and encourage stabilization and expansion of trade in the primary commodities that many Third World countries depend on for export earnings. Many also would like to see more IMF control over the creation, distribution, and management of global liquidity, and more Fund authority over worldwide capital flows, the domestic policies of reserve-currency countries, and external debt issues. The positions taken by the Third World blocs in the United Nations Conference on Trade and Development, the U.N. General Assembly, and the Fund's Interim Committee and its annual meetings point in the same direction.

These critics argue that at its birth, the Fund was expected to deal with problems of the developed countries. Since no major industrial country currently uses Fund resources or is expected to tap them in the near future, the Fund should now cater to its new, Third World, clientele.

The Fund staff rejects allegations of a vested interest in restoring external balances at the expense of other objectives such as employment and growth. The IMF maintains that its stabilization programs are designed to ensure domestic price stability and a sustainable external balance, and are, in fact, the very ingredients of increased domestic production, more jobs, and larger incomes. By improving the allocation and use of internal resources like capital and labor, Fund programs help a country increase its productive capacity over the long term.

Additionally, the Fund has adapted its role and its policies to the perceived needs of its LDC membership by developing special facilities such as the buffer stock financing facility, the extended fund facility, the subsidy account, the supplementary financing facility, the cereal imports facility, the Trust Fund, and the latest structural adjustment facility.

DEFINING RESPONSIBILITIES

The debate here seems largely a matter of nuance and emphasis rather than basic philosophy. The Fund's argument is that, within the Bretton Woods framework for postwar stability and development, its global task has been to serve as a monetary and financial agency, dealing with short-term gaps in external payments, exchange fluctuations, and capital flows. Its added responsibility for economic expansion and larger productive capacity in the Third World, the IMF emphasizes, must be achieved by encouraging balanced growth in international trade and by evening out short-term capital movements, not by dispensing aid.

Economic stabilization under the IMF's standard "monetarist" model sees short-term external balance as a precondition for long-term growth. But many liberal critics insist that IMF programs must speed up economic growth and thereby achieve a viable balance of payments by stimulating supply instead of reducing demand. They believe that growth is a condition for adjustment.

According to these critics, the Fund's model subverts LDC's development strategy in many ways. Essentially, they claim that the IMF view blames inflation on excess aggregate demand while the real culprits are structural bottlenecks in the agricultural, foreign trade, and public sectors; supply shortages due to unused capacity; and other nonmonetary problems common in developing countries. Thus combating inflation and external imbalances by choking off demand—by devaluing currency, reducing credit subsidies and imports, and raising taxes—results in depressing the economy instead. Economic stability requires removing supply bottlenecks by reallocat-

ing investment, cutting taxes, and somehow restraining prices and wages.

But the record of the IMF shows that as the nature and causes of the initial problems differ widely in different countries, so do the Fund's policy recommendations. A 1986 Fund staff study, *Fund-Supported Adjustment Programs and Economic Growth,* by Mohsin S. Kahn and Malcolm D. Knight, reiterates that Fund-supported adjustment programs comprise three distinct features: demand-side policies aimed at cooling an overheated economy, supply-side measure designed to expand domestic output, and exchange-rate incentives to improve a country's external competitiveness. For example, IMF programs in Gabon, Panama, Peru, and South Korea during the late 1970s and early 1980s did emphasize demand restraint. But similar programs in Burma and Sri Lanka encouraged an increase in the rate of public investment and the liberalization of imports. In Gabon, Panama, Peru, South Korea, and Sri Lanka, the objective was to increase supply by using excess capacity, improving external competitiveness, or boosting private or public investment.

According to a 1985 Fund report, *Adjustment Programs in Africa,* IMF staff members Justin B. Zulu and Saleh M. Nsouli show that IMF programs in 21 African countries strove to tailor each country's adjustment policies to that country's specific circumstances. While most programs aimed at increasing growth, reducing inflation, and improving balance of payments, considerable flexibility was shown with regard to budgetary deficits, credit expansion, inflation rates, and import volume. According to the same study, all stabilization programs in recent years have emphasized both supply- and demand-oriented policies. The former, addressing exchange rates, prices, interest rates, investment incentives, and efficiency of public enterprises, have all been conducive to growth.

A review of some 94 Fund-supported programs in 64 countries during the 1980–1984 period, prepared by Charles A. Sisson and published in the March 1986 issue of *Finance and Development,* shows a distinct variety of approaches to the adjustment problem and a wide range of policy measures. Although nearly all programs contained limits on credit expansion and government current expenditures, only 55 per cent included measures related to currency values and external trade liberalization; 41 per cent required a cap on or reduction in consumer subsidies; and a mere 28 per cent dealt with budgetary transfers to nonfinancial public enterprises. Even some of the Fund's more knowledgeable critics, such as the economist Graham Bird, clearly admit that "it is far too simplistic and inaccurate to claim that the Fund is a doctrinaire monetarist institution."[2]

Critics who concede that the Fund's primary objective is restoring short-term external balance still assail its approach to adjustment. They maintain that the Fund perceives LDC balance-of-payments deficits, foreign-exchange shortages, budgetary gaps, supply crunches, declining rates of productivity, inflation, and black markets to be largely of domestic origin—the result of economic mismanagement, overspending, exorbitant social welfare programs, and price controls. Domestic inflation and balance-of-payments deficits, in turn, are allegedly traced by the Fund to excessive consumption, insufficient investment, excessive import levels reflecting increased aggregate demand and caused by large budget gaps and loose credit, and anemic export earnings due to domestic inflation and overvalued currencies.

These critics maintain that LDC external imbalances are in fact frequently caused by a host of other external factors beyond LDC control that have nothing to do with domestic waste or inflation: oil prices, artificially stimulated rapid growth through easy credit, worldwide inflation, declining demand for commodities, deteriorating terms of trade and protectionism, rising real rates of interest on foreign debt, and poor harvests. The Fund is thus blamed for believing that deficits—no matter how they are

---

[2]Graham Bird, "Relationship, Resource Uses, and the Conditionality Debate," in *The Quest for Economic Stabilization,* ed. Tony Killick (New York: St. Martin's Press, 1984), 179.

caused—call for adjustment, and that adjustment must focus on the deficits, whether temporary or persistent.

The Fund is also often accused of identifying the adjustment's success with improvements in the trade or current account balance— an interpretation that the critics see not only as tautological but also as harmfully misleading. For improvements in the trade balance, they argue, result overwhelmingly from cuts in imports, not necessarily in big increases in exports. Such drastic and unsustainable cuts in foreign purchases not only limit LDC's current and future output levels, they also hurt LDC trading partners, who end up losing markets. The real adjustment, say the critics, must be structural, involving such permanent changes as a shift in the composition of production and demand to boost export earnings and reduce dependence on imports.

The Fund's critics are right in claiming that it always insists on adjustment regardless of the nature or origin of the external balance. But the Fund also has an equally valid position in arguing that the need for adjustment is a pragmatic necessity, not the reflection of any dogma. In the March 1986 issue of *Finance and Development,* IMF Managing Director Jacques de Larosière observes that countries with soaring inflation, enormous fiscal deficits, huge and wasteful public sectors, money-losing public enterprises,

distorted exchange rates, and low interest rates are unlikely to mobilize domestic savings or attract foreign investment, and are bound to crowd out domestic resources in a way that will hurt growth. Without adjustment, writes Fund staff member Wanda Tseng, external and internal imbalances eventually will deplete the country's international reserves, erode its international creditworthiness, dry up access to foreign funds, and result in the stoppage of needed imports.[3]

With regard to the origin of external deficits, Fund critics seem bent on constructing a general thesis out of isolated cases. Some, but not all, balance-of-payments gaps are clearly caused by factors outside a country's control. In the case of Jamaica, for example, even one of the Fund's most astute critics admits that during the 1972–1980 period domestic policies and structural factors were the prime culprits behind the excess demand and the worsening payments position. Nor was imported inflation found to be a "major cause" of the island's deteriorating economy. In general, the authorities declined to adopt unpopular adjustment measures necessitated by their own profligate fiscal and monetary policies. Another IMF critic attributed Indonesia's 1965–1966 crisis mainly to hyperinflation between 1962 and 1966 resulting from government deficit financing. Even in Kenya between 1974 and 1981, where major

[3]Wanda Tseng, "The Effects of Adjustment," *Finance and Development,* December 1984, 2–5.

external factors—mainly the two oil shocks—were at work, domestic monetary forces and the mismanagement of the coffee and tea boom had to bear their share of responsibility.[4]

The critics, however, seem to have a strong point in arguing that, for most of the deficit-ridden LDCs, the external shocks of the 1970s and the early 1980s almost totally altered the fundamental assumptions on which their medium-term economic planning was based. A completely different type and direction of adjustment was required for many of these countries, such as a much bigger shot of capital and much more stimulation of supply, instead of routine belt tightening.

IMF BIASES

A much stronger and more vituperative attack is aimed at the Fund's conditions for making its resources available. The main condition—a "viable" payments position—is defined as a current account deficit that can be sustained by capital inflows on terms compatible with a country's development prospects without resorting to restrictions on trade and payments, which add to rather than correct the existing distortions.

Almost all critics agree on the need for some conditionality. The quarrel, then, is about the types of conditions needed. At the macroeconomic level, the IMF's "draconian" approach and "shock treatment" are blamed for hindering economic growth, raising unemployment, lowering the already low Third World standards of living, ravaging the poorest of the poor, and seriously undermining the country's capacity for realistic adjustment.[5] Even in countries committed to adjustment and stabilization, the critics point out, formidable constraints—internal political friction, inadequate central financial control mechanisms, pressure groups or broader public resistance, and bureaucratic inefficiencies—make Fund measures hard to swallow.

Fund-prescribed microeconomic remedies are considered by the critics particularly ill-conceived, if not downright harmful. Devaluation is regarded as inherently regressive because it raises the costs of essential imports, leaves untouched exports subject to extremely low supply elasticities, and adds to domestic inflation. Higher interest rates are judged irrelevant in the context of Third World economies because so much credit goes to the public sector, because private sav-

---

[4]Jennifer Sharpley, "Jamaica, 1972–80," Mary Sutton, "Indonesia, 1966–70," and Tony Killick, "Kenya, 1975–81," in *The IMF and Stabilization,* ed. Tony Killick (New York: St. Martin's Press, 1984).

[5]See Chuck Lane, "Dunning Democracy," *The New Republic,* 4 June 1984, 9–12; and Richard E. Feinberg and Valeriana Kallab, eds., *Adjustment Crisis in the Third World* (Washington, D.C.: Overseas Development Council, 1984).

ers are usually few and insignificant, and because capital flight has little to do with interest-rate differentials. Reduced real wages, lower subsidies for the poor, and cutbacks on other social welfare programs are regarded as the nemeses of sociopolitical stability. Credit restrictions are thought to reduce employment rather than inflation.

The IMF responds by arguing that conditions are neither rigid nor inflexible and that they are designed jointly with the member country. IMF conditions are applied flexibly as well, with varying socioeconomic circumstances taken into account. The periodic review of Fund programs confirms the agency's interest in ensuring sufficient flexibility. Further, the IMF's approach to balance of payments does not work only through demand deflation and real-income reduction. The relationship between monetary factors and external imbalances is important, but the IMF approach embraces all aspects of economic policies, bearing on both demand and supply conditions. Finally, although restoring the external balance is admittedly a Fund objective, it is not the sole purpose of adjustment. The IMF believes that adjustment ultimately encourages high employment and long-term growth by balancing aggregate demand and supply better.

Fund programs are also often blamed for their allegedly high social and economic costs. The critics argue that, despite its best efforts, the IMF can hardly avoid politics. National strikes, riots, political up-

heavals, and social unrest in Argentina, Bolivia, Brazil, the Dominican Republic, Ecuador, Egypt, Haiti, Liberia, Peru, Sudan, and elsewhere have been attributed directly or indirectly to the implementation of austerity measures advocated by the IMF.

The companion charge of undermining national sovereignty and political democracy in Third World countries follows from the social frictions and imbalances that austerity allegedly brings. LDC governments add that the Fund does not quite appreciate the political risks involved in applying the IMF recipe.

Conditionality is also thought to undermine fair income redistribution. The argument maintains that the Fund's adjustment programs almost always require a cut in both public and private consumption, in order to transfer resources to investment and the export sector. Critics frequently argue that the heaviest and most immediate burdens of adjustment are likely to be passed by the upper and middle classes to the poor. The Fund's alleged insistence on reducing or eliminating food and other consumer subsidies is further attacked on the ground that these policies are in fact a rational means of internal income redistribution in countries lacking an effectively progressive tax system or adequate social security schemes.

Fund supporters argue that blaming the IMF for fomenting political unrest merely confuses cause and effect. Many countries do not come to the IMF until the seeds of political turmoil are firmly rooted in their soil. Indeed, economics-related civil disturbances are hardly unknown in countries without Fund programs—witness Iran, Nigeria, South Africa, and Tunisia. And scores of countries adjusting with the IMF's assistance have been remarkably stable. Of the 67 countries that carried a stabilization program at some period between 1980 and 1983, critics can single out only the 10 mentioned previously as having experienced serious turmoil—not all of it Fund-related. Nevertheless, the unrest that can be blamed on the IMF must be considered a minus for adjustment policies.

Finally, the Fund is charged with harboring biases toward capitalism and against government planning and economic intervention. Worse, it is called an agent of neocolonialization for the West. More moderate critics accuse the Fund of an ideological slant that results in the scrapping of public enterprises, the abandonment of price controls, the reduction of food subsidies and free medical and educational facilities, and the elimination of social services from already deprived populations.

The Fund is also alleged to discriminate in its treatment of poor and rich members. LDC supporters claim that the Fund opposes as distortions of the free market such policies as exchange restrictions, wage-price controls, rationing, and subsidies when pursued by the developing countries. Yet the IMF is virtually impotent in the fight against similar practices by its industrial members. Critics additionally see a perceived asymmetry in treatment between reserve-currency centers (and surplus countries) on the one hand and the rest of the world on the other. This asymmetry is considered not only inconsistent in itself, but also crucial in shifting the onus of adjusting external imbalances to deficit LDCs. Reserve-currency countries like the United States, it is alleged, cannot be pressured by the IMF to adjust, and can continue their profligate ways year after year.

Finally, critics see an IMF political bias that is reflected in sympathy and leniency toward regimes pivotal to the economic, military, strategic, or geopolitical interests of the United States or other major Fund shareholders, and toward countries with international economic clout because of enormous debts that threaten the global monetary system.[6] To prove this political bias, critics such as staff members of the Center for International Policy claim that proposed IMF loans to "countries from the wrong side of the track," including Grenada before the U.S. invasion,

[6]See, for example, Amir Jamal, "Power and the Third World Struggle for Equilibrium," in *Banking on Poverty: The Global Impact of the IMF and World Bank,* ed. Jill Torrie (Toronto: Between the Lines, 1983); and Ismaïl-Sabri Abdalla, "The Inadequacy and Loss of Legitimacy of the IMF," *Development Dialogue,* 1980, no. 2: 25–53.

Nicaragua, and Vietnam, have been vetoed by major shareholders for "technical reasons." Credit for others, such as El Salvador and South Africa, is routinely approved.

Yet Fund members today include countries with distinctly nonmarket philosophies. Any penchant toward the market simply reflects the belief that market allocations are more efficient. On the question of discriminatory treatment of the poor, the dividing line is not poverty but the balance-of-payments situation. Surplus or reserve countries may indeed escape the Fund's strict discipline. After all, they have no need for Fund resources. But this is a choice open also to poor countries, which can decide not to approach the IMF. Further, some of the rich deficit countries that have drawn on the Fund in the past, such as Great Britain, France, and Italy, have been similarly treated.

It is no secret that the IMF statutes and covenants expect the Fund to promote a world of free markets, free trade, and unitary exchange rates under a multilateral payments system. To allow any different course of action would place the IMF in violation of its legal mandate.

Yet not only do such centrally planned economies as China, Hungary, Romania, and Yugoslavia enjoy full IMF membership and make ample use of its resources without any encumbrances or impositions, but some left-of-center govern-

ments, in fact, have in the past benefited more from Fund assistance than supposedly favored regimes. By one key measure, Jamaica, under then Prime Minister Michael Manley's democratic socialist regime in 1979, was the world's largest recipient of Fund resources, receiving 360 per cent of its quota compared with only 64 per cent for other developing countries.[7]

The Fund adamantly maintains that its Articles of Agreement specifically prohibit political considerations for the use of its resources. Yet the charges of political bias deserve closer scrutiny. The Fund's ability to maintain absolute neutrality is, to be sure, affected by the interests of influential member governments, by the decisions of the executive board to grant or deny loans to a given country, and by the evaluation reports and recommendations of staff missions on a country's underlying economic conditions.

Major shareholding governments obviously have political, strategic, and economic interests in their own zones of influence or involvement and do not wish to separate economic from political and other considerations. The U.S. Congress, for example, explicitly requires that the American executive director at the Fund vote in a prescribed manner in regard to certain countries and regimes. Other major governments may have similar predilections, but are not quite prepared to legislate them.

---

[7]Sharpley, "Jamaica, 1972–80," in *IMF and Stabilization,* 160.

The executive board has a mixed position. Its members are appointed or elected by developed or developing member governments, to whom they are beholden. They, too, cannot be purely apolitical robots. They lobby for their views among their colleagues; they try to win over management and staff; and they endeavor to protect the political and other interests of their constituencies. At the same time, board members are required and expected to uphold the Fund's basic objectives and to ensure the proper functioning of the international monetary system. In neither of these two capacities can the executive directors as a whole be found to be practicing a distinct, or immutable, political bias. The burden of proof is still on the critics to show that many IMF decisions are made deliberately according to political considerations. Significantly, the IMF staff has never been accused of partisan political bias.

The issue of inherent bias against the poor is more intractable. In general, allegations that the Fund's reluctance to suggest specific national redistributive priorities is of no help to the poor and the powerless may have a certain moral validity. It is also true that the objective of better income distribution, or at least of proportionate sacrifices, is not explicitly included in a country's letter of intent as a condition for Fund assistance. But claims that the IMF is indifferent to such factors are grossly unfair.

More important, the critics' ardent contention that the cost of adjustment is always borne disproportionately by the poor has seldom been supported by any statistical evidence. Rather, there is usually an a priori presumption that Fund programs aggravate income inequities because the rich and the strong see to it that they avoid the effects of the stabilization measures. The arguments have been at best theoretical, and usually anecdotal. The countless books, articles, speeches, and statements critical of the Fund contain not a single piece of empirical information or statistical data showing that Fund-supported programs have, in a clear and convincing manner, aggravated internal income-distribution patterns.

Moreover, the impact of IMF programs on income distribution essentially depends on how the program is implemented by national authorities. In the Fund's view, any other approach would entangle the IMF directly in microeconomic policy measures closely related to a country's social and political choices. Such involvement probably would be vehemently resisted by most countries, and would also violate the Fund's own mandate and guidelines.

In addition, the Fund believes that changes in income distribution as such cannot be performance criteria in adjustment programs because this area is so difficult to quantify. The numbers can be affected by methods of classifying income recipients. Further, few programs last long enough to allow a comprehensive study of their distributional implications, particularly where necessary information on consumption, government transfers, nonmonetary sources of income, and personal income levels is inadequate or unreliable—as is generally the case in developing countries. Finally, the Fund maintains that any given domestic distributional system is the product of deep-rooted economic, social, political, and cultural phenomena going back decades, if not centuries. Fund programs, being of relatively limited scope and duration, cannot be expected to make much of a dent in the system.

In the absence of clear-cut evidence and good data, theoretical arguments do assume importance. In the short run, stabilization programs can worsen income distribution. But the story scarcely ends there. The distributional outcome of a cut in government outlays, for example, depends on where the specific reductions are made. A reduction of food subsidies to urban workers could help the rural poor by raising farm prices. A tax on urban services and amenities could likewise redistribute income from workers in modern industries—a minority in the labor force—to the rural poor. Moreover, a reduction in inflation itself tends to favor poorer groups because they can rarely adjust their incomes to rising prices.

An IMF study, *Fund-Supported Programs, Fiscal Policy, and Income Distribution,* concludes, after presenting some case studies, that Fund programs have not been directed against the poor; often, in fact, policies have been designed to protect low-income groups as much as possible. Even when total consumption has been reduced through prudent demand-management policies, high-income groups probably have been hit hardest. The elimination of large general subsidy programs has inflicted some hardships on the population as a whole, including the poor. But the study calls such programs "inefficient and ineffective" mechanisms for redistributing incomes.

SOME SUCCESS STORIES

Some Fund detractors are quick to denigrate the IMF's achievements in the Third World and cite Mexico in particular as a blatant example of the failure of the adjustment formula. More moderate critics admit that Fund programs have succeeded in improving the balance of payments in several countries. But they contend that other significant benefits have not followed.

Yet the overall track record of IMF programs shows some noteworthy accomplishments. An independent 1984 study by the German Federal Parliament, *The Conditionality Policy of the IMF,* shows that although the current account deficits of all non-oil-developing countries (NODCs) tended to expand between 1970 and 1980, most Fund-assisted countries managed to close those gaps perceptibly. The inflation rate for all NODCs increased during that period, while the tempo in countries with adjustment programs was slower. Countries undergoing adjustment experienced sharper decreases in short term growth than the group as a whole, but their long-term expansion rates were above average. Finally, the report noted, the increase in real consumption in program countries was only slightly less on average—4.3 per cent as opposed to 4.7 per cent annually—than in the whole group.

According to the aforementioned 1985 IMF study of the 21 African countries where the IMF had an ongoing program from 1981 to 1983, economic growth targets were achieved in about one-fifth of the countries, inflation targets were reached in roughly one-half of the cases, and the balance-of-payments goals were reached in about two-fifths of these states.

At first glance, improvements under Fund-supported programs may show that the IMF's advice is often better suited to containing inflation and rectifying external imbalances than to fostering growth. But some short-term consolidation in the growth tempo may in fact be necessary for longer-term expansion. And although the success stories may not be numerous or seem spectacular or even truly impressive to the hostile critics, they nonetheless tend to contradict the allegations that Fund programs bring few, if any, benefits to LDCs. Moreover, these detractors frequently fail to ask where these countries would be without the IMF.

Still, it is disturbing that, despite its valiant rescue efforts across the Third World, the IMF is hard pressed to show more than a few clearly viable programs out of the roughly three dozen under its wing. Why haven't the programs done better?

One answer is that the IMF's latest perennial clients have been among either the poorest LDCs with large balance-of-payments disequilibriums, or the newly industrializing countries with gargantuan external debts. Adjustment has been made more difficult by outside factors such as high energy costs, high interest rates, world recessions, and protectionism.

Second, IMF programs often bring some concealed problems into the open, making partial success look like a setback and partial recovery like a retrogression. In a country living beyond its means, the real causes of payments difficulties—such as overvalued currencies, artificially low prices, and virtual rationing, as evidenced by shortages and black markets—are rarely acknowledged. When Fund programs begin to remove some of the existing distortions and dislocations through cost-price adjustments, the economic weaknesses that these policies hid or suppressed begin to emerge for all to see.

Third, the worse a country's problems, the harder it will be for IMF programs to succeed. The host government's cooperation is crucial as well. A 1984 Fund study showed a "striking" correlation between the success of IMF programs and the observance of policy measures by the governments concerned.[8]

Fourth, most of the Fund-assisted countries that have been less than successful are those that had long postponed adjustment efforts. As stabilization is delayed, distortions become solidified, and rectification becomes correspondingly costlier and more painful. It literally pays economically, socially, and politically to go to the IMF early.

In no other North-South debate has the so-called dialogue of the deaf been so evident as in that over the IMF. The biggest reason for the critics' persistence is surely the Fund's patchy track record. The increasing number of cases where disbursement of standby credits has been suspended because of noncompliance with Fund criteria, and the growing number of members declared ineligible for further assistance because of long overdue financial obligations, show that the path of the Fund-supported programs has been neither short nor smooth.

Indeed, in spite of prolonged use of Fund programs by certain members, economic imbalances persist for many internal and external reasons. Fund successes in other countries also have often been temporary.

But if the IMF cannot or will not influence domestic priorities, such as the size of military budgets or the pattern of income distribution, that have a major impact on the economy, why, the critics ask, impose an austerity program that skirts these problems? The same question is prompted by the IMF's inability to do much about external problems, such as protectionism or foreign recessions, that lie beyond the control of deficit LDCs and that can often make or break a country's prospects. If the IMF's conditional assistance produces no more than certain short-term improvements in the country's external balances and some temporary reductions in the rate of inflation at the cost of growth, full employment, social welfare, and self-reliance, is it worth the attendant sacrifices?

Convincing answers to these questions are not easy to come by because all these critical inquiries seem to miss two crucial points. First, what other choices do LDCs facing deteriorating debt and development problems have? Second, putting aside the merits of the critics' arguments or of the Fund's defense, are there other practical and effective policies that the IMF, as presently constituted, can pursue?

Debt-strapped countries incapable of paying their external bills and unable or unwilling to adopt Fund-supported adjustment programs have three alternatives: repudiate external debt altogether and seek to

---

[8]Justin B. Zulu and Saleh M. Nsouli, "Adjustment Programs in Africa," *Finance and Development,* March 1984, 7.

start afresh; seek bilateral accommodations with bondholders; or go it alone.

An outright repudiation, or even a debt moratorium, obviously would release resources for more urgent outlays. But it might close off larger and more valuable access to foreign reserves, assets, credits, markets, and technology. For this reason, even the poorest African countries assembled for the July 1985 Organization of African Unity summit refused to endorse any suggestion of wholesale default. Nor did Cuban Premier Fidel Castro's similar proposal for Latin America attract any takers.

The second alternative is appealing, but except for a very few lucky and resourceful countries, foreign creditors usually ask LDC debtors to accept the Fund's discipline before engaging in debt renegotiations or extending new credits. The consequences of doing nothing, the third alternative, would be further economic deterioration and perhaps a need for stricter adjustment efforts. In the Fund's view, the costs of nonadjustment by any measure will probably greatly exceed those of adjustment.

The IMF, in its turn, can adapt to external realities and the critics' challenges in four ways: by increasing its resources and expanding both the scope and the number of its special LDC facilities to serve its Third World members better; by revising its rules and statutes to become more adjustment-oriented toward its developed members and comparatively more finance-directed toward LDCs; by abdicating its structural adjustment role in the LDC economies in favor of the World Bank; or by doing nothing.

A Fund with twice as much liquidity could accommodate its LDC members with less painful adjustment programs. The Fund also could revise its rules to improve more decisively its role in overseeing the exchange-rate system, its surveillance capabilities over the surplus and reserve-currency countries, and its management of international liquidity.

The Fund staff has already recommended improvements in the design of adjustment measures in favor of low-income groups. These include exchange-rate changes that provide adequate incentives for the agricultural sector dominated by small farmers, greater access to domestic credit markets, taxation of global income, expansion of tax bases, replacement of quotas by tariffs, and the provision of basic skills and vocational training for unemployables.[9]

In addition, the Fund could get out of medium-term or Extended Facility financing—an activity that may duplicate the World Bank's structural adjustment loans. This step would free the Fund to concen-

---

[9]Charles A. Sisson, "Fund-Supported Programs and Income Distribution in LDCs," *Finance and Development,* March 1986, 36.

trate on its exchange-related functions and operations.

The fourth alternative—and perhaps the easiest—is for the Fund to do nothing. But the status quo includes the current and thorny problem of the repayment of the Fund's past loans, some of which are now technically in default. Without fresh efforts and initiatives, the number of countries in arrears will steadily rise. Further, the continued attacks on the Fund, if not properly dealt with, may further tarnish and distort the Fund's image, discourage some member governments from seeking badly needed IMF help because of domestic political opposition, and weaken and erode world public support for the Fund's surveillance, guidance, and assistance.

Meanwhile, the difficulty for the IMF in adopting any of the first three alternatives remains its members' inability to agree on either the need for fundamental revision of the current trade and exchange regime or the nature of critical procedural changes in the system's implementation. Most developed countries repeatedly have rejected such basic Third World proposals as a system of target zones for keeping major currencies in leash, a doubling of IMF quotas, larger LDC access to Fund resources, periodic issues of the Special Drawing Rights (SDRs), the IMF's reserve currency, a link between SDRs and development finance, a grant to LDCs of 50 per cent of the vote on all Fund decisions, the reactivation of the Trust Fund for fresh lending to poorer countries, and the establishment of a new interest-rate facility.

And the LDCs deem unacceptable such rich-country suggestions as giving greater publicity to the outcome of Fund consultations with members, extending the techniques of enhanced surveillance, assuring that commercial banks continue to play a big role in providing international reserves, and increasing World Bank-IMF collaboration in the design of conditionality.

Memories of the past create the uneasy feeling that, without a major new financial crisis, the Fund's principal shareholders and their bankers may not have enough incentive to accommodate poorer countries. Some concerned observers actually believe that such a crisis is already on the horizon. Averting disaster requires genuine debtor-creditor cooperation—no matter which side has a more valid position or better arguments.

Any new initiative must synthesize the positions of the two groups. The chances of reaching this consensus, in turn, would be greatly enhanced if the sparring partners could agree upon several fundamental postulates. First, LDC debtors must admit that the bulk of their credit needs must be reasonably conditioned. The debtors must also be willing, in exchange for fresh inflows of foreign credit, management, and technology, to adopt certain genuine domestic economic reforms.

The industrialized creditors must accept the fact that no matter how economically necessary adjustment conditions are, they must be politically palatable and operationally feasible and must offer a clear promise of growth in addition to economic stability. Also needed are improvements in the workings of the international exchange system, a multilateral trading regime where the handicaps of different players are properly reckoned with, and a system of resource transfers based on both country needs and global competitiveness. Such measures as multiyear reschedulings of debts, the reduction of interest rates, or some eventual debt write-offs might be part of the solution.

Serious North-South negotiations in the framework of the meetings of the Fund's Interim Committee and the joint Bank/Fund Development Committee—or a new global monetary conference—may offer new possibilities for such an approach. Without them, the expectations of critics and the Fund's capacity to meet these expectations will remain far apart. The persistence and poignancy of the attacks on the Fund—and eventually on the World Bank, once its inevitable conditionality begins to bite—will further damage the prestige and influence of both organizations at a time when their involvement in the Third World is more necessary than ever to ensure global economic stability and growth.

15

THE GATT AND THE REGULATION OF TRADE BARRIERS: REGIME DYNAMICS AND FUNCTIONS

Jock A. Finlayson and Mark W. Zacher

During the latter stages of World War Two the United States and the United Kingdom began extensive bilateral discussions concerning the shape of the postwar international economic order. One outcome of these discussions and subsequent multilateral negotiations was the creation in July 1944 of the International Monetary Fund and its associated rules regarding exchange rates and the balance of payments.

SOURCE: Reprinted from *International Organization*, Vol. 35, No. 4, Jock Finlayson and March Zacher, "The GATT and the Regulation of Trade Barriers: Regime Dynamics and Functions," by permission of The MIT Press, Cambridge, Massachusetts. ©1981 the Board of Regents of the University of Wisconsin System.

Almost four years later, in March 1948, over fifty countries signed the Havana Charter for the International Trade Organization (ITO). The charter contained a comprehensive set of rules designed to regulate the policies of national governments in several trade-related issue areas, and included chapters dealing with tariff and nontariff barriers, restrictive business practices, economic reconstruction and development, and intergovernmental commodity agreements.[1]

The U.S. Congress failed to approve American participation in the ITO; ironically, the most fervent proponent of a comprehensive code of international law to govern trade policies was itself largely responsible for the demise of the ambitious ITO scheme.[2] All that remained after years of intensive negotiations was a trade agreement negotiated in October 1947, "designed to record the results of a tariff conference that was envisioned at the time as being the first of a number of such conferences to be conducted under the auspices of the ITO."[3] The 1947 conference had been held at the urging of U.S. officials anxious to take advantage of the president's tariff-cutting authority before it expired. The results were codified in the General Agreement on Tariffs and Trade (GATT); which consisted of the tariff concessions agreed to by the twenty-three signatories and most of the trade barrier rules that later were incorporated into the commercial policy chapter of the ITO Charter. These trade barrier rules were included to ensure that the tariff concessions would have legal status and not be undermined by other trade measures before the comprehensive ITO entered into force. When the ITO failed to materialize, the GATT was transformed from a temporary agreement into a normative-institutional framework in which governments pursued multilateral regulation and discussed trade policy.

Had the ITO actually become the global trade-policy forum and legal framework that it was envisioned to be, one could perhaps speak of *the* postwar international trade regime. The GATT, however, was never intended to be the basis for the postwar trade order and was not even conceived of as an international organization.[4] Thus, a large number of trade matters are neither dis-

---

[1]For a comprehensive analysis of the ITO, consult W. A. Brown, *The United States and the Restoration of World Trade* (Washington, D.C.: Brookings, 1950). Also useful, especially for the perspective of a U.S. participant in the negotiations, is Clair Wilcox, *A Charter for World Trade* (New York: Macmillan, 1949).

[2]This fascinating story is told in William Diebold, *The End of the ITO,* Essays in International Finance no. 16 (Princeton University, 1952).

[3]Kenneth Dam, *The GATT—Law and International Economic Organization* (1970; New York: Midway Reprint, 1977), p. 11.

[4]In fact, in the technical legal sense it can be argued that the GATT is not even an international organization today. Dam, *The GATT,* p. 335; John H. Jackson, *World Trade and the Law of GATT* (Indianapolis: Bobbs-Merrill, 1969), pp. 119–22.

cussed in, nor subject to regulation and supervision by, this peculiar and entirely accidental international institution. We suggest that the GATT is at the center of a particular international trade regime, which has for the most part been concerned with one international trade issue area, namely, trade barriers, which are *state* policies or practices that impede the access countries enjoy to each other's markets for their exports. Other trade matters, such as prices and earnings deriving from the export of primary commodities or the effect of private business practices on trade—which were both brought within the ambit of the ITO—were not addressed by the 1947 General Agreement. They have not since been brought within the GATT's regulatory-consultative framework to any significant extent.

The GATT regulatory framework has been virtually coterminous with what we term the global (or quasiglobal) trade barriers regime. Several UN bodies (e.g., the General Assembly, UNCTAD, and FAO) have concerned themselves with barrier issues, but their deliberations have not been particularly influential and have certainly not resulted in binding legal instru-

ments. Insofar as these bodies have affected treaty obligations in the issue area, it is largely because they have been taken into account by national negotiators at the GATT. There are, of course, many regional or bilateral accords on trade barriers, but not only do they link small numbers of states, they have often been shaped to conform with GATT rules. The fact that the number of states associated with the GATT is just over one hundred has detracted somewhat from the labeling of the GATT as the global trade barriers regime.[5] However, the only important trading states not in the GATT are several communist countries (especially the USSR), and some outsiders accept many GATT rules in any case.

Our objectives in this essay are to describe the GATT trade barriers regime, to assess its strength, and to explore some of the regime's functions in international trade and political relations. We are not seeking to explain why the regime changed over time, although some insights on this matter are inevitably included. . . . [this essay offers] analyses of how each of the seven substantive and procedural norms has increased or decreased in importance since 1947 and how their

---

[5]GATT, *Basic Instruments and Selected Documents* (hereinafter *BISD*), 26th Supp., 1980, p. viii. Countries with full membership rights and obligations are known as contracting parties, of which there are currently 85. Two countries have acceded provisionally. A third category, which at present includes 30 countries, is referred to as "Countries applying the General Agreement on a *de facto* basis." These are former colonies that have not yet decided whether to join the GATT. They generally do not participate in GATT affairs except during trade rounds. Interviews, Ottawa, September 1980.

relative significance has shaped the procedural mechanisms and the programs (i.e., rules and rule implementation).

Our rationale for organizing the [essay] around the norms is that they constitute the fundamental or underlying structure of a regime. One dimension of the regime excluded from the section is principles. Principles generally apply to many issue areas, and it is beyond the scope of an essay of this length to examine the variety of beliefs of fact, causation, and rectitude that have impinged on the trade barriers regime.

This section will highlight a major problem in the analysis of regimes. While the influence of norms at different times shapes the programs, it is the characteristics of these programs which provide the first and best evidence of their changing relative importance. It is virtually impossible to escape this problem of circularity, although efforts to explain interrelationships among factors and to gather additional evidence on states' policies in the issue area can lessen it.

REGIME DYNAMICS: EVOLUTION OF FRAMEWORK AND PROGRAMS

The central substantive and procedural norms of the GATT trade barriers regime have been relatively few in number. They have varied in importance to the regime at particular times, and the salience of some of them has changed quite markedly over the almost three and a half decades since the signing of the General Agreement in 1947. The substantive norms concern nondiscrimination, liberalization, reciprocity, the right to take "safeguard" action, and economic development. The procedural norms relate to multilateralism and the role of states with "major interests" in trade relations. The regime programs, which have been affected by these norms, are discussed after an overview of each norm, and include rules concerning the utilization of nontariff barriers (NTBs), tariff "bindings," and various rule-implementation activities.

Substantive Norms

1. Universal Application of Trade Barriers: The Nondiscrimination Norm

The former Director-General of GATT, Eric Wyndham-White, has written that the principle of nondiscrimination was the "cornerstone" of the GATT.[6] In the immediate postwar era it was regarded as the crucial GATT norm, if only because the immensely powerful United States saw it as necessary for both the expansion of its own trade and the forestalling of hostile economic blocs. However, nondiscrimination

---

[6]Eric Wyndham-White, "Negotiations in Prospect," in C. Fred Bergsten, ed., *Toward a New World Trade Policy: The Maidenhead Papers* (Lexington, Mass.: D.C. Heath, 1975), p. 321.

has since suffered severe and regular blows, which have had a significant cumulative effect. Most of the original GATT rules regarding nondiscrimination remain "on the books"; but they are often disobeyed, and the GATT does little to promote their implementation. The norm still has a role in the regime; but it tends to be important in fewer trade contexts and is in general a less powerful restraint on behavior than once was the case.

The basic GATT commitment to nondiscrimination—or "unconditional most-favored-nation" (MFN) treatment, as it is usually termed—appears in Article I:1 of the General Agreement and requires that "any advantage, favour, privilege, or immunity granted by any contracting party to any product originating in or destined for any other country shall be accorded immediately and unconditionally to the like product originating in or destined for the territories of all other contracting parties." This MFN clause applies to all tariffs, whether or not a concession has been negotiated, as well as to all other GATT rules. The fact that unanimous consent is required to amend Article I underlines the importance attached to nondiscrimination at the time of GATT's formation. Additional statements of the nondiscrimination obligation appear in a host of other articles of the General Agreement.[7]

Despite the importance of the norm in 1947, many exceptions to it were accepted. The British and French refused to dismantle their extant preference schemes, and the U.S. was consequently forced to agree to a permanent exception (Article I:2) allowing for their continued existence, although preference margins (i.e., the difference between the MFN and preferential tariff rates) were frozen. Another exception, which in retrospect appears enormously significant, permitted discrimination in the form of customs unions, free trade areas, and "interim" arrangements during a period of transition. Article XXIV of the General Agreement recognizes "the desirability of increasing freedom of trade by the development, through voluntary agreements, of closer integration between the economies of the countries parties to such agreements." The U.S. and other countries concerned about the weakening of the nondiscrimination norm insisted that, in order to be eligible for the Article XXIV exception to MFN, proposed schemes would have to require the abolition of tariffs and other restrictions on "substantially all trade" among participants. In addition, trade barriers for each member of a free trade area and for a union could not, "on the whole," be more restrictive after the formation of such schemes than they were before.[8]

---

[7]For example, in Article XIII:1 (nondiscriminatory application of quantitative restrictions), Article XVII:1 (state trading practices), and Article XVIII:20 (economic development measures). For a fuller list, see Jackson, *World Trade*, pp. 255–56.

[8]Ibid., pp. 502–503; Dam, *The GATT*, pp. 276–83.

Other exceptions in the General Agreement allow discrimination in connection with quotas imposed to safeguard the balance of payments, the imposition of antidumping and countervailing duties against dumped or subsidized goods, and the withdrawal of previous "concessions" in retaliation for the "nullification or impairment" of any benefits enjoyed by a contracting party.[9]

Throughout the history of the GATT regime the major source of erosion of the nondiscrimination norm has come from "regional" (and other) trade arrangements that involve discrimination in the use of trade barriers against nonmember contracting parties. Most have been presented by proponents as basically meeting the rather strict criteria spelled out in Article XXIV but, according to one legal scholar, of the dozens of schemes put before GATT members for examination and approval only one, the 1965 United Kingdom-Ireland Free Trade Area, has been in essentially complete accord with the article's requirements.[10] The drafters of the General Agreement had no conception of the popularity that political and economic arguments in support of "economic regionalism" would attain in later decades; nor could they foresee what this trend would portend for the "sacrosanct" MFN obligation in the GATT.

Undoubtedly the most important regional scheme to be considered by GATT members was the EEC customs union outlined in the Treaty of Rome. Because the United States announced its unambiguous political backing for the "discriminatory" EEC plan—as it had done previously in connection with West European discrimination against "dollar area" imports and with the European Coal and Steel Community scheme of the early 1950s[11]—the legal issue of whether the proposed customs union conformed with GATT rules was fudged, and the EEC went into operation in 1958 without obtaining the formal approval of the GATT membership. The GATT committee scrutinizing the Treaty of Rome concluded that "examination and discussion of the legal issues involved . . . could not usefully be explored at the present time."[12] A precedent was thus set: the nondiscrimination norm notwithstanding, regional trade arrangements would not have to conform to GATT rules, and multilateral supervision of regional schemes would be lax since the "rules" were implicitly discarded. Thus the European Free Trade Area in the 1960s, the free trade treaties between the EEC and other developed West European states, and the enlargement of the EEC itself in the 1970s have undermined the MFN obligation, partly because participants perceive little

---

[9]Articles XIV, VI, and XXIII, respectively.
[10]Dam, *The GATT*, p. 290.
[11]*BISD*, 2nd Supp., 1954, pp. 101–109.
[12]*BISD*, 7th Supp., 1959, pp. 69–71.

need to meet the GATT rules regarding regional exceptions to MFN.

But regional trade among developed countries was not the only preferential onslaught the nondiscrimination norm had to bear. Beginning with the EEC's "reverse" preferential arrangements with former African colonies, codified in the Yaoundé Convention of 1963, a potpourri of EEC-LDC preferential schemes has sprung up, the most recent being the second Lomé Convention of 1979 between the enlarged Community and fifty-eight African, Caribbean, and Pacific LDCs.[13] These arrangements violate the GATT's original rules regarding regional exceptions to MFN. Many GATT members—including the United States since the early 1960s—have voiced sharp opposition to the Community's myriad preference schemes with LDCs and "Mediterranean" states but, as the Curzons comment, "too many members of GATT had preferential leanings of one kind or another" by the mid-1960s for there to exist a workable political consensus to reassert the primacy of nondiscrimination over preferences of various kinds.[14] Discriminatory preferences were recognized in the Tokyo Round "framework" agreement, which accepted the permanent legitimacy of the Generalized System of Preferences (GSP) for LDCs. (The GSP violation of nondiscrimination had earlier been authorized by a ten-year GATT waiver in 1971.) Intra-LDC preferences, also authorized temporarily by a 1971 waiver, were similarly accorded permanent legal status as a result of the Tokyo Round.[15]

At the very least this proliferation of regional, developed-developing country, and intra-LDC trade preferences has "greatly lessened the amount of trade" covered by the nondiscrimination norm.[16] Over one-fifth of the world's trade now takes place within a huge West European preferential trade zone.[17] In

---

[13]Alfred Tovias, *Tariff Preferences in Mediterranean Diplomacy* (London: Macmillan, 1977); *Lomé II,* Overseas Development Institute Briefing Paper no. 1 (London: ODI, 1980).

[14]Gerard and Victoria Curzon, "The Management of Trade Relations in the GATT," in Andrew Shonfield, ed., *International Economic Relations of the Western World, 1959–71,* volume 1: *Politics and Trade* (Oxford: Oxford University Press, 1976), p. 231.

[15]*BISD,* 18th Supp., 1972, pp. 24–28 for the 1971 waivers. See Tracy Murray, *Trade Preferences for Developing Countries* (London: Macmillan, 1977), for an analysis of GSP, and H. Espiel, "GATT: Accommodating Generalized Preferences," *Journal of World Trade Law* 8 (May-June 1974), for a discussion of GATT's response to the GSP. See *BISD,* 26th Supp., 1980, pp. 201–11 for the Tokyo Round decisions on GSP and preferences among LDCs.

[16]Robert E. Baldwin, *Beyond the Tokyo Round Negotiations,* Thames Essay no. 22 (London: Trade Policy Research Centre, 1979).

[17]Rachel McCulloch, "Trade and Direct Investment: Recent Policy Trends," in Rudiger Dornbusch and Jacob A. Frenkel, eds., *International Economic Policy: Theory and Evidence* (Baltimore: Johns Hopkins University Press, 1979), p. 90.

1955, about 90 percent of GATT trade took place at MFN tariff rates; this had fallen to 77 percent by 1970,[18] and to perhaps 65 percent in 1980.[19] . . . That a further lessening in the influence of the nondiscrimination norm and a further relative reduction in the proportion of GATT trade conducted on an MFN basis will result, seems inevitable.[20]

Finally, another trend clearly unfavorable to nondiscrimination in the GATT regime is the growing popularity of "voluntary" export restraints (VERs) as instruments of trade control.[21] The increasing resort to VERs stems significantly from the GATT's generally permitting only nondiscriminatory emergency import controls (discussed under "the safeguards norm," below). VERs, on the other hand, allow for selectivity in taking action against the (alleged) sources of "market disruption,"[22] and for this reason are attractive to some states.[23] Although with the excep-

tion of the textile-restraint accords VERS are not undertaken within the GATT regime (a testimony to weakness in the regime, to be sure), the general trend contributes to the erosion of nondiscriminatory trade.

The various currents that have undermined the norm of nondiscrimination in the GATT have not succeeded in completely stripping it of influence. Several key trading nations—the U.S., Canada, Japan, and a few others—continue to pay homage to it. Moreover, the very low industrial tariffs prevailing in most West European countries tend to lessen the trade significance of preferential European arrangements,[24] while the structure of donor countries' GSP schemes indicates that the volume of trade affected has not been and is not likely to be high.[25] However, we find it difficult to dissent from the conclusion of one eminent observer, that it is becoming increasingly "difficult to sustain that the unconditional most-favored-nation clause

---

[18]Curzon, "Management of Trade Relations," p. 229.

[19]Interviews, Ottawa, September 1980.

[20]*MTN Studies,* vol. 4, p. 4; Stephen Krasner, "The Tokyo Round: Particularistic Interests and Prospects for Stability in the Global Trading System," *International Studies Quarterly,* 23 (December, 1979), pp. 500–24.

[21]C. Fred Bergsten, "On the Non-Equivalence of Import Quotas and 'Voluntary' Export Restraints," in Bergsten, ed., *New World Trade Policy,* p. 242; OECD, *Policy Perspectives for International Trade and Economic Relations: Report by the High-Level Group on Trade and Related Problems* (Paris, 1972), p. 82.

[22]Bergsten, "On Non-Equivalence"; Jagdish Bhagwati, "Market Disruption, Export Market Disruption, Compensation and GATT Reform," in Jagdish Bhagwati, ed., *The New International Economic Order: The North-South Debate* (Cambridge: MIT Press, 1977).

[23]Curzon, "Management of Trade Relations," pp. 274–78.

[24]McCulloch, "Trade and Direct Investment," p. 90.

[25]Murray, *Trade Preferences,* passim.

is a basic pillar of the international trading system."[26]

2. Reduction of Trade Barriers: The Liberalization Norm

The norm of liberalization or free trade is often regarded as central to the GATT regime, but it did not have the paramountcy of nondiscrimination in the immediate postwar years. Liberalization was regarded as important by many American officials, but it was not a primary goal of most other industrial and developing countries. Following European recovery in the late 1950s the norm achieved a fairly high profile (particularly in the manufactures sector), but receded somewhat in importance in the 1970s. The decline of support for freer trade has been reflected not so much in the results of the Tokyo Round, which in fact made some progress in reducing nontariff barriers, as in actions and agreements taken outside the GATT, which in many instances contravene GATT rules and escape its supervision. The norm remains relevant to trade in manufactured products among the industrial countries and to trade in unprocessed commodities, but outside these areas protectionism has had a significant impact.

Although the Preamble of the General Agreement refers to reductions in trade barriers as one means to achieve economic growth, full employment, and increasing incomes, the signatories recognized that domestic stabilization and full employment took precedence over liberalization. This was enshrined in Article XII, and was implicit in "the many loopholes in the name of balance-of-payments difficulties, domestic unemployment, and the lack of effective demand."[27] Support for liberalization in the immediate postwar years was not widespread, and this was reflected in the first set of tariff negotiations.

When the General Agreement was drawn up in 1947, an initial "round" of tariff negotiations was undertaken simultaneously by twenty-three countries. A large number of tariff reductions ("concessions" in GATT parlance) were negotiated between pairs of countries (123 in all), and those by the U.S. were quite extensive.[28] . . . It was not until the late 1950s that a more "positive" attitude toward freer trade became pervasive.[29] As the Curzons comment, this development "had its roots in the fundamental change in the economic environment between 1947 and 1958": economic recovery in Europe and growth elsewhere, as well as the "technological and industrial explosion of the 1960s," combined to generate a much larger

[26]White, "Negotiations," p. 323.
[27]Curzon, "Management of Trade Relations," p. 148.
[28]V. Meyer, *International Trade Policy* (London: Croom Helm, 1978), pp. 137–38.
[29]Curzon, "Management of Trade Relations," pp. 149–50; Dam, *The GATT,* p. 57.

"political constituency" for freer trade.[30]

The sixth GATT tariff conference (the Kennedy Round) began with a ministerial agreement on the key objectives in May 1963 and did not conclude until June 1967. It is generally regarded as the most successful exercise in trade barrier liberalization in the GATT's history.[31] . . . Sentiment in most developed non-EEC countries—especially the U.S.—strongly favored a major multilateral exercise in tariff reductions in order to mitigate the apparent and feared trade division occasioned by European integration.[32] After protracted haggling over the formula for making linear tariff reductions and what products to exclude, sixteen industrial countries did make linear cuts of almost 40 percent on manufactured products.[33] Large tariff reductions were accepted by the four major participants—the U.S., EEC, the U.K., and Japan.[34] Important, but far smaller, reductions in agricultural duties were also agreed

to by the major countries, on the order of 20 percent,[35] but their effect was undermined by nontariff obstacles in the sector. Finally, for the first time since 1947 an important nontariff barrier to trade, antidumping measures, was subject to negotiation in a GATT trade round.[36]

While the norm of trade barrier liberalization enjoyed perhaps its greatest support in the closing years of the 1960s (particularly from industrial countries), the 1970s witnessed a marked resurgence of strongly protectionist pressures in most developed countries, especially in the period since the 1973–74 oil crisis and the ensuing recession. Sectors complaining loudly about import competition included both older, capital-intensive heavy industries (e.g. steel, shipbuilding) and light, standardized manufactures and consumer durables (e.g. textiles and clothing, footwear, and electrical manufactures). Two points of relevance to the GATT regime and the liberalization

---

[30]Curzon, "Management of Trade Relations," pp. 149–50.

[31]Curzon, "Management of Trade Relations," p. 170; Ernest H. Preeg, *Traders and Diplomats: An Analysis of the Kennedy Round of Negotiations Under the General Agreement For Tariffs and Trade* (Washington, D.C.: Brookings, 1970), p. 12.

[32]Ibid., p. 29.

[33]Canada, New Zealand, South Africa, Australia, and the LDCs were not participants in the linear tariff negotiations. Dam, *The GATT,* pp. 72–73.

[34]Derived from Preeg, *Traders and Diplomats,* pp. 208–11 (Tables 13–1, 13–2, 13–3, 13–4).

[35]Ibid., p. 251.

[36]On the Antidumping Code consult Dam, *The GATT,* pp. 174–77; and Peter Lloyd, *Anti-dumping Actions and the GATT System,* Thames Essay no. 9 (London: Trade Policy Research Centre, 1977). See also the first report of the GATT committee of signatories, *BISD,* 17th Supp., 1970, pp. 43–46.

norm stand out.[37] First, the "new protectionism" largely relies on various nontariff obstacles to imports, both because they are more effective protective devices than tariffs (which operate through the price system) and because tariffs have been markedly reduced and usually "bound" during GATT negotiations. Many of these protectionist measures are patent violations of GATT nontariff barrier rules, especially the GATT prohibition of quotas, but are taken outside the regime and thus are not subject to multilateral scrutiny. The best-known examples are VERs, which involve often secret accords between an importing country and firms or the government in exporting countries to restrict exports to prescribed levels over a period of time. Second, the recent protectionism has focused on manufacturers and has hit hardest at developing countries, especially new industrializing countries, which have expressed increasing concern about this trend and the GATT's failure to secure implementation of its rules.[38] Trade liberalization in textiles and clothing, a key export sector for LDCs and the only sector subject to special GATT supervision,[39] has been undermined by practices and policies in developed countries taken under the rubric of the GATT textile arrangements. . . .

A continuing commitment to trade barrier reduction is evidenced by the tariff cuts negotiated in the Tokyo Round and in the serious efforts to tackle NTBs through new

---

[37]Recent treatments of the current protectionist drift include Bela Balassa, "The 'New Protectionism' and the International Economy," *Journal of World Trade Law* 12 (September-October 1978); Susan Strange, "The Management of Surplus Capacity," *International Organization* 33 (Summer 1979); and R. Blackhurst, N. Marian, and J. Tumlir, "Trade Liberalization, Protectionism and Interdependence," *GATT Studies in International Trade* no. 5 (November 1977). The next two paragraphs draw heavily on Balassa. He estimates that industrial countries' "new" protective measures affected 3–5% of world trade, or $30–50 billion, in 1976 and 1977, and that, partly as a result, world trade growth was more than halved in 1977 over 1976 (pp. 418, 429).

[38]*BISD*, 25th Supp., 1979, pp. 32–33; *BISD*, 26th Supp., 1980, pp. 276–79.

[39]Following the establishment of a Working Party on "Market Disruption" in 1959, a Long-Term Arrangement Regarding International Trade in Cotton Textiles (LTA) was agreed to in 1962, under the auspices of the GATT (which struck a committee to administer the Arrangement); the LTA was extended for three years in 1967 and again in 1970. A broader arrangement to ensure the so-called "orderly expansion" of trade in virtually all classes of textiles and clothing, the Multi-Fibre Arrangement (MFA), was negotiated in 1973 and renegotiated to cover the period 1978–82. Membership in the committee and participation in the various textile agreements have been open to both members and nonmembers of GATT. For evaluation and description of these schemes, consult Dam, *The GATT*, pp. 296–315; Strange, "Surplus Capacity," pp. 310–18; and H. Taake and D. Weiss, "The World Textile Arrangement: The Exporters' Viewpoint," *Journal of World Trade Law* 8 (November-December 1974). For the contrasting views of exporters and importers on the impact and utility of the recent MFA, see GATT Doc. COM.TEX/15, 5 February 1980, and *BISD*, 26th Supp., 1980, pp. 340–53.

codes that improve on existing GATT rules. However, the scope of this commitment and its importance vis-a-vis other regime norms are unclear. In agriculture, there is little likelihood that the strong belief in "the sanctity of internal farm policies" will soon disappear.[40] The proliferation of VERs and extralegal restrictions on exports from developing to developed countries, and the failure to bring these practices within the regime's system of multilateral surveillance, are testimony to the fragility of the liberalization norm in the GATT. Ironically, many LDCs are now strong proponents of more liberal trade policies, having gone through a long period when import-substitution industrialization was popular.[41] They are constantly pressing the advanced industrial countries to liberalize access for LDC exports within GATT forums.[42]

3. *Exchange of Trade Concessions: The Reciprocity Norm*

Reciprocity, long identified as a central norm of the GATT regime, has had a major influence on rules concerning trade barriers and on rule interpretation. The notion that a country that benefits from another country's lowering of trade barriers should reciprocate, preferably to an equivalent extent, has had a profound impact on almost all agreements in the GATT. But since the advent of linear tariff negotiations and NTB codes in the 1960s, the norm has been more difficult to operationalize; and with the symbolic waiver of the reciprocity requirement for developing countries in 1965, the GSP in 1971, and the "enabling clause" in 1979, it has suffered some weakening. However, despite these trends there can be little doubt about the continuing importance of reciprocity in trade bargaining within the GATT. . . .

While observers are unanimous in proclaiming the influence of the reciprocity norm, no one knows quite what it means in concrete terms. The text of the General Agreement is not particularly helpful in clearing up the confusion since it only alludes briefly to the norm. Article XXVIII bis, added in 1955, states that negotiations are to be conducted "on a reciprocal and mutually advantageous basis. . . ."

---

[40]T. E. Josling, *Agriculture in the Tokyo Round Negotiations*, Thames Essay no. 10 (London: Trade Policy Research Centre, 1977), p. 11.

[41]Bela Balassa, *The Structure of Protection in Developing Countries* (Baltimore: Johns Hopkins Press, 1971); Carlos Diaz-Alejandro, "Trade Policies and Economic Development," in Peter Kenen, ed., *International Trade and Finance: Frontiers for Research* (Cambridge: Cambridge University Press, 1975).

[42]"The representative of a developing country stated that even though his country had liberalized almost completely its trade regime and imports had consequently greatly expanded, difficulties of access impeding the expansion and diversification of exports were being experienced in some developed country markets." *BISD*, 26th Supp., 1980, p. 277 (Report of the Committee on Trade and Development, November 1978).

In practice, "trade coverage" has been used to determine reciprocity in the GATT; it involves measuring the volume of imports "covered" by an agreed tariff cut. In the Rounds, "the custom grew up of attempting to balance the trade coverage of concessions made by each party to a particular negotiation."[43] The depth of tariff cuts has also been considered in calculations of reciprocity since the early 1960s.[44]

Most observers argue that reciprocity is a requirement imposed on trade negotiators by fundamentally political imperatives.[45] Governments feel compelled to justify their tariff "concessions" to instinctively mercantilist domestic audiences by pointing out that major trading partners have made at least equivalent "sacrifices." As one critic has lamented, governments "cannot ignore the pervasive belief that, when a country grants a tariff concession, it incurs a cost that must be compensated."[46] Clearly, this way of thinking about reducing trade barriers owes little to liberal economic theory, which stresses the benefits accruing to the country

that lowers barriers, even unilaterally. There are macroeconomic arguments in favor of reciprocity, such as the view that with a "balanced" increase in imports and exports a deficit in the balance -of-payments and a net rise in unemployment are less likely. These considerations certainly affect governments' broad bargaining strategies; however, it is the political salience of reciprocity that stands out.[47] As Kenneth Dam has commented, the GATT's trade bargaining vocabulary is suggestive of a political battle: "an original tariff reduction is a 'concession,' whereas a reciprocal reduction is 'compensation.' Even the word 'round' suggests a competition in which one side must 'win,' a boxing match with two parties locked in combat."[48]

The major effect of the reciprocity norm (in tandem with the "major interests" procedural norm) is that it assures that rules reflect the interests of the major trading nations in GATT Rounds. Since reciprocity dictates that states receiving tariff reductions for their exports be able to offer lower bar-

[43]Dam, *The Gatt,* p. 59.

[44]Curzon, "Management of Trade Relations," p. 160.

[45]Ibid., p. 159; John Evans, *The Kennedy Round and American Trade Policy: The Twilight of GATT?* (Cambridge: Harvard University Press, 1971), pp. 24–25; Harry Johnson, *Trade Negotiations and the New International Monetary System* (Geneva: Graduate Institute of International Studies, 1976), pp. 16–18.

[46]Evans, *Kennedy Round,* p. 25.

[47]Curzon, "Management of Trade Relations," pp. 158–59; Johnson, *New Monetary System,* pp. 16–18. Johnson notes (p. 23) that flexible exchange rates undermine the "balance-of-payments rationale for . . . reciprocity." Johnson has elsewhere contrasted the liberal and instinctive mercantilist ways of viewing tariff reductions: "An Economic Theory of Protectionism, Tariff Bargaining, and the Formation of Customs Unions," *Journal of Political Economy* 73 (1965): 256–82.

[48]Dam, *The GATT,* p. 65.

riers and markets to their negotiating partners, leverage on barrier reductions requires that states have both large domestic markets and a high volume of trade with countries whose barriers they want lowered. And since the industrialized states have the biggest domestic markets and are each other's major trading partners, they—particularly the U.S., the EEC, and Japan—have shaped the GATT's rules in large part to serve their commercial goals.[49] These states have the ability to offer "reciprocal" concessions and are consequently reciprocity's strongest adherents.

A more specific effect of the norm of reciprocity with its strongly mercantilist cast is that GATT members rarely reduce tariffs unilaterally. Even tariffs that have "no intrinsic economic value" can serve as bargaining chips with which a country can help to satisfy its trading partners' need for reciprocity without hurting its own economic interests.[50] Reciprocity had a comparable effect on negotiations in the 1960s over the removal of quantitative restrictions: certain states took the position that they would not end practices contrary to GATT rules unless they were compensated with reciprocal concessions.[51] The lesson is that any barrier reduction has a price.

While problems in determining reciprocity have arisen in negotiations over linear cuts and the NTB codes, the norm has not lost its significance. Concerning the bargaining over linear reductions in the Kennedy Round, the Curzons remark that a balance of concessions between any two large traders remained "as central as ever to the bargaining process."[52] Commercial policy officials have testified that the expectations that all major trading powers had to offer roughly comparable concessions exercised a tremendous influence in negotiations of the NTB codes during the Tokyo Round.[53] Although the difficulties of measuring reciprocity were magnified in the case of NTB negotiations, no one was prepared to abandon the concept. . . .

4. Waiving Rules in Cases of Economic Difficulty: The Safeguard Norm

"Exceptions," "loopholes," "escape clauses," or "safeguard clauses" in international agreements give states the flexibility not to comply with certain rules when

---

[49]Golt (*GATT Negotiations*) pictures the Tokyo Round as essentially a triangular bargaining process among the "big three," with Canada, the LDCs, and a few other countries occupying minor roles except when specific issues (e.g., tropical products for the LDCs) were discussed. Preeg similarly discusses the Kennedy Round as if the only players of consequence were the U.S., Japan, the EEC, and the U.K., the latter not then a member of the Community.

[50]Evans, *Kennedy Round*, pp. 24, 31.

[51]Dam, *The GATT*, p. 19.

[52]Curzon, "Management of Trade Relations," p. 161; Dam, *The GATT*, pp. 68–77.

[53]Interviews, Ottawa, September 1980; interview, U.S. trade officials, November 1980.

changes in the domestic or international environment mean that compliance would seriously undermine the well-being of part or all of their population. Such exceptions threaten the order that nations are trying to promote, but on the other hand little order would be possible if states felt they were locking themselves into rigid compliance with all the substantive rules of an accord. In the case of the GATT, it has been noted that without the exceptions the signatories "would not have signed the Agreement in the first place."[54] However, the exceptions did not simply give members the right to opt out at will: specifying criteria for the exercise of the right and procedural hurdles did pose some constraints. Since the founding of GATT these constraints have been eroded through interpretation and lack of collective action. Strictures on the taking of safeguard action still do exist, but they have frequently been applied in a less stringent fashion than one would expect from a reading of the General Agreement.

In the General Agreement a number of trade spheres are exempted *permanently* from GATT regulations. These are government procurement practices, from the MFN rules; customs unions and free trade areas, from the MFN rules; agriculture and fisheries, from the prohibition on quotas (provided domestic production control is practiced); export subsidies on primary products, from the prohibition on export subsidies; and actions taken in connection with national security imperatives and policies related to health, safety, and public morals, from GATT rules generally.[55] In addition, thanks to the "grandfather clause," states only accede to the GATT "provisionally," and are thereby allowed to continue trade practices domestically legislated at the time of accession.[56] However, this section focuses on GATT authorizations to take safeguard action or waive compliance with particular substantive rules *on a temporary basis*—as a result of "emergency," "extraordinary," or "exceptional" situations. These can be classified under the headings of balance of payments, economic development, market disruption, and other "exceptional circumstances."[57] (Economic development is treated in detail under the next norm, special and differential treatment for developing countries.)

A crucial exemption or escape clause is provided for countries whose balance of payments is in

---

[54]Curzon, "Managment of Trade Relations," p. 152.

[55]Articles III:3, XXIV, XI:2, XVI:3, XX, XXI.

[56]Jackson, *World Trade*, pp. 60–64.

[57]These other minor, temporary escape clauses concern the withdrawal or modification of tariff concessions (Article XXVIII) and the authorization of "exceptional" duties in cases where dumping or subsidization allegedly occurs (permitted by Article VI, the Kennedy and Tokyo Round Antidumping Codes, and the Tokyo Round Subsidies/Countervailing Duties Code).

deficit. Article XII permits the imposition of quantitative restrictions—generally prohibited in Article XI—to safeguard the balance of payments. Article XVIII:B provides more generous treatment of LDCs in this regard, and its provisions were further liberalized in the Tokyo Round.[58] Up through the 1950s the developed West European countries used the safeguard extensively while employing quotas and exchange restrictions during economic recovery.[59] In fact, the Balance of Payments Committee was the most active body in GATT during these years.[60] Since the early 1960s developed states in payments difficulties have tended to eschew quotas and instead impose tariff surcharges, since they are easier to administer and dismantle.[61] (These surcharges violate Article II, but members have usually been willing to grant waivers under Article XXV.)[62] Since the mid-1960s the LDCs have been the only states to employ quotas frequently because of payments deficits, usually under the generous provisions of

Article XVIII:B.[63] The criteria in this article have been applied rather loosely to LDCs, but they have still exerted a constraining influence on their policies.

The right to waive the rules in cases of market disruption (Article XIX) is the most important escape clause or safeguard provision in the General Agreement. It stipulates that GATT members can impose quotas or alter bound tariffs if three conditions are met: first, actual or threatened "serious injury" to a domestic industry resulting from GATT obligations is shown; second, the parties concerned consult; and third, the import restraints are imposed in a nondiscriminatory fashion. Resort to emergency restraints under Article XIX has become more frequent and the use of quotas more popular.[64] However, this legal way of meeting threats from low-cost producers has tended to be replaced by approaches that violate the General Agreement and stretch the accepted scope of safeguard action. Countries have increasingly tended to abjure invok-

---

[58]*BISD,* 26th Supp., 1980, pp. 205–209.

[59]Gerard Curzon, *Multilateral Commercial Diplomacy* (London: Michael Joseph, 1965), p. 137.

[60]Interview, Ottawa, September 1980.

[61]Balassa, "The 'New Protectionism,' " p. 422; Dam, *The GATT,* pp. 33–34.

[62]Dam, *The GATT,* pp. 32–34; Curzon, "Management of Trade Relations," pp. 217–20. See the report of the Working Party that examined a 1971 Danish surcharge, where it was concluded that, although "not explicitly covered by any provision of the GATT," the Danish surcharge was consistent with the "spirit" of GATT. It was further noted: "Quantitative restrictions provided for in Article XII would have had a more serious effect on the interests of its trading partners." *BISD,* 19th Supp., 1973, pp. 129.

[63]For example, all the contracting parties having recourse to quantitative restrictions under the balance-of-payments safeguard provision in 1976, 1977, 1978, and 1979 have been LDCs, and all have done so under Article XVIII.

[64]GATT Doc. L/4679, "Modalities of Application of Article XIX," 5 July 1978.

ing Article XIX when establishing import restraints because of doubts about their ability to show "serious injury," their perceived need to impose the restraints "selectively" against certain countries, and their wish to avoid retaliation (under Article XIX:3[a].[65] A common tactic has been to negotiate often-secret "voluntary export restraints,"[66] which are undoubtedly more common than invocations of Article XIX. In the Tokyo Round the developing countries and Japan pushed for a new safeguards code to curb the arbitrary shelving of GATT rules, but the negotiations came to naught—largely because of the EEC's insistence on the right to apply restraints "selectively." The consensus on the right of states to take safeguard action to prevent market disruption remains strong, but there are serious differences on the conditions under which it is legitimate and on the extent of multilateral control desirable.

In designing an international agreement states try to anticipate all of the situations in which they might want waivers, but normally they recognize their foresight is limited. In the General Agreement this recognition appears in Article XXV:5, which states that "in exceptional circumstances not elsewhere provided for in this Agreement," obligations may be waived by two-thirds majority of the votes cast. This has been termed "the equivalent of a large hole in the hull below the water line,"[67] and has been used on almost sixty occasions to exempt contracting parties from a variety of GATT obligations, usually on a temporary basis (or so it is thought).[68] GATT members have often interpreted "exceptional circumstances" in a flexible and vague fashion. Many essentially permanent waivers have been granted, especially with respect to agricultural policies and quotas inconsistent with Article XI[69] and preference

---

[65]Jan Tumlir, "A Revised Safeguard Clause for GATT?" *Journal of World Trade Law* 7 (July-August 1973), p. 405 and passim; Gerald Meier, "Externality Law and Market Safeguards: Applications in the GATT Multilateral Trade Negotiations," *Harvard International Law Journal* 18 (Summer 1977), pp. 496–97, 523; Bhagwati, "Market Disruption."

[66]Bhagwati, "Market Disruption," p. 169; Meier, "Externality Law," p. 523.

[67]Curzon, "Management of Trade Relations," p. 152.

[68]Waivers are listed in the cumulative index, *BISD*, 26th Supp., 1980, pp. 387–92. Jackson *(World Trade,* p. 548) argues that waivers were intended to be temporary, but have become permanent in many cases.

[69]In 1955, the U.S. obtained a waiver to permit the use of import quotas regardless of whether production controls were employed, as required by the Agricultural Adjustment Act. This was "a grave blow to GATT's prestige" (Dam, *The GATT,* p. 260), and was the first major step to remove agriculture from GATT rules. Jackson *(World Trade,* p. 548) notes that because of the size of the U.S. market, the impact of this waiver "on world trade has probably been more extensive" than that of any other. The Community's Common Agricultural Policy has no doubt been infinitely more disruptive, but it is not covered by a waiver. Evans notes that "Community producers are insulated from the effect of any price competition with the outside world" *(Kennedy Round,* p. 84).

schemes inconsistent with Article I but not acceptable under Article XXIV (customs unions and free trade areas). The membership evidently has regarded and still regards such an open-ended waiver as providing a needed element of flexibility in the regime.

The GATT's provisions to permit the taking of safeguard action have grown somewhat obsolete since 1947. It is doubtful, for example, that the industrial countries fully anticipated the extent to which certain of their economic sectors would require protection to survive. Similarly, the drafters of the General Agreement would probably be surprised at the incidence of severe payments imbalances in certain countries. Unanticipated trends and events have increased the size of the "holes" provided by the GATT's safeguard rules, as in the frequently loose application of safeguard provisions. More important, however, has been the tendency to avoid multilateral supervision by taking actions outside the regime framework. This has *de facto* broadened the scope of safeguard action in the trade barrier issue-area.

5. Special Treatment of LDC Trade: The Development Norm

The norm obligating the developed countries to provide special treatment to the trade of developing nations in order to assist their eco-nomic development has grown gradually in importance since the founding of the GATT. In the late 1940s and early 1950s it played a minor role in the trade regime, in part because of the demise of the International Trade Organization (with its extensive provisions on economic development). From the mid-1950s to the mid-1960s it slowly achieved greater prominence as a result of the significant increase in the number of Third World GATT members and the heightened political sensitivity of the western countries to their demands. . . .

A large number of newly independent underdeveloped countries joined the GATT in the early 1960s, and pressure to broaden the scope of the norm of special treatment intensified. The creation of UNCTAD in 1964 facilitated this Third World campaign to reform GATT rules. In February 1965, a new chapter on trade and development—known as Part IV of the General Agreement—was added.[70] Part IV strengthened the norm of special treatment and was a victory of at least a symbolic nature for the developing countries. It consists of three articles, none of which imposes binding obligations on the developed contracting parties,[71] but which taken together articulate a significant *symbolic* acceptance of the special character of LDC's rights and obligations within the regime. Perhaps the best

[70]GATT Press Release 962 (1966).

[71]Jackson describes the legal obligations contained in Part IV as "soft" (*World Trade,* p. 647). Dam notes that the new chapter contains "a great deal of verbiage and very few precise commitments" (*The GATT,* p. 237).

known element of the new chapter on trade and development is Article XXXVI:8, which states that "The developed contracting parties do not expect reciprocity for commitments made by them in trade negotiations to reduce or remove tariffs and other barriers to the trade of less-developed contracting parties." Article XXXVII spells out "commitments" accepted by developed countries to reduce trade barriers (including internal taxes) "currently or potentially of particular interest to less-developed countries." However, this is qualified by the phrase "to the fullest extent possible," which makes it impossible to regard these "commitments" as binding "obligations."[72]

In recent years efforts have been made to strengthen the relative importance of the economic development norm in the GATT, with respect both to LDCs' ability to deviate from certain rules related to imports and to the conditions under which their exports enjoy access to developed-country markets. LDCs have proposed that "in any new safeguard system, special rules should be provided for developing countries, including the general rule that these countries be excluded from the application of safeguard measures by developed countries."[73] Predictably, this suggestion has gone nowhere, since the developed countries regard certain Third World countries as the major source of "market disruption." LDCs have achieved greater success in their attempts to benefit from discriminatory trade preferences. As noted earlier, waivers to permit both the General System of Preferences and intra-LDC trade preferences were obtained in 1971. Under the GSP each industrial country has established preferential tariffs for particular LDC imports, although the effects have been quite limited. After the conclusion of the Tokyo Round, the contracting parties accepted an "enabling clause" that permits "differential and more favorable treatment" of developing countries. This decision made "legal" both the GSP and trade preferences among LDCs, and thus obviated the need for further waivers for these schemes.[74] It also granted LDCs greater latitude to use trade barriers for developmental purposes. . . .

The Tokyo Round appears to have enshrined special treatment of LDCs as a central norm of the regime, although the effect on trade bargaining is unclear. It remains questionable whether the GATT regime, which is focused on trade barrier reduction and regulation in pursuit of mutual commercial advantages, will prove to be a hospitable forum in which new practices can be developed to guide

---

[72]Ibid., p. 239.

[73]*Tokyo Round*, p. 93.

[74]*BISD*, 26th Supp., 1980, p. 203; "GATT: A Legal Guide to the Tokyo Round," *Journal of World Trade Law* 13 (September-October 1979), pp. 443–44.

North-South economic relations.[75] To date the industrialized states have made concessions at the normative level and the level of very general rules, but the concrete effects of their "sacrifices" have been very modest.

Procedural Norms and Mechanisms

At the heart of the procedural component of a regime are the norms that provide guidelines as to how decisions are to be made. The mechanisms, which Young has described as the "institutional arrangements specialized to the resolution of problems of social choice arising within the framework of particular regimes,"[76] are shaped by the norms. Hence the impact of procedural norms on actual regime programs is mediated by the mechanisms. Our analysis will focus on the evolution of the two central procedural norms and their impact on mechanisms and regime programs, but first it is necessary to provide an overview of the GATT's institutional mechanisms.

The GATT's two most important institutions are the annual meetings of contracting parties and the Council (open to all states). Under the Council—which meets at least six times a year—there are a variety of committees and *ad hoc* working parties, which monitor and make recommendations on particular issues. There are also two different types of dispute settlement bodies. Panels of Conciliation are composed of experts appointed by the Director General, and they are charged with submitting specific proposals for resolving conflicts. Working Parties are more "political" and include representatives of the two disputants as well as outside parties; they are supposed to encourage agreement between the conflicting parties. Since the 1960s Working Parties have been used more frequently than Panels.[77] In addition, there are now committees that will oversee the new NTB codes; these are limited to signatories.

In large part, the permanent institutions are concerned with rule implementation (including dispute settlement) and general reviews of trade relations, but the Council and the annual meetings of contracting parties also deal with amendments to the General Agreement and "decisions" that establish policy directions for the organization. Amendments to the most-favored-nation clause and the tariff schedules (Articles I and II) and Article XXX require unanimity; amendments to other articles require the approval of a two-thirds majority, but only become effective for those coun-

---

[75] See Sidney Golt, *Developing Countries and the GATT System*, Thames Essay no. 13 (London: Trade Policy Research Centre, 1978).

[76] See Young, in this collection.

[77] Jackson, *World Trade*, chapter 8; Dam, *The GATT*, chapter 19; Hudec, *Adjudication of International Trade Disputes*, pp. 1–25.

tries accepting them.[78] "Decisions" can be taken by a simple majority. Voting in the meetings of contracting parties and the Council is not common, and there is a strong preference for operating by consensus.[79]

While this ongoing network of GATT bodies is mainly charged with the promotion of rule implementation, it is the periodic conferences (seven since 1947) or "Rounds" that are responsible for rule making. The administrative aspects of these conferences are handled by a committee-of-the-whole, the Trade Negotiations Committee, but specific accords on tariffs and nontariff barriers are formulated by two or more states. During the first five conferences, between 1947 and 1962, the mode of decision making was dominantly bilateral, and the agreements were "the result of essentially bilateral concessions, which accumulate and are automatically made multilateral by the most-favored-nation clause."[80] With the advent of linear tariff cuts and the formulation of NTB codes in the Kennedy and Tokyo Rounds, an important multilateral element has been introduced. However, trade agreements still depend on a group of states coming together voluntarily—and not on a decision of a particular deliberative body. GATT rounds resemble more a

stock exchange than a legislature. The participants operate within the framework of certain rules, but "deals" are generally made between two or among a limited number of states. It is this feature that sets off the GATT from most other international organizations.

1. Collective Decision Making: The Multilateralism Norm

Certain of the substantive norms identified above are clearly in conflict (e.g., liberalization vs. safeguards), and in the case of the two procedural norms this is even more true. Multilateralism signifies the willingness of governments to participate in rule-making conferences and to allow multilateral surveillance of, and even a degree of control over, their trade policy. It symbolizes regime members' acceptance of the proposition that they have a legitimate interest in each other's policies and behavior. What we call the major interests norm, on the other hand, stems from a contrasting belief that participation in certain aspects of decision making ought to be restricted to those most affected or most influential, or both, in respect of the issue being dealt with. That a tension exists between these two procedural norms is obvious.

Two major aspects of decision making are identified here: rule

---

[78]Jackson, *World Trade,* pp. 77 and 122–23.

[79]Gerard and Victoria Curzon, "GATT: Traders' Club," in Robert W. Cox and Harold K. Jacobson, eds., *The Anatomy of Influence: Decision-Making in International Organization* (New Haven: Yale University Press, 1973), p. 302.

[80]Ibid., p. 314.

making and the promotion of rule implementation. The latter category in turn includes several distinct types of activity, of which we discuss three: the monitoring of state behavior, the interpretation of rules, and the settlement of disputes. In the case of the multilateralism norm, its impact on rule making in the GATT was minimal until the advent of linear tariff negotiations in the mid-1960s and, especially, the deliberations concerning nontariff codes of conduct. Insofar as the promotion of rule implementation is concerned, the multilateralism norm has exercised an important influence on the monitoring of behavior, although this has declined somewhat in the past decade or so. Rule interpretation and dispute settlement have also been affected by the belief in multilateral procedures in the regime, but here the competing major interests norm has perhaps been dominant. We first discuss the role of multilateralism in rule making, then the indicators and evolution of the norm with respect to rule implementation.

Rule making (i.e., the negotiation of binding agreements concerning tariffs and NTBs) was dominantly bilateral in character during most of the GATT's first two decades. Tariff conferences typically "commenced as networks of bilateral negotiations"[81] (discussed under the major interests norm, below).

Near the close of negotiations, a "last-minute balancing" of "offers" and "concessions" would occur in order to get countries that would benefit secondarily from the nondiscriminatory application of agreed tariff reductions to "pay" for these benefits.[82] This constituted the only multilateral element in rule making. However, the development of linear tariff negotiations and, even more so, the growing importance of NTBs in recent bargaining rounds have introduced a stronger component of multilateralism into decision making in the GATT. True, the major trading states continue to dominate the rule-making process, but more regime members now participate in any given negotiation, particularly in the case of NTBs.

The impact of the belief in multilateral supervision and decision making is perhaps easiest to adduce from the monitoring of behavior, which is the major aspect of rule implementation in the regime. In connection with this, mention should be made of both the consultation and the notification requirements of the GATT. The General Agreement contains a host of provisions that obligate members to consult, if requested by other members, in the case of such actions as the modification of tariff schedules, actions taken to support "infant industries," the imposition of emergency quotas, and many other

---

[81]Dam, *The GATT,* p. 61.
[82]Ibid., pp. 62–63.

matters. Jackson lists nineteen "clauses" that require consultations between contracting parties or between a party initiating a certain action and the membership as a whole.[83] Frequent consultations clearly facilitate the close monitoring of behavior by the membership. . . .

The GATT's numerous notification requirements are also indispensable to the close monitoring of behavior that lies at the heart of effective rule implementation. Contracting parties are obligated to *report* (which involves more than simply *consulting*) regularly on actions taken under certain "escape clauses," such as those permitting the formation of customs unions and free trade areas (Article XXIV), the furtherance of economic development (Article XVIII), and the safeguarding of the balance of payments (Article XII). In addition, once waivers are granted, recipients are in most cases required to make annual reports and generally show that they are in compliance with the terms of the waiver. Further, notifications and the provision of information are required not only in relation to escape-clause actions and waivers, but in connection with many other aspects of state behavior in the trade barrier field. . . .

Although the extent of compliance with these notification obligations has varied over time and between individual provisions, the record has in fact been reasonably good.[84] Compliance with the obligation to provide information concerning trade barrier policies helps immeasurably to increase the transparency of policy in this issue area. Observers of the GATT often argue that improving the quality and quantity of information about international trade policy has been one of the regime's major contributions.[85] More importantly, without the provision of data and information concerning members' trade policies, behavior could not be effectively monitored and therefore the ability to implement regime rules would suffer.

Multilateral rule implementation has also involved the interpretation of regime rules by GATT bodies. Students of the GATT are often "struck by the extent to which 'legalism' was dominant in the drafting of the original General Agreement . . . and . . . 'pragmatism' has governed the interpretation and administration of GATT rules."[86] Most GATT members have preferred a pragmatic, flexible approach to rule interpretation, but on many occasions this has not been inconsistent with multilateral decision making. The numerous GATT bodies that have existed over

---

[83]Jackson, *World Trade,* pp. 164–65.
[84]GATT Doc. MTN/FR/W17.
[85]Jackson, *World Trade,* p. 124.
[86]Dam, *The GATT,* p. 4.

the years have frequently reinterpreted GATT rules in light of changing circumstances and state preferences. Legal scholars have expressed some dismay at the tendency "informally" to reinterpret rules and even to ignore the rules in certain instances, a tendency that has become more marked since the early 1960s.[87] However, the fact that a rather pragmatic approach to rule interpretation has existed in the regime does not vitiate the argument that rule interpretation has exhibited a multilateral character. Moreover, it must be emphasized that many "reinterpreted" rules have in fact achieved the status of new, although uncodified, law in the GATT.[88]

Another dimension of multilateral rule interpretation relates to the various decisions of the contracting parties. The granting of waivers is the most obvious example of collective decision making that may involve rule interpretation in some cases. For example, the several waivers permitting states to impose tariff surcharges for balance-of-payments reasons, in spite of their illegality under GATT rules, indicates that the membership has "reinterpreted" GATT obligations.[89] Similarly, waivers to permit LDCs to benefit from preferences have amounted "to new thrusts of regulation designed to support completely new policies."[90] GATT members also make collective decisions that have the effect of altering, reinterpreting, or adding to the corpus of regime rules.

Finally, rule implementation has also manifested a degree of multilateralism in connection with dispute settlement. Article XXIII authorizes the contracting parties to consider complaints from a GATT member about the behavior of another member. Upon investigation, a ruling or recommendation may be handed down. In the 1950s in particular, GATT Panels quite successfully addressed a number of disputes. Since then, the use of adjudicatory bodies has declined and members have instead relied on bilateral settlement techniques or, alternatively, have resolved their differences in the context of Working Parties, where matters are generally settled with only limited reference to existing rules. Nonetheless, between 1947 and 1977 some thirty collective "decisions of sorts" were issued by the membership or subsidiary bodies in

---

[87]Hudec, *Ajudication of International Trade Disputes;* John H. Jackson, "The Crumbling Institutions of the Liberal Trade System" *Journal of World Trade Law* 12 (March-April 1978), and "Governmental Disputes in International Trade Relations: A Proposal in the Context of GATT," *Journal of World Trade Law* 12 (Jan.-Feb. 1979); Thomas Roschke, "The GATT: Problems and Prospects," *Journal of Law and Economics* 12 (1977).

[88]Jackson, *World Trade,* p. 757.

[89]Dam, *The GATT,* pp. 30–32.

[90]Jackson, *World Trade,* pp. 30–31.

instances of disputes between contracting parties.[91] However, as discussed below, dispute settlement in the GATT has tended to be highly bilateral during most of the regime's history.

In assessing the evolution of the multilateralism norm, it must be admitted that the monitoring and surveillance of members' compliance with GATT rules have suffered from the proliferation of actions taken outside the regime's framework (e.g., VERs), from the extremely superficial scrutiny given to many regional trading arrangements that harm the trade interests of nonparticipants, and from the marked inclination to treat much agricultural trade as a special sector to which GATT disciplines do not apply. In addition, the conscious encouragement of bilateral dispute resolution by many regime members has limited the scope for multilateral decision making in relation to dispute settlement. Thus, while multilateralism has grown more prominent in the rule-making process in the GATT, the impact of the norm on the various facets of rule implementation has at the same time suffered some attenuation.

2. Trading Interests and Decision-Making Roles: The Major Interests Norm

What we call the major interests norm of the GATT reflects the belief

of many members that those with the most obvious stake in a given issue or negotiation should exercise paramount influence in related decision making. To some extent it also signifies a belief, or perception, that the most powerful states have, almost by definition, the largest stakes in regime negotiations and activities, and therefore are entitled to exert a degree of influence proportionate with this role. In addition, the "efficiency" benefits of conducting decision making among the parties most concerned also appear to have supported states' acceptance of the norm. The Curzons suggest that bilateral negotiations have been "the key to GATT's relative success as a forum for tariff negotiations" because they limit "the effective negotiators to those who have a genuine interest in the subject under discussion . . ."[92] Restricting the number of participants in decision making also ensures that the fragile multilateral machinery is not overloaded with matters that can more easily be settled in a bilateral or limited multilateral context.

This major interests norm has been important in shaping both rule making and rule implementation throughout the GATT's history. Its impact has clearly been diminished in the former case by the introduction of more multilateral rule-making techniques, but it has remained extremely important for

[91]Robert Hudec, *Ajudication of International Trade Disputes,* Thames Essay no. 16 (London: Trade Policy Research Centre, 1978), p. 5.

[92]Curzon, "GATT: Trader's Club," p. 134.

most aspects of regime activity and continues to enjoy the support of many regime members, especially the most powerful.

Prior to the 1956 conference it was agreed that countries could join together to request concessions on products of which they *collectively* were the major suppliers to an importing country.[93] By the time of the Dillon Round (1960–62), it was accepted that a country supplying more than 10 percent of a product to an import market would be asked to "reciprocate" or "pay" for a concession received on this product, although it would not itself negotiate such a concession, that task being restricted to the importing country and the principal supplier.[94] In general, however, it must be recognized that GATT tariff bargaining procedures "served to reinforce as well as to reflect the bilateral character of pre-Kennedy Round trade negotiations."[95] Thus, small countries, especially LDC's, that did not have large import markets to "offer" and that were not major suppliers of most traded goods were effectively stripped of significant influence in the negotiation of tariff reductions.

With the advent of linear, across-the-board tariff reductions in the Kennedy Round and the growth of interest in negotiating NTB codes, this bilateral technique was discarded for a greater degree of multilateralism. But the ability of those few countries that are the major suppliers of most products and that possess the largest import markets to determine the extent of linear tariff cuts, the sectors to be excluded from such cuts (e.g., textiles, agriculture), and the new rules governing the use of NTBs, remains striking.[96] The crucial bargaining now occurs in a *"petit sommet"* of a few states, where such essential issues as the tariff-cutting formula to be adopted or the outline of a new subsidies agreement will be resolved.[97] In the view of observers of the Tokyo Round, the "big three" (the U.S., the EEC, and Japan) are an overwhelming presence during most facets of contemporary trade barrier negotiations in the regime,[98] although there has been some modest sharing of influence—especially in NTB code negotiations.

The major interests norm has also influenced the monitoring of state behavior, which is the most important aspect of rule implementation in the regime. For example, supervision of countries' compliance with the rules and their general behavior is explicitly bilateral according to GATT articles dealing with emergency import restrictions (Article XIX), the modification of past tariff bindings (Article

---

[93]*BISD*, 4th Supp., 1956, p. 80.
[94]Curzon, "Management of Trade Relations," p. 173.
[95]Dam, *The GATT*, p. 62.
[96]Ibid., pp. 61–77; *MTN Studies*, vol. 2, pp. 34–35.
[97]Curzon, "Management of Trade Relations," p. 205.
[98]Golt, *GATT Negotiations*, passim.

XXVIII), and the alleged "nullification or impairment" of benefits accruing to a member under the General Agreement.[99] The absence of guaranteed multilateral surveillance in regard to emergency actions taken against imports causing "market disruption" is particularly significant in this context. Several observers have criticized the paucity of multilateral supervision and control of countries' behavior in imposing emergency import restrictions, which is occasioned by the "bilateral" negotiating bias of Article XIX.[100] And, of course, the proliferation of extralegal "voluntary" export restraints and "orderly" marketing schemes outside the regime's supervisory framework is also a telling indication of certain states' eagerness to "regulate" behavior in a bilateral setting, where major interests and the superior leverage of the powerful are given freer rein than in the GATT.

It is evident that rule interpretation and dispute settlement should be discussed together, for while there is no formal provision for nonmultilateral rule interpretation or reinterpretation in the GATT, nonetheless the strongly bilateral character of dispute settlement in the regime may lead to highly informal types of rule interpretation on the part of two or a small number of concerned states. Of major importance here is GATT members' *obligation* to seek bilateral resolution of a dispute before invoking the regime's multilateral machinery (Article XXII).[101] A bias in favor of "containing" disputes through bilateral or limited multilateral discussions is striking.[102] The norm of reciprocity has clearly affected the approach taken toward disputes in the GATT and has supported the major interests norm in this area. Observers note that the central goal of dispute settlement in the regime is not to develop a sophisticated jurisprudence or to ensure that behavior is perfectly consonant with the rules, but rather to restore the previous "balance of advantages"—that is, reciprocity.[103] This has irked legal scholars and several smaller GATT members, who fear that resolving disputes according to the major interests and reciprocity imperatives puts weaker powers at a disadvantage and undermines the integrity of the rule system.[104] The Tokyo Round accords appear to reflect a more multilateral approach to dispute settlement, but it is unclear whether the pattern established in the

---

[99]Curzon, "Management of Trade Relations," p. 205.

[100]Jan Tumlir, "A Revised Safeguards Clause for GATT?" *Journal of World Trade Law* 7 (July-August 1973), p. 407; Bhagwati, "Market Disruption."

[101]Curzon, "Management of Trade Relations," p. 205.

[102]Curzon, "GATT: Traders' Club," p. 316.

[103]Curzon, "Management of Trade Relations," p. 206.

[104]Hudec, *Adjudication of International Trade Disputes;* George A. Maciel, *The International Framework for World Trade: Brazilian Proposals for GATT Reform* (London: Trade Policy Research Centre, 1977), pp. 11–12.

1950s—when multilateral techniques of adjudication were quite successful and popular—will once again develop in the regime.[105] One is entitled to be skeptical.

In sum, while rule making in the regime has become more multilateral in character since the mid-1960s, the monitoring of behavior and other elements of rule implementation have been increasingly affected by the competing major interests norm. The ongoing battle between the procedural norms of multilateralism and major interests warrants close scrutiny by students of the GATT, since the balance between them provides in some respects an index to the strength of the regime.

Conclusion

This discussion has highlighted a number of major characteristics of the GATT trade barriers regime; these are in turn of some interest for the study of regimes generally. Three basic conclusions emerge from the analysis of GATT's normative structure and evolution. First, it must be emphasized that it is the norms of a regime, and the importance the most influential members attach to them, that largely determine the regime's rules and rule implementation as well as its decision-making mechanisms. In the case of the GATT's procedural norms, their impact on regime programs is mediated through their effect on the decision-

making mechanisms, a point of some import for students of international organizations who seek to understand why decision-making bodies evolve in certain ways and how they are related to the broader structure of international collaboration in various issue areas.

Second, recognition of the fact that the relative importance of regime norms varies over time is critical for an adequate understanding of regime evolution. These normative dynamics are a major cause of changes in regime programs. The reasons for the rise and fall of regime norms are of course to be found in the shifting power resources and policy objectives of regime members, particularly the most influential ones. But changes in the relative significance of norms do not necessarily indicate that the regime has "broken down" or ceased to regulate state behavior effectively, at least if the interdependence norms continue to exert some influence in the regime.

Third, norms do not live in isolation; many are either mutually supportive or to some extent in conflict. Rule making can in some senses be conceived as the product of a "dialectical struggle" between conflicting norms, leading sometimes to "victories" by one norm but more frequently to tradeoffs and compromises. Of course underlying the "victory" or "defeat" of a given norm are the views, priorities, and relative strengths of the states that comprise the regime's

[105]Hudec, *Adjudication of International Trade Disputes*, pp. 7–11.

membership. Nonetheless, interesting tensions are bound to exist as a result of conflicts among regime norms. In the case of the GATT, the development norm is manifestly incompatible with certain other regime norms, nondiscrimination and reciprocity in particular. Another interesting set of tensions exists between liberalization on one hand and reciprocity and nondiscrimination on the other. Reciprocity, while in some respects a political necessity if barrier reduction is to succeed, does work to constrain progress toward liberalization by ensuring that concessions requested by state A will only be offered by state B to the extent that B can in turn obtain concessions from A. Nondiscrimination supports liberalization because it extends all negotiated reductions to all regime members, but it also limits the willingness of countries to liberalize because of their fear that "free riders" who do not contribute will nonetheless benefit as a consequence of the MFN obligation.[106] . . .

Some norms are also mutually supportive. The relationship between reciprocity and the major interests norm—both of which derive from generally prevailing beliefs and practices in the international system—is one example. The nondiscrimination norm has helped to strengthen multilateralism by increasing the number of GATT members with a commercial stake in any bilateral or limited multilateral trade bargain. Others could be enumerated, but the point is clear: norms affect each other, and the tradeoffs or mutually supporting relationships that may develop help to determine the rules and rule implementation of a regime.

By serving to promote constraint within the context of an evolving code of rules, the GATT has greatly contributed to the growth of trade—or the promotion of interaction.[107] In addition, a measure of predictability has been introduced into international trade relations by the fact that the resolution and avoidance of trade disputes has been a notable feature of the regime. A significant depoliticization of trade relations appears to have been one legacy of the GATT's existence. Whether the regime will continue to perform in an effective way the various functions discussed above is of course open to question. However, there can be little doubt that the GATT has had an important role in the evolution of postwar international trade relations.

---

[106]William Cline et al., *Trade Negotiations in the Tokyo Round* (Washington, D.C.: Brookings, 1978), p. 30.

[107]Between 1948 and 1973, the volume of world trade increased sixfold, growing at an average annual rate of 7%. This growth rate surpassed that of world production, which was also growing rapidly. Since 1973, growth rates have slowed, but trade has generally continued to expand faster than production. See ibid., pp. 7–19, and Richard Cooper, *The Economics of Interdependence* (New York: McGraw-Hill, 1968), chap. 3.

16

NEW DEVELOPMENT APPROACHES AND THE ADAPTABILITY OF INTERNATIONAL AGENCIES: THE CASE OF THE WORLD BANK

William Ascher

The World Bank and the other international financial agencies are continually being called upon to adopt new orientations, which entail different actions and often different objectives. Understanding how such agencies respond to these demands for change, whether for better or for worse, is important for both practical and theoretical reasons. The practical questions—which changes are viable, how does one effect changes in the international economic regime through reorientations of these agencies—have no simple answers. Yet it is important to anticipate the kinds of reorientation that are doomed to failure, for efforts to achieve them waste resources. It is equally important to know whether such efforts should be directed at the nation states that at least formally control the agencies or at the agencies' leadership or staffs. If and when a leadership wishes to dedicate its agency to the pursuit of a given approach, what is the best way to proceed?

From a theoretical perspective, the "paradox" of the international financial agencies is that, although they are by definition the creatures of agreements among sovereign states, they are also among the most formally institutionalized features of the international economic regime. They have large professional-technical staffs, full-blown bureaucratic structures, and ingrained routines, all of which may be influenced by a variety of professional and organizational norms distinct from nation-state interests. Consequently, while it can be argued that "every international organization at some points finds itself limited by the very principle which gives it being,"[1] it can also be argued that "regimes may assume a life of their own, a life independent of the basic causal factors that led to their creation in the first place."[2]

SOURCE: Reprinted from *International Organization*, Vol. 37, No. 3, William Ascher, "New Development Approaches and the Adaptability of International Agencies: The Case of the World Bank," by permission of The MIT Press, Cambridge, Massachusetts. Copyright ©1983 by the Massachusetts Institute of Technology and the World Peace Foundation.

[1]Samuel P. Huntington, "Transnational Organizations in World Politics," *World Politics* 25 (April 1973), p. 339.

[2]Stephen D. Krasner, "Regimes and the Limits of Realism: Regimes as Autonomous Variables," *International Organization* 36 (Spring 1982), p. 499.

PROPOSALS FOR CHANGE IN WORLD BANK PRACTICE

The many changes in the priorities and strategies of the international financial agencies proposed by governments, private organizations, "development theorists," and officials of the agencies themselves, can be classified into four categories.

The first involves changes in the *priorities* of economic objectives. The alleviation of poverty has been more heavily emphasized through a greater attention to the promotion of employment; a reorientation of investment to the social sectors rather than to the productive or physical infrastructure sectors (one variant is the "basic needs" approach); a reorientation of investment to rural development rather than to industry; and the "graduation" (i.e., disqualification from aid and concessional loans) of the wealthier less developed countries. The institutional (i.e., administrative) development of agencies in borrower nations has also received more attention.

The second category involves changes in economic growth strategy. These changes emphasize relieving the agricultural bottleneck to economic growth and relieving the energy bottleneck, through massive financial support for a shift to renewable energy resources. They also concentrate research on appropriate (i.e., generally smaller-scale, energy-conserving) technologies.

The third category seeks the inclusion of various *noneconomic* criteria: a greater concern for the ecological effects of economic development; concern for human rights violations; greater agency involvement in population planning and control; and greater appreciation of and support for the role of women in development.

The final category recognizes changes in the North-South balance. It seeks to rebalance the economic strengths of developing and industrial nations through the promotion of a "New International Economic Order" based on support prices for raw material exports and greater volumes of financial resource transfers to the Third World, and the substitution of major currencies and gold with special drawing rights (SDRs) as the major form of international exchange. It also includes attempts to increase the decision-making autonomy of the borrowing nation vis-à-vis the international financial agency (which, in a sense, "upholds" the criteria established by contributor countries) through more flexible standby agreements that recognize political constraints on and differing socio-economic objectives of borrowing governments, and general (rather than project-specific) loans, either for balance-of-payments amelioration or structural adjustment.[3]

---

[3]The proposals, and part of the literature, are summarized in P. Alston, "Human Rights and the New International Development Strategy," *Bulletin of Peace Proposals*

Three points must be made about this barrage of claims for new departures. There is considerable overlap (e.g., poverty alleviation through rural development and the economic strategy of relieving the agricultural bottleneck); some changes situated within different categories of this classification may be regarded by some as comprising a "package." Furthermore, none of these proposals ought to be considered as superior to the current priorities and practices simply by virtue of the fact that it has been put forward by some organization or individual as an improvement. Each has formidable critics as well as advocates. Finally, in terms of how legitimate or imperative these proposals will be perceived to be, the authoritativeness of those who proposed them is seldom clear-cut. The status of proposals articulated by international notables (such as Brandt Commission members), the international financial agencies' Executive Directors (who formally represent one or several member nations), and government financial officials (such as a Delfim Neto or a

C. Fred Bergsten) falls somewhere between "mere" advice and binding dictum; the issue of what constitutes an imperative proposal is at the heart of the problem of determining whether and how the international financial agency should adapt.

HESITANT REACTIONS TO DEMANDS FOR CHANGE

To a certain degree the World Bank has indeed reoriented its efforts. Whether the extent of change is regarded as impressive or disappointing depends both on one's opinion of the wisdom of the new orientations and on one's expectations about the adaptability of large international organizations. But it is clear that there has been significant resistance on the part of the World Bank to changing its priorities and to adopting the practices required to pursue new strategies. Irrespective of the merits of any of the proposed departures, it is generally accepted that the Bank only changes its orientations slowly.[4] The World Bank began its experi-

10 (Fall 1979), pp. 281–90; C. Fred Bergsten, *Managing International Economic Interdependence: Selected Papers of C. Fred Bergsten 1975–1976* (Lexington, Mass.: Lexington Books, 1977), chap. 23; Robert W. Cox, "Ideologies and the New International Economic Order: Reflections on Some Recent Literature," *International Organization* 32 (Spring 1979), pp. 257–302; J. Dolman and J. van Ettinger, eds., *Partners in Tomorrow: Strategies for a New International Order* (New York: Dutton, 1978); Independent Commission on International Development Issues (Brandt Commission), *North-South: A Program for Survival, The Report of the Independent Commission on International Development Issues under the Chairmanship of Willy Brandt* (Cambridge: MIT Press, 1980); and U.S. Department of the Treasury, *United States Participation in the Multilateral Development Banks in the 1980s* (Washington, D.C., 1982).

[4]See Robert Asher and Edward Mason, *The World Bank since Bretton Woods* (Washington, D.C.: Brookings Institution, 1973), chaps. 14, 20, 21; and Bettina Hürni, *The Lending Policy of the World Bank in the 1970s* (Boulder, Colo.: Westview Press, 1980), chaps. 1 and 2.

ments in integrated rural development, explicit employment promotion, urban sites-and-services upgrading, and human resources development much later than did the national governmental development agencies such as USAID. The Bank has yet to adopt modifications of its cost-benefit analysis to give greater weight to poverty alleviation (the so-called "social pricing" or "social rate of return analysis") as standard procedure despite a management campaign that began in the early 1970s. Some proposed criteria, such as the borrower's human rights performance, have been rejected altogether. Others, such as the concerns for ecological impact, population planning, and the role of women, have been acknowledged as relevant but the manpower devoted to pursuing these concerns is slight and the impact of these criteria on project selection and design is very difficult to detect.

Who is responsible for the Bank's limited responsiveness to these proposed changes? Formally, all significant Bank decisions must be approved by the Executive Directors. In practice, though, the decisions of the Bank's staff and management on project approval and policy advice—undoubtedly the two most important components of the Bank's work—have become increasingly independent of the intervention of the Executive Board despite its status as the oversight body representing the member countries. . . .

In practice, the Executive Directors veto a project only under extraordinary circumstances and have virtually no opportunity to initiate the consideration of specific projects. Thus, although the Executive Directors are naturally involved in the discussions on changing Bank procedures, they are of limited importance in the shaping of the projects that constitute what the Bank actually does. Moreover, the Bank's policy advice to borrower governments, which comes as a more-or-less informal part of the "dialogue" that accompanies project discussions and economic survey missions, is also largely beyond the sphere of the Executive Board. This minor impact of the Executive Board on decisions over specific project lending and macroeconomic policy advice limits its influence to general issues of the Bank's own financing, lending rates and terms, interorganizational relations, and so on. While these issues are of considerable importance, particularly to the overall volume of transfers from the North to the South, they have little to do with the development orientations of borrower countries. We must look elsewhere to find the sources of resistance to the reorientations of national development strategy that comprise so many of the proposals relevant to the World Bank's operations.

It has been suggested that where an international agency's oversight is weak, the qualities of that agency's executive leadership will determine its dynamism, innovativeness, and success. Robert Cox has argued that "the quality of executive leadership may prove to be the most critical single determinant of the growth in scope and authority of international organizations."[5] There is little doubt that prominent and dynamic individuals such as Robert McNamara can move centralized institutions such as the World Bank in distinctive ways.

However, it would be misleading to assume that the World Bank of the 1970s was Robert McNamara writ large. Cox also notes that the degree to which the executive head can control the organization—and hence the degree to which the organization's responsiveness or resistance to a new departure can be explained as that of the executive leadership—is variable. He maintains that the executive's control depends on staff loyalty, geographic balance, and the absence of "interest groups" within the organization.[6] To these factors should be added the sheer volume of uncertainty that the executive leadership and staff confront. Insofar as the executive leadership can neither clarify its own policy guidelines with enough precision to eliminate the staff's uncertainty as to how the executive would resolve each detailed issue nor intensively monitor the staff's deliberations on these issues, the executive must delegate discretion where the volume of uncertainty is high. Here we see the

irony, from the perspective of its executive leadership, of the expansion of World Bank operations. The proliferation and increasing complexity of projects has reduced the capacity of the Executive Board to oversee the Bank's operations with any mastery; at the same time, the Bank's executive leadership has lost some of its mastery over the staff's work as well. The World Bank leadership has tried to minimize the incidence of technically bad decisions resulting from this delegation by maintaining the technical quality of the staff, but it is more difficult to ensure that the staff is like-minded with the senior management than that it is competent.

The result of the leadership's inability to specify or to monitor all of the staff decisions that constitute the World Bank's operations is that the staff itself has considerable discretion to accept or to resist new approaches, even if these approaches are "sponsored" by the executive leadership. This discretion is often difficult to demonstrate, because the distinction between what originates from the Bank's management and what from the staff is never clear-cut; only extreme acts of blatant "defiance" would be easy to discern as demonstrating discretion, and yet these are understandably rare. Nevertheless, some evidence confirms

---

[5]Robert W. Cox, "The Executive Head: An Essay on Leadership in the ILO," *International Organization* 23 (Spring 1969), pp. 205–30.

[6]Ibid., p. 230.

March and Simon's view that the subordinates' ability to absorb uncertainty is the basis of their power vis-à-vis superiors.[7]

> The person who summarizes and assesses his own direct perceptions and transmits them to the rest of the organization becomes an important source of informational premises for organizational action. The "facts" he communicates can be disbelieved, but they can only rarely be checked. Hence, by the very nature and limits of the communications system, a great deal of discretion and influence is exercised by those persons who are in direct contact with some part of the "reality" that is of concern to the organization.[8]

Much of what the World Bank staff member does falls outside explicit guidelines. This would be less important if the Bank merely appraised project proposals submitted to it by borrowing entities; but the Bank is heavily involved in "project identification," the process whereby promising project ideas are generated and become the focus of proposal preparation, often with the technical assistance of the Bank itself. When a Bank mission visits a country, potential project ideas are identified in such an informal, unstructured, judgmental way

that it is implausible to say that the project selection is deduced from Bank policy, even if the staff members regard themselves as acting "within" the guidelines of Bank policy as articulated by its management. Staff members reported in interviews that project identification is the phase least bounded by Bank policy. Even if the five-year country planning document (the "country program paper") calls for an emphasis in certain sectors, projects in these sectors will not be pursued if the relevant staff find them insufficiently promising and other sectors may be emphasized if the staff become enthusiastic about project possibilities in these sectors.

Similarly, the Bank country economists' advice to borrower governments on emerging economic problems necessarily outstrips the existing policy guidelines already codified as Bank policy. Moreover, the staff member "on the firing line" is the primary contact between the Bank as an institution and the borrower government; his or her judgment as to how far the borrower government can be pressed to accept the Bank's stated objectives on project design and macroeconomic policy cannot easily be second-guessed. In several

---

[7]The attitudes reported in the following analysis were explored through 60 formal interviews with World Bank personnel during 1980, reviews of internal Bank memoranda and the project documents of selected countries in each of the World Bank's six regional divisions, and numerous informal discussions with Bank officials and staff. This research was greatly facilitated by a fellowship from the Council on Foreign Relations and the cooperation of the IBRD Projects Advisory Staff.

[8]March and Simon, *Organizations,* p. 165.

prominent cases (which here have to go unnamed), the country programs division (division chief and staff) has dramatized the borrowing government's opposition to ecological and poverty-alleviation concerns in ways that are consistent with their own value preferences.

The guidelines specific to each country are as much the work of the Bank staff (professionals without managerial responsibility) as they are of the Bank's management. The country program staff rather than the review offices within the Bank produce the first draft of the "country program paper"—the fundamental planning document for the Bank's position vis-à-vis each borrower country. The staff member responsible for the detailed analysis of a specific economy has an enormous informational advantage over the managerial reviewer, who must keep abreast of developments in many nations. The feasibility of a project idea or macroeconomic policy is seen as often hinging on "details" best known by the country specialist. Examples that emerged from interviews included whether a particular government ministry was capable of efficiently administering the project or policy; the availability of an adequately skilled workforce; the net effects of myriad subsidies and exemptions in distorting prices; and the strength of governmental commitment to the project or policy. Consequently, the generalist manager is in a poor position to overrule the better-informed country specialist. Much of what the staff believes necessarily becomes Bank policy.

The general policies of the Bank originate, in part, from the thinking going on within the Bank itself, an utterly unsurprising observation considering the reputations of Bank personnel and the sheer magnitude of the "brain trust" employed by the Bank. Inasmuch as the World Bank staff is an important source of development thinking in its own right, some of the impetus for new approaches comes from the staff itself. It is not particularly useful to try to assess the importance of any particular institution in originating development approaches, given that ideas circulate widely throughout the development community. However, it is quite safe to say that the Bank staff has been deeply involved in development thinking. Therefore the premise that the orientation of the Bank is imposed from the top is clearly inadequate in accounting for the positions taken by the Bank leadership and staff. Hürni argues that the Bank president's speeches "are an expression of a kind of intellectual consensus within the Bank."[9] But the diversity of opinion represented by the theorists mentioned above belies the possibility of consensus and certainly implies that no one in the Bank would presume that there is just one definitive or authoritative development approach to be

---

[9]Hürni, *Lending Policies*, p. 80.

implemented as a matter of course. The Bank president also listens to outside sources, but the fact that such outside advice is itself influenced by the Bank's massive body of theoretical work and practical experience highlights the diversity of channels by which the views of the Bank staff mold the very policies they are called upon to implement.

The staff member can, consciously or unconsciously, convert personal disagreement with policy into technical caveats about the applicability of the policy in specific cases. Interviews showed those staff members most skeptical about the validity of the objectives of the "basic needs approach" (i.e., attending to the nutritional, educational, and housing needs of the population even if the economic payoff is only the delayed result of human resource improvement) were most likely to question the technical feasibility of basic-needs-oriented projects (from their administrative difficulties to their targeting for the truly poor). This, again, is not surprising, because there is no ironclad separation between the choice of objectives to pursue and the assessment of the difficulties of achieving them.

The staff can also block the pursuit of a particular objective in a disarmingly indirect way, by discrediting the procedures deemed necessary to pursue it though without attacking the objective itself. The most striking example has been the resistance to "social rate of return" analysis, or "social pricing,"

an elaboration of cost-benefit analysis designed to give greater weight to the alleviation of poverty by allowing greater rates of return to projects that channel benefits to low-income recipients. Although social pricing has been championed for many years by prominent economists, including the Nobel laureate Jan Tinbergen, and considerable efforts have been made to gain its acceptance as regular Bank procedure since at least 1973, the opposition within the Bank has pressed its objections fiercely. That these objections are not without technical merit is the point: whether the staff's objections to social pricing are wholly technical or stem from opposition to the objectives it serves, the technical objections can be made credibly enough to untrack the timely adoption of the approach. Interviews revealed that several staff members simply refused to gather or apply the statistics necessary to accomplish the social-rate-of-return analysis on the grounds that the data were insufficiently precise.

The task of assessing the work of the international financial agency is made enormously more difficult by the fact that the personnel are (at least arguably) of unsurpassed quality. We generally base appraisals of past actions either on contrasts between actual performance and what could have been or on a "theoretical" assessment of the approaches taken, evaluated according to the "state of the art" as formulated by authorities of the highest reputation. Lacking obvious cases for comparison or any means for estimating reliably what could have been, performance appraisal for institutions like the World Bank and the International Monetary Fund (IMF) is rarely feasible; theoretical appraisal is the only viable choice. However, as long as the staffs of the international agencies can claim to hold the highest level of expertise, theoretical assessment comes uncomfortably close to sheer second-guessing. Thus any outside critique of the approaches taken by the World Bank or the IMF can be deflected by the argument that the staff knows best and the critique itself is faulty. It is to the credit of the staffs of these institutions that this argument is not always made. Yet the possibility makes outside criticism inevitably disputable.

ROLE SETS

Why would a World Bank staff member oppose or promote a new development strategy within the range of discretion established by organizational constraints? The straightforward model of the staff member as bureaucrat, which would explain behavior in terms of career advancement or perhaps of defense of the agency itself or subunits within it, is not irrelevant. Interviews revealed that the Bank staff members who regard punctual, technically tight work as the most important criterion for promotion within the Bank were also most critical of strategies for the direct alleviation of poverty, on the grounds that proposal preparation

and assessment are more time-consuming and less rigorous for poverty-alleviation than for more traditional projects.

Career incentives do not provide a sufficient explanation. Case studies of project work and policy advice for six countries (Egypt, Brazil, Sri Lanka, Mali, Kenya, and the Philippines) demonstrated ample instances of staff actions regarded by the staff members themselves as endangering their chances of promotion. In one case, a staff economist opposed a large dam project that had the enthusiastic backing of the division chief and the regional director; in another case, several program staff raised ecological concerns over a highway project when it was clear that the divisional *esprit de corps* depended on minimizing these concerns. Some staff members are active in the staff association, PARTAC, despite their own perception that senior management frowns on such activity.

Nor is it sufficient to presume that Bank staff are motivated solely by intraorganizational politics, the defense of the Bank against the world outside, or either of these in combination with careerist motives. Although Bank staff often express pride in and loyalty to the World Bank and the division in which they work, the examples cited above imply that other motives sometimes override organizational unity.

Beyond the staff members' status as members of the organization, their other attributes also figure in organization theory. First, the

World Bank staff are professionals. As economists or engineers, they are professionals bound by the ethics and standards of the discipline. In contrast to generalist bureaucrats, who owe their standing almost exclusively to their position within the organization, World Bank professionals are likely to hold a set of values derived from membership in the profession. These values may or may not clash with the values pursued by the organization or implicit in what the organization calls upon the professional to do.[10] Whereas bureaucrats can define their role as pursuing the objectives specified by the institution, professionals in bureaucracy have an additional layer of disciplinary standards and objectives that enter into their role conception. This does not mean, of course, that the objectives and rules of discipline are necessarily defined clearly or interpreted uniformly. But it does mean that professionals may experience conflict between the behavior they are called upon to pursue on behalf of the organization and the standards they interpret as consistent with professional obligations. They can object righteously.

Further, the fact that the World Bank staff are regarded (by themselves and by most others) as top-level experts considerably increases the "legitimacy" of noncompliance to agency dictates. It is difficult for the World Bank professional to defer meekly to the expertise of other authorities on development strategy; it is not clear that superior expertise exists. Therefore, many of the professionals in these institutions see their role as including the responsibility to formulate development strategies for particular countries, to question the strategies espoused by other sources of development thinking (e.g., the Brandt Commission), and to redefine the tasks assigned to them if their own expertise tells them that other approaches are superior.[11]

Moreover, the criticism of staff decisions made by the agency's management is also akin to second-guessing, although it obviously has more formal authority than criticism from outside the institution. Interviews did not reveal any belief on the part of Bank staff that the individuals who rise to managerial positions do so because of superior expertise as professionals; rather, promotion is seen as the result of managerial promise along with efficient (but not brilliant) work.

Finally, the growing recognition that development is not simply a technical process, nor economics a value-free discipline, has made clear to the staff of the World Bank that in making decisions they serve as much as intellectuals as technical specialists. This is not a comfortable recognition, because it

---

[10]Francis Rourke, "Bureaucracy in Conflict: Administrators and Professionals," *Ethics* 70 (Fall 1960), pp. 220–27.

[11]Brandt Commission, *North-South*.

clashes with the more soothing view of the economist or engineer as a neutral scientist and the international civil servant as a neutral expert and implementer. As we shall see with respect to the staff's views on the propriety of pursuing the intellectual-activist role, there is still reluctance to accept it. Nonetheless, the awareness that agency decisions are value-laden further bolsters the legitimacy of staff who choose to defend their own views of development against opinions from outside *or* within the agency. The typical result, however, is not staff who relish the opportunity to impose their views on the world but rather individuals with a profound ambivalence toward the conflicting roles of development thinker and neutral civil servant.

RELUCTANCE TO CHANGE

The rather peculiar position of the World Bank staff member, as a top-level expert in an international civil servant's position requiring value choices, gives rise to several forms of reluctance to enact new adaptations.

Resistance to New Criteria

Many professionals in the World Bank have been reluctant to incorporate new considerations in formulating development strategies if they require modes of analysis less rigorous than the traditional economic framework. The economist called upon to make decisions on the rate of return of a project will often balk at including factors for which only shaky data exist, such as the environmental cost, the indirect effects on the creation of employment, or the eventual benefits of administrative development. The most illuminating example can be found in the slow adoption of social pricing, mentioned above. The internal debate, reflected in published articles and a flurry of memoranda circulated within the World Bank when the approach was presented and tested, was intense. The parameters for weighting the utility of benefits going to individuals of different income levels were criticized as being, in the final analysis, arbitrary and judgmental.[12] The method's advocates retorted that it is equally if not more arbitrary and judgmental to assign the same utility to a "dollar's worth" of benefit regardless of who receives it.[13]

According to interview responses, however, the arbitrariness of the social pricing parameters was not the major cause of concern. It was, rather, the objection that the

[12]See Bela Balassa, "The Income Distribution Parameter on Project Appraisal," in *Economic Progress, Private Values, and Public Policy,* ed. by Bela Balassa and Richard Nelson (Amsterdam: North Holland, 1977), pp. 217–232.

[13]Squire and van der Tak, *Economic Analysis,* Ian Little and J. A. Mirrlees. *Project Appraisal and Planning for Developing Countries* (London: Heinemann, 1974); and Organization for Economic Cooperation and Development, *Manual of Industrial Project Analysis* (Paris: OECD, 1969).

income distribution data and project-impact estimates for which the method called were little more than guesswork, thus requiring the staff member to assume responsibility for analysis far less rigorous than usual. To this complaint the Bank's response was "try your best; estimates are better than nothing; we understand that the data are intrinsically shaky." Yet the Bank management's assurances that the weaknesses of these estimates were inevitable, and would not be held against the staff responsible for them, were not enough to overcome the reluctance. This is consistent with the interpretation that the staff react as much to the threat to their professional norms and standing as to the bureaucratic risk of being shown to be wrong.

The obvious lesson of the experience of social pricing in the Bank is that the implementation of a seemingly straightforward shift in priorities may involve arduous technical adjustments. Their acceptance as legitimate techniques will require even more time, adding to the delay in adopting the new orientation. Unless and until development strategies can be converted into decision-making procedures acceptable to the professional norms of those entrusted with using them, the implementation of these strategies is bound to meet resistance. On a different level, it may also be argued that the incorporation of concerns for which sound procedures have

not yet been developed is, indeed, simply premature.

A more general lesson is that any new approach can be construed as a threat to the professional integrity of a perfectionist staff. Any new consideration can be viewed as mitigating the cold calculus of economic viability; hence, these considerations can be viewed as pretexts to erode standards. New approaches also call for untested analytic procedures and, of course, there can be professional gratification in pioneering new techniques. Yet this possibility is diminished by the widespread belief that the Bank has to set an example of technical solidity in every project it sponsors, because the Bank's "demonstration effect" ought to be the demonstration of the importance of well-designed and administered development projects. This is a laudable objective, but it should be recognized that it trades off against innovation and the demonstration effect of innovation.

The final component of the staff members' qualms about adding new criteria (e.g., equity, environmental protection, human rights) to the desiderata of development is that the increasingly "cluttered" agenda obscures the Bank's priorities as an institution, thus leaving the staff more exposed in having to make its own value judgments. Although the Bank acknowledges the importance of these concerns, through speeches, the establishment of units within the organization (e.g., the Office of Environmental Affairs), and exhortations in the operations manual, it never makes clear in a general way how much weight should be given to any particular aspect relative to all the others. It is hard to imagine how the Bank could proceed otherwise, given the variable salience of such factors in specific cases (e.g., in some cases administrative development is a critical issue, in others it is irrelevant and ecological concerns are important). In attending to the particular case, the staff, particularly in the crucial early stages of project identification, are left to balance these priorities with—from their perspective—inadequate signals from above. This also threatens the professional caliber of the staff member's work: more considerations to attend to, with the same level of staffing, mean less rigorous attention to any one of them. Yet the most troubling aspect seems to be how the lack of institutional guidelines exacerbates the ambivalence of the staff's role of civil servant-intellectual. One interview respondent summarized the broad sentiment:

> Every few years there is a new factor that we must take into account, but we are not given more time or staff to accommodate it. This makes me think that the Bank's senior management is responding to outside pressures by delegating the hard choices to us. I don't have any clear understanding of whether we are supposed to pay lip service to, say, the environment or the role of women in development, or to

take them seriously. Even worse, I don't know to what extent the Bank wants me to take any one of these things seriously when they conflict with one another. I can make up my own mind on this, but am I supposed to?

Resistance to the "Bargainer" Role

Some development concerns require the international financial agency staff to pressure borrower governments, sometimes defying or at least challenging the wishes of these sovereign powers. It might be said that any conditions attached to a loan constitute such pressure, but one can distinguish between conditions intended to assure the payback of the loan (although the actual default of World Bank or IMF loans has not been a problem, given the disastrous consequences for a government that fails to pay back such a loan) and other conditions. A further distinction can be made between conditions intended to enhance the effectiveness of the project or program to which the loan is devoted and additional conditions imposed by the agency using the granting of the loan as leverage. At various points in the project-preparation cycle for a World Bank loan the staff can, with varying degrees of subtlety, exercise leverage. They are most hesitant to engage in this kind of pressure, beyond even the pragmatic limitation of maintaining a constructive "development dialogue" rather than confrontation with the borrower government. It can be forcefully argued that the World Bank can legitimately impose its own conditions on loans to sovereign powers, because its Executive Board represents member countries and because the Bank has been mandated to invest its funds to promote development.[14] Professionals who define their roles as "technical," however, are often reluctant to participate in such "political" acts as pressuring and negotiating with national governments even when they accept the right of the Bank to do so. This reluctance, rather than being manifested in outright refusals to carry out the Bank's work, is generally revealed in a less obvious hesitance and distaste for asserting the priorities of the Bank (to the degree that these are clear) when the borrower government seems unenthusiastic about them. Staff members taking such a position can defend themselves, with some justification, by citing the importance of governmental enthusiasm for a project as a requisite for its success; yet there is generally a sizable set of projects that a government wants enough to be willing to accept the Bank's recommendations on proj-

ect design or macroeconomic policy in order to secure their funding.

Resistance to Political Analysis

Deciding how far to press borrowing governments to adopt new development directions requires an understanding of the political constraints under which these governments operate. Yet this is true even for deciding whether a straightforwardly economic project is viable. Hürni points out that "no external project financing can be successful without very strong, permanent local and national commitments."[15] However, the attractiveness of the neutral civil-servant role model, reinforced by the stricture in the Bank's Articles of Agreement (Article IV:10) that "The Bank and its officers shall not interfere with the political affairs of any member; nor shall they be influenced in their decisions by the political character of the member or members concerned," discourages the Bank staff from devoting much overt effort to political analysis. Ironically, Bank staff necessarily exercise political judgments in assessing whether conditions they suggest or demand can muster sufficient political sup-

---

[14]Michael Hoffman, then Director of the World Bank's International Relations Department, wrote in "The Challenges of the 1970s and the Present Institutional Structure," in *The World Bank Group, Multilateral Aid, and the 1970s,* John P. Lewis and Ishan Kapur, eds. (Lexington, Mass.: Lexington Books, 1973): "The Bank can do practically anything it wants to do in pursuit of its objectives (except default on its bonds). The Executive Directors are not only the institution's governing board but its supreme court for interpreting the Articles of Agreement and their implications for operational work. . . . The important issues to discuss are not whether the Bank can do this or that but whether it should and how" (p. 17).

[15]Hürni, *Lending Policies,* p. 11.

port from the borrowing government; and the denials by Bank staff and managers that they take political considerations into account must be interpreted in light of the obviously delicate situation the Bank faces in dealing with sovereign governments. The problem is that in not fully acknowledging the legitimacy of taking politics into account, Bank staff are reluctant to make their political analyses explicit or systematic. Thus assessments of creditworthiness (which have an undeniable political component insofar as stronger governments can better guarantee loan paybacks), willingness to tolerate more poverty-alleviating project designs, and the administrative capacity to undertake a given project efficiently are made without the explicit political assessment that, by contrast, commercial banks increasingly rely on. Without such analysis, the Bank's overtures are not only riskier (since the ad hoc political assessment may be wrong) but also more timid insofar as ignorance in dealing with a largely uncharted political situation imposes greater restraint on Bank staff who recognize the limitation.

EXPLANATIONS OF BANK STAFF RESISTANCE TO CHANGE

Although the staff member's view of innovations is inevitably rooted in personal outlook and ideology, some of the variation in the Bank staff's disposition to accept or resist new approaches can be accounted for by a combination of where they are situated within the organization (with bureaucratic politics and unit-specific role sets determining different orientations) and the professionalist-intellectual outlook shared, but to varying degrees, by Bank professionals in general. The fact that different kinds of units recruit different types of staff unavoidably obscures the precise weighting of these aspects.

World Bank units can be distinguished on classic lines as "line" and "staff" units, depending on whether they have direct responsibility for project development and approval. Of course, many "staff" units are involved in the project cycle of identifying, evaluating, and supervising project work, but only in advisory, monitoring, research, or other support capacities. The "line" units, in turn, are either *projects divisions,* responsible for the design and appraisal of specific projects, usually in one geographic region and one or only a few functional sectors (e.g., the East Africa Agricultural Projects Division); or *programs divisions,* responsible for the development of, and Bank-governmental relations over, the Bank's portfolio of projects in one or a few countries (e.g., the Brazil Program Division).

In general, projects personnel are more "role-conservative" than programs staff in several respects.

First, they resist giving greater emphasis to poverty alleviation. The project staff's two most common arguments are that the Bank is slighting growth in order to pursue distribution, even in countries where nearly all are poor, and that the staff time required to design and supervise a project to ensure that it reaches the poor is excessive in the context of the needs to meet deadlines, appraise traditional projects, and meet quantitative lending targets.

Second, they resist employing social pricing. Whether or not the "technical" objections serve to rationalize a rejection of the priority to alleviate poverty, projects staff advance justifications quite distinct from opposition to poverty alleviation when they explain their opposition to social pricing. They maintain that social pricing requires them to make up data, guess at parameters, and thus produce unprofessional analyses. When confronted with the retort that standard economic rate-of-return analysis is equally if not more problematical inasmuch as it omits entirely the distributional considerations that a utility-maximizing cost-benefit calculation must include, they typically respond that economic rate-of-return analysis *is* incomplete from this perspective but openly and honestly so, and thus has more professional integrity.

Third, they question the propriety of "bargaining" between Bank staff and borrower-government officials. Project staff members are more likely to accept the view that Bank staff are civil *servants* employed by the member countries, particularly when they are designing and evaluating projects, to serve

the government of the borrower country. They are more likely to accept the degree of poverty orientation of a given project as being at the discretion of the borrowing government rather than a matter of compromise between Bank and government officials. Of course, projects staff have less opportunity to engage in this bargaining themselves and, in having to work on projects in a relatively large number of countries, may be more likely to presume that the Bank does not have deep enough insight into a particular country to make a constructive contribution by pressuring its borrower government. On the other hand, while the programs staff do not exaggerate their competence in understanding political complexities, they are more likely to accept that the dialogue between the Bank and the borrower government is a legitimate vehicle for the Bank to press—tactfully—for its objectives.

Fourth, they are more skeptical as to whether the other relatively new concerns of the Bank either warrant greater effort or require changes in project design. These concerns—ecology, "appropriate technology," the role of women, etc.—are rejected or minimized either on the grounds that competent project engineers and economists already take them into account adequately ("Do these 'appropriate technology' advisors have to tell us to use the right technologies—what do you think project appraisal is, besides deciding whether the technology is appropriate?") or on the grounds that these concerns ought to be kept secondary to the "main work" of economic growth.

Personnel in "staff" (as opposed to "line") positions were divided in supporting or opposing new Bank orientations and the roles they required. However, for "staff" personnel these issues were consistently more salient. To be sure, line personnel expressed opinions for or against these initiatives and, if opposed, explained how they could circumvent them. Yet line personnel were far less likely than staff personnel either to proselytize for a new approach or to oppose it "publicly" within the organization by circulating memoranda expressing their opinions; their concern was for the integrity of their own work. "Staff" personnel were more likely to take part in crusades for or against particular initiatives. . . .

CONCLUSIONS

The practical implications of this analysis speak to the question posed in the introduction: which strategies are viable, who determines their success, how should one go about ensuring their adoption? I have argued that the viability of a development objective or strategy to be implemented through the World Bank depends not only on the acquiescence of the obvious international actors—the nation states through their formal institutional representation and their various pressures—but also on its congruence with the professional role models of the relevant staff. If the staff perceives the strategy or ob-

jective as a "decline in standards," as requiring them to become more "political" vis-à-vis the borrower governments, as requiring yet-to-be-perfected techniques, or simply as clashing with their principles, its viability is doubtful unless altered role models can be quickly inculcated, new incentives provided, or rapid staff turnover undertaken. Rather than conceiving of development objectives and strategies as nation-state agreements to be imposed upon the international financial agency, it is more useful, as well as more accurate, to view them as the products of a formulation of policy in which the international financial agency participates as much as it does in implementation. Timing also becomes important, both in spacing out the shifts to new goals and orientations to permit sufficient time for accommodation and in allowing enough time for a new approach to be incorporated before judging it as a success or failure.

The conclusion of greatest theoretical importance is that development objectives and approaches as implemented by the World Bank cannot be usefully viewed as mere manifestations of bargained agreements among nation states. Apart from the difficulty of identifying just what approaches or objectives have been "agreed to" at the many high-level conferences since Bretton Woods, the practical autonomy and wide discretion of the World Bank make it unlikely that any approach we could identify as representing such an agreement would survive intact if it ran counter to the values and interests of the World Bank as an institution. It may be impossible to say for any given case whether a new initiative is or is not in the interest of the most powerful nation state or states. But because the rejection or acceptance of development approaches is often tied so clearly to the learning process of how to "design development" with professional integrity, it is highly unlikely that the evolution of development approaches would also run parallel to the evolution of state interests. The answer to the question "Where do the objectives and approaches of the international development community come from?" must be complicated: many voices, only some representing nations' interests, influence the search for a better package of strategies. The testing of these strategies may be severely constrained by the organizational interests and role conceptions of those called upon to implement them. Such testing means appraising whether a given strategy seems to foster development of sufficient speed and balance to satisfy the expectations of feasible development. Insofar as these expectations often tend to be overly ambitious, we may expect that the abandonment of old development strategies for new ones will be an enduring pattern apart from the evolution of state interests and shifts in the balance of power.

There is no a priori reason to believe that the behavior of the World Bank is typical of international agencies as a whole. Rather than assume that the theoretical perspective useful for understanding the World Bank is of general utility, it is more fruitful to ask under what conditions the same dynamics are likely to hold.

In one important respect the World Bank differs from certain other international agencies in which the problem of national identification and rivalry creates a high level of conflict and debate.[16] Because of the cosmopolitan training of top economists and engineers, the personnel in professional positions in the World Bank behave very much alike, whether they be Indian, English, Argentine, or Canadian. The World Bank mirrors the ideological divisions of the international "development community." Thus the ideological division within the Bank is not a conflict between North and South as much as between the Chicago School and the Sussex School.

However, regardless of the presence or absence of national rivalries within an international agency, the scope of autonomy of the agency vis-à-vis its overseers, and of the staff vis-à-vis its executive leadership, is still the central theoretical issue. What dimensions of the functions, structures, and staffing of

---

[16]See Robert S. Jordan, "What Has Happened to Our International Civil Service? The Case of the United Nations," *Public Administration Review* (March/April 1981), pp. 236–45.

international agencies are relevant to whether the agency is indeed an "autonomous variable" in the international political-economic system? This exploration of how and why World Bank staff members exercise relative autonomy provides clues to the relevant dimensions. These correspond quite straightforwardly to the conditions March and Simon identify as contributing to the uncertainty of either performing staff functions or monitoring them.

1. Lack of clarity of the priorities of organizational objectives. In the absence of clear-cut priorities, the signals from the organization's leadership are more likely to be ambiguous; the inability to reduce the set of "reasonable" options to those corresponding to clearly ranked objectives leaves greater scope for staff discretion and greater importance in choosing from among these options; and the leadership of the organization and the oversight representatives are in a weaker position to reject the work of subordinates as inconsistent with the organization's mandate.

The lack of clarity of priorities is obviously not a fixed characteristic, as it depends on the initiatives taken by the agency's leadership, the external pressures on the agency, and the perception-altering feedback from the agency's own behavior. Yet lack of clar-

ity may have some enduring correlates, most notably the number of objectives regarded as ultimate ends in themselves. The more objectives, the less likely that the priorities will be clear or consensually accepted.

There is ambiguity as to whether the World Bank has a higher priority to serve a regulative as opposed to a supportive role vis-à-vis borrower countries. The ambiguity gives Bank staff the room to resist leadership signals to be more assertive; but, ironically, this reluctance also represents inhibition rather than strength in dealing with the outside world. Clear objectives and priorities may limit the staff's power within the organization but strengthen the organization with respect to its environment. Thus we can speculate that International Monetary Fund personnel have an easier time than World Bank staff members in justifying their involvement in dictating terms to sovereign nations; the IMF's mandate to preserve and strengthen the international monetary system, ostensibly for the good of all members of the international community, can be invoked over the claim of autonomy of any particular government. Interestingly, IMF staff members can still avoid being "political" despite the difficulty of maintaining that the Fund's activities are free of political implications, for the Fund is necessarily at odds with governments seeking emergency loans at the least internal political cost. As the IMF's confrontations with the governments of Jamaica, Peru, and a host of other nations indicate, the Fund is notable—or notorious—for its reluctance to compromise, to depart from its firm a priori principles, or to admit tacitly that its economic criteria can be superseded by political considerations. Whether this reluctance is partly due to the "technician" mindset that prevails at the Fund, or can be entirely explained by the IMF's watchdog role, remains to be determined.

2. The difficulty and complexity of accomplishing the organization's mandate. Insofar as the agency's task becomes one of grappling with apparently or actually intractable problems, uncertainty increases and the bases for monitoring weaken. Thus, for example, the staff of the International Telecommunications Union, facing rather straightforward and technically surmountable tasks, are far less likely to become embroiled in a drawn-out debate on funda-

mental issues of how to approach the agency's tasks.

3. Organizational size. The larger the organization, the more difficult it is to monitor all the decisions of its personnel. For international organizations consisting of little more than nation-state representatives and tiny secretariats to serve them, such as OPEC or GATT, the opportunities for autonomy or defiance are obviously limited.

4. The number of "boundary" personnel. William Evan points out that organization staff who mediate between the organization and its environment not only are more prone to adopt the perspectives of other organizations thus increasing the diversity of goals held within the organization, but also are more capable of monopolizing information concerning the organization's dealings with the outside world.[17]

5. The number of decision points. The greater the number of decisions, large and small, that an organization must make, the more difficult it is for managers and overseers to monitor decisions. The World Bank's decisions on the whole range of project design and pol-

---

[17]William M. Evan, "An Organization-Set Model of Interorganizational Relations," in *Interorganizational Relations,* Evan, ed. (Philadelphia: University of Pennsylvania Press, 1978), pp. 85–86.

icy advice are considerably more numerous than the decisions taken by the International Monetary Fund, where the decisions to extend credit and to impose a usually small number of loan conditions are sufficiently limited—and important enough—to permit and to warrant careful scrutiny by the IMF leadership and Executive Directors.

6. *The reputation of personnel.* The justifications that World Bank personnel can offer to themselves and to others for resisting directives depend heavily on their claim to top-level status within their professions. Other international agency personnel (or, for that matter, foreign service professionals) may face similar dilemmas resulting from multiple objectives, unclear guidelines, and demands to violate professional norms, but their credibility in departing from orders from above suffers unless they enjoy as much repute as or more repute than their superiors. Specialized expertise reinforces the claim to top-level status, inasmuch as "generalists" have greater difficulty in establishing themselves as experts. By the same token, the absence of suspicion that national rivalries are responsible for the international civil servant's position within the agency also reinforces his or her claim to expertise, inasmuch as such suspicion could offer an alternative explanation for the staff member's having "made it."

There is no a priori reason to expect that all international agencies will have the capabilities to behave with sufficient autonomy to require treatment as international "actors." However, there are theoretical bases for analyzing the potential for autonomy and the motivation to exercise it. Once the potential is recognized for a given agency, these capabilities can be assessed through the organizational theories that account for the adaptive patterns of the World Bank.

17

UNCTAD'S FAILURES: THE RICH GET RICHER

Robert Ramsay

It is common knowledge that the United Nations Conference on Trade and Development (UNCTAD) has failed to do what it was set up to do—to narrow the ever-widening gap between rich and poor countries. There has, however, been remarkably little examination of the real reasons underlying its failure. Yet an understanding of just why UNCTAD has failed throws considerable light on the general decline of the North-South debate. In particular, it casts considerable doubt upon the validity of trying to rectify the maldistribution of wealth between rich and poor *countries* without examining the maldistribution of wealth between rich and poor *people*. Is the lack of any real probe into UNCTAD just an accidental omission, or is there a reluctance to face the unpalatable facts that underlie the organization's failure?

Most people who have had contact with UNCTAD write it off as a bizarre institution that deals in generalities. Its bizarre nature became all too apparent at its previous conference (UNCTAD V, in 1979), when five thousand people assembled in Manila under the most lavish conditions imaginable—for a discussion on world poverty. The contradiction was accentuated by the nebulosity of the policy speeches, and by the manner in which the speakers all congratulated one another and applauded each others' platitudes. By the end of UNCTAD V, the deficiencies of the organization were obvious—yet when delegates met to review the situation they made no real proposals for change. Government representatives renewed the contract of the Secretary General, which was tantamount to expressing their satisfaction with the way the organization was functioning, or failing to function.

At [the next conference], the policy speeches were just as nebulous, but the applause and congratulatory statements died down after the first day or two: people simply abandoned the pretense of a great success. All the same, it would be surprising if delegates were to make any real proposals for change [after this].

The failure of UNCTAD is often attributed to the "group system"

SOURCE: Reprinted from *International Organization*, Vol. 38, No. 2, Robert Ramsay, "UNCTAD's Failures: The Rich Get Richer," by permission of The MIT Press, Cambridge, Massachusetts. Copyright ©1984 by the Massachusetts Institute of Technology and the World Peace Foundation.

(whereby the arguments advanced are those of groups of countries and not those of individual countries) and to the inefficiency of the UNCTAD secretariat. Both these factors do call for comment, but what really needs examining is not so much the failure of UNCTAD as the failure of governments—*of rich and poor countries alike*—to show any real concern. It is this latter failure which illuminates not only the relationship between North and South but also the relationship between rich and poor people.

THE GROUP SYSTEM

The member states of UNCTAD are grouped into three "political parties." *Group B* is comprised of the industrialized countries, members of the OECD, the *Group of 77* is comprised of the developing countries (being a fusion of Groups A and C, which covered developing countries in different regions), and *Group D's* members are the socialist countries of Eastern Europe. There are also a couple of "independent members," China and Israel. Within the groups, there are enormous differences. Even in Group B, levels of prosperity and economic systems differ to a marked degree; the common factor is that all members are relatively prosperous market-economy countries. The Group of 77 embraces a much more diverse collection of countries, ranging from the oil-producing countries, through rapidly industrializing countries like

India and Brazil, to small impoverished countries like Nepal and Niger. The one thing these countries have in common is that they all classify themselves as "developing."

Unlike most national political parties, these international parties lack any coherent political philosophy. Logically, the Group of 77 might be expected to produce a body of proposals, but interests within the group are so divergent that the member countries can usually reach a uniform position only by phrasing their proposals in terms so general that they could not be used as a basis for serious negotiations. In fact, it is no secret that many of the 77 speakers who made "demands" at UNCTAD VI were aiming to produce press reports for domestic consumption rather than to provoke international discussion. Besides, the Group of 77 has one serious disadvantage when it comes to policy making: it has no secretariat.

The Group B countries generally confine their role to opposing any proposal for change. Although most of them realize that a more equitable distribution of wealth would be in the *long-term* interests of a healthy world economy, in the short term any change would adversely affect some of the B countries. The ones likely to be affected call for, and obtain, the support of the others in the name of "Group solidarity" (it being understood that on some future occasion reciprocal support will be obtained). Even when the Group B countries put forward "positive proposals" of their own, these are usually of a cosmetic nature designed to conceal their underlying resistance to change.

The Group D countries play very little part in the North-South debate. The problems, they claim, are attributable to the former colonial activities of the Group B powers (and to the current activities of the Group B corporations). They are consequently a matter for settlement between B and the 77. Nevertheless, the D countries generally support the 77, as does China.

Thus, if any specific proposals are to come forth, they could only come from the international civil servants who comprise the UNCTAD secretariat. But whereas national civil servants work to the instructions of the politicians in power, on the international scene there is no party in power and there is no cabinet to direct policy; the UNCTAD secretariat works on its own—often with peculiar results, and frequently with no results at all.

UNCTAD could have become a better forum for debating North-South issues had it been equipped with a competent secretariat to produce sound policy proposals. Unfortunately, most of the secretariat's reports have been notable for little but their length, verbosity, and obscurity, often being issued too late to be even read, let alone considered, before the relevant meetings.

Insofar as it has enunciated any general philosophy, the secretariat has talked about the need to "change the structure of the world economy" and proposed "development strategies" to bring about a "New International Economic Order" (but all in the vaguest terms). Few of the secretariat's proposals have served as a basis for taking specific action. As an inevitable consequence, most UNCTAD discussions have degenerated into an exchange of generalities. Even when the secretariat has proposed specific action, its proposals have read far too much like election speeches. Promising too many things to too many people, proposals emphasize advantages and ignore disadvantages instead of arguing the pros and cons of different courses of action, which is so essential for sound policy formulation.

Although UNCTAD officials talk of their various successes over the years in the form of international conventions, agreements, and resolutions, most of these contain more than a fair quota of vague language, and much of the consensus relates to minor rather than major matters. The "successes" have a certain value in demonstrating the procedures that could be used if ever governments were to get down to serious business, but considerably less value from the point of view of substance.

PROBLEMS IN THE SECRETARIAT

Among government delegates, it is common to attribute UNCTAD's failure to the failure of the secretariat, but, as already noted, the real question relates to the lack of any move by governments to change the secretariat.

When the secretariat was set up, what was needed was a small, cohesive body of senior officials who could clarify the issues in different sectors of the world economy and point out what could, and what could not, be achieved by intergovernmental action. It was essential that the top officials be *knowledgeable* not only as regards specific sectors of the economy but also as regards the way in which governments function. They had to be people, that is, with some appreciation of the difference between an academic thesis and a policy proposal upon which governments can take action, and also people with some basic administrative ability.

As it turned out, the qualities most needed were the most lacking. The high salaries and diplomatic status inevitably attracted individuals who were more interested in the salary and status than in the job itself. Many officials treated their Geneva appointments as little more than a comfortable way of spending their last years before retirement.

As a result, the secretariat has been not so much *administered* as *allowed to drift*. People have been hired with no real qualifications to serve the organization; others have been engaged to undertake assignments that could not possibly serve the organization's aims; others have arrived at the Palais des Nations to find themselves pitifully underemployed. Staff are permitted to develop all sorts of proposals for "further studies," proposals that are designed to serve not so much the interests of the developing countries as the personal needs of the staff in justifying extensions of their employment contracts. Vast sums of money are wasted on unnecessary work (and on paying people who do not really work at all), and on the inevitable worldwide air travel to which so many UN officials become addicted. But at the same time, there is considerable penny-pinching in areas where expenditure is really needed: professional staff have to work without even the most elementary reference facilities.

The result is the well-known stream of poor-quality documentation that flows into the in-trays of government delegates. Many of these reports should have been suppressed without being submitted, but senior officials tend to insist on publishing everything that can be published—as if the sheer volume of paper were an indicator of productivity. Yet the obscurity that permeates so many reports may not be entirely accidental: many officers feel, at least subconsciously, that if they are obscure, no one will ever be quite sure just what they are saying, and hence no one will ever say that their findings are wrong. The same attitude applies to the length of documents and the delays if delegates receive long documents at the last minute, there is a fair chance that they will never read them—and hence not criticize their authors. Even more serious, though, is the tendency of the top officials to tamper with the few good reports that are produced. Being political survivalists at heart, they erase points that might cause difficulties for particular countries (and hence the "election speech" character of so many UNCTAD reports).

As in other UN bodies, there is virtually no internal evaluation. The work of staff members is periodically evaluated on several counts and must be rated according to the standard UN ratings of Outstanding, Very good, Adequate, Somewhat below standard, and Poor. However, supervisors have been instructed that "Adequate" is deprecatory and would give a staff member the right of appeal, so even officials who can recognize poor work when they see it end up by rating all staff work as "Outstanding" or "Very good."

Faced with a growing reputation for inefficiency, many of the top officials do what incompetent civil servants do all over the world: they turn to matters of organization and procedure. But, as always, no amount of reorganization can compensate for a basic lack of competence. At the same time, many officials turn away from the policy issues for which the organization was established and bury themselves in technical assistance projects. Most of these projects are of dubious value to the recipient developing countries but of decided financial value to the bureaucrats and to the vast army of "experts" who have made technical assistance their profession.

The growing inefficiency of the secretariat has been accompanied by a decline in the number and the caliber of delegates attending UNCTAD meetings. Governments see little point in sending large numbers of high-caliber people to discuss the sort of generalities tabled for consideration. There has been a marked tendency to leave attendance to Geneva-based staff, who are inevitably jacks-of-all-trades who cannot discuss specific subjects in depth. Delegates from the capitals are much more numerous in summer than in winter, which suggests that some may not be traveling to Geneva to attend the UNCTAD meetings so much as using UNCTAD as an excuse to take trips to Europe. In turn, the decline in delegate quality has had an adverse effect upon the secretariat, as officials see little point in producing in-depth proposals for discussion by generalists. A vicious circle of cause and effect has set in, leading to the organization's ever-increasing ineffectiveness.

INACTION IN THE MEMBER GOVERNMENTS

However, all of these facts have been well known to government delegates for some time—and, it must be presumed, to government officials in the capitals. The laxity of work in Geneva's Palais des Nations has even been described in vivid terms in the press. Why, then, are there no signs of concern?

From time to time, delegates from countries that supply most of the funds (such as the United States) complain of the expense and wastage—but always in such a way as to suggest that they want to have a complaint on record rather than any real investigation and change. When delegates met to review the debacle of UNCTAD V, they made a number of proposals: for example, that the secretariat's future reports should be short (32 pages), action-oriented, and issued "on time." But these demands had been made so many times before, and ignored so many times, that the likelihood of any change was minimal. Besides, the delegates' idea of getting documents "on time" is that governments should receive them *six weeks* before a meeting, which is totally insufficient for the formulation of a national viewpoint on any issue of significance. Did the delegates not expect (or did they not *want*) the secretariat to come up with any proposals of significance?

All the evidence points to an overwhelming desire on the part of governments to prevent any change in the status quo, under which rich people get steadily richer and poor people, at least comparatively, get steadily poorer. The attitude of the Group B countries is both evident and comprehensible, since these are the countries that would suffer from any change. What is harder to understand, even allowing for the divergent interests that make it dif-

ficult for the Group of 77 to arrive at a common policy, is the 77's restraint in pressing for changes in the economic system that keeps their countries in a state of poverty. Occasionally, delegates from the 77 deliver a forceful opening statement, which suggests that they are about to move from generalities to specifics, but then fail to follow it up. Like the American delegates who complain about wastage, the 77 often give the impression of wanting to get a statement on record rather than to bring about any real change. Thus, in many UNCTAD debates, one sees the Group B countries defending the status quo, the 77 refraining from attacking it, and Group D sitting and watching.

The Group B countries have an easy task in defending the status quo in sectors where the proposals consist of generalities. All they have to do is to respond with their own, equally vague, generalities and they can be sure that nothing concrete will emerge. It is when specific proposals are advanced that the true intensity of Group B's opposition to change becomes apparent.

For the most part the B government delegates respond to specific arguments with evasive generalities. Professing to agree on the need for reaching an international consensus, they fail to show any signs of being prepared to accept a consensus on any terms but their own. The more reactionary statements are generally made by business organizations (which have been known to distort proposals to make them easier to attack). In private discussion, the government delegates dissociate themselves from organizations that "only speak for the private sector," yet in their public statements they never give any indication that they are not in entire agreement.[1]

Outside the conference rooms, the Group B countries go further. They have been known to send envoys to complain to governments of developing countries whose delegates they regard as troublemakers. Some have even involved "difficult" governments in potentially profitable contract negotiations, which effectively prevents them from speaking out at a meeting while negotiations are in progress.

The main effect of the Group B tactics has been to drive militancy *underground*. The governments of the 77 have become tired of the intransigence and prevarication they meet in UNCTAD, and individual delegates have become reluctant to be identified and harassed as troublemakers. Consequently, develop-

ing countries that are big enough, or that have sufficient bargaining power by virtue of their resources, avoid participating in any depth in UNCTAD debates and quietly go ahead and take unilateral action. The Latin American countries, for example, have maintained a low profile in UNCTAD debates on cargo entitlements for national fleets while passing their own cargo reservation laws. Countries in Africa and Asia are now doing the same.

However, the failure of the 77 to attack the existing economic order more vigorously can only be partly explained by the manner in which the 77 militancy has been driven underground. After all, comparatively few of the members of the 77 have sufficient commercial strength to be able to act unilaterally, and even the strongest of them can take only a limited amount of unilateral action. For a true explanation, one must look deeper than the superficial conflict between rich and poor *countries* and examine the underly-

---

[1]Some business organizations that can claim to be international (by virtue of the geographic spread of their membership) have official consultative status with UNCTAD; otherwise, they usually try to have representatives attached to their government delegations. The extent of the influence of such business interests has been the subject of specific comment in UNCTAD (see the secretariat report *Open Registry Fleets,* TD B/C.4/220 [Geneva, 3 March 1981], especially p. 15). Prior to UNCTAD V, the secretariat made a very limited proposal for cargo-sharing in *regular* bulk traffic with developing countries. As the concept of cargo-sharing had already been accepted in the liner trades (which are regular), it would have been difficult to oppose this proposal on grounds of logic or equity. Nevertheless, an association of tanker owners circulated counterarguments against a so-called "UNCTAD proposal to introduce cargo-sharing into *all* bulk trades." As most bulk trades are irregular, the association had no difficulty in painting an horrific picture of the practical difficulties that would arise. By exaggerating proposals, business organizations can strengthen the arguments against any international action whatsoever.

ing conflict between rich and poor *people*. For the status quo does not so much benefit rich countries as rich people, whether they are in rich or poor countries.

RICH PEOPLE AND THE STATUS QUO

There is a strong community of interest between the rich people of the rich countries and the rich people of the poor countries. The governments of poor countries are virtually all controlled by rich people, who have more in common with the rich people who control the Group B corporations than they have with their own poverty-striken fellow countrymen.

In international warfare, there is universal contempt for quislings, those who work with occupying forces to the detriment of their nation's interest. In international business, however, it is quite common for *economic* quislings to assist foreign corporations to exploit their own countries. Such people exist in all countries, but it is in the poor countries that the results are so tragic.

It is in the national interest of a poor country to pay as little as possible for imports and services such as shipping, to obtain as much as possible for exports, and to obtain the greatest possible involvement of its nationals in ventures operated by transnational corporations on its own territory. However, economic quislings will agree to pay more than necessary for imported goods and services (or agree to unneces-

sary imports) and to accept less than necessary for exports, and will allow a corporation to treat their country like an economic colony—*provided* that they themselves are "looked after" by the corporation. In fact, the main reason why the rich of the rich countries are so successful in maintaining their grasp on the world's wealth and wealth-producing activities is that there are so many rich and would-be-rich people in the poor countries who are only too willing to collaborate with them. "Economic colonialism" depends just as much upon economic quislings as upon economic imperialists.

Once one perceives the underlying labyrinth of personal interests and pressures, it becomes apparent that the formal debates between rich and poor countries in UNCTAD are little more than mock battles between the rich people of the rich countries and the rich people of the poor countries, stage-managed by the rich people of the secretariat. All of the participants have a vested interest in seeing that UNCTAD does nothing to change the status quo.

Yet none of them would want to see the organization abolished. If UNCTAD did not exist, it would be harder to resist pressures to set up some other organization, one that might turn out to be effective. As things stand, the leaders of the rich countries can pacify some of their left-wing pressure groups by talking about their efforts in UNCTAD to help the poor countries, and the rich leaders of the poor countries can talk about their efforts in UNCTAD to obtain a greater share of the world's wealth for their people. Though established to help *poor countries,* UNCTAD has ended up by serving the interests of *rich people.*

It is impossible to solve the international problem of poverty without tackling the issue of rich and poor people—and yet the question of personal enrichment is one that simply cannot be raised, let alone answered, in international bodies. Any attempt to raise this issue meets objections on the grounds that such questions constitute unjustifiable interference in the domestic affairs of sovereign states. At UNCTAD V, the people who met in such lavish conditions to discuss world poverty all behaved as if they believed the maldistribution of personal wealth to be totally irrelevant when considering the maldistribution of international wealth.

In actual fact, nothing could be more relevant. The reason is obvious: governments and corporations that oppose any redistribution of the world's wealth are all controlled by *people,* people who are in a position to reward those who do them favors and to exert pressure on those who do not. When people fight to preserve the wealth of their country or their corporation, it is because they expect to be rewarded for their efforts. The rewards sought by the UNCTAD delegates who defend the status quo (or who refrain from attacking it) are relatively modest: they are just bureau-crats who are seeking promotion. But the delegates are only the tentacles of a vast hierarchy of vested interests, headed by people whose rewards from the status quo are very substantial, and who can offer substantial rewards to those who cooperate with them and exert substantial pressure on those who do not. Indeed, it is impossible to understand the failure of the North-South debate merely by examining the substantive issues; one must look at the underlying labyrinth of personal interests and pressures.

So long as people are free to enrich themselves excessively, they will continue to apply excessive pressure to preserve a status quo that enables rich people to get richer. The failure of the North-South debate can ultimately be traced back to the failure to curb excessive *personal* enrichment. The machinery for dealing with North-South issues will continue to fail so long as it is geared to do no more than examine the superficial issues between rich and poor countries.

THE FAILURE TO CURB EXCESSIVE PERSONAL ENRICHMENT

However, while excessive personal enrichment cannot be curbed by international action, it is also the one issue upon which absolutely no initiative can be expected from national policy makers. The reason is simply that anyone who is sufficiently powerful to influence national policies is inevitably well-to-do, if not rich—someone who has already collected a fair share of the rewards and who is hoping for more. And there are very few politicians or civil servants in the world who want to abolish their own perks and privileges. Even leaders of trade unions and left-wing political parties become rather attached to the joys of living at the top. Outside the circles in which government policies are formulated, the effects of excessive personal enrichment are largely unstudied. Scholars steer well clear of the subject, perhaps out of fear of offending people who could help their future careers.

Certainly, there has been public comment on Third World elites who enrich themselves while neglecting their communities, but always with the innuendo that this is a problem endemic to developing countries. Yet it is obvious to anyone who has moved around in the bureaucracies of business, industry, and government that exactly the same thing is occurring in the industrialized countries, albeit in a less blatant form.

High salaries, status symbols, and fringe benefits have ceased to be rewards for competence and effort and have become ends in themselves. They divert administrative and managerial talent away from the task of improving the productive capacity of society and into incessant power struggles to get to the top, creating a whole new breed of power-seekers who are more competent at manipulating themselves into well-paid, prestigious positions than they are at performing the functions involved. The worst aspect is that government planning officers, whose sole function should be to determine what is best for their country, have become notorious for favoring policies that will maximize their own roles and minimize those of their rivals. Whether the policies happen to be good or bad for the country has become a secondary consideration. The same applies a fortiori to the planners in international organizations.

It is true that the money spent "rewarding" the top people would make little difference to the standard of living if redistributed in cash throughout the community. However, it *would* make a significant difference if invested on the factory floor to increase productivity and improve working conditions. Moreover, people who are free to use their decision-making powers to make life comfortable for themselves soon *cease to care* how comfortable or uncomfortable life may be for the rest of the community, and the money they siphon off for lavish living arouses the hostility of the work force. A hostile work force, in turn, discourages outside investment. Thus, the failure to curb excessive personal enrichment, whether in rich or poor countries, ultimately leads to poor national planning and administration, mismanagement, a hostile work force, and insufficient investment— a perfect formula for failure.

Given the vested interests, though, if there is to be any revolt against excessive personal enrichment it could only come from outside the established corridors of power. Such a revolt, in fact, could only come from the sort of popular pressures that stopped the war in Vietnam and forced governments to take up issues of human rights.

The need for some such revolt is greatest in the poor countries, for they suffer from the greatest gap between rich and poor people, the greatest economic failures, the greatest instability, and the greatest lack of investment. The inequitable distribution of wealth *within* poor countries also provides rich countries with a sound reason for refusing aid, since they can argue that benefits would only end up in the hands of the ruling elites. In fact, aid to the Third World has been cynically defined by some disillusioned field experts as "taxing money out of the pockets of the poor of the rich countries in order to fill the pockets of the rich in the poor countries."

However, it is in the poor countries that such a revolt is least likely to occur, because most of them lack the democratic structure needed for popular protests, and most lack the middle classes of reasonably educated people from whom such protests are most likely to arise. In any event, it is the rich of the rich countries who set the basic pattern for lavish living-at-the-top. If excessive personal enrichment were to be forced out of fashion in the rich countries, it would soon cease to be the fashion elsewhere.

THE DECLINE OF THE NORTH-SOUTH DEBATE

The North-South debate is fading toward oblivion because the conflict between rich and poor countries was never really the fundamental issue, and the debate has now reached the point where the participants can no longer pretend that they are making progress. Initially, the debate had a strong appeal to those who felt motivated to do something about poverty, but after years of talking the poverty continues.

The basic problem in tackling poverty is that one cannot examine the question of *poverty* unless one also examines the question of *wealth*—though that is just what national politicians try from time to time to do by advocating a "war on poverty," whereby they can pander to public feelings of pity without pointing accusing fingers at their rich constituents. One might conceivably wage war on wealth, but to speak of waging war on poverty is meaningless. It is for this reason that wars on poverty invariably fade from public notice after the first flurry of political speeches.

Unlike wars on poverty, the North-South dialogue at least recognizes the relevance of wealth when dealing with poverty—but it is the delightfully vague wealth of the rich countries, or the even vaguer wealth of "the West." Treating the issue in terms of rich and poor *countries* implies that the poor countries (including their upper layers of very rich people) should enjoy a monopoly on world pity, while the rich countries (including their masses of poor people) should take all the blame. While it is common for countries to be called rich or poor if the majority of their citizens are rich or poor, it is the poverty of poor *people,* not poor countries, that should arouse sympathy, and it is the avarice of rich *people,* not rich countries, that calls for examination.

There will be no solution to the international problem of "poor countries" until governments take action to restrain excessive personal enrichment. And governments are only likely to take action if popular pressure forces them to do so.

CHAPTER VII

Social and Humanitarian Activities

The most varied and yet least known activities of international organizations are in the social and humanitarian issue area. Many goals such as those of universal literacy, adequate nutrition, and proper health care are widely shared. The methods of implementation are also considerably less controversial than operational activities in the security and economic issue areas. States are less inclined to disagree over the promotion of sanitary facilities than they are over international trade barriers. Consequently, support for these efforts is generally high. The World Health Organization (WHO) is almost universally applauded for its efforts at eradicating certain diseases. The United Nations High Commissioner for Refugees has twice been awarded the Nobel Peace Prize for its work. Some of the most effective work of international organizations takes place in this issue area.

Even though there is consensus on many international organization activities, controversy is far from absent. The most prominent example of conflict is the withdrawal of several states from the United Nations Scientific, Educational, and Cultural Organization (UNESCO). As that organization questioned press freedom and acted on other issues with political overtones, some Western members objected that the organization had gone beyond its original mandate of promoting literacy and cultural exchanges. Indeed, the same cleavages that are apparent in the economic realm manifested themselves in UNESCO. Other social issues also generated conflict between member-states. A recent conference on population problems produced a heated debate over the use of abortions to limit further population growth. In another instance, various meetings on the status of women have produced some bitter controversies as states seek to reconcile differing cultural perspectives on the role of women in societies.

The articles in this section focus on two of the most controversial issues that international organizations have sought to address: human rights and regulation of health-related products. Setting international standards for human rights is a difficult task at best, complicated by the tremendous political and cultural diversity in the world. Western states

320

have emphasized individual, political, and civil rights in their formulations, while Third World states have often noted the primacy of group rights in the economic and social realm. Reconciling these positions has been slow, but some notable successes are apparent. Forsythe traces the activities of the United Nations in the human rights field over the past forty years. It may be discouraging to realize that human rights violations are a common practice in many states of the world today. Yet, it must be remembered that prior to World War II, little or no international standards of human rights conduct existed. Given also that it takes several generations for norms to become embedded in international society, it may surprise the reader that real progress has been made in this area. Forsythe's analysis is useful both in pointing out the various actions already taken as well as the limitations that international organizations still face in the promotion of human rights around the globe.

Another notable activity of international organizations has been the attempt to regulate the behavior of transnational corporations through the establishment of codes of conduct. Much of the emphasis in the United Nations has been concerned with national development and the impact that large, foreign corporations can have on that process. Yet, equally important have been the efforts to enhance the health and well-being of the world's population by regulating the sale and use of certain products from those corporations. Sikkink details the most successful of these efforts in her article on the international regulation of infant formula products. Her insightful analysis will allow the reader to get a good view of the work of the WHO and the United Nations Children's Emergency Fund (UNICEF) as well as the critical role of nongovernmental organizations in the development of policy in this area. The most important contribution of this article is her analysis of the conditions that allowed for such a successful regulatory effort. This should provide the reader with some basis for judging the likelihood that similar international codes will arise on other products such as pharmaceuticals. Undoubtedly, in the coming years, codes of conduct to improve health and safety will become a prominent and controversial item on the agendas of international organizations.

18

THE UNITED NATIONS AND HUMAN RIGHTS, 1945–1985

David P. Forsythe

Between 1945 and 1985 there has been a marked change in the treatment of human rights at the United Nations. On the foundation of a few vague references to human rights in the UN Charter there has evolved an International Bill of Rights indicating numerous obligations of increasing salience. This core of global rules has been supplemented by a series of particular human rights instruments, some with special control mechanisms. Once the subject of human rights seemed idealistic and abstract, but by the 1980s there was growing attention through an increasing array of UN organs to specific countries and patterns of behavior such as torture and people who have disappeared. The subject of human rights has not faded away like that of military coordination under the Security Council nor has it remained on the back burner like the Trusteeship Council. Rather it has emerged more and more as one of the subjects to which member-states give great attention, if not always for the same reasons.

Considerable debate exists at the United Nations over the signifi-cance of this change in the treatment of human rights. Clearly, the institutional and procedural changes in the field of human rights have been striking. It also seems clear that there is some legal significance to these changes. At least it now can be said that states have accepted a number of new legal obligations and that numerous "cases" exist which can be used as "precedent" should actors choose to do so in pursuit of human rights values. Ambivalence begins to set in when one tackles the subject of the practical significance of these changes for the condition of human rights beyond UN meeting rooms. There is considerable disagreement about what constitutes progress in human rights and how to discern it. Debate also exists over whether events at the United Nations constitute a global regime on human rights.

Attention will be given first to the more striking institutional and procedural changes at the United Nations concerning human rights to be followed by a discussion of some of the reasons why these changes have occurred. In these first two sec-

SOURCE: Edited and abridged with permission from *Political Science Quarterly*, Vol. 100, No. 2, Summer 1985, pp. 249–67.

tions evidence will be presented which should help correct a widespread misunderstanding about the UN and human rights. The third section will tackle the difficult subject of the significance of the changes. What can one realistically expect from the United Nations on human rights issues? What has the UN achieved measured against this standard of expectation? If the conclusion is ambivalent, both optimistic and pessimistic, perhaps this will prove understandable in a complex and uncertain world.

AN OVERVIEW

There are a variety of views on the historical evolution of the United Nations and human rights.[1] Most observers agree on three early stages, each lasting about a decade. From 1945 or 1947 to 1954 human rights diplomacy at the UN focused on the drafting of norms— the elaboration of the Charter provisions on human rights. From about 1954 to around 1967 optimists say human rights diplomacy turned to indirect protection or promotion efforts through seminars and publications of various studies on human rights problems in general, without naming countries or specific patterns of behavior. Pessimists see this period as one of inaction despite a supposed UN action plan on human rights. This view has some merit, although numerous persons at the UN were active on several human rights matters. The Eisenhower administration, however, traded away much activity on human rights at the UN in return for the demise of the movement in the U.S. Congress for a "Bricker amendment" to the Constitution which would have limited executive authority in foreign affairs.[2] A third stage clearly starts around 1967 when activity at the United Nations began to target selective protection of rights in specific countries like South Africa and Israel. Shortly after, this concern for specifics was broadened to other targets. At one point these efforts at protection became almost global, especially after the two major Covenants—or treaties—on human rights came into legal force. Most countries were not guaranteed freedom from some type of "UN" supervision of their rights record. Whether there will be a fourth stage beyond these three is a matter of debate.

---

[1]Howard Tolley, Jr., "The United Nations Commission on Human Rights," unpublished manuscript, read by permission; Theo C. van Boven, "United Nations and Human Rights: a Critical Appraisal," in Antonio Cassese, ed., *UN Law/Fundamental Rights* (Alphen aan den Rijn: Sijthoff & Noordhoff, 1979), 119–136; Karel Vasak, ed., *The International Dimensions of Human Rights,* vols. 1–2 (Paris: UNESCO, 1982).

[2]James Frederick Green, an advisor to Eleanor Roosevelt, confirms that the "Action Plan" was a diplomatic device to deflect criticism away from the U.S. policy shift. Interview with author, Atlanta, Ga., 1984.

Because the definition of most historical eras is partly arbitrary, I will speak simply of before and after the mid-1960s. Before the 1960s there was a certain "timidity" on the part of member-states in approaching the human rights issue, and almost all expectations were low about utilizing the United Nations to act on human rights questions.[3] The superpowers had not been terribly interested in international human rights at the start of the San Francisco Conference in 1945, although the U.S. responded to nongovernmental organization (NGO) pressures enough to get Article 55 placed in the Charter to give a legal basis to human rights activity. This climate of opinion controlled events at the United Nations during its first years. The UN Humans Rights Commission, an instructed body reporting to the Economic and Social Council (ECOSOC), issued a self-denying ordinance in 1947 holding that it had no authority to hear specific complaints about human rights violations. The commission functioned basically as a research and drafting organ. As part of its action (or inaction) plan of the 1950s, states were asked to voluntarily report on their rights policies. Reports were generally self-serving and not subjected to careful review. When the commission's Subcommission on the Prevention of Discrimination and the Protection of Minorities, composed of experts uninstructed by their states' governments, had a rapporteur who became assertive and tried to push an analytic summary drawn from state reports, the subcommission buried the project. Western states sought the termination of the commission's subgroups and ironically succeeded in stopping the one on freedom of information. The one on discrimination and minorities was barely saved by other coalitions.[4] The one on women continued as a separate commission. Sporadic resolutions on particular subjects like forced labor did not change the dominant pattern of this early period which was marked more by lip service to human rights than by specific protection efforts.

The Universal Declaration of Human Rights was adopted in 1948.

---

[3]M. E. Tardu, "United Nations Response to Gross Violations of Human Rights: the 1503 Procedure," *Santa Clara Law Review* 20 (Summer 1980): 559; and Van Boven, in Cassese, 122. For a good overview of the early climate of opinion at the UN see Leon Gordenker, "Development of the UN System" in Toby Trister Gati, ed., *The U.S., the UN, and The Management of Global Change* (New York: New York University Press, 1983), 11–21.

[4]The fight to save the subcommission was led by Chile, Mexico, and the Philippines. The Soviet bloc gave its support. Those voting to keep alive the subcommission were: Afghanistan, Argentina, Burma, Byelorussia, Chile, Colombia, Czechoslovakia, Denmark, Dominican Republic, Ecuador, Egypt, Ethiopia, Haiti, Indonesia, Iran, Iraq, Liberia, Mexico, Pakistan, Paraguay, Peru, Philippines, Poland, Saudi Arabia, Syria, Ukraine, Soviet Union, Uruguay, Venezuela, Yemen, Yugoslavia. *United Nations Yearbook 1951* (New York: United Nations, 1954).

The two major Covenants were negotiated (one on civil and political rights, the other on economic, social, and cultural rights). These instruments came to have considerable salience legally and politically. However necessary this drafting was, in this first period it was accompanied by considerable foot-dragging. Even Eleanor Roosevelt, the U.S. representative to the Human Rights Commission, argued repeatedly that the Declaration was not intended to be legally binding.[5] The Covenants, while substantially completed by 1954, were not approved by the General Assembly and opened for signature until 1966, and did not reach the number of required adherences for entry into legal force until 1976. Most states seemed anxious about accepting specific and binding obligations and did not want the UN Human Rights Commission or other organs of the UN to be assertive in the cause of human rights.

Prior to the mid-1960s, however, a number of other human rights instruments were developed. Concern with labor rights and slavery carried over from the time of the League of Nations. New legal instruments were created concerning refugees, genocide, women's political rights, and the rights of the child. Toward the end of this first period treaties were drafted on prevention of racial discrimination and discrimination in education. It was as if states could not help themselves from drafting documents proclaiming high-minded goals, even if their specific policies fell short of the standards they were approving. Many states failed to submit required reports to the Committee on the Elimination of Racial Discrimination (CERD) after adhering to the treaty.[6]

In the second twenty years of the United Nations the situation changed markedly. Efforts increasingly moved from the general and the abstract to the specific and the concrete. Some drafting efforts continued—for example, on a special instrument concerning torture. The UN accepted the principle of the permissibility of individual petitions and created several mechanisms to deal with them. Increasingly UN bodies used publicity to pressure specific states. Targets were not limited to South Africa and Israel, or even Chile. Increasingly across the UN system there was a fragile but persistent movement toward improved supervision of states' policies on human rights. More and more human rights treaties came into legal force and var-

---

[5]General Assembly, Third Committee, Summary Record, A/C.3/SR.89, 30 September 1948. See further A. Glenn Mower, Jr., *The United States, The United Nations, and Human Rights: The Eleanor Roosevelt and Jimmy Carter Eras* (Westport, Conn.: Greenwood Press, 1979).

[6]Thomas Buergenthal, "Implementing the Racial Convention," *Texas International Law Journal* 12 (Spring/Summer 1977): 187–222. While this Convention came into legal force in 1969 and now has over 120 adherences, it was not until 1982 that ten states permitted individual petitions and thus brought that part of the treaty into legal force.

ious agencies tried to see that they were implemented.

The Human Rights Committee

The UN Covenant on Civil and Political Rights came into legal force for adhering states in 1976. Since then the number of states that are bound under the treaty has grown to about seventy-five. These elect an eighteen member committee of uninstructed persons to review state reports and to hear individual petitions from persons whose state has accepted an optional protocol permitting such action (about thirty at the time of this writing). The committee does not take instructions from UN bodies, but it reports to the General Assembly and interacts with the UN Secretariat. By most accounts since 1978 the committee has been energetic and assertive, seeking to make the review process as rigorous as possible, but staying within the bounds of a generally cooperative attitude toward states.[7]

In 1980 an important discussion arose about the authority of the committee in the light of Article 40, paragraph 4 in the Civil-Political Covenant. This reads: "The Committee shall study the reports submitted by the States Parties to the present Covenant. It shall transmit its reports, and such general comments as it may consider appropriate, to the States Parties. The Committee may also transmit to the Economic and Social Council these comments along with the copies of the reports it has received from State Parties to the present Covenant."

A majority of the thirteen members participating in the debate wanted to give considerable scope to the word "study" and not be deterred from vigorous action by the word "general." This majority was made up of Third World as well as western members. Clear support for an active committee came from Ecuador, Jordan, Tunisia, and Senegal, as well as West Germany and Norway. The members from Eastern Europe—especially from the USSR, East Germany, and Romania—were a distinct minority. Eventually a compromise statement was reached: "general comments" would be addressed to state parties; the committee could comment on the implementation of the Covenant; protection of human rights was a proper subject for the committee, not just promotion; the committee could take up the sub-

---

[7]Dana D. Fischer, "Reporting Under the Covenant on Civil and Political Rights: The First Five Years of the Human Rights Committee," *American Journal of International Law* 76 (January 1982): 142–153. Under Article 41, states may declare that the Committee is authorized to receive complaints from other states. Too much can be made of this subject. The history of other instruments—for example, the European Convention on Human Rights—shows that states are reluctant to make such legal claims. Similar political claims can already be made in the General Assembly or Human Rights Commission.

ject of "the implementation of the obligation to guarantee the rights set forth in the Covenant. . . ;" the committee might later consider further what duties it would undertake; the Secretariat would be asked to make an "analysis" of states' reports and the pattern of questions by members. Subsequently other comments by members indicated that many would continue to push for a serious review process and that an attempt would be made to be systematic in order to establish patterns over time.[8] If this compromise seemed in the short run a concession to the East Europeans, it contained ample language to legitimize expansive and assertive action by the western and Third World members. Since 1980, "general comments" has been used to interpret the Covenant in a specific way.

In 1981 the committee publicly criticized Uruguay for its treatment of certain individuals. The committee in effect rejected a report from Chile and criticized the inadequacies of several other reports. The committee also requested the Secretariat to put pressure on Zaire for its failure to file a report on time. Many states have been questioned closely about their reports and policies; frequently additional information is requested and provided. Aside from the Soviet Union and its close allies, the nature of questioning does not usually follow ideological alignments. At one point in 1983 the member from Yugoslavia seemed very tough on the subject of Nicaragua's treatment of Miskito Indians. At another point the member from West Germany was exceedingly tough in addressing the presenter of the report from France. The member from Tunisia led the effort to put pressure on Zaire.[9]

The Human Rights Committee has not functioned for very long. Its authority, procedures, and impact are still in flux. It seems clear thus far that the majority on the committee, irrespective of turnover, intend to have as much impact as the committee can generate. National laws in Sweden and Senegal have been changed apparently as a result of committee questioning.

The Human Rights Subcommission

The United Nations Subcommission on Prevention of Discrimination and Protection of Minorities has become over time an uninstructed body on human rights in general, functioning under the Charter under whatever mandates might be received from its parent commission, ECOSOC, or the General Assembly, and under whatever

---

[8]Covenant on Civil and Political Rights, Committee on Human Rights, Summary Record, CCPR/C/SR.201, 24 March 1980; CCPR/C/SR.231, 24 July 1980; CCPR/C/SR.232, 23 July 1980; CCPR/C/SR.253, 28 October 1980; CCPR/C/SR.260, 4 November 1980.

[9]*United Nations Chronicle* 20 (January 1983): 105; 20 (July 1983): 92–95; 20 (November 1983): 57–64.

initiatives it might seize for itself.[10] On the one hand its membership has not been that different from its instructed parent which elects its twenty-six members. In 1982, according to the index of Freedom House, ten members came from "Free" nations, seven from "Partly Free," and nine from "Not Free."[11] Many individuals have served as instructed representatives of a state and at another time as supposed uninstructed members of the subcommission. This is a prevalent personnel pattern not limited to Eastern European delegations and one that reappears in the Human Rights Committee as well. On the other hand the members of the subcommission have been so assertive at times that superior bodies have found it necessary to suppress the subcommission's activity, ignore its projects, change its mandates, or change its membership. The subcommission has been more willing to use public pressure on states than its superiors and has also sought to do as much as possible on a number of specific problems like detained or disappeared persons. It has tried a variety of procedures to improve its efficacy, such as instituting working groups on particular problems which meet before regular sessions. The working group on slavery has been notable in this regard. It is the U.N. body of first recourse for private communiques under important resolutions, and it has performed that review with seriousness of purpose since 1972. At times the subcommission has attempted direct, public, and specific protection; for example, it sent a telegram to the government of Malawi concerning a violation of human rights.

Once, there was some fear that the expansion of the subcommission's membership and thus an increase in Third World members would dilute or slant its activity. This does not appear to have happened. In the 1980s members from Eastern Europe, joined by the one from Pakistan, tried to establish the principle that the subcommission would act only by consensus. This would have given a blocking role to a minority which might wish to curtail the persistently assertive subcommission. This move was rejected, with a number of Third World members lining up with western members.[12] The subjects taken up by the subcommission, the states criticized, and the resolutions passed do not show a simple East-West or North-South bias. At

---

[10]See further in Tolley, "The United Nations Commission."

[11]"Free" countries were Belgium, Costa Rica, France, Greece, India, Nigeria, Norway, Peru, United Kingdom, United States. "Partly Free" were Bangladesh, Egypt, Mexico, Morocco, Panama, Sudan, Zambia. "Not Free" were Argentina, Ethiopia, Ghana, Iraq, Pakistan, Rumania, Syria, Soviet Union, Yugoslavia. There is much controversy about the accuracy of this Index.

[12]Lanne Wiseberg, ed., *Human Rights Internet Reporter,* 9 (September-November 1983): 58–59.

the time of this writing the subcommission seemed as serious and assertive as in the past, and as seriously circumscribed.

The Human Rights Commission

The United Nations Human Rights Commission is an instructed body elected by ECOSOC and now comprised of 43 states. Using the rating system of Freedom House, one finds that in 1982 the commission was made up of 17 states classified as "Not Free," 10 as "Partly Free," and 16 as "Free."[13] If 63 percent of the states making up a human rights body show major deficiencies in their own records concerning civil and political rights, one might reasonably expect that body to be less than enthusiastic in its activity. This assumption, however, is not completely substantiated by the facts.

If one looks at the last decade of the commission, after the drafting of the Covenants and later after two expansions of its membership, it can be said that doctrinal disputes over the relationship of socioeconomic and civil-political rights—and over which had priority—gave way to an increasing focus on the protection of specific civil and political rights.[14] During the 1980s

the West has become increasingly successful at enlisting majority support for new implementation measures to protect civil and political rights. In 1980 the Commission for the first time indirectly condemned an Eastern bloc ally by passing a resolution calling for withdrawal of foreign forces from Kampuchea. In the following two sessions, the Commission denounced foreign intervention in Afghanistan. The West also narrowly succeeded in getting Commission action on Poland and Iran in 1982. [There were also] several important Western-sponsored resolutions adopted by consensus—involving the appointment of special rapporteurs on mass exoduses and summary or arbitrary executions and studies on the role of the individual in international law.[15]

The key to these and other developments within the commission has been the role of Third World states which are truly nonaligned. They have voted their concern for self-determination in Kampuchea and Afghanistan, and they have also voted for economic rights and

---

[13]"Free:" Australia, Canada, Costa Rica, Cyprus (Greek sector), France, West Germany, Greece, Italy, Netherlands, United Kingdom, Denmark, Fiji, India, Japan, Peru, United States. "Partly Free:" Panama, Philippines, Uganda, Uruguay, Zimbabwe, Brazil, Gambia, Mexico, Senegal, Zambia. "Not Free:" Algeria, Bulgaria, Ethiopia, Jordan, Rwanda, Syria, Zaire, Argentina, Byelorussia, China, Cuba, Ghana, Pakistan, Poland, Togo, Soviet Union, Yugoslavia. See comment in footnote 11.

[14]Philip Alston, "The alleged demise of political human rights at the UN: a reply to Donnelly," *International Organization* 37 (Summer 1983): 537–546; van Boven in Cassese, 90.

[15]Tolley, "The United Nations Commission."

against racial discrimination.[16] Some Third World states like Senegal have been vigorous and balanced in their attention to human rights violations. Evidently a number of Third World states are genuinely interested in human rights, even civil and political rights. Daniel Patrick Moynihan, the former U.S. Ambassador to the United Nations, noted that one of the merits in framing issues in terms of human rights, rather than democracy pure and simple, was that a state did not have to be a democracy to pursue the subject with some real interest.[17] Of course some Third World states of various ideological stripe have sought to limit the activity of the commission. For example, Pakistan, India, and Ethiopia have all taken restrictive positions in commission debates at one time or another. And any Third World state will seek to block attention to its own transgressions.

Yet in the final analysis Third World support for western positions, and vice versa, has allowed the commission to do as much as it has. Since 1978 the commission has been publishing a "Black List" of states which have been the subject of private complaints as noted confidentially by the subcommission. Over time this list has shown considerable balance.[18] To be sure, it is correct to observe that this "Black List" is a very weak form of pressure; specifics about the subject of the complaint are not provided. A working group of the commission has been focusing in a balanced way on states in which persons "disappear" by forceful action.[19] A summary statement about the commission seems accurate:

> Representatives continue to assert the principle of non-intervention when it suits their national interest, but in practice most members of the Commission have supported some initiatives to protect the human rights of citizens against violation by their own governments . . . the Commission has systematically reviewed confidential communications alleging violations by members . . . the Commission has expanded its concern for violations far beyond the early narrow focus on South Africa and Israel and has

---

[16]Ibid.

[17]Daniel Patrick Moynihan, *A Dangerous Place* (Boston: Little, Brown and Co., 1978), 281.

[18]Through the spring of 1984 the following states had been targeted: Albania, Argentina, Benin, Bolivia, Burma, Chile, Equatorial Guinea, Ethiopia, Greece, Indonesia, Iran, Malawi, Nicaragua, Paraguay, South Korea (not a UN member), South Africa, Uganda, Uruguay, Soviet Union.

[19]Through the spring of 1982 the following states had been targeted: Argentina, Bolivia, Brazil, Chile, Cyprus, El Salvador, Ethiopia, Guatemala, Guinea, Honduras, Indonesia, Iran, Lesotho, Mexico, Nicaragua, Philippines, Sri Lanka, Uganda, Uruguay, Zaire, South Africa, Namibia. Interestingly, the Working Group was made up of three "Not Free" states (Ghana, Pakistan, Yugoslavia) and two "Free" ones (Costa Rica, United Kingdom).

reviewed allegations involving over thirty states. Members and NGOs now disregard the former taboo against attacking states by name in public debate and make sweeping public indictments. After thirty years, the Commission has become the world's first intergovernmental body that regularly challenges sovereign nations to explain abusive treatment of their own citizens.[20]

The Economic and Social Council

(ECOSOC) receives the reports of the Human Rights Commission as well as state reports under the U.N. Covenant on Economic, Social, and Cultural Rights—a treaty now in legal force in about eighty states. In this part of the United Nations system there does not at first glance seem to be striking change in the treatment of human rights. The conventional wisdom has been that on human rights ECOSOC functions as a "post office," carrying mandates from one body to another.[21] A recent analysis by an insider argued that ECOSOC was still giving "very superficial scrutiny" to state reports on socioeconomic rights and had failed to develop or borrow standards by which to observe violations.[22] Yet within ECOSOC several further points can be noted, even if

ECOSOC votes reflect decisions made in the commission or subcommission.

In the late 1960s Third World states pushed for specific attention to human rights violations by South Africa and Israel in many parts of the United Nations system. Stimulated by reports not only from the Human Rights Commission but also from the U.N. Special Committee on Decolonization, ECOSOC passed E/RES/1235 in 1967. This resolution—originally intended only for situations of racism, colonialism, and alien domination but amended by the West to include other human rights violations—authorized ECOSOC's suborgans to deal with specifics revealing a pattern of gross violations of human rights. The following year an effort to close the barn door failed; ECOSOC again refused to limit the scope of 1235 to only some violations of human rights, and thus the Human Rights Commission and its subcommission were authorized to take up specific patterns with full publicity.[23]

Three years after the passage of 1235, ECOSOC adopted E/RES/1503 which permitted its suborgans to deal with private communications alleging violations of human rights. This resolution permitted NGOs as well as individuals—any-

---

[20]Tolley, "The United Nations Commission."

[21]James Frederick Green, "Changing Approaches to Human Rights: The United Nations, 1954 and 1974," *Texas International Law Journal* 12 (Spring/Summer 1977): 223.

[22]Alston, "The alleged demise." See also his "The United Nations' Specialized Agencies and Implementation of the International Covenant on Economic, Social and Cultural Rights," *Columbia Journal of Transnational Law* 18 (1979): 79–118.

[23]Tardu, "United Nations Response."

one with direct and reliable knowledge—to lodge an allegation confidentially with the Secretariat, which then passed a sanitized version to the subcommission for possible future action.

The result of these two resolutions in ECOSOC was to make possible the expanded activity of the Human Rights Commission and Subcommission. Specifics could be pursued and private information could be formally utilized. There was both a public and a confidential process, although the two did not always remain distinct. The point worth stressing is that certain Third World and western states succeeded in authorizing more serious attention to human rights. An effort by the East Europeans and other Third World states to keep the process limited to the international pariahs was not successful. The margin of success for the majority was very small on both resolutions. The key to the majority, in addition to western states, was certain Third World states which sought a balanced approach to human rights protection.[24]

General Assembly

Much has already been written about the General Assembly and its standing committees regarding human rights. A widespread impression, supported by a number of facts, is that the Assembly has "politicized" human rights by employing double, unfair, or unacceptable standards. Israel is publicly and harshly criticized by a special committee made up of three states that do not even have formal diplomatic relations with the Jewish state. Yet the Soviet Union's gulag is never formally condemned by the UN bodies discussed in this article. The litany about the tyranny of the majority in the General Assembly is too well known to require restatement. Considerable attention has also been given to the view that the majority has tried to erase serious attention to civil and political rights by elevating social and economic rights to a place of exclusive priority.[25]

I will suggest a counter thesis and give just one example as evidence. Much is wrong with the General Assembly's treatment of human rights. Politics controls; equity suffers. Increasingly, however, one sees in the Third Committee on Social and Humanitarian Affairs the same alignment on votes that one finds in other UN bodies—namely, ECOSOC and the Human Rights Commission. The result is improved balance in the treatment of human rights produced by the western and Third World coalition noted earlier. Take the following example.

In 1982 in the Third Committee there was another doctrinal debate about the priority of rights. As the

---

[24]Ibid.

[25]Jack Donnelly, "Recent Trends in UN Human Rights Activity: Description and Polemic," *International Organization* 35 (Autumn 1981): 633–655.

representatives of both New Zealand and Senegal noted, the debate was about the balance between individual and collective socioeconomic rights. An Irish resolution emphasized the former, a Cuban the latter. The crux of the matter came down to whether each resolution could be adopted without distorting amendments, thus signifying that each type of right had importance. The Cuban resolution was voted upon first and adopted by 104-1 (U.S.) with 24 abstentions (mostly western). The Irish resolution was finally adopted 75-30-22. Voting with the West in the majority were 46 nonaligned states.[26] A similar alignment carried the day on paragraph 12 of the Irish resolution which authorized a study of the mandate for a possible High Commissioner for Human Rights.

As on any vote in any political body, no one simple reason explains a coalition. The list of those voting for the Irish resolution does not reflect a club of the pure on civil and political rights. Paraguay, for example, voted for it. Despite the fact that the Cuban resolution was assured passage and the Irish was not, the end result was that individual civil and political rights received equal formal endorsement. This was made possible by the number of Third World states that were not prepared to endorse in principle a one-sided approach to human rights.

Security Council

The Security Council has not been generally linked to the protection of human rights. But, on the two occasions when the Council reached a "decision" in relation to the Charter's Chapter VII concerning enforcement action, the real issue at stake was human rights. The decision in the 1960s to consider Ian Smith's Unilateral Declaration of Independence in Rhodesia as a threat to peace meriting mandatory economic sanctions was a decision designed to implement the right to self-determination for the majority in what was to become Zimbabwe. That right is the first right listed in each of the two general UN Covenants on Human Rights. The decision in the 1970s to consider arms traffic with South Africa as a threat to the peace requiring a mandatory ban on such traffic was an indirect approach to the subject of apart-

---

[26]Bahamas, Barbados, Botswana, Burma, Chad, Colombia, Costa Rica, Cyprus, Democratic Kampuchea (represented by the Pol Pot faction), Djibouti, Dominican Republic, Ecuador, Egypt, El Salvador, Fiji, Gabon, Guatemala, Ivory Coast, Jamaica, Kenya, Lesotho, Liberia, Malawi, Mali, Mexico, Morocco, Nepal, Niger, Papua New Guinea, Paraguay, Peru, Philippines, Senegal, Sierra Leone, Singapore, Somalia, Sri Lanka, Sudan, Thailand, Trinidad and Tobago, Tanzania, Upper Volta, Uruguay, Venezuela, Zambia, Zimbabwe. Voting with the East Europeans in the minority were: Afghanistan, Algeria, Angola, Argentina (under military rule), Congo, Cuba, Democratic Yemen, Laos, Libya, Madagascar, Mongolia, Pakistan, Syria, Vietnam. Other states abstained, including Ethiopia and Nicaragua. A/C.3/37/SR.60, December 1982, 7, 17–19.

heid as a gross violation of internationally recognized human rights, and perhaps as a violation of self-determination as well. Especially with regard to South Africa and Namibia, the Council has called upon states to implement the principles contained in the Universal Declaration of Human Rights. As a member of the Secretariat has observed, in these actions the Council "treated respect for the basic provisions of the Declaration as a legal obligation of States as well as of their nationals."[27]

THE REASONS

It can be seen from the preceding incomplete synopsis that the United Nations has changed with respect to human rights. What are the underlying reasons for this change? At least five sets of factors contributed to this modification.

States' Foreign Policies

A view with some popularity in the 1980s is that events unfold at the United Nations according to a struggle between the United States and the rest of the world.[28] Therefore, any progress on human rights questions results from the quality of the diplomacy of the U.S.-led West. This view is overstated, al-

though it is correct in a certain sense.

The Soviet bloc, joined by some Third World states, has been consistently hostile to international civil political rights and to any meaningful UN review process. The Soviet interpretation of human rights under Marxism, one that is inhospitable to the prima facie meaning of UN instruments, is stated openly.

> The political freedoms—freedom of the press, of expression, of assembly—are interpreted from class positions as conditions of the consolidation of the working people and the spread of socialist ideology which rules out the 'freedom' of anti-socialist propaganda, the freedom to organize counter-revolutionary forces against the fundamentals of socialism.[29]

Thus the individual has the right to say and do only what the party-state decrees is progressive for socialism. The Soviet-led socialist bloc will try to avoid real supervision of its rights policies by a non-socialist review body. The Soviet Union has maintained this dual position from 1947 when it opposed having the UN Human Rights Commission made up of uninstructed individuals, and 1948 when it first tried to postpone and then finally abstained on the vote on the Uni-

---

[27]Egon Schwelb and Philip Alston, "The Principal Institutions and Other Bodies Founded Under the Charter," in Vasak, ed., *The International Dimensions*, 262.

[28]Richard Bernstein, "The United Nations vs. The United States," *New York Times Magazine*, 22 January 1984, 18. (On human rights see especially 25–26).

[29]Vladimir Kartashkin, "The Socialist Countries and Human Rights," in Vasak, ed., *The International Dimensions*, 633.

versal Declaration, to the 1980s when it argued that the UN Human Rights Committee should have no real control over states' interpretation of the Civil-Political Covenant. The member of that committee from East Germany even argued that the committee had no right to take any action whatsoever when a state failed to submit a required report.[30] On issue after issue during the first forty years of the United Nations, the Soviet Union and its allies, joined occasionally by such non-Marxist authoritarian states as Pakistan and the Philippines, tried to suppress attention to international civil-political rights and to vitiate real UN supervision of rights policies.

The Soviets and their shifting bedfellows on human rights have not always, or even fundamentally, triumphed at the United Nations because of two factors. First, other states have displayed an equally persistent interest in a different interpretation of civil and political rights (as well as a real interest in socio-economic rights) and have fought for a genuine review process at the UN. One thinks primarily of the Scandinavian states, but also at times the United States, the rest of the western coalition, and some Third World states.

Second, a self-serving interpretation equal to that of the Soviets by some U.S. administrations has offset the Soviet position and in a dialectical process caused a number of states to seek a compromise leading to a certain type of progress. If the Soviet Union consistently displayed a double standard in favor of socialist states, so the United States at times manifested a double standard in favor of authoritarian and capitalist states aligned with it. When a rapporteur for the subcommission wrote a report criticizing economic relations which supported the governing junta in Chile after 1973, the United States helped suppress it.[31] When resolutions were introduced in various UN organs criticizing gross violations of human rights in El Salvador and Guatemala, the United States voted against them.[32] At one point the U.S. voted against a commission study on the right to food,[33] and the U.S. was the only government to vote against World Health Organization voluntary guidelines designed to protect mothers and infants from questionable marketing practices by the Nestlé Corporation. The Reagan administration likes to publicly castigate leftist governments such as Cuba's while remaining silent about mass political murder by governments of the right such as Argentina's. U.S. Ambassador Jeane Kirkpatrick had written approvingly of such double

---

[30]CCPR/C/SR.201, 24 March 1980, 4–5.
[31]Tolley, "The United Nations Commission."
[32]*United Nations Chronicle*, 20 (June 1983): 28.
[33]*United Nations Chronicle*, 20 (July 1983): 80.

standards.[34] Thus an American double standard, an American self-serving bias could be and was observed at the United Nations.[35] This provided a counterpoint to the Soviet position.

Because some states were genuinely interested in a cosmopolitan human rights program and sought a compromise between the self-serving positions of the superpowers, states' foreign policies greatly contributed to the alteration of the United Nations' record on human rights. State hypocrisy, narrow self-interest, and blatant double standards, along with more cosmopolitan forces, combined to produce a certain progress over time.[36]

Nongovernmental Organizations (NGO)

One of the main reasons why the United Nations record on human rights is different in the 1980s from the earlier days is because of the activity of nongovernmental international organizations. Groups such as Amnesty International, the International Commission of Jurists, the International League for Human Rights, and others have been creative and energetic in keeping the pressure on states to acknowledge and then implement international human rights standards.

NGO information started various UN organs down the path of a slow but eventually interesting treatment of human rights violations in Equatorial Guinea in the 1970s. Confidential NGO information was provided to the subcommission, and eventually the commission sent a rapporteur for an in-country visit which led to a public report critical not only of the fallen regime but of the current one as well. NGO pressure after the passage of E/RES/1235 quickly broadened the subcommission's focus beyond Israel and South Africa; information was submitted on Greece then under military rule and also on Haiti. NGOs successfully pushed for passage of E/RES/1503 permitting confidential communiques of broad scope. They kept the pressure on states to do something about the growing problem of torture, and pushed successfully for a special group on disappeared persons. NGO reports are

---

[34]Jeane Kirkpatrick, *Dictatorships and Double Standards* (Washington, D.C.: American Enterprise Institute, 1982).

[35]If the American double standard was particularly pronounced during the Reagan administration, in fairness it should be noted that in 1974 Rita Hauser, a former representative to the UN Commission, testified in Congress that the U.S. frequently used a double standard at the UN House of Representatives, Committee on Foreign Affairs, *Report of the Subcommittee on International Organizations,* "Human Rights in the World Community: A Call to Leadership," (Washington, D.C.: U.S. Government Printing Office, 1974), 10, 11. See also Tolley, "The United Nations Commission."

[36]On the subject of how state hypocrisy can lead to beneficial change, see Louis Henkin, "The United Nations and Human Rights," *International Organization* 19 (Summer 1965): 514.

used openly by the Committee of Experts under the Racial Discrimination Convention. In the Human Rights Commission their information is referred to formally by Secretariat reports. In the Human Rights Committee it is now acknowledged that members can informally use NGO reports as a basis for questioning the accuracy of state reports.[37]

Nongovernmental organizations have been so active on human rights at the United Nations that various states have threatened to curtail their activity, sometimes succeeding, but more often failing. The Soviet Union, for example, tried unsuccessfully to exclude NGO reports from ECOSOC and its suborgans.[38] Other threats have been made (by Argentina and Iran, for example) to deny a NGO group consultative status, but these have not been carried out. The very fact that NGOs are attacked suggests that these groups are taken seriously by states. Several observers believe that NGO activity is essential for continued efforts at protecting human rights.[39]

Secretariat

Members of the Secretariat have contributed to the changing United Nations record on human rights, from the Secretary-General down through the Directors (now Assistant Secretaries-General) for Human Rights to the Secretariat officials who service the various human rights working groups. The five Secretaries-General to date have been supportive of human rights to varying degrees. On a number of occasions the Secretary-General has used his good offices for quiet diplomacy designed to correct some human rights problem.[40] Publicly they have endorsed the cause. . . . The head of the human rights division (now centre) in the Secretariat has also always been a westerner. . . .

Uninstructed Individuals

Individuals, especially those on the subcommission and the Human Rights Committee must be given credit for contributing to increased efforts at specific protections.

---

[37]The literature on NGOs has grown voluminously. Particularly enlightening for this essay were: Virginia Leary, "A New Role for Non-governmental Organizations in Human Rights," in Cassese, 197–210; Nigel S. Rodley, "The Development of United Nations Activities in the Field of Human Rights and the Role of Non-Governmental Organizations," in Gati, 263–282; Chiang Pei-Leng, *Non-Governmental Organizations at the United Nations: Identity, Role, and Function* (New York: Praeger Publishers, 1981).

[38]Alston, in *Santa Clara Law Review*, 559.

[39]David P. Forsythe, *Human Rights and World Politics* (Lincoln: University of Nebraska Press, 1983).

[40]B. G. Ramcharan, "The Good Offices of the United Nations Secretary-General in the Field of Human Rights," *American Journal of International Law* 76 (January 1982): 130–141.

There are other uninstructed bodies not given adequate attention in this article because of lack of space: the Committee of Experts under the Racial Discrimination Convention, the Commission on Women, the Commission on Discrimination Against Women, the Committee of Experts, the Freedom of Association Commission of the International Labor Organization, and the office of the High Commissioner for Refugees (HCR). The HCR is perhaps the UN uninstructed agency given the highest marks for its human rights work and its merits extended analysis. On all these bodies there have been individuals keenly interested in the protection of human rights. They have generated some influence, impossible to measure in the aggregate. A number of these persons have come from the Third World.

World Public Opinion

One can certainly overstate the importance of the hoary idea of world public opinion. Even so, I think it prudent to note what other scholars have observed. "National political leaders have to reckon with the possibility, and on occasion the reality, that powerful voices in their own societies will echo the words of the General Assembly, as they have done on issues of colonialism, human rights . . . and humanitarian assistance."[41] If this is what is meant by world public opinion, then there is probably a process at work that bears noting and merits more research attention in the future.

It seems highly probable, but not proven in all cases, that various public groups draw some of the inspiration and legitimacy for their human rights activity from United Nations resolutions, declarations, and conventions. Various groups in Eastern Europe refer to these documents, as well as to others such as the Helsinki Accord. Human rights groups in Argentina did the same in addition to relying on human rights instruments under the Organization of American States. Obviously there is some overlap between what is called world public opinion and the impact of nongovernmental organizations. Yet there exist some groups and private citizens who do not act directly through the United Nations system but who are active at home in demanding that their governments abide by global, United Nations standards on human rights. In that sense there is something which passes for world public opinion, weak and uneven in distribution, but extant and possibly even growing. There is fragmentary evidence that even in closed societies governments are asked by some of their citizens to observe the human rights standards endorsed at the United Nations.

THE SIGNIFICANCE

The significance of United Nations activity on human rights can

---

[41]Gordenker, "Development of the U.N. System," 33.

be discussed according to immediate and long-term effects. The immediate impact is usually slight, for the United Nations does not primarily bring about direct protection, although such efforts exist from time to time: telegrams to Malawi; public reports about specific individuals in Uruguay; public debates about specific policies, states, and persons; special reports about Equatorial Guinea. These efforts of direct protection will continue; states, individuals, and groups will pressure the United Nations to take short-term action on particular problems.

There is not much evidence, however, that such human rights protection activity by the UN bodies discussed in this article has had much impact on target states, at least in the short run. In some cases negative and public approaches have backfired, as when Augusto Pinochet's Chile in the 1970s used United Nations pressure about human rights violations to produce a national plebiscite endorsing his military regime. While one can chart some cosmetic change in South Africa in terms of abandonment of petty apartheid, it is difficult, if not impossible, to find decisive change in the states targeted by the United Nations for human rights abuses, much less information which would allow one to attribute any change directly to the United Nations. Furthermore, when a ruling group is determined to consciously violate human

rights, it is doubtful that any international arrangement short of armed intervention will bring an end to these violations. Witness Greece under the colonels, Argentina under the junta, the USSR since 1917.

The bulk of United Nations activity on human rights is not designed to produce short-term change. The Human Rights Committee's main activity is to produce a record of *patterns* over time drawn from states' reports and members' questions. Under E/RES/1503, confidential communications and the subcommission's analysis are supposed to deal with patterns of gross violations of human rights. The commission's publication of a "Black List" devoid of specifics is designed to focus on certain states *over time*. What would be required for successful direct protection? The authority to command violating parties to do otherwise? The ability to enforce such a command? Overwhelming political pressure directed to human rights violations to the exclusion of other interests? No United Nations human rights body has such authority and power. Only the Security Council comes close, and even its power to enforce is tenuous as seen in the history of economic sanctions on Rhodesia.

Those most familiar with the United Nations and human rights understand that the organization does not normally utilize its authority and power for direct protection.[42] As a general rule, only

[42]See especially John Gerard Ruggie, "Human Rights and the Future International Community," *Daedalus,* 112 (Fall 1983): 93–110, and N. G. Onuf and V. Spike Peterson,

states and a few international agencies have the capacity to attempt direct protection: the European Court and Commission on Human Rights, the Inter-American Commission on Human Rights, the International Committee of the Red Cross, and the United Nations High Commissioner for Refugees.[43] The United Nations' primary raison d'etre in the human rights field is long-term and can be viewed in two ways. One can say that the sum total of UN activity is supposed to socialize or educate actors into changing their views and policies on human rights over time toward a cosmopolitan human rights standard as defined by United Nations instruments. Or one can say that the sum total of UN activity is to dispense or withhold a stamp of legitimacy on member-states according to their human rights record.

A version of the latter view has gained some currency in American circles in the 1970s and 1980s. Am-

bassadors Moynihan and Kirkpatrick, among others, have charged that the United Nations is a dangerous place where a majority attempts to delegitimize the western democracies while legitimizing their own violations of civil and political rights in the name of economic development.[44] This article demonstrates that the Moynihan-Kirkpatrick thesis is essentially correct when applied to Soviet bloc and some Third World states, but that it is not accurate as a description of the over-all United Nations record on human rights.

It does seem correct to highlight the socialization process and the dispensing of legitimacy, which are two sides of the same coin, as the main activity of the United Nations in the human rights area. It can be persuasively argued that in some cases—for example, Anastasio Somoza's Nicaragua, the Shah's Iran, perhaps Ferdinand Marcos's Philippines—the ruling regime lost its legitimacy in the eyes of important

---

"Human Rights and International Regimes," *Journal of International Affairs* 37 (Winter 1984): 329-f. See also Henkin, "The United Nations and Human Rights"; Tardu, "United Nations Response"; Helge Ole Bergesen, "The Power To Embarrass: The UN Human Rights Regime Between Realism and Utopia," paper presented to the International Political Science Association (IPSA) World Congress, Rio de Janeiro, Brazil, August, 1982; and N. G. Onuf and V. Spike Peterson, "Human Rights from an International Regimes Perspective," paper presented to ISA convention, Mexico City, April 1983.

[43]Direct protection has never been defined legally or analytically. It may be a phenomenon known when seen but resistant to precise definition. All international regimes or agencies that seek direct protection activities depend to some extent on state cooperation. This dependence does not denigrate direct protection. See Onuf and Peterson, "Human Rights and International Regimes." The key is that a human rights actor trying direct protection seeks immediate and specific change either by command—the European Court of Human Rights—or by diplomatic action—the European and Inter-American Commissions—or by administrative action combined with diplomacy—the ICRC and HCR.

[44]Moynihan, *A Dangerous Place,* 11; and Jeane Kirkpatrick, *The Reagan Phenomenon* (Washington, D.C.: The American Enterprise Institute, 1983).

actors because of human rights violations. The United Nations' definition of human rights, along with other international standards and actors, probably contributed to the process.[45]

The examples above might suggest that primarily non-Marxist authoritarian states have the most to fear from attention to international standards of human rights. Certainly the major democratic states have shown periodic discomfort about their close alignments with human rights violators. Yet it also seems true that Marxist states have problems of legitimacy and do not fare well when international sources of legitimacy are denied. Surely those who rule Poland have not been helped by persistent condemnation by the International Labor Organization (ILO), not to mention sporadic censure by the UN Human Rights Commission. There are a number of Soviet specialists who believe that achieving international legitimacy is still a pressing problem and priority for the Soviet Union itself,[46] not to mention Nicaragua under the Sandinistas.

The importance of United Nations activity on human rights lies in this long-term socialization process in which one source of legitimacy is given or withheld according to human rights performance. Any number of states are in need of the United Nations' stamp of approval, or in need of avoiding its disapproval, although all have other sources of legitimacy such as their own traditions, performance, and internal procedures. A feature which weakens United Nations impact is the disorganized state of its human rights endeavors. The various rights agencies are not well coordinated *inter se* or with the General Assembly.

At some point the long-term effects of the UN must become short-term if the organization is to show real impact on states and individuals. Socialization and manipulation of legitimacy must change specific behavior and must lead to direct protection by some actor if the United Nations is to manifest real significance for human rights. In a few situations this linkage can be demonstrated. In the case of *Filartiga* v. *Peña Irala* in the United States, a federal court held torture to be prohibited by customary international law, using United Nations instruments and actions as part of its legal reasoning.[47] This case opened the possibility of spe-

---

[45]Moynihan talks of the UN as a repository of "ideological authority," 12. For a discussion of international human rights as a new standard of legitimacy with the potential to transcend debates over democratic capitalism versus authoritarian Marxism see Forsythe, *Human Rights,* chap. 6.

[46]Seweryn Bialer, "The Soviets May Actually Want a New Cold War," *The Washington Post National Weekly Edition,* 6 February 1984.

[47]U.S. Court of Appeals, 2nd Circuit, 30 June 1980, No. 79-6090. 630 F. 2nd 876. A synopsis can be found in *The American Journal of International Law,* 75 (January 1981): 149–153.

cific prosecution for torturers of any nationality who appear in the jurisdiction of the United States. Other courts in the U.S. have also used United Nations instruments and activity on human rights as part of their decisions.[48] Other states beyond the U.S. show some influence from UN instruments in their legal and administrative decisions.[49] Politically it is clear that various groups and individuals refer to events at the United Nations to justify their existence and activity, and it is highly likely that in areas like the Southern Cone of South America in the 1980s the United Nations—along with other bodies—had a real if indirect impact on human rights and even the structure of national politics.

A smattering of evidence suggests that United Nations activity on human rights can have some real impact over time in changing behavior by contributing to direct protection by national authorities. Other evidence suggests that in other situations United Nations activity has very little, if any, impact.[50]

19

CODES OF CONDUCT FOR TRANSNATIONAL CORPORATIONS: THE CASE OF THE WHO/UNICEF CODE

Kathryn Sikkink

On 25 January 1984 one of the world's largest food corporations, Nestlé, signed an unprecedented agreement with its nongovernmental critics. Nestlé pledged to implement fully the WHO/UNICEF In-

SOURCE: Reprinted from *International Organization*, Vol. 40, No. 4, 1986, Kathryn Sikkink, "Codes of Conduct for Transnational Corporations: The Case of the WHO/UNICEF Code," by permission of The MIT Press, Cambridge, Massachusetts. Copyright © 1986 by the World Peace Foundation and the Massachusetts Institute of Technology.

[48]This has been especially true on refugee and immigration matters. See Gilburt D. Loescher and John A. Scanlan, "The Global Refugee Problem: U.S. and World Response," *The Annals,* 467 (May 1983). More generally see James C. Tuttle, ed., *International Human Rights Law and Practice* (Philadelphia: American Bar Association, 1978).

[49]See especially Louis Henkin, ed., *The International Bill of Rights: The Covenant on Civil and Political Rights* (New York: Columbia University Press, 1981), chap. 13.

[50]In an important study Ernst Haas shows that ILO activity in behalf of freedom of association failed to alter the policies of a number of states, especially those in Eastern Europe. See Ernst Haas, *Human Rights and International Action* (Stanford, Calif.: Stanford University Press, 1970).

ternational Code of Marketing of Breast-milk Substitutes, which the World Health Assembly had adopted in May 1981. In return the company's critics, represented by the International Nestlé Boycott Committee (INBC), recommended a suspension of the seven-year international consumer boycott of Nestlé products.[1]

The agreement was the culmination of an often novel interaction among international organizations, transnational corporations, national governments, and a transnational grass-roots movement of church groups, health workers, political activists, and consumer organizations. The WHO/UNICEF code is one of the few successful efforts to date to get an international code, and the final joint agreement between Nestlé and the INBC is even more unusual: a formal agreement between a corporation and its nongovernmental critics by which the corporation guarantees to abide by a voluntary code of conduct worked out in an international organization.

In the political economy literature of the 1980s it has become unfashionable to speak about "codes of conduct" for transnational corporations (TNCs); codes seem the vestiges of an unrealistic optimism about a New International Economic Order. Indeed, the literature on the issue reveals that very little has been written recently about ongoing efforts to regulate the international operations of TNCs.[2] Declining interest in codes may have resulted in part from the stagnation perceived in two of the largest and most visible efforts at codes: the general code of conduct being negotiated by the UN Commission for Transnational Corporations, and the transfer of technology code considered within UNCTAD. However, codes in more narrowly defined issues, such as the WHO/UNICEF code and the subsequent agreement for the code's implementation, may provide insights into future patterns of TNC regulation.[3] In this article I shall examine the WHO/UNICEF code, emphasizing its implica-

---

[1]World Health Organization, *International Code of the Marketing of Breast-milk Substitutes* (Geneva, 1981); "Joint Agreement, International Nestlé Boycott Committee and Nestlé," 25 January 1984, signed by Carl Angst, executive vice president of Nestlé, S.A., and William L. Thompson, stated clerk of the United Presbyterian Church, representing the International Nestlé Boycott Committee.

[2]Exceptions include John Robinson, *Multinationals and Political Control* (New York: St. Martin's, 1983), and Bart Fisher and Jeff Turner, eds., *Regulating the Multinational Enterprise: National and International Challenges* (New York: Praeger, 1983). In addition, legal journals have given considerable attention to codes, for example, the special issue of the *American Journal of Comparative Law* 30 (Autumn 1981) devoted to an examination of codes of conduct.

[3]Often called the Infant Formula Code, the code applies to "any food being marketed or otherwise represented as a partial or total replacement for breast-milk, whether or not suitable for that purpose." I thus refer to it as the WHO/UNICEF code and to the entire debate as the baby food debate rather than the infant formula debate.

tions for other international code efforts.[4]

1. CODES OF CONDUCT AND AN EMERGING INVESTMENT AND TNC REGIME

The WHO/UNICEF code will be discussed as an instrumentality developed within an emerging regime for investment and transnational corporations.[5] I shall argue that the code is a high-water mark for agreements possible within the current normative consensus because of a convergence of conditions favorable to its adoption. While new regimes for both trade and monetary issue areas emerged after 1945, as part of the Bretton Woods system,

new principles, norms, rules, and procedures to govern international investment or the activities of international firms attracted little attention (excluding the stillborn ITO Charter). By the late 1960s and early 1970s, however, this attitude was changing as Third World countries (and some developed countries) began to demand increased national and international control over TNCs.[6]

An active and sustained interest in TNCs on the part of the United Nations has been a feature of the 1970s and 1980s. The most significant UN resolution on the subject, passed in 1972 in ECOSOC, formally recognized the importance of TNCs for the United Nations and recommended the formation of a

---

[4]For other aspects of the baby food controversy, see Wolfgang Fikentscher, "United Nations Codes of Conduct: New Paths in International Law," *American Journal of Comparative Law* 30 (Autumn 1982), pp. 590–93, on legal implications. Prakash Sethi, *The Righteous and the Powerful: Corporations, Religious Institutions and International Social Activism—The Case of the Infant Formula Controversy and the Nestlé Boycott* (Marshfield, Mass.: Pitman, 1985), examines the issue in relation to the business literature. See also James E. Post, "Assessing the Nestlé Boycott: Corporate Accountability and Human Rights," *California Management Review* 27 (Winter 1985), pp. 113–31.

[5]Regime theorists have never shown how specific agreements relate to the larger regime. In this case it seems absurd to speak of an "infant feeding regime," though in the future it may be possible to speak of a "hazardous substance regime" of which the Infant Formula Code is a part. For the time being it is more useful to think of all current code efforts for transnational corporations as specific instrumentalities or agreements within the normative framework of the emerging regime for investment and TNCs.

[6]In the late 1960s many countries began to assert increased control over the TNC activities. Nationalization is the most dramatic, but not necessarily the most characteristic, form of host-country control, which can also involve policies, legislation, and provisions on such basic issues as monitoring and screening investors, ownership, and divestment, technology transfer, taxation, disclosure, investment guarantees, and dispute settlement. One survey reveals that of 29 less developed countries, 22 adopted regulations on transnational corporations during the period 1967–80; seven had legislation relating the TNCs prior to 1967; and only one has no such regulation. See United Nations, Centre on Transnational Corporations (UNCTC), "National Legislation and Regulations Relating to Transnational Corporations" (New York, 1981).

group of eminent persons to study the issue and make recommendations. This ECOSOC resolution laid the groundwork for subsequent UN actions on TNCs, among them the opening of negotiations on codes of conduct.[7] After the Group of Eminent Persons issued its report in 1974, a plethora of code efforts was initiated both inside and outside the UN system. A few have already been adopted; most are still being discussed or are under negotiation. The various efforts to regulate TNCs through codes of conduct fall into four main categories. First, industry codes, adopted either by a single company or more often by an industry or sector, are often "preemptive codes"—responses to criticism of industry practices, they attempt to ward off external regulation by showing that the industry is capable of regulating itself. Examples include the International Council of Infant Formula Industries (ICIFI) code on infant food marketing, adopted in 1975, and the code of the International Federation of Pharmaceutical Manufacturers Associations on the marketing of pharmaceutical products. At a more general level, both the International Chamber of Commerce (in 1972) and the U.S. Chamber of Commerce (in 1975) have published voluntary codes of conduct designed to guide the operations of their member companies.[8] Some industries are making efforts short of actual codes to respond to their critics by means of "dialogue groups" aimed at developing guidelines for corporate behavior. One such group, for example, has been discussing the export and marketing of pesticides.[9]

Second, regional governmental codes are efforts by groups of countries to develop common policies and harmonize existing practices with regard to the treatment of foreign investment or the behavior of corporate actors. Such codes include all rules on investment and TNCs involving more than bilateral agreements and yet less than global organization.[10] The two best-known examples are the Andean Investment Code and the OECD Guidelines for Multinational Enterprises.

Third, international codes of narrow scope often address a single in-

---

[7]See Werner J. Field, *Multinational Corporations and U.N. Politics: The Quest for Codes of Conduct* (New York: Pergamon, 1980), p. 18.

[8]International Chamber of Commerce, "Guidelines for International Investment" (Paris, 29 November 1972); U.S. Chamber of Commerce, "Elements of Global Conduct for Possible Inclusion in Individual Company Statements" (Washington, D.C., January 1975).

[9]"Guidelines for Advertising Practices in the Promotion of Pesticides Products in Developing Areas of the World." October 1983, prepared by the Agricultural Chemicals Association Dialogue and accepted by the National Agricultural Association, Washington, D.C.

[10]Robert Grosse, "Codes of Conduct for Multinational Enterprises," *Journal of World Trade Law* 16 (September-October 1982), p. 147.

dustry or even a specific aspect of a particular product. While the best-known example is the WHO/UNICEF code on baby foods, a similar code for the marketing of pharmaceutical products has also been discussed. Work is also going forward, in the Food and Agriculture Organization, on a draft international code for the distribution and use of pesticides.[11]

Finally, international codes of broad scope set standards for TNCs as a group rather than for specific industries or sectors. These codes are characterized by general (often vague) language and provisions. The broadest is the code currently being negotiated in the Commission on Transnational Corporations, which includes provisions for most aspects of TNC as well as governmental behavior. Other broad-scope codes include the ILO Tripartite Declaration of Principles Concerning Multinational Enterprises and Social Policy; the UNCTAD Set of Multilaterally Agreed Equitable Principles and Rules for the Control of Restrictive Business Practices; and the Transfer of Technology Code under consideration in UNCTAD.

These various attempts at international regulation share sufficient characteristics that one can envision them as components of a new investment/TNC regime. Most national and international efforts to regulate TNCs stress not "delinking" but rather the need to "harmonize" the activities of corporations with the economic and development goals of states. They seek to limit the potentially harmful aspects of TNC activity and ensure a higher net benefit for host countries. In this sense the underlying principle of the emerging TNC regime resembles the principles that have characterized the trade and monetary regimes—reconciliation of the needs of the capitalist international economic system with domestic social and economic policy. The compromise involved is what John Ruggie has called "embedded liberalism."[12] A multilateral, negotiated framework for TNCs and investment within which to resolve problems is still being constructed.

While the emerging regime provides an overall normative structure, the particular form and nature of attempts at regulation—the instrumentalities adopted in each issue area—are not predetermined by the general framework. Outcomes (specific agreements) thus depend on process-level factors that vary from one issue to another. The agreements that develop within regimes can be explained in part by factors that modify the cost-benefit calculations

---

[11]FAO, "Draft International Code on the Distribution and Use of Pesticides" (Rome, February 1984).

[12]John Ruggie, "International Regimes, Transactions, and Change: Embedded Liberalism and the Postwar Economic Order," *International Organization* 36 (Spring 1982).

of important actors.[13] The WHO/UNICEF code is perhaps the most detailed and restrictive agreement possible within the current normative consensus, because the convergence of favorable conditions created a significant demand for its adoption among key actors.

The favorable factors that contributed to the adoption of the WHO/UNICEF code can be divided into broad categories of issue, actor, and setting. Among the issue characteristics, the specificity of the issue and the high level of consensual knowledge contributed to code development. Among actor characteristics, I shall focus on three groups of actors: governments, industry, and nongovernmental organizations (NGOs) that criticized industry's marketing practices. What is especially significant in the baby food debate is that from the beginning a group of relatively unified and well-informed NGOs was heavily involved in the issue and in the code process. Most previous work on regimes has virtually ignored the role of nonstate actors in the formation and transformation of regimes. The baby food case illustrates the opportunities for nonstate actors (in this case, transnationally organized nongovernmental, nonprofit organizations) to alter the incentive structure for major actors and help create a demand for new agreements within the regime. The characteristics of the baby food industry in general, and Nestlé Corp. in particular, made these companies more susceptible to public pressure and, in the case of Nestlé, to a consumer boycott. Characteristics of the setting and timing of debate, in particular the speed of the code-building process, the commitment of WHO/UNICEF staff, and the extensive involvement of all interested parties in consultation and negotiation but not in actual drafting, also contributed to the successful completion of a detailed code.

In subsequent sections, after discussing the background to the WHO/UNICEF code, I shall discuss each of these characteristics in greater detail. . . . Finally, I shall discuss some implications of the baby food issue for the general development of codes of conduct for transnational corporate activities. . . . The WHO/UNICEF code is significant not only because it is one of the few successful code efforts to date but also because, within some business and government circles, it is being discussed as a harbinger.[14] Kenneth L. Adelman, when U.S.

---

[13]Cf. Robert O. Keohane, "The Demand for International Regimes," *International Organization* 36 (Spring 1982).

[14]Adopted UN codes includes UNCTAD's Set of Multilaterally Agreed Equitable Principles and Rules for the Control of Restrictive Business Practices, adopted by the UN General Assembly in 1980 (TD/RBP/CONF/10/Rev. 1); the Tripartite Declaration of Principles Concerning Multinational Enterprises and Social Policy, passed in November 1977 by the ILO Governing Body; the WHO/UNICEF Code for the Marketing of

deputy representative to the United Nations, wrote that "it appears that the infant formula drive was just the opening skirmish in a much larger campaign. . . . And this larger campaign could reach beyond regulation of pharmaceuticals to encompass United Nations codes on hazardous chemicals, transborder data flow, and an array of so-called consumer protection activities."[15]

One business service that monitors international organizations has warned its clients that "unless chemical and pharmaceutical [corporations] . . . carefully monitor developments in hazardous substances policy in the interim and deftly work to counter their growing critics, they may be faced . . . with the sort of fast-paced, hard-hitting, emotional code building exercise that confronted infant formula manufacturers."[16] An examination of the baby food code will help us to evaluate whether such sweeping judgments are justified.

2.   THE BACKGROUND OF THE WHO/UNICEF CODE

Infant formula was developed as a consumer product to respond to changing lifestyles and high incomes in the developed world. As birth rates in the developed world declined, however, markets expanded only slowly, and producers began to export to and market in the Third World. They gave little thought to the impact of their product in a new context. But illiteracy, poverty, contaminated water, and the absence of facilities to sterilize and refrigerate transformed a product relatively safe in the First World into a potentially hazardous substance in the Third.[17] Despite mounting scientific evidence and criticism of the impact of corporate marketing, industry refused to acknowledge responsibility for what seemed at times an inevitable misuse of the product it was aggressively promoting.

Although some infant formula TNCs began to locate production facilities abroad, subsidized milk production and export subsidies for dried milk exports in the European Economic Community (EEC) led many to maintain production units in Europe and the United States, supplying Third World markets through exports. These firms competed for market share primarily through minor product differentiation and intensive marketing and advertising, including mass media campaigns, free samples, free gifts

---

Breastmilk Substitutes; and the FAO/WHO Code of Ethics for International Trade in Food, adopted by the Codex Alimentarius Commission in 1979.

[15]Kenneth L. Adelman, "Biting the Hand That Cures Them," *Regulation*, July–August 1982, p. 16.

[16]International Organization Monitoring Service, Bulletin 82–02 (11 January 1982), p. 6.

[17]See, for example, D. Surjano et al., "Bacterial Contamination and Dilution of Milk in Infant Feeding Bottles," *Journal of Tropical Pediatrics*, 1979.

to doctors, and donations of supplies and equipment to hospitals and clinics. Sales personnel attired as nurses, the so-called "mothercraft nurses," promoted infant formula directly to new mothers in hospitals, clinics, and home visits.[18]

The issue first came to public attention in the early 1970s when health workers in Third World countries began to document significantly higher morbidity and mortality rates among bottle-fed as compared to breast-fed infants.[19] International organizations were actively involved in the issue from the outset. In the early 1970s the UN Protein Calorie Advisory Group warned that poverty, unsanitary conditions, and illiteracy could lead to abuse of infant formulas. It recommended careful supervision of the marketing and use of breast-milk substitutes. The Twenty-Seventh World Health Assembly, in 1974, passed a resolution that urged "member countries to review sales promotion activities on baby foods and to introduce appropriate remedial measures, including advertisement codes and legislation where necessary."[20]

Although international organizations had embraced the infant formula issue before activist groups became involved, the involvement of nongovernmental organizations (NGOs) speeded up and strengthened activity and ensured more complete implementation of the code once adopted. Church and consumer organizations helped generate public debate. They began to publicize the issue, focusing on the role of Nestlé, a company that accounted for approximately 40 percent of infant formula sales in developing countries. The British development organization War on Want published a pamphlet in 1974 entitled *The Baby Killers,* which the Swiss Third World Action Group translated into German and retitled *Nestlé Kills Babies.* Nestlé inadvertently provided the activists with a prominent public forum when it sued the Third World Action Group for defamation and libel.[21]

In 1977 a U.S. group, the Infant Formula Action Coalition (INFACT), was formed and initiated a consumer boycott of Nestlé to pressure the company into changing its marketing practices.

---

[18]James Post and Edward Baer, "Demarketing Infant Formula: Consumer Products in the Developing World," *Journal of Contemporary Business* 7 (Autumn 1978), p. 22; Andy Chetley, *The Baby Killer Scandal* (London: War on Want, 1979), pp. 94–95.

[19]S. J. Plank and M. Milanesi, "Infant Feeding and Infant Mortality in Rural Chile," *WHO Bulletin* no. 48 (1973), p. 48; H. Kananneh, "The Relationship of Bottle Feeding to Malnutrition and Gastroenteritis in a Pre-Industrial Setting," *Environmental Child Health,* December 1972; D. B. Jellife, "Commerciogenic Malnutrition," *Nutrition Review* 30 (1972).

[20]Resolution WHA27.43, *Handbook of Resolutions and Decisions of the World Health Assembly and the Executive Board,* 4th ed. (Geneva, 1981), 2:58.

[21]From case materials prepared by Professor James E. Post of Boston University, "Nestlé Boycott (A)," Graduate School of Business, Stanford University, 1981, p. 9.

Increased domestic concern led Senator Edward Kennedy (D.-Mass.), chairman of the U.S. Senate Subcommittee on Health and Scientific Research, to call hearings on "The Marketing and Promotion of Infant Formula in the Developing Nations." At a meeting in 1978 between Senator Kennedy and representatives of the infant formula industry, all parties agreed that an international approach should be taken; they requested a World Health Organization meeting.

The joint WHO/UNICEF consultative meetings on the issue, held in Geneva in 1979, included not only representatives from governments and international organizations but also industry executives, health experts, and NGO and consumer activists. In May 1980 the World Health Assembly gave the WHO secretariat a mandate to prepare a code of conduct regulating industry behavior. Twelve months later the World Health Assembly adopted the Code of Marketing for Breast-milk Substitutes prepared by the secretariat. The vote was 118 in favor, 3 abstentions, and one (the United States) against.

The code, adopted as a recommendation nonbinding on member governments, is a fairly specific, detailed set of guidelines. It restricts the more aggressive forms of marketing and advertising but does not limit the sale of infant formula. It calls for a prohibition on the use of mothercraft nurses to promote formula, bans direct advertising of breast-milk substitutes, prohibits distribution of free samples to mothers, and requires product labels to acknowledge the superiority of breast feeding and warn about the dangers of improper preparation. The code forbids the use of health care facilities for the promotion of baby food and limits company donations and gifts to hospitals and health care personnel. In addition, it specifies that companies shall not pay employees any commissions or bonuses on sales of infant formula.

NGO field monitoring has determined that, although significant violations still occur, industry marketing of baby foods and hospital feeding practices for infants have changed substantially since the code was adopted.[22] One activist referred to the result as a "minor revolution in infant feeding practices in the Third World."[23] Mothercraft nurses and mass media advertising have been virtually eliminated, while gifts, free sampling, and blatant misrepresentation of the benefits of formula feed-

---

[22]See INFACT, *Monitoring Report: Infant Foods Industry,* July–August 1984: "Thirteen Nation Field Data and Analysis of the International Babyfood Industry Marketing Activity with Reference to Industry Obligations under the International Code of Marketing of Breast-milk Substitutes." I have also used my field interviews, conducted in Central America December 1981–January 1982.

[23]Interview with Edward Baer, Interfaith Center on Corporate Responsibility, New York, 15 April 1982.

ing are much rarer than they used to be.[24]

Almost three years after the adoption of the code, Nestlé and its NGO critics signed a joint agreement that expressed Nestlé's commitment to abide by four final aspects of code implementation: a limit on the supply of free formula to hospitals, no personal gifts to health professionals, hazard warnings on labels, and no written materials to mothers and health care staff that omit the hazards of formula feeding and the benefits of breast feeding.

The WHO/UNICEF code, while extremely limited in scope, is one of the most successful code efforts to date, in terms both of the detail of its provisions and of the degree of its implementation. Why should this particular attempt at regulation have proved so successful?

3. EXPLANATIONS FOR THE CODE'S SUCCESS

The emerging regime for international investment and international enterprises may have created the general context for the code debate. But it was the special convergence of favorable characteristics of issue, actor, setting, and timing that resulted in a detailed code being successfully completed and implemented.

a. Issue Characteristics: Consensual Knowledge

The infant formula issue had several unique characteristics that help explain how the code developed. First, the issue was inherently emotional, and it was posed in such a way as to highlight the conflict between increased corporate sales and the well-being of infants in developing countries. Industry sources believed that the emotional nature of the issue colored the dispute. "Once an issue reaches the emotional plane (as when infant formula manufacturers were accused of killing babies) facts tend to become secondary and even the most brilliantly compiled scientific evidence has little or no impact on public opinion," said one *Business International* article.[25]

More interesting than how emotionalism skewed the debate away from "facts" is how an industry that had long cultivated the image of "mother's helper" was put on the defensive for endangering the health of infants. The issue shows that debates and actions within the UN system have the potential to delegitimize previously accepted practices and to create new consciousness about problems, especially where a high level of consensual knowledge exists.[26] In this sense, industry's intransigence

---

[24]Post, "Assessing the Nestlé Boycott," p. 121.

[25]"Lessons from the Anti-Infant Formula Campaign," *Business International*, 5 February 1982, p. 8.

[26]See Inis L. Claude, Jr., "Collective Legitimation as a Political Function of the United Nations," in Leland M. Goodrich and David A. Kay, eds., *International Organizations: Politics, Process* (Madison: University of Wisconsin Press, 1973), pp. 209–21.

when faced with an increasing level of consensual knowledge on the part of health professionals and NGOs contributed to the move toward an international code.[27]

Public health experts uniformly agreed that breast feeding is far superior to bottle feeding and that improper bottle feeding contributes to infant mortality and malnutrition.[28] Prestigious pediatricians estimated that in 1978 about ten million cases of infant malnutrition were occurring yearly in developing countries as a direct and indirect result of mothers ceasing to breastfeed their children. Improper infant feeding practices resulted in one to three million infant deaths per year. In addition, breast feeding was on the decline, and there was significant agreement that one important reason for that decline was misleading sales promotion of formula.[29] Industry representatives argued that although breast feeding was superior, no clear scientific evidence linked advertising to changes in infant feeding practices—but they found little support from health experts familiar with conditions in developing countries.

The high level of consensual scientific knowledge contributed to WHO/UNICEF action on the issue, swelling the ranks of industry critics with medical and scientific groups. When the companies refused to change marketing practices, organizations such as the American Public Health Association, the Ambulatory Pediatrics Association, and the National Council for International Health became endorsers of the WHO process and the Nestlé boycott. But it is not enough to say that consensual knowledge contributed to the development of the WHO/UNICEF code. Rather we need to ask how the political struggle surrounding the issue permitted a role for knowledge and learning within the debate. Not only was there a greater degree of consensual knowledge in the infant formula debate than in many code negotiations, but the interests that favored

---

[27]Ernst Haas has defined consensual knowledge as "a body of beliefs about cause-effect and end-means relationships among variables (activities, aspirations, values, demands) that is widely accepted by the relevant actors irrespective of the absolute or final truth of these beliefs." Quoted in Robert Rothstein, "Consensual Knowledge and International Collaboration: Some Lessons from the Commodity Negotiations," *International Organization* 38 (Autumn 1984).

[28]A study by the São Paulo School of Medicine in 1979, for example, monitoring babies of low-income families, found that 32% of bottle-fed babies suffered from malnutrition compared to 9% of breast-fed babies; 23% of the bottle-fed babies and none of the breast-fed babies had to be hospitalized. Research in Chile has shown that Chilean babies who were bottle-fed during the first three months of life suffered three times the mortality rate of those who were exclusively breast-fed. Reported in *Washington Post*, 21 April 1981.

[29]D. B. Jellife and E. F. P. Jellife, *Human Milk in the Modern World* (Oxford: Oxford University Press, 1978). See also Ambulatory Pediatrics Association, "Statement by the Board of Directors on the WHO Code of Marketing of Breast-milk Substitutes," *Pediatrics* 68 (September 1981).

a code were able to introduce code-supporting knowledge.[30]

The perception of WHO as a technical and professional organization with low "politicization" increased the impact of consensual scientific knowledge from credible health sources in the case of the baby food debate. Moreover, scientific consensus had begun to form before the debate began providing a substantial base of information that shaped a highly-charged dispute.

All parties presented scientific material, but industry positions generally relied on in-house or industry-sponsored research. Critics of industry practices, on the other hand, were able to draw on a wide variety of independent scientific sources.[31] NGOs also reprinted and distributed material originally produced by international organizations, such as the seminal article on the issue which had first appeared in the *WHO Bulletin*.[32] Robert Rothstein has pointed out that bureaucrats often serve as key conduits or bridges between producers and users of knowledge. In the infant formula debate not only bureaucrats but also NGOs diffused, publicized, and dramatized the information that supported the code effort.[33]

In the development and adoption of the code delegates clearly "learned" about the role of advertising in infant nutrition—learning that many of them did not possess before the debate began. But consensual knowledge and learning had a wider significance in the issue. Learning, on the part of such nongovernmental institutions as hospitals as well as governments, was also important in the implementation of the code's provisions.

b. Actor Characteristics

i. Industry and Market Structure

The major companies involved in the baby food debate derived only a fraction of their total sales from infant formula, and the code's mar-

---

[30]"The political implications of the consensual knowledge (especially interpretations of its effect on national interests) and the specific bargaining configuration must interact in a fashion that permits or facilitates diffusion and subsequently agreement on new policies." Rothstein, "Consensual Knowledge," p. 755.

[31]For a summary of scientific literature distributed by activists, see Interfaith Center on Corporate Responsibility (ICCR), *Breast Is Best* (New York, n.p., n.d.), and Infant Formula Action Coalition, "Policy vs. Practice: The Reality of Formula Promotion" (Minneapolis, May 1979). The latter juxtaposes quotations from scientific studies and health professionals with baby food company statements.

[32]Plank and Milanesi, "Infant Feeding," pp. 203–10.

[33]Other NGO publications and flyers that served to highlight, publicize, and circulate authoritative information on the issue include ICCR, "What the International Health Agencies Recommend about Baby Formula Promotion: Excerpts and Recommendations" (n.d.); "What Health Personnel Say about Infant Formula Promotion in the Third World" (n.d.); and "Excerpts from Documents: WHO/UNICEF Meeting on Infant and Young Child Feeding, Geneva, Switzerland, October 9-12, 1979," *ICCR Brief,* January 1980.

keting limitations actually affected only a fraction of infant formula sales. In 1978 worldwide sales of formula amounted to approximately $1.5 billion, of which an estimated $600 million were in the developing world. Nestlé's global sales in 1978 approached $10 billion, of which formula accounted for approximately $400 million.[34] Critics confronted a relatively small number of companies that devoted only a portion of their activities to the marketing of infant formula in developing countries.

Moreover, despite increasing limitations on company advertising, the baby food market continued to expand throughout the controversy. James Post estimates that by 1983 the global market for infant formula products probably exceeded $4 billion, with developing nations accounting for about 50 percent of the total. Since 1978 the total market had more than doubled. "This growth does not mean that the WHO Code has failed," Post argues. "Rather, it simply means that there has been continued population and market growth while, at the same time, there has been an improvement in the quality of competitive conduct."[35] It seems likely that regulating an industry in a constantly increasing market will be easier than regulating an industry whose market is shrinking. In the baby food case, increased regulation may have slowed market expansion, but it caused no absolute decline in sales.

The companies lobbying against the code often did not agree on strategy. Early in the campaign one U.S. formula producer, Abbott Laboratories, refused to join the International Council of the Infant Food Industry and criticized the ICIFI code of ethics as weaker than the Abbott code of marketing. Later Nestlé would exceed the marketing changes of other companies as a result of pressures from the infant formula campaign and agreements with boycott leaders.

Nestlé, the leader in the industry, held approximately 40 percent of the infant formula market in developing countries. Certain characteristics made the company particularly vulnerable to one of the strategies chosen by the consumer critics—a consumer boycott of Nestlé products. (The boycott began and was always strongest in the U.S. market but eventually spread to nine other industrialized countries.) Most of Nestlé's products are food products, many of them clearly identifiable not only by brand but also by parent company (Nescafé, Nestea, Nestlé Crunch, Nestlé Tollhouse Chips, etc.) and easily replaceable with alternative

---

[34]Post, "Assessing the Nestlé Boycott," p. 121, and Robert Ball, "Nestlé Revs up Its U.S. Campaign," *Fortune,* 13 February 1978, pp. 80–90. In 1978 Nestlé employed more than 140,000 persons in fifty plants and operated in more than fifty nations. Worldwide sales approached $10 billion—47% in Europe, 20% in the United States, 20% in the Third World. The company ranked 19th of *Fortune's* foreign 500.

[35]Post, "Assessing the Nestlé Boycott," p. 121.

products. Nestlé had also invested heavily in a corporate image based on high-quality products, which accusations that the company's products led to increased infant mortality in the Third World obviously threatened with long-term damage.

Before the boycott, Nestlé had targeted the United States as the primary market for corporate growth. The corporation intended to double sales and increase U.S. operations until they were approximately 30 percent of worldwide sales, both through expanding existing market lines and, in particular, through mergers.[36] There are indications that Nestlé eventually reached agreement with its critics not only because its sales were directly hurt but also because a new senior management team wanted to turn its attention to more pressing business problems, in particular mergers and acquisitions in the U.S. market.[37]

ii. The Role of Nongovernmental Organizations

The important NGO actors in the baby food debate included the Inter-Faith Center on Corporate Responsibility (ICCR), the organization that had initiated work on the issue in the United States through stockholders' resolutions by its church members; the International Organization of Consumers Unions (IOCU), an umbrella organization based in The Hague for consumer organizations around the world; and INFACT, the U.S. organization that organized and coordinated the Nestlé boycott. In addition, these three groups helped form and worked with the International Baby Food Action Network (IBFAN), which eventually brought together 100 groups working in 65 countries on issues of infant nutrition. The International Nestlé Boycott Committee, formed by INFACT and the U.S. National Council of Churches and representing 87 of the 120 national organizations that had endorsed the boycott in the United States and Canada, took responsibility for negotiations with Nestlé. U.S. and Canadian churches and religious orders were especially active in the committee and in ICCR.

The resources of NGOs working on the infant formula issue were severely limited. INFACT, for example, began in Minneapolis, Minnesota, as a group of twenty volunteers and one paid staff member. Though INFACT grew in size and sophistication over the years, its total budget for the seven-and-one-half-year period it waged the boycott probably never exceeded $3.5 million.[38]

The NGO coalition supporting the boycott was loosely knit, bring-

---

[36]By the mid-1970s Nestlé had nearly $2 billion in sales in the United States, and company plans called for a doubling of U.S. sales to $4 billion by 1982 (from over 20% to over 30% of Nestlé worldwide sales), by a combination of internal growth and energetic acquisitions. Post, "Nestlé Boycott," and Ball, "Nestlé Revs up."

[37]Post, "Assessing the Nestlé Boycott," p. 124.

[38]"Nestlé Boycott Being Suspended," *New York Times*, 27 January 1984.

ing together groups and individuals of various political persuasions and interests. Some elements had limited goals, others saw the infant formula campaign as one part of a larger political change. The number of full-time core activists was small, and the coalition relied heavily on volunteers, church groups, and the networks of endorsing organizations to spread news of the boycott.

The strengths of NGO actors were fourfold. First, they strengthened and used to their advantage the emotional and consensual characteristics of the issue. Second, the organization of a loose but nonetheless effective transnational network enabled them to gather and disseminate information internationally and to organize different forms of resistance to company policies in different settings. Third, they had the capacity to bring economic, moral, and political pressure to bear on TNCs in order to change their interest calculations and engage them in making and implementing international rules. Fourth, they were able to hold a disparate coalition together for over seven years of boycott, to present a unified front, and to prevent significant defections.

NGOs operated both inside and outside the UN system. They made their positions felt effectively within WHO and UNICEF, through participation in meetings,

lobbying of delegates and officials, and the publication and distribution of materials. But it was activities outside the United Nations, especially the Nestlé boycott, stockholders' resolutions, and publicity campaigns, that proved decisive in getting a final agreement. The combination of NGO activities inside and outside international organizations was particularly productive.[39]

The single most effective tactic of these groups was their ability to alter the interest calculations of companies and some national governments. Changes in TNC behavior on the infant formula issue were motivated more by increasing activism than by concerns over national law or WHO censure. For example, the industry group, ICIFI, was formed and adopted its voluntary marketing code of ethics in 1975 only a few days before the beginning in Switzerland of Nestlé's suit against the Third World Action Group over the pamphlet Nestlé Kills Babies. In December 1977 the Bristol Myers Company announced changes in its marketing of infant formula as a result of a two-year court battle, with church groups owning shares of its stock, over alleged false and misleading statements in the company's proxy material.

Perhaps the most powerful incentive for industry to change was the Nestlé boycott. Although

---

[39]Thierry Lemaresquier, "Beyond Infant Feeding: The Case for Another Relationship between NGOs and the U.N. System," *Development Dialogue* (1980), pp. 120–25.

Nestlé has never revealed how much damage the boycott inflicted, its actions indicated that it took the boycott very seriously. Nestlé's main antiboycott strategist, Rafael Pagan, conceded that "it is hard to quantify the effects of a prolonged controversy of this nature on the bottom line. However, we estimate that the implementation of the WHO Code alone will cost Nestlé $10–20 million. The cost in executive time and effort has been high. The impact on employee morale and on the corporation's image was quite substantial."[40] Boycott leaders argued that the boycott succeeded because it increased the costs for Nestlé while a Third World campaign simultaneously reduced the benefits that Nestlé received from violating the code.[41] According to one source, the boycott was the most "devastating attack [ever mounted] on corporate advertising in the Third World." *Business International* warned that consumer movements need to be taken seriously; they are developing effective international networks that allow them to draw world attention to sin-gle issues and spread information about regulations in the industrial world to other regions.[42]

Industry approached first voluntary codes and then action in international organizations as ways of diffusing public criticism and avoiding economic boycott. Initially both Nestlé and the American companies supported the idea of an international code of marketing. The infant food industry itself, after consultations with Senator Kennedy, requested international action on the baby food issue. Moreover, the issue was taken to WHO as a result of an industry decision, not of a request from governments or NGO lobbyists. Industry, it seems clear, saw the movement into international forums as an alternative to responding to activists' attacks.[43] . . .

iii. Government Positions

The strength of the code vote (118 in favor, 1 against, and 3 abstentions) underlined the seriousness with which many countries, especially in the Third World, viewed the problem. Third World

---

[40]Rafael D. Pagan, Jr., president, Nestlé Coordination Center for Nutrition, Inc., "Issue Management: No Set Path," before the Issues Management Association (Roosevelt Hotel, New York City, 7 November 1983).

[41]Interview with Douglas Johnson, executive director of the Infant Formula Action Coalition, New York, 5 December 1984.

[42]*Business International,* 17 October 1980.

[43]Some in the business community feel that codes of conduct will continue to proliferate and that corporations must get involved in their development. John Kline, for example, argues that "a carefully structured participatory role [in code exercises] could turn challenge into opportunity, benefiting both individual corporations and the broader objective of an open international economic system." Kline, "Entrapment or Opportunity: Structuring a Corporate Response to International Codes of Conduct," *Columbia Journal of World Business* 15 (Summer 1980), p. 6.

governments faced general demands to protect their domestic economies and societies from destabilizing forces and to reassert national control over TNCs' activities. More specifically, a consensus existed that breast-milk substitutes contributed little to national economies, used scarce foreign exchange, and by increasing infant morbidity and mortality generated unnecessary health care and hospital costs.

At the WHO Executive Board meeting in January 1980, and at the World Health Assembly in May 1980, government representatives from both less-developed and developed countries passed a consensus resolution calling for an international code of marketing for breast-milk substitutes. They requested that the director general prepare such a code "in close consultation with member states and with all other parties concerned."

The initial U.S. position at the May 1980 assembly opposed the development of a baby food marketing code. Domestic NGO lobbying pressured the U.S. government to reconsider its position during the assembly meeting, and eventually the United States supported the final resolution calling for a draft code. Subsequently the United States developed an interagency taskforce, chaired by the Department of Health and Human Services and including the State Department, the Agency for International Development, the National Institute of Health, and ACTION, the umbrella agency incorporating the Peace Corps and VISTA, to develop U.S. recommendations for the code. The taskforce gave priority to the health issues involved; it participated in building the code, although not totally in accordance with NGO recommendations. The eventual U.S. position was in part a result of top officials' commitment to the health aspects of the issue[44] and in part a response to more "strategic" concerns. On the strategic level one U.S. government memo pointed out that "it is clear that virtually all of the 156 member nations of the WHO are intent that there will be a code. . . . Key Europeans and developing countries [feel] that any weakening of the Code is unacceptable." The memo's author raised the concern that the "U.S. would be completely isolated in its position which could have deleterious effects in terms of support we would need (from such countries as Mexico, Nigeria, Algeria, India, Norway, Sweden, Kenya, and Jamaica) on other important issues, such as those involving Egypt and Israel."[45]

The active support of such European countries as Sweden and Norway and the acquiescence of all

---

[44]To protest the U.S. "no" vote, two senior AID officials resigned. They were Stephen Joseph, a pediatrician and the highest-ranking health professional at the agency, and Eugene Babb, deputy assistant administrator for food and nutrition.

[45]U.S. Department of Health and Human Services (DHHS). Memorandum, "WHO Code of Marketing of Breastmilk Substitutes—Decision" (October, 1980), p. 3.

of the other Western nations was important in the code's adoption. The Netherlands and Switzerland, both major exporters of baby food, supported a code. West Germany, the United Kingdom, France, Australia, and Canada offered little opposition to the code's content, but they believed strongly that the code should be adopted not as a regulation but as a recommendation. The Third World used regulation vs. recommendation as a bargaining tool. Fred Sai of Ghana, the highly respected professional who helped chair the preliminary meetings, warned that if the World Health Assembly saw the issue as a contest between a West that wanted to protect its industry and the South, the code would certainly be adopted as a regulation.[46]

The WHO secretariat, aiming for a code based on a consensus of member governments, made efforts throughout the code-building process to accommodate the demands of the United States and other countries. The new Reagan administration sent its assistant secretary of state for international organizations, Elliot Abrams, to Geneva to discuss the code with WHO's director general, Hafdan Mahler. Abrams told Mahler that the United States would vote for a recommendation to member governments, and WHO went on record favoring a recommendatory code.[47] As a result of industry lobbying, however, the Reagan admin-

istration reversed its decision at the last minute and cast the sole vote against the code. This reversal caused some resentment among code supporters who felt that they had bent over backward to incorporate U.S. concerns. In retrospect, the episode was an early indication of what would become, during the Reagan administration, characteristically abrupt and confrontational U.S. behavior in international forums.

c. Setting Characteristics

WHO and UNICEF's reputations as technical agencies, as mentioned above, created greater receptivity for the body of scientific data that tended to support regulation. Staff in the two organizations were concerned with the problem and committed to finding a solution. Once the process was underway, they helped move the code along quickly.

Timing also was important to the success of the code. The WHO/UNICEF code took only eighteen months from initial conceptualization to final vote. Speed prevented extended lobbying that might have diluted code provisions. The pace resulted from the initial convergence of almost all the major actors around the idea that a code was desirable. In addition, the process was accelerated by the practice of WHO and UNICEF staffers drafting the code and negotiaters modifying the

---

[46]U.S. Department of State, telegram from U.S. Mission in Geneva (no. 12065), September 1980.

[47]Post, "Assessing the Nestlé Boycott," p. 120.

prepared text. By the time that industry and the new U.S. administration began to have serious misgivings, they were too late to block the momentum for a code.

The WHO/UNICEF code was developed in a process that allowed full participation to governments, experts, industry, and critics.[48] The extensive involvement of all major actors in negotiations contributed to the development of detailed, meaningful regulations. WHO and UNICEF ensured the participation and consultation of all interested parties while limiting the actual drafting to the secretariats. The result was rapid and relatively consensual.

The final negotiations between Nestlé and the INBC were carried out at UNICEF in New York. Although UNICEF denies that it served as a mediator or arbitrator,[49] its presence in the negotiations clearly provided a face-saving way for Nestlé to reach an agreement with groups that the company had previously characterized as "irresponsible." UNICEF's role as a facilitator of the negotiations and the final agreement between Nestlé and its critics was also a departure from the customary activities of international organizations.[50]

The final joint agreement between Nestlé and the INBC guarantees that the corporation will abide by a voluntary code of conduct worked out in an international organization. The only parallel cases might be found where trade unions work to have references to codes of conduct included in their contracts with companies.[51] In both cases the activities of nongovernmental organizations create opportunities to implement a code beyond those envisioned when the codes were adopted.

It is important to stress this interaction of characteristics. The international forum, WHO, was more open to an issue characterized by a high level of consensual knowledge;

---

[48]Lemaresquier, "Beyond Infant Feeding," p. 120.

[49]Interview with Kathleen Cravero, UNICEF, New York, 10 January 1985.

[50]As a result of the negotiations between INBC and Nestlé, UNICEF and WHO were requested to clarify a portion of the code which states that infant formula companies could donate supplies to hospitals for infants who "have to be fed on breastmilk substitutes." WHO argued that the code was written and adopted by governments, and thus only the governments could further interpret it. Eventually, however, WHO developed a plan, presented by Dr. David Tejada, assistant director general of the organization, whereby WHO and UNICEF agreed to give technical advice to governments who would in turn develop the requested definitions based on that advice. Both Nestlé and the INBC agree to cooperate fully in the implementation of the Tejada Plan. See Minutes of the Joint Press Conference between Nestlé and INBC to announce the termination of the Nestlé Boycott, 4 October 1984 (Mayflower Hotel, Washington, D.C.).

[51]On the role of labor and trade unions in the adoption and implementation of codes at the regional and international level, see Robinson, *Multinationals and Political Control.*

the NGO actors used to their advantage both the emotional and the consensual characteristics of the issue and the susceptibility of corporate actors to public pressure; the speed of the process prevented key actors, especially a new U.S. administration, from undermining the negotiations.

4. IMPLICATIONS OF THE WHO/UNICEF CASE

Can the baby food code provide a model for codes for TNCs? Certain attributes of the process may be reproducible in other forums and issue areas, but the baby food code may nonetheless be a special case.

Collaboration between actors in the case was largely the result of the focused and consensual nature of the issue and the ability of nongovernmental groups to change the interest calculations of industry. One can argue that related events were largely responsible for the success of the UNCTAD code on restrictive business practices. There also, consensual knowledge was important—most participants, governments and industry alike, agreed that restrictive business practices had negative economic effects. Moreover, U.S. law already held American companies to standards higher than the code's in their overseas operations, giving U.S. business and the U.S. government an incentive to work for the adoption

of international norms. In the absence of such norms, U.S. businesses felt that they would be at a significant disadvantage vis-à-vis competitors based in other countries.

One determinant of future code efforts will be the business community's experience with these early codes. Indeed, many business groups view the WHO/UNICEF code and subsequent agreements as important precedents for UN regulation of TNCs. Opinion within the business community ranges from alarm (codes are an unacceptable encroachment on a firm's freedom of operation) to moderation (codes provide both opportunities and problems for TNCs).

The pharmaceutical industry in particular is on the defensive because it believes itself targeted for the next round of regulation.[52] Moderate attitudes have led some industry groups to meet criticism early in the hope of diffusing demands for strong codes in the future. In October 1983, for example, the Agricultural Chemicals Association Dialogue Group, composed of industry and NGO representatives, negotiated the Guidelines for Advertising Practices in the Promotion of Pesticides Products in Developing Areas of the World.

More generally, however, it is puzzling that corporate response has been so strong to a relatively minor code on an extremely narrow

---

[52]Harry Schwartz, "Perspective on the Third World," *Pharmaceutical Executive,* March 1982, pp. 13–16.

topic, especially when the infant formula industry initially supported the code. The solution to the puzzle lies in the nature of the modern corporation. Flexibility in export and marketing strategies is one of the essential requirements of a corporation, and the detailed, specific marketing regulations of the WHO/UNICEF code, applied to a wider range of TNC products and exports, could seriously hamper the TNC's ability to organize its activities globally.

The ability to organize worldwide depends in part on the maintenance of legitimacy or ideological hegemony.[53] The emerging TNC regime rests on a compromise between domestic stability and an open economy, the balance between the two based in part on a continuing belief in the overall benefits of an open international system and the specific benefits of TNC activity. TNCs increasingly view attacks as cutting into the legitimacy of their operations, which they believe will undermine their flexibility and scope. They take the struggle for political legitimacy very seriously; a token of that seriousness is the title of a session at a recent corporate conference— "The War of Ideas: The Struggle for Moral Legitimacy."[54]

5. CONCLUSIONS

The baby food debate indicates, more than anything else, that blanket statements about the future of codes of conduct are not possible. Nevertheless, the case alerts us to certain factors that may be common to other cases. First, it seems clear that too little attention has been given to nonstate actors and their impact in building codes. Most codes not only address nonstate actors (TNCs) but also depend on nonstate actors as well as states for implementation and monitoring. In the case of the WHO/UNICEF code the activities of nongovernmental groups, in particular transnational activist groups, were essential to the final outcome.

International organizations, WHO and UNICEF, played crucial roles in building the code, as arena, as grantor of legitimacy, creator of consciousness, and center of debate. Their importance to this case has been recognized even by the severest critics of the United Nations. Adelman points out, critically, that "the drive for international regulation of infant formula and pharmaceuticals surely would exist in a world without the U.N. . . . But it would not have an institutional, concrete locale. It is the

[53]Robert Cox, "The Crisis of World Order and the Problem of International Organization in the 1980s," *International Journal* 35 (Spring 1980), discusses the role of international organization in the institutionalization of hegemony—the universalization of norms proper to a structure of world power—and also the possibility that international institutions may become vehicles for the articulation of a coherent counterhegemonic set of values.

[54]Public Affairs Council, Program for Conference, "Activist Groups at the International Level" (Hilton Hotel, New York City, 21–22 April 1982).

U.N.'s organization and resources that give substance to what might otherwise be merely an abstract wish."[55] Other conservatives have also focused on the baby food case because it illustrates the UN capacity to open a space for new ways of thinking about problems and to generate momentum toward solutions to these problems. The WHO/ UNICEF code is a fait accompli, however; it has set in motion a global reordering of infant feeding practices and transnational marketing schemes. The debate over the WHO/UNICEF code emphasizes some of the opportunities for action within the UN system, action that can save children's lives, modify global marketing strategies, and al-

ter national health care practices. The case illustrates not only the potential for action but also the potential for creating or removing legitimacy.

Progress toward the international regulation of TNCs and negotiated agreements at the international level is bound to be slow and difficult. To ensure that international regulation actually leads to different TNC and state behavior will be even more difficult. The special conditions that led to an agreement on infant formula are unlikely to be duplicated. Still, opportunities exist within the UN arena for unexpected and vital developments on the regulation of transnational corporations.

---

[55]Adelman, "Biting the Hand," p. 16.

CHAPTER VIII

Regional and Nongovernmental Organizations

The first seven sections of this book have concentrated almost exclusively on those organizations that have a universal or potentially universal membership composed of sovereign states. Although such organizations receive primary attention, important activities are also performed by other types of organizations. Many of these organizations are composed only of states in a particular geographic area; the Organization of American States is one example of a regional organization. Some international organizations have a membership of nongovernmental, national organizations rather than sovereign states; Amnesty International is a well-known example of an INGO (International Nongovernmental Organization). The articles in this section are selected to acquaint the reader with some of the work performed by regional and nongovernmental organizations.

Regional, instead of global, organizations are formed because the issues to be addressed may only be of interest to states in a particular geographic area, or those states may share common cultural, political, or economic characteristics that facilitate cooperation better on a regional than a global level. Two of the most enduring and broad-based regional organizations are the EEC (European Economic Community) and the CMEA (Council for Mutual Economic Assistance or Comecon). The EEC is a collection of Western European states that has taken steps to harmonize and integrate their respective economies; one collective policy is a common external tariff levied on goods imported from a state outside of the EEC. If the EEC were a state, it would have a larger GNP than the United States or any other state. Similarly, the CMEA is the communist and East European counterpart to the EEC. Composed of the Soviet Union and its allies, Comecon serves to coordinate economic policy and facilitate trade among members. Each of these regional organizations has a counterpart in the security area, with virtually the same membership, in NATO and the Warsaw Pact respectively.

The first article looks at the interrelationship of the EEC and CMEA. Cutler's analysis points out the differences in the organizations and traces the changes in their interrelationship that have occurred in recent decades. Most significantly, he notes the role that law, politics, and economics play in affecting the character of the interactions between the two organizations. Finally, Cutler outlines four future scenarios for the economic relations between Eastern and Western Europe. If greater cooperation is achieved between these regional organizations, there could be a significant impact on the world market, not to mention the political implications of economic ties between military adversaries.

Blondel's article on the ICRC (International Committee of the Red Cross) provides a glimpse of the workings of perhaps the best known and one of the oldest (it was started in 1863) international nongovernmental organizations. National units of the ICRC are as visible in blood drives in the United States as they are on nightly television, giving relief aid to victims of civil strife in Beirut. This selection provides the reader with some historical perspective on the changing activities of the Red Cross as well as the role that international humanitarian law plays in those activities. Blondel also lists several obstacles that the ICRC must face in gaining access to those who need their help. Although the analysis is specifically targeted to the Red Cross, many of the problems mentioned are common to private international organizations. Lack of resources and the absence of cooperation from states are but two difficulties that plague Amnesty International and a host of other nongovernmental organizations.

20

HARMONIZING EEC–CMEA RELATIONS

Robert M. Cutler

Recent developments have taken the question of relations between the European Economic Community (EEC) and the Council for Mutual Economic Assistance (CMEA, unofficially known as Comecon) off the diplomatic back burner. Some of the reasons for the CMEA's current interest in the question are economic: most CMEA countries continue to have difficulties with their hard currency debt, and it

---

SOURCE: *International Affairs* 63 (Spring 1987).

may appear that formal relations between the two economic blocs can help to open the EEC up to Eastern imports, thus increasing the CMEA countries' hard currency earnings. Also, since 1980 the volume of trade between the two blocs has been increasing, and some in the East may think that this makes the absence of formal inter-bloc relations illogical. Yet some in the West have suggested that because the present arrangements seem to be working satisfactorily, formal inter-bloc links would have little practical value. Clearly, there are also political motives: it is only since the accession to power of Mr. Mikhail Gorbachev that these new moves have occurred.

This article aims to analyse recent developments in order to gain a perspective on the costs and benefits to both the EEC and the CMEA of formal organizational relations. To this end, some recent historical background is necessary.

THE 1970s

During the 1960s, the EEC and the CMEA both paid more attention to their own integration processes than to relations with each other. But in the course of the decade, economic policy-makers in the CMEA countries came to realize that the technological modernization of their own countries would

require Western imports and credits. Certain East European countries (most notably Hungary and Czechoslovakia, but others as well) reached out for improved economic relations with the West. Their push in this direction gave the Soviet Union—which was itself much less dependent on foreign trade—reason to worry whether such an attraction to the West might undermine Eastern bloc cohesion.

In the late 1960s, international flows of trade, communications and tourism increased markedly between the two halves of Europe. By the end of the decade it was clear that capitalist economic and commercial organizations were willing, on a broad scale, to take into account the idiosyncrasies of socialist state planning. As the East European economies adapted to West European organizations and procedures, diverse changes were introduced into the national economic, administrative and planning systems of the East European states. This heterogeneity made the coordination of national economic plans among CMEA members increasingly difficult. The Soviet invasion of Czechoslovakia in 1968 reinforced not only the bloc's political but also its economic cohesion.[1]

In the years immediately after the invasion, initiatives for integration within the framework of

[1] For a detailed discussion of the particular East European foreign trade reforms, see Harriet Matejka, *Trade control in Eastern Europe* (Geneva: Éditions Médécine et Hygiène, 1978); for concise analysis of their political effect on the bloc, see Andrzej Korbonski, 'Détent, East-West trade, and the future of economic integration in Eastern Europe,' *World Politics,* Vol. 28, No. 4 (July 1976), pp. 568–89.

the CMEA increased markedly. By 1971, this reintegration found expression in the CMEA's adoption of its Complex Programme of Socialist Economic Integration. This document was intended to serve as a set of guidelines for the development of economic integration within the Eastern bloc, with a time horizon of about two decades. But although some economic coordination was accomplished, it was hardly of the degree envisaged in the Complex Programme itself. The Complex Programme seems to have been part of an overall political and economic programme encompassing both foreign and domestic policy, through which Mr. Leonid Brezhnev sought to consolidate his political primacy. East European countries participated in the accelerating drive to integration, while at the same time being allowed to open up somewhat to the West. Greater integration of the CMEA into the world economy contributed to the further development of cooperation within the Eastern bloc: the CMEA's International Bank for Economic Cooperation, which came into operation in January 1964, provided access to international credit markets for financing imports of Western technology, while its International Investment Bank, which opened in

January 1971, promoted intra-bloc joint ventures.[2]

Changing Soviet Views in the Early 1970s

In the early 1970s, at a time when both Western and Eastern Europe were putting out feelers for greater inter-bloc economic cooperation, Soviet perspectives on world politics, and on 'international imperialism' in particular, were undergoing an important shift. As early as the 1969 World Communist Conference in Moscow, Soviet thinking about West European domestic politics was beginning to change in favour of a renovated 'united front' policy, under the slogan of the 'democratic alternative,' which advocated joint political and social action by communists with other left-wing forces. This approach was confirmed and elaborated at an April 1973 conference in Moscow organized by Yuri Krasin, prorector of the Central Committee's Academy of Social Sciences, and held at the Academy, which has played a significant role in managing relations with foreign communists. According to this viewpoint, the expansion of the EEC would help to realize the 'democratic alternative' by mobilizing the working classes and the intermediate social strata

---

[2]On the Complex Programme, see Peter Marsh, 'The integration process in Eastern Europe, 1968 to 1975,' *Journal of Common Market Studies,* Vol. 14, No. 4 (June 1976), pp. 311–35, esp. pp. 322–7. For a comprehensive review of the CMEA's institutional developments during this period, see Zbigniew M. Fallenbuchl, 'East European integration: COMECON,' in US Congress, Joint Economic Committee, *Reorientation and commercial relations of the economies of Eastern Europe* (Washington, DC: US Government Printing Office, 1974), pp. 79–134, esp. pp. 96–122.

of the EEC member states. It therefore followed that the pursuit of the 'democratic alternative' should be taken up not just in the various national parliaments in Western Europe but in the European Parliament as well.[3]

In fact the Soviet analysis of West European integration held four facets: economic, political, military, and financial and monetary. It was the last of these (which is also the most often overlooked) which in fact dominated the Soviet view of West European integration in the early 1970s. Soviet attention was focused in the context of the realization that the United States was, at least economically, no longer the systemic hegemon of international imperialism, but one of three centres, the other two being the EEC and Japan. Soviet scholars introduced a distinction between economic micro-integration (such as transnational cooperation between enterprises) and economic macro-integration (such as intergovernmental cooperation on economic policy). This led them to accept what might be called political macro-integration in Western Europe—intergovernmental cooperation in political affairs. This they interpreted to be the result of attempts to resolve the 'contradictions' of economic macro-integration and micro-integration. Curiously, the Soviet scholars seemed not to consider military and industrial micro-integration in Western Europe as part of West European economic integration in general. They were more worried about military macro-integration, and consequently paid more attention to such institutions as the West European Union, the Eurogroup, and the Independent European Planning Group.[4]

As a result the military, the political and the economic aspects of West European integration became separated from each other in Soviet thinking. Soviet scholars acknowledged the possibility of political integration in Western Europe, without being forced to conclude that military integration would follow. This attitude was in clear contrast

---

[3]The proceedings of the 1973 conference were published in *Opyt i perspektivy sovmestnykh deistvii kommunistov i sotsialistov: materialy nauchnoi konferentsii, sostoiavsheisia v AON pri TsK KPSS, 18–19 aprelia 1973 goda* [The experience and perspectives of joint activities of communists and socialists: materials of a scientific conference, held in the academy of social sciences attached to the CC CPSU, 18–19 April 1973] (Moscow: AON pri TsK KPSS, 1974). A summary of the general evolution of Soviet perspectives on the West during this period is in Jerry F. Hough, 'The evolution in the Soviet world view,' *World Politics*, Vol. 32, No. 4 (July 1980), pp. 509–30; but for a view contesting Hough's interpretation of that evolution, see Hannes Adomeit, 'Soviet perceptions of Western Europe integration: ideological distortion or realistic assessment?' *Millennium*, Vol. 8, No. 1 (Spr. 1979), pp. 1–24.

[4]For a fuller version of this argument, see Robert M. Cutler, 'The view from the Urals: West European integration in Soviet perspective and policy,' in Werner G. Feld, ed., *Western Europe's global reach* (New York: Pergamon, 1980), pp. 80–119.

to the bad old days when the EEC was considered the European pillar of NATO and any move towards even political integration was seen as an American-inspired attempt to institutionalize the division of Europe by building up that pillar. This was a Hobson's choice, of course: it was not clear whether the Soviet Union would prefer—if it had to choose—a Western Europe with an independent military force or one that supported the United States in NATO.

This change in Soviet thinking towards Western Europe, under way since the middle to late 1960s, was catalysed in May 1971 when the Federal Republic of Germany (FRG) floated the Deutschmark on international currency markets. Then in June, a summit meeting between Georges Pompidou, the French President, and Edward Heath, the British Prime Minister, cleared away the political obstacles to eventual British entry into the EEC. In August, the issue of currency and financial integration in Western Europe drew even more attention in both East and West when US President Richard Nixon unilaterally removed the dollar from the gold standard and imposed a ten per cent surcharge on all import duties. Following on as it did from the deterioration of the fixed exchange rates established at Bretton Woods, this move was interpreted by Soviet analysts as forcing the West European powers to recognize their common cause against the 'dollar zone' in international commerce and compelling them, in their defense against the American currency, to enter into a 'joint float,' the first step on the road to a European Monetary System (EMS).

The quick succession of these events led Soviet analysts to take a very close look at integration moves in Western Europe. In mid-1971 Andrei Anikin, one of the most creative members of the Institute for World Economy and International Relations (IMEMO) in Moscow, wrote in *Kommunist:* 'The transition from an agreed-upon tariff policy to the tasks of deepening economic unification makes the currency problem especially urgent for the "Common Market." '[5] The question whether the EEC was indeed a political reality came to be argued in Soviet analyses in terms of whether the nascent EMS had any chance of succeeding. The success of the EMS would clearly be an instance of political macro-integration, since it would require intergovernmental cooperation over not just an economic issue but a fundamentally political one as well. The EMS question, in turn, came to be argued in terms of the question whether gold had been 'demonetized'—whether gold would remain a standard for comparing the prices of national currencies. That was why Nixon's

---

[5] A. Anikin, 'Valiutnyi krizis kapitalizma: prichiny i posledstviia [Capitalism's currency crisis: causes and consequences],' *Kommunist,* 1971, No. 10 (July), p. 95.

move to take the dollar off the gold standard made such an impression on Soviet thinkers.

Debates took place between specialists in the Soviet international affairs community—not just in IMEMO and the Academy of Sciences' family of research institutes, but also in the various research institutes attached to government ministries concerned with national and international finance.[6] These debates were extremely pointed and argumentative; at times they reached the level of polemic, with specialists attacking one another by name (which is not extraordinary in domestic policy debates, but almost never occurs in debate over international policy) and accusing each other in print of being nothing less than un-Marxist. The eventual result was confirmation of the view that Western Europe was emerging as an independent

entity from under American tutelage.[7] In January 1972, a conference of the International Working Group on Capitalist Integration was held at IMEMO, and some of the conference's results were published authoritatively in *Pravda*.[8] Other ideas that had circulated at the conference were published in *Pravda* over the signature of Georgii Ratiani, a former diplomat who had become a researcher at the Institute of World History and a leading international affairs journalist in Moscow.[9]

All this set the stage for Brezhnev's remark in March 1972, during a speech to the Trade Union Congress, that:

> The Soviet Union by no means ignores the existing situation in Western Europe, including the existence of an economic grouping of capitalist countries such as the 'Common Market.' We are care-

---

[6]For an in-depth examination, see Alain Rémy, 'Le rôle de l'or dans l'économie monétair occidentale: analyses soviétiques,' Thèse pour le doctorat de troisième cycle (Université de Paris I—Panthéon-Sorbonne, Oct. 1981).

[7]A. V. Kozlov, 'Sovremmennyi valiutnyi krizis i mezhimperialisticheskie protivorechiia (SShA-Zapadnaia Evropa) [The contemporary currency crisis and interimperialist contradictions (USA-Western Europe)],' Diss. kand. ekon. nauk (Moskovskii finansovyi institut, 1975).

[8]A full page of articles on the subject of the conference, 'prepared by the scientific workers of IMEMO,' was published under the general headline 'Mir kapitalizma: v tupike protivorechii [The world of capitalism: in the blind alley of contradictions],' in *Pravda*, 16 Feb. 1972, p. 4. The conference proceedings themselves were subsequently published in Polish: Jerzy Bartosik and Zdislaw Nowak, eds., *Procesy integracyjne w systemie współczesnego kapitalizmu* (Poznán: Instytut zachodni, 1973).

[9]Ratiani's series of five articles was published in early 1972 under the general title 'Partnery i soperniki [Partners and rivals],' in *Pravda*, 18, 21 and 25 Jan. and 2 and 9 Feb. 1972, p. 4 of each issue. Information on his career is in Iurii Zhukov, 'K chitateliu [To the reader],' pp. 3–12 of Georgii Ratiani, *Na blizhnem i dal'nem zapade: kniga vtoraia [In the near and far West: book two]* (Moscow: Pravda, 1980), a posthumously published collection of his journalism that also reprinted that series.

fully observing the activity of the 'Common Market' and its evolution. Our relations with the participants of this grouping will, needless to say, depend on the extent to which they recognize the interests of the member states for the Council for Mutual Economic Assistance.[10]

A similar statement by Brezhnev on 21 December was circulated in Helsinki by the Soviet delegation to the Conference on Security and Cooperation in Europe (CSCE). This statement was probably motivated by a desire, among other things, to contradict the assertions by certain Western politicians and leaders of opinion that the Helsinki talks were designed to fragment Western Europe and/or to pry West Germany away from the rest of the European Community. Soviet policymakers were also probably aware of the deadline set by the Treaty of Rome (1 January 1973) for the Community members' decision on whether to transfer the authority to make a common foreign trade policy to the Community's executive organs. In the absence of a definite decision to that effect, the authority to make foreign trade policy would remain with the individual member states. The Soviet Union, anticipating further problems in promoting exports to the EEC, may have felt an addi-

tional motivation for direct dealings with the EEC.[11]

Subsequent Developments in the 1970s

In 1973, the chairman of the CMEA Executive Committee visited Copenhagen while 'on vacation' and met the Danish prime minister, who was serving at the time as president of the EC Council of Ministers. This was a curious move, as the CMEA chairman should properly have gone to Brussels if he had wished to explore contacts with the EEC. Little came of this hesitant initiative, however, possibly because the Soviet Union came to realize that the EEC's introduction of a common trade policy would have little effect on Soviet foreign trade.

By the mid-1970s, Soviet actions with respect to the EEC had clearly lost any independent initiative and had become principally reactive. CMEA integration provided a certain scope for an inter-bloc approach to handling trade issues, but to move from a network of bilateral trade links to one regulated by the integration organizations themselves would have implied, first, that the CMEA member countries' foreign trade was susceptible to supervision by the organization as a

---

[10]'Rech' tovarishcha L. I. Brezhneva [Speech of Comrade L. I. Brezhnev],' *Pravda*, 21 March 1972, p. 2.

[11]Robert Legvold, 'Four policy perspectives: the Soviet Union and Western Europe,' mimeographed (Cambridge, Mass.: Harvard University, Russian Research Center, Jan. 1976), pp. 7–21.

whole and, secondly, that the EEC recognized the CMEA as an equal. The EEC desired neither of these things, and the smaller CMEA countries, not wishing their national trade to be regulated by their integration organization, tacitly supported the EEC's contention that the CMEA executive organs had no juridical authority to sign such an agreement. Official CMEA policy was that bilateral agreements between the EEC and individual CMEA members should not be signed. However, international economic developments during the 1970s—especially hard currency requirements resulting from the oil shocks—forced the smaller CMEA members to seek and sign such agreements. As the Soviet Union could not keep the other CMEA members in line, its policy was constantly on the defensive.

The EEC and the CMEA actually exchanged drafts of an inter-bloc agreement in 1976.[12] However, negotiations were complicated by the question of Soviet and East European access to fishing grounds within the 200-mile maritime economic zone claimed by the EEC. The Soviet Union, on the verge of being locked out of the Community's waters in early 1977, ceased attempts to deal exclusively through the EC Council of Ministers and sought to come to terms directly with the Commission. In Brussels, the Soviet fisheries minister sidestepped questions from the Western press as to whether this meant that the Soviet Union now recognized the EC Commission. The answer soon came as Soviet ships moved out of the Community's waters, effectively blocking de facto recognition of the EEC. Ships of the EEC member countries left Soviet waters, and Brussels gave the Soviet fisheries minister a cold reception. By the middle of 1977 the fisheries issue was a political stand-off. This notwithstanding, general discussions between the EEC and the CMEA continued throughout 1978, and by 1979 they had actually arrived at a common text for a formal agreement, with the exception of a few political issues that required resolution at the highest level. Before those matters could be resolved, however, Soviet forces marched into Afghanistan. EEC-CMEA contacts, like so many other East-West contacts, fell apart.

To summarize. On the West European side, three parallel developments became increasingly manifest during the 1970s: the development of European Political

---

[12]For a good summary of formal inter-bloc developments in the 1970s (which does not, however, mention the fisheries issue), see Max Baumer and Hanns-Dieter Jacobsen, 'EC and COMECON: intricate negotiations between the two integration systems in Europe,' in Feld, ed., Western Europe's global reach, pp. 110–24; also John Pinder, 'Economic integration and East–West trade: conflict of interests or comedy of errors?' Journal of Common Market Studies, Vol. 16, No. 1 (Sept. 1977), pp. 1–21.

Cooperation (EPC); the development of CSCE, which in Basket II had a strong component relating to the expansion of international trade; and the EC Commission's assumption of responsibility for Community foreign trade policy.[13] Moreover, these developments were largely independent of any American coaxing. Indeed, in the early 1970s American and Japanese competition motivated the EEC member states to harmonize their trade policies with one another. EEC protectionism directed against Eastern Europe declined during this period, but grew stronger again during and after the 1975 recession. Because the CSCE involved trade and security, the EC Commission had also to be concerned with security issues. As the decade progressed, the Commission became more and more involved in European Political Cooperation. (Today the Commission acts virtually as a member state within EPC.)

The Soviet position of the 1970s, that there should be an overarching framework regulating relations between the two organizations, was undermined both by the East Europeans and by events. Today there are all manner of EEC agreements with CMEA member countries over such individual issues as agriculture and steel. Moreover, the very extension of bilateral economic cooperation between the two blocs over the course of the 1970s, such as Franco-Polish economic relations or Bulgaro-German economic relations, has created a self-sustaining structure of cooperation that does not depend on formal coordination between the two integration organizations. Indeed, it seems now that such formal coordination would be as likely to restrict as to promote further economic cooperation. The Soviet Union itself no longer has a policy on this matter. Having sought unsuccessfully to construct a policy without giving in on principles, its moves over the last ten years have become essentially reactive and aimed at damage limitation.

EEC-CMEA RELATIONS TODAY

The invasion of Afghanistan ruptured a dialogue between the two organizations that had been continuing, albeit in fits and starts, throughout most of the 1970s. However, by March 1981 the commissioner with responsibility for external affairs of the European Communities, Wilhelm Haferkamp, had written to express a willingness to resume talks. Not until the CMEA summit in Moscow in June 1984 did the CMEA respond with a

---

[13]For a survey of the thorny question of a common export credit policy, see Peter Marsh, 'Development of relations between the EEC and CMEA,' in Avi Shlaim and G. N. Yannopoulos, eds., *The EEC and Eastern Europe* (Cambridge: Cambridge University Press, 1979), pp. 57–61.

statement that improved relations were desirable, and a formal reply was not made until June 1985, when, in Brussels, the Polish ambassador to Belgium delivered to Commission President Jacques Delors an invitation to visit CMEA headquarters in Moscow. Later that month, the West European foreign ministers decided to explore cautiously the possibility of reinstating talks without jeopardizing the established relations between the EEC and individual CMEA member countries. In July 1985 the EEC therefore sent a request to the CMEA for more details.

The CMEA answered in September, with a letter offering vague promises that the Community's bilateral relations with the East European countries would not be endangered by the establishment of inter-bloc relations. The EEC wanted more specific assurances, however, and on 31 January 1986, while offering the CMEA a positive response, it also sent letters to the smaller East European members of CMEA, inviting their opinions on the establishment of diplomatic relations between the two organizations.[14]

Three types of factors—legal, economic, and political—obstruct the road to an EEC-CMEA accord. After these have been examined it will be possible to enumerate the possible outcomes of current contacts and to assess their respective probability.

Legal Factors

The EEC and CMEA are not equivalent organizations. Differences in their 'juridical personalities' under international law, and particularly in the competences of the executive organs under their respective charters, account in no little part for the failure in the early 1970s to establish relations between the organizations. These differences emerge from, for example, the two organizations' treatment of the Generalized System of Preferences (GSP) of the United Nations Conference on Trade and Development (UNCTAD). On the West European side, the EEC itself revised its own tariff schedule under GSP in order to promote imports from the less developed countries; but on the East European side, the CMEA member states, not the CMEA itself, revised the national, not the organization's, tariff schedules. To take another example, at the UNCTAD negotiations on the Common Fund for commodities, the Soviet Union strongly resisted the idea that the EEC should be able to become a member of the Common Fund just as a state could: this would have entailed legitimizing a certain juridical personality of the EEC under international law. In

---

[14]For a detailed chronology of recent developments, see Sophie Verny, 'CEE-CAEM: le problème de la reconnaissance mutuelle,' *Courrier des Pays de l'Est,* Apr. 1986, No. 305, pp. 34–7.

the end the EEC was allowed to contribute capital to the Common Fund, but not to vote in decisions that it might take.

The CMEA, by contrast, enjoys none of these competences. Indeed, the authority of the CMEA Executive Committee is not regularized, and can be revoked without notice by its member states. The Soviet delegate to the Sixth Committee of the UN General Assembly has even suggested that any international organization should be able to invoke its internal statutes in order to decline to fulfil the commitments of any treaty or other agreement that it might sign.[15] Yet if the CMEA Executive Committee has authority to act on behalf of the member states only when they give it specific permission to do so in the individual instance, then it is legitimate to wonder against whom a complaint could be made in the case of non-fulfilment by the CMEA.

In the light of international law, the CMEA appears to be seeking the benefit of all the rights that flow from being an international organization (and an actor in the international community) without the obligation to fulfil any of the concomitant duties—since the authority of the CMEA's executive organs is conditional upon the will of the member states, and these may at any moment not only reappropriate that authority but also subsequently decline to execute the CMEA's obligations as non-binding on themselves as states. In its research functions, its coordination of national economic activities and its membership, the CMEA is much more like the Organization for Economic Cooperation and Development than the EEC.[16]

Until very recently, Soviet specialists on international law have ignored the accumulated case law of the EEC, which is nevertheless very important for how the EEC deals with the rest of the world. The most recent Soviet legal literature, however, recognizes the EEC's distinct juridical personality; and it is certainly no longer true, as had been suggested by a special (Soviet) rapporteur to the International Law Commission, that the EEC is a unique intergovernmental organization, not 'international' but 'supranational' and therefore having neither a substantive standing under customary law nor a normative standing under the law of treaties.[17]

---

[15]See UN General Assembly, *Official records,* A/C.6/SR.1403 (6 Oct. 1973), A/C.6/SR.1489 (31 Oct. 1974), A/C.6/32/SR.38 (7 Nov. 1977).

[16]The hegemon of the Eastern bloc—the Soviet Union—is a member of the CMEA, yet the United States is not a member of the EEC; however, the United States *is* a member of the OECD. For development of this argument, see John Pinder, 'The political economy of integration in Europe: policies and institutions in East and West,' *Journal of Common Market Studies,* Vol. 25, No. 1 (Sept. 1986), pp. 11–12.

[17]See, for example, UN General Assembly, 'Report on the Most-Favored-Nation Clause, by Mr. Nikolai Ushakov, Special Rapporteur,' A/CN.4/309 and ADD.1 and 2 (11

The Gulf Cooperation Council (GCC) is largely modelled on the EEC and, indeed, entertains relations with it.[18] The Soviet Union has accommodated the GCC and has even encouraged both North and South Yemen to draw closer to it. Perhaps it is these developments that have led the Soviet Union to drop its objections to the EEC under international law.

Economic Factors

Because the various CMEA member states have different trade patterns, the impact of any EEC-CMEA arrangement would vary in each case. CMEA countries that export raw materials generally have no problems with the EEC, because these materials are simply either traded or not traded. Other CMEA members mainly export industrial manufactured goods, such as industrial consumer goods, processed food, or machinery and equipment; while still others—Hungary, for example—are both industrial and agricultural exporters.[19]

It is typically countries in the latter two categories that feel their exports—shoes from Hungary or textiles from Romania—would be enhanced by a lowering of tariff barriers. Representatives of these countries, which feel injured by protectionist measures in agriculture as well as by industrial tariffs, maintain that in their view a general agreement with the EEC is desirable, and that the two organizations should recognize each other as a precondition to increasing the possibilities for actual cooperation. However, such countries frequently already have bilateral arrangements and developed marketing networks with Western Europe. Although West Germany is inclined to view the prospect of formal inter-bloc ties favourably, there is stiff resistance to this both among the national governments of other EEC member states and among the Eurocrats in Brussels.

Furthermore, for the EEC, trade with the CMEA is much more important for its political and strategic aspects than for its economic aspects; whereas the CMEA countries see such trade as economically important, not so much in quantitative terms—since most of their trade is with members of their own bloc—as in qualitative terms, since it could be an important source of advanced technological inputs. Because of this contrast be-

---

and 12 Apr. and 8 May 1978), in *Yearbook of the international law commission,* Vol. 2, pt. 1, p. 9.

[18]Giampaolo Calchi Novati, 'The EEC and the Gulf Cooperation Council,' *Politica Internazionale* (English edn.), Spr. 1985, Vol. 4, No. 1, pp. 110–18.

[19]For elaboration, including a discussion of other forums (e.g. GATT) where the East Europeans make known their demands, see John Pinder. 'The Community and Comecon: what could negotiations achieve?' *World Today,* Vol. 33, No. 5 (May 1977), pp. 176–85.

tween the positions and interests of the members of the two blocs, the CMEA's desire for greater openness on the part of the EEC—its insistence on the ending of import quotas—is not accompanied by any willingness to offer similar concessions. Indeed, the CMEA cannot make any such concessions, because this would promote the abolition of state trading monopolies in the Eastern bloc, thereby creating conditions for the disestablishment of statist economic planning.

Political Factors

Some in Western Europe hesitate to encourage any kind of contact with the CMEA, because they fear that any agreement might somehow enable the Soviet Union to supervise, control, or otherwise place limits upon the foreign trade activity and sovereignty of the smaller East European countries. This fear was voiced in the early 1970s and is still echoed today; however, it seems unfounded, for under current CMEA procedures it is hard to see how Soviet control could be put into practice. In talks within the CMEA, instructions given to national delegations are very flexible, except where national interests are at stake. There they are rigid. As early as 1962, for example, Romania was able to prevent the adoption of Nikita Khrushchev's plan for CMEA-wide 'superministries' that would have limited the members' autonomy. It follows that so long as the principle of unanimity continues to hold sway in CMEA councils, a real basis will be hard to find for the fear that Soviet economic influence may limit the sovereignty of the East European countries. It is questionable, therefore, whether any agreement between the CMEA and the EEC could make such limitation possible.

But political problems arising from the international legal considerations mentioned above remain. One question for the West Europeans is, with whom would they sign an agreement? The CMEA Executive Committee does not have the regularized statutory powers to sign such agreements. (The question of assigning responsibility on the CMEA side is therefore an open and non-trivial question.) Nevertheless, the CMEA has signed such agreements collectively on behalf of its member states on several occasions in the past, the member states having empowered the organization's Executive Committee, *in each particular case,* to do so on their behalf. For example, Soviet scholars often cite the agreement on economic cooperation signed by the CMEA's Executive Committee with Finland in 1973;[20] similar agreements have also been signed with Mexico, Iraq, and Yugoslavia.

---

[20]A good overview, and still current, is Henryk De Fiumel, 'The Council for Mutual Economic Assistance in international relations,' *Studies on International Relations* (Warsaw), Vol. 7 (1976), pp. 68–77.

But none of these is more than a framework agreement: the signatories commit themselves only to seek to attempt to fulfil certain goals for the extension of trade and commercial contacts. Such an agreement therefore embodies only general terms, the fulfilment of which depends upon specific subsequent negotiations. It is little more than a multilateral device for coordinating the bilateral long-term agreements that the CMEA member states sign individually with third countries.

In the abstract, such an agreement with the EEC could promote the East European countries' autonomous bilateral ties. However, in the past the Soviet Union has been the moving force behind the Eastern bloc's initiatives on this type of agreement. To the extent that that remains the case, such an agreement could serve to increase the coordination of national economic planning among some, if not all, CMEA members. The autonomous development of existing bilateral economic ties between East and West European states, on the other hand, could encourage an economic integration process in Eastern Europe that would exclude overt coordination with the Soviet Union.

EEC-CMEA RELATIONS IN THE FUTURE

It is possible to distinguish four possible outcomes of the current contacts between the two organizations: (1) an umbrella framework agreement, (2) the establishment of a joint statistical office, (3) an agreement in principle, and (4) no agreement at all.

An Umbrella Framework Agreement

Let us suppose that some interorganizational agreement establishes an institutional framework along the lines of the Franco-Soviet model (in which a multiplicity of councils and committees seek to regulate and facilitate commercial contacts between the parties). If the CMEA were to seek some such joint council with the EEC, some in Western Europe might fear that this would create a basis for the Eastern bloc to interfere in the affairs of EEC members. But it is at least as likely that this would also permit the West European countries to 'interfere' in the affairs of CMEA members. Indeed, that is precisely what happened after Helsinki through the follow-up conferences instituted by the CSCE Final Document. Although the Soviet Union thought it could use the document—as well as the process of its formulation—to divide Western Europe from the United States (and the West European states from one another), Basket III, on humanitarian issues, has given the Western countries the standing under international law to concern themselves with human rights in the Soviet Union. Moreover, the Helsinki accords gave rise to a wave of dissent in the CMEA countries in the late 1970s that was wholly unanticipated in both East and West. From this experience it would seem unlikely that Western Europe has much to fear from an EEC-CMEA joint commission.

Establishment of a Joint Statistical Office

After the failure in the early 1970s to establish strong, institutionalized formal relations, some rather more modest proposals were put forward, including one to establish a central statistical office to gather and exchange economic data, which might also facilitate trade contacts. Although this is a much more practical approach, the Geneva-based UN Economic Commission for Europe already fulfils precisely this function, and it is doubtful whether a duplication of that effort would promote further cooperation.

An Agreement in Principle

An agreement in principle would be entirely symbolic. Yet even this possibility encounters obstacles. The CMEA still does not like the EEC's supranational status, and the EEC rightly hesitates to confer on the CMEA the appearance of equality. An agreement in principle fits rather well with recent Soviet preferences for European security. Even more than in the early 1970s, Soviet moves today seem less mo-

tivated by the desire to establish practical and effective relations than by that to create a political atmosphere. The whole of Soviet policy in Europe in the 1970s, at CSCE, in the negotiations over Mutual and Balanced Force Reductions, and in the strategic arms limitation talks (SALT) suggests this pattern of motives.[21]

No Agreement

There is always the possibility that the present situation will continue and that no agreement will be struck between the EEC and the CMEA. It is unlikely that the absence of any agreement will make much difference. Without an agreement, relations will continue to develop along present lines, with the EEC seeking to aid the East European countries piecemeal to increase their autonomy in trade matters through accords on limited issues. Commercial contacts between states (Franco-Polish, Bulgaro-German, etc.) will be no more restricted by the absence of an agreement than they are now, and their recent development has been prodigious.

CONCLUSION

Underlying the issue of EEC-CMEA relations is the question of competing political visions of Europe. Despite calls for all-European

---

[21]See Robert Legvold, 'The problem of European security,' *Problems of Communism*, Vol. 23, No. 1 (Jan.–Feb. 1974), pp. 13–33, for this argument.

economic cooperation, the Soviet Union has given no evidence of regarding an interbloc economic agreement as the means for creating a united Europe 'from the Atlantic to the Urals.' An interbloc economic agreement would, in fact, only reinforce the East-West division of Europe, confirming the boundaries of the two blocs by regulating the EEC's autonomous penetration of the CMEA countries. Yet for the European Communities, the ultimate vision of Europe remains one of a genuinely transcontinental entity, organic and whole. There is a clear parallel between the EEC's approach to relations with the European Free Trade Association (EFTA) and its approach to the CMEA. EFTA's members ended up signing individual free trade agreements with the Community, which refused steadfastly to sanction any formal agreement with EFTA as an organization. This experience seems almost a conscious model for the EEC's treatment of the prospect of relations with the CMEA.[22]

If the EEC recognizes the CMEA, it is unlikely to be a recognition on equal terms. The EEC countries have little to gain economically from formalizing relations with the CMEA. However, such relations do have a role to play in the political construction of Europe. If the EEC countries succeed

in increasing their penetration of Eastern Europe in the long run, then the only way for the Soviet Union to maintain the region as a buffer zone would be for it to encourage a certain amount of economic and perhaps even political cooperation in Eastern Europe, independent of Soviet participation. Recent events cannot be encouraging in this regard: the Soviet Union has never been warm to attempts to construct all-Balkan cooperation, and at a time of very poor superpower relations in late 1983 and for much of 1984 it put the chill on a putative 'Berlin-Budapest-Bucharest axis' that sought expanded political contacts with Western Europe. Still, such a development cannot be ruled out in the long run: who in 1957 would have thought that the Soviet Union would ever entertain the prospect of formal political relations with the EEC? If distinct and autonomous East European movement towards regional economic and political integration does develop, however, it will certainly not be discernible before the twenty-first century.

In the late 1940s, the Soviet Union supported the still-born idea of the International Trading Organization (ITO), which was to have been a part of the Bretton Woods system. In 1956, it proposed to the UN Economic Commission for Europe that a European Trading Or-

---

[22]I wish to thank Baard Bredrup Knudsen at the University of Oslo for this insight. See also his 'Europe between the superpowers,' *Cooperation and Conflict*, Vol. 20, No. 1 (1985), pp. 91–112.

ganization should be created, and it lobbied unsuccessfully for a similar initiative at the CSCE meetings in the 1970s. Thus the Soviet Union has historically favoured the creation of new international organizations, and of legal and procedural frameworks for the regulation of international trade, while seeking consistently to break the capitalist countries' hold on whatever international economic institutions they dominate. This attitude helps to explain the Soviet Union's behaviour at UNCTAD, the positions it has articulated in the UN International Law Commission, and its general approach to international trade law. Soviet policy-makers have traditionally been less concerned with maximizing their maximum possible economic gain than with minimizing their maximum possible political loss.

Yet the experience of the East European countries demonstrates that those international economic institutions will adapt to some aspects of centralized statist planning,[23] whereas recent attempts to reinvigorate coordination by the CMEA of Eastern bloc economic activity have run into significant obstacles. The revision of intra-CMEA pricing rules, motivated by Soviet interests in the mid-1970s, forced the smaller CMEA countries to turn to world markets to satisfy their needs for energy and raw materials. But it was precisely these commodities that through their extraction, refinement, and trade formed the basis for the CMEA's earlier successes in promoting Eastern bloc economic cooperation. Economic managers in some of the smaller CMEA countries now see long-term advantages emerging from their need for hard currency, because this requires them to become internationally competitive in other export markets. It should come as no shock to hear even East European planners remark that the CMEA has been transformed from an integration mechanism into a disintegration mechanism. Having failed to delegitimize the EEC, the Soviet Union seems to wish to enlist its aid to relegitimize the CMEA.

---

[23]See Valerie J. Assetto, *The Soviet bloc in the IMF and the IBRD* (Boulder, Colo.: Westview, 1986).

21

GETTING ACCESS TO THE VICTIMS: ROLE AND ACTIVITIES OF THE ICRC

Jean-Luc Blondel

1. THE GENESIS OF THE ICRC

The genesis of the International Committee of the Red Cross (ICRC) is characteristic of its development and of all of its activities: it was born in a *time of war* as a result of a *private initiative*. In a time of war, true, but not as a support of war. On the contrary, because it works close to the fighting, it sees and meets the victims of war, whom it endeavours to assist and protect.

The ICRC was established in early 1863 to put into effect the measures proposed by Henry Dunant in his work *A Memory of Solferino* (1862), namely:

- to induce all States to create permanent national societies for the relief of wounded soldiers;

- to persuade all States to agree by treaty to respect the neutrality of army medical personnel.

These two aims were rapidly achieved at the time owing to the prevailing goodwill of States and the sensitization of public opinion to the suffering caused by war. It was, however, but the beginning of a vast movement which was to gain increasing momentum while preserving the essential motivation which had given birth to it, namely, the protection and assistance of the victims of conflicts and disasters.

2. ACCESS TO THE VICTIMS

The title of this article implies that *access* to the victims is not always easy. The obstacles are political, technical and economic. Since its foundation in 1863, the ICRC has had to face numerous and ever-varying difficulties. This can be illustrated by a few current examples.

In the *Republic of South Africa,* where its presence has been continuous since the end of 1978, the ICRC continues to make visits (as it has done since 1969) to persons sentenced under the state security law. The less the protection available to the persons it assists, the more important it considers its intervention. It has therefore asked the Government for regular access

SOURCE: Reprinted from "Getting Access to the Victims: Role and Activities of the ICRC," by Jean-Luc Blondel, from *Journal of Peace Research*, Vol. 24, No. 3, by permission of Norwegian University Press, Oslo.

to all persons detained under the state of emergency, and has undertaken negotiations for permission to visit persons sentenced for public violence in connection with the internal disturbances. By mid-1987, those efforts have not yet been successful.

While the ICRC is not allowed access to *all* the victims of the unrest in South Africa, in other cases it is denied access to entire countries. Thus, with the exception of two brief missions carried out in 1980 and 1982, the ICRC has until recently been consistently refused permission to pursue its activities inside *Afghanistan*. However, it opened a hospital in Peshawar (June, 1981) and one in Quetta (July, 1983) where Afghan refugees in Pakistan may receive care. It is allowed access, albeit too rarely, to prisoners held by the Afghan resistance movement, but the activities it is able to carry out on their behalf fall far short of the protection to which all the victims of the conflict, which has been going on since 1979, are entitled under the Conventions. In February 1987, however, the ICRC was allowed to resume its protection and assistance activities in Kabul itself.

Another obstacle, actually more technical than political, is *distance*. In order to reach starving civilians or to visit prisoners, long stretches of rough terrain must often be covered, sometimes even on foot. Some regions can be supplied only by air. Thus, relief activities in *Angola, southern Sudan, Ethiopia* and, in 1979–80, along the border between *Thailand* and *Kampuchea,* required the establishment of vast and complex transportation systems.

These observations bring to mind another difficulty, *lack of resources*. Relief operations in major emergencies require people and equipment on a large scale, and are therefore very costly. Moreover, emergencies go on forever, or rather, they recur. Emergency action should be followed by socio-economic reconstruction and development work, but this is far from being the rule. Under the sway of emotion and bolstered by public opinion, donor countries or agencies generally offer considerable financial and material aid during the first phase of a relief operation. Economic problems emerge later, when public and government interest wanes. The difficulty of financing ICRC activities in Africa and in the Middle East provides a good illustration of this point.

It is easier to launch an operation than to maintain it once financial support diminishes. However, perseverance, tenacity, and continuity are precisely what is required in the case of assistance to conflict victims. The ICRC is characterized by activities which *last*. More and more frequently now, it works in one country for several years, either because there is no substantial abatement in the disturbances (Israel and the occupied territories, Lebanon, the Philippines, El Salvador, etc.) or because it likes to keep contacts in as many countries as possible in regions which are calmer but none the less also breed tension (and where its regional delegations cover several countries at once, as in New Delhi, Hong Kong, Lagos, Harare, Bogota, etc.).

It is not unusual for the ICRC to have to deal with power changes in countries or regions beset by conflicts or even revolutions. Thus, the ICRC maintained delegations in Zimbabwe, Iran and Nicaragua despite the considerable political changes which recently swept those countries. In order to maintain its activities on behalf of the persons affected by these changes, the ICRC, for purely humanitarian reasons, maintains a policy of constant political neutrality.

In order to understand the motivation behind that policy, characterized by both *caring* (assistance to victims) and *impartiality* (political, ideological and religious neutrality), it is helpful to trace its origin. The humanitarian commitment of the ICRC stems from a history rife with trials and tribulations. A knowledge of the institution's birth and development provides a better understanding of today's ICRC and its resolve to have access to all the victims of conflicts.

3. THE FIRST YEARS

The ICRC, comprising at the outset five persons belonging to a Genevese circle of 'philanthropists,' saw itself merely as the promoter of an idea. At first glance, nothing marked it out for direct intervention in prisoner camps or among the civilian victims of com-

bats.[1] Such work 'in the field' was in fact not to be systematically undertaken by the ICRC until the early 1900s, although the Committee sent occasional missions to the front as early as 1864.

'Relief societies' were constituted and, as of 1872, adopted the *red cross* as their emblem.[2] They were to intervene in time of war and, gradually, also in time of peace. The ICRC itself was to remain an institution active primarily in time of armed conflict, which was to make it a special body within the world of the Red Cross and within the international political community. The ICRC is, in fact, a *private Swiss institution* whose delegates are exclusively Swiss citizens. It is none the less totally independent from the Swiss Government (as it is from all other governments), and all its activities are governed by the strict principle of neutrality (political, ideological and religious). The ICRC is *international* by its field of activity and its financing which is ensured, for the most part, by voluntary government contributions (the States signatory to the Geneva Conventions).

Although the National Societies rapidly grew and flourished, often giving rise at the same time to improved army medical structures, the development of what was later to be called *international humanitarian law* (IHL) had yet to be undertaken. This practical preoccupation was soon to lead the ICRC to its involvement in the field.

While the first humanitarian Conventions concluded in Geneva in 1864[3] guaranteed respect for armies in the field—shelter and care for troops whatever their nationality—no provisions had been made enabling prisoners to communicate with their families or, inversely, for families to receive information about prisoners. It was in response to this need that the ICRC opened, during the Franco-German war in 1870, an *Agency for the Wounded in Armies* soon to be followed by an *Agency for Prisoners of War* responsible for the establishment of lists of prisoners and for the exchange of letters and, later, packages. To ensure the distribution of relief consignments (then provided by the families or by the authorities of the native country of the prisoners of war), the ICRC sent delegates to prison hospitals and camps. This initiative was to become a tradition as the ICRC undertook an increasing number of humanitarian activities in the very midst of conflicts. It thus organized large-scale assistance operations for prisoners of war during the First World War (yet still with no firm base in any convention!).

In addition to the wounded in armies and prisoners of war, the ICRC was deeply concerned about another category of victims, namely civilians, who were very poorly protected, yet increasingly affected by hostilities in which they took no part. During the inter-war period, the ICRC spared no effort to enhance the protection of civilians. Unfortunately, of the proposals made by the ICRC from 1923 onwards, only the provisions concerning prisoners of war were to be adopted by States, who signed a Convention on the subject in 1929 (Convention Relative to the Treatment of Prisoners of War). It would take another cruel war to bring the States to accept—at least partially—responsibility for the protection of civilians. During the same period, the ICRC carried out several relief operations, particularly in the following conflicts:

- *The Russian Civil War* (1917–1921), where ICRC intervention took the form of a large-scale international relief operation on behalf of Russian refugees. This was the departure point for a refugee assistance scheme which engendered the *Office of the High Commissioner for Refugees*. The representatives of High Commissioner Nansen were, for the most part, ICRC delegates. The ICRC took advantage of the infrastructure used to repatriate prisoners at the end of the First World War, and proved particularly useful wherever a neutral intermediary was necessary.

- *The war between Italy and Ethiopia* (1936), which marked the beginning of ICRC assistance, especially medical, to areas outside Europe.

- *The Spanish Civil War* (1936–1938), during which the ICRC carried out large-scale relief operations to aid civilians while simultaneously engaging in difficult activities concerned with prisoners and hostages on both sides (visits, exchanges). These operations also demonstrated the need to establish humanitarian norms for internal conflicts.

4. THE SECOND WORLD WAR AND THE GENEVA CONVENTIONS

The relief services set up by the ICRC during the Spanish Civil War were still functioning in 1939. They rapidly became the core of the relief network in operation during the Second World War. The legal basis (the prisoner-of-war code of 1929) upon which the ICRC was able to base its activities was in fact quite limited in that it granted the ICRC only the right to establish an Agency for Prisoners of War and to take humanitarian initiatives. ICRC activities were nevertheless considerable: the Agency built up a file containing 40 million cards, and it received and sent more than 50 million communications. It ensured the dispatch and distribution of 36 million packages, and its delegates carried out more than 11,000 visits to places of detention (ICRC 1948).

However, the work of the ICRC encountered numerous obstacles, even in the countries which were Parties to the Conventions of 1929.[4] Germany thus threatened many times to close off its prisoner-of-war camps to ICRC delegates. Japan availed itself of every opportunity to hamper the Committee's activities, thereby preventing any real monitoring. Finally and most

importantly, owing to the absence of treaty provisions, the ICRC was unable to undertake effective action for civilians exterminated in concentration camps or threatened by bombing.

After the war was over, the Diplomatic Conference of 1949, which was to adopt what are today known as the *Geneva Conventions*, granted a number of specific rights to the ICRC, particularly:

- *To visit* and interview without witnesses *prisoners* of war (126:III) and civilian detainees or internees (76 and 143:IV) (Arabic numerals refer to the article quoted; Roman numerals to the Convention).

- *To provide relief* to civilians in occupied territories (59 and 61:IV).

- *To trace missing persons* and transmit family messages to prisoners of war (123:III) and civilians (140:IV).

- *To offer its services* to facilitate the establishment of hospital (23:IV) and safety (14:IV) zones and localities.

- *To receive applications for assistance* from persons entitled to protection (30:IV).

- To function, in case of need, as a *substitute for the Protecting Power* (10:I, 10:II, 10:III, 11:IV).

- To send to the parties to the conflict, by virtue of its *right of initiative,* any humanitarian proposal, in situations both of international armed conflict (9:I, 9:II, 9:III, 10:IV) and of non-international armed conflict (common Art. 3), (Sandoz 1979).

The latter point is particularly important to the ICRC. Since the Second World War, the situations of conflict in which it takes action have evolved considerably. Traditional wars between regular armies have been joined by growing numbers of often lethal internal conflicts of which civilians are the first victims. Article 3 common to the four Conventions, in itself a 'mini-convention,' gives the ICRC a legal basis, unfortunately not always possible to invoke, to offer its services to help the victims of internal armed conflicts.[5] It is on this basis that it works in numerous countries, including El Salvador, Nicaragua, Angola and Mozambique, to mention but a few examples.

5. VISITS TO 'POLITICAL DETAINEES'

However, there are other tragic situations in which no conventions exist to support humanitarian action, namely, internal disturbances and tensions, in which the ICRC has constantly carried out its activities. Whereas visits to prisoners of war and civilian internees are based on the Third and Fourth Conventions, those to persons detained in connection with internal disturbances and tensions—sometimes defined as 'political detainees'—fall outside the scope of these Conventions and of their additional Protocols adopted in 1977. They have their 'legal' basis in the Statutes of the International Red Cross as approved by an International Conference of the Red Cross. In 1928, these Statutes recognized the right of the ICRC, as a neutral and independent intermediary, to offer its services to States, without being accused of exceeding its competence or interfering in matters of national sovereignty.[6] However, States have no obligation to accept the activities of the ICRC and can refuse or put an end to them without breaching the *law*. This was the case, for example, of Greece between 1967 and 1971.

Visits to 'political detainees,' which first took place in Russia in 1918 and in Hungary in 1919, became regular only after the end of the Second World War.

Since then, the ICRC has visited more than half a million detainees in 95 countries. Its visits are governed by the observation of very strict conditions. Its delegates visit places of detention only if they are assured of being allowed to:

- see all the detainees, register them, and talk to them freely (interviews without witnesses);
- have access to all the places of detention;
- repeat the visits as necessary.

Respect for *all* these conditions is a prerequisite of all ICRC visits.

The visits carried out by the delegates have a purely humanitarian purpose. Concerned with preserving, by its neutrality, the confidence of all, the ICRC does not become involved in the political problem at the root of the disturbances and unrest, nor does it take a stand on the *reasons* for detention. It is mainly concerned with the material and psychological *conditions* of the detainees (accommodation, food, family visits, treatment during interrogation and detention), which it seeks to improve by its activities.

The ICRC carries out this work discreetly. Its reports to the authorities are confidential and it does not make public comments on its observations. However, if any Government publishes a partial or inaccurate version of any of its reports, the ICRC reserves the right to publish the full report.

These visits to 'political detainees' constitute a unique activity of this nature at the international level. It makes an essential contribution to the protection of prisoners. Individuals are particularly ill-protected in the above-mentioned situations, which are covered by the inalienable standards of human rights but not by IHL. Post-war conflicts are also characterized by another dimension which blurs the strict distinction between 'war' and 'peace.' Within a single country, fighting goes on alongside areas where there is peace and where disturbances and attacks break out only sporadically. Such situations are particularly frequent in countries in which economic conditions were already precarious before the outbreak of the conflicts.

6. COMPREHENSIVE ASSISTANCE

Modern warfare not only affects its direct victims: it has disastrous side effects on the civilian population, destroying its fragile equilibrium, particularly in relation to food and medical care. The approach to such situations can be no less than comprehensive and requires protection corresponding to the diversity of needs.

The ICRC has thus undertaken large-scale relief operations in countries simultaneously afflicted by armed conflicts and natural disasters.

In recent years, Africa has naturally remained the major setting of such large-scale ICRC activities, partly because of the extent of its armed conflicts, internal disturbances and domestic unrest, and partly because of the size of the relief operations which had to be undertaken there, mainly to assist Angola, Uganda and Ethiopia.

In Ethiopia since 1977, the ICRC has carried out activities arising from the conflict with Somalia over the Ogaden. From 1983, however, most of its activities have focused on assisting the victims of the internal conflicts in the north of the country (Tigre, Eritrea, northern Wollo and northern Gondar), whose fate has worsened considerably as a result of the drought.

The continuation of hostilities and the persistence of the drought have increased the number of displaced persons in the conflict zones. In October 1985, at the height of the crisis, the ICRC assisted over 800,000 persons.

Beginning in May 1985, seed has been distributed along with food, to enable the assisted populations rapidly to achieve self-sufficiency and to return home. Beginning late it 1985, owing to a general improvement in the situation, the ICRC was able to reduce the volume of relief distributed.

In recent years, the ICRC has carried out other long-term food relief operations, particularly in Uganda, Angola, El Salvador, Nicaragua, the Philippines and Lebanon.

The progress of such operations has been frequently slowed down or hampered by security problems and logistic difficulties in addition to the reluctance of certain parties to allow the ICRC to function according to its criteria.

The importance of conformity with the ICRC conditions for visits to detainees has already been stated. In the case of relief operations, the ICRC will undertake them only providing it has direct access to the victims to be assisted, that is, specifically on condition that it is allowed to:

- make surveys in the area to determine the urgency of the needs and identify the categories and numbers of beneficiaries;

- organize and supervise the distribution of relief.

The need for strict management by a neutral and impartial agency is clear. Relief dispensed in regions of conflict can become a political gambit if it is diverted to benefit the combatants, to the detriment of the victims for whom it is intended. Moreover, the ICRC is determined to safeguard its independence. It is willing to coordinate its activities with those of the responsible authorities or other relief agencies, but it refuses to subordinate blindly its contribution to a government programme. Such programmes tend to be conceived to benefit strategic and political interests rather than the people directly affected by the conflict.

Moreover, as already mentioned, the armed conflicts in which the ICRC takes action no longer resemble traditional wars between armies: these have been superseded by wars in which the distinction between civilians and armed forces has become less clear. Economic stagnation, the major disruption of an already unhealthy environment (malnutrition, underdeveloped health services), administrative anarchy and socio-economic upheaval accompanying today's conflicts exacerbate the fate of civilians, far more vulnerable than armies, and make hunger and disease often more lethal than weapons. The vital needs of civilians are frequently greater in scale than those of the wounded and prisoners who, in the past, were the war victims who had priority. The ICRC has had to take this new situation into account and adapt its operational activities, particularly in the medical sphere, to the increasing numbers and new needs of the victims.

In a temporary situation (earthquake, flood, limited conflict), an emergency operation can sustain civilians during a short period and enable them to weather the crisis, albeit at great expense (trucks, aeroplanes, numerous expatriate personnel, etc.).

However, when situations remain uncertain, as today on the border between Thailand and Kampuchea, in Afghanistan, Angola, Ethiopia, etc., the problem can no longer be approached in the same manner. Solutions must be found which are less costly and better adapted to local needs. Attention must be given to digging wells, to cultivation, construction and the use of all local resources, with the aim of rendering the population self-sufficient as rapidly as possible.

Once vital needs have been covered for the time being (basic food, medical care and shelter), assistance directed towards the long-term satisfaction of those needs provides an excellent opportunity to teach the population notions of hygiene, public health and mother and child care, all of which may bring beneficial consequences long after the emergency situation has abated. Such activities must, however, be undertaken only with the full support of the people concerned and with all due respect for their traditions and lifestyles. It is

within this wide spectrum of aims that the ICRC is increasingly active today in the face of chronic medical emergencies, without however embarking on long-term development programmes.

7. LAW, HUMANITARIAN AID AND THE SETTLEMENT OF CONFLICTS

Too many emergency situations drag on, however, because the belligerent parties lack the sincere will to negotiate solutions conducive to ending the conflict. A keen observer of ICRC activities in Thailand wrote that:

> To the ICRC it seems that today more and more governments are abjuring compromise and are seeking to use its offices and those of other humanitarian organizations as a way of postponing, perhaps indefinitely, difficult political compromises in favor of continual, uncompromising, ever-encroaching war (Shawcross 1984, p. 428, see also Rufin 1986).

These considerations, although not alone sufficient to challenge all humanitarian action, merit reflection. They touch upon an essential aspect of the humanitarian activity of the ICRC, which strives to relieve the suffering of victims by all possible means without ever sacrificing them to political considerations. One might even ask whether the contribution of humanitarian action does not, in alleviating the tragic fate of civilians, decrease the pressure on governments to negotiate a political solution to the differences which oppose them. That suspicion should above all arouse the concern of States and intergovernmental agencies. Neither the ICRC nor any of the other numerous non-governmental organizations can resolve the conflicts that cause the human suffering necessitating their intervention.

These observations bring us back to our point of departure. The ICRC, striving in the midst of conflicts to curb their effects and assist their victims, is well aware of the horror of warfare and has no greater desire than to see it cease. However, the settlement of differences which underlie conflicts remains a highly political task. In that respect, the ICRC can at most aspire, by acting as a neutral intermediary between the parties to the conflict and by helping to maintain some humanity in the midst of the fighting, to foster a climate favourable to negotiations.

The ICRC sees its work above all within the framework of international humanitarian law, the full respect of which would already greatly reduce many of the ills of war. A high official of the ICRC said in that respect that:

> The main problem is to *ensure compliance with,* rather than development of, the existing law. If the States would only observe the rules which have already been laid down, 80% of our problems would be solved. Observance of the existing body of law is a more important issue than further development of it. Governments and peoples should not be led to believe that more law could be a remedy. What is needed is greater political will to comply with the existing norms (Moreillon in Bedjaoui 1986, pp. 56–57. Emphasis added.).

Law is meaningful only insofar as it is complied with. The ICRC strives to ensure compliance both through the dissemination of the law and through the careful monitoring of its application in the course of armed conflicts.

NOTES

1. The ICRC staff currently includes over six hundred employees working in Geneva and about 450 collaborators sent on mission from headquarters, not counting some 2,000 employees engaged locally. In 1978, the ICRC had 18 delegations. By late 1986, that number had grown to 37, spread across the world.

2. During its war against Russia, Turkey, on 16 November 1876, informed the Swiss Federal Council, depository of the Geneva Convention of 1864, that it had adopted a new emblem, the *red crescent.* Turkey nevertheless agreed to respect the red cross emblem displayed by Russian troops. It was not until 1929 that the red crescent was officially recognized as having the same protection value as the red cross.

3. *Geneva Convention of 22 August 1864 for the Amelioration of the Conditions of the Wounded in Armies in the Field.* On the development of humanitarian law, see the article by Jacques Meurant in this issue.

4. It should be recalled that, because the Soviet Union had not signed the Convention of 1929, the ICRC was unable to undertake any relief operations on behalf of German prisoners of war in Soviet hands or of Soviet prisoners in German camps.

5. The paragraph concerning ICRC work in Article 3 reads as follows: *'An impartial humanitarian body, such as the International Committee of the Red Cross, may offer its services to the Parties to the conflict.'*

6. The International Conference of the Red Cross meets in principle every four years. It brings together all the delegates of the International Movement of the Red Cross and Red Crescent (the ICRC, the League of Red Cross and Red Crescent Societies, the National Societies) and representatives of the States Parties to the Geneva Conventions.

   The Twenty-Fifth Conference, held in Geneva in October 1986, revised the Statutes of the Movement. Article 5, which concerns the mandate of the ICRC, states in particular:

   '(The role of ICRC is) *to endeavor at all times—as a neutral institution whose humanitarian work is carried out particularly in time of international and other armed conflicts or internal strife—to ensure the protection of and assistance to military and civilian victims of such events and of their direct results.'*

   Further: *'The International Committee may take any humanitarian initiative which comes within its role as a specifically neutral and independent institution and intermediary, and may consider any question requiring examination by such an institution.'*

7. It should be noted that these conditions are analogous to those which the Third Geneva Convention provides for prisoners of war (Article 126).

REFERENCES

Bugnion, Franqis, *The Emblem of the Red Cross. A Brief History.* Geneva: ICRC.

Boissier, Pierre 1985. *History of the International Committee of the Red Cross. 1: From Solferino to Tsushima.* Geneva: Henry Dunant Institute.

Durand, André 1984. *The International Committee of the Red Cross. 2: From Sarajevo to Hiroshima.* Geneva: Henry Dunant Institute.

Durand, André 1981. *History of the International Committee of the Red Cross.* Geneva: ICRC.

Deming, Richard 1982. *Heroes of the International Red Cross.* Geneva: ICRC.

Dunant, Henry (1862) 1986. *A Memory of Solferino.* Geneva: ICRC.

Freymond, Jacques 1976. *Guerres, Révolutions, Croix-Rouge, Réflexions sur le rôle du Comité international de la Croix-Rouge.* Geneva Institut Universitaire de Hautes Etudes Internationales.

International Red Cross Handbook 1983. Twelfth Edition. Geneva: ICRC and LRCS.

The International Committee of the Red Cross and Internal Disturbances and Tensions. ICRC Protection and Assistance Activities in Situations not covered by International Humanitarian Law 1986. Geneva: ICRC.

ICRC, *Annual Report*. Geneva: published every year.

ICRC 1986. *Five Years of Activity 1981–1985*. Geneva.

Jmed Marcel 1982. *The Warrior Without Weapons*. Geneva: ICRC.

Junod, Sylvie 1984. *Protection of the Victims of Armed Conflict Falkland-Malvinas Islands* (1982). *International Humanitarian Law and Humanitarian Action*, Geneva: ICRC.

ICRC 1948. *Report of the ICRC on its Activities during the Second World War (September 1, 1939-June 30, 1947)*, 3 vols. Seventeenth International Red Cross Conference. Stockholm. Geneva: ICRC.

ICRC 1981. *Kampuchea: Back from the Brink. The ICRC Report and its 15 Months Joint Action with UNICEF in Kampuchea and Thailand*. Geneva: ICRC.

Macalister-Smith, Peter 1985. *International Humanitarian Assistance. Disaster Relief Actions in International Law and Organisation*. Dordrecht: Martinus Nijhoff.

Bedjaoui Mohammed, ed. 1986. *Modern Wars: The Humanitarian Challenge. A Report for the Independent Commission on International Humanitarian Issues*. London and New Jersey: Zed Books Ltd.

Moreillon, Jacques 1973. *Le Comité international de la Croix-Rouge et la protection des détenus politiques*. Lausanne: L'Age d'Homme.

Pictet, Jean 1979. *The Fundamental Principles of the Red Cross, Commentary*. Geneva: Henry Dunant Institute.

Pictet, Jean 1985. *Une institution unique en son genre: Le Comité international de la Croix-Rouge*. Geneva: Henry Dunant Institute, and Paris: Ed. A Pedone.

Rufin, Jean-Christophe 1986. *Le Piège. Quand l'aide humanitaire remplace la guerre*. Paris: J.C. Lattès.

Sandoz, Yves 1979. 'Le droit dìnitiative du CICR,' *German Yearbook of International Law*, vol. 22, pp. 352–373.

Shawcross, William 1984. *The Quality of Mercy: Cambodia, Holocaust and Modern Conscience*. New York: Simon and Schuster.

Siegrist, Roland 1985. *The Protection of Political Detainees—The International Committee of the Red Cross in Greece 1967–1971*. Montreux: Editions Corbaz.

Veuthey, Michel 1983. *Guérilla et droit humanitaire*, Geneva: ICRC.

CHAPTER IX

The United States and the United Nations

Since the inception of the United Nations, public opinion in the United States has consistently supported the existence of the organization as well as U.S. membership in it. Yet, there has been persistent criticism of the United Nations by the American public and various political leaders. Most of that criticism centers on the inability of the United States to marshal support for its own policy positions. On several occasions, the United States has been the sole negative vote against an overwhelming majority in the General Assembly or Security Council. There is even a vocal minority in the United States that has denounced the international body and called for an American withdrawal similar to the action taken earlier with the International Labor Organization (ILO) and more recently with UNESCO.

American criticism of the United Nations is not a new phenomenon. During the 1950s, conservatives and isolationalists labeled the organization as a tool of communist influence. This claim was made despite a fairly consistent majority for Western interests in the General Assembly. The frustration with the U.N. police action in Korea and the series of Soviet vetoes in the Security Council no doubt contributed to this dissatisfaction. In the next decade, the Western majority faded in the wake of an explosion in U.N. membership following decolonization. A new Third World majority, often seemingly aligned with the Soviet Union and its allies, left the United States more frequently on the losing end of most formal votes. This turn of events strengthened the arguments of those who claimed U.N. decisions were inimical to American interests.

Criticism of the United Nations has continued to the present. Actions such as the continuing condemnations of Israel have served to isolate the United States on several issues in the organization and to arouse opposition at home. The occurrence of spy activities by Soviet members of the U.N. Secretariat has also given the organization a black eye among the American populace.

Despite the criticism of the United Nations in the United States, each remains dependent upon the other. The United Nations receives about one fifth of its regular budget from the United States, more than any other member; significant voluntary contributions add to this total. Furthermore, the United States' position as a superpower and economic giant means that the organization relies on its membership and support to give credibility and strength to international decisions. The United States also looks to the United Nations to legitimize American policies and further its interests; American use of the organization during the Cuban Missile Crisis and following the seizure of American hostages in Iran illustrates that the organization can be a useful policy tool. Various peacekeeping efforts have also served United States interests in preserving peace and international security.

If there remains a strong mutual interest between the United Nations and the United States, the logical points of examination are the bases for American criticism of the organization and the validity of those claims. The article by John Ruggie covers the major American objections to the United Nations. Focusing on security issues and the administrative performance of the United Nations, he is able to identify both the events that sparked American criticism and the standards by which those actions have been judged. From his analysis, it is evident that it is probably unrealistic and unreasonable to expect an organization of over 160 diverse members to adhere to the dictates or policy interests of any one of its members, the United States in particular. Furthermore, Ruggie implies that observers may have unrealistic expectations about what the United Nations is capable of accomplishing. That organization is inherently limited by the powers and missions assigned to it by its membership. The blame for its failures or inadequacies must lie as much with its members as with the organization itself.

Donald Puchala evaluates the criticism that the United Nations acts in contradiction to American interests. Admittedly, his analysis concentrates heavily on the ways in which the organization promotes American interests and ideals. Yet, the points he makes are too often ignored. With all the criticism of the United Nations in the media and political forums, the reader needs to be reminded of the various U.N. actions that directly serve U.S. interests. Furthermore, there needs to be recognition that even when decisions do not correspond to the American position, the actions often are either largely symbolic or have been significantly moderated by American lobbying efforts in the organization.

In this last section, it is perhaps important to remember that international organizations are neither the incompetent bureaucracies that some claim nor the panacea for all global problems. In evaluating international organizations, it is important to go beyond the myths that dominate our conception of these entities and look for the activities that international organizations do well and those in which they fall far short of expectations. It is the task of the future to expand the scope of the former and work to correct the flaws of the latter.

22

THE UNITED STATES AND THE UNITED NATIONS: TOWARD A NEW REALISM

John Gerard Ruggie

Quantitatively, international governmental organizations (IGOs) are still an expanding force in international affairs. Qualitatively, however, the world of IGOs is not in good shape. Indeed, there is widespread talk these days about a crisis of multilateralism, especially but not exclusively in the context of the United Nations.[1] With regard to peace and security, the UN secretary general himself has remarked that the organization's machinery functions so poorly that the international community finds itself "perilously near to a new international anarchy."[2] North-South economic negotiations in the United Nations have been stalemated for a decade, and the decade-long Law of the Seas negotiations failed to produce a universally acceptable treaty. The administrative performance of the United Nations and its agencies is said by many critics to be inferior, the salary and benefit levels inflated. Many of its technical agenices are accused of having become thoroughly politicized. There is a pervasive sense that the system as a whole is somehow out of control.

Nowhere are these feelings as pronounced as they are in the United States. Contrary to popular myth, there never was a "golden age" in U.S.-UN relations—not even when the General Assembly tended to favor "our" issues and "our" side, often by a predictable majority of nearly ten to one; when the Soviet Union was effectively isolated; and when no large, cohesive bloc of Third World states existed.[3] Moreover, there have been previous periods of irritation. It is

SOURCE: Reprinted from *International Organization*, Vol. 39, No. 2, 1985, John Gerard Ruggie, "The United States and the United Nations: Toward a New Realism," by permission of The MIT Press, Cambridge, Massachusetts. © 1985 by the Massachusetts Institute of Technology and the World Peace Foundation.

[1]See the speech, "What Future for Multilateralism?" by UN Secretary-General Javier Pérez de Cuéllar, delivered to the Geneva Diplomatic Club and the Centre d'études pratiques de la négociation internationale in Geneva, 3 July 1984, reproduced as UN Press Release SG/SM/3574, 9 July 1984; and the 1984 *Report of the Secretary-General on the Work of the Organization* (A/39/1).

[2]*Report of the Secretary-General on the Work of the Organization, 1982* (A/37/1), p. 5.

[3]Indeed, the morning after the U.S. Senate ratified the UN Charter by a vote of 89 to 2, James Reston reported in the *New York Times:* "It was a grim-appearing Senate that rolled the 'ayes' on the final count this evening. Despite the long parliamentary debate in the chamber on the subject, and despite its overwhelming approval at the

no exaggeration to say, however, that a fundamental reassessment of U.S. ties with the United Nations and its agencies is under way today. Unfortunately, this reassessment has been dominated to date almost exclusively, both inside the government and in the broader public arena, by those for whom the problems of multilateralism are often a vindication of the efficacy of unilateralism. Congressional supporters of the United Nations these days are few in number and low in profile.[4] The executive branch has been, if anything, more uniformly critical of the United Nations.[5] The nongovernmental constituency of the United Nations has lagged badly, in resources, organi-zation, and lobbying skills, behind those who oppose much of what the organization does.[6] The academic community, from which one would hope for the dispassionate analyses that should inform policy debates, has barely been heard from at all.[7]

The purpose of this article is to begin to rectify the abdication of responsible comment by the aca-demic community. It is not an aca-demic treatise about the United Nations but a contribution to the current policy debate by an Amer-ican academic who has studied the United Nations closely for some time. Professional students of inter-national organization can perform, it seems to me, two valuable public services. One is to remind the pub-

---

end, there was no sense of a job finished but merely of a difficult job just beginning" (29 July 1945, p. 1).

[4]As a result, an amendment by Senator Nancy Kassebaum of Kansas to cut the U.S. contribution to the United Nations by $500 million over four years drew a two-thirds majority in the Senate, though it was not approved by the House. An amendment by Senator Robert Kastens of Wisconsin, requiring an annual State Department report to the Senate detailing the voting pattern of individual UN members, was approved by the Congress and is now law, the idea was to hold other countries accountable for their UN voting in the reckoning of U.S. foreign aid.

[5]President Reagan's first reaction was favorable to Ambassador Lichtenstein's invi-tation that members of the United Nations "seriously consider removing themselves and this organization from the soil of the United States"—a position associated in the past with a tiny minority of ultraconservatives. Recently, though, the administration has taken a more constructive position than several critics in the Congress.

[6]Most effective in this regard has been the Heritage Foundation, a conservative think tank in Washington, D.C. Not many UN bodies have escaped criticism from its "United Nations Assessment Project Study," which issues frequent broadsheets that have had a discernible impact in shaping official U.S. attitudes toward the United Nations during the early phases of the first Reagan administration and receive extensive coverage by the national press. A recent summary of the foundation's position is contained in Bur-ton Yale Pines, ed., *A World without a U.N.: What Would Happen if the U.N. Shut Down* (Washington, D.C.: Heritage Foundation, 1984).

[7]A major exception is the debate over UNESCO, in which both physical and social scientists have spoken out. For one such contribution, by a distinguished student of international organization, see Harold K. Jacobson, testimony before the Human Rights and International Organization Subcommittee, Committee on Foreign Affairs, U.S. House of Representatives, 25 April 1984.

lic how severely the contemporary world system and the exigencies of politics within it circumscribe the capacity of international organizations to effect any measure of collective governance. The other is to help pinpoint specific organizational problems and shortcomings that governments and international officials can influence and control. In short, the academic community can help engender realistic expectations and offer proposals for institutional reform.

I focus on two areas of concern, one because it constitutes for the American public the irreducible raison d'être of the United Nations, and the other because it has been the object of much of the congressional criticism of the organization. The first is the role of the United Nations in the maintenance of international peace and security—ultimately, for the American public, why the United Nations exists. For critics the organization is at best ineffective in this area; at worst, it contributes to rather than helps resolve international disputes. The other area of concern is the administrative performance of the UN system, including the specialized agencies. Here, the criticisms are that the United Nations comprises so bloated and inefficient a bureaucracy, and that the agencies have so politicized their technical tasks and

deliberations, that the United Nations as a whole accomplishes too little of what it was designed to accomplish (and at great expense). No assessment of the relationship between the United Nations and the United States can, however, limit itself to the United Nations alone; hence I briefly take up the recent performance of the United States in relation to the organization.

THE MAINTENANCE OF PEACE AND SECURITY

For the governments assembled in San Francisco, the primary purpose of the United Nations was to "maintain international peace and security."[8] Some two hundred international conflicts later, the goal still appears elusive. What has been the record, what are the problems, and what the prospects? In the record we can distinguish three types of UN activities: normative development concerning the nonuse of force, nonintervention, and peaceful change; the creation of specific international rules governing levels and types of national armaments; and the management of actual conflicts among states.

In the first area, development of a normative presumption against the use of force, the United Nations can best be thought of as a source

---

[8]Article 1.1 of the UN Charter continues, "and to that end: to take effective collective measures for the prevention and removal of threats to the peace, and for the suppression of acts of aggression or other breaches of the peace, and to bring about by peaceful means, and in conformity with the principles of justice and international law, adjustment or settlement of international disputes or situations which might lead to a breach of the peace."

for the legitimation of certain standards of national behavior. Here its contribution is weak. For instance, it took nearly thirty years of effort merely to define interstate aggression. Specific cases of aggression tend to be condemned, but not uniformly so and rarely if the conflict opposes two nonaligned states. The use of force in support of decolonization actually enjoys some degree of legitimacy, though what constitutes "colonialism" has become increasingly ambiguous. Moreover, the status of international law appears to have reached a particularly low point in recent years. For the moment, progress toward a more robust, international normative order remains constrained by the East-West and North-South struggles, and to some extent it is also and intricately connected with progress toward the resolution of conflicts in the Middle East and southern Africa.

In the second area, the creation of international rules governing levels and types of national armaments, the United Nations serves as both an arena and a catalyst for actual negotiations. The pattern of outcomes is fairly consistent: no discernible impact on the rate of growth of existing arsenals, nuclear or conventional; a substantial role in helping proscribe the spread of nuclear weapons either to additional states (Non-Proliferation Treaty and IAEA safeguards) or to extraterritorial settings (deep seas, outer space, atmosphere); and a more limited role in prohibiting the development of entirely new weapons systems (biological weapons as well as environmental modification). This pattern follows quite closely the managerial capacity of the concert of major powers to affect outcomes in each of these domains.

The third area, management of actual conflicts among states, involves two distinct tasks: the peaceful resolution of disputes and UN enforcement action. Here the United Nations serves as a forum for concerted action and as an actor in its own right. With respect to peaceful resolution, it was widely appreciated from the start that superpower disputes would not readily lend themselves to accommodation in the veto-governed Security Council. Where UN efforts have been least effective, however, is in conflicts between two nonaligned countries; there seems to exist in the international community an extremely high level of tolerance for such disputes. In the aggregate, UN efforts at peaceful resolution have been most effective in cases where a Western nation (other than the United States) or a nation aligned with the West has initiated a dispute with a non-aligned state.[9]

---

[9] A good compendium and analysis of cases can be found in Mark W. Zacher, *International Conflicts and Collective Security, 1946–77* (New York: Praeger, 1979); and a more up-to-date statistical overview in Ernst B. Haas, "Regime Decay: Conflict Management and International Organizations, 1945–1981," *International Organization* 37 (Spring 1983).

The ability of the United Nations to settle or even isolate disputes reached, with the important exception of the 1973 Arab-Israeli conflict, a nadir by the mid-1970s. It has not improved much to this day. This decline in efficacy roughly coincided with several developments: the arrival in the United Nations of many more developing countries, guarding their newly acquired sovereignty and making consensus more difficult to achieve; the constraint that U.S. military involvement in Vietnam placed on U.S. initiatives in the Security Council for dealing with conflicts elsewhere; and American success in marginalizing the role of the Soviet Union in such critical areas of conflict as the Middle East, thus ensuring Soviet opposition in the Security Council to international approval of U.S.-negotiated settlements. The revival of Cold War rhetoric in the 1980s worsened an already bad situation.

Virtually by default, therefore, the focus of UN activity in the peaceful resolution of disputes has shifted to the secretary general. At the present time the only open channel of communication to the Soviet Union concerning the withdrawal of their troops from Afghanistan runs through the office of the secretary general. Similarly, in the Iran–Iraq war, it was the secretary general's office that first brought the matter before the Security Council, repeatedly sent mediators to the region, corroborated damage done to civilian targets, documented the use of poison gas, and, most recently, reached an agreement with the two sides to refrain from deliberate military attacks on purely civilian centers. "Unfortunately," as the *Washington Post* noted in an editorial, "the political side of the UN"—for which we may read governments seated in the Security Council—"has consistently dillydallied."[10]

As for enforcement action under Chapter VII of the UN Charter, it was a dead letter in 1945 and is likely to remain so for the foreseeable future. In recognition of this fact, Dag Hammarskjöld and his staff back in the 1950s invented the more modest notion of peacekeeping forces.[11] These forces have been deployed in a dozen or so instances—in the past, generally to

---

[10]*Washington Post*, 2 April 1984. As a result, the secretary general simply informed the Security Council of the June 1984 agreement on civilian centers, making no attempt to obtain its concurrence—an indication of his fear for the viability of the agreement once subjected to American-Soviet maneuvering in the Security Council.

[11]Brian Urquhart, UN undersecretary general in charge of peacekeeping, has defined the concept as "the use by the United Nations of military personnel and formations not in a fighting or enforcement role but interposed as a mechanism to bring an end to hostilities and as a buffer between hostile forces. In effect, it serves as an internationally constituted pretext for the parties to a conflict to stop fighting and as a mechanism to maintain a cease-fire." Urquhart, "International Peace and Security: Thoughts on the Twentieth Anniversary of Dag Hammarskjöld's Death," *Foreign Affairs* 60 (Autumn 1981), p. 6.

control conflicts attending decolonization that threatened to become globalized along East-West lines. On the whole, peacekeeping has been a success story for the United Nations, as even some of the fiercest critics of the organization are obliged to concede.[12] Of late, however, governments have shown some reluctance to use this instrument. Their reluctance in the first instance reflected an almost uniform reaction against Hammarskjöld's attempt to transform the United Nations into a more active peace organization, as exemplified by his direction of the Congo operation. Subsequently, it became compounded by the growing paralysis of the Security Council and the growing irrelevance of the General Assembly to peace and security issues. Most recently there has been a greater resort on the part of the major powers to the use of national forces in attempted peacekeeping roles, including the ill-fated multinational force in Lebanon, which both resulted from and contributed to the marginalization of the UN peacekeeping instrument.

What can we conclude from this brief survey of the record to date? Where do we go from here?

When the United Nations works on matters of peace and security, it works to insulate and contain, to provide an environment within which governments can undertake measures to deal with underlying issues. This proposition is as true of nonproliferation as it is of peacekeeping. Taking an issue to the United Nations is, therefore, only the beginning of collective conflict management, not the end. If governments with the means to do so do not follow through, no issue can be resolved.[13] The United Nations has not worked at all well in the peace and security area of late because governments have failed to exercise their influence and provide support in behalf of collective efforts. The normative authority of the organization has been dissipated, and its decision-making arenas are in disarray.

A reversal of this desultory state of affairs can be led only by the permanent members of the Security Council, in particular by the

---

[12]The Heritage Foundation report on the subject (Roger A. Brooks, "U.N. Peacekeeping: An Empty Mandate" [Washington, D.C., 20 April 1983]) appears to imply in its subtitle that lack of jurisdiction is part of the problem; the report, however, proceeds as if no such constraint existed. It also contains numerous factual errors. For the UN response to it, presumably drafted by Urquhart, see "United Nations Peacekeeping: Comments on Heritage Foundation Publication." UN Department of Public Information, Press Section (New York, June 1983).

[13]Again, the nub of the problem is alluded to by the critics: "In terms of American interests, the United Nations' peacekeeping operations have been convenient; however, they may also have provided the United States with excuses to postpone those hard decisions of national security that it must eventually make." (Patrick J. Garrity, "The United Nations and Peacekeeping," in Pines, *A World without a U.N.*, p. 155.) The point is well taken, but surely it cannot be offered as a criticism of UN peacekeeping!

two superpowers. The United States and the Soviet Union have similar, or at least complementary, interests in resolving a number of disputes in which they are not themselves involved—Iran–Iraq being a prime example. Indeed, a window of opportunity may now exist in the peacekeeping field, for the multinational force experiment in Lebanon has failed. . . . Tacit agreement or behind-the-scenes efforts by the United States and the Soviet Union to support UN attempts to resolve conflicts from which neither can hope to gain any advantage would not only serve to rejuvenate the peace and security mechanisms of the organization but perhaps also contribute to an easing of the current tension between the two superpowers. One highly visible indication of superpower support for UN peacekeeping would be the inclusion under appropriate circumstances of U.S. and Soviet contingents in UN peacekeeping forces.

Specific institutional reforms in the functioning of the Security Council are also required, but they are meaningless in the absence of substantive agreement and will be achieved more readily in the wake of substantive agreement.

ADMINISTRATIVE PERFORMANCE

If the public at large has been disappointed by the United Nations in the field of peace and security, government officials in the United States are particularly exercised by its administrative performance. Assessing the United Nations in such terms, however, is no easy task, because there is very little systematic evidence to go on, and even if there were, it is difficult to know what to compare the United Nations to. No other organization anywhere operates on the basis of six official languages, with 159 autonomous constituencies and programs in just about every country in the world. Nonetheless, I focus on those issues which most concern U.S. policy makers: budgetary and personnel policies, and the politicization of the specified agencies.

Budgetary Policy

Total annual contributions (assessed and voluntary) to the UN system now stand at roughly $4 billion. The United States is the largest contributor, paying about one-fourth of the total, almost as much as the next four contributors combined (Japan, the Federal Republic of Germany, Sweden, the Netherlands). The three Soviet republics are ranked seventh, contributing slightly over $160 million. On a per capita basis, the United States ranked eighteen h in 1982, contributing less than $4.50 per man, woman, and child, or half the contribution of Switzerland (which is not a UN member), about 12 percent of the per capita contribution of Norway, and less than Gabon and several other developing countries. The Soviet Union ranked sixty-fifth, contributing less than fifty cents per capita.[14] Ultimately, whether the United Nations is worth this level of expenditure on the part of the United States depends on important value judgments about what $1 billion, or $4.50 per capita, ought to purchase in terms of U.S. and UN objectives, compared to other means that may be available to achieve the same ends. In purely financial terms, though, the United States obtains a return on its investment, directly through procurement in the United States by UN agencies (especially UNDP, UNICEF, and General Services, all of which are located in the United States, are headed by Americans, and purchase a sizable portion of all UN goods and services), and indirectly by virtue of being the site of UN headquarters. According to widely cited estimates, the United Nations contributes some $700 million per year to the economy of the New York metropolitan region alone.[15]

Quite apart from the level of overall contributions to the United Nations are the issues of the efficiency and effectiveness of UN programs. Program planning and budgeting are still largely pro forma

activities in the United Nations, systematic program and project evaluation is in its infancy, and the machinery for project auditing is inadequate. Although fragmentary data exist and anecdotal evidence is adduced in support of all manner of claims, it is, as a result, quite simply impossible to make a systematic, comprehensive assessment.[16] That this is so indicates a major weakness. It suggests that wastage, duplication of effort, and slack management exist, particularly in the economic and social sectors, where UN activities have grown fastest in recent years and which account for some nine-tenths of the entire expenditures of the system. Equally serious is the extreme fragmentation of programs and projects in the economic and social sectors, so that it is sheer euphemism to refer to a UN "system" at all.

In the final analysis, however, the hostility that the budgetary policies of the United Nations has aroused in some circles is not due to size, growth, and inefficiency alone. An important political issue is also at stake: the asymmetry between financial contributions and control over budgetary allocations. This is-

[14]Permanent Mission of Sweden to the United Nations, "Total Contributions of Member States to the United Nations System, 1982" (New York, October 1983).

[15]Elliott L. Richardson, testimony before the Human Rights and International Organization Subcommittee, Committee on Foreign Affairs, U.S. House of Representatives, 27 September 1983. The figure is also used by the New York City Commission for the United Nations.

[16]For a well-informed and objective analytical overview of some of these issues, see Maurice Bertrand, "Political, Conceptual, and Technical Constraints on the Effectiveness of the United Nations" (paper presented at the Ford Foundation Conference on International Organizations, New York City, 7–8 November 1984).

sue pits "have" against "have not" nations; the former account for the overwhelming share of contributions and the latter for the overwhelming share of votes. The problem is endemic, and mutal restraint is the only mutually beneficial solution. The UN secretariat has, however, contributed to the problem on more than one occasion. It has done so by being unduly responsive to certain highly contentious legislative mandates adopted by the General Assembly, for example, on Palestinian and southern African problems and in connection with aspects of the New International Economic Order. It has exploited and even initiated such mandates for its own ends, to expand its bureaucratic tasks and generate revenue. More simply, the secretariat has secured increases in its own salaries and benefits in excess of comparable remuneration at national levels.

Personnel Policy

The ideal form of an international civil service was diluted in the United Nations right from the start. The great powers began immediately to jostle for senior secretariat positions for their nationals. The Soviet Union persistently accused Trygve Lie, the first secretary general, of pro-Western bias, in an effort to inspire fear along with the awe in which he already held the Soviet Union. And McCarthyism in the United States spilled over to impugn the loyalty of U.S. citizens working for the United Nations. Hence current American criticism of UN personnel policy cannot in all good conscience claim that there was ever a period in which staffing in the United Nations was not in substantial measure subject to "political" factors. The major difference between past and present is that the developing countries now play a much larger role in the international politics of UN personnel.[17]

The very principle of an international civil service is denied, however, by Soviet staffing practice. The Soviet Union oversteps the already diluted standards of propriety by considering UN secretariat officials of Soviet nationality to be mere extensions of the Soviet state apparatus. The USSR does not allow its nationals to accept permanent contracts from the United Nations. Soviets in the secretariat are required to maintain extraordinarily close links with their UN Mission. The Soviet Union appears to target for its nationals specific positions in the secretariat which are particularly useful for its own propaganda and intelligence-gathering purposes. Sometimes these activi-

---

[17]Recruitment, of course, is not a complete free-for-all but is governed by Article 101 of the Charter. The article calls for "the highest standards of efficiency, competence and integrity" with due regard to the importance of wide geographical distribution, which now is itself a composite of membership, financial contribution, population, and other factors.

ties go well beyond routine monitoring of publicly available sources of information. There is little that the United Nations can do directly to compel the Soviet Union to desist. It is disconcerting, however, when senior secretariat officials, given the opportunity to take a principled stand, side with Soviet practice instead.

Apart from the questions of who gets what post and what is done to advance the cause of particular candidates or nationalities is the issue of staff performance once on the job. Here the situation is analogous to the cost-effectiveness of UN programs: very little of a systematic and comprehensive nature is known, and in a well-managed organization more would be known. The United Nations is beginning to develop the form of a personnel policy by requiring competitive examinations at the lowest entry levels on the professional ladder and by periodic routine evaluations of performance for all professional levels thereafter. But there still exists no effective personnel policy in substance, leading to staff qualifications and performance that have the secretary general himself concerned.[18]

The Specialized Agencies

Traditionally, activities of the specialized agencies have received little public notice. Of late, however, they have become the object of considerable media and official scrutiny. In the United States this shift has been prodded by several criticisms. The first is that the agencies have become thoroughly politicized and have therefore compromised their technical missions. This argument is not without merit, yet the issue is more complex than it appears at first glance. Great care must be taken to distinguish between two very different kinds of politicization. One, concerning the principles governing an issue area, is inevitable and legitimate; the other, concerning the introduction of extraneous political issues into an issue area, is neither. Take, as an illustration, the case of the International Telecommunication Union. The basic rules concerning allocation of the frequency spectrum and registration of frequency bands were determined by the industrialized countries to suit their particular needs, on a first-come, first-served basis. As the frequency spectrum has become more crowded, both because of the rapid growth of telecommunications services and the trebling of membership in the ITU, the developing countries (not surprisingly) have challenged the prevailing principles of allocation. They have sought to replace them with principles that more effectively protect their own long-term interests.

To challenge a principle of allocation in any social system is, of course, an act of "politicization,"

---

[18]*Report of the Secretary-General on the Work of the Organization, 1983* (A/38/1).

particularly when the challenge is accompanied by rhetorical flourishes, as it is in the case in the ITU, calling for a "new international information and communication order." There is nothing whatever perverse or illegitimate about this activity, however; Americans would do precisely the same were the United States in the disadvantaged position. Appropriate compromises will, we may presume, be worked out in such contexts, as indeed they are beginning to be in the ITU.[19]

The threshold of admissibility is crossed, however, when governments or groups of governments seek to exploit a technical forum purely for the pursuit of political objectives that have no direct bearing on that realm. Even at the height of the Cold War, East and West managed to circumscribe their ever-present desire to engage in this practice; but the developing countries seem to have been less successful in restraining themselves. In some ultimate sense, everything may well be related to everything else in international politics; acting on this premise in UN agencies, however, produces organizational paralysis, not reform.

The recent UNESCO crisis has brought to public attention another problem afflicting the specialized agencies: once executive heads are appointed, there are relatively few effective internal checks and balances on their behavior. The UNESCO case may be extreme, combining, as it apparently does, autocratic leadership, gross cronyism, the explicit abandonment of impartiality, and questionable financial practices.[20] Still, the more general problem is potentially present in all UN agencies: effective and accountable leadership depends too much on individual professionalism and integrity and not enough on institutionalized restraints. Existing restraints, such as they are, are inadequate for two reasons. First, executive heads are not responsible on a day-to-day basis to any legislative body or executive board; both meet too infrequently to perform such a supervisory role. Second, there exists a symbiotic relationship between the executive heads of international agencies and officials in national ministries who serve as delegates to the governing bodies of those agencies. The two can be of enormous assistance to each other in allocating resources and advancing their respective careers. As a result, the governors are not always eager to govern, and the sole mechanism of accountability that does exist can be too easily compromised.

A third and final point of contention concerns the perennial problem of overlap and duplication in the programmatic activities of UN

---

[19]Paul Lewis, "Geneva Parley Agrees on a Radio Plan," *New York Times,* 12 February 1984.

[20]Gordon Crovitz, "Auditing M'Bow: Where the Trail Should Lead," *Wall Street Journal,* 8 March 1984, and personal interviews.

agencies. The record shows that interagency coordination is marginally more effective today than it was in the past. The record also shows, however, that the problem ultimately cannot be solved at the interagency level. After all, it was not international bureaucrats but national governments that established (as one example) no fewer than four international agencies dealing with food and agriculture alone. Nor is it only officials of international agencies who ignore requests by various central UN organs to coordinate their activities in similar domains. The governing boards of the separate agencies, consisting of national officials, jealously guard the piece of institutional turf for which they are responsible, even against the wishes of their own foreign offices for more efficiency and less duplication.

One constant theme runs through this discussion of UN budgetary and personnel policies, as well as the special problems of the agencies. The United Nations may have become too much of a bureaucracy in the current, pejorative sense of the term, but it is not enough of a bureaucracy in the classic, analytical sense: a system of rationalized authority and administrative relations, capable of rising above particularism and personalism, following generalized rules of procedure, and held strictly accountable on the basis of objective performance criteria. To some extent the United Nations is prevented from becoming more "bureaucratized" in this latter, positive sense by the very nature of the international polity and the particular alignments that prevail within it. Nonetheless, resolution of some of these problems is possible, particularly in budgetary and management techniques, as well as personnel and career development policy.[21] If the proper lessons are learned from the UNESCO affair, it may become possible to invent and institute more effective governing structures in UN agencies as well.

U.S. POLICY

American power and resources first breathed life into the many postwar multilateralist schemes, including the United Nations. Subsequently, the United States and the United Nations worked in tandem, over the opposition of the major colonial powers, to catalyze and facilitate decolonization. For the first quarter century or so, U.S. foreign policy included a routine if not central part for the United Nations. It is ironic, therefore, that the United States now plays the multilateral game less effectively than many other states. American leaders tend to focus blame exclusively on the United Nations, but a dispassionate assessment also calls for

---

[21]For a brief review of recent attempts in this regard, see *Issues before the 39th General Assembly of the United Nations* (New York: United Nations Association of the USA, 1984), chap. 7.

an examination of the posture and performance of the United States.

One is struck first of all by the inability of the United States to define and maintain any kind of strategic orientation toward the United Nations. The Soviet Union looks to the organization as a vehicle to delegitimize the postwar international order constructed by the capitalist nations, while retaining its own political prerogatives to act unconstrained by multilateral obligations. The Third World seeks to liquidate the remnants of colonialism and upgrade its position in the international division of labor. The small European states support the United Nations as a potential agency of peaceful change in the face of international forces over which they have no control. Their larger European neighbors see the United Nations as a forum that to some extent endows them with a status and influence they no longer enjoy in the world at large. But what of the United States? Put simply, the visions being debated in UN forums today are the visions of others, not our own. Few can recall the last time the United States initiated a major new action in the United Nations. Our posture toward the organization recently has oscillated wildly between accommodationism, rejectionism, and pragmatism, but at no time has it been guided by a clear strategic concept of the potential contribution of the United Nations to the kind of world order we desire.

American ambivalence toward the United Nations is reflected in and reinforced by the radically divergent political persuasions and personal styles of recent U.S. permanent representatives. Additional problems arise because the U.S. permanent representative is not simply an ambassador but also a member of the president's cabinet. In theory, this arrangement should enhance the importance of the United Nations in the highest circles of the U.S. government. In practice, it gives the permanent representative merely the hope or the illusion of influence in Washington, often to the detriment of his or her job performance in New York. Moreover, cabinet rank puts far too much visibility and pressure on the permanent representative in the domestic political arena; the essence of effective diplomacy requires that an ambassador be shielded from such exposure. Finally, having the permanent representative in the cabinet gives those who would use the United Nations to abuse the United States a direct line into the White House. There is no reason why Americans should be so obliging.

U.S. ambivalence toward the United Nations is reflected in another attribute of our representation at the United Nations. Only intermittently does America engage in the kind of political give-and-take at the United Nations at which Americans excel in their domestic legislative bodies—and when we do, we surprise ourselves (but not others) with our successes. Were we to choose to become more extensively engaged in UN corridor politics, however, we would be handicapped by Washington's relative neglect of U.S. missions to the United Nations in the designing of attractive career lines for foreign service officers and their counterparts in other agencies of the U.S. government.

Despite the many strains, there continues to exist a reservoir of goodwill and support for the United Nations in the American public. Public support is not as strong as it was in the past. According to a Roper Poll commissioned by UNA–USA and conducted in mid-1983, however, respondents felt, by a margin of two to one, that the United Nations is compatible with U.S. interests, not inimical to them. A majority, moreover, favored maintaining or increasing the present level of U.S. involvement in the United Nations rather than decreasing it.[22] It seems, therefore, that the current malaise about the United Nations is more pronounced among decision-making elites in the United States than it is within the public at large. The posture and performance of those elites is in fact, as I have suggested, part of the problem.

CONCLUSION

The theme that emerges from these considerations is unlikely to satisfy opponents of the United Nations; nor is it likely to make any remaining idealist supporters happy. Critics will see it as too friendly, and friends as too critical. The problems, however, are far too important to be left either to uncritical friends or unfriendly critics. Any crisis of multilateralism is a crisis of humankind, for the human agenda is coming to be dominated by more, not fewer, issues of global proportions. International institutions can resolve none of these issues on their own, but neither can national states resolve them without international institutions. For better or worse, then, we are condemned to improve existing international institutions or to invent new ones to take their place.

I have discussed only two dimensions of the vast and complex UN system.[23] The pattern adduced in this context, however, can probably be generalized: the effectiveness and efficiency of the United Nations must be substantially enhanced, but any improvement in the current state of affairs will require detailed reviews of individual organizations, program areas, and even programs. In other words, the current policy debate must shift from symbols to specifics. Greater satisfaction with the United Nations by the United States will also require a greater sense of vision and con-

---

[22]Results of the 1983 Roper Poll commissioned by UNA–USA. "Directions for the UN: US Public Opinion on the United Nations," background paper prepared by UNA–USA (New York, September 1983).

[23]A close examination of recent UN activities in the economic sector, especially the increasingly ritualistic "negotiations" between North and South, together with recommended changes, can be found in Jagdish N. Bhagwati and John Gerard Ruggie, eds., *Power, Passions, and Purpose* (Cambridge: MIT Press, 1984).

sistency in the policies and tactics of this country. If the intellectual capital necessary to help bring about these shifts is to be available, and if the quality of public discourse in this domain is to be raised, professional students of international organization and journals will have to play their part—which is to rejuvenate the systematic study of the structure and functioning of institutions in the contemporary world system.

23

AMERICAN INTERESTS AND THE UNITED NATIONS

Donald J. Puchala

For more than 35 years it has been the policy of the United States to support the United Nations by participating in multilateral policy-making, by favoring and furthering institutional growth, and by helping to finance general UN activities and special programs. The American government's positive posture toward the United Nations has met with public approval as evidenced in opinion polls, widespread mass media endorsement, and political party platforms. U.S. presidents of both parties have reaffirmed our commitments to international organizations. "The ideals of the United Nations," former Secretary of State Alexander Haig told the 36th U.N. General Assembly, are "also American ideals. The Charter embodies American principles. It will always be a major objective of our statecraft to make the United Nations an instrument of peace."[1]

Continuing support for the United Nations and deepening involvement in its processes, policies, and programs remain in the American national interest. Yet criticisms of the United Nations and questions about U.S. participation are presently being voiced by some analysts of American foreign policy.[2] Their main argument is that the United States is currently sub-

SOURCE: Reprinted from *Political Science Quarterly*, Vol. 97, No. 4, Winter 1982–83, pp. 571–588, by permission of the author.

[1]Alexander M. Haig Jr., "A New Era of Growth," *Current Policy*, No. 314 (21 September 1981), p. 1.

[2]Juliana Geran Pilon, "The United States and the United Nations: A Balance Sheet," *Backgrounder* No. 162 (Washington, D.C.: The Heritage Foundation, January 1982).

jected to considerable rhetorical abuse in the U.N. General Assembly and other large multilateral forums where majorities of countries are pressing for world political and economic changes that appear to be inimical to American interests. In addition, the critics contend that the United Nations seems to operate on a double standard by condemning actions of the West while condoning similar behavior by the East. While America is ridiculed and slighted, the critics say, our government continues to pay a substantial share of the organization's bills. Do we get our money's worth from the United Nations? What has the world organization done for the United States lately?

In addition to legitimate questions and concerns, some of the current criticism of the American involvement in the United Nations is ideologically slanted and motivated, in part, by domestic politics in the United States. Such criticism must be interpreted, therefore, in terms of where it is coming from. Furthermore, some bemoaning of the United Nations stems from wishful thinking about the end of American global dominance and the passing of Western cultural universalism. Such positions are symptoms of a broader dissatisfaction with trends in world affairs. However, venting frustrations by attacking the United Nations hardly seems appropriate since the organization cannot alter the fact that the world is mostly non-American, non-Western, and non-Caucasian.

With regard to the more reasoned criticisms, it should be emphasized that there are two fundamental flaws in American critics' assessments. First, they tend either to misrepresent or misperceive the nature of the international organization, attributing to it capabilities it does not have. This enables critics to decry the United Nations for being unable to perform according to the impossibly high standards they themselves have established. Second, critics confuse rhetoric with performance. Clearly, much of the harsh language spoken in U.N. deliberative organs nowadays tends to be anti-American or anti-Western, and much of it is unfair and untrue. But, as is the case of most parliamentary bodies, the weakest members shout the loudest, the most radical seek the most attention, and the most paranoid are the most critical. In these respects, U.N. forums are almost archetypical. Rhetoric is important, but so is performance. Looking at the record, when actual U.N. decisions and programs of action are examined, what emerges in fact is a marked congruence between U.N. policies and U.S. preferences.

Despite this, there are still plausible and very real questions to be asked about the United States and the United Nations. There are also problems about the latter that even supporters identify. The questions deserve a reasoned response, and the problems call for corrective action by the United Nations itself. Both of these points will be addressed in this paper.

THE UNITED NATIONS TODAY: REFLECTIONS OF A DANGEROUS AND FRAGMENTED WORLD

Those who have called the United Nations "a dangerous place" are correct only in that it is a microcosm of the cleavages, contentions, insecurities, and volatilities of a very dangerous world.[3] Rivalry between superpowers, the nuclear specter frustrating efforts at disarmament, racial, ethnic and class antagonisms, and festering, explosive political issues are some of the stuff of U.N. affairs. Governments go to the United Nations to deal with matters that divide them, but they do not often reach lasting agreements because incompatibilities beneath such issues are real. There is no remedial magic in the Security Council or the General Assembly. Conflicts between the United States and the Soviet Union are no more soluble within the United Nations than without, and Cold War issues in general remain practically immune from U.N. influence. Yet governments do sometimes find accommodation through multilateral diplomacy there, and when they do, the world becomes incrementally *less* dangerous—as, for example, with Zimbabwe, earlier in the Suez, in the area of nuclear testing and non-proliferation, in the Latin American nuclear free zone, and in the creation of the U.N. Interim Force in Lebanon.

Governments also go to the United Nations to deal with matters that unite them. Many of the most pressing problems of our planet are transnational in origin and impact, and most defy unilateral solutions. Preserving peace among nations; facilitating international commerce; protecting the global environment; ordering the use of the seas, airways, and airwaves; alleviating hunger; and accommodating global movements of information, resources, and people are beyond any single country's capacities. These are tasks for collective action, and governments have assigned many of them to the United Nations.[4] Global policies toward global problems are not easily or quickly formulated at the United Nations because consensus is critical for enforcement, and this is elusive in a fragmented, politically-charged world. Nevertheless, when consensus is reached —as, for example, in the General Agreement on Tariffs and Trade's (GATT) trading rules, the International Monetary Fund's (IMF) lending rules, the United Nations Conference on Trade and Development's (UNCTAD) commodities program, the Food Aid Convention and the International Fund

---

[3]See Abraham Yeselson and Anthony Gaglione, *A Dangerous Place: The United Nations as a Weapon in World Politics* (New York: Grossman Publishers, 1974), and Daniel Patrick Moynihan, *A Dangerous Place* (New York: Berkley Books, 1980).

[4]United Nations Secretariat, Department of Economic and Social Affairs, Office of Financial Affairs, *Proposed Medium-Term Plan for the Period 1984–1989* (A/36/6, in press).

for Agricultural Development's (IFAD) rural development program, the allocation of airwaves, and important aspects of the Law of the Sea—the world becomes less anarchic, more predictable, and thus safer.

The United Nations is not a world government, and there is no evident desire by its members to have it evolve toward greater supranationality. Most Americans hardly want yet another level of political authority reaching down into their lives. But along with recognizing that the organization is not an independent power "beyond the nation-state," it must also be accepted that the international organization has limited capabilities. It has no power beyond that which its members grant it, and no legitimacy beyond that which its members accord it. Furthermore, as an association of sovereign states, each one equal under international law, majority rule, consensus, or unanimity must be the principles of U.N. decision-making. Where majority rule prevails, no member can hope to be part of a winning coalition on every decision, and the organization is therefore bound to make policies that some members will not agree with. When policy is formulated by consensus, as it is most frequently at the United Nations, compromises produce "common denominator" agreements acceptable to all members but often

less than ideal for most. Where unanimity is the rule, decisions will often not be made at all, and impasse will prevail. In addition, because U.N. members are sovereign states, enforcing the organization's decisions is ultimately a national matter for each of them. The United Nations cannot compel any member to act or react in any specified manner. Nor can it move militarily, politically, financially, or otherwise onto the territory or into the domestic affairs of any member state unless it is specifically invited. In light of this, the answer to the question, "Why didn't the United Nations do something?" is often simply that the member states had not given it either the authority or the power.

U.S. PREFERENCES AND U.N. POLICY: A LOOK AT THE RECORD

Talk in the United Nations is too often substituted for action, mainly because action demands consensus, while talk requires only wordsmiths, mass media agents, and attentive home-country audiences. At the present time, some of the talk is critical of the United States, but this was not always so. During the 1950s, much U.N. rhetoric was anti-Communist as Western Europe, Latin America, and much of the rest of the membership echoed Washington's themes.[5] There is

---

[5]Thomas Hovet Jr., *Bloc Politics in the United Nations* (Cambridge: Harvard University Press, 1960), *passim.*; Hayward R. Alker, Jr. and Bruce M. Russett, *World Politics in the General Assembly* (New Haven, Conn.: Yale University Press, 1965), pp. 50–54, 70–80.

also some reason to expect that the present anti-American volume will diminish in years ahead, partly because time puts the Western colonial period further and further into history and as events focus attention on the expansionist tendencies of other types of regimes, particularly the Communist ones. Furthermore, economic development in coming years will create more and more states with interests—and economic and political systems—akin to ours so that gaps in perception and interests between the West and the South could narrow appreciably. Even today the so-called "newly industrializing countries" (NICs) are increasingly uncomfortable with the more radical themes, demands, and accusations of the Group of 77 (G-77), and the anti-American utterances of the NICs are accordingly subdued. During the next two decades many more newly industrializing countries will emerge, and present ones will look, behave, and increasingly sound like the more developed Western countries.

The United States could not afford to tolerate the changes made against it at the United Nations and resolve merely to ride out the present rhetorical storm if there were a direct connection between what extremist orators say at the General Assembly and what the United Na-

tions actually does in policy and program. But this connection is at best tenuous and in some cases non-existent. U.N. programs (as opposed to U.N. rhetoric) reflect the consensus that produced them, and consensus usually requires wooing the United States. Little of substance can happen in the U.N. system without American cooperation—and little happens without American resources—so that it is not very surprising that negotiators often defer to United States preferences. Examples abound:

• Security Council resolutions are frequently modified to court the approval of the United States, as was the case with Iraq's compromises on the 1981 resolution that protested the Israeli air attack on the Iraqi nuclear reactor.[6]

• A similar episode in 1981 concerned a Security Council resolution of condolence for three Nigerian soldiers killed in U.N. service in Lebanon. The American government preferred not to have the resolution single out Israel for condemnation, and strong contrary stands by other members of the Security Council eventually gave way to the American position.[7] When U.S. approval cannot be ob-

---

[6]Resolution 487 (1981); see also *Issues Before the 36th General Assembly of the United Nations* (New York: United Nations Association of the United States, 1981), pp. 18–19; *New York Times*, 20 June 1981, pp. 1, 4–5.

[7]Dorothy Rabinowitz, "Reagan's 'Heroine' at the U.N.," *New York Magazine* 20 July 1981, p. 38.

tained, an American veto is sufficient to kill any possibility of Security Council action.

• On questions of economic development, American influence is linked to its resources, and American preferences consequently often prevail. A case in point is the Third World stance on the question of world economic restructuring, a stance which was modified dramatically between the Sixth and Seventh Special Sessions of the General Assembly after it became apparent that the United States was not going to support schemes of redistribution nor be swayed by confrontational tactics.[8]

• Similarly, the agreement on an International Development Strategy (IDS) for the U.N. Third Development Decade was a bargained compromise that took into account American preferences for free trade and open markets, American insistence that agriculture be a central target of development, and the American posi-

tion that first responsibility for development rests with the less developed countries themselves.[9]

• The final form of the Integrated Commodities Program agreed to by UNCTAD was largely a concession by the Group of 77 to the American position.

• Earlier, the conciliation or "cooling off" mechanism which modified UNCTAD decision-making by moving it away from straightforward majority voting was another case of American preferences taking precedence over G-77 desires.[10]

• The system of "graduation" linking eligibility for assistance to levels of economic development, agreed upon at the June 1980 meeting of the Governing Council of the United Nations Development Program (UNDP), was yet another G-77 concession to an American position.[11]

• The voluntary rather than binding nature of the U.N. Code for Restrictive Business

[8]Branislav Gosovic and John Gerard Ruggie, "On the Creation of a New International Economic Order: Issue Linkage and the Seventh Special Session of the UN General Assembly," *International Organization* 30 (1976), pp. 320ff.

[9]United Nations, Department of Public Information, *International Development Strategy for the Third United Nations Development Decade* (New York: United Nations, 1981).

[10]Richard N. Gardner, "The United Nations Conference on Trade and Development," *International Organization* 22 (1968): 114–20.

[11]Cf. Statement of Elliot Abrams, Assistant Secretary of State for International Organization Affairs, before the Subcommittee on Foreign Operations, House Committee on Appropriations, 97th Cong., 1st Sess., 12 May 1981, pp. 490–511.

Practices is yet another deference to American preferences, and work on the Code of Conduct for Transnational Corporations also appears to be evolving in directions that American firms and the U.S. government can accept.

• The U.N. Interim Force in Lebanon was accepted largely in the form that the United States proposed.

More generally speaking, throughout its 35-year history, the organization's principles and most of its actions have been consistent with U.S. interests.[12] Americans, for example, certainly have no trouble with the U.N. principle of *self-determination*. Woodrow Wilson was its early American champion, and the rapid and peaceful dissolution of our fledgling "colonial empire" was its embodiment in policy. The *illegitimacy of armed intervention* is another U.N. principle that Americans can readily accept, though our own record as regards "gunboat diplomacy" is somewhat blemished. The promotion of *peaceful change* is a cornerstone of American diplomacy; it is also a first principle of the United Nations. *Protecting and promoting human rights* are central to American political theory, just as they are central among U.N. objectives. Conflict resolution through *negotiations, mediation, conciliation and adjudication* are main elements of the American political process and are also prominent in U.N. decision-making. That human affairs should be ordered by *codes of law* rather than contests of power is another tenet of both American and U.N. political thinking.

U.N. PRINCIPLES AND PRACTICES

Principles are fine, but what about practice? To be sure, there is considerable disparity between the principles held by the United Nations and the domestic and international practices of some of its members. But the day-to-day actions of the organization and the behavior of some of its members should not be confused. In fact, the United Nations itself has expressed disapproval of some of its members' actions. During the 1950s, France and the United Kingdom were censured for their invasion of Egypt, as was Israel; similarly, the Soviet Union was censured for its invasion of Hungary.[13] The 1960s saw the beginning of public U.N. disapproval of apartheid in South Africa, Ian Smith's usurpation in Rhodesia, and Chilean denial of human rights. In the 1970s, U.N. members decried the atrocities of Idi Amin's Uganda and the genocide perpetrated by the government of Kampuchea. More recently, the

---

[12]Flora Lewis, "The Value of the U.N.," *New York Times,* 23 May 1982, p. E23.

[13]United Nations, Department of Public Information, *Yearbook of the United Nations, 1956* (New York: United Nations, 1957), pp. 25–62, 67–89.

General Assembly voted sharp disapproval of the Khomeini regime's imprisonment of U.S. diplomats; it condemned the Soviet Union's invasion of Afghanistan by an extraordinary majority of 104 to 18; and it censured Israel for its de facto annexation of the Golan Heights.[14]

These condemnations are important because they forcefully assert the limits of the international community's tolerance. Yet sanctions against deviant members are only a very small part of U.N. activities. Through the years, actions to strengthen the international community in areas of peacekeeping and peaceful change, economic development, and the preservation of the earth's resources have been primary concerns. Here again, in most of these areas there has been a close correlation between U.N. policies and American preferences.

In Defense of Peaceful Change

In the realm of peacekeeping, the United Nations has on several occasions inserted international military contingents to monitor and enforce ceasefires between warring countries and factions. . . . The primary purposes of these U.N. missions have been to deter renewed fighting, to gain time for diplomacy, and to discourage external, and especially superpower, intervention that could escalate into larger wars.

The United States has supported each of the peacekeeping ventures, and the results of these missions have largely supported the American interest. The different ventures in the Middle East, particularly UNEF II, bought some of the time American statesmen required in order to promote Egyptian-Israeli reconciliation. The Congo operation contained anarchy in Central Africa and thwarted Soviet interference. The mission to Cyprus has discouraged two NATO allies from open warfare, and the diplomatic time purchased by the monitored ceasefire may presently be yielding first conciliatory results.

In each of these cases, escalation was controlled, and frequently, "keeping the superpowers out" mainly meant preventing Soviet intervention. The Russian refusal to pay U.N. assessments for peacekeeping operations caused considerable financial stress for the organization. Yet it also denied the Soviet Union legitimacy as a mediator and the opportunity to share credit for peacekeeping successfully executed. American support for U.N. peacekeeping, on the other hand, has enabled the United States to participate in the diplomacy of conciliation both preceding and following peacekeeping episodes. (This has been especially important for American policy in the Middle East.) The United States initially challenged the So-

---

[14]See S/RES/46 (1979); A/RES/ES-6/2, A/RES/35/37; *New York Times,* 18 December 1981, pp. 1, 3.

viet Union on the question of payment for peacekeeping operations, but when the so-called "Article 19 Crisis" threatened to destroy the United Nations, the issue was left unresolved, and Washington announced that it, too, would henceforth support only those U.N. peacekeeping missions that were in the American interest. To date, however, the U.S. government has continued to support all U.N. peacekeeping activities. U.N. Ambassador Jeane Kirkpatrick recently indicated that the Reagan Administration "would like to see the role of the U.N. in promoting and preserving and maintaining peace expanded."[15]

Threats to peace nowadays come as often from terrorists, guerrillas, mercenaries, and other transnational trouble-makers as from hostilities between governments. The United Nations is devoting considerable effort to finding ways to control such lawlessness. Nevertheless, building international consensus has been difficult because groups abhorred as "terrorists" by some are acclaimed as "freedom fighters" by others. There is widespread agreement, however, that innocent people should be protected from indiscriminate violence, and toward this end the United Nations has drafted conventions concerning airline hijacking, the protection of diplomats, and the taking of hostages. Basically, these commit sig-

natories either to prosecute or extradite captured terrorists. A U.N. committee is presently drafting a convention against the recruitment, use, financing, and training of mercenaries. Naturally these codes are only as effective as individual governments permit, but many are adhering because proscriptions against terrorism are in almost everyone's interest. Since Americans abroad seem particularly vulnerable to terrorism and are disproportionally chosen as targets, U.S. citizens benefit by whatever deterrents the United Nations can contrive. For example, incidents of aerial piracy involving Americans dropped off markedly since the adoption of the Hijacking Convention in 1977.

Decolonization

Decolonization has been the primary concern in the U.N. principle of peaceful change. In historical perspective, the end of the great European overseas empires represents a world-political change of monumental proportion and import. In a period of less than 30 years, the entire structure of the international state system changed; distributions of power and wealth among states altered; the agenda of diplomacy changed; and global affairs became truly "global" for the first time. Despite its enormity, the change from a world of a few em-

---

[15]"U.S. Positions to Change Under Reagan, Reflect More Realism," *Diplomatic World Bulletin*, 6 April 1981, p. 2.

pires to a world of many states was unexpectedly peaceful, quite unlike the decolonization of the Americas during the eighteenth century when Great Britain and Spain were ejected at considerable cost in human lives. Some wars of independence in the 1950s and 1960s—in Algeria, Indochina, and Angola, for example—were long and bloody. Nevertheless, most of Africa, South Asia, the Pacific, and the Caribbean moved to self-government without much bloodshed.

The story of the role of the United Nations in twentieth-century decolonization has been told many times.[16] To monitor the *Declaration on the Granting of Independence to Colonial Countries and Peoples,* the U.N. General Assembly appointed a Special Committee on Decolonization in 1962. For nearly two decades this "Committee of 24" has been overseeing the decolonization process and pushing it forward by prodding imperial powers toward planned, orderly withdrawals. The United Kingdom and France have not entirely appreciated the Committee's zeal, and the United States has lost its enthusiasm for it as well. Yet in many ways the United Nations has been but a handmaiden to history, since colonialism had already lost

legitimacy, and the ability to maintain empires was drained from Western Europe during World War II. During the 1960s and 1970s, the Committee of 24 put the "handwriting on the wall" in bold script while counseling haste and order in the midst of what might otherwise have been delay and chaos.

Except for a brief flirtation with imperial grandeur at the end of the nineteenth century, anti-imperialism has been a main tenet of American foreign policy. The United States broke away from the British empire; self-determination was part of Wilsonian idealism; American refusal to endorse the reconstitution of empires after World War II was a source of inter-allied dissension in wartime diplomacy.[17] In light of U.S. tradition, decolonization was something that Americans could understand and welcome. And *peaceful* decolonization was even more welcome, since this spared the United States countless agonizing decisions about policies toward NATO allies on the one hand and contestants in colonial struggles on the other. The United States had difficulties with the Committee of 24, and usually abstained because the issues raised continually forced choices between Western allies and advocates of co-

---

[16]David A. Kay, *The New Nations in the United Nations, 1960–1967* (New York: Columbia University Press, 1970); David A. Kay, "The United Nations and Decolonization," in *The United Nations: Past, Present and Future,* James Barros, ed. (New York: Free Press, 1972), pp. 143–70; Rupert Emerson, *From Empire to Nation* (Boston, Mass.: Beacon Press, 1967), pp. 308–28.

[17]Robert Beitzell, *The Uneasy Alliance: America, Britain and Russia, 1941–1943* (New York: Alfred A. Knopf, 1972), pp. 142–43.

lonial independence. Had these been choices about battles, rather than resolutions, where our allies were losing, the American dilemma would have been infinitely greater. The battles were far fewer because the United Nations guided peaceful decolonization, a fact sometimes forgotten.

There is no denying that some of the new countries that emerged from decolonization are now among the harshest critics of the United States. Collectively they compose the Group of 77, now about 121 strong, vocally volatile, politically and economically impatient, outwardly single-minded, and narrowly self-interested.[18] They are also highly dependent upon the West financially, commercially, and technologically, and almost powerless in their efforts to effect changes on the issues that interest them most—world economic restructuring, independence for Namibia, the abolition of apartheid in South Africa, and statehood for the Palestinians.

On economic questions the fundamental division between the United States and the Group of 77 stems from relative wealth: The industrialized countries of the so-called North are rich and the less developed nations of the South are poor, in many cases very poor. Southern ideologies center on doctrines of equality, and restructuring schemes involving international leveling reflect the poorer countries' economic conditions and aspirations.[19] These will probably temper as economies develop. At this juncture the United States may either contribute to the pace and scope of Southern development, or remain passive and watch it happen anyway, albeit more slowly and haphazardly. Contributing to Third World development by accommodating some of the interests of the Group of 77 may not yield immediate political gains for the United States, since allies are no longer to be bought and the appeal of non-alignment grows as dangers in the East-West relationship mount. Contributing to development, however, will establish economic partnerships and international market relationships where two-thirds of the world's people live, work, and consume, and, consequently, where marketing and investing opportunities are vast. Western Europe and Japan seem to understand this much better than the United States, as does the Soviet Union. Those who promote Marxist revolutions make their views most convincing where people are miserable and frustrated, and the more strained the relationship between the United States and the Group of 77, the slower the probable course of

---

[18]Robert L. Rothstein, *The Weak in the World of the Strong: The Developing Countries in the International System* (New York: Columbia University Press, 1977), pp. 3–72.

[19]Roger Hansen, "The Political Economy of North-South Relations," *International Organization* 29 (1975): 925–47.

development and the greater the likelihood of revolutions in the Third World.

The major political questions in U.S. relations with the Group of 77—Namibia, apartheid, and Palestine—are complex and dangerous since each could escalate into a large-scale war. Namibia is an issue of self-determination, a decolonization matter with international legal implications. Apartheid is fundamentally a question of human rights denied by a racist doctrine enforced by an obstinate regime. The "Palestine Question" involves issues of self-determination, conflicting territorial claims and security interests, disagreements about the legitimacy and representativeness of the Palestine Liberation Organization (PLO), and broader matters having to do with ways and means to a comprehensive Middle Eastern settlement. On each of these issues, the United States has the opportunity to exercise considerable influence because it is able to deal directly with almost all contending parties. If there are keys to peaceful settlement, Washington certainly holds several of them. However, U.S. effectiveness resides in a willingness to accept and an ability to play the mediator's role or, where that is not possible, to protect opportunities for institutions like the United Nations to do so.[20]

Economic Development

The bulk of the United Nations' current work is in the realm of *economic development*. Here, U.N. policies and programs emerge not only from American and G-77 dispute, but from negotiating processes that involve the rest of the Western countries, sometimes some of the eastern countries (increasingly China), and often officials of the U.N. Secretariat and specialized agencies. Contrary to what North-South rhetoric might suggest, there has been substantial agreement between North and South at the United Nations on development issues and considerable activity at the operational level. Since the United States has been party to most of the development agreements and, indeed, author of some of them, it is more appropriate to explain *why* they are in the American interest rather than to ask whether they are.

U.N. planning for global development is a decade-by-decade effort. In 1980, the United Nations, having entered its Third Development Decade, negotiated and published a very ambitious plan to guide its agencies and member governments toward 1990. Bearing in mind that the plan lists aspirations only, that it obligates no one, and that its goals are loftier than its accomplishments will be, Ameri-

[20]Oran Young, *The Intermediaries: Third Parties in International Crises* (Princeton, N.J.: Princeton University Press, 1967), pp. 50–115.

cans might nonetheless ask whether they would welcome the future that U.N. planners project. The U.N. International Development Strategy assigns "primary responsibility for the development of developing countries" to "those countries themselves," though it also encourages increased North-to-South financial flows and transfer of technology. It envisions a world of increased economic interdependence, "an open and expanding trade system," and "the realization of the dynamic pattern of comparative advantage." It also calls for enhanced cooperation among less developed countries under the rubric of "collective self-reliance" and a more efficient allocation of industrial production globally. Responsibility for world economic growth and well-being is assigned to developed and less developed countries jointly because "in an interdependent world economy, it is the responsibility of all Governments to contribute to the goals and objectives of the Strategy." Linkages between agricultural and industrial development are affirmed, and less-developed country (LDC) investment in agriculture, agrarian reforms, national food policies, and the eradication of hunger are called for. Linkages between development and improved social conditions are also acknowledged, and population, health, and education policies are prescribed, as well as special efforts on behalf of women, children, and youth. "The ultimate aim of development," according to the plan, "is the constant improvement of the well-being of the entire population." According to the IDS, a number of institutional reforms are in order, especially in international monetary affairs, where less developed countries are seeking more influence over decision-making.[21]

If the IDS for the Third Development Decade represents the United Nation's interpretation of the New International Economic Order (NIEO), a slogan which has raised so much alarm in the West, it may surprise many Americans to find little in it that is particularly objectionable. Passions surrounding the acronym NIEO have distracted many in the United States from actually studying the substance of the U.N. development plan. Clearly, some of its aspirations are controversial. How much more aid would be needed, whose technology would flow to whom on what terms, how much of whose industrial production would be relocated and how fast, and what kinds of institutional reforms would be feasible in light of American interests remain to be determined. But these are matters for negotiation rather than confrontation, and, indeed, the West holds most of the bargaining chips: The industrial countries need only say "no" to Third World demands when such

---

[21]United Nations, *International Development,* pp. 1–27.

denials are reasoned to be in the western interest.

Furthermore, the controversial issues are not the central features of the development strategy, which centers upon improved well-being for poor countries and poor people and calls for greater international cooperation to accomplish this. The IDS does not seek the redistribution of the world's wealth, nor would the West ever permit this. It does, however, look to a narrowing of the income gap between industrialized and less developed countries in the context of a general increase in world prosperity through the development of new resources, productive capacities, and markets. What the United Nations aspires to in its development planning is notably different from what G-77 extremists advocate. It will also turn out to be different from what some extremists in the West believe they can accept.

Whether or not the development strategy succeeds will depend upon U.N. members' separate and collective policies and actions. Meanwhile, a great many development programs are currently underway under U.N. auspices. For example, as a result of the World Food Conference in 1974, an International Fund for Agricultural Development was established, partly financed by the United States, but mostly by Arab countries. IFAD has been paying particular attention to small farmers in poor countries. Rural development efforts of the World Bank under Robert McNamara's presidency were also focused on small farmers. Projects financed by the UNDP are primarily intended to develop economic infrastructure—roads, dams, port facilities, public utility systems, and training schools—that are essential to economic modernity, but unattractive to private investors. Efforts have been mounted by the United Nations Industrial Development Organization (UNIDO) to encourage Third World investors to keep funds in their own countries and to encourage inflows of foreign funds. UNIDO is also promoting the development of indigenous industrial technologies. UNCTAD is seeking stabilized markets for internationally traded agricultural and mineral commodities which are mainstays among Third World exports and crucial exchange earners. The International Labor Organization (ILO) is pressing for development oriented directly toward meeting basic human needs such as food, shelter, sanitation, health facilities, and education. With the exception of activities like famine relief and aid to children via UNICEF, little of what the United Nations is doing in development can be interpreted as doling international welfare. Economic development is a multi-faceted process with each phase and element related to every other one; U.N. programs are directed toward welding these interrelationships.

The United Nations is promoting development in the Third World, and development is taking place.

By many indicators, growth in the South has been outpacing growth in the North, although, of course, huge income gaps remain.[22] Whether what the United Nations is doing is in the American interest depends upon whether economic development in the Third World is in the American interest. Aside from all the obvious economic reasons why better-off people make better neighbors, customers, borrowers, and partners, there are political reasons for encouraging development. The correlation between economic desperation and political turmoil is very high, and turmoil in Third World countries tends either to promote local demagogues with "quick fixes" (and usually anti-Western ideologies) or to invite outside meddling. Neither of these is particularly welcome to the United States. In addition, there are domestic political costs to pay in the United States as a result of turmoil in Third World countries, as Americans tend to be quite divided about how our government should respond to such situations.

Preservation of the Earth's Resources

Increasingly, the United Nations has been led by its members into issues concerning the disposition of the global commons. The commons are those domains possessed by no nation but used by many or all. These include the high seas, regional seas, the seabed, international river basins, the atmosphere, the ionosphere, and outer space. A generation ago the exploitation of many of these common domains was technologically unfeasible, and their despoilation was unimaginable. Yet today we can mine the oceans and the moon, direct electronic signals and laser beams through the ionosphere, and travel in outer space. We can also pollute the oceans, change the rains to acid, destroy the earth's ozone layer, squander reserves of fresh water, contaminate the atmosphere with radioactivity, and station nuclear weapons on the floor of the sea and on platforms orbiting in outer space. Moreover, because some countries are more technologically able to accomplish these feats than others, there is danger that the exploitable commons will disappear as the pioneers scramble to extend their national jurisdictions. There is also danger that present-day polluters will pass on a highly contaminated earth to future generations.

The thrust of U.N. efforts on issues of global commons has been to attempt to regulate these domains under international law. Some law-making via treaty, convention, and code has been directed toward forestalling the closure of the com-

---

[22]Martin M. McLaughlin, ed., *The United States and World Development Agenda, 1979* (New York: Praeger Publishers for the Overseas Development Council, 1979), pp. 149–82.

mons by guaranteeing access to all countries regardless of present power positions or technological prowess.[23] This, for example, has been a major element in U.N. efforts to institutionaliz[e] the principle that the oceans are the "common heritage of mankind." Forestalling closure is also a key element in negotiations concerning the allocation of radio and television frequencies, considered at the World Administrative Radio Conference in 1979.[24] A similar issue has been the parceling of satellite space in the earth's geostationary orbit. In 1980, U.N. members concluded the Agreement Concerning the Activities of States on the Moon and Other Celestial Bodies, stipulating that neither the moon's surface nor its subsurface shall become the national property of any state. Outer space as well as the seabeds were previously demilitarized by U.N.-sponsored treaties in 1967 and 1971. As esoteric as some of these matters may appear, they are but hints of the world affairs of the future fashioned by advancing technology. Current efforts to establish legal regimes are attempts to provide means for future conflict resolution by adjudication rather than by force.

Legislation concerning environmental matters in the United Nations is designed to elicit commitments from states either to refrain from polluting or to cooperate in clean-up efforts. By U.N. agreement, for example, ocean-going oil tankers are regulated by international law, and owners are held responsible for pollution their ships may unleash. A major U.N. treaty, the Treaty Banning Nuclear Tests in the Atmosphere, in Outer Space and Under Water, attempts to slow the nuclear arms race, but also stems contamination by radioactivity in the atmosphere and the oceans. Ocean contamination is also the target of the U.N. Environmental Program's emphasis on regional seas, where activities are underway to combat pollution in the Mediterranean, the Caribbean Sea, the Red Sea, the Persian Gulf, the Gulf of Guinea, and other areas of the Pacific.[25] All of these programs involve commitments to common action by littoral states, and all are funded by international trusts established to finance U.N. environmental activities. In 1977 the United Nations also adopted a Plan of Action to Combat Desertification at the perimeters of the Sahara, as well as a global plan to

---

[23]Seyom Brown, et. al., *Regimes for the Ocean, Outer Space and Weather* (Washington, D.C.: Brookings Institution, 1977).

[24]*Issues Before the 34th General Assembly of the United Nations* (New York: United Nations Association of the United States, 1979), p. 115.

[25]Conference of Plenipotentiaries of the Coastal States of the Mediterranean Region for the Protection of the Mediterranean Sea Against Pollution from Land-based Sources, 1980, *Final Act* (New York: United Nations, 1980); *Issues Before the 35th General Assembly*, pp. 103–04; *Issues Before the 36th General Assembly*, p. 107.

preserve the earth's fresh water resources.[26]

American interest in the global commons is consistent with the intent and direction of U.N. efforts. Americans use the global commons much more than other peoples. The United States would probably benefit from a short-run scramble to close off the commons and parcel it into national jurisdictions. Since our technology permits us to exploit now what others can only hope to exploit in the future, we would for a time command the lion's share of the parcelled commons. But there should be no doubt that such a policy would invite challenge and conflict in the future—much as colonizers' territorial conquests in the past invited later decolonization. A commons regulated by law, protected from contamination, and exploited under a regime which allocates shares among users, including the United States and other industrialized countries, promises greater international tranquility by providing an equitable division of benefits between present and future generations. Far from contradicting American beliefs in free market behavior (since abusive exploitation is regulated even in our own country), U.N. programs concerning the global commons affirm the fundamental American belief that law and not force must be the basis of public order.

AMERICA'S FUTURE AT THE UNITED NATIONS: CRITIC, SUPPORTER, LEADER

The U.N. system of international organization that emerged after 1945 was for the most part the product of American idealism, imagination, and political creativity. Others read our cues, accepted our visions, followed our lead, and took steps away from traditional international anarchy not only because they believed that the United States was powerful, but because they also believed that the United States was right. A great mistake of those who specialize in rewriting the history of the postwar era is to attribute America's leadership, or "hegemony" as some call it, solely to its power. Certainly, the United States was powerful, and its might was widely respected, particularly by the Soviet Union and its allies. Among non-Communist countries, America's moral leadership was equally compelling. Washington's initiatives were accepted and acclaimed because they were viewed as legitimate, with legitimacy flowing from projected values that people almost everywhere could accept: freedom, human dignity, the rule of law, anti-imperialism, non-

---

[26]*Report of the United Nations Conference on Desertification, Nairobi, Kenya, 29 August–9 September, 1977*, A/CONF, 74/36; *Report of the United Nations Water Conference, Mar del Plata, Argentina, 14–25 March, 1977*, U.N.P. Sales No. E.77.11.A.12; see also *Yearbook of the United Nations 1977*, pp. 509–14, 553–63.

aggression, and peaceful change. U.S. endorsement gave a critical measure of legitimacy to the United Nations, and in this sense it very much still needs American approval.

The organization also needs the United States as an anchor. The United States remains among the very few countries in the world that both share the values upon which the United Nations was founded and is capable of acting in the interest of world order. Without the United States, the United Nations becomes a parade of small countries largely unable to act upon their aspirations, plus some Communist states that continue to reject the principles of the organization. When eastern countries use the United Nations at all, they attempt to use it solely as an instrument of their revolutionary foreign policies, and they almost always fail. We may applaud this failure, but if that is all we can expect from international organizations, the world would indeed be a more dangerous place. The United Nations requires American power and authority behind its programs for world order and peaceful change.

The United Nations also needs a constructive critic, sympathetic to its goals but realistic about its shortcomings. The United States must take on the critic's role, as indeed it has already, both to protect our national interests and to keep the organization true to its original purposes. In many ways the United Nations is less than most of its supporters would like it to be, and emphasizing its accomplishments must not distract us from looking at the organization's problems. As Vice President George Bush told the United Nations Association in 1981, there is an urgent need for an "immediate and meaningful reduction in political rhetoric throughout the U.N. system," since it is impossible to politicize every issue and still hope to create humanitarian and developmental programs that benefit the international community.[27] The primary victim of the harsh rhetoric exchanged in U.N. forums is the organization itself, for it loses credibility and efficiency when it turns into a multinational shouting match.

Moreover, the United Nations must be protected against straying from its own ideals, or from being used by overzealous members for ends that are not prescribed in its charter. Recent attempts by some in UNESCO, for example, to push international authorities toward limiting freedom of the press distort U.N. principles concerning the free flow of information. Similarly, the "double standards" evident especially in the General Assembly and the persistent scapegoating of a few governments do little either to advance the causes of the accusers or to enhance the stature of the

---

[27]Hon. George Bush, "Address by Vice President Bush at UNA/USA," United Nations Association of the United States, New York, 25 May 1981, transcript, p. 5.

United Nations. Such behavior contributes only to polarization; it is wholly out of place in an institution chartered to promote international conciliation.

That U.N. activities are costly, that budgets need to be more tightly controlled in times of economic austerity, and that such controls have been less than effective in international organizations in recent years are all true. Former Secretary General Kurt Waldheim's call for "no-growth" budgeting for the next biennium and his insistence that program administrators make their priorities explicit are steps in the right direction. So, too, are expanded Secretariat efforts at evaluation and assessment and more deliberate attempts to terminate ineffective or redundant activities. Much more such monitoring and control are necessary in the U.N. administration, however, and some of this could be prompted by donor countries such as the United States, watching and questioning the ways in which their contributions are used.

If the United Nations needs the United States to do all these things, it is also true that in these last decades of the twentieth century, the United States also needs the United Nations, for the organization has become a legitimizer in its own right.[28] Most members currently respect the United Nations, accept commitments contained in its policies and programs, adhere to U.N.-inspired conventions and codes, and accord authority to resolutions that follow from consensus. The United States must therefore watch what happens at the United Nations very closely. For the United States, as for other countries, power plus legitimacy remain the keys to leadership. As underlined throughout this article, American values and foreign policy interests are largely consistent with U.N. principles and policy directions. A more positive U.S. official attitude, then, together with greater willingness to work within the organization, more flexibility and imagination in parliamentary diplomacy, and indeed more diplomacy and less unilateral posturing, could help recreate a situation where American foreign policy works in tandem with U.N. objectives to build legitimacy for both. It is time again to identify the United States with the goals and aspirations of most of the peoples of the world. The United Nations is one place where this can be done.

---

[28]Inis L. Claude, Jr., *The Changing United Nations* (New York: Random House, 1967), pp. 73–104.

APPENDIX A

The Covenant of the League of Nations*

The High Contracting Parties

In order to promote international co-operation and to achieve international peace and security
    by the acceptance of obligations not to resort to war,
    by the prescription of open, just and honourable relations between nations,
    by the firm establishment of the understandings of international law as the actual rule of conduct among Governments,
    and by the maintenance of justice and a scrupulous respect for all treaty obligations in the dealings of organised peoples with one another,
Agree to this Covenant of the League of Nations.

Article 1

1. The original Members of the League of Nations shall be those of the Signatories which are named in the Annex to this Covenant and also such of those other States named in the Annex as shall accede without reservation to this Covenant. Such accession shall be effected by a Declaration deposited with the Secretariat within two months of the coming into force of the Covenant. Notice thereof shall be sent to all other Members of the League.

2. Any fully self-governing State, Dominion or Colony not named in the Annex may become a Member of the League if its admission is agreed to by two-thirds of the Assembly, provided that it shall give effective guarantees of its sincere intention to observe its international obligations, and shall accept such regulations as may be prescribed by the League in regard to its military, naval and air forces and armaments.

3. Any Member of the League may, after two years' notice of its intention so to do, withdraw from the League, provided that all its international obligations and all its obligations under this Covenant shall have been fulfilled at the time of its withdrawal.

---

*The texts printed in italics indicate amendments adopted by the League.

Article 2

The action of the League under this Covenant shall be effected through the instrumentality of an Assembly and of a Council, with a permanent Secretariat.

Article 3

1. The Assembly shall consist of Representatives of the Members of the League.

2. The Assembly shall meet at stated intervals and from time to time as occasion may require at the Seat of the League or at such other place as may be decided upon.

3. The Assembly may deal at its meetings with any matter within the sphere of action of the League or affecting the peace of the world.

4. At meetings of the Assembly, each Member of the League shall have one vote, and may have not more than three Representatives.

Article 4

1. The Council shall consist of Representatives of the Principal Allied and Associated Powers, together with Representatives of four other Members of the League. These four Members of the League shall be selected by the Assembly from time to time in its discretion. Until the appointment of the Representatives of the four Members of the League first selected by the Assembly, Representatives of Belgium, Brazil, Spain and Greece shall be Members of the Council.

2. With the appproval of the majority of the Assembly, the Council may name additional Members of the League whose Representatives shall always be Members of the Council; the Council with like approval may increase the number of Members of the League to be selected by the Assembly for representation on the Council.

2. *bis. The Assembly shall fix by a two-thirds majority the rules dealing with the election of the non-permanent Members of the Council, and particularly such regulations as relate to their term of office and the conditions of re-eligibility.*

3. The Council shall meet from time to time as occasion may require, and at least once a year, at the Seat of the League, or at such other place as may be decided upon.

4. The Council may deal at its meetings with any matter within the sphere of action of the League or affecting the peace of the world.

5. Any Member of the League not represented on the Council shall be invited to send a Representative to sit as a member at any meeting of the Council during the consideration of matters specially affecting the interests of that Member of the League.

6. At meetings of the Council, each Member of the League represented on the Council shall have one vote, and may have not more than one Representative.

Article 5

1. Except where otherwise expressly provided in this Covenant or by the terms of the present Treaty, decisions at any meeting of the Assembly or of the Council shall require the agreement of all the Members of the League represented at the meeting.

2. All matters of procedure at meetings of the Assembly or of the Council, including the appointment of Committees to investigate particular matters, shall be regulated by the Assembly or by the Council and may be decided by a majority of the Members of the League represented at the meeting.

3. The first meeting of the Assembly and the first meeting of the Council shall be summoned by the President of the United States of America.

Article 6

1. The permanent Secretariat shall be established at the Seat of the League. The Secretariat shall comprise a Secretary-General and such secretaries and staff as may be required.

2. The first Secretary-General shall be the person named in the Annex; thereafter the Secretary-General shall be appointed by the Council with the approval of the majority of the Assembly.

3. The secretaries and staff of the Secretariat shall be appointed by the Secretary-General with the approval of the Council.

4. The Secretary-General shall act in that capacity at all meetings of the Assembly and of the Council.

5. *The expenses of the League shall be borne by the Members of the League in the proportion decided by the Assembly.*

Article 7

1. The Seat of the League is established at Geneva.

2. The Council may at any time decide that the Seat of the League shall be established elsewhere.

3. All positions under or in connection with the League, including the Secretariat, shall be open equally to men and women.

4. Representatives of the Members of the League and officials of the League when engaged in the business of the League shall enjoy diplomatic privileges and immunities.

5. The buildings and other property occupied by the League or its officials or by Representatives attending its meetings shall be inviolable.

Article 8

1. The Members of the League recognize that the maintenance of peace requires the reduction of national armaments to the lowest point consistent with national safety and the enforcement by common action of international obligations.

2. The Council, taking account of the geographical situation and circumstances of each State, shall formulate plans for such reduction for the consideration and action of the several Governments.

3. Such plans shall be subject to reconsideration and revision at least every ten years.

4. After these plans have been adopted by the several Governments, the limits of armaments therein fixed shall not be exceeded without the concurrence of the Council.

5. The Members of the League agree that the manufacture by private enterprise of munitions and implements of war is open to grave objections. The Council shall advise how the evil effects attendant upon such manufacture can be prevented, due regard being had to the necessities of those Members of the League which are not able to manufacture the munitions and implements of war necessary for their safety.

6. The Members of the League undertake to interchange full and frank information as to the scale of their armaments, their military, naval and air programmes and the condition of such of their industries as are adaptable to warlike purposes.

Article 9

A permanent Commission shall be constituted to advise the Council on the execution of the provisions of Articles 1 and 8 and on military, naval and air questions generally.

Article 10

The Members of the League undertake to respect and preserve as against external aggression the territorial integrity and existing political independence of all Members of the League. In case of any such aggression or in case of any threat or danger of such aggression, the Council shall advise upon the means by which this obligation shall be fulfilled.

Article 11

1. Any war or threat of war, whether immediately affecting any of the Members of the League or not, is hereby declared a matter of concern to the whole League, and the League shall take any action that may

be deemed wise and effectual to safeguard the peace of nations. In case any such emergency should arise, the Secretary-General shall, on the request of any Member of the League, forthwith summon a meeting of the Council.

2. It is also declared to be the friendly right of each Member of the League to bring to the attention of the Assembly or of the Council any circumstance whatever affecting international relations which threatens to disturb international peace or the good understanding between nations upon which peace depends.

Article 12

1. The Members of the League agree that if there should arise between them any dispute likely to lead to a rupture they will submit the matter either to arbitration or *judicial settlement* or to enquiry by the Council, and they agree in no case to resort to war until three months after the award by the arbitrators *or the judicial decision* or the report by the Council.

2. In any case under this article the award of the arbitrators *or the judicial decision* shall be made within a reasonable time, and the report of the Council shall be made within six months after the submission of the dispute.

Article 13

1. The Members of the League agree that whenever any dispute shall arise between them which they recognize to be suitable for submission to arbitration *or judicial settlement,* and which cannot be satisfactorily settled by diplomacy, they will submit the whole subject-matter to arbitration *or judicial settlement.*

2. Disputes as to the interpretation of a treaty, as to any question of international law, as to the existence of any fact which, if established, would constitute a breach of any international obligation, or as to the extent and nature of the reparation to be made for any such breach, are declared to be among those which are generally suitable for submission to arbitration *or judicial settlement.*

3. *For the consideration of any such dispute, the court to which the case is referred shall be the Permanent Court of International Justice, established in accordance with Article 14, or any tribunal agreed on by the parties to the dispute or stipulated in any Convention existing between them.*

4. The Members of the League agree that they will carry out in full good faith any award *or decision* that may be rendered, and that they will not resort to war against a Member of the League which complies therewith. In the event of any failure to carry out such an award *or decision,* the Council shall propose what steps should be taken to give effect thereto.

Article 14

The Council shall formulate and submit to the Members of the League for adoption plans for the establishment of a Permanent Court of International Justice. The Court shall be competent to hear and determine any dispute of an international character which the parties thereto submit to it. The Court may also give an advisory opinion upon any dispute or question referred to it by the Council or by the Assembly.

Article 15

1. If there should arise between Members of the League any dispute likely to lead to a rupture, which is not submitted to arbitration *or judicial settlement* in accordance with Article 13, the Members of the League agree that they will submit the matter to the Council. Any party to the dispute may effect such submission by giving notice of the existence of the dispute to the Secretary-General, who will make all necessary arrangements for a full investigation and consideration thereof.

2. For this purpose, the parties to the dispute will communicate to the Secretary-General, as promptly as possible, statements of their case with all the relevant facts and papers, and the Council may forthwith direct the publication thereof.

3. The Council shall endeavour to effect a settlement of the dispute, and if such efforts are successful, a statement shall be made public giving such facts and explanations regarding the dispute and the terms of settlement thereof as the Council may deem appropriate.

4. If the dispute is not thus settled, the Council either unanimously or by a majority vote shall make and publish a report containing a statement of the facts of the dispute and the recommendations which are deemed just and proper in regard thereto.

5. Any Member of the League represented on the Council may make public a statement of the facts of the dispute and of its conclusions regarding the same.

6. If a report by the Council is unanimously agreed to by the members thereof other than the Representatives of one or more of the parties to the dispute, the Members of the League agree that they will not go to war with any party to the dispute which complies with the recommendations of the report.

7. If the Council fails to reach a report which is unanimously agreed to by the members thereof, other than the Representatives of one or more of the parties to the dispute, the Members of the League reserve to themselves the right to take such action as they shall consider necessary for the maintenance of right and justice.

8. If the dispute between the parties is claimed by one of them, and is found by the Council, to arise out of a matter which by international law is solely within the domestic jurisdiction of that party, the Council shall so report, and shall make no recommendations as to its settlement.

9. The Council may in any case under this article refer the dispute to the Assembly. The dispute shall be so referred at the request of either party to the dispute provided that such request be made within fourteen days after the submission of the dispute to the Council.

10. In any case referred to the Assembly, all the provisions of this article and of Article 12 relating to the action and powers of the Council shall apply to the action and powers of the Assembly, provided that a report made by the Assembly, if concurred in by the Representatives of those Members of the League represented on the Council and of a majority of the other Members of the League, exclusive in each case of the Representatives of the parties to the dispute, shall have the same force as a report by the Council concurred in by all the members thereof other than the Representatives of one or more of the parties to the dispute.

Article 16

1. Should any Member of the League resort to war in disregard of its covenants under Articles 12, 13 or 15, it shall, *ipso facto,* be deemed to have committed an act of war against all other Members of the League, which hereby undertake immediately to subject it to the severance of all trade or financial relations, the prohibition of all intercourse between their nationals and the nationals of the Covenant-breaking State, and the prevention of all financial, commercial or personal intercourse between the nationals of the Covenant-breaking State and the nationals of any other State, whether a Member of the League or not.

2. It shall be the duty of the Council in such case to recommend to the several Governments concerned what effective military, naval or air force the Members of the League shall severally contribute to the armed forces to be used to protect the covenants of the League.

3. The Members of the League agree, further, that they will mutually support one another in the financial and economic measures which are taken under this article, in order to minimise the loss and inconvenience resulting from the above measures, and that they will mutually support one another in resisting any special measures aimed at one of their number by the Covenant-breaking State, and that they will take the necessary steps to afford passage through their territory to the forces of any of the Members of the League which are co-operating to protect the covenants of the League.

4. Any member of the League which has violated any covenant of the League may be declared to be no longer a Member of the League by a vote of the Council concurred in by the Representatives of all the other Members of the League represented thereon.

Article 17

1. In the event of a dispute between a Member of the League and a State which is not a member of the League or between States not members of the League, the State or States not members of the League shall

be invited to accept the obligations of membership in the League for the purposes of such dispute, upon such conditions as the Council may deem just. If such invitation is accepted, the provisions of Articles 12 to 16 inclusive shall be applied with such modifications as may be deemed necessary by the Council.

2. Upon such invitation being given, the Council shall immediately institute an enquiry into the circumstances of the dispute and recommend such action as may seem best and most effectual in the circumstances.

3. If a State so invited shall refuse to accept the obligations of membership in the League for the purposes of such dispute, and shall resort to war against a Member of the League, the provisions of Article 16 shall be applicable as against the State taking such action.

4. If both parties to the dispute when so invited refuse to accept the obligations of membership in the League for the purposes of such dispute, the Council may take such measures and make such recommendations as will prevent hostilities and will result in the settlement of the dispute.

Article 18

Every treaty or international engagement entered into hereafter by any Member of the League shall be forthwith registered with the Secretariat and shall, as soon as possible, be published by it. No such treaty or international engagement shall be binding until so registered.

Article 19

The Assembly may from time to time advise the reconsideration by Members of the League of treaties which have become inapplicable and the consideration of international conditions whose continuance might endanger the peace of the world.

Article 20

1. The Members of the League severally agree that this Covenant is accepted as abrogating all obligations or understandings *inter se* which are inconsistent with the terms thereof, and solemnly undertake that they will not hereafter enter into any engagements inconsistent with the terms thereof.

2. In case any Member of the League shall, before becoming a Member of the League, have undertaken any obligations inconsistent with the terms of this Covenant, it shall be the duty of such Member to take immediate steps to procure its release from such obligations.

Article 21

Nothing in this Covenant shall be deemed to affect the validity of international engagements, such as treaties of arbitration or regional understandings like the Monroe doctrine, for securing the maintenance of peace.

Article 22

1. To those colonies and territories which as a consequence of the late war have ceased to be under the sovereignty of the States which formerly governed them and which are inhabited by peoples not yet able to stand by themselves under the strenuous conditions of the modern world, there should be applied the principle that the well-being and development of such peoples form a sacred trust of civilisation and that securities for the performance of this trust should be embodied in this Covenant.

2. The best method of giving practical effect to this principle is that the tutelage of such peoples should be entrusted to advanced nations who, by reason of their resources, their experience or their geographical position, can best undertake this responsibility, and who are willing to accept it, and that this tutelage should be exercised by them as Mandatories on behalf of the League.

3. The character of the mandate must differ according to the stage of the development of the people, the geographical situation of the territory, its economic conditions and other similar circumstances.

4. Certain communities formerly belonging to the Turkish Empire have reached a stage of development where their existence as independent nations can be provisionally recognised subject to the rendering of administrative advice and assistance by a Mandatory until such time as they are able to stand alone. The wishes of these communities must be a principal consideration in the selection of the Mandatory.

5. Other peoples, especially those of Central Africa, are at such a stage that the Mandatory must be responsible for the administration of the territory under conditions which will guarantee freedom of conscience and religion, subject only to the maintenance of public order and morals, the prohibition of abuses such as the slave trade, the arms traffic and the liquor traffic, and the prevention of the establishment of fortifications or military and naval bases and of military training of the natives for other than police purposes and the defence of territory, and will also secure equal opportunities for the trade and commerce of other Members of the League.

6. There are territories, such as South West Africa and certain of the South Pacific Islands, which, owing to the sparseness of their population, or their small size, or their remoteness from the centres of civilisation, or their geographical contiguity to the territory of the Mandatory, and other circumstances, can be best administered under the

laws of the Mandatory as integral portions of its territory, subject to the safeguards above mentioned in the interests of the indigenous population.

7. In every case of mandate, the Mandatory shall render to the Council an annual report in reference to the territory committed to its charge.

8. The degree of authority, control or administration to be exercised by the Mandatory shall, if not previously agreed upon by the Members of the League, be explicitly defined in each case by the Council.

9. A permanent Commission shall be constituted to receive and examine the annual reports of the Mandatories and to advise the Council on all matters relating to the observance of the mandates.

Article 23

Subject to and in accordance with the provisions of international Conventions existing or hereafter to be agreed upon, the Members of the League:

(a) will endeavor to secure and maintain fair and humane conditions of labour for men, women and children, both in their own countries and in all countries to which their commercial and industrial relations extend, and for that purpose will establish and maintain the necessary international organisations;

(b) undertake to secure just treatment of the native inhabitants of territories under their control;

(c) will entrust the League with the general supervision over the execution of agreements with regard to the traffic in women and children, and the traffic in opium and other dangerous drugs;

(d) will entrust the League with the general supervision of the trade in arms and ammunition with the countries in which the control of this traffic is necessary in the common interest;

(e) will make provision to secure and maintain freedom of communications and of transit and equitable treatment for the commerce of all Members of the League. In this connection, the special necessities of the regions devastated during the war of 1914–1918 shall be borne in mind;

(f) will endeavour to take steps in matters of international concern for the prevention and control of disease.

Article 24

1. There shall be placed under the direction of the League all international bureaux already established by general treaties if the parties to such treaties consent. All such international bureaux and all commissions for the regulation of matters of international interest hereafter constituted shall be placed under the direction of the League.

2. In all matters of international interest which are regulated by general Conventions but which are not placed under the control of international bureaux or commissions, the Secretariat of the League shall, subject to the consent of the Council and if desired by the parties, collect and distribute all relevant information and shall render any other assistance which may be necessary or desirable.

3. The Council may include as part of the expenses of the Secretariat the expenses of any bureau or commission which is placed under the direction of the League.

Article 25

The Members of the League agree to encourage and promote the establishment and co-operation of duly authorised voluntary national Red Cross organisations having as purposes the improvement of health, the prevention of disease and the mitigation of suffering throughout the world.

Article 26

1. Amendments to this Covenant will take effect when ratified by the Members of the League whose Representatives compose the Council and by a majority of the Members of the League whose Representatives compose the Assembly.

2. No such amendments shall bind any Member of the League which signifies its dissent therefrom, but in that case it shall cease to be a Member of the League.

APPENDIX B

The Charter of the United Nations

We the peoples of the United Nations determined

to save succeeding generations from the scourge of war, which twice in our lifetime has brought untold sorrow to mankind, and

to reaffirm faith in fundamental human rights, in the dignity and worth of the human person, in the equal rights of men and women and of nations large and small, and

to establish conditions under which justice and respect for the obligations arising from treaties and other sources of international law can be maintained, and

to promote social progress and better standards of life in larger freedom,

and for these ends

to practice tolerance and live together in peace with one another as good neighbors, and

to unite our strength to maintain international peace and security, and

to ensure, by the acceptance of principles and the institution of methods, that armed force shall not be used, save in the common interest, and

to employ international machinery for the promotion of the economic and social advancement to combine our efforts to accomplish these aims.

Accordingly, our respective Governments, through representatives assembled in the city of San Francisco, who have exhibited their full powers found to be in good and due form, have agreed to the present Charter of the United Nations and do hereby establish an international organization to be known as the United Nations.

CHAPTER 1

Purposes and Principles

Article 1

The Purposes of the United Nations are:

1. To maintain international peace and security, and to that end: to take effective collective measures for the prevention and removal of threats to the peace, and for the suppression of acts of aggression or other breaches of the peace, and to bring about by peaceful means, and in conformity with the principles of justice and international law, adjust-

ment or settlement of international disputes or situations which might lead to a breach of the peace;

2. To develop friendly relations among nations based on respect for the principle of equal rights and self-determination of peoples, and to take other appropriate measures to strengthen universal peace;

3. To achieve international cooperation in solving international problems of an economic, social, cultural, or humanitarian character, and in promoting and encouraging respect for human rights and for fundamental freedoms for all without distinction as to race, sex, language, or religion; and

4. To be a center for harmonizing the actions of nations in the attainment of these common ends.

Article 2

The Organization and its Members, in pursuit of the Purposes stated in Article 1, shall act in accordance with the following Principles.

1. The Organization is based on the principle of the sovereign equality of all its Members.

2. All Members, in order to ensure to all of them the rights and benefits resulting from membership, shall fulfill in good faith the obligations assumed by them in accordance with the present Charter.

3. All Members shall settle their international disputes by peaceful means in such a manner that international peace and security, and justice, are not endangered.

4. All Members shall refrain in their international relations from the threat or use of force against the territorial integrity or political independence of any state, or in any other manner inconsistent with the Purposes of the United Nations.

5. All Members shall give the United Nations every assistance in any action it takes in accordance with the present Charter, and shall refrain from giving assistance to any state against which the United Nations is taking preventive or enforcement action.

6. The Organization shall ensure that states which are not Members of the United Nations act in accordance with these Principles so far as may be necessary for the maintenance of international peace and security.

7. Nothing contained in the present Charter shall authorize the United Nations to intervene in matters which are essentially within the domestic jurisdiction of any state or shall require the Members to submit such matters to settlement under the present Charter; but this principle shall not prejudice the application of enforcement measures under Chapter 7.

CHAPTER 2
Membership

Article 3

The original Members of the United Nations shall be the states which, having participated in the United Nations Conference on International Organization at San Francisco, or having previously signed the Declaration by United Nations of January 1, 1942, sign the present Charter and ratify it in accordance with Article 110.

Article 4

1. Membership in the United Nations is open to all other peace-loving states which accept the obligations contained in the present Charter and, in the judgment of the Organization, are able and willing to carry out these obligations.

2. The admission of any such state to membership in the United Nations will be affected by a decision of the General Assembly upon the recommendation of the Security Council.

Article 5

A Member of the United Nations against which preventive or enforcement action has been taken by the Security Council may be suspended from the exercise of the rights and privileges of membership by the General Assembly upon the recommendation of the Security Council. The exercise of these rights and privileges may be restored by the Security Council.

Article 6

A Member of the United Nations which has persistently violated the Principles contained in the present Charter may be expelled from the Organization by the General Assembly upon the recommendation of the Security Council.

CHAPTER 3
Organs

Article 7

1. There are established as the principal organs of the United Nations: a General Assembly, a Security Council, an Economic and Social Council, a Trusteeship Council, an International Court of Justice, and a Secretariat.

2. Such subsidiary organs as may be found necessary may be established in accordance with the present Charter.

Article 8

The United Nations shall place no restrictions on the eligibility of men and women to participate in any capacity and under conditions of equality in its principal and subsidiary organs.

CHAPTER 4
The General Assembly

Composition
Article 9

1. The General Assembly shall consist of all the Members of the United Nations.

2. Each Member shall have not more than five representatives in the General Assembly.

Functions and Powers
Article 10

The General Assembly may discuss any questions or any matters within the scope of the present Charter or relating to the powers and functions of any organs provided for in the present Charter, and, except as provided in Article 12, may make recommendations to the Members of the United Nations or to the Security Council or to both on any such questions or matters.

Article 11

1. The General Assembly may consider the general principles of co-operation in the maintenance of international peace and security, including the principles governing disarmament and the regulation of armaments, and may make recommendations with regard to such principles to the Members or to the Security Council or to both.

2. The General Assembly may discuss any questions relating to the maintenance of international peace and security brought before it by any Member of the United Nations, or by the Security Council, or by a state which is not a Member of the United Nations in accordance with Article 35, paragraph 2, and, except as provided in Article 12, may make recommendations with regard to any such questions to the state or states concerned or to the Security Council or to both. Any such question on which action is necessary shall be referred to the Security Council by the General Assembly either before or after discussion.

3. The General Assembly may call the attention of the Security Council to situations which are likely to endanger international peace and security.

4. The powers of the General Assembly set forth in this Article shall not limit the general scope of Article 10.

Article 12

1. While the Security Council is exercising in respect of any dispute or situation the functions assigned to it in the present Charter, the General Assembly shall not make any recommendations with regard to that dispute or situation unless the Security Council so requests.

2. The Secretary-General, with the consent of the Security Council, shall notify the General Assembly at each session of any matters relative to the maintenance of international peace and security which are being dealt with by the Security Council and shall similarly notify the General Assembly, or the Members of the United Nations if the General Assembly is not in session, immediately the Security Council ceases to deal with such matters. .

Article 13

1. The General Assembly shall initiate studies and make recommendations for the purpose of:
a. promoting international cooperation in the political field and encouraging the progressive development of international law and its codification;
b. promoting international cooperation in the economic, social, cultural, educational, and health fields, and assisting in the realization of human rights and fundamental freedoms for all without distinction as to race, sex, language, or religion.

2. The further responsibilities, functions, and powers of the General Assembly with respect to matters mentioned in paragraph 1 (b) above are set forth in Chapters 9 and 10.

Article 14

Subject to the provisions of Article 12, the General Assembly may recommend measures for the peaceful adjustment of any situation, regardless of origin, which it deems likely to impair the general welfare or friendly relations among nations, including situations resulting from a violation of the provisions of the present Charter setting forth the Purposes and Principles of the United Nations.

Article 15

1. The General Assembly shall receive and consider annual and special reports from the Security Council; these reports shall include an account of the measures that the Security Council has decided upon or taken to maintain international peace and security.

2. The General Assembly shall receive and consider reports from the other organs of the United Nations.

Article 16

The General Assembly shall perform such functions with respect to the international trusteeship system as are assigned to it under Chapters 12 and 13, including the approval of the trusteeship agreements for areas not designated as strategic.

Article 17

1. The General Assembly shall consider and approve the budget of the Organization.

2. The expenses of the Organization shall be borne by the Members as apportioned by the General Assembly.

3. The General Assembly shall consider and approve any financial and budgetary arrangements with specialized agencies referred to in Article 57 and shall examine the administrative budgets of such specialized agencies with a view to making recommendations to the agencies concerned.

Voting

Article 18

1. Each member of the General Assembly shall have one vote.

2. Decisions of the General Assembly on important questions shall be made by a two-thirds majority of the members present and voting. These questions shall include: recommendations with respect to the maintenance of international peace and security, the election of the non-permanent members of the Security Council, the election of the members of the Economic and Social Council, the election of members of the Trusteeship Council in accordance with paragraph 1 (c) of Article 86, the admission of new Members to the United Nations, the suspension of the rights and privileges of membership, the expulsion of Members, questions relating to the operation of the trusteeship system, and budgetary questions.

3. Decisions on other questions, including the determination of additional categories of questions to be decided by a two-thirds majority, shall be made by a majority of the members present and voting.

Article 19

A Member of the United Nations which is in arrears in the payment of its financial contributions to the Organization shall have no vote in the General Assembly if the amount of its arrears equals or exceeds the amount of the contributions due from it for the preceding two full years. The General Assembly may, nevertheless, permit such a Member to vote if it is satisfied that the failure to pay is due to conditions beyond the control of the Member.

Procedure

Article 20

The General Assembly shall meet in regular annual sessions and in such special sessions as occasion may require. Special sessions shall be convoked by the Secretary-General at the request of the Security Council or of a majority of the Members of the United Nations.

Article 21

The General Assembly shall adopt its own rules of procedure. It shall elect its President for each session.

Article 22

The General Assembly may establish such subsidiary organs as it deems necessary for the performance of its functions.

CHAPTER 5
The Security Council

Composition

Article 23

1. The Security Council shall consist of fifteen Members of the United Nations. The Republic of China, France, the Union of Soviet Socialist Republics, the United Kingdom of Great Britain and Northern Ireland, and the United States of America shall be permanent members of the Security Council. The General Assembly shall elect ten other Members of the United Nations to be nonpermanent members of the Security Council, due regard being specially paid, in the first instance to the contribution of Members of the United Nations to the maintenance of international peace and security and to the other purposes of the Organization, and also to equitable geographical distribution.

2. The non-permanent members of the Security Council shall be elected for a term of two years. In the first election of the non-permanent members after the increase of the membership of the Security Council from eleven to fifteen, two of the four additional members shall be chosen for a term of one year. A retiring member shall not be eligible for immediate reelection.

3. Each member of the Security Council shall have one representative.

Functions and Powers

Article 24

1. In order to ensure prompt and effective action by the United Nations, its Members confer on the Security Council primary responsibility for the maintenance of international peace and security, and agree that in carrying out its duties under this responsibility the Security Council acts on their behalf.

2. In discharging these duties the Security Council shall act in accordance with the Purposes and Principles of the United Nations. The specific powers granted to the Security Council for the discharge of these duties are laid down in Chapters 6, 7, 8 and 12.

3. The Security Council shall submit annual and, when necessary, special reports to the General Assembly for its consideration.

Article 25

The Members of the United Nations agree to accept and carry out the decisions of the Security Council in accordance with the present Charter.

Article 26

In order to promote the establishment and maintenance of international peace and security with the least diversion for armaments of the world's human and economic resources, the Security Council shall be responsible for formulating, with the assistance of the Military Staff Committee referred to in Article 47, plans to be submitted to the Members of the United Nations for the establishment of a system for the regulation of armaments.

Voting

Article 27

1. Each member of the Security Council shall have one vote.

2. Decisions of the Security Council on procedural matters shall be made by an affirmative vote of nine members.

3. Decisions of the Security Council on all other matters shall be made by an affirmative vote of nine members including the concurring votes of the permanent members; provided that, in decisions under Chapter 6, and under paragraph 3 of Article 52, a party to a dispute shall abstain from voting.

Procedure

Article 28

1. The Security Council shall be so organized as to be able to function continuously. Each member of the Security Council shall for this purpose be represented at all times at the seat of the Organization.

2. The Security Council shall hold periodic meetings at which each of its members may, if it so desires, be represented by a member of the government or by some other specially designated representative.

3. The Security Council may hold meetings at such places other than the seat of the Organization as in its judgment will best facilitate its work.

Article 29

The Security Council may establish such subsidiary organs as it deems necessary for the performance of its functions.

Article 30

The Security Council shall adopt its own rules of procedure, including the method of selecting its President.

Article 31

Any Member of the United Nations which is not a member of the Security Council may participate, without vote, in the discussion of any question brought before the Security Council whenever the latter considers that the interests of that Member are specially affected.

Article 32

Any Member of the United Nations which is not a member of the Security Council or any state which is not a Member of the United Nations, if it is a party to a dispute under consideration by the Security Council, shall be invited to participate, without vote, in the discussion relating to the dispute. The Security Council shall lay down such conditions as it deems just for the participation of a state which is not a Member of the United Nations.

CHAPTER 6
Pacific Settlement of Disputes

Article 33

1. The parties to any dispute, the continuance of which is likely to endanger the maintenance of international peace and security, shall, first

of all, seek a solution of negotiation, enquiry, mediation, conciliation, arbitration, judicial settlement, resort to regional agencies or arrangements, or other peaceful means of their own choice.

2. The Security Council shall, when it deems necessary, call upon the parties to settle their dispute by such means.

Article 34

The Security Council may investigate any dispute, or any situation which might lead to international friction or give rise to a dispute, in order to determine whether the continuance of the dispute or situation is likely to endanger the maintenance of international peace and security.

Article 35

1. Any Member of the United Nations may bring any dispute, or any situation of the nature referred to in Article 34, to the attention of the Security Council or of the General Assembly.

2. A state which is not a Member of the United Nations may bring to the attention of the Security Council or of the General Assembly any dispute to which it is a party if it accepts in advance, for the purposes of the dispute, the obligations of pacific settlement provided in the present Charter.

3. The proceedings of the General Assembly in respect of matters brought to its attention under this Article will be subject to the provisions of Articles 11 and 12.

Article 36

1. The Security Council may, at any stage of a dispute of the nature referred to in Article 33 or of a situation of like nature, recommend appropriate procedures or methods of adjustment.

2. The Security Council should take into consideration any procedures for the settlement of the dispute which have already been adopted by the parties.

3. In making recommendations under this Article the Security Council should also take into consideration that legal disputes should as a general rule be referred by the parties to the International Court of Justice in accordance with the provisions of the Statute of the Court.

Article 37

1. Should the parties to a dispute of the nature referred to in Article 33 fail to settle it by the means indicated in that Article, they shall refer it to the Security Council.

2. If the Security Council deems that the continuance of the dispute is in fact likely to endanger the maintenance of international peace and

security, it shall decide whether to take action under Article 36 or to recommend such terms of settlement as it may consider appropriate.

Article 38

Without prejudice to the provisions of Articles 33 to 37, the Security Council may, if all the parties to any dispute so request, make recommendations to the parties with a view to a pacific settlement of the dispute.

CHAPTER 7
Action with Respect to Threats to the Peace, Breaches of the Peace, and Acts of Aggression

Article 39

The Security Council shall determine the existence of any threat to the peace, breach of the peace, or act of aggression and shall make recommendations, or decide what measures shall be taken in accordance with Articles 41 and 42, to maintain or restore international peace and security.

Article 40

In order to prevent an aggravation of the situation, the Security Council may, before making the recommendations or deciding upon the measures provided for in Article 39, call upon the parties concerned to comply with such provisional measures as it deems necessary or desirable. Such provisional measures shall be without prejudice to the rights, claims, or position of the parties concerned. The Security Council shall duly take account of failure to comply with such provisional measures.

Article 41

The Security Council may decide what measures not involving the use of armed force are to be employed to give effect to its decisions, and it may call upon the Members of the United Nations to apply such measures. These may include complete or partial interruption of economic relations and of rail, sea, air, postal, telegraphic, radio, and other means of communication, and the severance of diplomatic relations.

Article 42

Should the Security Council consider that measures provided for in Article 41 would be inadequate or have proved to be inadequate, it may take such action by air, sea, or land forces as may be necessary to maintain or restore international peace and security. Such action may include demonstrations, blockade, and other operations by air, sea, or land forces of Members of the United Nations.

Article 43

1. All Members of the United Nations, in order to contribute to the maintenance of international peace and security, undertake to make available to the Security Council, on its call and in accordance with a special agreement or agreements, armed forces, assistance, and facilities, including rights of passage, necessary for the purpose of maintaining international peace and security.

2. Such agreement or agreements shall govern the numbers and types of forces, their degree of readiness and general location, and the nature of the facilities and assistance to be provided.

3. The agreement or agreements shall be negotiated as soon as possible on the initiative of the Security Council. They shall be concluded between the Security Council and Members or between the Security Council and groups of Members and shall be subject to ratification by the signatory states in accordance with their respective constitutional processes.

Article 44

When the Security Council has decided to use force it shall, before calling upon a Member not represented on it to provide armed forces in fulfillment of the obligations assumed under Article 43, invite the Member, if the Member so desires, to participate in the decisions of the Security Council concerning the employment of contingents of that Member's armed forces.

Article 45

In order to enable the United Nations to take urgent military measures, Members shall hold immediately available national air-force contingents for combined international enforcement action. The strength and degree of readiness of these contingents and plans for their combined action shall be determined, within the limits laid down in the special agreement or agreements referred to in Article 43, by the Security Council with the assistance of the Military Staff Committee.

Article 46

Plans for the application of armed force shall be made by the Security Council with the assistance of the Military Staff Committee.

Article 47

1. There shall be established a Military Staff Committee to advise and assist the Security Council on all questions relating to the Security Council's military requirements for the maintenance of international peace and security, the employment and command of forces placed at its disposal, the regulation of armaments, and possible disarmament.

2. The Military Staff Committee shall consist of the Chiefs of Staff of the permanent members of the Security Council or their representatives. Any Member of the United Nations not permanently represented on the Committee shall be invited by the Committee to be associated with it when the efficient discharge of the Committee's responsibilities requires the participation of that Member in its work.

3. The Military Staff Committee shall be responsible under the Security Council for the strategic direction of any armed forces placed at the disposal of the Security Council. Questions relating to the command of such forces shall be worked out subsequently.

4. The Military Staff Committee, with the authorization of the Security Council and after consultation with appropriate regional agencies, may establish regional subcommittees.

Article 48

1. The action required to carry out the decisions of the Security Council for the maintenance of international peace and security shall be taken by all the Members of the United Nations or by some of them, as the Security Council may determine.

2. Such decisions shall be carried out by the Members of the United Nations directly and through their action in the appropriate international agencies of which they are members.

Article 49

The Members of the United Nations shall join in affording mutual assistance in carrying out the measures decided upon by the Security Council.

Article 50

If preventive or enforcement measures against any state are taken by the Security Council, any other state, whether a Member of the United Nations or not, which finds itself confronted with special economic problems arising from the carrying out of those measures shall have the right to consult the Security Council with regard to a solution of those problems.

Article 51

Nothing in the present Charter shall impair the inherent right of individual or collective self-defense if an armed attack occurs against a Member of the United Nations, until the Security Council has taken the measures necessary to maintain international peace and security. Measures taken by Members in the exercise of this right of self-defense shall be immediately reported to the Security Council and shall not in any way affect the authority and responsibility of the Security Council under the present Charter to take at any time such action as it deems necessary in order to maintain or restore international peace and security.

CHAPTER 8
Regional Arrangements

Article 52

1. Nothing in the present Charter precludes the existence of regional arrangements or agencies for dealing with such matters relating to the maintenance of international peace and security as are appropriate for regional action, provided that such arrangements or agencies and their activities are consistent with the Purposes and Principles of the United Nations.

2. The Members of the United Nations entering into such arrangements or constituting such agencies shall make every effort to achieve pacific settlement of local disputes through such regional arrangements or by such regional agencies before referring them to the Security Council.

3. The Security Council shall encourage the development of pacific settlement of local disputes through such regional arrangements or by such regional agencies either on the initiative of the states concerned or by reference from the Security Council.

4. This Article in no way impairs the application of Articles 34 and 35.

Article 53

1. The Security Council shall, where appropriate, utilize such regional arrangements or agencies for enforcement action under its authority. But no enforcement action shall be taken under regional arrangements or by regional agencies without the authorization of the Security Council, with the exception of measures against any enemy state, as defined in paragraph 2 of this Article, provided for pursuant to Article 107 or in regional arrangements directed against renewal of aggressive policy

on the part of any such state, until such time as the Organization may, on request of the Governments concerned, be charged with the responsibility for preventing further aggression by such a state.

2. The term enemy state as used in paragraph 1 of this Article applies to any state which during the Second World War has been an enemy of any signatory of the present Charter.

Article 54

The Security Council shall at all times be kept fully informed of activities undertaken or in contemplation under regional arrangements or by regional agencies for the maintenance of international peace and security.

CHAPTER 9
International Economic and Social Cooperation

Article 55

With a view to the creation of conditions of stability and well-being which are necessary for peaceful and friendly relations among nations based on respect for the principle of equal rights and self-determination of peoples, the United Nations shall promote:

a. higher standards of living, full employment, and conditions of economic and social progress and development;

b. solutions of international economic, social, health, and related problems; and international cultural and educational cooperation; and

c. universal respect for, and observance of, human rights and fundamental freedoms for all without distinction as to race, sex, language, or religion.

Article 56

All Members pledge themselves to take joint and separate action in cooperation with the Organization for the achievement of the purposes set forth in Article 55.

Article 57

1. The various agencies, established by intergovernmental agreement and having wide international responsibilities, as defined in their basic instruments, in economic, social, cultural, educational, health, and related fields, shall be brought into relationship with the United Nations in accordance with the provisions of Article 63.

2. Such agencies thus brought into relationship with the United Nations are hereinafter referred to as specialized agencies.

Article 58

The Organization shall make recommendations for the coordination of the policies and activities of the specialized agencies.

Article 59

The Organization shall, where appropriate, initiate negotiations among the states concerned for the creation of any new specialized agencies required for the accomplishment of the purposes set forth in Article 55.

Article 60

Responsibility for the discharge of the functions of the Organization set forth in this Chapter shall be vested in the General Assembly and, under the authority of the General Assembly, in the Economic and Social Council, which shall have for this purpose the powers set forth in Chapter 10.

CHAPTER 10
The Economic and Social Council

Composition

Article 61

1. The Economic and Social Council shall consist of fifty-four Members of the United Nations elected by the General Assembly.

2. Subject to the provisions of paragraph 3, eighteen members of the Economic and Social Council shall be elected each year for a term of three years. A retiring member shall be eligible for immediate re-election.

3. At the first election after the increase in the membership of the Economic and Social Council from twenty-seven to fifty-four members, in addition to the members elected in place of the nine members whose term of office expires at the end of that year, twenty-seven additional members shall be elected. Of these twenty-seven additional members, the term of office of nine members so elected shall expire at the end of one year, and of nine other members at the end of two years, in accordance with arrangements made by the General Assembly.

4. Each member of the Economic and Social Council shall have one representative.

Functions and Powers

Article 62

1. The Economic and Social Council may make or initiate studies and reports with respect to international economic, social, cultural, ed-

ucational, health, and related matters and may make recommendations with respect to any such matters to the General Assembly, to the Members of the United Nations, and to the specialized agencies concerned.

2. It may make recommendations for the purpose of promoting respect for, and observance of, human rights and fundamental freedoms for all.

3. It may prepare draft conventions for submission to the General Assembly, with respect to matters falling within its competence.

4. It may call, in accordance with the rules prescribed by the United Nations, international conferences on matters falling within its competence.

Article 63

1. The Economic and Social Council may enter into agreements with any of the agencies referred to in Article 57, defining the terms on which the agency concerned shall be brought into relationship with the United Nations. Such agreements shall be subject to approval by the General Assembly.

2. It may coordinate the activities of the specialized agencies through consultation with and recommendations to such agencies and through recommendations to the General Assembly and to the Members of the United Nations.

Article 64

1. The Economic and Social Council may take appropriate steps to obtain regular reports from the specialized agencies. It may make arrangements with the Members of the United Nations and with the specialized agencies to obtain reports on the steps taken to give effect to its own recommendations and to recommendations on matters falling within its competence made by the General Assembly.

2. It may communicate its observations on these reports to the General Assembly.

Article 65

The Economic and Social Council may furnish information to the Security Council and shall assist the Security Council upon its request.

Article 66

1. The Economic and Social Council shall perform such functions as fall within its competence in connection with the carrying out of the recommendations of the General Assembly.

2. It may, with the approval of the General Assembly, perform services at the request of Members of the United Nations and at the request of specialized agencies.

3. It shall perform such other functions as are specified elsewhere in the present Charter or as may be assigned to it by the General Assembly.

Voting

Article 67

1. Each member of the Economic and Social Council shall have one vote.

2. Decisions of the Economic and Social Council shall be made by a majority of the members present and voting.

Procedure

Article 68

The Economic and Social Council shall set up commissions in economic and social fields and for the promotion of human rights, and such other commissions as may be required for the performance of its functions.

Article 69

The Economic and Social Council shall invite any Member of the United Nations to participate, without vote, in its deliberations on any matter of particular concern to that Member.

Article 70

The Economic and Social Council may make arrangements for representatives of the specialized agencies to participate, without vote, in its deliberations and in those of the commissions established by it, and for its representatives to participate in the deliberations of the specialized agencies.

Article 71

The Economic and Social Council may make suitable arrangements for consultation with non-governmental organizations which are concerned with matters within its competence. Such arrangements may be made with international organizations and, where appropriate, with national organizations after consultation with the Member of the United Nations concerned.

Article 72

1. The Economic and Social Council shall adopt its own rules of procedure, including the method of selecting its President.

2. The Economic and Social Council shall meet as required in accordance with its rules, which shall include provision for the convening of meetings on the request of a majority of its members.

CHAPTER 11
Declaration Regarding Non-Self-Governing Territories

Article 73

Members of the United Nations which have or assume responsibilities for the administration of territories whose peoples have not yet attained a full measure of self-government recognize the principle that the interests of the inhabitants of these territories are paramount, and accept as a sacred trust the obligation to promote to the utmost, within the system of international peace and security established by the present Charter, the well-being of the inhabitants of these territories, and, to this end:

a. to ensure, with due respect for the culture of the peoples concerned, their political, economic, social, and educational advancement, their just treatment, and their protection against abuses;

b. to develop self-government, to take due account of the political aspirations of the peoples, and to assist them in the progressive development of their free political institutions, according to the particular circumstances of each territory and its peoples and their varying stages of advancement;

c. to further international peace and security;

d. to promote constructive measures of development, to encourage research, and to cooperate with one another, and, when and where appropriate, with specialized international bodies with a view to the practical achievement of the social, economic, and scientific purposes set forth in this Article; and

e. to transmit regularly to the Secretary-General for information purposes, subject to such limitation as security and constitutional considerations may require, statistical and other information of a technical nature relating to economic, social, and educational conditions in the territories for which they are respectively responsible other than those territories to which Chapters 12 and 13 apply.

Article 74

Members of the United Nations also agree that their policy in respect of the territories to which this Chapter applies, no less than in respect of their metropolitan areas, must be based on the general principle of good-neighborliness, due account being taken of the interests and well-being of the rest of the world, in social, economic, and commercial matters.

CHAPTER 12
International Trusteeship System

Article 75

The United Nations shall establish under its authority an international trusteeship system for the administration and supervision of such territories as may be placed thereunder by subsequent individual agreements. These territories are hereinafter referred to as trust territories.

The basic objectives of the trusteeship system, in accordance with the Purposes of the United Nations laid down in Article 1 of the present Charter, shall be:

Article 76

a. to further international peace and security;

b. to promote the political, economic, social, and educational advancement of the inhabitants of the trust territories, and their progressive development towards self-government or independence as may be appropriate to the particular circumstances of each territory and its peoples and the freely expressed wishes of the people concerned, and as may be provided by the terms of each trusteeship agreement;

c. to encourage respect for human rights and for fundamental freedoms for all without distinction as to race, sex, language, or religion, and to encourage recognition of the interdependence of the peoples of the world; and

d. to ensure equal treatment in social, economic, and commercial matters for all Members of the United Nations and their nationals, and also equal treatment for the latter in the administration of justice, without prejudice to the attainment of the foregoing objectives and subject to the provisions of Article 80.

Article 77

1. The trusteeship system shall apply to such territories in the following categories as may be placed thereunder by means of trusteeship agreements:

a. territories now held under mandate;

b. territories which may be detached from enemy states as a result of the Second World War; and
c. territories voluntarily placed under the system by states responsible for their administration.

2. It will be a matter for subsequent agreement as to which territories in the foregoing categories will be brought under the trusteeship system and upon what terms.

Article 78

The trusteeship system shall not apply to territories which have become Members of the United Nations, relationship among which shall be based on respect for the principle of sovereign equality.

Article 79

The terms of trusteeship for each territory to be placed under the trusteeship system, including any alteration or amendments, shall be agreed upon by the states directly concerned, including the mandatory power in the case of territories held under mandate by a Member of the United Nations, and shall be approved as provided for in Articles 83 and 85.

Article 80

1. Except as may be agreed upon in individual trusteeship agreements, made under Articles 77, 79, and 81, placing each territory under the trusteeship system, and until such agreements have been concluded, nothing in this Chapter shall be construed in or of itself to alter in any manner the rights whatsover of any states or any peoples or the terms of existing international instruments to which Members of the United Nations may respectively be parties.

2. Paragraph 1 of this Article shall not be interpreted as giving grounds for delay or postponement of the negotiation and conclusion of agreements for placing mandated and other territories under the trusteeship system as provided for in Article 77.

Article 81

The trusteeship agreement shall in each case include the terms under which the trust territory will be administered and designate the authority which will exercise the administration of the trust territory. Such authority, hereinafter called the administering authority, may be one or more states or the Organization itself.

Article 82

There may be designated, in any trusteeship agreement, a strategic area or areas which may include part or all of the trust territory to which the agreement applies, without prejudice to any special agreement or agreements made under Article 43.

Article 83

1. All functions of the United Nations relating to strategic areas, including the approval of the terms of the trusteeship agreement and of

their alteration or amendment, shall be exercised by the Security Council.

2. The basic objectives set forth in Article 76 shall be applicable to the people of each strategic area.

3. The Security Council shall, subject to the provisions of the trusteeship agreements and without prejudice to security considerations, avail itself of the assistance of the trusteeship Council to perform those functions of the United Nations under the trusteeship system relating to political, economic, social, and educational matters in the strategic areas.

Article 84

It shall be the duty of the administering authority to ensure that the trust territory shall play its part in the maintenance of international peace and security. To this end the administering authority may make use of volunteer forces, facilities, and assistance from the trust territory in carrying out the obligations towards the Security Council undertaken in this regard by the administering authority, as well as for local defense and the maintenance of law and order within the trust territory.

Article 85

1. The functions of the United Nations with regard to trusteeship agreements for all areas not designated as strategic, including the approval of the terms of the trusteeship agreements and of their alteration or amendment, shall be exercised by the General Assembly.

2. The Trusteeship Council, operating under the authority of the General Assembly, shall assist the General Assembly in carrying out these functions.

CHAPTER 13
The Trusteeship Council

Composition

Article 86

1. The Trusteeship Council shall consist of the following Members of the United Nations:

a. those Members administering trust territories;

b. such of those Members mentioned by name in Article 23 as are not administering trust territories; and

c. as many other Members elected for three-year terms by the General Assembly as may be necessary to ensure that the total number of members of the Trusteeship Council is equally divided between those Members of the United Nations which administer trust territories and those which do not.

2. Each member of the Trusteeship Council shall designate one specially qualified person to represent it therein.

Functions and Powers

Article 87

The General Assembly and, under its authority, the Trusteeship Council, in carrying out their functions, may:

a. consider reports submitted by the administering authority;

b. accept petitions and examine them in consultation with the administering authority;

c. provide for periodic visits to the respective trust territories at times agreed upon with the administering authority; and

d. take these and other actions in conformity with the terms of the trusteeship agreements.

Article 88

The Trusteeship Council shall formulate a questionnaire on the political, economic, social, and educational advancement of the inhabitants of each trust territory, and the administering authority for each trust territory within the competence of the General Assembly shall make an annual report to the General Assembly upon the basis of such questionnaire.

Voting

Article 89

1. Each member of the Trusteeship Council shall have one vote.

2. Decisions of the Trusteeship Council shall be made by a majority of the members present and voting.

Procedure

Article 90

1. The Trusteeship Council shall adopt its own rules of procedure, including the method of selecting its President.

2. The Trusteeship Council shall meet as required in accordance with its rules, which shall include provision for the convening of meetings on the request of a majority of its members.

Article 91

The Trusteeship Council shall, when appropriate, avail itself of the assistance of the Economic and Social Council and of the specialized agencies in regard to matters with which they are respectively concerned.

CHAPTER 14
The International Court of Justice

Article 92

The International Court of Justice shall be the principal judicial organ of the United Nations. It shall function in accordance with the annexed Statute, which is based upon the statute of the Permanent Court of International Justice and forms an integral part of the present Charter.

Article 93

1. All Members of the United Nations are *ipso facto* parties to the Statute of the International Court of Justice.

2. A state which is not a Member of the United Nations may become a party to the Statute of the International Court of Justice on conditions to be determined in each case by the General Assembly upon the recommendation of the Security Council.

Article 94

1. Each member of the United Nations undertakes to comply with the decision of the International Court of Justice in any case to which it is a party.

2. If any party to a case fails to perform the obligations incumbent upon it under a judgment rendered by the Court, the other party may have recourse to the Security Council, which may, if it deems necessary, make recommendations or decide upon measures to be taken to give effect to the judgment.

Article 95

Nothing in the present Charter shall prevent Members of the United Nations from entrusting the solution of their differences to other tribunals by virtue of agreements already in existence or which may be concluded in the future.

Article 96

1. The General Assembly or the Security Council may request the International Court of Justice to give an advisory opinion on any legal question.

2. Other organs of the United Nations and specialized agencies, which may at any time be so authorized by the General Assembly, may also request advisory opinions of the Court on legal questions arising within the scope of their activities.

CHAPTER 15
The Secretariat

Article 97

The Secretariat shall comprise a Secretary-General and such staff as the Organization may require. The Secretary-General shall be appointed by the General Assembly upon the recommendation of the Security Council. He shall be the chief administrative officer of the Organization.

Article 98

The Secretary-General shall act in that capacity in all meetings of the General Assembly, of the Security Council, of the Economic and Social Council and of the Trusteeship Council, and shall perform such other functions as are entrusted to him by these organs. The Secretary-General shall make an annual report to the General Assembly on the work of the Organization.

Article 99

The Secretary-General may bring to the attention of the Security Council any matter which in his opinion may threaten the maintenance of international peace and security.

Article 100

1. In the performance of their duties the Secretary-General and the staff shall not seek or receive instructions from any government or from any other authority external to the Organization. They shall refrain from any action which might reflect on their position as international officials responsible only to the Organization.

2. Each Member of the United Nations undertakes to respect the exclusively international character of the responsibilities of the Secretary-General and the staff and not to seek to influence them in the discharge of their responsibilities.

Article 101

1. The staff shall be appointed by the Secretary-General under regulations established by the General Assembly.

2. Appropriate staffs shall be permanently assigned to the Economic and Social Council, the Trusteeship Council, and, as required, to other organs of the United Nations. These staffs shall form a part of the Secretariat.

3. The paramount consideration in the employment of the staff and in the determination of the conditions of service shall be the necessity of securing the highest standards of efficiency, competence, and integrity. Due regard shall be paid to the importance of recruiting the staff on as wide a geographical basis as possible.

CHAPTER 16
Miscellaneous Provisions

Article 102

1. Every treaty and every international agreement entered into by any Member of the United Nations after the present Charter comes into force shall as soon as possible be registered with the Secretariat and published by it.

2. No party to any such treaty or international agreement which has not been registered in accordance with the provisions of paragraph 1 of this Article may invoke that treaty or agreement before any organ of the United Nations.

Article 103

In the event of a conflict between the obligations of the Members of the United Nations under the present Charter and their obligations under any other international agreement, their obligations under the present Charter shall prevail.

Article 104

The Organization shall enjoy in the territory of each of its Members such legal capacity as may be necessary for the exercise of its functions and the fulfillment of its purposes.

Article 105

1. The Organization shall enjoy in the territory of each of its Members such privileges and immunities as are necessary for the fulfillment of its purposes.

2. Representatives of the Members of the United Nations and officials of the Organization shall similarly enjoy such privileges and immunities as are necessary for the independent exercise of their functions in connection with the Organization.

3. The General Assembly may make recommendations with a view to determining the details of the application of paragraphs 1 and 2 of this Article or may propose conventions to the Members of the United Nations for this purpose.

CHAPTER 17
Transitional Security Arrangements

Article 106

Pending the coming into force of such special agreements referred to in Article 43 as in the opinion of the Security Council enable it to begin the exercise of its responsibilities under Article 42, the parties to the Four-Nation Declaration, signed at Moscow, October 30, 1943, and France, shall, in accordance with the provisions of paragraph 5 of that Declaration, consult with one another and as occasion requires with other Members of the United Nations with a view to such joint action on behalf of the Organization as may be necessary for the purpose of maintaining international peace and security.

Article 107

Nothing in the present Charter shall invalidate or preclude action, in relation to any state which during the Second World War has been an enemy of any signatory to the present Charter, taken or authorized as a result of that war by the Governments having responsibility for such action.

CHAPTER 18
Amendments

Article 108

Amendments to the present Charter shall come into force for all Members of the United Nations when they have been adopted by a vote of two-thirds of the members of the General Assembly and ratified in accordance with their respective constitutional processes by two-thirds of the Members of the United Nations, including all the permanent members of the Security Council.

Article 109

1. A General Conference of the Members of the United Nations for the purpose of reviewing the present Charter may be held at a date and

place to be fixed by a two-thirds vote of the members of the General Assembly and by a vote of any nine members of the Security Council. Each Member of the United Nations shall have one vote in the conference.

2. Any alteration of the present Charter recommended by a two-thirds vote of the conference shall take effect when ratified in accordance with their respective constitutional processes by two-thirds of the Members of the United Nations including all the permanent members of the Security Council.

3. If such a conference has not been held before the tenth annual session of the General Assembly following the coming into force of the present Charter, the proposal to call such a conference shall be placed on the agenda of that session of the General Assembly, and the conference shall be held if so decided by a majority vote of the members of the General Assembly and by a vote of any seven members of the Security Council.

CHAPTER 19
Ratification and Signature

Article 110

1. The present Charter shall be ratified by the signatory states in accordance with their respective constitutional processes.

2. The ratifications shall be deposited with the Government of the United States of America, which shall notify all the signatory states of each deposit as well as the Secretary-General of the Organization when he has been appointed.

3. The present Charter shall come into force upon the deposit of ratifications by the Republic of China, France, the Union of Soviet Socialist Republics, the United Kingdom of Great Britain and Northern Ireland, and the United States of America, and by a majority of the other signatory states. A protocol of the ratifications deposited shall thereupon be drawn up by the Government of the United States of America which shall communicate copies thereof to all the signatory states.

4. The states signatory to the present Charter which ratify it after it has come into force will become original Members of the United Nations on the date of the deposit of their respective ratifications.

Article 111

The present Charter, of which the Chinese, French, Russian, English, and Spanish texts are equally authentic, shall remain deposited in the archives of the Government of the United States of America. Duly certified copies thereof shall be transmitted by that Government to the Governments of the other signatory states.

IN FAITH WHEREOF the representatives of the Governments of the United Nations have signed the present Charter.

DONE at the city of San Francisco the twenty-sixth day of June, one thousand nine hundred and forty-five.

About the Author

Paul F. Diehl received his Ph.D. from the University of Michigan and is now Assistant Professor of Political Science at the University of Georgia. He is co-editor with Loch Johnson of *Through the Straits of Armageddon: Arms Control Issues and Prospects* (University of Georgia Press, 1987). Professor Diehl has written almost twenty articles on war and security issues; these have appeared in some of the leading journals in political science including *Journal of Conflict Resolution, Journal of Politics, Political Science Quarterly, Armed Forces and Society,* and *Journal of Peace Research.* He currently teaches courses on international conflict, international organizations, and nuclear war.

DEC 2 2 1995

A Note on the Type

The text of this book was set in 10/12 Times Roman, a film version of the face designed by Stanley Morison, which was first used by *The Times* (of London) in 1932. Part of Morison's special intent for Times Roman was to create a face that was editorially neutral. It is an especially compact, attractive, and legible typeface, which has come to be seen as the "most important type design of the twentieth century."

Composed by Weimer Typesetting Co., Inc.

Printed and bound by Malloy Lithographing, Inc.